Uncertainty and Enterprise

Uncertainty and Enterprise

Venturing Beyond the Known

AMAR BHIDÉ

OXFORD
UNIVERSITY PRESS

Oxford University Press is a department of the University of Oxford. It furthers
the University's objective of excellence in research, scholarship, and education
by publishing worldwide. Oxford is a registered trade mark of Oxford University
Press in the UK and certain other countries.

Published in the United States of America by Oxford University Press
198 Madison Avenue, New York, NY 10016, United States of America.

© Oxford University Press 2025

All rights reserved. No part of this publication may be reproduced, stored in
a retrieval system, or transmitted, in any form or by any means, without the
prior permission in writing of Oxford University Press, or as expressly permitted
by law, by license, or under terms agreed with the appropriate reproduction
rights organization. Inquiries concerning reproduction outside the scope of the
above should be sent to the Rights Department, Oxford University Press, at the
address above.

You must not circulate this work in any other form
and you must impose this same condition on any acquirer.

Library of Congress Cataloging-in-Publication Data
Names: Bhide, Amar, 1955– author
Title: Uncertainty and enterprise : venturing beyond the known / Amar Bhidé.
Description: New York, NY : Oxford University Press, [2025] |
Includes bibliographical references and index. |
Identifiers: LCCN 2024024085 (print) | LCCN 2024024086 (ebook) |
ISBN 9780197688359 (hardback) | ISBN 9780197688380 | ISBN 9780197688366 (epub)
Subjects: LCSH: Entrepreneurship | Financial risk management |
Risk management | Uncertainty
Classification: LCC HD61 .B52 2025 (print) | LCC HD61 (ebook) |
DDC 658.15/5—dc23/eng/20240930
LC record available at https://lccn.loc.gov/2024024085
LC ebook record available at https://lccn.loc.gov/2024024086

DOI: 10.1093/oso/9780197688359.001.0001

Printed by Integrated Books International, United States of America

The manufacturer's authorised representative in the EU for product safety is Oxford University Press España S.A. of El Parque Empresarial
San Fernando de Henares, Avenida de Castilla, 2 – 28830 Madrid (www.oup.es/en or product.safety@oup.com). OUP España S.A. also acts as
importer into Spain of products made by the manufacturer.

To Len Blavatnik
For his spontaneous generosity, decades of friendship, and tolerating my
first-time-out teaching in the Fall of 1988.

Table of Contents

Preface   ix

PART I: INVITATION TO THE VOYAGE

1. The Offering   3
2. Uncertainty as Doubt   10
3. Conjectures about Justification   23
4. Applications to Enterprise   33

PART II: FORMIDABLE OBSTACLES, FORGOTTEN BEACONS

5. Frank Knight: The Spark That Did Not Ignite   43
6. Practically Omniscient Microeconomics   52
7. Imperfect Market Theories: Realism without Fallibility   60
8. John Maynard Keynes: Help to Distraction   69
9. Herbert Simon: Faded Guiding Star   90
10. Daniel Ellsberg's Ambiguity: A Simplifying Side Trip   110
11. Kahneman and Tversky: Gaining Acceptance, Dropping Uncertainty   126
12. Richard Thaler & Co.: Building the New Behavioral Boomtowns   148

PART III: THE SPECIALIZATION OF ENTERPRISE

13. Including Uncertainty: Recapitulation and Preview   165
14. "Bootstrapping" Improvised Startups   176
15. Calculating Capitalists: VCs and Angel Investors   197
16. The Evolution of Dynamic Bureaucracies   217
17. The Dominions of Giants   232

viii   TABLE OF CONTENTS

PART IV: IMAGINATIVE DISCOURSE

18. The Aims of Discourse	259
19. The Devices of Discourse	268
20. Stories as Side Dishes	281
21. Spillovers from Popular Stories	298

PART V: CODA

22. The Case for Widening	315
Acknowledgments	335
Notes	337
References	383
Index	405

Preface

A hundred years after its 1921 publication, Frank Knight's *Risk, Uncertainty and Profit* has become an object of empty obeisance: Scholars bow to its novel construct, now called "Knightian uncertainty," but ignore it in their research. Many consider it a relic that modern approaches have made obsolete or an occult idea they cannot systematically study. Milton Friedman, Knight's doctoral student and famous Chicago colleague, rejected the utility of the category altogether.

Like most graduate students in business and economics, I did not encounter Knight's book in my courses and seminars. Even Richard Caves's Industrial Organization, a buffet that included some exotic dishes, kept it off the menu. Then, a few years after I joined Harvard Business School's entrepreneurship unit in 1988, Dean John H. McArthur summoned me to lunch. We talked about everything—except why we were lunching. After about three hours, John clarified: he had been reading my work and wanted to know "who was writing this stuff."

Following this (subtle) grilling, John sent me Knight's book with one of his trademark scribbled notes, suggesting it would resonate with me.

It certainly did. Knightian uncertainty—and the "judgments" it impels—became my lodestar. Throughout the 1990s, I included the terms *uncertainty* and *judgment* in the titles and texts of my articles.

But few took notice.

In 2000, I made Knightian uncertainty the organizing premise in *The Origin and Evolution of New Businesses.* Catchy stories and some summary data in that 1.66-pound, 432-page (with fine print) tome attracted attention, but not its Knightian framing (see Figure PR.1).

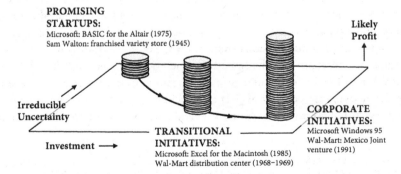

Figure PR.1 Investment, Uncertainty, and Profit
Source: *The Origin and Evolution of New Businesses* (Bhidé 2000, 4)

X PREFACE

I persisted with a concise article with implicit Knightian framing, replacing all mentions of uncertainty with "novelty aversion." This subterfuge did not sway journal editors, although Joseph Stiglitz cited the piece in his 2001 Nobel Lecture. Eventually, in 2006, *Capitalism and Society*, which I started and would edit for the next twelve years with Edmund Phelps, included the much-rejected piece in its inaugural issue.[1]

Robert Solow perceptively noted its underlying Knightian premise in his commentary (published with the article). "[Bhidé's] observations about 'novelty aversion' rang true," wrote Solow, "but I wonder if they are not symptomatic of a broader issue.... New propositions are not samples from some stationary stochastic process. They seem to present what used to be called Knightian uncertainty.... This is not dramatically different from Bhidé's take on the issue. The difference is that it suggests a general line of inquiry: is there a reasonable theory of reactions to Knightian uncertainty, possibly a 'behavioral' theory?"[*, 2]

But the 2006 piece, too, crashed soundlessly, although other articles published in the journal by more distinguished authors had staying power.[3]

My upbeat *Venturesome Economy*, whose unpropitious publication in 2008 coincided with a global financial collapse, contained scores of references to Knightian uncertainty. A key construct in this book—"venturesome consumption"—relied on the uncertain value of novel products. (In standard economics, consumers somehow know the utility they will get from new goods.)

Likewise, my 2010 *A Call for Judgment* argued that ignoring Knightian uncertainty had created a dangerously dysfunctional financial system.

After that argument was ignored, I gave up on financial and economic questions and focused on the development of productive knowledge and writing and teaching case histories of medical innovations.

In 2020, John Kay and Mervyn King published *Radical Uncertainty*, just as the Covid-19 pandemic made normal life impossible. Their engaging tour de force nonetheless secured the attention and success it deserved. Kay and King, joined by Tim Besley, then convened a global multidisciplinary group to continue the conversation under the aegis of the Hayek Seminars at the London School of Economics.

Stimulating seminar sessions (remotely, on Zoom) rekindled my interest in Knightian uncertainty. At the same time, memories of past futilities have convinced me of the need to update it significantly. I envision a modernization akin to reviving the concept of electric bicycles first proposed in the nineteenth century. Although inventors secured several patents in the 1890s, they did not

---

* The "possibly a 'behavioral' theory" puzzled me, but I did not dare ask Solow. Researching the development of behavioral economics for chapters 9–12 has provided a plausible answer—that Solow had a broader and historically more accurate understanding of "behavioral."

produce or sell many e-bikes. The concept has now become popular, but not by implementing nineteenth-century patents. The revival of the e-bike has needed new designs and technologies that improve functionality. The twenty-first-century e-bike has more range, reliability, and safety than its nineteenth-century predecessor. Any impactive renewal of Knightian uncertainty requires similar modernizing.

Or, to use a nautical analogy, we should sail *from* Knight's 1921 dock but not *on* Knight's 1921 ship.

Traditionalists may object. But if the proposed renewal alienates some of Knight's devoted loyalists, so be it. I prefer pragmatism. John McArthur, a visionary who put getting things done over abstract principle, would have approved, I think.

PART I

INVITATION TO THE VOYAGE

Notes:

1. Adapted from the Smithsonian's Open Access online collection. The image to the left (ca. 1750) is described as "Frame for the Title or the Dedication of a Music Book, or a Program of or an Invitation to a Concert." The image on the right (ca. 1883–1884) is John Henry Twachtman's *Woman on the Quay, Honfleur*.

2. Charles Baudelaire's poem "L'Invitation au voyage" was published in *Les Fleurs du mal* in 1857, a book denounced as *une outrage aux bonnes mœurs*—"an insult to good manners" or "morality" (Gotrich 2018).

3. As mentioned in the Preface, we sail from Knight's dock, not on Knight's ship. Hence, *Quai d'Knight*.

1

The Offering

Uncertainty fascinates and challenges. An entirely predictable existence would be unbearably dull. The excitement of climbing a mountain, organizing a movement, developing a new technology, or starting a business comes from not knowing what awaits us, from outcomes that we cannot fully control, and that nature or providence have not preordained. Our enthusiasm for new products and experiences demands the prospect of a surprise. But we also struggle against uncertainty. Daring mountaineers plan and prepare diligently, leaving as little to chance as they can. Human artifice has battled natural misfortunes since prehistory, building shelters against storms, cultivating crops to provide more reliable food than hunting or foraging, and digging wells for predictable water supplies. Yet uncertainty defies conquest. Bold or cautious, impulsive or deliberate, we constantly face choices whose consequences we cannot foretell.

Scientific and industrial revolutions made it easier for people to reduce the impact of bad luck. Between 1550 and 1650, one in five ships sailing between Portugal and India were lost because they relied on "dead reckoning"—crude guesswork—to navigate. John Harrison's pathbreaking clocks reduced sailors' uncertainties about their locations,[1] making long-distance trade more routine and reliable. Medical knowledge and instruments (such as stethoscopes and X-rays) made diagnoses more accurate. Interchangeable components, automation, and statistical defect control reduced variability in manufacturing. Actuarial science and annuity calculations reduced the risks of providing life insurance and pensions. New legal technologies and instruments (such as letters of credit) improved commercial predictability across time and distance.

Innovations in this millennium have continued to increase predictability. Medical research and diagnoses are less hit-or-miss: Genetic advances have helped biotech researchers find precise targets for drug development and physicians identify individuals with a high propensity for several diseases. DNA tests help track down murderers and rapists—and overturn the convictions of innocents. More accurate weather forecasts provide life-saving storm alerts. Businesses have benefited from Six Sigma techniques that can nearly eliminate defects. Big-data algorithms help Google and Facebook personalize advertising and airlines fill their airplanes profitably. Consumers can predict when their Amazon packages and Uber cars will arrive with surprising accuracy. Online

Uncertainty and Enterprise. Amar Bhidé, Oxford University Press. © Oxford University Press 2025.
DOI: 10.1093/oso/9780197688359.003.0001

4 UNCERTAINTY AND ENTERPRISE

marketplaces like Airbnb provide pictures and ratings that help price-conscious travelers find suitable accommodation more confidently.

Scientific discoveries and technological innovations have not, however, eliminated uncertainty. In medicine, reliable diagnoses of common afflictions such as sleep apnea and muscle cramps remain frustratingly elusive. Diagnostic imaging now provides reliable evidence of coronary heart disease, but the causes remain a puzzle. Early detection can create new uncertainties: mammography can locate tiny, incipient breast tumors, raising the question of when and what treatment is best. Tests for very early-stage prostate cancers raise similar questions. And despite high-tech medical testing, missed, wrong, or delayed diagnoses occur in up to one in seven hospital admissions in the United States.[2]

Airbnb pictures and reviews have not ended unpleasant surprises. The commercial success of ad-serving programs on Google and Facebook shows their superiority over blind advertising. Yet most ads I see are laughably unrelated to anything I would buy. The outcomes of entrepreneurial initiatives remain highly unpredictable. Despite nearly unlimited financial resources, vast troves of data, formidable analytical capabilities, and the savviest talent money can buy, Google and Facebook repeatedly fail to launch successful new products and services and instead rely on acquisitions to sustain their growth. Most businesses backed by the brightest and best venture capitalists (VCs) flop. Legendary VCs also often dismiss opportunities that later achieve stunning success.

And put aside radical uncertainties and life-altering possibilities. Nothing is certain under the sun. Our knowledge of the world—or our future wants—is incomplete and fallible. Nor can we be sure about others' opinions or wants. We can only imagine. Yet resolute action requires confidence in our individual and collective choices. Where does confidence come from, especially when we imagine something new? How do we justify judgments prone to mistake and disagreement?

Managing uncertainty also imposes costs. Techniques for making predictions about large groups and agglomerations often rely on standardized procedures and statistical models that ignore contextual and personal differences. These "one-size-fits-all" systems can cause widespread harm. Yet the experts who design or operate defective systems carry on, their power unchecked. People's frustration with unaccountable experts can empower authoritarian demagogues. Therefore, while technology increases the possibilities of predictability and control, it also raises difficult questions about when and how to rely on technical solutions and experts.

The kind of evidence used to justify uncertain choices poses related problems. Satisfying demands for "evidence-based" justification now often requires statistical validations and randomized controlled trials. This is sometimes prudent: it would be reckless for the US Food and Drug Administration (FDA) to authorize new vaccines without large-scale trials. In other instances, however, statistical justification is impossible or unwise: Supreme Court justices cannot base their rulings on a statistical model. Similarly, choices about whether and how to treat incipient breast tumors or early-stage breast cancers should consider individual patients' case histories, not just the results of clinical trials. But dogmatic reliance on statistics to resolve all kinds of uncertainties—and on experts who claim a supernatural capacity for such resolution—has become widespread.

1. Elusive Prospects

Given Frank Knight's stature—Knight is sometimes remembered as the father of Chicago economics—his classic book on uncertainty might seem an obvious source for insights. But extracting insights on significant contemporary issues isn't easy.

Briefly, Knight's 1921 book *Risk, Uncertainty and Profit* distinguished uncertainty from risk thus: Risk can be objectively calculated from historical statistics (as in constructing life expectancy tables) or from probability theory (like the chance of successive "heads" in a coin toss). Knight defined uncertainty by *exclusion*—as situations when we *cannot* calculate probabilities from statistical distributions or mathematical laws. For example, picking the Best Movie Oscar winner five years from now involves incalculable uncertainty because we cannot even know which films will be in the running then. Knight further attributed to entrepreneurs the crucial role of taking "responsibility" for uncertainty rather than risk (as explained in chapter 4). This attribution helped secure Knight's place as a pioneering researcher of entrepreneurship.

Knight's definition of uncertainty as the absence of calculable risks has immediate intuitive appeal, but this definition has also become a reason for its neglect. Most real-world situations and problems—which dish to order in a new restaurant, for example—don't naturally map into statistical distributions or mathematical calculations. We know this intuitively. But the very banality of this vast residual "nonrisk" space has encouraged interpretations that are hard to understand or apply.

Some present-day references, for example, restrict "true" Knightian uncertainty to "unknown unknowns." This restricted interpretation puts uncertainty in the metaphysical sphere, making practical application or analysis impossible.

Knight's exposition, which swings between the straightforward and the mystical, contributes to these obstacles. On the straightforward side, he calls uncertainty a "probability situation" in which "there is *no valid basis of any kind* for classifying instances" (italics in the original)[3] because "the situation is in a high degree unique."[4] Knight's "best example" pertains to "the exercise

6 UNCERTAINTY AND ENTERPRISE

of judgment," namely, the formation of opinions about future events, which "guide most of our conduct."[5] If our opinions about what will happen if we do something are favorable—and we have sufficient confidence in our opinions—we act.

But, adds Knight, the "ultimate logic, or psychology, of these deliberations is obscure, a part of the scientifically unfathomable mystery of life and mind. We must simply fall back upon a 'capacity' in the intelligent animal to form more or less correct judgments about things, an intuitive sense of values."[6] Fair enough; such mysteries of life and mind are indeed unfathomable. But practically, such language pushes uncertainty into a metaphysical realm, better suited for scholastic disputation. Economists—like other social scientists—have no interest in such disputes. They prefer to work with constructs they can observe and, better yet, measure.

What's more, as we see in later chapters, mainstream economic theories now make no distinction between "probability situations" that are, in Knight's words, "to a high degree unique" and those that are not. Uncertainty is banished to the unexaminable, occult world of unknown unknowns. Even in the entrepreneurial sphere, where promoters tout the distinctiveness of their ventures, mainstream theorists prefer to look at other matters, such as incentives and information asymmetries. And while economists might sympathize with Knight's claim that profit is impossible when the risks are known, their usual theories of profit do not include uncertainty.

Textbook economics also tells us little about justifying sincere, carefully reasoned beliefs and resolving honest disagreements. Standard theories focus on lying and cheating, and behavioral economists focus on thoughtless biases and blunders. The give-and-take of grounded yet imagined reasons about imagined possibilities are beyond their scope.

2. Unradical Aims

While my perspective and methods are unconventional, my project isn't radical. I aim to stimulate inquiry into neglected questions about the role of uncertainty in human affairs and improve our understanding of how to manage it. I do not offer grand theories or manifestos. Instead, I propose some conjectures about the justification of imagined choices illustrated by applications in entrepreneurship. My conjectures and applications also complement rather than challenge mainstream economics; I have no interest in overthrowing the results of its uncertainty-free theories. To return to the e-bike analogy of the Preface, I propose an electrically assisted bicycle, not an all-electric scooter. Instead of refuting existing theories, I focus on what mainstream economics can't easily examine or explain.

THE OFFERING 7

Thus, my uncertainty-based applications aim to show how and why self-financed founders, wealthy "angel" investors, venture capitalists, and large corporations occupy different entrepreneurial niches and often play symbiotic roles. I also show how imaginative uncertainty-reducing discourse—which is excluded from the purview of mainstream economic theories—helps entrepreneurs secure resources for their ventures. I do not, however, reexamine Knight's original thesis that true profit requires uncertainty. I believe that is a lost cause in economics—although I stress the dictum in teaching entrepreneurship to analytically obsessed business students.

My contextual, "abductive" reasoning and "narrative mode" discourse[7] may trouble economists and other social scientists more than my conjectures and applications themselves. I make no apologies. Facts that aren't numerical and evidence about unique circumstances affect what we routinely do and how confident we feel about our choices. They deserve a place in accounts of our economic and social conduct. That such facts and evidence resist mathematical or statistical treatment does not justify their exclusion. Much of human reasoning and discourse has, throughout human history, included such facts and evidence. Adapting how the older learned professions—law and medicine—use nonnumerical contextual data and "think in cases"[8] can broaden our understanding of human conduct.

But again, as with the results of mainstream economics, I aim to broaden, not attack, conventional methodologies. While discouraging careless observation and theorizing, the prevailing math, statistics, or nothing convention also limits the range of problems examined and the completeness of explanations. More acceptance of other approaches will broaden what economists and like-minded social scientists can explore and explain.

3. Crossover Readership

This book targets a crossover but not a mass audience. I hope to inform and persuade economists willing to consider approaches outside accepted paradigms and a select group of noneconomists. The latter include academics outside economics departments, policymakers, and practitioners with intellectual interests and scholarly dispositions.

Writing for this dual target poses challenges. Like other natural and social scientists, economists regard journal articles as the primary means for communicating scholarly ideas. As the philosopher of science Thomas Kuhn put it, scientific research is now usually reported in "brief articles addressed only to professional colleagues . . . whose knowledge of a shared paradigm can be

8 UNCERTAINTY AND ENTERPRISE

assumed and who prove to be the only ones able to read the papers addressed to them." In contrast, scientific books are "usually either texts or retrospective"; the scientists who write them are more likely to find their "professional reputation impaired than enhanced."[9] Worse, I explain things the professional economist already knows well and include intellectual histories that are not technically necessary. I offer no model or statistics. All this does not help me make my unconventional case to mainstream scholars.

In contrast, other readers may find even my simplified summaries of established economic ideas challenging. For the same reason, they should get more from the summaries than academic economists. And being less preconditioned by existing theory, other readers may more readily follow my reasoning. The absence of actionable prescriptions may disappoint practically minded readers, however. This book is not a "how-to"; I have long been skeptical of generalized remedies. Effective practice, I believe, must reflect specific circumstances.

Yet, a conceptually guided understanding of how the world generally works has practical value. Even "madmen in authority, who hear voices in the air, [distill] their frenzy from some academic scribbler of a few years back," as John Maynard Keynes wrote.[10] As it happens, I have no interest in stirring up madmen in authority, but I hope to raise questions that could help worldly readers develop their own practical insights.

Anticipating a diverse—if select—readership, I have organized this book into modular parts. After the introductory Part 1, you can read the next three parts sequentially or in any other order. For example, the practically minded reader could go to the applications in Parts 3 and 4 and then return to the more theoretical Part 2. The text also includes shaded boxes to enrich and enliven the main text through biographical sketches, in-depth examples, and technical explanations. The shaded boxes can be read in the order in which they appear, postponed for later perusal, or, depending on the reader's interests and expertise, skipped.

My language and presentation favor nonacademic readers. Besides simplifying the technical material and using shaded boxes, I have put many details in the endnotes. I use bullet points, numbered sections, and other visual markers to make the chapter structures transparent.* I also avoid long or made-up words, idiomatic references that might puzzle readers from outside the Anglosphere, and "maybes" and "perhapses" to qualify every argument (although I deeply mistrust certitudes). These choices may undermine my credibility with some academic readers. But I hope that even objectors will secretly like an easy-to-follow format and that its transparency will encourage refutations and corrective research.

---

* David Ogilvy's *Confessions of an Advertising Man* (1963) had numbered paragraphs, along with boxed articles. I have not gone that far.

THE OFFERING   9

To complete this prospectus for modernization: the following three chapters outline, in turn, how I modify Knight's concept of uncertainty, the conjectures that follow from my reconceptualization, and the applications of my conjectures to entrepreneurship. Taken together, the chapters in this part of the book distill the book's argument. But the value and pleasures of a book, like its devils, lie in its details, so I hope Part 1 stimulates rather than satisfies the reader's interest.

2

Uncertainty as Doubt

Returning to the electric bicycle analogy of the Preface: Modern e-bikes can go farther and provide smoother rides by using modern components. The better rides and modern components go hand in hand—producers select the components to provide the targeted improvements in the rides. Likewise, I have modified Knight's approach (described in this chapter) to support my conjectures about justifying uncertain choices (discussed in the next chapter) and the application of these conjectures to enterprise (discussed in chapter 4).

Table 2.1 summarizes three modifications discussed in this chapter. While I designed the modifications to support my modernization project—whose aims deviate from Knight's—they also maintain the spirit and some of the crucial features of Knight's construct, as we will see.

Table 2.1 Modifications to Knight's (1921) Construct

Knight's (1921) Construct	Modifications
Uncertainty as a *"situation,"* contrasted with numerical *"risk."*	Uncertainty as the *mental state* of *doubt*, contrasted with *confidence*.
Contextual information does not affect situational uncertainty.	Contextual information reduces doubts.
Explain preconditions for true *profit*.	Analyze *disagreements*.

1. Mental versus Situational Specification

Uncertainty as Doubt   Recall that Knight called uncertainty a "probability situation" produced by unique circumstances. I follow a more common use of uncertainty as a state of mind, namely doubt. In my usage, doubts can be about anything that we (or some authority we trust entirely) have not seen or cannot logically prove. Uncertainty is thus a personal ("subjective") mental state that covers future events that no one can observe before they occur. Doubts can also pertain to ignorance of existing or past conditions. Do I, or did I, have a

Uncertainty and Enterprise. Amar Bhidé, Oxford University Press. © Oxford University Press 2025.
DOI: 10.1093/oso/9780197688359.003.0002

mild Covid infection or a bad cold? Or when did Slovakia become an independent state?

Uncertainty goes beyond doubts about sharply defined "yes" or "no" conditions, like Covid infections or the date of Slovakian independence. It covers ranges (tomorrow's high and low temperatures), statistical distributions (next month's mean daily rainfall and its standard deviation), fuzzy states (how happy will sunny weather make me?), and broad "what is going on here" inquiries (why are so many people quitting their jobs?). We can also be uncertain about inferences, which may themselves be fuzzy. How "strongly" do dark clouds make it "prudent" to carry an umbrella? And, crucially for my book, uncertainty applies to assessing others' capacities and dispositions—including their integrity and expertise—and it also applies to our predictions of how they will act. We expect X will do such and such, but we cannot be sure. And to what degree can we rely on X's opinions and judgments?

Calling uncertainty a state of mind rather than an external "probability situation" produced by unique circumstances, as Knight did, puts uncertainty on a different plane. My specification of uncertainty is psychological, located within the individual; Knight's exists outside anyone's mind. Some other writers also follow Knight's example in referring to uncertain situations. Yet others use situational and mental uncertainty interchangeably.

As it happens, unique situations also often produce internal mental uncertainty. And Knight's original theory also assumed that situational uncertainty created psychological discomfort that some individuals (especially entrepreneurs) did not feel or were more willing to tolerate. For simplicity, I treat Knight's situational uncertainty produced by uniqueness—the source—as synonymous with mental uncertainty—its effect.[*]

Another difference arising from the mental state specification is what I contrast uncertainty *with*. Knight contrasts uncertainty with known statistical risk, as mentioned, treating both as situational. I contrast mental uncertainty with the mental state of confidence or conviction; and, as an extreme case of uncertainty, the absence of confidence. (A religious parallel would contrast complete faith in God with agnosticism.)[†]

---

[*] However, I also include doubts that can be reduced without any change in the external situation, for example, through persuasive discourse. Such methods for doubt reduction play an important part in my conjectures about justification and their applications to enterprise.

[†] In Knight's specification, "risk" can also produce certitude, and its absence, doubt. How frequently should we expect a coin, whose "fairness" has been established through repeated tosses, to land on heads? With certitude, in half the tosses on average. How about a visibly warped and previously untossed coin? Now we cannot be confident about any estimate. But Knight's risk can only produce one kind of certitude: the type resulting from calculated probabilities and statistical distributions.

12   UNCERTAINTY AND ENTERPRISE

Therefore, in my extension, we can feel confident about objectively unique one-off choices, such as selecting or discarding a mate.

Retained Features As in Knight's distinction, uncertainty as doubt is unrelated to known, confidently calculated numerical probabilities and their everyday connotations of risk. For example, bets on "zero" in an unrigged roulette wheel entail nearly double the probability of loss than bets on "black," with a more than seventeenfold larger payout. In ordinary language, we would call betting on zero a riskier gamble. But if we believe the roulette wheel spins to be fair (here and in Knight's specification), both bets have identical, zero uncertainty in the following sense. After numerous spins, 97.37 percent of bets on zero and 53.63 percent on black would lose. And we'd be nearly certain about that.

Roulette wheel bets also illustrate the connection between doubts and mistakes. Calculations of the distribution of roulette wheel spins have a single demonstrably correct result. But we rarely find undisputed correctness outside artificial mathematical puzzles and carefully constructed arrangements and devices, such as roulette wheels used in casinos. There is no correct mathematical calculation of the number of races or games a horse or football team will win in a season.

Doubts about correctness should be the logical default. True and certain knowledge, according to ancient Greek and Indian skeptics and many seventeenth- and eighteenth-century thinkers is impossible. As the Scottish Enlightenment philosopher David Hume argued, we cannot prove or know that what has happened before will keep happening. We cannot observe tomorrow's sunrise today and logically exclude an overnight rearrangement of the cosmos. Our extrapolations from past events result from animal instinct—blind faith in what Hume called the "uniformity of nature." This instinct eliminates doubts about continued sunrises but can sometimes mislead us.[*]

Sunrises apart, experience suggests that we should avoid certitudes. In criminal prosecutions, written confessions cannot eliminate the possibility that the confessor was coerced, wants attention, or seeks to protect someone else. And successful "beyond *reasonable* doubt" prosecutions do not remove all *possible* doubt about guilt. Similarly, diligently obtained data in medical research cannot eliminate doubts about safety or efficacy. For example, the

---

[*] Bertrand Russell's "inductivist turkey," raised on a farm, observes that no matter what, the farmer always feeds him at nine o'clock every morning. His inferred rule of always being fed at 9 a.m. works flawlessly—until Thanksgiving.

inadvertent exclusion of control variables in clinical trials can produce misleading results.

The Trials of Prozac

Prozac, Eli Lilly's blockbuster antidepression drug, did not initially outperform a placebo. But then the Lilly researchers developing Prozac learned that the trial had enrolled volunteers who had not responded to other antidepressants, perhaps because they had been incorrectly diagnosed as depressed. When researchers repeated the trial on patients who had responded to other tranquilizers, it outperformed a placebo and two existing tranquilizers.[1] Conversely, several antipsychotic drugs were marketed in the 1990s after clinical trials had "demonstrated a dramatic decrease in the subjects' psychiatric symptoms." Actual clinical use and later studies, however, suggested that the 1990s drugs were not better than cheaper antipsychotics that had been introduced in the 1950s and might even be worse.[2]

With doubt must come the possibility of error: juries may convict the innocent, and regulators can approve unsafe drugs. The possibility of error raises issues of justification that are at the heart of my project to update Knight.

Mistakes and misjudgments are also crucial to Knight's original theory of profit. Unique situations require Knight's entrepreneur to form judgments about what will happen. A correct judgment produces profit; a misjudgment, loss. But without the possibility of error, there is no possibility of profit or loss—and no "distinctive role" for the entrepreneur.

As in Knight's specification, the uniqueness of situations that produce doubt can be mundane. Developing a breakthrough driverless car is, of course, a unique situation. But a simple expansion of factory capacity (to use one of Knight's examples) also involves unique circumstances that are not amenable to statistical analysis. This mundane uniqueness thus becomes a source of doubt—and although Knight does not address this—raises issues of justification.

2. Contextual Evidence

Situational versus Statistical Sources My second modification expands the scope of uncertainty-reducing information. Knight focused on statistical data, such as actuarial tables used to calculate life expectancies; ample data about "like instances" turns predictions about distributions into nearly sure things. Although

14   UNCERTAINTY AND ENTERPRISE

technically "risky," there is little "uncertainty" about the predicted distribution. Statistically validated patterns have become the goal of much of economics, as mentioned. Unsurprisingly, the few modern economic texts that take Knightian uncertainty seriously define it as "*variability* that we find hard to describe by *objective probability distributions*" (italics added).[3] The "variability" in this definition is statistical—it excludes nonstatistical doubts about facts like the date of Slovakian independence and fuzzy "What is going on around here" inquiries.

Moreover, what makes statistical variability "uncertain" is the absence of statistical evidence. Statistical evidence to reduce statistical uncertainty is routinely sought with religious fervor. Furthermore, researchers and policymakers now strongly favor data produced by controlled trials—or, failing which, "natural experiments"—to make statistical inferences more dependable. We see this trend in randomized trials of new drugs and antipoverty programs, in telemetry and A/B tests of software and web designs, and in evaluating the adequacy of the capital buffers of financial institutions.

Swimming against this tide, my approach includes nonstatistical information and methods. I see no reason for their exclusion. We routinely consult data that does not map into a statistical series—and that isn't produced by trials and experiments—to reduce feelings of uncertainty. To borrow a simple example from Kay and King's *Radical Uncertainty*, statistics and probability distributions do not resolve (nonnumerical) doubts about the capital of Pennsylvania. An atlas tells us that the capital is Harrisburg, not Philadelphia.[4] Friedrich Hayek's classic 1945 paper suggests that context-specific, nonstatistical facts perform "eminently useful functions."[5]

Eminent Utility

Hayek distinguishes between "general rules" and "knowledge of the particular circumstances of time and place." The latter is often "regarded with a kind of contempt, and that anyone who by such knowledge gains an advantage over somebody better equipped with theoretical or technical knowledge is thought to have acted almost disreputably."[6]

Yet contextual knowledge plays a vital role in exploiting unexpected opportunities and coping with unforeseeable fluctuations in demand and supply, writes Hayek:

> We need to remember only how much we have to learn in any occupation after we have completed our theoretical training, how big a part of our working life we spend learning particular jobs, and how valuable an asset in all walks of life is knowledge of people, of local conditions, and special circumstances. To know of and put to use a machine not fully employed, or

somebody's skill which could be better utilized, or to be aware of a surplus stock which can be drawn upon during an interruption of supplies, is socially quite as useful as the knowledge of better alternative techniques. And the shipper who earns his living from using otherwise empty or half-filled journeys of tramp-steamers, or the estate agent whose whole knowledge is almost exclusively one of temporary opportunities, or the arbitrageur who gains from local differences of commodity prices, are all performing eminently useful functions.[7]

The kind of contextual knowledge I am especially interested in differs from that analyzed by Hayek, however. Hayek stresses the value of delegating decisions to the "man on the spot" whose knowledge cannot be "conveyed in statistical form" without "abstracting from [seemingly] minor differences ... in a way which may be very significant for the specific decision."[8] My argument includes contextual knowledge that people *can* communicate. This possibility is crucial in using contextual data to make and justify choices about imagined possibilities.

Types of Targets In my extension of Knight's construct—as in the real world—reliable inference does not have to be exclusively statistical or based on numerical distributions. Contextual information is rarely statistically analyzed; unique circumstances can make such attempts worthless. Instead, objective treatment of diverse contextual data in business, the law, and medicine usually relies on methods such as abductive, analogical, and heuristic reasoning (as we see in later chapters). Explanations, diagnoses, predictions, and proposals that do not reduce to a scientific law or the parameters of a statistical distribution are widely accepted; they can also be strongly preferred, depending on the "target"—what the uncertainty is "about."[9]

Contextual information and nonstatistical analyses usually predominate in resolving doubts about one-offs. In contrast, statistical data and analytical methods predominate when the doubts pertain to the attributes of a distribution. For example, assessing whether X committed a burglary requires contextual information, whereas assessing whether unemployment encourages crime requires statistical data. As it happens, respectable analytical techniques emphasize distributional uncertainties. These techniques are well suited to resolving questions about aggregates in disciplines such as macroeconomics, finance, epidemiology, criminology, and education. Yet, practical questions in business, the law, medical research, and healthcare often involve doubts about one-offs. In keeping with

16 UNCERTAINTY AND ENTERPRISE

the spirit of Knight's book, my conjectures and their applications tilt toward the
neglected analyses of one-offs.

Background Beliefs and Information Doubts about one-offs cannot however be reduced or resolved just through contextual information. Inferences
from specific facts typically also require generalizations and assumptions, often
working in the background. For example, analogies are often at the heart of legal
arguments. The outcome of case A, clearly different in its particulars, is nevertheless used to argue for a similar result in case B. The persuasiveness of the analogy
(B to A) depends on the similarity also applying to a broader class of cases—C,
D, E, and so on. Without some general principles of correspondence, analogical
justifications lack strength.[10]

Some of the background generalizations may be instinctive, self-
recommending intuitions. Or they may be incontrovertible rules of the game—as
in chess puzzles where the pawn can only advance by one square and the bishop
must only move diagonally. In yet other cases, the background generalizations
may be produced by direct, repeated experience (for example, that atlases contain reliable information about state capitals) or generalizations inferred from
analyzing large datasets (for example, that studies of large handwriting samples
support an expert's authentication of a signature on a will).

Conversely, reliable statistical inferences must fit specific circumstances, as
sensible statisticians recognize. Normal blood pressure ranges and the average
efficacy of treatments derived from studies of Caucasians may not apply to other
ethnicities. Overall mortgage defaults can be poor predictors of delinquencies
among older homebuyers. And insurers' models for storm coverage will result in
significant losses if climate change produces more extreme weather.[11]

Typically, the prominence of contextual data on the one hand and statistical
or scientific patterns on the other depends on the kind of target uncertainty.
Efforts to reduce one-off uncertainties—doubts about individual cases—stress
particular conditions, with generalizations, including statistical inferences,
working in the background. In contrast, reductions and resolutions of
uncertainties about distributions stress statistical models.

Murder and drug trials provide archetypal contrasts. Murder trials are prototypical examples of one-off uncertainties. Here, verdicts based on statistical
models would be unthinkable. Instead, prosecutors and defense lawyers present
case-specific, but typically objective,[12] evidence, such as eyewitness testimony,
texts and emails, financial records, and forensic data. Interpretations from these
different items of evidence depend on background generalizations of varying
tenability. For example, an intuitive but statistically unvalidated relationship between nervousness and truthfulness can undermine the credibility of witnesses

UNCERTAINTY AS DOUBT   17

who sweat or stutter. Similarly, according to a customary "practical postulate,"[13] the lack of a demonstrable motive can create "reasonable doubts" about guilt. Likewise, the reliability of forensic DNA and fingerprint evidence rests on scientific principles and statistically validated tests.

Trials of the efficacy and safety of new drugs—a prototypical case of distributional uncertainty—exemplify the statistics-first archetype. The FDA typically requires "at least two adequate and well-controlled studies, each convincing on its own, to establish effectiveness."[14] Approvals require statistically significant better outcomes for the drug over a placebo (or another "comparator")—without serious side effects. Several contextual factors, like the origin and development of the disease and the mechanism of how the drug works, also influence approval decisions, but these factors operate in the background.[15]

Technological, Conventional, and Experiential Influences Besides the target (whether one-off or distributional), know-how, conventions, rules, and norms also affect the relative prominence of contextual and statistical information. These factors also influence whether we treat a question as a one-off, and therefore, the role of contextual data in resolving doubts.

For example, statistical analysis has determined life insurance pricing and availability for over a hundred years. Knight used life insurance as the archetype of statistical risk, where actuarial data virtually eliminated doubt. But it was not always thus. "Underwriting practice in eighteenth-century life assurance was remote from modern actuarial science," writes historian Robin Pearson. "This appears remarkable given the great advances in probability theory during the century and the attention paid [by statisticians] to the problems of valuing annuities on lives and measuring the rates of mortality in sample populations." But the rudimentary "contemporary level of knowledge about health, disease and medicine" made it reasonable for insurers to regard the "subjective evaluation of an individual's constitution" as a "superior form of knowledge" to mortality statistics. Accordingly, "Each candidate for life insurance had to appear in person" before the directors of the insurance company. Policies had to be renewed each year—after interviews with directors.*

---

* These practices had serious drawbacks. Directors' interviews limited the number of policies sold and encouraged insurers to charge high rates to compensate for their limited diversification of risks. This reduced the demand for life insurance and the proportion of the population insured. And, UK insurers avoided Jewish and Irish applicants because of prejudices about their character (Pearson 2002, 1). In the United States, social and ethnic prejudices led to the formation "of a separate African American life insurance industry," according to historian Walter Friedman. "White-owned companies charged Black customers different premiums or refused to insure them at all" (email communication with author, August 31, 2009).

18 UNCERTAINTY AND ENTERPRISE

US and European lending practices provide a contemporary contrast. US lenders now mail more than three billion offerings for credit cards and other personal loans to US consumers yearly, and websites offer "instant-approval credit cards." The automated offerings rely on generic credit bureau scores, while fair-lending rules deter "discretionary overrides" of the scores by local lending staff. European regulations and conventions, in contrast, discourage lending based on standardized credit scores.[16] Thus, the rules dictate treating consumer lending mainly as a distributional question to be addressed through statistical analysis on one side of the Atlantic and as a more contextual borrower-specific question on the other.

Organizational conventions and practices also affect the relative prominence of statistical and contextual information. For example, large, bureaucratic lenders have reputations for "by-the-numbers" lending, relying mainly on statistical scores to assess the creditworthiness of small business borrowers.[17] In contrast, their smaller competitors will consider contextual facts and subjective character assessments. Similarly, large healthcare organizations are more prone to rely on statistical models than small physicians' practices.

Similarly, experience affects attention to contextual data. To take an extreme case, generations of people in Chile's Atacama Desert who had never seen rain there confidently assumed—with no consideration of current weather conditions or forecasts—they never would. In New England, where it rains frequently and unpredictably, people base their expectations of wet or dry weather in the next hour on live radar maps.

3. Doubts and Disagreements

Missing Information As mentioned, Knight analyzed situational uncertainty as a precondition for profit. Moreover, Knight focused on the extreme case of unmeasurable uncertainty—as contrasted with numerical risks—and did not attribute any significance to the in-between possibilities. According to Knight, uncertainty due to whatever degree of uniqueness was a precondition for profit, but the degree of uncertainty and uniqueness did not affect potential profit. In contrast, my modernization emphasizes the degrees of doubts and disagreements produced by the extent of missing information (and thus connects situational and mental uncertainty).

More missing information increases doubts, with the nature of the "more" depending on the targeted uncertainty. With questions about statistical distributions, more of the same kind of data produces more confidence, while less data increases doubt. For example, a large, randomized trial for a new medical treatment that enrolls thousands of patients will produce more convincing results than a trial on a few volunteers, which does not compare the treatment to a placebo. With one-off targets, in contrast, diverse types of data can be more persuasive than multiple observations of the same kind. In a murder investigation, for example, many instances of a suspect's fingerprints at the crime scene may be less persuasive than a few fingerprints and evidence of the suspect's DNA, blood, and bodily fluids (see Figure 2.1).

Unambiguous observations ("objective" facts) produce more confidence about both one-offs and distributions. For example, in criminal investigations, closed-circuit video recordings of a suspect's movements carry more weight than the recollections of an elderly eyewitness. Similarly, in medical trials, blood tests and biopsies are more persuasive than patients' self-reported feelings of wellness.

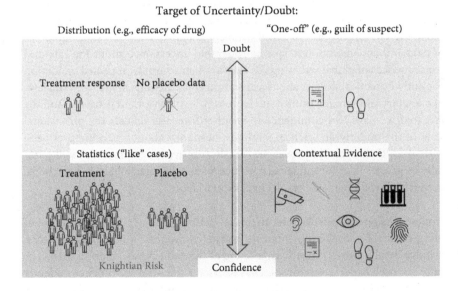

Figure 2.1 How Targets and Missing Information Affect Degrees of Doubts

Notes:

1. Knight's book limits risk—which precludes true profit—to the bottom left-hand quadrant. All other quadrants are uncertain and profit-permitting. The bottom right-hand quadrant in my scheme also has low uncertainty, although statistics don't reduce doubts there. And although I don't analyze this, that quadrant would also limit "true" Knightian profit.

2. Although not shown in the figure, contextual evidence requires background generalizations, and statistical data requires contextual interpretations to reduce doubt.

3. I have belatedly discovered a similar contrast that the late Cambridge historian and philosopher of science John Forrester had previously discussed between statistical reasoning and thinking in cases.[18]

20 UNCERTAINTY AND ENTERPRISE

Exclusions I focus on evidence that reasonable people expect to reduce doubts about the question at hand. For example, in a murder trial, forensic evidence that places a suspect at the scene of the crime is relevant, doubt-reducing information, and placebo results are relevant in drug trials. Self-evidently, the absence of forensic evidence or placebo results increases doubts. However, missing—yet objective—information about a suspect's zodiac sign should not affect reasonable jurors' doubts.

I also exclude what former US Defense Secretary, Donald Rumsfeld famously called unknown unknowns. While unknown unknowns can produce inchoate anxieties, I cannot see how they can affect degrees of doubt. Like ambiguity research (chapter 10), I focus on information that is known to be missing, thus avoiding some of the mystic connotations of uncertainty that some Knightian purists now demand.

Novelty and Prior Validation Unlettered shepherds, with no knowledge of astronomy, will treat future sunrises as certainties because they believe that, as far as sunrises are concerned, one day is exactly like the next. In contrast, because the circumstances are novel, trained scientists with access to terabytes of data and supercomputers face considerable uncertainty about the rate and consequences of global warming. To take another example, repeated validation has ended practical doubts about astronomical predictions made from the laws of planetary motion. In contrast, meteorology is still a work in progress, and the fact that we have less confidence in weather forecasts reflects the provisional state of the underlying science. Similarly, hesitancy about a vaccine produced with an mRNA technique never previously approved for human use will naturally be greater than for influenza vaccines made with tried and tested methods, even if both yield the same results in clinical trials.

Honest Disagreements Where there is doubt, there is the possibility of disagreements. Conflicting interests naturally promote such disagreements. A judge recalls two orthopedists, looking at the same X-ray, offering diametrically opposed expert testimonies. One asserted a fracture; the other confidently testified otherwise. The opposing testimonies of the experts may be entirely sincere—and indeed, their effectiveness will depend on their sincerity. Yet testimonies invariably align with which side pays the expert. Who would select an expert who won't support your case?

Crucially, for my purposes, disagreements can also arise without conflicting interests. Imagine a couple deciding where to celebrate their anniversary. Both genuinely want to please each other but disagree about how. And both may sincerely believe that going along with the other's wishes is more selfish than insisting, "It pains me to disagree, dear, but you really won't like it." While this

UNCERTAINTY AS DOUBT 21

example may exaggerate the mutual devotion of the typical couple, unselfish disagreement is not unusual: parents disagree on how to raise their children, business partners on whom to hire, physicians on treatments, jurors on verdicts, and meteorologists on weather forecasts.

Interpersonal Differences Given missing information, individuals with different temperaments and life experiences can interpret differently whatever evidence is available, even when (unlike paid expert witnesses) they have no personal stake. For example, criminal trials are rarely open and shut. If guilt or innocence were self-evident, no trial would be necessary. Instead, the prosecution presents evidence and arguments suggesting guilt, while the defense makes a case for reasonable doubt. But because the evidence is incommensurate, jurors cannot mechanically "add up" or "net out" their conflicting implications. Individual items can also have ambiguous implications. Sweating under hostile cross-examination may suggest that a witness is lying—or just nervous. Because temperaments, character traits, and differences in prior experiences affect how different individuals add up and interpret information, jurors screened for impartiality and evaluating the same evidence may still fail to reach a unanimous verdict.

Differences in backgrounds and beliefs can create strong disagreements about one-offs, such as murder trials. As mentioned, inferences about one-offs often rely on many kinds of information. Interpretations of the different information types require different background generalizations. Many of these generalizations are ad hoc rules of thumb derived from personal experience and idiosyncratic "abduction,"* not well-established scientific rules. Thus, there is more potential for differences in interpretation than in questions about distributions and aggregates. These questions can be analyzed through standardized statistical techniques, and relevant variables often have a widely accepted theoretical basis,

Degrees of Disagreements Controlling for differences in backgrounds and beliefs, conditions (such as the extent of missing information) that increase doubts also increase degrees of disagreement. For example, when relevant information is nearly complete, different individuals will be more likely to draw similar conclusions than when the gaps in information are large. Similarly, the novelty or newness of situations and unreliable models also increase doubts and disagreements. When there is no novelty (as in daily sunrises) or the accuracy of the predictive model is well established (as in models of planetary motion), there is little room for doubt. When everyone is equally sure, there can be no disagreement. In contrast, highly novel circumstances or erratic ("noisy") models provide scope for wide divergences in expert predictions about, for instance, global warming or tomorrow's weather.

* See shaded box on page 178, chapter 14, Abductive Inferences.

22   UNCERTAINTY AND ENTERPRISE

Conversely, controlling for information and novelty, wide interpersonal differences in attitudes and temperaments can increase disagreements. Confidence or skepticism in global warming models and the efficacy of masks in controlling airborne infections often correlate with political attitudes. Maverick personalities are prone to firm convictions. A friend shown an early prototype of the iPod by Steve Jobs recalls that the legendary innovator was supremely confident that Apple could "own music." My friend had his doubts. Similarly, after Jobs was diagnosed with pancreatic cancer in 2003—which led to his death in 2011—he rejected standard surgical treatments. Instead, Jobs followed a "strict vegan diet, with large quantities of fresh carrot and fruit juices" supplemented by acupuncture, herbal remedies, and "other treatments he found on the Internet or by consulting people around the country, including a psychic."[19]

Attitudinal differences can also produce disagreements. Highly incomplete information or novelty may attract thrill-seekers but repel the careful. Thus, in the earlier example about the couple celebrating their anniversary, one may want to try something new simply because it is new, while the other may favor an old tried-and-tested favorite.

How Disagreements Matter   Sometimes, disagreements may be practically unimportant. For example, experts remain divided about the results of Steve Jobs's dietary therapy for his pancreatic cancer. Memorial Sloan Kettering Cancer Center's Barrie Cassileth opines, "Jobs's faith in alternative medicine likely cost him his life . . . He had the only kind of pancreatic cancer that is treatable and curable . . . He essentially committed suicide."[20] However, surgical oncologist and Wayne State professor David Gorski offers a "best guess" that "Jobs probably only modestly decreased his chances of survival, if that."[21] Yet, practically, retrospective disagreements about whether Jobs essentially committed suicide cannot bring Jobs back to life.

Disagreements about what to do next may also not matter. Jurors in a criminal trial may have different beliefs about a defendant's guilt, and experts on FDA panels may have different opinions about the efficacy of a new drug. Yet jurors may all agree that the prosecution has satisfied the beyond-reasonable-doubt standard. Similarly, FDA experts with different opinions about the efficacy demonstrated in a clinical trial of a new drug may all agree that results are good enough to justify approval.

However, disagreements can pose serious problems, such as juries that fail to reach a verdict, the dissolution of marital and business partnerships, or compromises that leave everyone unhappy. These unpleasant possibilities can spur efforts and arrangements to reach agreements through justificatory discourse—the giving and taking of plausible reasons. The next chapter reviews conjectures about justification derived from the "uncertainty as doubt" extensions I just outlined.

3

Conjectures about Justification

What makes justification a suitable object for modernizing uncertainty? Justification is hardly uncharted territory. Knight's book said nothing about the topic, but justification has been studied since ancient times. Philosophers asked what justified beliefs. Aristotle and the Sophists analyzed rhetoric—how to justify claims. Justificatory argument was and remains at the heart of legal theory and practice. Scientific methodologies provide tools and rules for acceptable justification. Philosophers and historians of science study how scholars engage in justificatory discourse.

This modernizing project focuses on justifying practical, one-off, collaborative choices: I analyze how people—not the social scientists who study them—justify practical proposals and predictions. I emphasize their justifications of one-offs, not the general propositions on which scientific methods focus. And unlike courtroom arguments that also focus on specific cases, I am interested in cooperative, not adversarial, justifications: how devoted parents reconcile differences about raising their children, not the disputes of divorcing couples over child support.

In this chapter, I zero in on conjectures that go well beyond Knight's thesis about uncertainty and profit about

- The roles and challenges of justification.

- Supply and demand for justification.

- Routines that organizations use to evaluate and justify claims.

1. Roles and Challenges

Agreement and Other Functions Justificatory discourse (or hereafter and interchangeably, "justification") can produce agreements about one-offs, typically by *combining* evidence and giving and taking reasons. Evidence alone rarely resolves honest disagreements. To start with, crucial gaps in evidence can be large and unfillable. Crime investigators cannot invent the forensic evidence that the astute perpetrator carefully removed. Placebo outcomes for trials of personalized immunological therapies for untreatable blood cancers are practically unobtainable. Moreover, evidence is typically subject to differing

Uncertainty and Enterprise. Amar Bhidé, Oxford University Press. © Oxford University Press 2025.
DOI: 10.1093/oso/9780197688359.003.0003

24   UNCERTAINTY AND ENTERPRISE

interpretations. Therefore, jurors in legal trials rarely reach verdicts before they deliberate, notwithstanding the vast amount of data with which they have been presented.

Conversely, evidence-free arguments usually fail to produce a meeting of minds. They can sink into posturing and bloviating. Senators are fond of calling the US Senate the "World's Greatest Deliberative Body." Outsiders use the label ironically.

Combining evidence and reason can, however, produce a practically adequate convergence of views. Juries typically do reach unanimous verdicts after deliberations, sometimes after prodding by judges who urge jurors who say they are deadlocked to continue. In medicine, conferences that combine evidence— which is rarely decisive—with the diverse views of clinicians, researchers, regulators, and other professionals somehow produce guidelines that profoundly influence practice. Famously, attendees at the 1996 International AIDS Conference in Vancouver reviewed research on two treatments based on a combination of drugs. Conference attendees then endorsed a standard of care called "HAART," for "highly active antiretroviral therapy," based on multidrug combinations. Physicians switched tens of thousands of AIDS patients to HAART within weeks of the Vancouver conference, and "in just a few years, combinations (HAART) had a stunning effect in reducing death rates in the United States and in Europe."[1]

Overcoming disagreement is not the only possible function of justification, however. In fact, people often justify where there is no disagreement or after they reach an agreement. Unanimous Supreme Court judgments, which cannot be appealed, nonetheless include elaborate justifications. Uncontested medical diagnoses, property appraisals for residential mortgages, and expert reviews of grant applications also often include justifications.

Justifying uncontested decisions about uncertain one-offs has several advantages. Reasoned justifications secure legitimacy for decisions that could have been made differently—which is the case in most one-offs. Justificatory discourse can guide future decisions. Written-down judgments are essential in precedent-based common law. A record of the reasons for a patient's diagnosis or the approval of a small business loan provides a benchmark for later review. If the reasons cease to be valid, that provides a basis for reconsideration. And the process of justification—and the requirement for giving reasons—reduces the possibility of mistakes.

Justification unquestionably requires time and effort, but whether it can overcome disagreement or deliver the benefits of legitimacy, acceptance, benchmarking, and reduced mistakes is not guaranteed. As we see next, the exercise of authority usually requires less time and effort to resolve disagreements than justification. But authority does badly in other areas where justification can shine.

Authoritarian Alternatives   Coercive edicts and commands, sometimes backed by the threat of force, provide a time-honored alternative to voluntary agreement. While we may celebrate voluntary agreement and independent choice, we often simply do what we are told without discussion or argument. We drive on the specified side of the road and stop at red lights on deserted streets. Whatever our personal views about the benefits of masking and vaccinations in the Covid pandemic might have been, most of us followed masking rules and presented our vaccination certificates on demand.

Nonetheless, because authority is rarely absolute, reasoned justifications have an indispensable role. The rule of law depends on reason-giving and due process. In politics, populists bombard voters with reasons; opponents who ignore the reason-giving should not be surprised if they lose. In business, innovators cannot command consumers to buy breakthrough products. Consumers cannot work out the value of new products on their own—even a Steve Jobs must persuade buyers of the advantages of iPhones. Justification is also necessary to get the support of financiers and funding agencies and permissions from bosses and regulators. We must provide convincing reasons—make "warranted assertions," in the pragmatic philosopher John Dewey's terms—although we can rarely provide indisputable proof.

Even those with authority to command find an advantage in justifying and selling their judgments. Deliberations that recognize diverse views can promote solidarity, as Hirschman suggested in *Exit, Voice, and Loyalty*, and giving dissenters a hearing can legitimize disputed choices.[2] Alfred Sloan Jr., who created the modern General Motors after taking over the troubled, debt-laden, and disorganized company in 1920, wrote in his memoir that "an industrial organization is not the mildest form of organization in society." Sloan says he "never minimized the administrative power of the chief executive officer in principle when [he] occupied that position." But he "exercised that power with discretion" and "got better results by selling my ideas than by telling people what to do."[3]

Justifying decisions has advantages beyond securing the compliance of subordinates. Incomplete or ambiguous information often makes it impossible to deduce choices from well-founded premises. Instead, we often start with some impulse or inchoate instinctive inference. According to Oliver Wendell Holmes and other realist legal theorists, even judges determine outcomes before checking whether they follow established legal principles.[4] But spontaneous impulses, according to some behavioral theories, carry the defects of fast

26 UNCERTAINTY AND ENTERPRISE

thinking. The discipline of making a reasoned argument can force us to correct these defects. Justifying our intuitions can also help overcome our hesitations about our impulses.

Justificatory discourse magnifies these benefits. An influential recent book, *The Enigma of Reason,* claims that evolution has made individual reason-giving naturally "lazy" and subject to self-serving, "myside" biases.[5] Even if this claim is valid—and I am skeptical—our conditioning and training encourage us to correct these biases before we try to sell our arguments to potential skeptics. Sales training, for example, teaches anticipating every objection that buyers might raise. Litigators, expert witnesses, politicians, and executives sometimes learn the hard way to prepare for hostile questioning. People who make lazy, myside arguments risk losing credibility. And dialogue with questioners can also fill in blind spots we had not anticipated.

Giving and taking reasons certainly has limitations. Self-interest can close minds. "It is difficult to get a man to understand something, when his salary depends on his not understanding it," as Upton Sinclair wrote.[6] Instead of correcting initial impulses, groupthink can reinforce unfounded prejudices, as in the 1692 Salem witch trials.[7] Deliberations can also waste time and increase personal animosities, as common experience of business, faculty, or town-hall meetings suggests. Deliberations may also kill unconventional or unformed ideas, produce compromises no one wants, or trigger default rules such as reliance on authority or keeping the status quo.

Competition Competitive markets are often seen as effective, decentralized alternatives to top-down authority for resolving disagreements. For example, which is better: Apple's "walled garden" iPhones or Google's more open Android ecosystem? Let the market decide. US Supreme Court Justice Oliver Wendell Holmes applied the metaphor of competitive markets to political disagreements, declaring in a famous 1919 dissenting opinion,

> If you have no doubt of your premises or your power and want a certain result with all your heart you naturally express your wishes in law and sweep away all opposition. . . . But when men have realized that time has upset many fighting faiths, they may come to believe even more than they believe the very foundations of their own conduct that the ultimate good desired is better reached by free trade in ideas—that the best test of truth is the power of the thought to get itself accepted in the competition of the market, and that truth is the only ground upon which their wishes safely can be carried out.[8]

The federal system of government in the United States is commended for its state-level experimentation. "A single, courageous State," Supreme Court Justice Louis D. Brandeis wrote, can "serve as a laboratory; and try novel social and economic experiments."[9] Governments and private organizations can sponsor contests. In 1714, the UK Parliament passed an act "providing a public Reward for such Person or Persons as shall discover the Longitude at Sea."[10] The reward spurred a race eventually won by John Harrison's pathbreaking clock. In 1882, Paul Wallot won a contest that attracted two hundred architects to design the Reichstag for the recently unified Germany.[11]

Competition also however requires authority and justification. Due to the multibillion-dollar costs, only a few mobile phone systems can enter the market. Extensive internal deliberation and debate, adjudicated by organizational hierarchies, decide the designs of Apple's walled garden and Google's Android ecosystem. More open markets also require systems of property rights. Legislatures and courts specify these rights after justificatory discourse, and their enforcement requires the coercive authority of the state. Likewise, federal systems of government do not experiment with all possible policies; only those initiatives successfully promoted and justified in state legislatures get a chance. Deciding the terms—and winners—of prizes (such as the 1714 longitudinal prize) and architectural contests (like the 1882 Reichstag design) also requires deliberation and debate within the prize-giving bodies.

2. Demand and Supply

Evidentiary Weights The impossibility of indisputable proof raises a question that Knight did not address: How much evidence and explanation do we need to justify uncertain choices? Or, differently put, how much "irreducible" uncertainty and gaps in our knowledge can we tolerate? The tolerances are personal for autonomous choices such as Jobs's dietary treatment. But for interdependent or collective activities, rules and conventions affect acceptable uncertainty. A physician who prescribed esoteric diets to treat patients with pancreatic cancers would risk disbarment.

Stakes, Uniqueness, and Complexity The magnitude of the stakes—the cost of a mistake or misjudgment—affects the conventional demand for justification. With low stakes, little evidence or explanation is expected. Physicians will diagnose most sprained ankles based on a quick physical exam. But if there is some sign of serious injuries, physicians will order—and patients may demand—X-rays, which can show broken bones, and MRIs, which produce detailed images

28 UNCERTAINTY AND ENTERPRISE

of soft tissues. For life-threatening diseases such as AIDS, diagnostic protocols specify a sequence of well-calibrated laboratory tests.

Uniqueness magnifies the effects of stakes. We naturally delegate choices about low-stake, routine matters to experienced practitioners, who may, in turn, reflexively follow tried-and-tested conventions. Unfamiliar problems and initiatives often demand more justification, especially if the stakes are high. For example, the Food and Drug Administration (FDA) can exempt from clinical trials new medical devices that the FDA accepts to be incremental extensions of previous devices. But with drugs—where the slightest modification of molecular structures can radically alter outcomes—the FDA requires rigorous multiyear trials.[12]

Uniqueness or novelty can also reduce the supply of credible justifications. Novel solutions and exceptional circumstances reduce the reliability of statistical inference because the old data may not be like the new case. Novelty can also make the background principles, precepts, and rules of thumb used to form contextual, case-specific judgments obsolete. Advances in the scientific understanding of schizophrenia can undermine precedents about insanity defenses, and improved knowledge of Sudden Infant Death Syndrome (SIDS) has similar implications for "cot death" prosecutions. Similarly, Google launching a natural-language, artificial intelligence–based search product, or Boeing developing an electric airplane cannot depend just on lessons derived from their existing products.

Complexity can affect the demand and supply of justifications by making choices unique. Even if the individual elements of a complex choice are standard, their arrangement and interconnections may be unprecedented. Moreover, conflicting inferences suggested by the individual elements can introduce doubt. If in a murder trial, for example, motive, opportunity, forensic evidence, and so on, all point to guilt, then confidence about the overall inference will be high. However, if the individual inferences conflict, any overall conclusion will be difficult to justify.*

Cultural and Technological Influences Conservative attitudes toward new technologies, such as driverless cars or genetically modified foods and crops, encourage strict safety reviews, increasing the demand for justification. Conversely, venturesome attitudes reduce demands: If we crave novelty we are more willing

---

* Recall defense lawyer Johnnie Cochran's refrain in his successful closing argument to jurors in O. J. Simpson's double-murder trial in 1995: "If it doesn't fit, you must acquit." The prosecution had earlier asked Simpson to try on leather gloves the killer was believed to have worn. Simpson seemed to struggle to tug on the gloves, which may have shrunk from forensic testing conducted before the trial, and was heard by jurors to mutter, "Too tight." Cochran's refrain referred not just to the gloves but also sought to paint the prosecution's case as uneven. "Those gloves didn't fit," Cochran said in his closing. "The gloves didn't fit Mr. Simpson because he is not the killer" (details at Campbell 2020).

to take our chances. Progress is also a snowballing source of uniqueness. It creates opportunities for further advances whose success or failure cannot be predicted from historical data, thus reducing the supply of justification.[13]

3. Justificatory Routines

Organizational Specialization Individuals who bear the full consequences of their choices do not have to justify them. But autonomous decisions made by self-reliant individuals usually have low stakes—apart from the potential losses the decision-makers face. In contrast, public and private organizations can have both the responsibility and the capacity to make high-stakes choices and undertake high-stakes initiatives. Criminal courts, for example, can impose severe punishments—or can acquit people accused of heinous crimes. The FDA can approve or reject life-saving—or life-threatening—treatments. And companies in the pharmaceutical, semiconductor, and aerospace industries, like Merck, Intel, and Boeing, can invest shareholder funds in megaprojects where the stakes run into billions of dollars.

High stakes require or encourage organizations to use strict evaluation routines that embody a high demand for verifiable evidence. Organizations that serve a high-stakes public purpose face mandates that help reassure the public that these organizations will take their responsibilities seriously. For example, the 1962 legislation authorizing the FDA to evaluate the efficacy of new drugs required "adequate and well-controlled studies." Congress also made it clear that the studies would have to both randomly allocate patients to control and therapeutic groups and standardize criteria for judging effectiveness.[14] In contrast, local authorities that certify taxi drivers or hairdressers have broad discretion. Similarly, criminal trials follow structured rules and procedures that require prosecutors to establish "beyond reasonable doubt" guilt, while traffic court judges can, on cursory evidence, summarily fine drivers for speeding.

In business, the governance and managerial procedures of companies like Merck, Intel, and Boeing embody strict routines to scrutinize large investments in new drugs, semiconductors, and airliners. And because even modest modifications, such as a new logo on a McDonald's Happy Meal box, can have significant repercussions, seemingly trivial changes also face scrutiny. The strict routines help reassure stockholders that managers will make high-stakes choices responsibly. Small business owners can make such choices on impulse, but they lack the resources for high-stakes projects.

Bias against Uniqueness As mentioned, uniqueness or novelty reduces the supply of confidence-producing discourse. Therefore, the strict routines used by

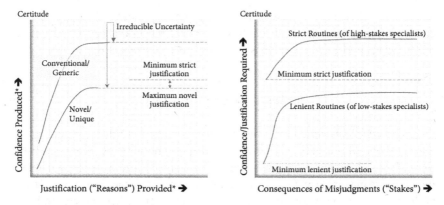

Figure 3.1 How Strict Routines Discourage Novel Deviations

* Irreducible uncertainty limits how much justification can be provided and, thus, how much confidence can be produced.

organizations specializing in high-stakes activities also reduce their tolerance for unique or novel deviations from conventional practices that cannot satisfy high justificatory standards (see Figure 3.1).

Process   Mainstream economics focuses on outcomes, not the process of choice. As we will see, heterodox scholars like Richard Nelson, Herbert Simon, and Sidney Winter analyzed decision-making processes, including routines, putting their work outside the mainstream. And even they typically modeled routines as computerized, algorithmic procedures without justificatory discourse or human give-and-take. Such discourse plays a critical role in my conjectures. In my conjectures—and in observed practice—strict routines for high-stakes choices often require extended deliberation, not just more evidence. Investment committees, juries, FDA panels, and professors making tenure decisions do not just vote on the evidence presented to them. They aim for consensus through discussion and debate. This aim of achieving consensus also favors choices that can be strongly justified and a multi-stage process that can reach agreement at an acceptable cost.

Staged Justifications

Drug development typically starts with cheap, quick in-vitro tests of potentially therapeutic molecules. It continues through increasingly costly and time-consuming in-vivo tests, animal experiments, and human trials. The human trials also proceed in phases designed to produce progressively more reliable evidence of efficacy and safety. The costs also progressively increase, but developers (or the FDA) can stop at any point if the evidence secured does not justify continuing. Even starting the process requires some evidence of a potentially desirable outcome. A murder trial is similarly the culmination of an uncertainty-reducing process starting with showing that a crime was committed, then identifying persons of interest, then suspects, then securing enough evidence to justify an arrest, and ultimately deciding whether to prosecute and for what charges. Here, too, starting and continuing the process must be justified by the evidence already accumulated.

Qualifications Individuals with charismatic authority (to use Max Weber's term) can ignore the usual requirements for justification. Founder-CEOs with larger-than-life personalities and a history of "seeing around corners," such as Apple's Steve Jobs and Tesla's Elon Musk, can wave aside questions about visionary, high-stakes schemes. Instead, they can follow nineteenth-century British prime minister Benjamin Disraeli's motto: "Never complain, never explain."

Executives with positional authority also have the power to act unilaterally. Uncharismatic CEOs with no record of astute dealmaking can negotiate multibillion-dollar acquisitions over dinner, relying on the pro-forma approval of pliant boards of directors. In the public sphere, FDA officials have the authority to override the recommendations of the expert panels they have appointed to evaluate clinical trial results.[15] Federal prosecutors have broad discretion in deciding whom to prosecute. Their decisions can technically be contested for selective prosecution or vindictiveness, but such challenges are difficult to sustain.[16]

Functional Reasonableness Besides the number of stages, several other variables characterize routines to evaluate and justify choices (see Table 3.1).

The designs are often "emergent"; they evolve after problems arise and because of changes in the organization's charter, purpose, or leadership. Nonetheless, justificatory routines that stand the test of time develop what Simon called "functional" rationality: they fit the stakes, uniqueness, and complexity of what the organizations usually do and the social zeitgeist. The next chapter reviews how functionally rational routines affect the conduct of commercial enterprise in technologically advanced and venturesome societies, exemplified by the United States.

32 UNCERTAINTY AND ENTERPRISE

Table 3.1 Design Variables

Matters requiring justification. What requires justification instead of being left to a boss with positional authority, a technical expert, or Hayek's knowledgeable "on-the-spot" decision-maker?

Case-specificity and evidence. To what degree are uncertainties resolved case by case rather than statistically? How much and what kind of evidence is allowed or required? How many items ("variables")? Are surrogate ("indirect") indicators and personal ("subjective") impressions allowed?

Extent of justifications. When and to what degree do the routines tolerate unresolved doubts? Who decides the degree? And how strictly do the generalizations supporting specific contextual or statistical inferences themselves require justification?

Evaluators and agreements. Who judges the adequacy of justification—one or several individuals? Internal or external reviewers? Interested parties or impartial outsiders? How much agreement (majority, supermajority, unanimity) do justifications aim to produce? And what is the default if agreements cannot be reached?

Procedures. Are reviews and deliberations quick or extended? Progressive or single-stage? Standardized and codified? Synchronous (as in jury deliberations) or asynchronous (as in peer reviews of grant proposals)?

4

Applications to Enterprise

The conjectures outlined in the last chapter derive their plausibility from everyday experience. As we will see in Part 2, they are also grounded in the ideas of some towering twentieth-century intellects, including John Maynard Keynes and Herbert Simon. But I cannot demonstrate their validity through logico-scientific methods (more on that in Part 4). Instead, I illustrate their utility through two entrepreneurial applications. The applications—analogous to the extended range and comfort of a modern e-bike—are covered in detail in Parts 3 and 4. In this chapter, I preview

- Why entrepreneurship is a suitable venue for my applications.

- The two applications, namely how uncertainty affects the specialization of entrepreneurial initiatives and the nature of entrepreneurial discourse.

- What lies ahead in the next parts of the book.

1. Why Entrepreneurship?

Surging Interest William Baumol's 1968 article in the *American Economic Review* lamented the absence of the entrepreneur from economic theory. The entrepreneur, Baumol wrote, had frequently appeared in the writings of classical economists but as a "shadowy entity without clearly defined form and function." Only Schumpeter and Knight had "infus[ed] him with life" and "assign[ed] to him a specific area of activity to any extent commensurate with his acknowledged importance." Subsequently, the entrepreneur had "virtually disappeared from the theoretical literature."[1]

The theoretical firm, Baumol continued, was now "entrepreneurless—the Prince of Denmark ha[d] been expunged from the discussion of *Hamlet*." The firm was assumed to "perform a mathematical calculation which yields optimal (i.e., profit maximizing) values for all of its decision variables." There was "no room for enterprise or initiative. The management group becomes a passive calculator that reacts mechanically to changes imposed on it by fortuitous external developments over which it does not exert, and does not even attempt to exert, any influence. One hears of no clever ruses, ingenious schemes, brilliant innovations, of no charisma or of any of the other stuff of which outstanding

Uncertainty and Enterprise. Amar Bhidé, Oxford University Press. © Oxford University Press 2025.
DOI: 10.1093/oso/9780197688359.003.0004

34 UNCERTAINTY AND ENTERPRISE

entrepreneurship is made; one does not hear of them because there is no way in which they can fit into the model."[2]

In my analysis, the developments in microeconomics during and after the 1930s (detailed in chapter 6) that excluded uncertainty from mainstream theory also banished entrepreneurship. Then, starting in the 1990s, business schools went on a hiring spree for new faculty to satisfy surging demand for entrepreneurship courses.[3] Many of the new faculty hired were capable, ambitious young economists. They secured tenure through prolific publications on entrepreneurial topics in top economics journals. Their success encouraged more such research (as discussed in chapter 13).

Complementary Potential The recruits did not, however, emphasize uncertainty in their research. Mainstream economics had continued down the explicitly uncertainty-free path it started on in the 1930s (reviewed in chapters 6 and 7). As we will see, the popular new specialties in economics focused on concerns about misaligned incentives, not doubts about misjudgments. And while young economists had ample scope for researching entrepreneurial topics, such as venture capital contracts, if they wished to get published in top journals (and thus tenure), they could not stray far from the mainstream. Baumol's Hamlet was now firmly in the kingdom—but without the doubts of Shakespeare's protagonist.

It is hard to imagine entrepreneurial initiatives that do not involve meaningful doubts about one-offs. Including such doubts thus offers a significant opportunity for scholarly inquiry grounded in real-world concerns. At the same time, we do not have to reject mainstream concerns about misaligned incentives. Including the conjectures about doubts and justification described in the last chapter can add to our knowledge of enterprise, coexisting with the research done using mainstream incentive-centric approaches.

2. Specialization and Discourse

Lost Cause Knight's 1921 book distinguished between uncertainty and risk for a reason: to propose that true profit requires bearing (taking "responsibility" for) uncertainty rather than risk. In Knight's theory, providing capital for risks that can be calculated from the laws of probability or statistical tables only earns the going market rate for risk-bearing. (*Conceptually*, according to Knight, the market rate of return must be excluded from true profit, although no one actually does this.) Moreover, responsibility for uncertainty is an entrepreneurial function, and the return for performing this function is the source of an entrepreneur's profit.[4]

Although I find Knight's "no-uncertainty, no-profit" thesis appealing, I see little hope of its acceptance in mainstream economics. As I show in Part 2, economics has well-established theories of profit that ignore uncertainty. Instead of debating the true nature of entrepreneurial profits, I try to show how my modified version of uncertainty helps explain the specialization of enterprise in the organizations that populate the entrepreneurial ecosystem and the role of entrepreneurial discourse.

Specialization When Knight's book was published in 1921, large, professionally managed firms were transforming the entrepreneurial landscape. Knight presciently saw the rise of large firms as an important development for entrepreneurship. But his as-it-was-happening account did not include historian Alfred Chandler's retrospective raison d'être of large corporations: realizing significant economies of scale and scope. Furthermore, Knight depicted decisions in large organizations as following a simple vertical order. Employees on lower rungs exercise judgment in routine matters, passing up nonroutine matters to bosses.

But economies of scale and scope demand more than simple hierarchies, as Chandler later documented. Businesses attempting to achieve these economies face severe coordination problems. Organizational pyramids and top-down control cannot ensure the alignment of the many parts and activities. Yet misspecification of small parts, like the O-ring seal in the space shuttle *Challenger's* rocket booster, can have catastrophic consequences. Large corporations cope, as best they can, by establishing intricate, consultative routines with inputs from specialized staff and multifunctional teams to complement hierarchical control. Strict routines also protect stockholders from managerial carelessness. This helps give public companies access to substantial permanent capital, enabling them to undertake complex megaprojects.

Routines to control mistakes and misjudgments also impose unintended but unavoidable restrictions. They discourage small projects whose profit potential cannot absorb the fixed planning and oversight costs. Requirements for objective evidence and consensus similarly deter initiatives with high uncertainty about customers, technologies, and competitors. For example, large corporations avoid highly novel projects, as mentioned, or more generally, initiatives where they cannot objectively evaluate paths to sustainable profits.

The unintended restrictions provide space for self-financed (or informally financed) entrepreneurs to undertake small, simple initiatives in unsettled markets and rely on their personal capacities to seize fleeting opportunities. Likewise, professional venture capitalists (VCs) and angel investors are not as spontaneous or ad-hoc as self-financed entrepreneurs, but their justificatory requirements are not as strict as those of large public corporations. These

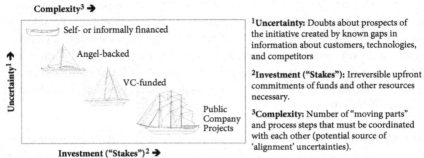

Figure 4.1 Map of Entrepreneurial Specialization[5]

"in-between" requirements encourage VCs and angel investors to specialize in ventures involving intermediate funding needs, uncertainty, and complexity (as shown in Figure 4.1).

This hypothesis about specialization emphasizes the value of a diverse entrepreneurial ecology. For example, venture capital alone cannot sustain widespread opportunities for material advancement and creative adventure. The underlying uncertainty-based reasoning likewise helps us see the advantages of often-mocked large-company routines. These routines do not just help the trains run on time. They undergird the development of railroads and are as indispensable for complex technological advances as time-consuming jury trials are for a civilized criminal justice system.

My hypothesis also suggests that economically significant initiatives cluster along a diagonal running from the northwestern to the southeastern corner of my map. Projects with high uncertainty and high resource requirements (the empty northeastern space in Figure 4.1) are natural nonstarters. Entrepreneurs cannot self-finance such projects, while in-house promoters cannot satisfy the strict routines of large organizations that have the necessary funds and coordination capacities. Conversely, when uncertainty is low (i.e., below the diagonal), so are the profit prospects—and thus also the scope for outside financing.*

Imaginative Discourse Entrepreneurial ideas emerge from a creative process that combines facts and imagination. Entrepreneurs do not merely observe or notice facts. They imaginatively interpret what they observe or notice. Imagination is particularly important in entrepreneurship that goes beyond simply buying

---

* The southwestern space is not empty, however. Founders of low-potential / low-uncertainty businesses—who just want to find jobs for themselves—cluster there (as discussed in chapter 14).

low to sell high. The innovative entrepreneur must imagine what could be and a plausible path for getting there. Almost by definition (and Knight's thesis), information gaps preclude deducing the desired destination and path through logic or statistical analysis. If sufficient information for logical or reliable statistical inference existed, there would be no opportunity for profit, as I keep reminding students in my entrepreneurship classes.

Moreover, promoters of an enterprise cannot just imagine desired future states and feasible paths. They must also persuade financiers, customers, employees, and others that their imagined scheme is worth supporting. Here, too, promoters cannot merely provide objective facts and signal their confidence in their ventures by putting their own money in them. They must also engage in imaginative discourse that is more writerly than logico-scientific, using figurative language, metaphors, and imagined events.

The discourse entails paradoxes: for example, adding imagined detail makes imagined futures and paths more believable. A detailed spreadsheet model with made-up but defensible numbers is better than not having a model. This is not a con job aimed at naive targets or the peddling of a trippy, hallucinatory fantasy. Imaginative justification and discourse are necessary to overcome the doubts that discourage hard-nosed investors from funding, astute employees from joining, and skeptical customers from buying the offerings of entrepreneurial ventures. Yet the justifications must be *groundedly* imaginative, not pure fantasy.

Broadening Mainstream Views   The kind of specialization shown in Figure 4.1—and the routines that help shape it—fall outside the scope of mainstream economic models in which no justification is demanded or supplied. These conventional models emphasize problems of slacking, lying, and cheating (controlled by aligning incentives) rather than misjudgments (controlled by justificatory routines).

Economic theories also typically ignore stories or other kinds of rich communication used to justify or share ideas. In textbook theories of decentralized markets, autonomous buyers and sellers have fully formed preferences and transact if the price is right. Or, as in Hayek's paper mentioned earlier, price changes coordinate dispersed producers and consumers: rising (or falling) prices alone evoke changes in supply and demand. Conversely, theories of hierarchical control posit top-down commands or ratification of subordinates' proposals.[6] In either case, there are no mutual doubts about fallible judgments, no anxiety about outcomes, and no constructive role for storylike discourse. According to these theories, persuasive *pathos* can only deceive.[7] Dialogue to forestall or correct coordination problems is also absent.

38 UNCERTAINTY AND ENTERPRISE

Excluding narrative-mode discourse (chapter 18) raises questions about the scope of economics. The Scientific Revolution attacked and replaced animism with naturalistic theories about inert objects that had no will of their own. Scientific economics brought the ethos of the natural sciences into the human sphere, modeling free markets without any actual free will (although it kept the Aristotelian concept of predestined striving). This unnatural naturalism limits our understanding of how we live and work together and our discourse about its improvement. Adding the sensibilities found in the humanities (particularly history and literature) and the law (which stresses human intentions, doubts, and imaginations) thus has both theoretical and practical value.

My book takes a few steps toward such broadening. According to an influential 'paradigmatic' view (reviewed in the next chapter), specific, archetypal problems and solutions shape normal scientific research. Concrete, internalized examples, not abstract constructs, guide what scientists actually do.[8] Similarly, even if mainstream economists question my general conjectures, I hope the concrete applications help broaden their acceptable problems and explanations in areas beyond entrepreneurship.

3. What Lies Ahead

Part 2 (chapters 5–12) describes how mainstream economic theories[*] obstruct an uncertainty-based view of enterprise, but some forgotten ideas provide helpful guidance. This is the most technical part of the book and the one in which the reactions of economists and noneconomists are most likely to diverge.

I hope economists excuse my simplified comparisons of mainstream and forgotten ideas. My intention isn't to disparage mainstream theories but rather to show how the forgotten theories could improve our understanding of the present-day world. Exploring the unfamiliar may also deepen economists' understandings of the familiar. As Rudyard Kipling's 1891 poem asks, "What do they know of England who only England know?"

Other readers may find the chapters a useful (if idiosyncratic and partial) introduction to important economic ideas, even if they struggle with unfamiliar terms and constructs. Both economists and noneconomists, I hope, find the intellectual histories and biographical sketches included in the chapters

---

[*] I rely on representation in National Bureau of Economic Research (NBER) working groups and in articles published in the top financial and economic journals as proxies for "mainstream" ideas. I do not, however, comprehensively review the mainstream specialties. I focus instead on placing my conjectures about uncertainty in mainstream "microeconomic" maps while saying little about macroeconomic aggregates.

stimulating. (Moreover, the modular structure allows readers who find the material gets too simplistic or confusing to skip ahead to Parts 3 and 4).

Part 3 (chapters 13–17) contains the first of the two applications summarized above, on the specialization of entrepreneurship. The chapters proceed down the "southeasterly diagonal" of Figure 4.1: chapter 14 covers self-financed entrepreneurs; chapter 15, ventures backed by angel investors and VCs; and chapters 16 and 17, projects undertaken by large public companies.

Part 4 (chapters 18–21) covers the role of imaginative discourse. The chapters are at once furthest from standard economics, prevailing popular views of storytelling, and my own beliefs before I started this book. The concluding chapter—a Part 5 coda—pleads for widening the field of view of economics, without abandoning existing ideas. It also examines broader social and political problems, beyond commercial enterprise, through the lens of uncertainty.

PART II
FORMIDABLE OBSTACLES, FORGOTTEN BEACONS

Compiled from images downloaded from the Smithsonian's Open Access collection. The bottom left image is Henry Wolf's *North-Easter*, 1908. The image to the top right is Miner Kilbourne Kellogg's *Lighthouse, Civitavecchia*, 1843.

5

Frank Knight: The Spark That Did Not Ignite

I shall conclude by recalling a conversation with Professor Ronald H. Coase when he and I were colleagues at the University of Virginia, where Frank Knight had visited for an extended period. Coase and I were walking along Mr. Jefferson's Lawn, and we had been discussing famous economists. Ronald said something like the following to me. "I can think of almost any famous economist, like '_____,' '_____,' or '_____,'" naming the obvious world-renowned figures in our discipline as evaluated from the perspective of the early 1960s, "and I can sort of imagine myself in their position of fame with a bit of luck, persistence, and effort. But I simply cannot imagine myself to be like Frank Knight. I guess that amounts to saying that Knight is a genius." I have always remembered that conversation because Coase put so well what so many of us feel when we think of the professor from whom we learned so much.

—James Buchanan (1982)

The historical tour in this and the other chapters of Part 2 aims to understand why Knightian uncertainty never took off and what could obstruct its modernization.[1]

Frank Knight and his 1921 book are a natural first stop. The legacy of the man and the book are curious. Revered by distinguished students, Knight was by all accounts an incomprehensible lecturer. Skeptical and cantankerous but not a hermit, Knight helped found the University of Chicago's legendary interdisciplinary Committee on Social Thought. His doctoral dissertation, published as *Risk, Uncertainty and Profit* became a classic—a dream result for any PhD student—but no other landmark publications or research followed.

How mainstream economics treated Knight's book is noteworthy. As mentioned, Knight's claims about uncertainty and profit never entered formal economics. Incongruously, his book's most enduring, if unnoticed, legacy seems to be its analysis of competition in the *absence* of uncertainty.[2] According to Nobel Laureate and Knight's Chicago student George Stigler, Knight's definition of perfect, uncertainty-free competition was "an enormously influential

---

Uncertainty and Enterprise. Amar Bhidé, Oxford University Press. © Oxford University Press 2025.
DOI: 10.1093/oso/9780197688359.003.0005

44 UNCERTAINTY AND ENTERPRISE

part of the book." Thanks to the book's "clear and succinct statement of neoclassical price theory . . . Lionel Robbins made it a basic text at the London School of Economics."[3] Yet Knight had analyzed uncertainty-free competition as a steppingstone to showing how true profit requires uncertainty. Stigler found this part of the book "lack[ing] substantive structure."[4]

The rest of this chapter discusses three possible reasons that Knight's ideas about uncertainty failed to catch on.

- Knight's writing style, possibly reflecting his haphazard education, is challenging.

- Knight did not follow through with his ideas about uncertainty.

- Mainstream economics developed a scientific paradigm—opposed by Knight—that became a formidable barrier to uncertainty-based research.

1. Problems of Writing Style

Knight's writing limits the influence of his book and thus of Knightian uncertainty. Even sympathizers call it "complex and difficult to interpret" and Knight's approach "murky."[5] Others are more scathing. Economists Stephen LeRoy and Larry Singell, for example, express "much sympathy for those who take away from *Risk, Uncertainty and Profit* the opinion that Knight simply had no very clear idea of what he was talking about." They scorn the book's imprecise writing and "extended Austrian-style disquisitions on the foundations of human knowledge and conduct." "Almost all readers," they assert, "will at times despair of extracting any core of original insight from the overripe fruit of Knight's prose."[6]

Knight's inaccessible prose style may reflect his background, the origins of his book, and his skeptical temperament. Knight had a haphazard early education; his teachers likely did not stress elegant prose. He wrote *Risk, Uncertainty and Profit* (RUP) as a PhD dissertation—an oeuvre that does not always require clear writing.

The Making of a Maverick

Frank Hyneman Knight, born in 1885, was the oldest of eleven children of an Illinois farm family. When Frank was twelve, his father took him out of school to work on the farm. Knight nonetheless read avidly, somehow propping books on the frame of a horse-drawn plow. Around that time, Knight was baptized, following the Evangelical custom—but influenced by a free-thinking humanist, he became a skeptical antidogmatist. This attitude would extend far beyond a distaste for organized religion (although he retained a deep interest in theology and delivered sermons in Unitarian churches).[7]

A contract he had earlier made with his father returned Knight to school when he turned eighteen. He enrolled at a high school in Kentucky, lodging with his mother's family, the Hynemans. His mother's younger brother, Uncle Lev, just seven years older than his nephew, became a "major influence."[8] Lev started a bicycle repair shop while still in school and started the Lexington Home Telephone Company in 1897. Knight worked there as a nighttime switch operator when he lived in the Hyneman home. Political economist (and leading Knight historian) Ross Emmett speculates that observing his uncle's telephone business might have influenced Knight's views of entrepreneurship and uncertainty.[9]

In 1905, the soon-to-be twenty-year-old started at a now-defunct religious college in eastern Tennessee. He left after two years, when the college faced severe financial difficulties, and found a secretarial position in Virginia for an employer who soon declared bankruptcy. A second secretarial position in Milligan College, another small Christian institution in eastern Tennessee, followed. Knight also taught shorthand and typing at Milligan—and took courses that earned him a bachelor's degree from the college in 1911. He then earned a second bachelor's (in the sciences) and a master's in German from the University of Tennessee.[10]

In 1913, Knight, now twenty-seven, won a scholarship for a PhD in philosophy at Cornell University. But, after a year, he switched to economics, banished from philosophy by a professor who had high regard for Knight's intellect but thought Knight's "ingrained skepticism" would "destroy the true philosophic spirit wherever he touches it."[11] Knight wrote his dissertation, "A Theory of Business Profit," and, on the promise of polishing and publishing it later, got a PhD in 1916. The following year, Knight submitted a version of the dissertation in an essay contest. It came in second to "The Results of Municipal Electric Lighting in Massachusetts," which one Edmund Lincoln had written for his Harvard PhD.[12]

In 1921, Houghton Mifflin published a revised and extended version of Knight's second-place essay per their agreement with the contest organizers. With this publication, as a book titled *Risk, Uncertainty and Profit*, Knight finally fulfilled the promise that had secured him a waiver from Cornell's rules for PhD degrees. By then, Knight had joined the economics faculty at the University of Iowa, where he would teach for ten years before moving to the University of Chicago.[13]

46   UNCERTAINTY AND ENTERPRISE

Knight's epistemological, ethical, and psychological qualifications make RUP's arguments difficult to disentangle. Thus, while Knight favored the aspiration of theoretical economics to become an exact science like physics, he acknowledged that it was a "human science." And because economic conduct is often not "rational or planned," this imposes "notable restrictions" on theoretical economics. The extensive acknowledgment of the "restrictions" and the paradoxes they produce often swamp Knight's main arguments in RUP.[14]

2. No Follow-Through

In 1927, Knight returned to the University of Chicago, where he had previously taught for two years. Cornell tried to lure him away from Chicago in 1928 and Harvard in 1929. But Knight continued teaching at Chicago until 1958 and remained there until he died[15] in 1972 at age eighty-seven. The university was hospitable to Knight's broad interests and appointed him Professor of the Social Sciences and Philosophy.[16]

Knight is "usually considered to be the founder of the Chicago school of economics."* His doctoral students included Nobel Prize winners and libertarian-conservative icons Milton Friedman, George Stigler, and James Buchanan. Knight cofounded the anticollectivist Mont Pelerin Society with a group Friedrich Hayek had convened that included Friedman and Stigler. Despite their "notoriously diffuse presentation," his lectures turned incoming "soft socialists," like Buchanan, into libertarians.[17] Hayek called Knight "the man who among Americans has probably done most to spread an understanding of the working of a free society."[18]

Yet Knight had a "deep ambivalence" about capitalist societies and refused to "extol the virtues of markets without drawing attention to their manifest limitations and sins." In a 1922 essay, he wrote that the "economic man is the selfish, ruthless object of moral condemnation."[19] Before the 1932 presidential election, Knight addressed the University of Chicago's Communist Club on why "those who want[ed] a change and wish[ed] to vote intelligently should vote

---

* Stigler (1985 *Preface*). Note the "usually." Moreover, Stigler (1985, 2) writes that Knight was "clearly the dominant intellectual influence upon economics students at Chicago *in the nineteen thirties*" (italics added). And Buchanan (1982, ix–x) pointedly calls Knight, "the primary intellectual source for the *original*, or *pre-Friedman*, 'Chicago school' of economics." Buchanan notes that "Knight put his stamp on several generations of students who learned *economics with philosophical overtones*" (italics added)—not a salient feature of cut-and-dried Friedmanite economic methodologies.

Communist."[20] According to Stigler, Knight relentlessly asserted that a "competitive enterprise system inherently leads to a cumulative increase in the inequality of the distribution of income." Friedman challenged this at "countless lunches." Each time, Knight would "make temporary concessions only to return to his standard position by the next lunch."[21]

Knight's heresies included methodology. In a biting *Journal of Political Economy* essay, he wrote that "the saying often quoted from Lord Kelvin [that] 'where you cannot measure your knowledge is meagre and unsatisfactory,'" was, in the social sciences, "misleading and pernicious ... Insistence on a concretely quantitative economics means the use of statistics of physical magnitudes, whose economic meaning and significance is uncertain and dubious ... The Kelvin dictum very largely means in practice, 'if you cannot measure, measure anyhow!' ... Perhaps we do not 'know' that our friends really are our friends; in any case an attempt to measure their friendship would hardly make the knowledge either more certain or more 'satisfactory'!"[22]

Here, too, Knight departed from Friedman's methodological approach. Under the emerging norms of disciplinary economics, that Friedman influenced, economists would only accept propositions they could logically deduce from first principles or verify through objective data. But the uncertainty-profit thesis, although intuitive, is purely definitional. Uncertainty and true profit, as Knight defines the terms, are both conceptual, not measurable. Their relationship, therefore, cannot be falsified or supported by objective data. Furthermore, Knight's "no uncertainty, no profit" formulation does not imply "more uncertainty, more profit."

Knight did not try to nurture a community to advance his ideas about profit and uncertainty. RUP was Knight's "only effort in this area. His subsequent career led elsewhere, so he did not engage with subsequent interpretations of this work."[23] Some scholars claim that Knight later renounced or downplayed his distinction between risk and uncertainty.[24] And unlike Milton Friedman, Knight was not interested in a broad audience which might have attracted attention to his work. Friedman produced a popular TV show, *Free to Choose*; wrote columns that went head-to-head with Paul Samuelson's; and advised presidents and prime ministers.

In contrast, writes Buchanan, Knight "did not address his words to the agents who might hold positions of governmental political power over others. Even in a remote conceptual sense, Knight was not an adviser to governments, a characteristic that, in itself, separates Knight from so many of his fellow economists, in his time and now."[25]

48   UNCERTAINTY AND ENTERPRISE

3. Paradigmatic Barriers

Overall, during his long career at Chicago, Knight and mainstream economics were ships sailing in opposite directions. The first sentence of Knight's 1921 book tells us that economics is "the only one of the social sciences which has aspired to the distinction of an exact science."[26] In subsequent decades, economics went much further in this direction. It adopted what the philosopher of science Thomas Kuhn called the "paraphernalia of specialization" that gives sciences their "prestige"[27] and a supporting "paradigm."

Paradigms, per Thomas Kuhn

According to Kuhn, who established its present-day meaning, scientific paradigms "define the legitimate problems and methods of a research field."[28] In the pre-paradigmatic stage, scientists record several facts and observations but with competing explanations fitting different facts. Paradigm-enabling breakthroughs combine "two essential characteristics." First, they explain a wide range of facts. This "achievement" is "sufficiently unprecedented to attract an enduring group of adherents away from competing modes of scientific activity." For example, gravitation explained the parabolic paths of cannonballs on Earth and the elliptical orbits of planets in the skies. Darwin's theory of evolution explained a vast diversity of life forms. A second essential characteristic is that the breakthroughs are "sufficiently open-ended to leave all sorts of problems for the redefined group of practitioners to resolve."[29] Modern physics and evolutionary biology began and did not end with Newton's and Darwin's contributions. They were seminal, not terminal.

The two characteristics enable research communities to undertake "normal science." Compelling, unified explanations legitimize agreements that researchers do not question. The "open-endedness" is also crucial because it gives researchers something to do. A breakthrough that solved everything would not; if breakthrough discoveries were a job requirement, few scientists would find employment.

Paradigms are typically tacit and unspoken, cultural rather than codified. They do not require a common acceptance or understanding of the basic assumptions or "axioms." What researchers do and how they do it defines their "paradigm." The doing produces agreements about pertinent problems, methods for solving those problems, and solutions the researchers consider acceptable.[30] Kuhn's scientists do not even need to make their axioms explicit "in order to know how to 'go on,'" writes the Cambridge philosopher of science John Forrester. "A paradigm is what you use when 'you don't have to have agreement about the axioms.'"[31]

Paradigmatic theories, writes Kuhn, are learned by the "study of *applications* including practice problem-solving both with a pencil and paper and with instruments in the laboratory. If, for example, the student of Newtonian dynamics *ever discovers* [italics added] the meaning of terms like 'force,' 'mass,' 'space,' and 'time,' he does so less from the incomplete though sometimes helpful definitions in his text than by observing and participating in the application of these concepts to problem-solution."[32]

The unspoken agreements and half-understood concepts, internalized through paradigmatic examples, profoundly influence normal scientific research. The agreements accelerate advances by aligning the efforts of many scientists, but they also discourage unconventional research. Only a confidence-shattering crisis, produced by the accumulation of observations contradicting basic, unquestioned assumptions, creates room for a new paradigm.[33]

Like communities in the natural sciences, economists developed and enforced conventions for acceptable methods and results. Deductive equilibrium models—mathematical derivations of what eventually happens under certain assumptions—"axioms"—emerged as the gold standard.

Axioms, Old and New

The dictionary, writes Marsay, defines an axiom as a "self-evident truth." This usage applies to much of Euclidean geometry, which starts with self-evidently valid assumptions. But in modern mathematics, axioms "are just those propositions about the truth of which mathematics is silent."[34] Economics has followed a similar progression. Like ancient geometry, it started with seemingly self-evident tendencies, like the desire for wealth (as stipulated by John Stuart Mill). Now, like modern mathematics, standard economic theory uses axioms as starting points for mathematical deduction. Any claim to real-world validity lies mainly in the correspondence of the deductions with observable statistical data. Moreover, economists, like other scientists, internalize their axioms by doing, by repeatedly solving "pencil and paper" problems, and by application. No deep understanding of what they really mean is required.

50 UNCERTAINTY AND ENTERPRISE

Initially, economists merely favored research that followed the emerging paradigmatic methods, but over time, they virtually required it. The top economics journals now summarily reject submissions without an equilibrium model or statistical tests of equilibrium models. And top journal publications make or break careers. According to University of Chicago economics Nobel prize winner, James Heckman, tenure committees often rely on counting papers published in the "top five" journals, instead of carefully reading the candidate's work.[35]

Moreover, observes Stanford economist David Kreps, economics is the only social science that has a robust and cohesive paradigm, although it isn't otherwise more scientific than the other social sciences. The paradigm provides "a way of approaching questions in the economic and social realm, which we [economists] apply the way religious missionaries apply the catechisms of their faiths, namely without doubt or question."[36]

Knight took a different approach. "For Knight, the primary role of economic theory," Stigler wrote in his 1985 tribute, was "to contribute to the understanding of how by consensus based upon rational discussion we can fashion a liberal society in which individual freedom is preserved and a satisfactory economic performance achieved.... That is why the larger part of Knight's writings are outside of technical economics; indeed, that is why Knight did not return to the subjects constituting the main contributions of RUP."[37]

Knight was "unawed by either the 'wisdom of the ages' or the potential censure of his peers in the academy," Buchanan writes. He "did not preach a gospel (despite the old University of Chicago saying that 'there is no God, but Frank Knight is his prophet'). There was, to him, no gospel to be preached. He made no effort to present the 'truth according to Frank Knight.' He taught that 'truth' was whatever emerged from the free discussion of reasonable men who approached the dialogue without prejudice and as good sports."[38]

Continues Buchanan, "As he himself acknowledged, and as many others have recognized, Frank Knight was essentially a critic. His work, aside from *Risk, Uncertainty and Profit*, can be interpreted as a series of long book reviews. His 'social function' was that of exposing the fallacies, nonsense, and absurdities in what was passed off as sophisticated-scientific discourse."[39]

Knight believed that the task for economists was "located squarely at the level of elementary common sense," not science, and had "a highly skeptical attitude" toward "empirical research." He would find "particularly disturbing" the old-fashioned image of man as a wealth maximizer that "the modern emphasis on empirical testability forces on the economist." The reemergence of *Homo economicus* reflects "retrogression into a simplistic and wrongheaded usage of the valuable insights that economic theory can offer. *Homo economicus* exists in every man, but one of Knight's most persistent themes through all his works is that there exist all sorts of other men (the romantic fool, the sportsman who enjoys the fray, the prejudiced ignoramus, the man who wants to be a 'better' man) alongside the rational maximizer of economic interest."[40]

Knight "categorically rejected the elitism too often met in the academy and at the same time reaffirmed his own faith in a society of free men. While he remained always pessimistic as to its potential realization, such a society was, for Knight, the only one worthy of serious consideration."[41]

For better or worse, Knight was on the wrong side of history. His 1921 prediction that "mathematical economics . . . seems likely to remain little more than a cult"[42] couldn't have been more wrong. Knight's long editorship helped put the University of Chicago's *Journal of Political Economy* (the *JPE*) in the very top tier—and he published many of his own math- and statistics-free articles in it. Now the *JPE* sternly enforces the discipline's methodological purity.

Instead of Knight's free-thinking, economics has "a well-developed orthodoxy," writes Kreps, himself a distinguished and largely mainstream scholar. Economists "respected and played by the same basic rules set forth by earlier generations" and had "a clear conception" of what they did and did not know and "how to work on things unknown." Kreps traces the rules and conceptions to a paradigm established in the 1950s and 1960s, which gave economics "remarkable unity and consensus" and the "ability, through unity, to defend itself and to arrogate to itself particular perks and benefits."[43] It also made economics "a monolithic and smugly self-satisfied scientific discipline."[44]

In my view, the economic paradigm did not follow the patterns of evolution that Kuhn had described in the natural sciences. Its foundational theories did not provide a unifying explanation for many inexplicable facts, and they did not resolve an intellectual crisis. However, they had paradigmatic features that attracted researchers: they provided agreement about core assumptions and many follow-on puzzles for further research—which Knight's book did not. They also conformed to the scientific aspirations of the discipline.

The next chapter examines a cornerstone of the economics paradigm and why it rejected Knightian uncertainty.

6

Practically Omniscient Microeconomics

Milton Friedman was characteristically direct about his erstwhile teacher's construct in his 1962 textbook:

> In his seminal work, Frank Knight drew a sharp distinction between *risk*, as referring to events subject to a known or knowable probability distribution and *uncertainty*, as referring to events for which it was not possible to specify numerical probabilities. I have not referred to this distinction because I do not believe it is valid. I follow L. J. Savage in his view of *personal probability*, which denies any valid distinction along these lines. We may treat people as if they assigned numerical probabilities to every conceivable event.[1]

Kenneth Arrow, a less blunt Nobel Prize–winning economist, had also previously written, "Knight's uncertainties seem to have surprisingly many of the properties of ordinary probabilities, and it is not clear how much is gained by the distinction."[2]

Friedman's claim that Knightian uncertainty excluded numerical estimates has been disputed.[3] But it conforms to the overall spirit of Knight's argument. Knight associated uncertainty with subjective opinions formed when situational uniqueness ("one-offs") makes objective calculation impossible. Knight also observed that the impossibility of objective measurement is ubiquitous. And everyday experience suggests that we often use words, not numbers, to express our opinions when we cannot make objective numerical predictions. Therefore, Friedman's impression that Knightian uncertainty excluded numerical estimates is understandably widespread.

That said, people do occasionally use numbers to express opinions about one-off possibilities. They may even offer monetary bets on them, like bookmakers offering odds on horse races. But for my modernization project, other aspects of opinions about one-offs are more consequential than their numerical expression. I am concerned about the fallibility and disagreements arising from missing information (e.g., wrongful convictions or hung juries in trials when the evidence is entirely circumstantial) and the implications for entrepreneurship. Friedman and Savage's personal probabilities and the microeconomics they support keep this out: they ignore ignorance, mistakes, and disagreements. Yet as we

Uncertainty and Enterprise. Amar Bhidé, Oxford University Press. © Oxford University Press 2025.
DOI: 10.1093/oso/9780197688359.003.0006

see in this chapter, this microeconomics has become paradigmatic. Specifically, the main sections of this chapter examine how

- Personal probabilities became a building block of the subjective expected utility (SEU) theory that

- Became a cornerstone of the modern economics paradigm, which in turn

- Conflicts with my modernization project.

1. The Development of Subjective Utility Theories

Objective to Subjective Choices The mid-nineteenth-century English philosopher John Stuart Mill had, as we will later see, described economics as the study of conduct directed to the acquisition of wealth—and monetary wealth is objective.[4] However, more than a century earlier, Swiss mathematician and physicist Daniel Bernoulli had introduced "ideas of utility and expected utility-maximizing behaviour."[5] Utility—as in the satisfaction derived from wealth or anything else—is naturally subjective, as is its "expectation."

By the end of the nineteenth century, economics had settled on subjective utility rather than objective wealth as the goal of human conduct that the discipline would analyze. However, the core expectation theories, derived from mathematics and statistics, remained objective. Based on analyses of games of chance, such as dice, or data, such as mortality tables, these theories analyzed questions about distributions: What proportion of bets on black in roulette will lose? Or what is the life expectancy of a sixty-year-old? Expectations about situationally unique one-offs remained a "scientifically unfathomable mystery of life and mind," as Knight had put it.

In 1954, Jimmie Savage (referred to by his initials "L. J." in the Friedman quote above) proposed a comprehensive theory that included one-offs in *The Foundations of Statistics*. The book was published when Savage was a professor in the University of Chicago's statistics department, which he had cofounded in 1949.[6] Simply put, the theory expects rational decision-makers to estimate quantified "utilities" of the outcomes of their choices (what satisfaction they expect to get) and the probabilities of each outcome. Multiplying utilities and probabilities leads decision-makers to their "best" option, which maximizes the multiplication result.

Savage's theory specified logical, self-recommending rules—or postulates as Savage called them—for such maximization. Following the postulates ensures that all utilities and probabilities are rational in the sense of being logically consistent. The theory also assumes what Knight had called "practical omniscience"—meaning that decision-makers assume they know everything they

54 UNCERTAINTY AND ENTERPRISE

need to know. At the same time, the theory does not require true omniscience—objectively correct assessments of utilities and probabilities. The source of the estimated probabilities—whether they are mathematically deduced, inferred from statistics, or just wild guesses—is also irrelevant. This makes Knight's distinction between subjective uncertainty and measurable risks irrelevant.

Landmark Synthesis Savage's theory did not come out of the blue. Widely considered a genius, Savage had, like Newton, "stood on the shoulders of giants." The giants included:

- Thomas Bayes, an eighteenth-century English clergyman and statistician. Bayes (1701–1761) formulated (but did not publish in his lifetime) what came to be known as Bayes' theorem—a rule for estimating probabilities from statistical distributions that incorporates prior knowledge.

- Frank Ramsey, a precocious British philosopher-mathematician. Ramsey (1903–1930) attacked the ideas of his mentor, John Maynard Keynes, about nonnumerical probabilities. Ramsey proposed expressing all probability estimates, including subjective guesses that have no statistical basis, as numerical betting odds (as we see in the next chapter).

- Bruno De Finetti, an Italian statistician-actuary. De Finetti (1906–1985) independently developed and clarified Ramsey's ideas about subjective probabilities in the 1930s.

- Hungarian-born mathematician John von Neumann[7] and the German-born economist Oskar Morgenstern. Von Neumann (1903–1957) and Morgenstern (1902–1977), who had both immigrated to the United States in the 1930s, made significant contributions to utility theory and several other topics in their 1944 classic *Theory of Games and Economic Behavior.*

2. Paradigmatic Cornerstone

Scientific Aspirations Savage has been credited with changing the "Kuhnian" paradigm in statistics.[8] Savage's theory also became a cornerstone of a paradigm that conformed to economists' goals of a physics-like science.

As I have argued in *Making Economics More Useful*, scientists, as opposed to engineers and humanities scholars, favor simple, universal propositions and precise models that produce "equilibrium" solutions. Newton's second law of motion, $F = ma$, and Einstein's law of mass-energy equivalence, $E = mc^2$, exemplify the gold standard; fuzzy historical or literary explanations for World War I or Hamlet's torment are the antithesis. Engineering blueprints, while precise, are also not scientific exemplars because of their granular detail and limited generality.

Subjective utility maximization had the desired scientific qualities. Savage expressed his postulates in precise mathematical terms. Calculating expected utility by multiplying the utilities of possible outcomes with their subjective probabilities is self-evidently unambiguous (and its resemblance to *Force = mass * acceleration* is noteworthy, if entirely coincidental).

Extensions and Application The theory also had Kuhnian "paradigmatic" potential for extension and elaboration. Discounting future utilities added a temporal dimension (as in the net present value calculations of future cashflows that became a staple of modern financial analysis). The theory could also be applied to make folklore about the invisible hand more precise: with unfettered competition, individual utility maximization would be the best way of matching what people wanted with what could be produced. At the same time, the inferences and assumptions of the theory provided an attractive target for skeptics: they enabled technical attacks on the invisible hand and rationality. Without such a target, advocates and skeptics alike could only make assertions.

Friedman, who had coauthored a 1948 paper with Savage that presaged Savage's more complete 1954 theory, became an enthusiastic promoter of utility maximization. Friedman's 1962 book (which endorsed Savage's rejection of Knightian uncertainty) was "one of the first textbooks to talk about expected utility" and became a "classic in graduate school [economic] education."[9] Other economists spread subjective utility maximization beyond microeconomics. Macroeconomists used the device in "rational expectations" theories and finance researchers in modeling the risks of portfolios. Business schools taught it in MBA programs in decision trees.

Decision Trees

When I attended Harvard's MBA program from 1977 to 1979, the school did not require coursework in economics. It still does not. However, the business school had a managerial economics department whose members had made pioneering contributions to decision theory. They included mathematicians and statisticians John Pratt and Howard Raiffa, and Robert Schlaifer, a PhD in ancient history. (The three had coauthored a seminal 1964 article on subjective probabilities.[10]) The department taught a required first-year course Managerial Economics, in which decision trees were a basic building block. Solving a decision tree required estimating the probabilities for alternative outcomes and the values realized—subjective utility maximization.

56 UNCERTAINTY AND ENTERPRISE

As a twenty-one-year-old who had just endured a five-year bachelor's or-deal at the Indian Institute of Technology, I was dazzled by decision trees and the brilliance of John Pratt, my section instructor. Many older classmates with real work experience but less math in college were not as enthusiastic. Decision trees taught through made-up cases also did not easily fit HBS's tradition of discussing real cases. Eventually, in the 1990s, the managerial economics department was disbanded (at the behest, it was rumored, of Dean John McArthur), and its flagship course was removed from the MBA curriculum.[11]

The new paradigm helped economics enter remote domains. Gary Becker (who won an Economics Nobel in 1992) used utility maximization to ana-lyze racial discrimination, crime, family relationships, and rational addic-tion and to argue that seemingly self-destructive choice could be considered utility-maximizing. Herbert Simon (whose 1978 Economics Nobel came four-teen years before Becker's) sharply observed that the choices of Becker's *Homo economicus* extended to the bedroom where "he would read in bed at night only if the value of reading exceeded the value (to him) of the loss in sleep suffered by his wife."[12]

Criticisms Skeptics, including Simon, have also wondered whether earlier and simpler constructs could not have provided the same explanations and predictions. Could subjective utility maximization, they ask, merely offer opportunities to display technical virtuosity and score difficulty points for math-ematical gymnastics?[*]

The practical applications have also attracted critical scrutiny. Savage had acknowledged that his utility maximization theory applied to a "small world" where decision-makers might conceivably anticipate and consistently, if not cor-rectly, estimate the probabilities of all outcomes.[13] Using the procedure for some-thing as simple as "planning a picnic," according to Savage, was "ridiculous."[14] As a young college student, Herbert Simon attempted to apply utility maximization while working for Milwaukee's recreation department. He concluded that this was "hopeless."[15]

---

[*] Simon's (1978c) Richard T. Ely Lecture delivered to the American Economic Association questions the value of mathematized maximization. Compelled by "a sense of fairness" Simon cites one of his own papers (Simon 1951) explaining why employment relations are so widely used in so-ciety. "My argument," Simon observes, "requires a theorem and fifteen numbered equations. . . ." In fact, "the rigorous economic argument, involving the idea of maximizing behavior by employer and employee, is readily translatable into a simple qualitative argument that an employment contract may be a functional ('reasonable') way of dealing with certain kinds of uncertainty" (1978c, 5).

Kay and King's *Radical Uncertainty* further argues that applications outside Savage's "small world" promote dangerous complacency, particularly in financial markets and macroeconomic policymaking.[16] They also point out that many outcomes (e.g., "winning the war on terror") are so fuzzy that specifying numerical probabilities and utilities is impossible.

3. Conflicts with Uncertainty Modernization

Subtle Omissions The disconnect between Savage's approach and my modernizing project goes beyond the impossibility of anticipating all outcomes or estimating numerical probabilities. For me, simpler omissions are problematic. Notably Savage's model ignores errors from obviously missing information about "known" unknowns—such as the absence of a radar map in predicting rain. As in Knight's preliminary analysis of uncertainty-free competition, Savage implicitly assumes "practical omniscience." But omniscience precludes profit (as Knight defines it) and produces an irreconcilable conflict between entrepreneurship and paradigmatic microeconomics.

Banishing Entrepreneurship from Microeconomics

Early-twentieth-century economists, according to Humberto Barreto, had treated the entrepreneur as "a key agent."[17] But after the 1930s, "rapid intellectual changes" in microeconomics that produced a "perfectly interlocking, self-contained model"[18] required banishing entrepreneurship. The choice between a model whose pieces "fit perfectly together to form a grand, unified whole" and entrepreneurship was "an 'either-or' proposition" with "no happy medium."[19]

As Barreto further observes, excluding entrepreneurship created a tension between the informal discussions and formal theories of economists like Milton Friedman. Informally, they painted a picture of "brave, buccaneering" entrepreneurs. In contrast, their formal theories reduced the buccaneer to an ordinary ship hand with no room for initiative and any real decision-making rendered empty by the absence of uncertainty.[20] Friedman's popular book and TV show, *Free to Choose*, thus celebrated enterprise, while his scholarly writing excluded it.

Ignoring Disagreements Besides excluding entrepreneurship—the main application of my proposed modernization—Savage's utility maximization model also deviates sharply from my general conjectures about collective

58 UNCERTAINTY AND ENTERPRISE

conduct (previewed in Part 1). As mentioned, I aim to analyze interconnected and collaborative enterprise rather than atomistic or autonomous entrepreneurship and, more generally, problems of agreement and justification. A microeconomics that assumes practical omniscience ignores how people form judgments about one-offs and the consequences of their disagreements.

Recall from earlier chapters that judgments about one-offs draw on diverse—and typically contextual—information. The information may be widely available and public, precisely described (though not necessarily as statistical distributions), and the implications obvious. Or the information may be private and confidential, hard to codify, and ambiguous in its implications. These attributes, in turn, affect disagreements and their possible resolutions.

For example, a racehorse's track record (for once, literally) naturally influences the odds offered and bets placed. But what about a young horse that has never raced before? Here, bookmakers and bettors will rely on other nonstatistical information. This information might include the horse's pedigree—whether it is the offspring of a famous champion, the times it has clocked in pre-race workouts, the look of the horse's gait, and gossip in racing circles. These considerations have, to varying degrees, ambiguous implications. Pedigree and gaits are both observable, but pedigree is more precisely described and has clearer implications for a horse's prospects than gait. Gossip isn't public, is difficult to codify, and has ambiguous consequences for betting odds: Might the gossip be false? Or, if true, is this gossip known to bookmakers who have already included it in their odds? If not, how inaccurate might their offered odds be? Private, hard-to-codify, and ambiguous information will, in turn, produce wider divergences of opinions and more disagreements. One bettor might take gossip seriously, while another may not.

Divergent opinions and disagreements may not obstruct arm's length trades between individual buyers and sellers. Differences of opinion can even help businesses and markets that rely on speculation. Bookmaking requires gamblers who disagree with the odds offered. Stock exchanges similarly depend on differences in judgments about values and future prices. An assured consensus would drive out the speculation that keeps trading cheap and active.

But disagreements can obstruct entrepreneurial initiatives that individuals cannot unilaterally undertake. As I argue in Part 3, promoters must overcome the doubts of investors and consumers. Without convincing justifications, promoters cannot "make the sale" regardless of the prices or terms they offer or how strongly or sincerely they believe in their schemes and products. Examining the interplay of doubts and justification can significantly improve our understanding of enterprise. But "practically omniscient" uncertainty-free microeconomics ignores these issues in entrepreneurship and, more broadly, in most other kinds of joint human activity.

7

Imperfect Market Theories: Realism without Fallibility

This chapter examines two theories that became popular after Savage's subjective utility helped constitute the discipline's paradigm. Although the theories questioned the "invisible hand," perfect-competition implications of the prevalent paradigm, both were assimilated into mainstream economics. The paradigmatic tent was apparently big enough to accommodate well-behaved skeptics. Both theories also excluded or neglected uncertainty. Roughly following the historical timeline, we see how

- Theories attributing profit to the market power of oligopolists (rather than Knightian uncertainty) flourished after the 1950s.

- "Information economics," which emerged in the 1970s, rejected the all-knowing actors of earlier microeconomics and, in principle, could have analyzed uncertainty. In practice, however, information economics research focused on asymmetric information and misaligned incentives.

- An article published in 1987 by the University of Chicago's flagship *Journal of Political Economy* radically reframed Knight's 1921 thesis to conform to the by-then-entrenched focus on asymmetric information and incentives.

1. Market Power (Oligopolistic Competition)

Profiting from Imperfections Perfect, profitless competition in Knight's theory requires perfect foresight—and thus the absence of uncertainty. But foresight alone cannot ensure perfectly competitive markets. Monopolization obviously suppresses competition. So does collusion. Adam Smith had bitingly observed, "People of the same trade seldom meet together, even for merriment and diversion, but the conversation ends in a conspiracy against the public, or in some contrivance to raise prices."[1]

According to then–HBS strategy professor Pankaj Ghemawat's historical account, formal research on monopolies starts with a "definitive analysis" published in Antoine Cournot's 1838 book.[2] After that, according to Ghemawat,

Uncertainty and Enterprise. Amar Bhidé, Oxford University Press. © Oxford University Press 2025.
DOI: 10.1093/oso/9780197688359.003.0007

economists focused on monopolies and did not pay much attention to oligopolies until the 1930s. In the 1930s, economists, many from the "Harvard School," argued that some industries had *structures* that allowed oligopolists (not just monopolists) to earn high profits. Edward Mason, for example, argued in a landmark 1939 article that industry *structures* (most notably the market shares of the leading firms) influenced firms' *conduct* (the firm's critical decisions). That, in turn, helped determine their profitability and other dimensions of their *performance*, like their efficiency and innovativeness.[3]

In the 1950s, Mason's colleague, Joe Bain, published empirical research suggesting that (1) concentrated industry structures (i.e., where the leading firms had high market shares) produced significantly higher profits, and (2) firms in industries with high barriers to entry (from patents, product differentiation, and economies of scale) could charge high prices. Bain's findings seeded a new subfield of economics called industrial organization (often called IO). IO researchers had published several hundred empirical studies by the mid-1970s[4] and offered graduate courses.[5]

In the 1970s, Michael Porter opened a new "business" front for IO. Porter is a Princeton-trained engineer (where he had also been a star golfer), Harvard MBA (and Baker Scholar), and PhD in business economics from Harvard (where Caves taught him IO and then supervised Porter's thesis). Joining the Harvard Business School (HBS) faculty after his PhD, Porter soon wrote a "Note on the Structural Analysis of Industries." The note attempted to "turn IO on its head by focusing on the business policy objective of profit maximization, rather than on the public policy objective of minimizing 'excess' profits,"[6] according to Ghemawat (whose PhD thesis advisers included Porter and Caves).

Instead of just using existing IO models, Porter constructed his now famous Five Forces framework. Porter recognized that economic models focused only on a few variables did not suit business decisions.[7] Like juries in a criminal trial, managers must consider many factors. Porter later recalled that his framework provided "an encompassing way to look at an industry."[8] Each "force" contained numerous factors that Porter expected—because of case studies, not statistics— would affect profitability.

Porter's framework provided the backbone of a new elective course that he offered, which I took in the fall of 1978. Unlike their lukewarm response to the required Managerial Economics course, my classmates enthusiastically welcomed Porter's elective.[9] A few years later, HBS made Porter's elective a required course. Porter's 1980 book *Competitive Strategy* became a runaway global success.

Paradigmatic and Practical Advantages The popularity of market power theories (and Porter's frameworks) deprived Knight's profitability-uncertainty thesis of the attention it might have attracted. I suggest below that both the

62 UNCERTAINTY AND ENTERPRISE

"Kuhnian" benefits IO provided to researchers and the commercially valuable tools and prescriptions it gave to practitioners explain this popularity.

IO researchers could define their dependent variable—profitability—in easily measurable ways, such as reported returns on equity and profit margins. Their independent variables—the presumed determinants of profitability, such as market shares of leading firms, R&D spending, and advertising expenditures—were also quantifiable. In other words, the conceptual building blocks of IO theories (e.g., performance, market structure, and conduct) had concrete, measurable counterparts. Moreover, measurable profits increased with their measurable determinants. This measurability gave IO ample scope for statistical testing, which was becoming a prerequisite for publication in prestigious economic journals.

Knight's specification of "profit," in contrast, was ephemeral. In Knight's theory, profit isn't merely what is left after payments for goods purchased or wages paid. It isn't even profit that excludes notional costs such as depreciation, imputed rent for premises belonging to the owners, and the unpaid supervisory services provided by the owners. It also excludes the notional cost and reward of bearing measurable and potentially diversifiable risk.

True profit earned after these notional adjustments is, therefore, itself unmeasurable, as is the uncertainty that produces it.* The uncertainty-profitability thesis is also definitional and therefore fails the test of falsifiability that many economists assert scientific theories must satisfy.

Knight also rejected the idea that expected profits increase with the degree of uncertainty. Instead, Knight argued uncertainty produces profits or losses depending on the correctness of the entrepreneur's judgments—and in the overall economy, total profits depend on how many individuals undertake uncertain projects, not on the correctness of their opinions. Knight further speculated that an oversupply of entrepreneurs competing for employees and other inputs usually makes the "true" total profit in the economy negative.

Knight's proposition was thus doubly disadvantaged. It failed the falsifiability test that some IO alternatives ostensibly passed. It also did not support Kuhn's "normal science." In contrast, IO allowed researchers to "extend" and "elaborate" their core assumptions in ways that conformed to paradigmatic norms. By the mid-1970s, IO researchers had produced hundreds of statistical studies, as mentioned.

---

* Using modern terms, Knight's specification of the profitability of a project requires a deduction for its imputed "cost of capital." And the cost of capital, according to modern theory, reflects only the "market" risks that diversified stockholders face. As a practical matter, owners of private companies often cannot sufficiently diversify their investments to the point where they eliminate their "idiosyncratic" risks. Even in public companies, there is no reliable method for diversifying away the idiosyncratic risks of individual projects. Yet according to Knight's theory, the actual possibilities and costs of diversification do not affect the "true" profit of a project—just as in modern finance theory, they do not affect a project's cost of capital.

Then, starting in the late 1970s, the subfield spawned research displaying mathematical virtuosity through the application of game theory.[10]

IO also provided practical tools. Here is how: the US Congress passed the Sherman Antitrust Act of 1890 to the monopoly power of railroad trusts. The 1914 Clayton Antitrust Act increased the government's capacity to break up big businesses, limit mergers, and control monopolistic pricing. Congress also created the Federal Trade Commission (FTC) to enforce the rules. The IO theories that emerged after the 1930s gave regulators analytical tools and justifications to force breakups and block mergers. Businesses also used these tools defensively to resist the Justice Department and the FTC. This defensive (and sometimes offensive) use provided academic economists with lucrative opportunities to provide expert testimony in antitrust trials.

Porter's IO extending framework became a staple of MBA programs. Managers, investment bankers, brokerage houses, and strategy consultants also used the framework extensively. Porter himself cofounded the Monitor Group, a strategy consulting firm.[*]

In contrast, Knight's theory of profit has never been used in expert testimony, teaching business courses, investment banking, stock brokerage, or consulting.

Ignoring Uncertainty and Entrepreneurship Unlike Savage's subjective utility maximization theory, IO (and Porter's framework) did not directly exclude uncertainty. Some of IO's game-theoretic variants produced what I would consider uncertainty-infused and contextually dependent results.[11] Uncertainty, however, did not explicitly feature on IO's research agenda. Perhaps uncertainty-free microeconomics, which occupied a more central position in the discipline, had kept the construct out of everyone's sight.

Foundational IO research also excluded entrepreneurship. Although IO did not have a "perfectly interlocking" model that required exclusion, many pioneers questioned the Invisible Hand of perfect competition. They sought to provide legitimacy and analytical support to the trust busting that had started as a populist reaction to railroad barons and other Gilded Age monopolists. Big Business, rather than entrepreneurs, naturally attracted reform-minded researchers' attention. Big Business also provided clients for academics who served as experts in antitrust lawsuits and for the consulting services of Michael Porter and his Monitor Company.

Paradigmatic methodological conventions favored research on large companies. Established businesses and mature industries provided more data

---

[*] The firm expanded rapidly for over two decades. Then, in 2012, after Monitor's controversial work for the Libyan dictator Muammar Gaddafi and borrowing from a private equity firm to pay its bills, Monitor's US subsidiary filed for Chapter 11 bankruptcy (Gleason 2012).

64   UNCERTAINTY AND ENTERPRISE

for statistical analysis than new and fledgling businesses. Researchers tried to explain endpoints that could be analyzed statistically, not the distinctive paths that exceptional entrepreneurs traversed to get there.[*]

2. Information Economics

Wasteful Imperfections Information economics, like IO, examines deviations from the perfect, profitless competition modeled in basic microeconomics. However, there are significant differences in the causes and consequences of the deviations.

In perfectly competitive—and profitless—markets, all resources are put to their most valued use, and customers' wants are satisfied to the greatest possible extent. "All that is is for the best," as Voltaire's Dr. Pangloss might say. In IO's *imperfectly* competitive markets, businesses with pricing power deliberately and wastefully underproduce. They maximize profits by charging more and selling less than they would under perfect no-profit / no-loss competition.

In information economics, imperfectly distributed information creates problems without monopolists or oligopolists exercising market power. Sellers of used cars know the actual condition of their vehicles, but buyers do not— and cannot be sure of the truthfulness of sellers. Job candidates know how good they are, but employers do not. Buyers can also exploit superior information: purchasers of life or health insurance know more about their habits and health than insurance companies. Detecting bad behavior, such as the carelessness of employees or the hypochondria of individuals covered by health insurance, can also be challenging.

These information asymmetry, incentive, and moral hazard problems, as economists call them, can discourage valuable, mutually beneficial transactions. They may even—in theory anyhow—stop markets from operating entirely. Information problems can also promote wasteful or unproductive expenditures, such as supervising and monitoring employees, which would otherwise be unnecessary. Spending merely to "signal" quality—by professionals on expensive suits and offices, for example—and negotiating complicated contracts to align

---

[*] For example, IO economists used statistics to claim that consumer "tastes" or "receptiveness to advertising" created barriers to entry that enabled the leading firms to dominate their markets. But I asked in my 2000 book, how could tastes or receptiveness to advertising explain why colas and chewing-gum makers built globally dominant brands while ginger ale and bubble-gum companies did not? It was likewise implausible that spontaneous changes in consumer tastes had catalyzed the expansion of Starbucks' coffee shops centuries after the availability of coffee. Analyzing what entrepreneurs did—Asa Griggs Candler in colas, William Wrigley in chewing gum, and Howard Schultz in coffee retailing—could have enriched IO. But IO economists could not have done this with statistics—it would have required abductive, case-specific speculation (Bhidé 2000, 311).

incentives could also be avoided. The dysfunctions do not necessarily produce "excess" profits, however. Buyers and sellers both lose.

Changing the Paradigm Information economics won wider academic acclaim than IO research on market structures. Three pioneers—George Akerlof, Michael Spence, and Joseph Stiglitz—shared the 2001 Nobel Prize in Economics. Other Nobel Prizes in Economics were then awarded for work on information problems (including issues of incentives, monitoring, and contracting) to Oliver Williamson, Oliver Hart, and Bengt Holmström. In contrast, just two Nobel Awards—to George Stigler in 1982 and Jean Tirole in 2014—cited contributions to studies of industrial structures and market power. Even here, Stigler's Nobel citation called him "the foremost originator of economics of information,"[12] and Tirole's game-theoretic contributions would not usually be classified as "structural" IO.

The enthusiasm for information economics might puzzle outsiders. It did not offer counterintuitive ideas like Ricardo's 1817 principle of comparative advantage: that countries should forgo making things in which they had absolute advantages if they were even better at making something else. Unlike Bain's IO research,[13] information economics did not uncover many surprising facts. The commercial possibilities and prescriptive implications were limited. No Porterian Five Forces framework was produced. Unlike the Efficient Market Hypothesis, information economics theories did not challenge common practices like trying to beat the market. And unlike John Maynard Keynes's fiscal theories or Milton Friedman's monetarism, they did not advance radical policy ideas.

Compared to everyday practices and beliefs, the new 1970s information economics seems old hat. The ancient warning "Don't buy a pig in a poke" flags information asymmetry issues. The sixteenth-century Gresham's Law, "Good money drives out bad," anticipated the essence of lemon market problems. Economists did not have to tell businesses about the advantages of signaling quality or incentivizing employees. Governments have long attempted to stop the sales of underweight or adulterated goods—the Pure Food and Drug Act passed by the US Congress in 1906 followed many state laws. Common law, dating back to an 1815 case,[14] excluded the "buyer beware" (caveat emptor) protection for sellers who refuse the inspection of their goods.

Yet Stiglitz justifiably titled his 2001 Nobel Lecture "Information and the Change in the Paradigm in Economics." Information economics gave economists a unified account for several disparate observations—the hallmark of a Kuhnian paradigm. Doing this through the mathematical models that economic communities had come to demand was difficult. Modelers had to find assumptions ("axioms") from which they could deduce interesting (if, typically,

66 UNCERTAINTY AND ENTERPRISE

already well-known) outcomes. These assumptions had to be as general as possible, plausible, and capable of producing a widely applicable "equilibrium" result. Modelers also had to specify mathematical steps between assumptions and outcomes. In contrast, structural IO models typically did not start with general assumptions about individual choices. Nor did they embody much mathematical wizardry (although later game-theoretic IO models did).

Information economics offered a broader challenge to the Panglossian perfection of standard microeconomics. The "best possible" outcomes in the new models could waste resources without any monopoly or oligopoly power. Consumers "overpay" for life and health insurance because providers incur expenditures that do not increase their profits. Stiglitz and other information economics stars argued that governments should take corrective action. In contrast, skeptical economists in Chicago and elsewhere argued that government interventions would do more harm than good. But regardless of ideological orientations, economists did not dispute the problems analyzed. The paradigmatic achievement of information economics also made it a popular hammer for many research nails—including entrepreneurship, as we will see in Part 3.

Avoidable Exclusion Information economics could, in principle, have also examined uncertainty. While earlier microeconomic models assumed practical omniscience, the newer approach did not. True, information economists usually modeled worries about concealed information rather than uncertainty, but the models could also have focused on ignorance and misjudgments. Indeed, Stigler "saw that regulation can be based on erroneous perception of real conditions."[15] Similarly, while much of Stiglitz's research had examined misaligned incentives and information asymmetries, he also published several papers modeling mistakes. His 2001 Nobel Prize Lecture noted,

> Even if individuals are well intentioned, with limited information, mistakes get made. To err is human. Raaj K. Sah and I, in a series of papers (1985, 1986, 1988a, b, 1991) explored the consequences of alternative organizational design and decision-making structures for organizational mistakes: for instance, whether good projects get rejected or bad projects get accepted. We suggested that, in a variety of circumstances, decentralized [organizations] have distinct advantages (see also Sah, 1991; Stiglitz, 1989d). These papers are just beginning to spawn a body of research; see, for example, Bauke Visser (1998), Amar Bhidé (2001), and Michael Christensen and Thorbjom Knudsen (2002).[16]

In practice, these were exceptions. Most information economists ignored uncertainty. Their models even excluded doubts about honesty and

IMPERFECT MARKET THEORIES   67

truthfulness: their protagonists assumed that, given the opportunity, lying and cheating were inevitable.

3. A Telling Deconstruction

In 1987, two economists, LeRoy and Singell, went beyond ignoring missing information and misjudgment; they reinterpreted Knight's thesis to fit an information asymmetry and moral hazard–based worldview.[17] Briefly, the LeRoy and Singell article claims that what Knight meant by uncertainty was situations where moral hazard or adverse selection caused insurance markets to collapse.

As it happens, Stigler's glowing introduction to the 1971 edition of Knight's RUP, had called insurance interpretations an "extreme caricature."[18] I have long found the LeRoy and Singell paper unconvincing and dismissed it in one paragraph in an earlier book.[19] I then wrote a more detailed critique in a working paper.[20]

But why even bother? Emmett calls the LeRoy and Singell article, published by the *Journal of Political Economy*, "the definitive Chicago School take" on "how the economist should approach uncertainty."[21] Yet, scholarly citations of LeRoy and Singell's article number just in the hundreds,[22] perhaps reflecting the now-limited interest in Knight's 1921 book. Akerlof's lemons paper[23], in contrast, has, at the time of this writing, more than thirty-nine thousand citations.[24] LeRoy and Singell's 1987 deconstruction could not possibly have produced the prolonged prior neglect of Knightian uncertainty. Their article's low citation numbers suggest that it did not stop economists who researched entrepreneurship more than twenty years later from using Knight's ideas either.

Yet more scrutiny (provided in my working paper) may help the interested and technically minded reader better understand what Knight attempted to convey. More importantly for this book, LeRoy and Singell's claim shows how strongly many economists reject the essence of Knight's construct. Their article exemplifies the gap between the current preoccupation with incentives and Knight's concerns about knowledge.[*]

Stiglitz and Stigler's pluralism respects uncertainties and mistakes, as well as incentives and moral hazard. Lesser enforcers of the new gospel demand unwavering monotheism. Pagan polytheism must be reinterpreted—as Thomas Aquinas did with Aristotle's theology—and what does not fit must be discarded. LeRoy and Singell channel the spirit of Aquinas in asserting that Knight's

---

[*] Edmund Phelps suggests that two "Austrian" icons, von Mises and Hayek, had similarly divergent mindsets: "The arguments of Hayek are knowledge-based, while those of Mises were incentive-based" (Phelps 2013, 125).

68   UNCERTAINTY AND ENTERPRISE

discussion of moral hazard and adverse selection in insurance markets was "a remarkable anticipation of the modern literature."[25]

The preoccupations that LeRoy and Singell reflect (which may have secured them the coveted imprimatur of the *Journal of Political Economy*[26]) have practical consequences. Publication in a top five journal may have exempted LeRoy and Singell's "definitive take" on uncertainty from careful reading or critical scrutiny.[27] Doctrinal commitments to misaligned incentives and information asymmetries—which the pioneers of information economics did not intend—have suppressed our understanding of the complementary roles of doubts about honest mistakes. Yet neglect also offers ample scope for new research. Specifically, analyzing *degrees* of uncertainty—interpreted in a broadened way—offers rich possibilities for entrepreneurship research, as mentioned in the Introduction, and as I try to show in Parts 3 and 4.

8

John Maynard Keynes: Help to Distraction

John Maynard Keynes's Depression-era thesis of how severe uncertainties can trigger systemic collapses attracted renewed interest after the 2008 global financial crisis. But attention to extreme, "We simply do not know" uncertainties—and their systemic consequences—hinders my modernization proposals. Like Knight's RUP, I focus on more routine uncertainty and its day-to-day implications. Keynes's earlier but lesser-known *Treatise on Probability* does support my project, however, as this chapter shows.

Specifically, we will see that

- Keynes and Knight shared iconoclastic views about probabilities—but had little else in common.

- Keynes's 1921 *Treatise* clarified the roles of nonnumerical probabilities and evidence. Both roles, which are muddied or absent in RUP, support the propositions of my updating project.

- The *Treatise*'s legacy, however, was its antithesis: skepticism about Keynes's ideas spurred the development of subjective utility maximization that excluded Knightian uncertainty (as we saw in the previous chapter).

- Keynes later invoked extreme uncertainty to explain systemic macroeconomic collapses. That claim has attracted broader interest, but its memorability draws away attention from more mundane uncertainty and its "micro" implications.

1. Unfriendly Iconoclasts

According to Peter Bernstein's *Against the Gods: The Remarkable Story of Risk*, Keynes and Knight were the first to seriously question whether "patterns of the past always reveal the path to the future."[1] Both Knight and Keynes, Bernstein observes, also "distrusted classical theories based on the laws of mathematical probability or assumptions of certainty as guides to decision-making."[2] Yet the two iconoclasts had little else in common, and their interactions were unfriendly.

Uncertainty and Enterprise. Amar Bhidé, Oxford University Press. © Oxford University Press 2025.
DOI: 10.1093/oso/9780197688359.003.0008

Worlds Apart

The first paragraph of "Dynastic Origins," the first chapter of Robert Skidelsky's magisterial biography of Keynes, introduces its subject thus:

> There was scarcely a time in his life when John Maynard Keynes did not look down at the rest of England, and much of the world, from a great height. He went to England's best school, Eton. He was an undergraduate and fellow of King's, one of Cambridge's top colleges. He served in the Treasury, the top home department of government. He was the intimate of one prime minister, and the counsellor of many. He was at the heart of England's economics establishment, and at the centre of its financial oligarchy. He was a member of the Bloomsbury Group, England's most potent cultural coterie. His communications with the educated public were always made from a position of unimpeachable authority. This position was largely achieved by the force of his dazzling intellect and by his practical genius. But he started life with considerable advantages which helped him slip easily into the parts for which his talents destined him. There was no nonsense about his being in the wrong place or having the wrong accent. Of his advantages the chief was being born at Cambridge, into a community of dons, the son of John Neville and Florence Ada Keynes.[3]

Keynes began lecturing on monetary economics at Cambridge in 1909. Although he had taken a couple of college courses, Keynes never received a degree in economics. His undergraduate degree, a first-class-honors "Tripos," was in mathematics. Nonetheless, writes Skidelsky, Keynes

> set out to destroy the argument of "classical" economics that a competitive market economy would always ensure full use of potential resources. He invented almost singlehandedly a new branch of economics, macroeconomics, to show why this was not true, and to justify active fiscal and monetary policy. The task of overturning orthodox theory seemed all the more urgent in the wake of the Great Depression of 1929–33. The result was *The General Theory of Employment, Interest and Money*, whose publication in 1936 is conventionally taken to be the start of the Keynesian Revolution.[4]

Knight, born two years after Keynes in 1885 and whom he outlived by twenty-six years, had quite a different life story and worldview. As mentioned, Knight was raised on a midwestern farm, kept out of school until he was eighteen, and attended obscure and now-defunct colleges in Tennessee before earning a PhD in economics from Cornell. Knight, as also mentioned, had profound misgivings about capitalism. But he was even more "reluctant to believe in doing good with power." As he declared in a 1950 presidential address to the American Economic Association, "When a man or group asks for power to do good, my impulse is to say, 'Oh, yeah, who ever wanted power for any other reason? and what have they done when they got it?' So, I instinctively want to cancel the last three words, leaving simply 'I want power'; that is easy to believe."[5]

Knight disliked Keynes "intensely," according to Bernstein. Ignoring conventional niceties about not speaking ill of the dead—Keynes had died in 1946—Knight's 1950 address also asserted, "The latest 'new economics' and in my opinion rather the worst, for fallacious doctrine and pernicious consequences is that launched by the late John Maynard (Lord) Keynes, who for a decade succeeded in carrying economic thinking well back to the dark age." (Knight's address also likened the "absolute authority" of the pope to that of Hitler and Stalin.) Earlier, in 1940, when the University of Chicago had awarded Keynes an honorary degree, Knight had protested strongly. Keynes's "very unusual intelligence, in the sense of ingenuity and dialectical skill," Knight complained, was "directed to false and subversive ends," posing "one of the most serious dangers in the whole project of education."[6]

Knight's jealousy, Bernstein suggests, likely contributed to his hostility. Keynes may have "annoyed" Knight because he had "carried the distinction between risk and uncertainty much further" than Knight himself. Moreover, writes Bernstein, Knight "must surely have been angered when he discovered that the sole reference Keynes made to him in *The General Theory of Employment, Interest and Money* was in a footnote that disparages one of his papers on the interest rate as "'precisely in the traditional, classical mould,' ... Only this, after Knight's pioneering explorations into risk and uncertainty fifteen years before."[7]

2. Useful Clarifications

Ambitious Treatise Keynes's *Treatise*, published in 1921—the same year as Knight's RUP—had also originated in a dissertation. However, Keynes's dissertation, which he wrote in his spare time while employed as a civil servant, had been submitted for a Fellowship at King's College, and not for a PhD in economics. Keynes's first Fellowship submission, in 1907, failed. The following year, a revised dissertation was successful. Philosophers W. E. Johnson and A. N. Whitehead served as examiners for both submissions.[8] The dissertation was set in proofs in 1913 after Keynes added sections on induction and statistical inference. But the *Treatise* wasn't published until August 1921 after Keynes had made

72 UNCERTAINTY AND ENTERPRISE

extensive corrections to the proof and paid his publisher £767 11s ($63,898 in 2022 US dollars[9]) out of his own pocket for twenty-five hundred copies.[10]

"Squarely intended as a contribution to the foundations of probability," the *Treatise* contained "little by way of economics,"[11] according to the overview of a special issue published by the *Cambridge Journal of Economics* to commemorate the 2021 centennial of Keynes's and Knight's books. Keynes's theory was "highly original" and "characteristically provocative," aiming to reclaim the subject from its narrow use by mathematicians. Knight was more of a "consumer" of the existing literature on probability, according to the overview. His contribution lay in "recognizing and exploring the consequences of there being something different about situations in which decision-makers do not have well-defined probabilities."

Keynes's *Treatise* treated probability as a branch of logic, taking it beyond prevailing frequency theories (that, for example, considered the proportion of smokers getting lung cancer as synonyms for probabilities). Relying on ordinary usage, Keynes asked, what made beliefs about what was "probable," reasonable or rational? Moreover, Keynes's question was about the reasonableness of beliefs in propositions rather than in the frequencies of events. The difference is subtle but important. For example, the extent of reasonable belief in the proposition that smoking poses more risks than speeding is related to, but not the same as, the relative proportions of smokers who die of lung cancer and fast drivers who die in car accidents.

Uncertainty itself did not feature prominently in Keynes's 1921 book. As the centennial special issue overview noted, "The word 'uncertainty' comes up only seven times in *A Treatise on Probability*, and then always in an innocuous, nontechnical sense."[12] The *Treatise* also mentions business (as a commercial activity) just twice and omits any reference to entrepreneurs or entrepreneurship. RUP's emphasis on uncertainty and entrepreneurs is explicit and emphatic. Keynes also took, unpersuasively and contra Knight, an objective view of probabilities. Nonetheless, as we will next see, the *Treatise* has shaped my updating of (subjective) Knightian uncertainties and their applications to enterprise through its examination of (1) nonnumerical probabilities and (2) the weights of evidence.[13]

Nonnumerical Probabilities Knight's book distinguished between confidence (or degrees of belief) in estimates and the estimates themselves. Knight further asserted—implausibly in my experience—that entrepreneurs always express confidence in their estimates as numerical ratios. Keynes argued that numerical measures were rarely justified, although he also took a degree-of-belief view of probability.

The *Treatise* bounds degrees of reasonable beliefs (in the probable truths of propositions) by the extremes of certainty and impossibility, designated by p = 1 and p = 0, respectively. But specific numbers for intermediate degrees, Keynes argues, are usually unjustified, although this is often done by equating probabilities of events with the frequencies of events. According to Keynes, numerical estimates for one-offs are especially questionable.

That underwriters "insure against practically any risk," writes Keynes, "shows no more than that many probabilities are greater or less than some numerical measure, not that they themselves are numerically definite." He further doubts whether "the process of thought, through which [the underwriter] goes before naming a premium, is wholly rational and determinate" and concludes that "the practice of underwriters weakens rather than supports the contention that all probabilities can be measured and estimated numerically."[14]

Probabilities, according to Keynes, also often cannot be numerically compared even if they can be ranked. For instance, we could judge proposition A as more likely than proposition B, just as we might assess movie X as more entertaining than movie Y. But without a consistent numerical scale, we could not say how many times A was more likely or X more entertaining.[15] Only exceptional conditions justified numerical estimates and comparisons, yet Keynes notes that "opportunities of mathematical manipulation" had secured numerical probabilities scholarly attention far "out of proportion to their real importance."[16]

Uses and Reservations My modernization focuses on entrepreneurial and other settings where numerical probabilities can be little more than figurative expressions of felt uncertainty ("doubts") about one-offs, sometimes in the language of betting odds. And the *Treatise*'s arguments about nonnumerical probabilities better suit my purposes than Knight's exposition. As mentioned, Knight implausibly (and inconsistently) asserts that entrepreneurs always numerically estimate the reliability of their opinions. I do, however, favor the subjectivity of Knight's construct and find Keynes's specification of an objective 0 to 1 scale awkward and unsuitable for my purposes.

Reservations

Despite Keynes's skepticism about numerical measurement, the *Treatise* sets bounds of p = 1 for "certainty" and p = 0 for "impossibility" for all probabilities. Keynes takes these bounds from deductive logic, which seeks to demonstrate certain truths:

> If a is [demonstrably] certain, then the contradictory of a is impossible. If a knowledge of a makes b certain, then a knowledge of a makes the contradictory of b impossible. Thus a proposition is impossible with respect to a given

74   UNCERTAINTY AND ENTERPRISE

premiss, if it is disproved by the premiss; and the relation of impossibility is the relation of minimum probability.[17]

Keynes's specification conforms to the traditional mathematical bounding of probabilities from 0 to 1—and by accommodating both deductive and probabilistic inference it supports Keynes's ambition of an integrated theory. Yet I find Keynes's bookending—setting numerical deductive bounds to a range of typically nonnumeric possibilities—awkward. It seems analogous to defining the Celsius scale by setting the temperature at which water abruptly shifts to steam as 100°C and to ice as 0°C. But the phase shifts from water to steam or ice are observable and scientifically explained; Keynes's jumps from probabilistic to deductive—at the top and bottom of his scale—are neither. The *Treatise* asserts that such discontinuities occur without example or explanation.

Putting aside the discontinuities at 0 and 1, I find Keynes's lower "impossibility" limit an unnatural counterpart to his upper "certainty" bound. Valid deductions seem more naturally contrasted with invalid deductions. Proving p cannot imply q does not establish that q is impossible or untrue. Indeed, negatives are typically unprovable. Keynes could have specified his lower bound as baseless inferences (that are neither probabilistic nor deductive) or as the intractable uncertainty (as in his later work).

In any case, neither a baseless nor an intractable lower bound suits my purposes. My uncertainty is a subjective psychological state. Its bounds are the states where confidence becomes complete "certitude" on the one side and doubts become utter "uncertainty" on the other. These bounds retain Keynes's skepticism about the numerical measurement of most probabilities—but without an inexplicable jump to numerical values at the extremes.*

---

*I am tempted to represent the lower limit of doubt by the Sanskrit *shunya*—the origin of the idea of the mathematical "zero" but which also has the nonnumerical connotation of "nothingness." But *shunya* would suggest occult interpretations, which I am anxious to avoid.

Evidentiary Weights My second use of the *Treatise* draws on its examination of the relationship between evidence and belief. My scaling of belief relies on its natural correlation, with more evidence raising confidence toward certitude and the absence of evidence pushing doubt toward uncertainty. My propositions about justificatory routines also extend what the *Treatise* says about the practical uses of evidence, as we will see.

According to the *Treatise*, rational belief in propositions should depend on the total amount ("weight") of evidence that the proposition relies on, not just the extent of differences between favorable and unfavorable evidence.[18] Keynes further suggests that practical decisions should consider the "completeness of the information upon which a probability is based," along with the "actual magnitude of the probability."[19,*]

Knight's 1921 book, in contrast, did not analyze evidentiary weight. Evidentiary weight is also usually excluded from mainstream models of rational choice. Considering the amount, completeness, and quality of evidence can, in fact, be seen as violating the basic assumptions of the models. But as mentioned in the previous chapter, the standard models pertain to an artificial "small world." Uncontroversial real-world practices support the intuitive reasonableness of Keynes's evidence-confidence nexus. In reducing doubts about one-offs, contextual evidence seems pivotal.

Medical and legal conventions illustrate how the amount and quality of evidence affect confidence about specific cases. As mentioned, protocols to diagnose life-threatening diseases require confirmatory tests, and the US Food and Drug Administration (FDA) strongly favors two sets of independent clinical trials for new drugs. Note that additional evidence can strengthen confidence even if it is less favorable. Two blood-glucose readings increase confidence in diagnosing diabetes, even if the second reading is closer to normal.[20]

In criminal trials, corroborated testimony carries more weight. Scottish law requires corroboration. The testimony of just one witness for the prosecution, however credible, must be supported by another witness. No person can be convicted of a crime "unless there is evidence of at least two witnesses implicating the person accused or charged with the commission of the crime."[21]

Civil cases exemplify the inadequacy of purely statistical evidence. Consider the classic "Blue Bus Company" example, constructed from an actual 1941 case (*Smith v. Rapid Transit*) tried in the Superior Court of the Commonwealth of Massachusetts: A car driving late at night is hit by a bus that does not stop after the accident. The injured car driver sues a local bus operator, the Blue Bus Company, for damages. The plaintiff establishes that the defendant operates 80 percent of the buses in the city and that the driver of the bus that hit the car was undoubtedly negligent. In principle, winning compensatory damages does not require proof beyond reasonable doubt. Plaintiffs only need to establish "a preponderance of the evidence," or in English law, "a balance of the probabilities."

---

* The pragmatist Charles Sanders (C. S.) Peirce had anticipated, Peden (2018) observes, Keynes's arguments about evidentiary weight. Peirce used, in his 1878 essay "The Probability of Induction," the example of estimating the proportions of red and black beans in a bag. Sampling one thousand beans would justify more confidence in the proportions than sampling just two beans, even if the proportions in both samples were identical. Peirce's essay, unlike Keynes's *Treatise*, however, took a firmly frequentist—or what he called the "materialist"—view of probability, not the "conceptualist," degrees-of-belief view favored by Knight and Keynes).

76 UNCERTAINTY AND ENTERPRISE

But statistical data alone do not establish preponderance or balance. In the actual 1941 *Smith v. Rapid Transit* case, the trial court judge refused to let the jury even consider the allegations because there was no "direct" evidence that one of the defendant's buses had hit the plaintiff. The Massachusetts Supreme Judicial Council upheld the trial court's decision: Even if the "mathematical chances" favored "the proposition that a bus of the defendant caused the accident," this was "not enough." A jury's "actual belief" in the proposition would require more "actual evidence." The case is not "unique," and "the Supreme Judicial Court's ruling is generally in line with the law as it was then, and as it is now."[22] Apparently, "naked statistical evidence" alone does not establish "preponderance" or the "balance of the probabilities."

Unlike Savage's model, the law distinguishes between one-off and distributional targets. Plaintiffs alleging that they have personally suffered discrimination must produce evidence about their specific circumstances. Statistical data can only provide supplementary support. Statistical claims can only lead in cases alleging class discrimination. Conversely, in lawsuits alleging discrimination against a group, plaintiffs must produce statistical evidence, while defendants cannot use individual examples to show their impartiality.

Similarly, as Keynes's thought experiment illustrates, logical a priori calculations may have, by themselves, little weight for resolving doubts about one-offs.

Keynes's Thought Experiment

Keynes proposed a hypothetical comparison of balls drawn from urns with known and inferred distributions:

> In each case we require the probability of drawing a white ball; in the first case we know that the urn contains black and white in equal proportions; in the second case the proportion of each colour is unknown, and each ball is as likely to be black as white. It is evident that in either case the probability of drawing a white ball is 1/2 but that the weight of the argument in favour of this conclusion is greater in the first case.[23]

Note: Knight had also proposed a similar thought experiment in RUP.[24] And forty years after the publication of Keynes's *Treatise*, Daniel Ellsberg published the results of surveys along the lines of Keynes's example (as we will see in a later chapter).

To slightly adapt Keynes's thought experiment, imagine calculating the odds of successive heads after tossing two different coins. One is a newly minted coin, and the other a coin that has been tossed many times (and landed heads as often as tails). In both cases, we would expect a one-in-four chance of successive heads; but we would have more *confidence* in these odds with the coin that has already been tossed many times: a minute asymmetry could bias how the new coin lands.

The thought experiments also show the subtle relationship between evidence, probabilities, and practical correctness. "Metaphorically," according to the *Treatise*, probabilities measure the *difference* between positive and negative evidence. But probabilities and the amount of evidence—the *sum* of the positive and negative information—are independent. Repeated tosses of a coin may not affect our expectations of successive heads—or they may increase or decrease the expected odds. Moreover, in principle, the alterations in the expected odds may be incorrect—a fluky run may produce the mistaken belief of a biased coin. Therefore, a proposition backed by more evidence, Keynes writes, "is not 'more likely to be right' than one of low weight."[25]

Realistically, however, we expect evidence to reduce rather than increase mistakes. Although the weight of evidence has "no theoretical connection with probable error," writes Keynes, it can have a "practical connection, namely, that high weight may be associated with low probable error." And in "scientific problems a large probable error is not uncommonly due to a great lack of evidence, and that as the available evidence increases there is a tendency for the probable error to diminish."[26] All things being equal, therefore, we might prefer propositions supported by more evidence, especially about one-offs.

Sufficiency and Relevance Keynes interprets Bernoulli's maxim "that we must take into account all the information we have" as an "injunction" that we should be guided by propositions for which "the evidential weight is the greatest."[27] But practical problems make following the injunction difficult. Evidence, like its associated probabilities, may not be comparable. Suppose I must choose between two novels: one written by an author I usually like and the other recommended by a critic whose reviews usually match my tastes. I cannot reasonably compare the probabilities of liking either novel. And if I take a neutral position—that I am as likely to enjoy one as much as the other—I cannot rely on the rule of favoring the one supported by more evidence. How can I compare the weight of my experience with the author's previous novels with the critic's previous recommendations? A whimsical choice based on the books' covers or titles would not be irrational.[28]

Relevance and sufficiency also pose practical problems in preferring more evidence to less. Changes in an author's writing style or a book reviewer's tastes can make historical evidentiary weight irrelevant; recall the inductivist turkey's unpleasant surprise on Thanksgiving. New scientific or technological knowledge can also alter relevance. Facts we now believe irrelevant can turn out to be pivotal—and vice versa. Physicians considered handwashing unrelated to

78 UNCERTAINTY AND ENTERPRISE

the probability of childbirth deaths before the mid-1800s—and then only reluctantly accepted the connection.

Conversely, we learned that disinfecting tables and doorknobs, initially expected to reduce the spread of Covid infections (caused by an airborne virus), was useless. And evolving medical techniques can severely reduce the relevance of evidence produced at great cost by clinical trials.

The Coronary Bypass Trial Controversy

René Favaloro, an Argentinian surgeon at the Cleveland Clinic, and his colleagues simplified, standardized, and helped disseminate "open heart" bypass surgery to treat coronary disease in the late 1960s. Bypass operations then multiplied from two thousand in 1969 to twenty thousand in 1971. A front-page story published in 1972 by the *Boston Globe* called the procedure "one of the most exciting and controversial operations ever developed."

However, the article also reported that some physicians were skeptical. Mass General Hospital's general director said that operating on everyone with angina would require "turn[ing] the whole hospital over to open heart surgery." Doctors could not be sure that bypass operations prolonged lives, and they could treat angina with medication, exercise, diet, and lifestyle changes "without resorting immediately to surgery."

An editorial in the British journal *Lancet* observed that "pioneer work at the Cleveland Clinic" had produced a "snowball," with major cardiac centers "organizing a production line" for the operations. But "without scientifically reputable appraisal of the results . . . we are at risk of making many serious errors of judgment."[29] What's more, Medicare legislation passed in 1965 required the US federal government to pay for surgeries performed on patients above age sixty-five. Typical costs of six thousand to ten thousand dollars per procedure "meant that the government faced enormous expenditures if bypass surgery grew unchecked."[30]

In 1973, the National Heart and Lung Institute[31] sponsored the Coronary Artery Surgery Study (CASS), a randomized trial to compare bypass operations and drug treatments. The CASS study enrolled fewer than eight hundred patients in fifteen hospitals, "reflecting a reluctance to enter patients into randomized trials."[32] Another randomized trial sponsored by the US Veterans Administration (VA) study similarly enrolled only about seven hundred patients in thirteen VA hospitals. One VA hospital, whose chief of surgery believed the study would be "an expensive and time-consuming effort without valid conclusions," did not participate.

The trials did not resolve much. The first results of the VA trial were published in September 1977, and those of the CASS trial—which had taken ten years and cost twenty-four million dollars—were published in November 1983. Harvard Medical School cardiologist Eugene Braunwald praised both studies in *New England Journal of Medicine* editorials. Critics cited the "crossover" problem: patients chosen for drug treatments had been switched to surgery during the trial period when drug treatments failed, but the trials credited their survival to drug treatments.[33] Bypass pioneer Favaloro argued that the survival of switched-over patients (many of whom were "difficult" cases) should have been counted as a success of surgery—and as failures of drug treatments.

The bigger problem, in my view, is that bypass techniques changed materially between 1979 (when the last patients in the CASS trial had been treated) and 1983, when the results were published. In the early 1980s, cardioplegic drugs had reduced mortality rates of bypass operations. Physicians also got better results by changing the blood vessels they used to bypass constricted coronary arteries. Therefore, even if the trials had somehow avoided the crossover problems or enrolled many more patients, the evidence they produced about past outcomes could not resolve future treatment uncertainties.

For more details about the controversy, see Jones (2000) and Bhidé, Datar, and Villa (2020).

The question of sufficiency—deciding how much evidence is enough and when to stop looking for more—also poses acute challenges.[34] Bernoulli's maxim, Keynes observes, might imply that we should maximize our evidence by "getting all the information we can." But it isn't easy to decide how far

> increasing the evidence ought to be pushed. We may argue that, when our knowledge is slight but capable of increase, the course of action which will, relative to such knowledge, probably produce the greatest amount of good, will often consist in the acquisition of more knowledge. But there clearly comes a point when it is no longer worth while to spend trouble, before acting, in the acquisition of further information, and there is no evident principle by which to determine how far we ought to carry our maxim of strengthening the weight of our argument. A little reflection will probably convince the reader that this is a very confusing problem.[35]

One scholar asks whether the unsolved problem "is sufficiently serious to undermine the relevance of the theory of evidential weight."[36] Another argues that "the question of when to stop gathering information is a pragmatic one"—implying that it's not worth studying.[37] Keynes himself hesitated about the practical

80 UNCERTAINTY AND ENTERPRISE

relevance of evidentiary weights,[*] remaining "uncertain" about "how much importance to attach" to the theory.[38] He called the question "highly perplexing, and it is difficult to say much that is useful about it."[39]

Routines as Antidotes My answer unapologetically focuses on "pragmatic," domain-specific routines that economists and decision theorists often ignore. Here, as in many practical matters, we must manage the problems of relevance and sufficiency without much guidance from a general theory.

Routines to reduce the risks of missing important considerations are age-old. Followers of Hippocrates in ancient Greece adopted the transformational idea of attributing disease to natural causes, not divine displeasure. Their revolutionary approach included a "highly sophisticated type of physical examination."[40] Physicians in French hospitals established basic steps—inspection (of tongues, eyes, ears, etc.), palpation, percussion, and auscultation—in the early nineteenth century.[41] In murder investigations, comprehensive postmortems help distinguish homicides from suicides and accidents. If the medical crime series *Silent Witness* is to be believed, no one ever dies from the initially most obvious cause. In banking, templates guide evaluations of the creditworthiness of borrowers. In business strategy, frameworks direct attention to the facts and factors that can affect the profits of a business. It is the comprehensiveness of Porter's Five Forces framework—not its predictions or prescriptions—that accounts for its widespread use, in my view.[†]

Routines and conventions also provide defaults for weak or ambiguous evidence. Physicians immediately remove polyps found during colonoscopies and biopsy them afterward but may merely monitor skin moles. Similarly, hospitals keep older patients who have suffered a fall for observation when scans show no evident brain damage but will send younger patients home. Judges instruct juries in criminal trials to acquit if the prosecutor's evidence is credible but not enough to eliminate reasonable doubt, as mentioned. Scottish law allows "not proven" verdicts, along with its more demanding two-witness requirement for criminal

---

[*] Keynes (1921, 84) writes that "it seems plausible to suppose that we ought to take account of the weight as well as the probability of different expectations. But it is difficult to think of any clear example of this, and I do not feel sure that the theory of 'evidential weight' has much practical significance." As it happens, decades after the *Treatise*'s 1921 publication, Alan Turing's cryptographers at Bletchley Park used the book's ideas about the weight of arguments to crack German wartime codes (Marsay 2016, 17). Perhaps not coincidentally Turing was a friend of Keynes, and Irving John Good, one of Turing's teammates, had been a student of Keynes.

[†] These routines do not guarantee consideration of all the material evidence since they cannot go beyond existing background knowledge and generalizations. Applications outside target domains can also be problematic. See my "Hustle as Strategy" critique (Bhidé 1986) of Porter's model.

convictions. In finance, high-tech investors often give the benefit of the doubt to unproven businesses, while the conventions of prudent banking require careful documentation of creditworthiness.

The defaults are not foolproof. Judicial requirements for overwhelming evidence can produce widely criticized outcomes; recall the outcry when OJ Simpson was acquitted of murder. Likewise, default rejection rules can deny credit to good borrowers. Nonetheless, default conventions seem more reasonable than coin-toss choices, especially if they embody previous experience.

My conjectures (chapter 3) further suggest that reasonableness depends on the consequences or "stakes." Routines designed for high stakes usually require more evidence and minimize harm when evidence is unavailable or ambiguous. In contrast, abnormal or pathological routines overdemand evidence for low stakes or under-demand evidence for high stakes. I further argue that variations in the demand for evidence promote a diverse entrepreneurial ecosystem (as was shown in Figure 4.1).

3. Unintended Legacy

Mixed Reception "There is much here," Keynes's preface to his *Treatise* noted, "which is novel and, being novel, unsifted, inaccurate, or deficient. I propound my systematic conception of this subject for criticism and enlargement at the hand of others, doubtful whether I myself am likely to get much further, by waiting." As it happens, the book got more criticism than enlargement, along with some praise. As we will also see, the *Treatise* did not reform mainstream ideas. On the contrary, challenges to its arguments helped strengthen the mathematized approaches that Keynes had questioned.

Early admirers of the *Treatise* included Bertrand Russell, the renowned philosopher, logician, 1950 Nobel Laureate in Literature—and imaginer of the inductivist turkey. Russell's review for the *Mathematical Gazette* described the *Treatise* as "the most important work on probability that has appeared for a very long time," which was "impossible to praise too highly."[42] Russell also however questioned Keynes's proposition that many probabilities are not numerically measurable and hoped for a "modified form" of the frequency theory.[43]

Keynes's assumption of "objective" probability relations also attracted skepticism. We can readily think of the numerical frequencies of "events" that traditional probability theories analyzed as objective. Keynes went further. He

82 UNCERTAINTY AND ENTERPRISE

asserted that probability relations broadly conceived also have an "objective" existence that we can naturally perceive or "cognize."

> When once the facts are given which determine our knowledge, what is probable or improbable in these circumstances ... is independent of our opinion. The Theory of Probability is logical, therefore, because it is concerned with the degree of belief which it is rational to entertain in given conditions, and not merely with the actual beliefs of particular individuals, which may or may not be rational.[44]

Keynes's protégé, Frank Ramsey, thought Keynes's perceived yet objective probability relations[45] implausible. Ramsey also resisted Keynes's demotion of numerical probabilities and their mathematical calculus to a corner of a broader domain of logical propositions. As Keynes wrote in a 1922 letter, "Ramsey and other young men at Cambridge are quite obdurate, and still believe that either Probability is a definitely measurable entity, probably connected with Frequency, or is of merely psychological importance and is definitely non-logical."[46]

Ramsey's Attacks and Alternative Ramsey proved a formidable critic. A second-year college student at Cambridge, Ramsey was about half Keynes's age when the *Treatise* was published. Keynes thought him "far and away the most brilliant undergraduate who has appeared for many years in the border-country between philosophy and mathematics." Like Keynes in 1905, Ramsey would take the mathematics Tripos exam in 1923—but while Keynes had ranked twelfth in the Tripos,[47] Ramsey stood first.

In a paper read to the Moral Sciences Club in Cambridge, Ramsey offered what he called a

> fundamental criticism of Mr. Keynes' views which is the obvious one that there really do not seem to be any such things as the probability relations he describes. He supposes that, at any rate in certain cases, they can be perceived; but speaking for myself I feel confident that this is not true. I do not perceive them, and if I am to be persuaded that they exist it must be by argument; moreover I shrewdly suspect that others do not perceive them either, because they are able to come to so very little agreement as to which of them relates any two given propositions.[48]

Donald Gilles calls this a "case of an argument which gains in strength from the nature of the person who proposes it. Had a less distinguished logician than Ramsey objected that he was unable to perceive any logical relations of probability, Keynes might have replied that this was merely a sign of logical incompetence, or logical blindness. . . . Ramsey, however, was such

JOHN MAYNARD KEYNES: HELP TO DISTRACTION   83

a brilliant mathematical logician that Keynes could not have claimed with plausibility that Ramsey was lacking in the capacity for logical intuition or perception."[49]

Instead of Keynes's objective but often nonnumerical probability relations, Ramsey proposed a theory of subjective probabilities. The theory expressed subjective estimates as numerical betting odds. "The old-established way of measuring a person's belief is to propose a bet, and see what are the lowest odds which he will accept. This method I regard as fundamentally sound," Ramsey argued. This was not "unreasonable" he claimed, "when it is seen that all our lives we are in a sense betting. Whenever we go to the station we are betting that a train will really run, and if we had not a sufficient degree of belief in this we should decline the bet and stay at home."[50]

Expressing subjective beliefs as betting odds allowed Ramsey to create a benchmark for their rationality. Rational beliefs and betting odds did not have to be objectively correct. Instead, Ramsey proposed consistency as the standard using the following test. An individual would offer bets, at odds reflecting her beliefs, to a counterpart who was allowed to choose the stakes. The beliefs failed the consistency test if the counterpart could choose stakes that gave the counterpart a sure profit. Otherwise, they passed the test. Ramsey also specified formal "laws of probability" to accompany the consistency of beliefs: Anyone who violated these laws "could have a book made against him by a cunning better and would then stand to lose in any event."[51]

Ramsey's theory applied both to inductive inferences about repeated events as well as to guesses about one-offs. Betting odds could, therefore, express—and numerically compare—all possible subjective beliefs.[52]

Ramsey, say some, "demolished" Keynes's *Treatise* "so effectively that Keynes himself abandoned it."[53] Others disagree; O'Donnell, for one, makes the following argument: Evidence of Keynes's surrender typically relies on a tribute that Keynes wrote in 1931; the twenty-six-year-old Ramsey had unexpectedly died the previous year after an attack of jaundice. While Ramsey had been unwavering in his criticism of the *Treatise*, Keynes was understandably gracious in his tribute to a dear friend who also happened to be a critic. But Keynes continued questioning the logic of universal numerical expression in his post-1931 work. Conceding the correctness of Ramsey's formal logic did not imply "any acceptance of Ramsey's subjectivized betting alternative."[54]

Regardless, whether Keynes surrendered to Ramsey's attacks is irrelevant. Ramsey's theories, and later work by De Finetti and then Savage, merged into subjective utility maximization—the foundation of modern microeconomics, as mentioned. Keynes did not try to develop or promote the ideas in his *Treatise*, turning his attention to macroeconomics in the 1930s. In his tribute to Ramsey,

84   UNCERTAINTY AND ENTERPRISE

the forty-eight-year-old Keynes had declared that "logic, like lyrical poetry, is no employment for the middle-aged."[55]

But the deceased Ramsey was no better placed to promote his theory, so why did it dominate?

Ramsey's theory wasn't more realistic. According to O'Donnell, Ramsey assumed "idealized beings" whose "rational betting" had "mathematical consistency across subjective universes of numerical probabilities."[56] Ramsey had criticized Keynes for assuming "non-existent probability relations" yet "endowed his own agents with non-existent superhuman powers."[57] Keynes "focused on how probabilities are used by real people in real domains," O'Donnell writes. "Any real human could appear to be thinking along the lines of Keynes's account, but no real human could possibly think (even 'approximately') in Ramsey's terms."[58]

To paraphrase Ramsey's attack on Keynes, I cannot imagine placing mental bets on everything under the sun, and I suspect that many others cannot either.

But although Ramsey's theories required implausible assumptions—and did not reliably predict or convincingly explain actual occurrences—they helped shape the subjective utility maximization paradigm (discussed in the previous chapter). Even information economics, which challenged the Panglossian results of mainstream microeconomics, assumed agents who maximize subjective utilities. Keynes's nonnumerical probability relations and evidentiary weights did not provide competing paradigmatic possibilities and opportunities for normal science. Like Knightian uncertainty, the *Treatise*'s ideas could not attract capable followers and fell by the wayside.

4. Extreme and Macro Uncertainties

Extra to Star   While the *Treatise* emphasized nonnumerical probabilities, it said almost nothing about the extreme, intractable uncertainty now often associated with Keynes (and, by extension, Knight). Keynes's 1921 book had just one suggestion of intractable uncertainty—about the inconsequential carrying of an umbrella for a walk:

> Is our expectation of rain, when we start out for a walk, always more likely than not, or less likely than not, or as likely as not? I am prepared to argue that on some occasions none of these alternatives hold, and that it will be an arbitrary matter to decide for or against the umbrella. If the barometer [i.e., air pressure] is high, but the clouds are black, it is not always rational that one should prevail over the other in our minds, or even that we should balance them,—though it will be rational to allow caprice to determine us and to waste no time on the debate.[59]

The example does not mention "uncertainty."[60]

Uncertainty stars in Keynes's 1936 *General Theory*, however. In a summary of his dense opus* in the February 1937 issue of the *Quarterly Journal of Economics*, Keynes writes,

> By "uncertain" knowledge, let me explain, I do not mean merely to distinguish what is known for certain from what is only probable. The game of roulette is not subject, in this sense, to uncertainty; nor is the prospect of a Victory bond being drawn. Or, again, the expectation of life is only slightly uncertain. Even the weather is only moderately uncertain. The sense in which I am using the term is that in which the prospect of a European war is uncertain, or the price of copper and the rate of interest twenty years hence, or the obsolescence of a new invention, or the position of private wealth-owners in the social system in 1970. About these matters there is no scientific basis on which to form any calculable probability whatever. We simply do not know. Nevertheless, the necessity for action and for decision compels us as practical men to do our best to overlook this awkward fact and to behave exactly as we should if we had behind us a good Benthamite calculation of a series of prospective advantages and disadvantages, each multiplied by its appropriate probability, waiting to be summed.[61]

Notice the switch from trivial rain showers to high-stakes European wars. Likewise, Keynes goes from "capricious" choices (of carrying umbrellas) to Benthamite (or what we might now call subjective utility or expected value) calculations. The "necessity for action," and presumably the stakes, "compel" these calculations, even when we have "no scientific basis" for estimating probabilities.

How "we manage in such circumstances to behave in a manner which saves our faces as rational, economic men" is also highly consequential in Keynes's theory. The most important of a "variety of techniques" and conventions, according to Keynes, are

1) Assuming that current conditions and trends will continue.
2) Assuming that "the existing state of opinion as expressed in prices and the character of existing output is based on a correct summing up of future prospects."

---

* Paul Samuelson's (1946) tribute, published in *Econometrica* after Keynes's death, called his *General Theory* "a badly written book, poorly organized; any layman who, beguiled by the author's previous reputation, bought the book was cheated out of his five shillings. . . . It is arrogant, bad tempered, and not overly generous in its acknowledgements. It abounds in mares' nests and confusions. . . . In short, it is a work of genius."

86 UNCERTAINTY AND ENTERPRISE

3) Conforming to the consensus: "Knowing that our own individual judgment is worthless, we endeavour to fall back on the judgement of the rest of the world which is perhaps better informed. That is, we endeavour to conform with the behaviour of the majority or the average."[62]

A "theory of the future," Keynes continues, "based on so flimsy a foundation is subject to sudden and violent changes":

> The practice of calmness and immobility, of certainty and security, suddenly breaks down. New fears and hopes will, without warning, take charge of human conduct. The forces of disillusion may suddenly impose a new conventional basis of valuation. All these pretty, polite techniques, made for a well-panelled Board Room and a nicely regulated market, are liable to collapse. At all times the vague panic fears and equally vague and unreasoned hopes are not really lulled, and lie but a little way below the surface.[63]

Knight's RUP (and Keynes's own *Treatise*) had none of this Sturm und Drang. RUP treats uncertainty in the "fundamental facts of life . . . as ineradicable from business decisions as from those in any other field."[64] His mundane examples include the "typical business decision" of "a manufacturer . . . considering the advisability of making a large commitment in increasing the capacity of his works."[65]

Keynes's *General Theory* focuses on abrupt changes in collective opinions, particularly in financial markets, with systemic macroeconomic consequences. In contrast, typical business decisions (such as the factory expansion decision) examined in Knight's RUP are "micro" choices. They mainly affect the individuals who make them. And unlike Keynes's unimaginable prospects for private wealth in thirty years, the sources of Knight's routine business uncertainties are themselves routine. For example, Knight attributes common business uncertainty about what and how much to produce to "known unknowns" about demand—what customers will want, how much they will pay, and so on. RUP only perfunctorily acknowledges unimaginable unknown unknowns—"occurrences so revolutionary and unexpected by any one as hardly to be brought under the category of . . . judgment at all"—for the sake of "completeness."[66]

Knight's 1921 book also had more modest aims. Keynes fiercely attacked prevailing theories of self-equilibrating economies, "accus[ing] the classical economic theory of being itself one of these pretty, polite techniques which tries to deal with the present by abstracting from the fact that we know very little about the future."[67] Published amid the Great Depression and in the aftermath of a stock market crash, the *General Theory* provided a rationale for large-scale macroeconomic interventions.

Knight laid out more business-focused and conservative aims in his book's preface. On the "technical" side, Knight offered a "fuller and more careful examination of the rôle of the entrepreneur" and "of the forces which fix the remuneration of his special function." On the "practical" side, Knight would answer the question of "what is reasonably to be expected of a method of [economic] organization" and emphasize both the defects of free enterprise as well as "the fatuousness of over-sanguine expectations from mere changes in social machinery."

Rise and Reframing Edmund Phelps calls Keynes's *General Theory* a "founding work" and "source-book" of "perceptive observations and theoretical suggestions" for modern macroeconomics.[68] Phelps's own influential theories about collective expectations (akin to Keynes's analysis of swings in public opinion) significantly extended and mathematized some conjectures in the *General Theory*.

Keynesian economics also dominated economic policy for over two decades after World War II.[69] In 1971, President Nixon declared he was "now a Keynesian in economics." Shocking conservatives, Nixon proposed fiscal stimulus to stave off a recession. At the start of his presidency in 1969, Nixon had proposed a balanced budget.

In the 1970s, however, when advanced economies suffered from "stagflation"—low growth plus high inflation—Keynesian theories became less popular.* Meanwhile, even earlier, Keynesians and neo-Keynesians had been developing deterministic models that excluded uncertainty, considering it mathematically inconvenient—and superfluous. The economists leading the reframing—Paul Samuelson being the most prominent[70]—held professorships at MIT and Harvard in Cambridge, Massachusetts (the "new" Cambridge). Holdouts from the "old" Cambridge resisted, however.

"Beginning in the mid-1950s, the 'war of the two Cambridges' animated the discipline," writes venture capitalist and (old) Cambridge economist William Janeway; by the late 1960s, "The war was over, unequivocally won by MIT and Harvard."[71] By the early 1970s, "The macroeconomics of Samuelson's neoclassical synthesis, universally and misleadingly termed Keynesian, had come to be

---

* Economists from the monetary school proposed regulating the money supply, while those from the "new classical school" argued that both Keynesian and monetary interventions were futile (Jahan and Papageorgiou 2014, 54). Central bankers did, however, attempt to manage collective inflation expectations—an indirect legacy of the *General Theory* that Phelps and others made a cornerstone of their macroeconomic theories.

88 UNCERTAINTY AND ENTERPRISE

intimately associated with large-scale econometric models."[72] Samuelson's synthesis "accommodated the Keynesian revolution by sleight of hand."

> The "Bastard Keynesians" of new Cambridge, as Keynes's student Joan Robinson provocatively called them, had appropriated the mantle of Keynesianism while abandoning the ontological core of Keynes's thinking.... Hy Minsky summarized his indictment of Samuelson's achievement: "the neoclassical synthesis became the economics of capitalism without capitalists, capital assets and financial markets."[73]

The determinism of uncertainty-free macroeconomics and its adherents' complacency disturbed skeptics, including Phelps. Former Fed chair Ben Bernanke and MIT economist Olivier Blanchard, Phelps recalls, had "crowed at a 2005 conference in Boston* that monetary policy had become a science: When money warrants tightening or loosening, experts will know it and act."[74] (In 2007 Bernanke had testified before Congress that "the impact ... of the problems in the subprime market seems likely to be contained."[75])

Prospects of and from a Revival The global financial crisis that erupted in September 2008 revived interest in Keynes's macroeconomics. Two months later, Harvard economist (and Republican adviser) Greg Mankiw opened his *New York Times* op-ed with this paragraph:

> If you were going to turn to only one economist to understand the problems facing the economy, there is little doubt that the economist would be John Maynard Keynes. Although Keynes died more than a half-century ago, his diagnosis of recessions and depressions remains the foundation of modern macroeconomics. His insights go a long way toward explaining the challenges we now confront.[76]

Mankiw's op-ed provided a Keynesian analysis of shortfalls in aggregate demand—but with no mention of uncertainty. And the full-blast macrointerventions unleashed after the 2008 crisis and again after the 2020 Covid pandemic have likewise aimed at sustaining demand.

A few economists had, however, stuck with Keynesian uncertainty, and the 2008 crisis brought them some attention and resources. Nominally, some of their research initiatives have included Knightian uncertainty, with which Keynesian uncertainty is now often bracketed. For example, the Institute for New Economic

---

* To celebrate Paul Samuelson's work, as it happens.

Thinking (INET) now sponsors the Knightian Uncertainty Economics program. According to its website, the program is "inspired by arguments advanced by Frank Knight, John Maynard Keynes, Friedrich Hayek, and Karl Popper about the inherent limits of what we can know about the future."[77]

For my modernization project, however, the conflation of Keynes's *General Theory* uncertainty and Knightian uncertainty is problematic. As discussed above, Keynes's uncertainty is extreme. It can produce stock market booms and busts with disastrous economy-wide effects. Knight focuses on how mundane uncertainties affect decentralized choices and the micro consequences of these choices for Main Street businesses, not financial markets. Additionally, conventions to cope with extreme uncertainty in Keynes's *General Theory* have dysfunctional consequences. My updating, in contrast, treats conventions and routines to justify and evaluate uncertain entrepreneurial initiatives as reasonable, practical necessities.

Yet some prominent heterodox researchers and programs favor the Keynesian focus. Notwithstanding its "Knightian" label, the INET program focuses on "the key implication" of uncertainty for "macroeconomics and finance theory." It aims to "develop formal macroeconomics and finance models and approaches to policy analysis."[78] Heterodox and bold indeed, but with no mention of concrete, individualized enterprises.

9

Herbert Simon: Faded Guiding Star

In principle, the methodology of behavioral economics delineates its scope. Herbert Simon—a pioneering polymath who won the 1978 Nobel in Economics—wrote (in 1987) that not all economists who "hold a behavioural point of view also hold a common theory, or are all preoccupied with examining the same parts of the economic mechanism." Instead, behavioral economics is "best characterized as a commitment to empirical testing of the neoclassical assumptions of human behaviour and to modifying economic theory on the basis of what is found in the testing process."[1]

In practice, the big tent Simon wrote about in 1987 has narrowed its attitude to rationality and uncertainty. The dominant view, based on Daniel Kahneman and Amos Tversky's research, now emphasizes mental failings that produce illogical choices. Some leading researchers, themselves presumably right-thinking, also promote "nudges" to protect the public from its feeblemindedness.* And like neoclassical and information economics, current behavioral research often ignores uncertainty.

To appreciate the nature of the currently dominant view, it will help to first examine what it eclipsed. Specifically, this chapter reviews how and why

- Knight had anticipated many of the biases and quirks studied by contemporary researchers—and noted how uncertainty magnified their effects. Knight also proposed a "middle way" methodology to limit the practical risks of theories that assume away biases, quirks, and uncertainty.

- Simon examined realistic reasonableness—rationality "bounded" by unavoidable limits to what we can know (i.e., uncertainty) and process.

- Simon's ideas, ignored by mainstream economics, provide useful steppingstones for my project.

---

* In the contemporary version of behavioral economics, "nudges" are ways of manipulating people's choices. "For example, putting fruit . . . near the cash register at a high school cafeteria is an example of a 'nudge' to get students to choose healthier options. An essential aspect of nudges is that they are not coercive: Banning junk food is not a nudge, nor is punishing people for choosing unhealthy options" (Max Witynski "Behavioral Economics Explained," uchicagonews, August 11, 2021, https://news.uchicago.edu/explainer/what-is-behavioral-economics)

Uncertainty and Enterprise. Amar Bhidé, Oxford University Press. © Oxford University Press 2025.
DOI: 10.1093/oso/9780197688359.003.0009

HERBERT SIMON: FADED GUIDING STAR   91

1. Knight's Anticipations and Antidotes

Unpredictable Responses to Uncertainty Knight rejected purely rational explanations of human conduct. Much of our economic behavior, Knight wrote, is "impulsive and capricious." Only a "small fraction of the activities of civilized man," according to Knight, seek to gratify "needs or desires having any foundation beyond the mere fact that an impulse exists at the moment in the mind of the subject."[2] We even choose longer-term objectives, such as getting an education, acquiring a skill, or making money, continues Knight, "more or less at random" with "the social situation furnish[ing] much of the driving power."

Knight's 1921 views were then unremarkable: doctrinal commitments to strict rationality did not solidify until after the 1930s. In earlier times, leading economists recognized the role of primal passions. Alfred Marshall wrote in his 1890 *Principles of Economics* that just as athletes "strain every nerve" to get ahead of competitors, a "manufacturer or trader is often stimulated much more by the hope of victory over his rivals than by the desire to add something to his fortune." Marshall urged economists to study such motives carefully because they could "alter perceptibly the general character of their reasonings."[3] Joseph Schumpeter's 1911 *Theory of Economic Development* credited innovation to entrepreneurs with "the will to conquer; the impulse to fight, to prove oneself superior to others, to succeed for the sake, not of the fruits, but of success itself."[4] And Keynes (who Marshall had mentored at Cambridge) wrote in his *General Theory*,

> A large proportion of our positive activities depend on spontaneous optimism rather than on a mathematical expectation, whether moral or hedonistic or economic. Most . . . of our decisions to do something positive, the full consequences of which will be drawn out over many days to come, can only be taken as a result of animal spirits—of a spontaneous urge to action rather than inaction, and not as the outcome of a weighted average of quantitative benefits multiplied by quantitative probabilities.[5]

Knight's 1921 book also anticipated ideas such as loss aversion and overconfidence, which have become mainstays of contemporary "behavioral economics"*—although the Knightian precedence is rarely acknowledged.[6] But

---

* A careful reader of Knight's book may be puzzled by his prediction that despite "rash statements by over-ardent devotees of the new science of "behavior," it was preposterous to suppose that it [would] ever supersede psychology (which is something very different)" (Knight 1921, 203). Knight was presumably referring to the then-new approach called "behaviorism"—pioneered by John Broadus Watson, Ivan Pavlov, and Burrhus Frederick Skinner—that attempted to explain all observed behavior as a response to external stimuli. In this theory, explanations based on unobservable mental states and processes were irrelevant. Knight's dismissal of this approach was prescient

92 UNCERTAINTY AND ENTERPRISE

there is a crucial difference between Knight and modern behavioral researchers on the effects of uncertainty on impulsive or erratic behavior.

Knight asserted that uncertainty often induces

> well-recognized deviations from the conduct which sound logic would dictate. Thus, it is a familiar fact, well discussed by Adam Smith, that men will readily risk a small amount in the hope of winning a large [amount] when the adverse probability (known or estimated) against winning is much in excess of the ratio of the two amounts, while they commonly will refuse to incur a small chance of losing a larger amount for a virtual certainty of winning a smaller. . . . To this bias must be added an inveterate belief on the part of the typical individual in his own "luck" . . . [and] the almost universal prevalence of superstitions. Any coincidence that strikes attention is likely to be elevated into a law of nature.[7]

Moreover, according to Knight, uncertainty tends to make conduct "erratic and extremely various from one individual to another."[8] In contrast, as I argue in a later chapter, contemporary behavioral research ignores the possibility that uncertainty may evoke or amplify erratic behavior.

"Middle Way" Methodologies Knight's justification for highlighting "erratic and extremely various" deviations from rational conduct also differs from why some leading behavioral researchers advance claims of rampant irrationality. The latter rely on widespread, self-harming or antisocial irrationality to promote policy "nudges." Nudges would have appalled Knight. His devotion to individual autonomy and freedom made him question even straightforward persuasion.

Knight's book does not "placard the unrealities of the postulates of theoretical economics . . . for the purpose of discrediting the doctrine." Rather, he defends "pure theory" as an essential step "toward a practical understanding of the social system." Just as perpetual-motion schemes do not "discredit theoretical mechanics, which is built upon the assumption of perpetual [frictionless] motion," so, also, we should not reject the unrealistic abstractions of economic theories. Knight, however, rebukes theorists who do not clarify the limitations of theoretical results and make "the corrections necessary to make them fit concrete facts. Policies must fail, and fail disastrously, which are based on perpetual motion reasoning *without the recognition that it is such*" (italics in original).[9]

---

but premature. It dominated US psychology in the 1920s and 1930s but was eventually superseded by "cognitive psychology"—which related behavior to mental processes and from which contemporary behavioral economics has evolved.

HERBERT SIMON: FADED GUIDING STAR   93

Knight recommends a "middle way" of "successive approximations": Start with abstract, general theory but constantly check the conclusions deduced against observations and revise accordingly.[10] Walter Vincenti[11] and other historians of technology have recorded a similar use of iteration in engineering: designers often start with general physical laws or concepts, which they then adapt to specific product requirements.

Like his uncertainty, Knight's "middle way" methodology did not follow the emerging norms and conventions of economics. As mentioned, the discipline has a strong "scientific" preference for concise ("parsimonious") general propositions over complex "technological" prescriptions optimized for particular times and places.[12] Friedman's famous 1953 methodological essay claims that an "important hypothesis" in economics explains much by abstracting "crucial elements from the mass of detailed and complex circumstances."[13]

Friedman's essay also advocates testing the predictions of parsimonious theories. This is not an innocuous norm. It sees changing theories to suit the facts—instead of rejecting hypotheses that fail testing—as an illegitimate procedure. The uncertain relationship between general theories and concrete circumstances makes "try-it, fix-it" efforts unavoidable in practical fields such as engineering, medicine, and business. But this goes against the predispositions of scientific economics.[14] Similarly, contextual and historical explanations of one-of-a-kind phenomena are apt to produce summary rejections from journal editors on the grounds of mere storytelling. Unsurprisingly, academic economists avoid Knight's middle-way iterations, along with uncertainty.

Implications for Modernization   Like Knight's theory, my conjectures recognize but do not require whimsical or impulsive behavior. However, the possibility of whim and impulse, magnified by uncertainty, increases the problem of trusting the quality of other people's judgments and the demand for justification. I also follow the spirit of Knight's middle-way synthesis of general propositions and contextual observation.

2. Simon's Realistic Reasonableness

Multidisciplinary Synthesis   Knight's observations about caprice and impulse, like those of other economists of his time, were improvised and ad hoc. This, however, changed after World War II with systematic research on individual and organizational "conduct" or "behavior" in the economic realm. Previously, behavior had been systematically studied mainly by sociologists, psychologists,

94 UNCERTAINTY AND ENTERPRISE

and physiologists (including the Russian experimentalist Ivan Pavlov, who accidentally discovered conditioned responses in dogs).*

Herbert Simon, a remarkable polymath, brought systematic behavioral research into economics. Simon's work, undertaken over sixty years, spans a formidable range of topics, methods, and insights. But much of it had a theme that ran against the omniscience of mainstream economics and saw a large part of economic behavior happening "inside the skin of firms."[15]

Polymathic Pioneer

Born in the American Midwest in 1916, Simon received a BA from the University of Chicago in 1936. According to a biographical entry in the *New Palgrave Dictionary of Economics*, Simon intended to major in economics but switched to political science after refusing to take a course in accounting that an economics degree required. His second-choice field left an enduring mark: political science attracted Simon to interdisciplinary thinking and to combining theory and practice.[16]

An undergraduate term paper created an interest in organizational decision-making. The paper also got Simon, after his graduation, a research assistantship studying municipal administration, "carrying out investigations that would now be classified as operations research." The research assistantship led to the directorship of a group at the University of Berkeley doing similar research. Simon concurrently enrolled in a PhD program at the University of Chicago, again in political science. In his three years at Berkeley, from 1939 to 1942, Simon took "doctoral exams by mail and moonlighted a dissertation on administrative decision-making."

In 1942, after funds for the Berkeley project had run out, a friend helped Simon return to Chicago to teach political science at the Illinois Institute of Technology. In 1949, Simon joined a new business school at the Carnegie Institute of Technology (now Carnegie Mellon University). "Our goal," Simon later recalled, "was to place business education on a foundation of fundamental studies in economics and behavioral science. We were fortunate to pick a time for launching this venture when the new management science

---

* Pavlov's research measured the saliva dogs produced when presented with food. The procedure inadvertently conditioned the dogs to drool whenever they encountered a researcher wearing a lab coat. Pavlov then used a bell to deliberately condition the same salivatory response. This discovery helped popularize the "behaviorism" mentioned in an earlier footnote. His other, less remembered but pioneering research of how the digestive system works won him a Nobel in Medicine in 1904 ("Ivan Petrovich Pavlov and Conditioned Reflexes," The Nobel Prize, accessed September 17, 2022, https://educationalgames.nobelprize.org/educational/medicine/pavlov/readmore.php).

techniques were just appearing on the horizon, together with the electronic computer."[17]

Carnegie Mellon later honored Simon with a University Professorship in Computer Science and Psychology, and Simon continued to work at Carnegie until he died in 2001 at age eighty-four. During his lengthy career, according to the *New Palgrave* biography, "Simon made important contributions to economics, psychology, political science, sociology, administrative theory, public administration, organization theory, cognitive science, computer science and philosophy." In 1975, four years before his economics Nobel, Simon and longtime collaborator Allen Newell won the Turing Award—the highest honor in computer science—for "contributions to artificial intelligence, the psychology of human cognition, and list processing."[18]

Yet, according to the *New Palgrave* biography, Simon's "main research interest remained the same: understanding human decision making" in ways that brought together "theory and reality," and his "vision for behavioural economics" grew out of "his early work in public administration and political science."[19] Notably, Simon's landmark book *Administrative Behavior*, published in 1947 and based on his doctoral dissertation, presented a "theory of human decision making which was broad and realistic enough to accommodate both those rational aspects of choice that have been the principal concern of the economist, and those properties and limitations of the human decision making mechanisms that have attracted the attention of psychologists and practical decision makers." Combining "economics and psychology, Simon laid the foundation for the later establishment of behavioural economics and for organization theory."[20]

Simon summarized his wide-ranging work in the Richard T. Ely Lecture delivered to the American Economic Association in 1978, in the Nobel Lecture he gave later that year, and in entries for the *New Palgrave Dictionary of Economics*. The following features, extracted mainly from Simon's summaries, are particularly relevant to my updating.

Kinds of Rationality Simon distinguishes between the dictionary meaning of "rational" and its narrower use in mainstream economics. In the dictionary, Simon notes, rational means "agreeable to reason; not absurd, preposterous, extravagant, foolish, fanciful, or the like; intelligent, sensible." In contrast, "The rational man of economics is a [utility] maximizer, who will settle for nothing less than the best."[21] For Gary Becker, a luminary of the mainstream view, any deviation from utility maximization is irrational, Simon observes.[22]

96 UNCERTAINTY AND ENTERPRISE

Simon believes that "almost all human behavior has a large rational component, but only in terms of the broader everyday sense of rationality, not the economists' more specialized sense of maximization." And he argues that most sociological, psychological, political, and anthropological theories assume the broader kind of rationality: "The view of man as rational is not peculiar to economics, but is endemic, and even ubiquitous, throughout the social sciences. Economics tends to emphasize a particular form of rationality—maximizing behavior—as its preferred engine of explanation."[23]

Functionally Rational Theories

According to Simon, the assumption of a general (nonmaximizing) rationality appears in functional theories throughout the social sciences. "Behaviors are functional" in these theories, Simon writes, "if they contribute to certain goals, where these goals may be the pleasure or satisfaction of an individual or the guarantee of food or shelter for the members of a society." Similarly, "Institutions are functional if reasonable men might create and maintain them in order to meet social needs or achieve social goals."[24]

Unlike standard economics models, Simon notes, functional theories aren't concerned with how variables are equilibrated at the margin. And they address qualitative questions: What makes buying flood insurance rational, not how much insurance homeowners buy. Or when and why firms hire employees rather than contractors, not what wages firms pay.[25]

Functional theories do not require a conscious pursuit of goals. The function served by an institution or pattern of behavior "provides the grounds for [its] reasonableness or rationality." The theories also often invoke evolutionary arguments to "explain the persistence and survival of functional patterns, and to avoid assumptions of deliberate calculation in explaining them."[26]

The theories typically go from empirical observations of institutions or behavior to asking what functions they perform. Consequently, they "may demonstrate the sufficiency of a particular pattern for performing an essential function" but not its "necessity." Differently put, rational arrangements are not inevitable. A functional theory can claim that an observed attribute of a system is "consistent with" some requirement for its "survival and further development" but not that the "same requirements could not be satisfied in some other way. Thus, for example, societies can satisfy their functional needs for food by hunting or fishing activities, by agriculture, or by predatory exploitation of other societies."[27]

Simon also distinguishes between "substantive" and "procedural" rationality.[28] Economics, says Simon, focused on the substantive and was "preoccupied with the *results* of rational choice rather than the *process* of choice." In contrast, "Neighboring disciplines of operations research, artificial intelligence and cognitive psychology" developed theories of procedural rationality. Likewise, operations researchers and economists turned into "management scientists" developed practical ideas on *how* to decide.[29]

Uncertainty and Computational Constraints The "classical model," wrote Simon, "calls for knowledge of all the alternatives that are open to choice. It calls for complete knowledge of, or ability to compute, the consequences that will follow on each of the alternatives. It calls for certainty in the decision maker's present and future evaluation of these consequences. It calls for the ability to compare consequences, no matter how diverse and heterogeneous, in terms of some consistent measure of utility."[30]

Simon observes that this model could fit "rational decision in static, relatively simple problem situations" but not in "complex, dynamic circumstances that involve a great deal of uncertainty."[31] A more realistic model would "describe how decisions could be (and probably actually were) made when the alternatives . . . had to be sought out, the consequences of choosing particular alternatives were only very imperfectly known both because of limited computational power and because of uncertainty in the external world, and the decision maker did not possess a general and consistent utility function for comparing heterogeneous alternatives."[32]

By "limited computational power," Simon does not mean faulty reasoning of the kind that might lead to a miscalculation in a simple game of tic-tac-toe. Instead, limitations arise in dealing with complexity, as in anticipating and evaluating the possibilities ten moves ahead in chess. "Uncertainty in the external world" similarly arises from inescapable ignorance—what people do not know or cannot easily find out—not unreasonable disregard of helpful information.* The constraints are, however, reducible: Standardized "openings," for example, help chess players anticipate possibilities without calculating them out.

---

* We can similarly regard the absence of a "general and consistent utility function" as an inescapable consequence of "internal" uncertainty about the satisfaction that alternative outcomes can provide before we have experienced the outcomes. This uncertainty in turn impels the need for the "venturesome consumption" of new products.

Moving the Bounds

Systematic learning—or accidental discoveries—can ease computational limits. Experience can reduce uncertainty about the satisfaction that alternative outcomes will provide, and technological advances help expand computational capabilities and improve procedural rationality. For example, Simon notes that the inventions of writing, printing, and computers

> represent basic changes in man's equipment for making rational choices—in his computational capabilities. Problems that are impossible to handle with the head alone (multiplying large numbers together, for example) become trivial when they can be written down on paper. Interactions of energy and environment that almost defy conceptualization lend themselves to at least approximate modeling with modern computers.
>
> The advances in man's capacity for procedural rationality are not limited to these obvious examples. The invention of algebra, of analytic geometry, of the calculus were such advances. So was the invention, if we may call it that, of the modern organization which greatly increased man's capacity for coordinated parallel activity. Changes in the production function for information and decisions are central to any account of changes over the centuries of the human condition.[33]

Simon called realistic reasonableness "bounded" rationality. In retrospect, the label was unfortunate. Technically, it refers to the limits or "bounds" to what humans can compute and know. Rationality is bounded, Simon writes, "when it falls short of omniscience. And the failures of omniscience are largely failures of knowing all the alternatives, uncertainty about relevant exogenous events, and inability to calculate consequences." No irrationality in the ordinary sense here.

But economists like Becker regarded any deviation from their standard assumptions as irrational, as mentioned—and Simon's label was more memorable than his repeated efforts to distinguish it from irrationality. As we will see in chapter 11, Kahneman and Tversky's perspective, which stressed defective reasoning, eclipsed Simon's "bounded rationality." Simon's catchy label then became a synonym for irrationality.

Satisficing Simplification Simon calls his early characterization of bounded rationality a "residual category." Then, in "A Behavioral Model of Rational Choice," published in 1955, Simon attempted a more "positive" account.[34] This paper, published in the *Quarterly Journal of Economics* (*QJE*), noted that standard "global rationality" required calculating all possible payoffs. But there was no evidence that "in actual human choice situations of any complexity, these computations can be, or are in fact, performed."[35] Actual decision-making, therefore, required simplification.

Simon proposed that the simplification occurred thus: "If the alternatives for choice are not given initially to the decision maker, then [s]he must search for them."[36] And as with evidentiary weight accumulation discussed in the previous chapter, searching requires rules for stopping. But someone who starts searching because she does not know what alternatives are available cannot know when she has found the best possible one.

Simon proposed a simple rule: Evaluate alternatives against an aspiration level, not an unknowable maximizing standard. When an alternative "satisfies" the aspiration, stop; otherwise, continue searching.[37]

This "search and satisficing theory," Simon writes, "showed how choice could actually be made with reasonable amounts of calculation, and using very incomplete information . . . without the need of performing [any] impossible . . . optimizing procedure."[38]

Neoclassical stalwarts also added search to maximizing models, dropping the omniscient assumption that decision makers choose from a deck of already known alternatives. In 1963, Chicago's George Stigler built a model (using as its example the purchase of a secondhand car) that included the cost and benefits of search. But Stigler's model, wrote Simon, "poured the search theory back into the old bottle of classical utility maximization, the cost of search being equated with its marginal return." This implausibly "required the decision maker to be able to estimate the marginal costs and returns of search in a decision situation that was already too complex for the exercise of global rationality." Nonetheless, Stigler's search paper, published eight years after Simon's, became "very influential," while Simon's satisficing gathered dust on a peripheral shelf of mainstream economics.[39]

Decision-Making in Business Firms Simon's heterodoxy included examining decision-making within business firms. His Nobel Lecture— "Rational Decision Making in *Business* Organizations" (italics added)— noted that according to "respected and distinguished figures," including Milton Friedman, "fundamental inquiry into rational human behavior in the context of business organizations is simply not (by definition) economics."[40] (Simon's Nobel Award delicately cited his "pioneering research into the decision-making process within economic organizations," avoiding the mention of business.)

In the fourth edition of his classic *Administrative Behavior*, Simon observed that markets were acclaimed as "the ideal mechanism for economic and social integration." But markets could only work efficiently alongside "efficiently managed business firms." And businesses and other organizations played at least as important a role as markets. "Visitors from another planet might be surprised to hear our society described as a market economy," wrote Simon. "They might ask why we don't call it an organizational economy. After all, they observe large agglomerations of people working in organizations. They encounter large business firms, public agencies, universities. They have learned that 80 percent or more of the people who work in an industrialized society work inside the skins of organizations, most of them having very little direct contact, as employees, with markets. . . . Our visitors might well suggest that, at the least, we should call our society an organization-and-market society."[41]

Yet neo-classical economics focused, Simon complained, mainly on markets.[42] Its theory of business firms was a "pitifully skeletonized abstraction," wrote Simon, in which firms consisted of "little more than an 'entrepreneur'" who seeks to maximize the firm's profits. The theory said nothing about "the motivations that govern the decisions of managers and employees." It did not "ask how the actors acquire the information required for these decisions, how they make the necessary calculations," or even "whether they [were] capable of making the kinds of decisions postulated by utility-maximizing or profit-maximizing theory."[43]

Simon's theories developed with Carnegie collaborators—notably Richard Cyert and James March—regarded businesses and other organizations as "machinery for coping with the limits of man's abilities to comprehend and compute in the face of complexity and uncertainty."[44] The theories postulated searches for satisfactory rather than utility or profit-maximizing alternatives. The organizational theories also envisioned *organizational* procedures for dealing with "social-psychological factors."[45] These included replacing global profit-maximizing goals with satisficing subgoals; "divid[ing] the decision making task among many specialists"; and "coordinating their work by means of a structure of communications and authority relations." These distinctively organizational procedures "fit the general rubric of 'bounded rationality,' "[46] not irrationality.

Simon offered intellectual and practical justification for studying business firms. Human behavior in business firms, Simon argued, "constitutes a highly interesting body of empirical phenomena that calls out for explanation."[47] He also suggested a practical policy reason: How firms respond to situations they find themselves in depends on the decision processes they employ. And policymakers cannot ignore the sensitivity of outcomes to decision processes—as neoclassical theories of the firm typically do. At the very least, before drawing any policy conclusions from neoclassical theories, we should "test how far our conclusions would be changed if we made different assumptions about the decision mechanisms at the micro level." If the conclusions don't change, "We will gain confidence in our predictions and recommendations." But "if the conclusions are sensitive to such substitutions, we [should] use them warily until we can determine which micro-theory is the correct one."[48] (Knight, as mentioned, had similarly warned about relying on reductive theory.)

Multifaceted Methodology Simon's theories form a constellation of related ideas, not a sharply defined model or compact formula. The ideas did not occur to Simon in one blinding flash—they accumulated through what Knight might have called a "middle way" process over many decades. The accumulation was also exceptionally eclectic.

An Eclectic Accumulation

From the beginning, Simon's research combined parsimonious first principles theories (that mainstream economics applauds) and granular field observations and case studies (that mainstream economics avoids).

Simon's 1947 classic, *Administrative Behavior*, sought to combine "rational aspects of choice that have been the principal concern of the economist, and those properties and limitations of the human decision-making mechanisms that have attracted the attention of psychologists and practical decision makers."[49] The book originated in Simon's field study of recreational facilities that he had conducted as a college student.[50] It was strongly influenced by Chester Barnard's 1938 book, *The Functions of the Executive*.[51] Barnard, an "intellectually curious" executive, had distilled "original theories" about organizational authority and employee motivation and had "provided a realistic description of organizational decision making." His numerous references to Barnard's work in *Administrative Behavior* attested—inadequately, Simon said in his Nobel Lecture—"to the impact he had on my own thinking about organizations."[52]

Research that Simon and his Carnegie colleagues performed in the 1950s, '60s, and '70s was similarly diverse, including the following:

- "Anthropological" studies on organizational decision-making. Simon cites his 1954 study of how large companies used accounting data and a series of studies, with Richard Cyert and James March, on specific policy decisions in several companies.[53]

- A case study in a business policy casebook that Simon and DeWitt Dearborn asked executives to analyze.[54] The analyses showed "identification with subgoals." The "perceptions of the principal problems facing the company described in the case" were "mostly determined" by the roles of executives. Sales executives identified sales problems while manufacturing executives saw problems in internal organization.[55]

- Laboratory and field evidence about individual decision-making. Some of this evidence showed that people did not maximize expected utilities even in "simple choice situations." Simon called this "negative evidence" of "what people *do not* do." Researchers had also produced "positive evidence about the processes that people use to make difficult decisions and solve complex problems."[56]

- Computer simulations. Simon and Allen Newell—and other researchers—built "information processing psychology" theories from the positive evidence. The theories, which typically used computer simulations for expression and testing, envisaged highly selective search through "immense" search spaces. Rules of thumb or "heuristics" guided the search to examine "only a tiny part of the total space." Satisficing criteria ended the search when satisfactory solutions were found.[57] The results showed, according to Simon, that choices depend on the heuristic process used. Process was, therefore, an essential factor in real-world decision-making—despite its avoidance in neoclassical theory.[58]

3. Sidelining Simon

Mission Unaccomplished Simon's 1978 Nobel Prize Lecture suggested his project was a promising work in progress. Although "theories of bounded rationality and the behavioral theory of the business firm" had played a "muted role in the total economic research activity during the past two decades," they had nevertheless "undergone steady development." But more was not to come. The "muted role," in fact, went silent.[59]

Simon's work with Carnegie colleagues anchored what Esther-Mirjam Sent calls the "old behavioral economics."[60] Other groups with different approaches and interests also contributed.

Diverse Contributors

Sent's 2004 article in the *History of Political Economy* identifies four groups of contributors to the "old behavioral economics":

- Carnegie researchers who "focused on bounded rationality, satisficing, and simulations," and Yale economists Richard Nelson and Sidney Winter, who "extended these insights at Yale," made the "most visible" contributions.

- Michigan researchers, led by Hungarian-born psychologist George Katona. "Whereas the Carnegie group [and Nelson and Winter] focused mainly on firm behavior, Katona's followers were interested in consumer behavior and macroeconomic issues."

- A group at Oxford that, with the "participation" of scholars from other British universities, "highlighted the importance of case studies, uncertainty, and coordination."

- Researchers from Scotland's Stirling University and other British institutions, who "stressed eclecticism and integration."

These groups, although diverse, "shared a dissatisfaction with mainstream economics and a desire to develop an alternative using insights from psychology," according to Sent.[61]

Some of these contributions had a significant impact—outside mainstream academic research in economics. For example, Kantona's group developed what became the University of Michigan's Consumer Sentiment Index. The index, published monthly, is included in the US Commerce Department's Index of Leading Economic Indicators, and unexpected changes in the index can move stock and bond markets. Nelson and Winter's *An Evolutionary Theory of Economic Change*, which extended the "Carnegie School's notion of routines as a 'key building block for organizational decision-making,'" became a "foundational text" in strategic management. The book, published in 1982, had received approximately 23,000 Google Scholar citations by May 2012,[62] and ten years later, an astounding 47,751 citations.

But, according to Sent's 2004 history (and other accounts), "Old behavioral economics never caught on in economics 'proper.'"[63] For example, Nelson and Winter's work, "foundational" in management and innovation research, and heterodox

104   UNCERTAINTY AND ENTERPRISE

"evolutionary" economics, received little acknowledgment in mainstream economic journals. They won well-deserved accolades, such as the Schumpeter Prize and Honda Prize, but no Nobel in Economics. Once colleagues at Yale's economics department, Nelson and Winter moved to professional schools, where presumably their work was better appreciated. Other "old" behavioral economics contributors, such as Katona's Michigan psychologists, were never in economics departments.

An Insider-Outsider Simon's relationship with the economic mainstream was complicated. His technical virtuosity in the discipline was unquestioned. Despite reservations, top economists took Simon's claims seriously. Robert Solow's 1958 review of a collection of Simon's essays (published in 1957 under *Models of Man—Social and Rational*) exemplifies this. Solow, then a thirty-three-year-old star of MIT's economics department (who had already published the papers that would win him an Economics Nobel in 1987), wrote that he had "no doubt" that economics had a "lot to learn" from Simon's models of "severely limited rationality." However, Solow's review also suggested that Simon exaggerated the rationality assumed in mainstream economics.[64]

Simon, in turn, did not dismiss the mainstream's recognition and respect even as he sharply questioned its ideas. "If I was an outsider to the economics profession as a whole," Simon writes in his memoir, "I was an insider to its elite."[65] The memoir includes what economist and historian Deirdre McCloskey calls Simon's "candid admission"[66] of his campaign for an Economics Nobel and the contribution of Simon's insider status to its success.[67] Simon also became a "duly certified member of the Econometric Mafia"[68] by placing his articles in top-tier journals like *Econometrica* and the *QJE* decades before his Nobel.

But Simon secured respect and honor rather than influence in economics. According to Alex Leijonhufvud, another insider-outsider iconoclast, Simon's Nobel showed a "curious contradiction" in the attitude of economists toward his contributions.

Nobel and Neglect

In a memorial volume published after Simon died in 2001, distinguished scholars recounted how Simon had influenced them. "Foremost," for the Stockholm-born macroeconomist and UCLA Professor Emeritus Leijonhufvud, was Simon's "stress on procedure, on process over end state." How "institutions and organizational structure shape process" also fit under this umbrella. In addition, Leijonhufvud had been struck by Simon's insistence, not just on empirically valid propositions, but also "*the kind* of empirical

HERBERT SIMON: FADED GUIDING STAR   105

knowledge that he considered to have some solidity." Running time-series regressions was not Simon's way, for example.[69]

Simon's way was not, however, the profession's way, Leijonhufvud observed. Despite Simon's lifelong efforts, neoclassical economics had become a "rigid and unforgiving" and "much more dogmatic" doctrine during Simon's career.[70] Leijonhufvud, a PhD from Northwestern's economics department, recalled how he had only gradually come around ("step by step") to Simon's views. His own experience gave Leijonhufvud hope that other economists would eventually come around, too, and that "the schizophrenia of Nobel and neglect [would] be resolved . . . in favor of a deeper and more pervasive influence of the thought of Herbert Simon."[71]

In about 1970, Simon, a self-taught psychologist,[72] moved his office from Carnegie's business school to its psychology department.[73] He had "heckled" his economist colleagues at the business school—a plurality of the faculty—"about their ridiculous assumptions." They, in turn, saw Simon as "the main obstacle to building 'real' economics in the school."[74] Elsewhere, too, Simon believed, "economists did not regard me as an economist."[75] The Nobel did not change this, according to Simon's 1991 memoir. He wrote in its Afterword, "My economist friends have long since given up on me, consigning me to psychology or some other distant wasteland."[76]

Paradigmatic Conflicts Simon's wide-ranging talents and interests may have limited his influence in any one sphere, including behavioral economics.[77] And in the behavioral sphere, the other contributors described earlier could not easily form a cohesive community. Simon and his Carnegie colleagues researching the behavioral theory of the firm had little in common with the Michigan psychologists surveying consumer attitudes, for example. But here I put aside such possibilities to highlight how Simon's ideas conflicted with the paradigmatic commitments of mainstream economists.

Behavioral Differences For me, the critical difference is behavioral: The gap between what Simon's routines and mainstream models assume about what people can *know* is less consequential than their assumptions about how incomplete knowledge affects what people *do*.

As Solow's review suggested, critics may exaggerate the omniscience they attribute to mainstream economics. Simon attacked the supposed omniscience repeatedly, as have Kay and King in *Radical Uncertainty*. My 2010 book also derided the "all-knowing beings" of modern financial theory. But, upon

106　UNCERTAINTY AND ENTERPRISE

reflection, how much omniscience does utility-maximizing behavior require? Plausibly, mainstream theory merely demands "practical omniscience," as Knight had put it. Theoretically rational decision-makers don't have to be oblivious to the incompleteness of their information. They can maximize based on what they know, coolly treating what they do not as "neutral" noise.

Moreover, research on ambiguity (see the next chapter) suggests that some decision-makers do ignore the incompleteness of information. We find examples of this disregard in real-world decisions as well. Calculations of cost-minimizing flight paths are also based on incomplete information about wind speeds and turbulence.[78] I have personally used best-guess spreadsheets to choose between buying and renting a home, fully aware of the unpredictability of housing markets and the impossibility of quantifying the joys and aggravations of homeownership.

In contrast, Simon's routines pertain to behavior that is emphatically and consistently sensitive to the incompleteness of information (or equivalently, the sufficiency of Keynes's 'evidentiary weights'). As mentioned, standard procedures—in legal trials, diagnostic medical protocols, reviews of mortgage applications, and employment reference checks—require efforts to secure satisfactorily complete information. Although they vary in the extent of their uncertainty aversion (and never expect *totally* complete information), the routines are certainly not uncertainty-neutral.

A Puzzle Simon's behavioral emphasis on incomplete information cannot, however, explain why mainstream economics excluded Simon's ideas about routines. Insiders like Solow and Leijonhufvud—and presumably Simon's Nobel Prize nominators—believed Simon was on to something. And, like utility maximization, Simon's theory relies on rational conduct. True, the information requirements of his routines aren't objectively determined. Yet, if routines are developed through extensive trial and error and produce acceptable results, they can be considered functionally reasonable. Routine-based decisions also have self-evident descriptive plausibility.

What then prevented routines from coexisting with utility maximization models in the way Einstein's relativity coexists with Newton's laws of gravitation?[79] As in earlier chapters, my explanation below for why mainstream economics ignored Simon's routines again uses Kuhn's ideas about the paradigmatic commitments of scientific communities.

Routines versus Economic Science As mentioned, scientific economics, like physics, favors universal models with concise "equilibrium" solutions. Subjective utility maximization conforms to these preferences (as does its multiperiod extension, commonly known as net present value). The simplicity and universality of utility maximization models also have attractions in MBA classrooms and other "practical" venues. In contrast, intricacy has severely limited the use of mathematical models that incorporate ambiguity or other kinds of Knightian uncertainty. They are largely absent from mainstream journals, and few business professors would dare expound on them in their classrooms.

The gap between Simon's routines and economists' paradigms is an even broader, virtually unbridgeable chasm. Routines resemble operas rather than algebraic equations with well-specified numerical inputs and outputs. Like the scores, librettos, choreography, and stage designs of operas, routines can have intricate, interrelated components. As with the multisensory, multiperiod outputs of opera performances, routines do not inevitably produce a clear, equilibrium answer. Some routines, such as jury deliberations and college admission procedures, do deliver sharp, yes-or-no decisions. But many other routines—such as those used to evaluate applications for commercial loans, venture capital funding, research grants, and job promotions—produce outputs that list strengths and weaknesses, suggest improvements, and provide justifications. Even with binary results, the character of the producers strongly influences what is produced, which is why the selection of jurors is often contested, and who is chosen to referee an academic paper or evaluate a grant proposal is so consequential.

Everyday examples, like the case studies Simon cited in his Nobel Lecture, also suggest consequential differences between routines. As Simon repeatedly emphasized—and everyday observation confirms—what is decided often depends on how decisions are made. Mathematized mainstream theories, in contrast, have no place for such procedural influences.

Like Knight's middle-way proposal, Simon's eclectic research program also transgressed methodological boundaries. Simon did use mathematical models and emphasized his commitment to the abstractions of scientific inquiry. But his research also reflected William James's favored combination of high-level "rationalism" and experiential, rather than statistical, "empiricism."

Combining Rationalism and (Traditional) Empiricism

The empiricists' world of "concrete personal experiences," William James observed in his 1907 lecture on pragmatism, "is multitudinous beyond imagination, tangled, muddy, painful, and perplexed."[*] In contrast, the rationalists' world is "simple, clean and noble. The contradictions of real life are absent from it. Its architecture is classic. Principles of reason trace its outlines, logical

---

[*] "Empiricism" in the social sciences is now associated with distilled statistical data, typically built around an abstract model, not direct personal experience. The "target" (per chapter 2) of empirical analysis is also usually a distribution, not a one-off.

108　UNCERTAINTY AND ENTERPRISE

necessities cement its parts. Purity and dignity are what it most expresses." But this latter world is just a "sanctuary in which the rationalist fancy may take refuge from the intolerably confused and gothic character which mere facts present. It is no *explanation* of our concrete universe, it is another thing altogether, a substitute for it, a remedy, a way of escape."[80]

James described his own "philosophic attitude" as one of "radical empiricism," as Knight also later did, contrasting it with "the half-way empiricism" that "dogmatically affirm[ed] monism as something with which all experience has got to square."[81] Yet James also favored abstractions when they had practical utility. James's pioneering work in psychology included broad generalizations.

Simon's rhetoric also had a strongly rationalistic flavor. He was an "indefatigable advocate for social science"[82] whose role he saw as "finding simple generalizations that will describe data approximately under some set of limiting conditions."[83] Simon likewise asserted that "to 'explain' an empirical regularity is to discover a set of simple mechanisms that would produce the former in any system governed by the latter"[84] and that any "uniqueness" in nature "cannot be accidental but must reveal underlying lawfulness."[85] At the same time, Simon drew on his personal observations in Milwaukee's Recreational Department, Chester Barnard's *Functions of the Executive* (which synthesized sociological theories with Barnard's experience in a telephone company), computer simulations, "anthropological" studies, and business cases.

Moreover, Simon took seriously the differences that close observation revealed. Unlike many contemporary theorists, he did not look for concrete cases just to support (or "motivate," in economist-speak) rationalist generalizations. His Nobel Lecture reported, for example, that studying the "actual processes of decision-making in organizational and business contexts" had provided "a multitude of facts" that were "uniformly consistent" with his behavioral model. But the case studies also showed significant variations in decision-making procedures within and across companies and situations— and what to do with these observations was a puzzle. No systematic methods had been developed for "distilling out from these individual case studies their implications for the general theory of the decision-making process."[86]

Therefore, while some of Simon's program fit the paradigm, as a whole it did not. Some of his quantitative methods, such as computer simulations, were borderline at best. Simulations allow researchers to make predictions from behavioral models that they cannot solve mathematically. But the results are sensitive to the numerical assumptions—a problem familiar to anyone who has worked with spreadsheet projections. Economists prefer the comfort, justified or not, of unique algebraic equilibrium solutions.[87] Simon also used engineering mathematics for some of his modeling,[88] recalling in his memoir that it had gradually dawned on him that he had been "a closet engineer since the beginning of my career."[89]

Other methods in Simon's toolkit, like field observations and business case histories, were beyond the pale. In my experience, many economists regard case studies and other accounts derived from specific instances as unscientific storytelling. Even those who see value in "anecdotal" data will not incorporate such methods into their research. Simon enthusiastically used case studies while recognizing their limitations: We could not expect "generalizations as neat and precise as those incorporated in neoclassical theory," he cautioned.[90]

The process by which Simon and a few kindred spirits studied process, therefore, also helped keep the "old" behavioral economics outside the mainstream. The "new" behavioral economics, spearheaded by two psychologists, Kahneman and Tversky, avoided these paradigmatic conflicts, as we will later see.

Guiding Modernization Recognizing that mainstream economics could not accept Simon's departures from its theories and methods, my conjectures and applications nonetheless follow and extend Simon's approach.

- Like Simon, I synthesize several kinds of hypotheses and observations, including case studies, to analyze organizational patterns and behavior, particularly of businesses.

- I assume reasonable behavior, as ordinarily understood. I do not exclude lapses from reasonableness, but, like Knight, I treat them as unpredictable outliers or noise. I also offer accounts of individual and collective behavior based on "functional" reasonableness—what benefit or purpose might a particular pattern serve? (These accounts do not, however, rise to the level of a proper scientific "explanation"—or rule out Panglossian rationalization.)

- I emphasize "procedural" reasonableness—and the variations in procedures—arising from "complex, dynamic circumstances that involve a great deal of uncertainty." And I analyze the nexus between procedures and substantive choices—showing *how* people and organizations choose affects *what* they do and avoid.

I take a narrower view of uncertainty than Simon, however. Simon's uncertainty includes unknown unknowns—possibilities that we cannot imagine—as well as known unknowns. I emphasize uncertainties when we know what we do not know. This more restricted source of uncertainty and its effects on behavior is informed by Daniel Ellsberg's work on ambiguity, examined in the next chapter.

10

Daniel Ellsberg's Ambiguity: A Simplifying Side Trip

Daniel Ellsberg is best known for his Vietnam War activism, not his academic research. Nonetheless, his one landmark contribution—a 1961 article, "Risk, Ambiguity and the Savage Axioms"—is worth a short side trip between the just-completed survey of Simon and the examination of Kahneman and Tversky's contribution to follow. Ellsberg documented how incomplete information, even about known unknowns (i.e., routine or simple uncertainty), encourages choices that contravene standard theories. My modernization project also relies on this simple source of uncertainty, making its intellectual history worth a look. Specifically, this chapter reviews how and why

- Ellsberg's efforts to find concrete support for Knightian uncertainty led him to propose "ambiguity" as one of its simple observable forms.

- Although later research repeatedly confirmed and extended Ellsberg's results, they were treated as just a "paradox," not a decisive refutation of standard, uncertainty-excluding theory.

- I rely on ambiguity as a simplified source of uncertainty.

1. Observing Uncertainty

Meteoric Trajectory Ellsberg, like Simon, grew interested in decision-making as an undergraduate and carried that interest into his doctoral research. His trajectory in economics was more meteoric than Simon's, blazing brightly and ending more quickly. Ellsberg's 1961 article (titled "Are There Uncertainties That Are Not Risks?") was published in the prestigious *Quarterly Journal of Economics* (*QJE*) while Ellsberg was still a doctoral student at Harvard. He hadn't even started writing his dissertation; typically, journal articles and books—including those of Knight, Keynes, and Simon—summarize or extend completed dissertations. But Ellsberg's article, now a "textbook reference" for the so-called Ellsberg Paradox, was his only significant contribution to academic research. Unlike Knight, Simon, and Keynes, whose academic research spanned decades,

Uncertainty and Enterprise. Amar Bhidé, Oxford University Press. © Oxford University Press 2025.
DOI: 10.1093/oso/9780197688359.003.0010

Ellsberg stopped soon after he started. He became better known for his 1971 leaking of the Pentagon Papers than for his 1961 paradox.

From Economics to Activism

Economics attracted Ellsberg when he was a Harvard College undergraduate and wrote an honors thesis on "Theories of Rational Choice under Uncertainty: The Contributions of von Neumann and Morgenstern." Graduating summa cum laude in 1952, Ellsberg secured a Fellowship to the University of Cambridge for a year, returned to Harvard to start a PhD in economics, and turned his undergraduate thesis into an *Economics Journal* (which Keynes had once edited) article. After passing his PhD oral exam—but before starting his dissertation—Ellsberg enlisted in the US Marine Corps in 1954. Discharged as a first lieutenant in 1957, Ellsberg returned to Harvard as a Junior Fellow in the Society of Fellows for two years and then resumed his PhD. As before, his research was on uncertainty. However, he now adopted a heterodox, Knightian perspective. His undergraduate thesis and *Economics Journal* article had been mainstream—as mentioned, the von Neumann and Morgenstern contributions that Ellsberg had written about in his undergraduate thesis are landmarks in the development of standard subjective utility theory.

Concurrently, after spending a summer as an analyst, Ellsberg became a full-time employee of the RAND Corporation in 1959. The Air Force had founded RAND in 1948 as a private nonprofit think tank based in Southern California to advise the government on military issues. At RAND, Ellsberg concentrated on nuclear strategy while continuing his Harvard research. At that time also, he came to know the preeminent decision theorists Jimmie Savage and Howard Raiffa, who were RAND consultants. Savage would generously serve as a sounding board for Ellsberg's skepticism of Savage's theories; Ellsberg would devote the first two paragraphs of the Acknowledgment to his dissertation testifying to the "intellectual debt" he owed to Savage.

Although Ellsberg had initially expected to become a professor of economics, he did not apply for any academic positions after completing his PhD in 1962. Instead, he kept his RAND job. In 1964, Ellsberg joined the Department of Defense to analyze the growing US military effort in Vietnam. The following year, he transferred to the State Department. Working at the US embassy in Saigon and accompanying troops on patrol, Ellsberg came to believe that the United States could not win the Vietnam War. He rejoined RAND in the United States to work on "US Decision-Making in Vietnam, 1945–68," a top-secret report for the US secretary of defense. The report

112 UNCERTAINTY AND ENTERPRISE

strengthened Ellsberg's opposition to the war, and in October 1969, he secretly photocopied it. Over the next eighteen months, he offered copies to several members of Congress, hoping they would make the report public. None would.

In June 1971, the *New York Times* began publishing articles based on leaked portions of the report, which came to be known as the Pentagon Papers. The Department of Justice secured a restraining order against the *Times* to stop further publication. The newspaper appealed and won in the Supreme Court and resumed publication. The government then arrested and charged Ellsberg for violating the Espionage Act, theft, and conspiracy. The charges could have resulted in a 115-year prison sentence. As it happens, the judge in Ellsberg's 1973 trial dismissed all charges on the grounds of governmental misconduct and illegal evidence gathering.

Ellsberg continued his activism, opposing the 2003 invasion of Iraq, the arrest of WikiLeaks founder Julian Assange, and the imprisonment of Chelsea Manning, who had leaked classified information to WikiLeaks. Ellsberg was awarded the Gandhi Peace Award in 1978, the Right Livelihood Award in 2006 for "putting peace and truth first, at considerable personal risk," and the Olof Palme prize in 2018 for "profound humanism and exceptional moral courage."

Critics, however, describe Ellsberg as an "egotist and a megalomaniac" who was "propelled by friendly patrons" in the Kennedy and Johnson administrations. He delayed leaking the Pentagon Papers because of "an enduring desire to be part of the Establishment. Harvard men such as McGeorge Bundy and Henry Kissinger pursued the kinds of careers that Ellsberg thought should be his by right, although they had a ruthless discipline he lacked. By the time the papers were published, Ellsberg had largely undermined his chances of becoming a senior policy official" because "his recognized brilliance" had been "overtaken by a reputation for being inefficient and unable to write."[1]

Ellsberg's autobiography, *Secrets: A Memoir of Vietnam and the Pentagon Papers*, published in 2003, does not even mention his 1961 *QJE* paper. However, in 2011, Ellsberg provided retrospective remarks to a fiftieth-anniversary symposium on his 1961 publication, which I draw on here.[2]

Finding a Behavioral Effect The introduction to his *QJE* paper lays out Ellsberg's purpose: to test whether Knightian uncertainty had any observable "behavioral significance." Citing Kenneth Arrow's observation that Knight's uncertainties produce "the same reactions in individuals as other writers attribute to risk," Ellsberg notes,

DANIEL ELLSBERG'S AMBIGUITY 113

There has always been a good deal of skepticism about the behavioral significance of Frank Knight's distinction between ... "risk," which may be represented
by numerical probabilities, and "unmeasurable uncertainty" which cannot.
Knight maintained that "uncertainty" prevailed ... when the decision-maker
was ignorant of the statistical frequencies of events relevant to his decision; or
when a priori calculations were impossible; or when the relevant events were
in some sense unique; or when an important, once-and-for-all decision was
concerned.

Yet the feeling has persisted that, even in these situations, people tend to behave "as though" they assigned numerical probabilities, or "degrees of belief," to
the events impinging on their actions. However, it is hard either to confirm or
to deny such a proposition in the absence of precisely-defined procedures for
measuring these alleged "degrees of belief."

What might it mean operationally, in terms of refutable predictions about
observable phenomena, to say that someone behaves "as if" he assigned quantitative likelihoods to events: or to say that he does not?[3]

Ellsberg started as a partial skeptic of the assumptions that excluded uncertainty from rational choice. Recall that consistency or coherence was the overarching benchmark for rational choice. Savage, building on the work of Ramsey,
De Finetti, von Neumann, and Morgenstern, had specified decision-making
rules ("axioms") that, if followed, ensured consistency. Savage's theories set
the stage for what became the accepted "neo-Bayesian" procedure for subjective utility maximization developed and enthusiastically promoted at Harvard
Business School (first by Raiffa and Schlaifer, then joined by Pratt after he moved
over from Harvard's statistics department).

Initially, Ellsberg accepted the reasonableness of Savage's axiomatic rules
but doubted the universality of their implications. The axioms implied that
subjective betting odds, expressed "in the same probabilistic terms as spins
of a well-balanced roulette wheel," could always be derived from observable
choices. Ellsberg suspected that numerical probabilities could not be derived for
decisions made under "Knightian" circumstances.[4]

Ellsberg also questioned another implication of Savage's rules. The rules implied that the quality of the information used to estimate probabilities—for example, whether it included observable statistical data—was irrelevant. Ellsberg
found this "hard to believe," although he found Savage's logic "compelling." As he
later recalled, "Like Knight (and Keynes, as I discovered only in researching my
doctor's thesis in 1962), it seemed to me that relative 'confidence' in one's information and estimates ... was a distinct variable that *ought to* [italics added] make
a difference in one's observed decisions."[5] And if relative confidence mattered,
decision-makers couldn't simply be maximizing probability-weighted payoffs.

114 UNCERTAINTY AND ENTERPRISE

Challenging Target Ellsberg's aim, like the targets of his skepticism, straddled the prescriptive and descriptive. To disprove the descriptive proposition that "swans are always white" merely requires finding some black swans. But, as the "ought to" suggests, Ellsberg was skeptical about Savage's theory of how rational individuals *should* always act and not just how they sometimes behave. He did not want to document what could be considered illogical or aberrant choices.[6]

Furthermore, Savage's theory did not require rational decision-makers to explicitly estimate numerical probabilities. Instead, conforming to Savage's axiomatic rules was claimed to result in decisions from which rational numerical odds could be inferred. To challenge the axioms, Ellsberg had to find decisions that established a negative—that rational numerical odds could not be inferred from the decisions.

That was not all. Savage chose axiomatic rules intended for double duty. The rules had a *prescriptive* purpose in establishing a benchmark for rationality: anyone who wanted to make consistent choices and maximize their utilities had to follow these rules. The rules were also supposed to be *descriptive* propositions in the following sense: Each was so naturally logical that every reasonable person would want to follow the rules. And like Simon, Savage expected that people wanted to behave reasonably.

From Prescriptions to Descriptions

In ordinary language, "prescriptions" are synonymous with "shoulds." They may be instrumental, as in recipes for a delicious dish, or moral or ethical, as in the rule of "doing unto others as you would have others do unto you." In other words, prescriptions can cover both means and ends.

Economists usually avoid ethical or what they now refer to as "normative" questions. Instead, they focus on what is called—confusingly for many—"positive" economics. In everyday language, we could say "positive" economics describes how things are rather than prescribing how they should be. For example, the claim that high taxes on alcohol reduce alcoholism is a "positive" proposition. Whether high taxes on alcohol are just or desirable is now called a "normative" question.

Other social scientists (e.g., psychologists) do not restrict "normative" theories to ethical questions—they can cover means, not just ends. Even in economics, "normative" also once included prescriptions. For example, Ellsberg's reference (below) to Savage's axiomatic rules as "normative maxims" did not include any ethical considerations. Moreover, modern economics, particularly finance, includes recipes for calculating option prices or the cost of capital that might previously have been called "normative."

I prefer "prescriptive" and "descriptive" instead of "normative" and "positive," allowing prescriptions to include ethical claims.

Even so, the line between my preferred categories isn't sharp. Descriptions select and organize facts to fit some account or theory—and the ethical values of the describer. Conversely, prescriptions can raise descriptive questions: Does sensitivity training change attitudes?

Indeed, Ellsberg's research focused on the "crossover" from prescription to aspiration. As Ellsberg put it in his *QJE* article, "propounders" of Savage's axioms "hoped that the rules will be commonly satisfied, at least roughly and most of the time, because they regard these postulates as normative maxims, widely-acceptable principles of rational behavior. In other words, people should tend to behave in the postulated fashion, because that is the way they would *want* to behave."[7]

Savage's 1954 book specified a demanding, want-based standard for questioning the validity of his prescriptive rules. Any empirical challenge would have to demonstrate violations of the rules by reasonable individuals who knew the rules and would not—after careful reflection—regret their violations. Savage's standard required Ellsberg to demonstrate a role for Knightian uncertainty that haste, or ignorance of Savage's rules could not explain.[8] Ellsberg would need to find examples of the "reflective choices of reasonable people" that violated Savage's axiomatic rules that the violators would not regret.*

Following a Hunch Ellsberg "intuited" that he would find unregretted violations in situations "where available information is scanty or obviously unreliable or highly conflicting; or where expressed expectations of different individuals differ widely; or where expressed [or felt] confidence in estimates tends to be low ... [like] the results of Research and Development, or the performance of a new president, or the tactics of an unfamiliar opponent." Borrowing from the psychological literature, Ellsberg called such conditions "ambiguous,"[9] and "ambiguity" a "special, extreme case" of Knight's more general uncertainty construct.[†]

---

* "What I was looking for," Ellsberg recalled in 2011, "were choices among gambles that would unequivocally show a behavioral effect of differences in information and subjective confidence that would show up in systematic and deliberate violation of ['rational' consistency benchmarks] by some persons that Savage would recognize as otherwise reasonable: ideally, Savage himself."

† Later in his dissertation, after he had reviewed Keynes's *Treatise*, Ellsberg also noted a close relationship between ambiguity and Keynes's "weight" of evidence that "cannot satisfactorily be expressed in terms of probabilities, "probable error," or the shape of a probability distribution" (Ellsberg 2001, 11).

116 UNCERTAINTY AND ENTERPRISE

After "endless trial and error with paper and pencil," Ellsberg designed two simple thought experiments to test reactions to ambiguity. He administered the tests in private conversations, to attendees of seminars he gave at RAND, and to faculty members at the Universities of Chicago, Harvard, Northwestern, and Yale.[10] Ellsberg's subjects included distinguished economists and decision theorists like Gerard Debreu, Paul Samuelson, Howard Raiffa—and Savage.

Many responses violated Savage's axiomatic rules and strongly suggested that choices under Knightian uncertainty (a) do not reflect or imply numerical probability estimates and (b) do consider the quality of information ("evidentiary weight").

Thought Experiments

In experiments conducted "under absolutely nonexperimental conditions,"[11] Ellsberg asked subjects to imagine bets on the color of balls drawn from hypothetical urns. Below, I summarize the first of his two experiments, condensed and modified for clarity.

Setup Ellsberg asked subjects to imagine two urns, both containing one hundred balls, which could be either red or black. One "ambiguous" urn contained unknown proportions of red and black balls. The other "known" urn contained fifty reds and fifty blacks. Subjects would place (imaginary) bets on balls randomly drawn from the urns, with a correct bet yielding a (hypothetical) prize of one hundred dollars and an incorrect bet of zero dollars.

Establishing Initial Indifference To start, Ellsberg asked subjects whether they would prefer to bet on the color of a randomly drawn ball, first from the urn known to contain fifty reds and fifty blacks and then from the "ambiguous" urn (where the proportions were unknown).

Subjects were usually indifferent between a bet on red or black in either urn. Their indifference "revealed" their expectation of an equal probability of drawing a red or black. This expectation was logical: For urns known to contain an equal number of reds and blacks, the objective probability of drawing either color—one in two—was the same as the implied subjective probability. There was also no reason to believe that the "ambiguous" urn would contain more reds than blacks (or vice versa). Hence, the "best guess" probability for drawing a red or black was also equal.

Did Ambiguity Matter? Ellsberg then asked his subjects for their preferences between the urns: Would they prefer to bet on a red ball drawn from the ambiguous or known urn? How about a bet on a black ball?

Now, only a minority were indifferent. A majority preferred betting on "unambiguous" urns (known to contain an equal number of red and black balls), while a few preferred betting on ambiguous urns.

The indifferent minority conformed to Savage's axiomatic rules: they continued to reveal expected 50:50 probabilities of red and black draws from both urns. But subjects who weren't indifferent, Ellsberg noted, were "simply not acting 'as though' they assigned numerical or even qualitative probabilities to the events in question." The choices (for or against the ambiguous urn) did not imply any belief or guess about whether the ambiguous urn contained more black balls than red balls or vice versa.

Preferences for or against ambiguous urns also suggested consideration of something beyond probability-weighted return. Asking subjects, in the "second round," which urn they preferred to bet on should not have changed their "initial" expectation of equal reds and blacks. If these initial expectations did not change—and given the same one-hundred-dollar prize from correct bets in both urns—the probability-weighted return ($50 = ½ × S100) on bets on both should also have been identical. According to Ellsberg, preferences between urns demonstrated a role for the quality of the information about their contents.

Checking for Regrets Finally, Ellsberg attempted to satisfy Savage's test for challenging prescriptive axioms: He explained to subjects who had preferred their "second stage" bets on known or ambiguous urns, how they had violated Savage's axiomatic rules, including the so-called sure thing principle.[12] (The details need not concern us here. What is relevant is that Ellsberg's subjects had the expertise to understand and accept their violations.) Ellsberg then checked (per Savage's test) whether his subjects regretted their violations. Would they make different choices if they had "plenty of time to reflect"?[13]

A minority "repented" their violations or did not violate to start with—they preferred to "apply the axioms [of rationality] rather than their intuition."[14] Savage and other "sophisticated and reasonable" people who had "previously felt a "first-order commitment" to their rationality postulates were "surprised" or "dismayed" that they now wished to violate them." Howard Raiffa "felt guilty" and "[went] back into further analysis."[15]

Other subjects "sadly but persistently, having looked into their hearts, found conflicts with the axioms and decided, in Samuelson's phrase, to satisfy their preferences and let the axioms satisfy themselves." Some, however, violated the rationality postulates "cheerfully, even with gusto."

Concerns about Trickery The experimental design also addressed problems of trickery or manipulation that Ellsberg had anticipated. "The

118   UNCERTAINTY AND ENTERPRISE

subject can always ask himself: 'What is the likelihood that the experimenter has rigged this urn?'" Ellsberg wrote. "Assuming that he has, what proportion of red balls did he probably set? If he is trying to trick me, how is he going about it? What other bets is he going to offer me? What sort of results is he after?"[16] Many contemporary experiments, I argue later, may well be tainted by such reactions or by contextual misdirection. But it is difficult to see how these problems could have materially affected answers to Ellsberg's straightforward, context-free questions. Moreover, the regret test gave subjects who might have felt tricked, a chance to change their minds.

Cautious Summation Ellsberg's *QJE* article concluded that in "information states," which could be "meaningfully identified as highly ambiguous," "many reasonable people tend[ed] to violate the Savage axioms." Their behavior was "deliberate and not easily reversed upon reflection," and "summarily to judge their behavior as irrational" was unjustified.[17]

Ellsberg's experiment avoided occult "unknown unknowns" and extreme uncertainty. As mentioned, Ellsberg had "intuited" several kinds of "ambiguities," such as "obviously unreliable or conflicting information" where uncertainties could have been extreme. But what he chose for his experiment—"relatively scanty information on some of the events compared to others"[18]—was extreme only in its simplicity. Information was "scant" in limited, well-defined ways: only the proportion of the colors of the balls in the "ambiguous" urns was unknown. And only ninety-eight two-color proportions were possible. Ignorance was hardly complete. Yet this limited ambiguity induced some die-hard subjective utility maximizers to unrepentantly discard their bedrock postulates.

Responses and Aftermath Ellsberg's *QJE* article made a splash but did not capsize or sink the accepted theory. Responses from leading theorists, Ellsberg recalls, were "respectful but mixed."[19] As mentioned, Ellsberg had tested Savage and Raiffa, who had both made "intuitive" choices that violated a fundamental axiomatic rule (the sure thing principle). Many of Raiffa's students at Harvard Business School (whom Raiffa himself tested) also violated the rules.

But Raiffa then persuaded himself and his students to change their choices, thereby inferring, Ellsberg reported in the *QJE*, "that people need more drill on the importance of conforming to the Savage axioms."[20] That drilling, by Raiffa and his HBS colleagues, continued through at least the fall of 1977, when I was a first-year MBA student, as mentioned.

Fifty years later, in 2011, Ellsberg recalled Raiffa's "religious faith" in the "validity and value" of his decision-making rules. That Raiffa could convince many subjects "to "correct" and "improve" their choices," Ellsberg continues, strengthened Raiffa's faith. "His confidence in the significance of [revised conformity] . . . seems never to have been undermined by the fact that all these subjects were his own students in class, dependent on him not only for their grades but for his respect and later recommendations."[21]

2. Just a Paradox

Survival of the Standard Prescription More than just faith protected the subjective probability prescription, however. Ellsberg's *QJE* article declared it aimed to improve and extend—not invalidate—Savage's rules. The rules usually worked fine, Ellsberg wrote: they only failed under unusual circumstances, namely under ambiguity. When Raiffa and others disputed even that limited claim, Ellsberg's response was restrained. He addressed some of the criticisms in his 1962 PhD dissertation—a "much elaborated and extended analysis" of the *QJE* paper[22]—and in a brief "Reply" published in the *QJE* in 1963. He sent a copy of his dissertation—which declared "changing minds" as its aim—to Savage and Raiffa, but it is unclear if they read it. Ellsberg also did not try to publish his dissertation until 2001 and did little to promote or defend his ideas as he concentrated on military policy.[23]

But perhaps the most crucial protection for Savage's rules came from the limitations of the alternatives. Savage's rules provided a comprehensive, understandable formula (which could be taught even to MBA students); the fact that they did not always work wasn't reason enough to abandon them. Ellsberg's *QJE* article (and subsequent doctoral dissertation) did try to provide an alternative to Savage's rules, but Ellsberg's rules did not provide a comprehensive, easily understandable substitute for rational choice.[24]

A few theorists started a cottage industry for modeling ambiguity but did not launch any Copernican Revolution to overthrow subjective probability theories. Copernican heliocentrism had compelling advantages that overcame the Catholic Church's brutal enforcement of its geocentric dogma that put the Earth at the center of the universe. Models of planetary motions with the sun at the center were simpler and more accurate than the convoluted epicycles of geocentrism, and simplicity and accuracy had practical advantages for maritime navigation. Mathematical models of ambiguity are more complex but without compensating benefits to practitioners or mainstream academic researchers. As mentioned, even information economists who challenged the prevailing

120   UNCERTAINTY AND ENTERPRISE

model of perfect competition typically assumed agents who estimate subjective probabilities.[25]

Ellsberg's finding, like an earlier empirical contravention of axiomatic maximization rules reported by the French economist Maurice Allais, was therefore put aside as a "paradox." Ellsberg, however, rejected the label.

What Paradox?

Ellsberg's opening remarks at the Symposium on the 50th Anniversary of the Ellsberg Paradox held in 2011:

> "I learned long ago to try to resist requests by laymen who have heard of an 'Ellsberg paradox' to explain to them what it is. There's no way to describe my argument that doesn't lead to the query, 'So, what's the paradox?' Convincing them that they do not always act as if they assigned precise numerical probabilities to uncertain events needs no demonstration for nearly anyone (other than ordained Bayesian statisticians) . . . The puzzle for them is why [this] commonsense proposition [is] described as paradoxical."[26]

> "Since I agree with them on this, I can only say, 'You're right, there is no Ellsberg 'paradox.'" I've never used that term (except in quotes). But to explain why others have. . . I go on to explain that a very, very smart statistician, L. J. Savage, convinced himself 60 years ago and went on to convince several generations of smart students and followers that this commonsense understanding—that not all uncertainties can be expressed adequately by precise numerical probabilities . . . or even by a complete ordering of relative likelihoods—was unsound."[27]

> "The people who found my early results 'paradoxical' were no fools. . . . I've still never met anyone smarter in my life than my RAND colleagues L. J. Savage or Howard Raiffa. And, their writings were brilliant and persuasive, to me, too. That's precisely what makes the ensuing controversy significant and interesting, above all to those who knew them or their work."[28]

Descriptive Advances While mathematical modeling "lay dormant" because researchers "simply couldn't address" the technical issues, descriptive and experimental research on ambiguity progressed.[29] By 1992, according to Camerer and Weber's survey, several "stylized facts" had emerged.

Stylized Facts

Camerer and Weber's 1992 survey of empirical research reported that:

- Systematically researched variants of Ellsberg's informal thought experiments had consistently found ambiguity aversion, including in experiments offering real money (albeit in small amounts) as prizes.

- Subjects were willing to forgo 10 to 20 percent of probability-weighted prizes to avoid draws from ambiguous urns.

- Ambiguity aversion was uncorrelated with risk aversion.

- Competence (knowledge, skill, and comprehension) could offset ambiguity aversion.

- Gambles with low probabilities of gain and high probabilities of loss could increase a *preference* for ambiguity.

Ellsberg's Regrets Ellsberg's Symposium remarks expressed satisfaction that his findings had "been widely replicated with unusually consistent results." But Ellsberg regretted that the later ambiguity experiments had been confined to scanty information. Experiments with other kinds and sources of ambiguity, he suggested, "shouldn't be hard."[30] More importantly, he lamented that most researchers focused on ambiguity avoidance, neglecting any preference for ambiguity. "For the record," Ellsberg complained, he had "never personally regarded the phenomenon I was investigating as 'ambiguity aversion,' though that is often wrongly attributed to my own views and writings and to the general subject."[31] In Ellsberg's view, affinities for ambiguity are as significant as aversion to ambiguity.

Affinity + Aversion

In his 2011 remarks, Ellsberg recalled that his *QJE* article had

> repeatedly mentioned that some subjects deliberately and consistently chose the more ambiguous alternative (see 651, 653, 654, 663, 667), rather than choosing to "avoid ambiguity." I made it clear, I thought (apparently wrongly) that I regarded these choices—which also violated the Savage axioms—as no less reasonable nor theoretically and empirically noteworthy than the opposite behavior.[32]

To be sure, I reported that these subjects constituted a small minority of respondents in my unscientific samples . . . but in context they were just as significant and supportive to my principal argument—that "ambiguity" was relevant to choice and regularly led to responses that violated the Savage axioms . . . as the so-called ambiguity averse choices, which are empirically more numerous in these particular examples.

I should have emphasized the last clause in the *QJE* article, but my failure to do so doesn't fully explain to me why nearly all later research has focused only on "ambiguity aversion," nor why most expositions have wrongly attributed the same preoccupation to me. It is as if the comments noted above—noting the occurrence of patterns of choice that clearly contradict "ambiguity aversion" . . . had never appeared in the article. My long-term complaint is not about the mischaracterization of my own exposition but about the general failure to explore this phenomenon in subsequent experiments and analysis.

3. Keeping Uncertainty Simple

Definitional Controversy To conclude this side trip, it will help to discuss the definitional controversies that Ellsberg's ambiguity construct provoked. "Defining ambiguity is a popular pastime in decision theory," Camerer wrote in 1995.[33] One "reductionist" approach treated ambiguity as "second-order" probability—subjective probability distributions about probability distributions. This view did not, however, capture even the simple ambiguity of red and black ball bets in Ellsberg's experiments. And how could someone whose choices did not embody consistent first-order probabilities estimate second-order distributions?[34]

A "pragmatic" alternative was to define ambiguity in a way that captured its "psychological essence." Ellsberg's definition of ambiguity—the "quality depending on the amount, type, reliability, and 'unanimity' of information, giving rise to one's degree of 'confidence' in an estimate of relative likelihoods," was, according to Camerer, a "typical if messy" example of a pragmatic definition. Camerer favored "a slightly pithier definition: ambiguity is known-to-be-missing information, or not knowing relevant information that could be known." Thus, in Ellsberg's classic experiment, the composition of the "ambiguous" urn was relevant missing information that could be known but was not. And known-to-be-missing information had psychological ramifications: "Not knowing important information" could be "upsetting and scary," making "people shy away from taking either side of a bet."[35]

Besides missing information about probability distributions, such as the composition of Ellsberg's ambiguous urn, Camerer's definition included other kinds of ambiguity-producing missing information. For example, disagreements among experts could produce ambiguity because of missing information about the most believable expert.[36] And Camerer connected his definition to Keynes's weight of evidence: If we consider weight as the difference between available and conceivable information, we can consider it as the amount of known-to-be-missing information.[37]

But is "ambiguity" *true* Knightian uncertainty—or at least, as Ellsberg had framed it, a part or observable form of uncertainty? Most decision theorists today consider ambiguity as a synonym for uncertainty. A minority, however, argue that Ellsberg's urn experiments do not capture "proper" or "fundamental" Knightian uncertainty. They maintain that "fundamental uncertainty pertains to situations in which information does not exist at the time of the decision, while ambiguity refers to missing information that could be known."[38]

Implications for Modernization Notwithstanding the definitional disputes, specifying uncertainty as a mental state produced by known-to-be-missing information is valuably versatile for my purposes. Missing information can create many kinds of doubts. They can range from "Will customers buy my new product?" to "Is Osama Bin Laden hiding in the Abbottabad compound?" And like the doubts it creates, the missing information can be numerical and statistical (e.g., the results of clinical trials) or qualitative and contextual (e.g., the testimony of an eyewitness).

Often, we can at least order or rank the extent of missing information. Clinical trials may enlist many or few patients, and a criminal investigation may or may not find eyewitness testimony. Our degrees of doubt will reflect the extent of missing information. Thus, at least conceptually and qualitatively, we can analyze degrees of uncertainty.

Specifying uncertainty as doubt produced by missing information does exclude unknown unknowns and unimaginable possibilities. But I regard the exclusion as an advantage. We cannot order the extent of unknown unknowns and analyze the uncertainty they produce. And as mentioned, to put Knightian uncertainty to practical use, I want to exclude the occult connotations of unknown unknowns. Moreover, in common usage, uncertainty blends knowledge and ignorance—neither bright sunshine nor impenetrable darkness but a hazy twilight. Confronting uncertain options requires some awareness of what we don't know.[39] Paranoia about unknown unknowns cannot support reasonable conduct and theories about such conduct.

While my specification may technically deviate from Knight's definition of uncertainty, it maintains its crucial association with error. As Knight repeatedly

124   UNCERTAINTY AND ENTERPRISE

pointed out, uncertainty creates possibilities of mistakes that are the source of entrepreneurial profit. Judgments based on simple, known-to-be-missing information are likewise fallible in entrepreneurship and beyond.

Additionally:

— I share Ellsberg's interest in psychological *affinities* for uncertainty. Such affinities may seem irrational. Why would anyone prefer less information and an increased chance of error? But now, invert the question. Would we want to know the surprise endings of movies in advance or only undertake sure things? Affinities for uncertainty can also serve the public good. As mentioned in my introduction, exciting challenges can stimulate scientific discoveries, technological advances, and the venturesome consumption that sustain innovation. And affinities for uncertainty—which research (cited above) suggests is uncorrelated with responses to measurable risk—may be a prerequisite for entrepreneurship.[40]

Of course, there are circumstances, often ones with high stakes, where we would denounce acting without sufficient information—in a criminal prosecution based on flimsy evidence or a coronary bypass operation performed without a diagnostic angiogram, for example. But equally, we do not applaud indecision in emergencies because there wasn't enough information to avoid error. Similarly, we would expect missing information to attract entrepreneurs, yet we'd want strong ambiguity aversion in a safety inspector of a nuclear power plant. In other words, we cannot easily specify any correct or normal level of affinity or intolerance toward uncertainty and possible error without consideration of goals, stakes, and circumstances.

— It does not require dramatic, high-stakes uncertainties to evoke idiosyncratic responses. The missing information in Ellsberg's urn experiments was transparent and straightforward. Nonetheless, the subjects' reactions ranged from avoidance to indifference to attraction. The variety of reactions remained in later experiments, which elicited monetary responses by asking, "How much would you be willing to pay to draw from the urn of your choice?"

We find differences in attitudes toward uncertainty in everyday decisions: whether to try exotic cuisines and buy the latest gadgets or stick with the tried and tested. Career choices similarly reflect our tastes for ambiguity. Some occupations, such as undercover drug operations, require a high tolerance for ambiguity; others, such as auditing accounts or expense reports, demand intolerance.*

— Differences in attitudes toward missing information can hinder joint activity even when there are no differences in information or interests. The

---

* At the same time, individuals who seek ambiguity in one domain may avoid it in another. For example, polar explorers may stick to bland meat-and-potato meals at home.

same missing information that excites an entrepreneur may repulse potential financiers. What's more, aligning financial incentives cannot close this psychological/behavioral gap: it requires reducing the amount of missing information, either naturally with time or by securing more information.

— Mathematical modeling that has, after decades of effort, failed to produce an understandable, unified formula for dealing with ambiguity is unlikely, in my view, to do so in the foreseeable future. Instead, I describe how routines help us cope with uncertainty and analyze the procedural or functional rationality of the routines, as Simon might have put it. And, again, following Simon, I am particularly interested in how procedures and routines affect organizational sensitivities to missing information. This relationship is as crucial to the specialization of enterprise as are differences in individual sensitivities.

Now back to the newer uncertainty-excluding behavioral economics.

11

Kahneman and Tversky: Gaining Acceptance, Dropping Uncertainty

The *International Encyclopedia of the Social Sciences* identifies "two major perspectives within behavioral economics." One perspective "follows and extends the work of the psychologists Kahneman and Tversky." It demonstrates, through experiments, "the extent to which human behavior deviates from neo-classical norms, where the latter are used as the benchmark for economic rationality. By such standards individuals are found to be largely irrational, but such behavior might possibly be corrected through education or government intervention." The other, second perspective, based on earlier work by Simon, assumes individuals to be "largely rational and intelligent, developing procedures and institutions that best suit their individual needs given the constraints that they face."[1]

The *Encyclopedia*'s broad-brush contrast seems valid, but as I argued in a previous chapter, Simon's work did not frame a "major perspective" in behavioral economics and never became mainstream. In this chapter, we see how and why the perspective based on Kahneman and Tversky's (hereafter K-T) research became well established. We also see how the now-mainstream perspective ignores uncertainty and other critical features of Simon's approach, such as satisficing organizational routines. The success of the new behavioral economics is, therefore, an unhelpful development for my project.

The main sections of this chapter show how

- Behavioral economics, reflecting the K-T perspective, boomed after the 1980s.

- K-T's research on biases, which had a paradigmatic and practical appeal that Simon's work had lacked, established a foothold for the new behavioral boom.

- K-T strengthened and broadened the foothold by developing prospect theory and propositions about framing. Like the earlier biases research, prospect theory and framing propositions were also uncertainty-free.

Uncertainty and Enterprise. Amar Bhidé, Oxford University Press. © Oxford University Press 2025.
DOI: 10.1093/oso/9780197688359.003.0011

1. The New Behavioral Economics Boom

Out of the Wilderness The announcement of the 2002 Nobel Prize in Economics noted that, in 1954, Edwards had "introduced decision-making as a research topic for psychologists" and Simon had proposed an approach based on bounded rationality. But "research in cognitive psychology [had] not come into its own until Daniel Kahneman and Amos Tversky (deceased in 1996) published their findings on judgment and decision-making." Although "adhering to the tradition of cognitive psychology," their "research ha[d] equally well been directed towards economists." One 1979 article even had the "highest citation count of all articles published in *Econometrica*, by many considered the most prestigious journal in economics." Therefore, while other psychologists had also helped us "better understand how people make economic decisions," Kahneman's work with Tversky stood out as "the most influential" and had been "a major source of inspiration behind the recent boom of research in behavioral economics and finance."*

The announcement's reference to a "recent" boom is notable. As mentioned, the old behavioral economics had never caught on. Simon's Nobel did not save his work from neglect, while other behavioral researchers faced downright hostility. Then, starting in the 1990s, attitudes quickly changed to acceptance.

Hostility to Acceptance

In their 2004 preface to *Advances in Behavioral Economics*, Colin Camerer, George Loewenstein, and Matthew Rabin wrote,

> Twenty years ago, behavioral economics did not exist as a field. There were scattered works by authors such as Duesenberry, Galbraith, Katona, Leibenstein, and Scitovsky, which received attention, but the general attitude of the field toward psychology was one of hostility and skepticism. Many economists simply didn't think it was necessary to try to model psychological limits (since errors would be extinguished by market, advice, evolution, etc.), or that it was even possible to do so parsimoniously. The older two of us experienced this hostility first-hand, from faculty members during graduate school, and later even more extremely when we attempted to publish. In fact, until about 1990, it was not uncommon to get a paper returned

---

* Nobels are not awarded posthumously, so Tversky, who had died in 1996, was not eligible for the prize in 2002. However, as the announcement—and Kahneman's Nobel Lecture—makes clear, Kahneman secured his Nobel mainly for his joint work with Tversky.

128   UNCERTAINTY AND ENTERPRISE

from a journal (usually after a delay of about a year) with a three sentence referee report saying "this isn't economics." Fortunately, hostility switched to curiosity and acceptance rather rapidly and completely in the past few years.

George Akerlof, who won an Economics Nobel for his pioneering work in information economics (chapter 7) and whose classic 1970 lemons paper was not behavioral, had become a behavioral enthusiast. In 1994, Akerlof and Robert Shiller (who would win a Nobel for contributions to behavioral finance in 2015) began organizing annual conferences in behavioral macroeconomics sponsored by the NBER.[2] Then, in 2001, Akerlof titled his 2001 Nobel Lecture "Behavioral Macroeconomics and Macroeconomic Behavior."

Noting the Akerlof lecture and accolades won by young stars of the new behavioral economics,[3] Sent's 2004 historical review concluded,

> Behavioral economics is now the topic of Nobel lectures. The NBER hosts conferences on behavioral economics. Graduate programs such as the one at the University of Chicago organize behavioral seminars. Behavioral economists hold positions at prestigious institutions such as Harvard University. The field is represented by journals, anthologies, and associations. And the *New York Times* publishes popular pieces about the rise of behavioral economics. In short, behavioral economics has arrived.[4]

Blending Psychology and Economics As suggested in the chapter on Simon, the absence of a cohesive Kuhnian community and paradigm enfeebled the old behavioral economics. Spanning disparate disciplines—business and public administration, operations research, psychology and sociology, and different methods ranging from case studies to computer simulations—the old behavioral economics was a hodgepodge. The new behavioral economics was a simpler blend of standard economics seasoned with psychological research. Moreover, psychology was a palatable seasoning. Like economics, psychology had scientific aspirations, and economic theories had long incorporated psychological ideas.

Yet, although psychology was potentially easier to blend into mainstream economics than the disparate ingredients of the "old" behavioral economics, there were also serious difficulties. During the first half of the twentieth century, economists had lost interest in psychology (see Addendum: Kindred Disciplines, Drifting Apart). Moreover, academic psychology, unlike economics, had not developed a cohesive paradigm. By the middle of the twentieth century, it had branched into about a dozen specialties.[5] Even the one specialty—cognitive psychology—which became the main ingredient that K-T blended into the new behavioral economics, had emerged as a complex admixture during and after the 1950s.

Cognitive Admixture

Many pioneers of the cognitive psychology "revolution" that overthrew the dominance of behaviorism (made famous by Ivan Pavlov and B. F. Skinner, as described in the Addendum) considered their achievement a Kuhnian paradigm shift.[6] This is debatable. Behaviorism might have had a paradigm defining its scope and methodologies. But it wasn't replaced by another such paradigm. Attacks on behaviorism came from many directions, including linguistics, animal experiments on learning, human factors engineering, cybernetics, artificial intelligence, and Simon and Allen Newell's information processing theories.[7] None dominated, so cognitive psychology emerged more as a broad category than a cohesive specialty.[8]

This admixture could not easily blend into economics. Popularizing a new behavioral economics that assimilated cognitive psychology was far from inevitable. As I argue next, K-T created the base formula for assimilation. They selected easily blended components of the cognitive psychology admixture and melded them in ways mainstream economists could accept.[9]

"Mapping" Bounded Rationality Kahneman titled his Nobel Prize Lecture, "Maps of Bounded Rationality: Psychology for Behavioral Economics." The "bounded rationality" in the title suggested continuity with Simon's earlier prize-winning work, but the features that Kahneman's map depicted were sharply different. As mentioned, the boundedness of Simon's bounded rationality had nothing to do with irrationality. At the risk of belaboring this point, here is what Simon wrote in a 1991 letter to the *Scientific American*, explaining his "preference for the phrase 'bounded rationality' over 'stupidity' ":

> I coined the phrase many years ago to serve as a contrast with the unboundedly rational person of classical economics, who chooses optimal behaviors without concern for the superhuman feats of computation required to select them. Real-world economic behavior is to an important extent shaped by *limits on our knowledge and on our ability to compute the consequences of our actions*. . . . It does not connote cynicism about human nature unless it is cynical to believe that not all human beings have godlike intelligence. (Italics added)[10]

130   UNCERTAINTY AND ENTERPRISE

Contrast this with the first four sentences of Kahneman's prize lecture:

The work cited by the Nobel committee was done jointly with Amos Tversky (1937–1996) during a long and unusually close collaboration. Together, we explored the psychology of *intuitive beliefs and choices* and examined their *bounded rationality*. Herbert A. Simon (1955, 1979) had proposed much earlier that decision makers should be viewed as boundedly rational, and had offered a model in which utility maximization was replaced by satisficing. Our research attempted to obtain a map of bounded rationality, by exploring the *systematic biases* that separate the beliefs that people have and the choices they make from the optimal beliefs and choices assumed in rational-agent models.[11] (Italics added)

Differently put, Kahneman's map shows danger zones where Intuition often mugs Reason, while Simon's map displays pathways around informational and computational barriers faced by reasonable decision-makers making reasoned choices.

But why would mainstream economics favor K-T's systematic biases over Simon's moderate deviations from unrestricted rationality? My explanation below follows the sequence of their three programs of research. I emphasize the first and catchiest program, on heuristics and biases, and then briefly examine their two subsequent projects, on "prospect theory" and "framing."

2. Heuristics and Biases

Origins Kahneman links this research to his early interest in cognitive illusions that accelerated through his collaboration with Tversky and culminated in a highly influential article published in *Science*.

Illusions to Biases

Kahneman collected cognitive illusions from an early age, like a young Darwin collecting beetles. He found his first—which he named the "illusion of validity"—as a conscript in the Israeli military, serving in the psychology branch. Kahneman had been conscripted in 1954 after his bachelor's degree, with a psychology major, from Jerusalem's Hebrew University.

After completing his military service in 1956 and more coursework at Hebrew University, Kahneman earned a PhD in psychology from the University of California in Berkeley. Returning as a psychology lecturer in

1961, Kahneman set up a vision lab at Hebrew University to study perception and attention.[12] He also researched motivation in children, asking simple questions instead of traditional "procedures that can be described only by long lists or by convoluted paragraphs of prose."[13]

In 1969, he began collaborating with a younger colleague, Amos Tversky. Tversky, like Kahneman, had a bachelor's from Hebrew University, majoring in philosophy and psychology, and had served in the Israeli military as a paratrooper in 1956 and commander of an infantry unit in the 1967 war. Tversky, too, had earned a PhD in psychology from the United States, at the University of Michigan, under the supervision of Ward Edwards—a psychologist who had once collaborated with Savage—and mathematical psychologist Clyde Coombs.[14] Like Kahneman, Tversky undertook experiments before starting their collaboration but on intuitive judgment rather than vision.

Their first joint project used a questionnaire administered at a meeting of the Mathematical Psychology Association. The questionnaire, Kahneman later recalled, "consisted of a set of questions, each of which could stand on its own—this was to be another attempt to do psychology with single questions."[15] The results published in a 1971 paper ("Belief in the Law of Small Numbers") purported to show that even trained scientists have strong but fundamentally erroneous intuitions about the laws of chance: "We submit," Kahneman and Tversky wrote, "that people view a sample randomly drawn from a population as highly representative, that is, similar to the population in all essential characteristics."[16] Consequently, they expect even small samples (from the same population) to be more similar than sampling theory predicts. Thus, this "representation hypothesis describes a cognitive or perceptual bias."[17]

A 1972 paper, based on a questionnaire administered to fifteen hundred Israeli college-preparatory high school students, placed the "representation hypothesis" in a broader class of "heuristics" used to "replace the laws of chance." The heuristics "sometimes yield reasonable estimates and quite often do not." Specifically, according to the "representativeness" heuristic, people judge event A as more probable than event B if A is more similar "in essential properties to its parent populations."[18]

In another "technical report," also published in 1972, K-T investigated biases arising from what they called the "availability" heuristic, proposing that people "use the number of relevant instances that [can] be readily retrieved or the ease with which they come to mind" as "major clues" in estimating probabilities. They offered the example of estimating whether words were more likely to start with a "k" or have "k" in the third position. To answer such questions, claimed K-T,

132 UNCERTAINTY AND ENTERPRISE

> People often try to think of words beginning with "k" (e.g., key) and of words that have "k" in third position (e.g., like), and then compare the number or the ease with which the two types of words come to mind. Obviously, it is easier to think of words that start with a "k" than of words with a "k" in the third position. Indeed, the majority . . . judged the former event more likely despite the fact that there are three times as many words with a "k" in the third position.[19]

In 1974, K-T published what Kahneman called a "progress report on our study of judgment under uncertainty."[20] It reviewed three heuristics—representativeness, availability, and anchoring—that could explain a dozen systematic biases. The biases included neglect of base rates (the overall distribution of occurrences, such as the overall mortality rates from Covid-19 infections), overconfident predictions, and overestimates of the frequency of events that are easy to recall.[21]

Expecting interest in the biases beyond psychology, K-T successfully sought publication in *Science*[22]—a prestigious peer-reviewed journal for research in all scientific fields (which also publishes commentary on issues of interest to the broad scientific community). Their earlier work had targeted psychology journals.

The article "spawned a large literature in cognitive science, philosophy, and psychology"[23] and by 2023 had been cited over fifty thousand times, according to *Google Scholar*.[24]

Paradigmatic Coexistence Although their *Science* article became "a standard reference as an attack on the rational-agent model," K-T's heuristics and biases program was surprisingly well suited to coexist with the mainstream economics paradigm.

Its grounding in cognitive psychology gave the K-T program more cohesion than the old behavioral economics, which spanned many disciplines and research traditions. As importantly, the cognitive psychology K-T used was itself simple and narrow, perhaps even shallow.[25] They could not directly establish the existence of bias-producing heuristics. Instead, K-T asserted that (unobservable) heuristics caused biased responses, relying in part on similar explanations for optical illusions. (For example, mistakenly seeing clearer images as closer.) Their labeling of the heuristics (as "representativeness," "availability," and "anchoring") was also ad-hoc. As Kahneman (writing with Shane Frederick) later put it, "The goal of the heuristics and biases program in its early days was to understand intuitive judgment under uncertainty, not develop a unified theory of it. Judgment heuristics were described as a collection of disparate cognitive procedures."[26]

The simplicity made the K-T program more accessible to mainstream economists than the complex simulations that Newell and Simon used in their information processing psychology.[27] That K-T did not provide a deep theory or complex explanation for their heuristics saved economists the trouble of learning psychology. Economists could treat heuristics as a dispensable construct and focus on the biases. The single-question method similarly helped economists easily understand the results.

The "empiricism" of the surveys also mirrored the reductionism of modern econometrics rather than the old-fashioned empiricism favored by William James and embodied in some of Simon's observational methods. Likewise, K-T presented their results in the summarized statistical forms that economists used in their research.* The anthropological studies, business cases, and computer simulations Simon and old behavioral economics scholars used had unfamiliar, often qualitative outputs.

Moreover, the K-T surveys could be cheaply and quickly administered to many subjects in practically any venue, such as professional meetings and classrooms. The results could, in principle, be easily replicated—and because the samples were large, the results could produce the all-important statistical significance. The experiments that K-T, like many other psychologists, had previously undertaken were more complex and time-consuming, and they could only be done in laboratories or laboratory-like settings.[28] This limited the number of subjects. Tversky's own experiments between 1965 and 1970 always had just seven or eight subjects, for example.[29] Statistical significance was, therefore, virtually impossible.[30]

K-T's methods may also have resonated with the introspection that John Stuart Mill had recommended for economics and which many contemporary economists still implicitly use to check their theories. As Kahneman, who attributes "the unusual attention" their *Science* article received "as much to the medium as to the message," recalled,

> Amos and I had continued to practice the psychology of single questions, and the *Science* article—like others we wrote—incorporated questions that were cited verbatim in the text. These questions, I believe, personally engaged the readers and convinced them that we were concerned not with the stupidity of

---

* By 1970, Simon (1991d, 326) writes, all "empirical work" in economics was "synonymous with 'econometrics.'"

134 UNCERTAINTY AND ENTERPRISE

Joe Public but with a much more interesting issue: the susceptibility to erroneous intuitions of intelligent, sophisticated, and perceptive individuals such as themselves.[31]

Prescriptive and Descriptive Conformity The heuristics-and-biases message did not challenge the core prescriptive *or* descriptive claims of mainstream economics and decision theory. On the prescriptive side, K-T and other new behavioral economics researchers took the standard model as their benchmark for rationality—how people *should* behave. The recognition of many biases *required* the standard rational-agent benchmark. And when K-T and other new behavioral economists diagnosed practical problems or offered solutions, these aimed to increase conformity to the standard model.

The descriptive coexistence is subtler: Recall from the last chapter that Savage and Raiffa claimed their prescriptive rules also described how reasonable people would *want* to behave or, after drilling in MBA classrooms, *would* behave. K-T's heuristics-and-biases program sidestepped Savage and Raiffa's descriptive claim. Where Simon had used "heuristics" as rules of thumb for making conscious decisions, K-T began using the term in 1971 for an intuitive response.[32] Their theory was silent on what reasonable decision-makers would want to do or would do after due reflection or training. Their model purported to describe and explain what people intuitively or reflexively did. Their account did not, therefore, conflict with the mainstream description in any fundamental way.[33] It merely added another facet.

In contrast, Ellsberg challenged claims about what reasonable people would want to do by interviewing willful violators of Savage's rules for rational choice. Simon raised a more fundamental question: why would reasonable decision-makers, aware of the limitations of their knowledge and computing abilities, ever want to follow an unrealistic utility maximization prescription? And on the assumption that people are usually reasonable, Simon predicted that they would settle on—possibly after some trial and error—functionally reasonable heuristics and routines. Simon's satisficing model of procedural rationality thus posed a head-on descriptive challenge to mainstream rationality that K-T's heuristics-and-biases did not.

Crucial Exclusions K-T used the mainstream model as their benchmark for showing biases; their scope was also naturally mainstream. Specifically, unlike Simon, who had a strong interest in businesses and other organizations, K-T only studied the heuristics and biases of individuals. This follows the focus of traditional microeconomics, whose usual "theory of the firm" is really an anthropomorphized account of an individual decision-maker—a make-believe "entrepreneur" (as Baumol pointed out).[34]

Like standard economics, K-T said nothing about the process of decision-making or decision-making routines—another hallmark of Simon's behavioral theory. Variations in decision-making processes reported in case studies (which, as mentioned, Simon thought called for further examination) were also ignored in K-T's single-question method—as they are in standard econometric research.

There were no Knightian superstitions about luck or Keynesian "animal spirits" in the K-T heuristics program. Words like feelings, emotions, hopes, anxieties, and fears are missing from their *Science* article. Freud's psychoanalytic ideas—which mainstream economists typically rejected—are also excluded, although Kahneman had studied with David Rappaport, a psychoanalytic theorist, in 1958.*

Perhaps most significantly, the 1970s heuristics-and-biases program, like Savage's 1954 utility theory and Milton Friedman's 1962 price text, did not distinguish between risk and uncertainty. K-T entitled their 1974 *Science* article, "Judgment under Uncertainty: Heuristics and Biases." But there was no uncertainty of the sort previously examined by Knight, Keynes, Simon, and Ellsberg.

K-T undoubtedly knew about the difference between risk and uncertainty.[35] But their research, which used standard probability and rational agent theory as its benchmark, required the benchmark's exclusion of uncertainty. Judgments about uncertain choices and results cannot be proven wrong—their correctness is itself uncertain. To document bias and error, K-T had to pose questions that had—or were assumed to have—objectively correct answers. To establish that a heuristic could produce misestimates of probabilities required an objective probability distribution. Showing an overconfidence bias required specifying the confidence a rational agent would have. But even the mildest forms of uncertainty (e.g., because of missing information about known unknowns) make the correctness of answers uncertain. And without objective, unambiguous correctness, bias or error cannot be established.†

Memorable Marketing A further reason for the success of the "heuristics and biases message," according to psychologists Thomas Gilovich and Dale Griffin, was its packaging: "Demonstration studies were designed as much like

---

* Kahneman says he had then studied the seventh chapter of Freud's *Interpretation of Dreams* "like a Talmudic text" and had "tried to derive from it experimental predictions about short-term memory" (Kahneman 2003b).

† Unable to accommodate uncertainty, K-T seem to have waved away the relevance of its distinction from risk. In their 1972 paper on the "representativeness" heuristic, they wrote, "Although our experimental examples were confined to well-defined sampling processes (where objective probability is readily computable), we *conjecture* that the same heuristic plays an important role in the evaluation of uncertainty in essentially unique situations where no 'correct' answer is available" (Kahneman and Tversky 1972, 451, italics added). I leave it to the reader to imagine what incentive or bias, if any, that conjecture might reflect.

136 UNCERTAINTY AND ENTERPRISE

cocktail party anecdotes as traditional cognitive psychology studies, making them magnets for academic lecturers and textbook writers alike. Scenarios involving feminist bank tellers ... made the lessons of the heuristics and biases tradition memorable."[36]

Tom and Linda

A fictitious graduate student, "Tom W," is an early example of the vivid characters K-T created for their experiments. They described Tom to their subjects as having

> high intelligence, although lacking in true creativity. He has a need for order and clarity, and for neat and tidy systems in which every detail finds its appropriate place. His writing is rather dull and mechanical, occasionally enlivened by somewhat corny puns and by flashes of imagination of the sci-fi type. He has a strong drive for competence. He seems to feel little sympathy for other people and does not enjoy interacting with others. Self-centered, he nonetheless has a deep moral sense.

K-T also gave their subjects nine fields that Tom could be studying.[37] Simplifying, K-T found their subjects' predictions of Tom's field of study strongly correlated with the stereotypical expectations of personalities in that field but not with enrollments in the field. For example, K-T's subjects predicted that Tom was more likely to be studying computer science (whose stereotype he fit) rather than humanities, even though enrollments in humanities were greater. This result reflected reliance on the representativeness heuristic and the bias of base rate neglect, claimed K-T.

Another famous K-T experiment described "Linda" to subjects as

> Thirty-one years old, single, outspoken and very bright. She majored in philosophy. As a student she was deeply concerned with issues of discrimination and social justice and also participated in antinuclear demonstrations.

K-T also gave subjects possible descriptions of Linda, including, "Linda is a bank teller," and "Linda is a bank teller and active in the feminist movement."[38] K-T reported that more subjects expected Linda to be a feminist bank teller than merely a bank teller—even though bank tellers should include feminists. They called this a "conjunction fallacy," again reflecting, as in the Tom W. experiment, subjects' reliance on a representativeness heuristic.

Critics have challenged the Linda experiment, now considered "the most controversial example in the representativeness literature."[39] But it undoubtedly contributed to the memorability of K-T's heuristics and biases program. As Gilovich and Griffin put it, although it would not have spread without substance, "It is difficult to overestimate the impact of style in the program's success. . . . A medium of communication that included stories and personality sketches was well-suited to the message."[40]

K-T complemented catchy examples with astute rhetoric. Consider the following sentences from the introductory paragraph to their 1974 *Science* article: "This article shows that people rely on a limited number of heuristic principles which reduce the complex tasks of assessing probabilities and predicting values to simpler judgmental operations. In general, these heuristics are quite useful, but sometimes they lead to severe and systematic errors."[41]

The claim that heuristics help simplify complex tasks follows the spirit of Simon's explanation of satisficing routines. It also allows K-T to reject interpretations of their work "as a broad attack on human rationality."

Defending Bias Hunts

Kahneman's autobiographical Nobel essay includes a spirited defense against accusations of "spreading a tendentious and misleading message that exaggerated the flaws of human cognition."[42]

"Amos and I always dismissed the criticism that our focus on biases reflected a generally pessimistic view of the human mind," Kahneman recalls. Asserting that critics commonly confuse "the medium of bias research with a message about rationality," Kahneman cites attacks on the "position of the letter k" experiment on the availability heuristic mentioned earlier. Some critics used the experiment "as an example of our own confirmation bias, because we had demonstrated availability only in cases in which this heuristic led to bias. But this criticism assumes that our aim was to demonstrate biases, and misses the point of what we were trying to do. Our aim was to show that the availability heuristic controls frequency estimates even when that heuristic leads to error—an argument that cannot be made when the heuristic leads to correct responses, as it often does."[43]

But consider again the sting in the tail, that heuristics "sometimes lead to severe and systematic errors." If "sometimes" is taken to mean "not often," and if the errors pertained merely to misjudging the position of "k" in words, who would care? But that is not the usual interpretation, even among scholars. For example, Sent, a behavioral economist with a PhD from Stanford, was undoubtedly aware

138   UNCERTAINTY AND ENTERPRISE

that K-T's experiments were designed to produce errors. Yet Sent reported (in a scholarly journal) that K-T had found that "systematically erroneous judgments were rampant."[44] Similarly, cognitive scientists Mercier and Sperber observe that experiments have repeatedly shown that human reasoning is "flawed,"[45] that people make "egregious mistakes," and that their reasoning is "systematically biased."[46]

As it happens, egregious mistakes and systematic biases suit Mercier and Sperber's argument in their *Enigma of Reason* and the research agendas of many other scholars. But might not K-T's dramatic language of "severe and systematic errors" have evoked and justified interpretations of rampant, egregious mistakes? Consider too the confident rhetoric—"This article shows that people rely on a limited number of heuristic principles" that can produce "severe and systematic errors." No feeble attribution of errors to mental shortcuts here. K-T also play to scientists' preferences for concise generalizations; they lump many shortcuts into "a limited number of heuristic principles." Might not such unhedged generalizations, presumably vetted by the referees of a top scientific journal, have evoked an indisputable law of nature?[*]

Kahneman concedes that "the name of our method and approach created a strong association between heuristics and biases, and thereby contributed to giving heuristics a bad name, which we did not intend." Perhaps. But on balance, did not the "strong association," possibly promoted by K-T's rhetoric, also serve K-T's cause, and make the new behavioral economics a popular and academic success?[†]

Contrast with Simon's Heuristics Simon regarded heuristics as components of routines used to cope with his version of bounded rationality. As with the boundedness of his rationality, there was nothing unreasonable or impulsive in his heuristics to capture people's imaginations.

Simon's heuristics also served as building blocks for the information processing theories and cognitive psychology he developed with Allen Newell. As mentioned, their theories conceived of minds as flawless computers but with limitations to memory and processor capacities, and they used computer simulations to model problem-solving procedures. "Heuristics" encoded in the

---

[*] Their first joint paper, published in 1971, similarly asserted that "most psychologists have an exaggerated belief in the likelihood of successfully replicating an obtained finding." Furthermore, their "strong intuitions" were "wrong in fundamental respects" yet were "applied with unfortunate consequences in the course of scientific inquiry." But K-T's 1971 claim of a "representation hypothesis" that "describes" a "cognitive or perceptual bias" did not confidently assert causality.

[†] Unaware of the "old" behavioral economics before this writing, I, too, had associated K-T's research—and behavioral theories—with unreasonableness. Hence my puzzlement at Solow's suggestion, mentioned in the Preface, of a possible behavioral theory lurking behind my 2006 article. I thought I had avoided any unreasonableness in that article. I now realize that Solow's comment reflected a historically correct view of "behavioral."

simulation programs were designed to find "satisficing" solutions after searching small parts of immense problem spaces. K-T's heuristics, in contrast, were presented as the mental equivalents to simple, unconscious rules that we might use, sometimes mistakenly, to judge distances (e.g., "what's clearer is closer").

These features of Simon's heuristics made their catchy packaging difficult. Routinized physical examination and its embedded heuristics aren't exciting. Inferring an infection by feeling swollen lymph nodes is useful but much less newsworthy than attributing diagnostic errors to stereotyping or "availability" misjudgments. Classroom demonstrations of cognitive biases excite students. Discussions of routines bore them. Likewise, the rules of Simon and Newell's computerized search simulations were hardly the stuff of cocktail-party anecdotes.*

Practical Appeal Although K-T positioned their heuristics-and-biases program as primarily descriptive, they did highlight its prescriptive implications. For Kahneman, it was a "fact of life that human beings often make cognitive errors," while psychology could help design "tools or education to help human beings correct these cognitive errors."[47] Social psychologists endorsed the heuristics-and-biases message because it fit their agenda of alleviating social problems.[48]

Government and foundation funding encouraged practical goals.[49] During World War II, psychologists worked on the "human engineering" of military machines. Dramatic increases in government funding for psychology research after the war ended continued "human engineering" for nonmilitary applications. Private foundations, set up in the early twentieth century, already supported "social engineering" research.

In 1907, the widow of a railroad magnate founded the Russell Sage Foundation for "the improvement of social and living conditions in the United States." As we will see, the foundation would play a central role in assembling a community of scholars who built on K-T's research. Russell Sage's support only started, however, in the mid-1980s. That was over a decade after K-T published the 1974 *Science* article on their heuristics-and-biases research.

Meanwhile, the two psychologists had completed (or nearly completed) two other research programs mentioned earlier—namely the development of "prospect theory" and propositions about "framing." These two projects, particularly prospect theory, helped bridge the earlier heuristics-and-biases program to "proper" economics. That bridge would help a convoy of behavioral researchers

---

* Simon and Newell's work did provide a foundation for the artificial intelligence models that captured the public imagination seventy years later. But this pioneering contribution is rarely remembered.

140   UNCERTAINTY AND ENTERPRISE

enter mainstream economics, as we will see. But first let's examine the construction of the two-spanned bridge.

3. Prospect Theory and Framing

A Conservative Prospect A history of behavioral economics calls K-T's prospect theory an "extended version of their heuristics and biases theory."[50] I see it as a major, stand-alone advance. Mainstream economics could treat biases—attributed to unconscious shortcuts—as peripheral curiosities. Moreover, the psychological theory of heuristics was entirely verbal. But by 1970, according to Simon, "mathematics had taken over economics," and "the simplest theory had to be clothed in mathematical garb before it could receive any serious attention."[51]

Prospect theory was more directly economic through its close connection with utility maximization. Moreover, it did not radically reject the standard theory and came dressed in acceptably formal mathematical clothes. K-T did not achieve this simply by extrapolating their heuristics-and-biases program. Their remarkable feat of designing and marketing a seemingly revolutionary, subtly conservative product was a five-year-long project.

The Painstaking Development of Prospect Theory

K-T's prospect theory, published in *Econometrica* in 1979, resulted from a five-year project. After their paper on judgment appeared in *Science* in 1974, Tversky proposed that they study decision-making. Tversky, writes Kahneman, was "already an established star" in that field, but Kahneman "knew very little" then. Tversky suggested that Kahneman read chapters from *Mathematical Psychology*, a 1970 text Tversky had previously coauthored.[52]

Kahneman found the book's discussion of utility theory, which expressed utility as *levels* of wealth, puzzling. Although conventional, this expression seemed "unnatural and psychologically unlikely" to Kahneman. He proposed using *changes* in wealth as "carriers of utility" with "no inkling that this obvious move was truly fundamental, or that it would open the path to behavioral economics." Assuming that people care more about changes than levels implied what K-T would later label "loss aversion"—which Kahneman believes was their "most useful contribution to the study of decision making."[53]

In under a year, K-T wrote up what they called "value theory," which focused on changes rather than levels of wealth (or some other valued *desiderium*). After presenting this theory at a conference in the spring of 1975, K-T spent the next three years, Kahneman recalls, "exploring interesting implications of our theoretical formulation and developing answers to all plausible objections."[54]

K-T chose a new and deliberately "meaningless" name, calling it "prospect theory" instead of "value theory" because "having a distinctive label would be an advantage." They targeted publication in *Econometrica*: "The identical paper, published in *Psychological Review*, would likely have had little impact on economics."[55] As it happens, their prospect-theory paper stood out even in distinguished *Econometrica* company.

Kahneman suggests an anthropological advantage their paper enjoyed:

> Prospect theory was a formal theory, and its formal nature was the key to the impact it had in economics. Every discipline of social science, I believe, has some ritual tests of competence, which must be passed before a piece of work is considered worthy of attention. Such tests are necessary to prevent information overload, and they are also important aspects of the tribal life of the disciplines. In particular, they allow insiders to ignore just about anything that is done by members of other tribes, and to feel no scholarly guilt about doing so. To serve this screening function efficiently, the competence tests usually focus on some aspect of form or method, and have little or nothing to do with substance. Prospect theory passed such a test in economics, and its observations became a legitimate (though optional) part of the scholarly discourse in that discipline.[56]

Kahneman's parenthetical "though optional" suggests a further Kuhnian explanation for the inclusion of prospect theory in mainstream economics. Despite appearances, it was "normal" science that extended rather than overthrew prevailing theory. Framed as a descriptive theory, it posed no prescriptive threat—and descriptively, it could serve as a complementary special case to explain phenomena such as preferences for the status quo. Economists, therefore, did not have to rip up their microeconomic texts or lecture notes to take it seriously.

Prospect theory was also methodologically conservative. Like their 1974 *Science* paper on heuristics, K-T's 1979 *Econometrica* paper did not trouble economists with deep or unfamiliar psychological theory. Adam Smith had written about loss aversion—a basic premise of prospect theory—centuries ago. And unlike Simon's satisficing computer simulations, replacing levels with changes needed technical virtuosity but no radical modeling moves.[57]

While working within the limits of normal economic science defused potential hostility, the novelty of prospect theory attracted supporters by creating

142   UNCERTAINTY AND ENTERPRISE

new opportunities for "within-the-paradigm" research. An accepted theoretical model made bias-and-anomaly hunting respectable—descriptions of phenomena, however interesting, can be challenging to publish unless they are attached to some theory.[58] The popularity of prospect theory also paved the way for more within-the-paradigm behavioral theorizing that boomed during and after the 1990s. As Camerer and Loewenstein put it in their introduction to a 2004 compilation of *Advances in Behavioral Economics* (mentioned earlier), most of the papers in the compilations changed just "one or two assumptions in standard theory in the direction of greater psychological realism. Often these departures [we]re not radical at all because they relax[ed] simplifying assumptions that are not central to the economic approach."[59]

Prospect theory kept the exclusions of K-T's heuristics-and-biases program, helping its assimilation into mainstream economics. It omitted procedures, routines,[60] and decision-making within organizations. Uncertainty was now more explicitly excluded. Prospect theory modeled choices that, like coin tosses, had known probability distributions. Excluding uncertain one-offs or choices with missing information (like unspecified red-and-black balls in the Ellsberg urns) was not strictly necessary. However, uncertainty would have made the theory unwieldy, complex, and heterodox. Without uncertainty, prospect theory could be positioned as a simple variant of standard theory. It could also be easily explained in textbooks and classroom lectures, increasing its mainstream appeal.*

Role of Framing K-T completed prospect theory in the 1977–1978 academic year when they were both at Stanford and, around that time, began their project on the study of framing. Framing challenges the standard assumption that people only care about objective consequences, disregarding how options are presented or "framed." The assumption is manifestly implausible; if it were true, ancient Greeks would not have developed and studied rhetoric, twentieth-century

---

* The psychologically questionable assumption that decision makers know the value of all expected outcomes had similar assimilation advantages. It conformed to the convention (which I have attacked in earlier work on venturesome consumption) of assuming that people have well-defined utility functions for all possible outcomes, and it sidestepped potentially intractable mathematical complications of recognizing that they do not.

marketers would not have invented advertising, and contemporary websites would not contain clickbait.[61]

K-T's contribution was to systematically show framing effects through questionnaire experiments and using prospect theory to frame their framing results. As in their heuristics-and-biases project, K-T constructed vivid examples that excluded uncertainty.

Framing Uncertainty-Free Choices

Kahneman writes that they showed framing effects by "constructing two transparently equivalent versions of a given problem, which nevertheless yield predictably different choices." One vivid example was the " 'lives saved, lives lost' question."[62] As reported in their 1981 paper published in *Science,* K-T posed two versions of the question to students at Stanford—whose faculty Tversky joined in 1978—and the University of British Columbia—whose faculty Kahneman joined, also in 1978.

In the first framing, K-T offered students a choice between two public health programs to deal with an epidemic threatening six hundred lives: one program would save two hundred lives; the other had a one-third chance of saving all six hundred lives and a two-thirds chance of saving none. Presented thus, 72 percent were risk averse—they preferred the program that would save two hundred lives for sure, although the "probability-weighted" value of the other option was the same, namely two hundred survivors. In a second version, subjects were told that one program would result in four hundred lives lost, while the other had a two-thirds chance of six hundred lives lost and a one-third chance of no deaths. Now, 78 percent favored risk-taking: the certain death of four hundred was less acceptable than a two-thirds chance of six hundred casualties. Yet the two problems were "effectively identical." The difference was just in the framing, as lives saved in the first and lives lost in the second.[63]

Notice that to make the two framings "transparently equivalent" (and perhaps to help produce "predictably different choices"), K-T excluded uncertainty: they specified the odds of deaths and survival as precise, known probabilities. In other experiments, framed problems were riskless. Yet, as we see later, critics have questioned whether subjects in such experiments adduce contextual uncertainty to the questions they are asked and whether their responses reflect uncertainty-infused interpretations.

144 UNCERTAINTY AND ENTERPRISE

Cultivating a Community Framing also played a significant role in K-T's own success. Unlike Watson and Crick's double-helix DNA model and Mendel's Laws of Inheritance K-T's results did not just speak for themselves. They did have natural paradigmatic advantages over Simon's old behavioral economics, but as argued, they were also well packaged and marketed by K-T. Moreover, as we see in the next chapter, K-T helped construct the community that produced a broad-based behavioral economics boom—and this community, rather than just K-T's ideas, presents a challenging obstacle to my uncertainty modernization project.

Addendum: Kindred Spirits, Drifting Apart

Aspirational Kinship Academic psychology shares the scientific aspirations of academic economics. The *Encyclopedia Britannica* calls psychology a *"scientific* discipline that studies mental states and processes and behavior" (emphasis added). Since about the nineteenth century, psychology has "self-consciously modeled itself upon successful sciences such as physics, chemistry, and biology."[64] And while academic economics has been more physics-like in mathematizing its theories and models, academic psychology is well ahead in controlled experimentation; Herbert Simon calls experimental psychology "the most 'scientific' of the social sciences."[65]

Psychology, like economics, did not always have these scientific aspirations. The *Encyclopedia Britannica* traces the origins of psychology to the speculations of philosophers. Thinkers like Aristotle, Augustine, Aquinas, Descartes, Hume, and Kant—usually called philosophers because of their metaphysical concerns—also offered theories of human and animal psychology.[66] The 1876 launch of *Mind: A Quarterly Review of Psychology and Philosophy*[67] exemplifies the connection between the two disciplines.

However, psychology's link with experimental physiology rather than philosophy shaped its emergence as a scientific discipline in the nineteenth century—and its influence on economics. The two founding figures of psychology, Germany's Wilhelm Maximilian Wundt (1832–1920) and the American William James (1842–1910), had medical degrees and undertook laboratory experiments. Wundt is considered the "father of experimental psychology" and "exerted enormous influence on the development of psychology as a discipline."[68] James taught one of Harvard University's first courses in psychology, The Relations between Physiology and Psychology, in 1875 and established the first experimental psychology laboratory in America.[69] (Unlike Wundt, however, James also relied on introspection, which he defined as "the looking into our own minds and reporting what we there discover."[70] This more speculative philosophical approach shaped his "theories of the self" and views in *The Will to Believe*.[71])

In the early twentieth century, psychology forked into Freudian and behaviorist branches. The Freudian fork focused on interpreting dreams and the subconscious and became a popular mode of clinical therapy. Academic psychology, however, embraced behaviorism. One of its founders, John B. Watson, "argued that psychology as a science must deal exclusively with directly observable behavior in lower animals as well as humans." Likewise, B. F. Skinner (who became a leading figure in Harvard's psychology department after William James) "explicitly excluded mental life, viewing the human mind as an impenetrable 'black box,' open only to conjecture and speculative fictions."[72]

146   UNCERTAINTY AND ENTERPRISE

Influence on Economics   Besides the aspirational similarities, economics embodied psychological ideas. As a science of human conduct, economics could not avoid psychology. For example, the philosopher-psychologist and preeminent mid-nineteenth-century British economist John Stuart Mill (1806–1873) called economics a "psychological" science. And, while Mill emphasized wealth-seeking, as mentioned, he described the scope of the discipline in distinctly psychological language. Economics, Mill wrote (italics added),

> does not treat of the whole of man's *nature* as modified by the social state, nor of the whole conduct of man in society. It is concerned with him solely as a being who *desires* to possess wealth, and who is *capable of judging* of the comparative efficacy of means for obtaining that end. . . . It makes entire abstraction of every other *human passion or motive*; except those which may be regarded as perpetually antagonizing principles to the desire of wealth, namely, *aversion* to labour, and *desire* of the present *enjoyment* of costly *indulgences*.[73]

Notice how psychology permeates Mill's stipulations and not just his language. Mill assumes that (1) the desire for wealth is a common and important part of human nature, (2) humans can evaluate alternative means for accumulating wealth, and (3) aversion to labor and the desire for consumption can offset the desire for wealth accumulation.[*]

Mill's psychology-infused economics relied on introspection and firsthand observation, not controlled experiments. In economics, as in any social science, Mill wrote, "It is seldom in our power to make experiments."[74] But "the desires of man, and the nature of the conduct to which they prompt him, are within the reach of our observation. We can also observe what are the objects which excite those desires. The materials of this knowledge every one can principally collect within himself."[75]

Later in the nineteenth century, economists applied the experimental findings of German psychologists. For example, Gustav Theodor Fechner conceptualized and measured "just noticeable differences"—the minimum change in a stimulus that individuals can detect. The British economist Francis Ysidro Edgeworth used Fechner's concept to develop his "diminishing marginal utility" theory.[76]

Drifting Apart   Mainstream economists resisted the early-twentieth-century rise of Freud's theories that deviated sharply from the cut-and-dried experimental

---

[*] Mill does *not* claim this as a complete characterization of human nature or behavior. Although no economist "was ever so absurd as to suppose that mankind are really thus constituted," Mill (1844, 139) writes, "This is the mode in which science must necessarily proceed." As mentioned, Knight made a similar argument for assuming rational conduct.

psychology of the nineteenth century. Even Keynes was, surprisingly, a skeptic. Some of his fellow Cambridge "apostles" thought Freud's theories were "one of the decisive scientific advancements of the century."[77] Keynes's protégé Frank Ramsey spent six months in Vienna for psychoanalysis.[78] Keynes's London friends were important lay disseminators of the new psychology.[79] What's more, Keynes's economics emphasized the role of emotions and animal spirits. Yet while acknowledging Freud's "genius," "scientific imagination," and "abundance of innovating ideas" with "shattering possibilities," Keynes pointed out that "when it comes to the empirical or inductive proof of his theories, it is obvious that what we are offered in print is hopelessly inadequate to the case—that is to say, a very small number of instances carried out in conditions not subject to objective control."[80]

Other economists and social scientists were even more disdainful.

Behaviorism, the more academic psychological fork that became popular in the 1920s and 1930s, was, in principle, aligned with the scientific aspirations of economics. But paradoxically, the scientific premise of behaviorism may have encouraged economics to keep its distance from psychology. According to Floris Heukelom's history, Paul Samuelson was "inspired by behaviorism" to argue that "only observed behavior by individuals should be used as a basis for scientific reasoning." Samuelson's "revealed preference" theory assumed that people's preferences could be inferred from their choices. Therefore, economics did not have to investigate internal states of mind.[81]

12

Richard Thaler & Co.: Building the New Behavioral Boomtowns

We can compare K-T's three research projects that we just reviewed to Meriwether Lewis and William Clark's epic eight-thousand-mile-long trek, hailed as the first big step in the westward expansion of the United States. Lewis and Clark produced maps of uncharted land, rivers, and mountains. But westward expansion also required others to settle in the West. Similarly, K-T's pioneering research created a boom, as we will see in this chapter, because

- Richard Thaler and other younger economists, supported by the Russell Sage Foundation, formed a strong, cohesive community that built on the base K-T had established.

- The community expanded the scope of behavioral research to finance while maintaining its cohesion and links to K-T's foundational ideas.

- Criticisms and alternatives could not disturb the dominance of the community or deflect behavioral economics from K-T's uncertainty-free path.

1. Strong, Cohesive Community

Capable Followers While, as mentioned, the technical virtuosity of K-T's *Econometrica* article earned them the respect and attention of economists, they remained primarily psychologists. And psychologists could not by themselves create a community whose work mainstream economists would accept. Acceptance required economic researchers capable of publishing in top economics journals. As often happens with new movements, young economists played a significant role in creating this new community, although some established stars like Akerlof were also supportive. Richard Thaler played a leading part through his research and through other younger researchers he helped attract.

Uncertainty and Enterprise. Amar Bhidé, Oxford University Press. © Oxford University Press 2025.
DOI: 10.1093/oso/9780197688359.003.0012

A "Sharp and Irreverent" Ringleader

In a warm and generous tribute to Thaler, Kahneman recalls that "sometime in 1976, a copy of the 1975 draft of prospect theory got into Dick's hands, and that event made a significant difference to our lives." The ideas in the draft had resonated with Thaler, then an assistant professor at the University of Rochester's business school. When Thaler learned that K-T would be at Stanford in 1977–1978, he secured an appointment at NBER's Stanford office. That started what Kahneman calls "the second most important professional friendship in [his] life." Thaler, a "young economist, blessed with a sharp and irreverent mind," Kahneman writes, had already "trained his ironic eye on his own discipline and had collected a set of pithy anecdotes demonstrating obvious failures of basic tenets of economic theory in the behavior of people in general—and of his very conservative professors in Rochester in particular." Thaler and Kahneman became friends at Stanford and "ever since had a considerable influence on each other's thinking."[1]

Kahneman also believes that his interaction with Thaler

> was a major factor in my receiving the Nobel Prize. The committee cited me "for having integrated insights from psychological research into economic science. . . ." Although I do not wish to renounce any credit for my contribution, I should say that in my view the work of integration was actually done mostly by Thaler and the group of young economists that quickly began to form around him starting with Colin Camerer and George Loewenstein, and followed by the likes of Matthew Rabin, David Laibson, Terry Odean, and Sendhil Mullainathan. Amos and I provided quite a few of the initial ideas that were eventually integrated into the thinking of some economists, and prospect theory undoubtedly afforded some legitimacy to the enterprise of drawing on psychology as a source of realistic assumptions about economic agents. But the founding text of behavioral economics was the first article in which Thaler (1980) presented a series of vignettes that challenged fundamental tenets of consumer theory. And the respectability that behavioral economics now enjoys within the discipline was secured, I believe, by some important discoveries Dick made in what is now called behavioral finance, and by the "Anomalies" columns that he published in every issue of the *Journal of Economic Perspectives* from 1987 to 1990.[2]

The Anomalies column, according to Camerer, Loewenstein, and Rabin's preface to *Advances in Behavioral Economics*, was "critical" in drawing attention to behavioral economics. It helped to shift many economists from the attitude of "if it works, don't try to fix it" to "it's broken; how can we fix it?"[3] Thaler was also emphatic about the widespread prevalence of anomalies

150   UNCERTAINTY AND ENTERPRISE

and errors. Where K-T had claimed that heuristics "sometimes" produce misjudgments, Thaler asserted that "mental illusions should be considered the rule rather than the exception."[4]

Camerer, Loewenstein, and Rabin (like Kahneman) also acknowledge the "unusual and vital role" of Eric Wanner. Wanner did not do any behavioral research., but as a program officer at the Sloan Foundation and then as president of the Russell Sage Foundation, Wanner worked closely with Kahneman, Tversky, and Thaler to support and influence the behavioral economics boom.

An "Unusual and Vital Role"

Wanner started as an assistant professor in Harvard's psychology department after his PhD in 1969 but left academia in 1976 to join Harvard University Press as an editor. He started the Cognitive Science Series at the press, whose advisory board included K-T. In 1982, Wanner moved to the Sloan Foundation as a program officer. There, Wanner proposed applying cognitive science to economics. In 1983, the Sloan Foundation made the first grant for its new "behavioral economics" program. The grant funded Thaler's sabbatical to work with Kahneman at the University of British Columbia.[5]

In 1986, Wanner was appointed president of the Russell Sage Foundation, which had a smaller endowment than the Sloan Foundation. At Sage, according to Camerer, Loewenstein, and Rabin, Wanner made a "big bet," seeing in "behavioral economics the chance for a small foundation to have a big impact in social science and to broaden the language of economics to say more about poverty. He funded research in behavioral economics and invited many behavioral economists to the foundation as fellows in residence." Another "brilliant" Sage Foundation investment was in "biannual 'summer camps,' to teach behavioral economics to advanced graduate students in economics and other social sciences." The camps were "hugely effective in conveying a body of knowledge that campers could not get in Ph.D. courses at their home schools" and "created a social network of students from around the world."[6]

No educational and network-building investment like the one that Wanner coordinated had been undertaken around the old behavioral economics. Thus, while the new behavioral economics had intrinsic advantages over the old, its boom was also strategically engineered.

2. Broadening the Scope

Behavioral Finance As Kahneman's 2002 Nobel announcement noted, behavioral finance was a prominent part of the "recent" behavioral boom. Finance had not interested Simon and the other "old" behavioral economics researchers. Finance also did not feature prominently in K-T's work. Then Thaler, working "predominantly in financial economics in the 1980s," "systematically connected Kahneman and Tversky's biases" to anomalies in financial markets.[7] Thaler's first "Anomalies" column in the *Journal of Economic Perspectives* mentioned earlier was on the so-called January effect in stock markets. In 1993, he edited *Advances in Behavioral Finance* for the Russell Sage Foundation, a collection of papers from the second half of the 1980s.[8] Younger stars, such as Harvard's Andrei Shleifer, who won the John Bates Clark medal in 1999, also researched behavioral finance in the 1990s.[9]

Finance was a strategic choice. In 1985, Kahneman, Thaler, and Wanner (then still at the Sloan Foundation) decided to promote research that would focus, in Wanner's words, on the "contribution of psychology and other behavioral sciences to the study of financial markets," because "financial markets are often considered the most efficient of markets and thus might be thought to be the most immune to non-rational factors."[10]

After Wanner moved to Sage, the foundation funded behavioral finance workshops at the National Bureau of Economic Research (NBER). Thaler (then at Cornell and later at Chicago)[11] and Shiller (then, as now, at Yale) organized the first such workshop in July 1991.[12] Initially held in small meeting rooms at the NBER's office near Harvard, the workshops attracted a few highly engaged participants. Some, like Shleifer, were acclaimed as rising stars in mainstream finance and economics. Top-tier journals would often later publish the papers they presented in the workshops. Eventually, behavioral finance became mainstream, and the workshops moved to large, packed conference halls. (A wide-eyed outsider, I regularly attended the workshops through the 1990s before they became popular.[13])

Finance was methodologically attractive. K-T and other researchers studying judgment and framing undertook experiments with a few hundred subjects. The incentives and subjective interpretations of the subjects and questions researchers openly designed to generate a desired result were controversial. Behavioral finance researchers, in contrast, could analyze databases of "objective" stock prices with hundreds of thousands of records to produce statistically significant results.

Behavioral finance also secured academic respectability from the rationalist theories that had emerged in earlier decades. Hitherto, financiers and many academics (including, as mentioned, Keynes) believed that fear and greed made

152   UNCERTAINTY AND ENTERPRISE

markets prone to irrational fluctuations, but researchers could not objectively establish this. And just as Savage et al.'s utility maximization provided a benchmark for K-T's critiques of rationalist decision theory, the rationalist financial theories defined a target for behavioral finance.

Creating a Target for Behavioral Finance

Rationality in finance is often associated with the University of Chicago, particularly the 1970 "efficient markets" paper published by Eugene Fama (who incongruously shared an Economics Nobel with Shiller in 2013). But significant contributions—many Nobel Prize–winning—have been made by researchers at other universities. These include Simon's colleagues at Carnegie, Franco Modigliani and Merton Miller, Paul Samuelson (MIT), William Sharpe (UCLA), John Lintner (Harvard), Jan Mossin (Norwegian School of Economics and Business Administration), and Steve Ross (Yale). Their research provided a benchmark for the rational pricing of financial assets, against which behavioral finance researchers could show "anomalous" risk-adjusted returns earned by investing in some "behavioral" effect.

Indeed, many of the arguments I heard at NBER's behavioral finance workshops in the 1990s were about whether behavioral strategies actually produced any "excess" returns. Were the higher returns merely fair compensation for taking more risk? Such arguments are not resolvable because what should be considered risk is debatable. Nevertheless, to argue for excess profit, finance behavioralists needed a benchmark to risk-adjust returns and databases of stock prices for statistical analyses. As it happened, believers in market rationality at Chicago and elsewhere had already created models for risk-adjusting returns and set up large databases (which the rationalists expected would help establish rationality).

The underlying psychological theory remained thin. Some financial behavioralists rhetorically invoked K-T's heuristics or prospect theory. Other researchers loosely suggested that feelings and emotions caused financial markets to stray from rational benchmarks. On occasion, Thaler did not even try to explain the anomalies he reported in his column. But financial economists, rationalist or behavioral, cared more about econometric validity than the underlying psychological theory.

Methodological commitments to econometrics encouraged a similar disregard for uncertainty on both sides. Rationalist benchmarks assumed that a stable statistical process, like the repeated spins of a roulette wheel, generated market prices. Likewise, the behaviorists too had to assume a stable statistical process, like the spins of a systematically biased wheel, which generated predictable "anomalies" such as the "January effect." If prices fluctuated without rhyme or reason, on the unpredictable whim of "Mr. Market" (to borrow from Warren Buffett's metaphor), statistical demonstrations of predictable anomalies would be impossible. Scientific behavioral research would not have added much to the traditional lore about fear and greed. Moreover, unpredictable fluctuations would be indistinguishable from Fama's efficient market outcomes.[14]

Practical Benefits Behavioral finance research had attractions outside academia. Financial journalists could dress up commonsensical advice (e.g., keep calm when markets are in turmoil) in scientific terms. Behavioral finance also helped active investment managers justify their fees. The efficient markets hypothesis had put them on the defensive against low-cost "indexed" funds. A theory that claimed markets were inefficient, with stock prices deviating systematically according to behavioral principles, provided an argument for active management. And just as Michael Porter had started the Monitor Company on the back of his Five Forces framework (chapter 7), some behavioral researchers attempted to exploit the commercial possibilities of predictable financial anomalies. Thaler, for example, cofounded Fuller & Thaler Asset Management in 1993 to "capitalize on cognitive biases such as the endowment effect, loss aversion and status quo bias."[15]

Other Extensions While strategically important, finance was just one of several settlements for the new behavioral economists. For example, behavioralists studied intertemporal choices and strategic bargaining— both of which mainstream economists had long analyzed—and fairness and altruism, which had not been prominent mainstream topics. Behavioral economists made mainstream theories more psychologically realistic and analyzed previously neglected issues in realistic ways. For example, behavioral researchers studied why people "live for the day," excessively discounting future outcomes (and thus don't save enough), or why they don't do what they had planned to do.

The applications of the new behavioral research fit the existing economic specializations, particularly labor economics (e.g., wage setting) and macroeconomics (e.g., saving rates). The theories also prompted innovative policies designed to help people overcome their weakmindedness or short-termism. Thaler and his law school collaborator, Cass Sunstein, provided attractive packaging, calling the interventions "nudges" and "libertarian paternalism." In 2010, the UK government established a Behavioural Insights Team (BIT), unofficially known as the "Nudge Unit." By 2018, according to the OECD, more than two

154 UNCERTAINTY AND ENTERPRISE

hundred institutions worldwide were "applying behavioural insights to public policy."[16]

While the new settlers encamped broadly, they continued the basic approaches that had helped K-T and Thaler gain acceptance in mainstream economics. The psychology invoked in theories to explain behavior now more frequently included feelings and emotion, but psychology per se often remained perfunctory and sometimes even absent. Many well-known papers relied on mathematical wizardry to derive their results—and excluded uncertainty. For example, they assumed that people know their future wants (e.g., financially secure retirement) but lack the willpower (e.g., saving instead of consuming) to secure these wants. The "be careful what you wish for because you might get it" problem, arising from uncertain future wants, was not high on the theoretical or policy nudges agenda.

3. Alternatives and Dissents

Smith's Experimental Economics Behavioral and experimental economics are often confused. Understandably so: both try to provide realistic accounts of behavior, often emphasizing intuitive or subconscious judgments and choices. Additionally, both rely mainly on studying the behavior of experimental subjects.[17] These similarities may explain why the Nobel committee awarded the 2002 Economics Prize to Vernon Smith for his pioneering contributions to experimental economics—the same year it honored Kahneman's work in behavioral economics.

But there are also significant differences between Smith's and Kahneman's work and in the specialties they pioneered.

Smith's experiments observe trading behavior as a function of (a) an "environment" that motivates subjects' trading through monetary rewards and (b) an "institution" defined as the "messages and rules of the market," which are "often computer controlled."[18] Uncertainty, often arising from incomplete information, is built into the experimental design. In contrast, K-T's survey experiments assumed that environments and institutions did not shape behavior. And, as mentioned, K-T's survey designs excluded even mundane "missing information" uncertainty.

Smith's research on experimental markets, which he has continued for seven decades, has produced a formidable body of work. Although much of this work is outside my scope, two striking results do relate to my purposes.

First, repeated trading in experimental markets for consumption goods (bought for one-time use) produced prices that conform to the predictions of mainstream economics. Crucially, researchers deliberately gave subjects incomplete information, and subjects undoubtedly had limited cognitive capacities and possibly biased intuitions. Yet, to use Simon's terms, the procedural rationality of Smith's experimental markets overcame the bounded rationality of the individual traders. Trading also corrected whatever K-T biases might have existed. "Poorly informed, error-prone, and uncomprehending human agents," Smith writes, produce outcomes "traditionally thought to require complete information and cognitively rational actors."[19]

However, not all experimental market designs converged to prices predicted by the rational paradigm. In Simon's terms, what was decided depended on how it was decided.

A second striking experimental result was the poor performance of trading in resalable assets, such as stocks or bonds. Bubbles—with prices far above their fundamental value—formed and collapsed in such assets. This happened even when all traders had complete information about the interest or dividends the asset would generate—and knew that all other traders had this information. This result which went beyond Keynes's bubbles that occur because future profits are highly uncertain (chapter 8) surprised Smith.[20]

Smith then "proposed a brilliant explanation for the bubble and crash pattern" for assets that are not bought for immediate consumption. "All traders might well be rational, but if this rationality is not common knowledge, traders might speculate in the pursuit of capital gains, and bubbles might arise."[21] Smith also discovered that designing market rules and structures to prevent asset bubbles was much more challenging than getting the prices of consumption goods right.

Returning to my overall argument: these difficulties suggest how mutual uncertainty about mental capacities and temperaments affect collective outcomes, even when there is no asymmetric information. Moreover, arm's-length trades and terse market messages often cannot control dysfunctional interactions. Detailed justifications and dialogue can become crucial for cooperative action (although Smith's experiments do not examine or show this).

Elster's Mechanisms Elster's critique of the "Excessive Ambitions" of the social sciences provides another helpful perspective on behavior.[22] Elster argues that economics and other disciplines that study human conduct cannot produce the kind of reliable general laws that the natural sciences deliver: "There are simply very few well-established general laws in the social sciences. The 'law of demand'—when prices go up, consumers buy less—is well supported, but as laws go it is pretty weak," writes Elster. The law predicts the direction of the change in demand but not its magnitude.[23]

156 UNCERTAINTY AND ENTERPRISE

Social science can instead identify "mechanisms," which Elster defines as "frequently occurring and easily recognizable causal patterns that are triggered under generally unknown conditions or with indeterminate consequences."[24] Proverbs summing up folk wisdom of general principles or situations suggest such mechanisms, often in

> mutually exclusive pairs. On the one hand, we have "Absence makes the heart grow fonder," but on the other "Out of sight, out of mind." On the one hand we may think that forbidden fruit tastes best, but on the other that the grapes beyond our reach are sour. On the one hand, "Like attracts like," but on the other "Opposites attract each other." On the one hand, "Like father, like son," but on the other "Mean father, prodigal son." On the one hand, "Haste makes waste," but on the other "He who hesitates is lost." On the one hand, "To remember a misfortune is to renew it," but on the other "The remembrance of past perils is pleasant."[25]

Either side of such paired proverbial mechanisms—or both—can be "triggered under generally unknown conditions or with indeterminate consequences." At most, we know that one pair member will be triggered, "but we cannot tell which." Moreover, "Some people may not be subject to either member of these mechanism pairs," while in other cases, "simultaneous triggering of two mechanisms with oppositely directed effects" makes the net effect indeterminate.[26]

The indeterminacy of Elster's paired proverbs* thus mirrors Knight's observation that uncertainty makes conduct "erratic and extremely various from one individual to another."[27] This indeterminacy differs greatly from K-T's *predictable* biases, documented in uncertainty-free circumstances. Additionally, in my interpretation, indeterminacy creates mutual doubts. A cannot predict what B will do and vice versa, even when A has no doubts about B's incentives or information. Their collaboration thus often requires justificatory discourse, with reason-giving and taking.

Gigerenzer's Critiques Gerd Gigerenzer, who received his PhD in psychology from the University of Munich in 1977, has unwaveringly criticized the research that K-T pioneered and is the only critic to whom K-T ever responded. Behavioral

---

* Enthusiasm for the indeterminacy of paired proverbial wisdom is not universal. In 1946, a young Herbert Simon had attacked Gulick and Urick's then-classical theory of administration in "The Proverbs of Administration," published in the *Public Administration Review*. Simon's article claimed, disapprovingly, that the basic principles of the Gulick and Urick theory "were not principles at all, but proverbs, full of wisdom, but always occurring in mutually contradicting pairs" without specifying "when and under what circumstances, which proverb is valid." Urick, Simon recalls, "never forgave me for this attack but Gulick became quite friendly in later years. Presumably he made allowance for the hubris of a young man" (Simon 1991d, 269–270).

economics, writes Gigerenzer, "began with the intention of eliminating the psychological blind spot in rational choice theory," but has "ended up portraying psychology as the study of irrationality." It portrays people as having systematic cognitive biases that are "persistent" and "costly in real life—meaning that governmental paternalism is called upon to steer people with the help of 'nudges.' "[28]

Yet there is little evidence that "alleged biases are potentially costly in terms of less health, wealth, or happiness."[29] Hundreds of studies have found little evidence that "irrational" attention to framing is costly.[30] In fact, a "bias bias"—the tendency to spot biases even when there are none—taints much of the research in behavioral economics. The bias bias mistakes "random error for systematic error" and confuses "intelligent inferences with logical errors."[31] In reality, psychological research suggests that people "appear to have largely fine-tuned intuitions about chance, frequency, and framing."[32]

Bias-Bias Examples

The "overconfidence bias" and framing effects are noteworthy targets for Gigerenzer's critique. Gigerenzer cites DeBondt and Thaler's (1995) claim that "overconfidence" is "perhaps the most robust finding in the psychology of judgment and choices."[33] But results are highly sensitive to how researchers frame their questions. For example, asking, "Are you a better driver than average?" (to which more than half of respondents tend to say "yes") subsumes the unposed question—how "better"? If good driving means avoiding accidents, more than half of drivers can objectively regard themselves as better than average. The number of accidents per person has a skewed distribution, and about 80 percent of US drivers have fewer accidents than the average number of accidents. Designing questions to evoke overconfident responses— or interpreting the results as such—suggests that the problem comes from the "bias bias" of researchers rather than from the minds of subjects.[34]

Similarly, Gigerenzer attacks K-T's evidence for framing effects. Recall that K-T used the "lives saved–lives lost" questions to construct "transparently equivalent versions of a given problem" that "yield predictably different choices." Gigerenzer argues that K-T's two framings are not equivalent; there are subtle yet important differences in wording. Remove the differences, and the framing effect disappears. More generally, sensible listeners should "expect that what and how the speaker communicates is relevant." They can anticipate that "a speaker is likely making an unspoken recommendation when using a positive frame for an option, whereas a negative frame likely indicates a warning." Therefore, "The ability to listen carefully and pay attention to how messengers frame messages" indicates "intelligence, not bias."[35]

158 UNCERTAINTY AND ENTERPRISE

On the positive side, Gigerenzer has followed Herbert Simon's path of studying heuristics to cope with bounded rationality in its Simonian sense—namely, limits to what we can know and process. He argues that "fast and frugal" heuristics, designed for specific tasks, are crucial when information or time is scarce. Even when choices are routine (as in prioritizing emergency room patients or granting bail), professionals often cannot and do not rely on a complex statistical model. They use simple decision protocols with yes/no forks and without any probability estimates.[36]

Gigerenzer also argues that good "biased" heuristics can be superior to unbiased but erratic models. Darts that consistently hit the dartboard just to the right of the bullseye beat unbiased hits scattered far away.[37] (The late and legendary economist Ziv Griliches once jokingly suggested random selection of students to Harvard's PhD program because "randomness eliminates bias.") And Gigerenzer questions why "consistency" in following the rules of deductive logic or probability theory should be a benchmark for rationality. Heuristics well adapted to specific tasks can be "inconsistent" across different tasks. And there are no recorded examples of "money pumps," operated by Ramsey's imaginary "cunning bettor" (chapter 8), bankrupting violators of axiomatic rationality; money pump arguments are just "logical bogeymen."[38]

Daunting Obstacles

As we end this survey, it will not surprise readers that I agree with Gigerenzer's claim that behavioral researchers often exaggerate mental defects, confusing "intelligent inferences with logical errors."[39] This does not at all mean that I believe people are reliably reasonable. Like Adam Smith, Marshall, Schumpeter, Knight, Keynes, and Simon, I agree that emotions and caprice often drive human conduct. But like Simon, Ellsberg, Gigerenzer, Kay and King, and several K-T critics, I reject using uncertainty-free benchmarks. We live in a world infused with ambiguity and one-offs, both trivial and consequential. Statistical risks are the exception, not the rule. Accordingly, we rely on conventions, authorities, social media "influencers," abduction, contextual inference, and Simon- or Gigerenzer-style heuristics, not statistical models or logical deduction. Uncertainty, even about simple known unknowns, makes this reasonable, not a behavioral error or bias.

Simple uncertainties can also make it impossible to numericize confidence. I may, if asked, incorrectly guess that Rome is south of New York, using the heuristic (as Gigerenzer points out) that warmer places are usually closer to the equator. But I would have no rational basis whatsoever to offer a numerical estimate of my confidence in my guess. I would not even know what it means to say that I am 40 percent confident rather than 60 percent confident. However, I might make up a number to be polite to a behavioral researcher—without fearing money-pump exploitation by Ramsey's cunning bettor.

Uncertain wants pose similar problems. When researchers ask subjects how much they would pay for some implausible experience, such as kissing their favorite movie star, they receive whimsical responses anchored to some irrelevant piece of data just planted in the subject's mind by the researcher, such as Social Security numbers. Does this show people are irrationally susceptible to framing, as researchers claim? Or that they blurt out the first thing that comes to mind to earn their five dollars for participating in the experiment? ("Snappy answers to stupid questions," a long-ago feature from *Mad* magazine, came to mind when I heard about the kissing experiment at a Columbia seminar.)

Uncertain wants can also preclude logical standards for "now" against "later" choices. We cannot know now what we will want in the future.[40] We cannot even know after the fact whether we justifiably sacrificed our future wants for current pleasures. If I splurge on an expensive car, I may jeopardize my long-term financial security. Or if I work long, unpleasant hours, I could retire early. But even assuming these expectations are correct, how can I know when the time comes if I made the right choice? Yet that is what behavioral models of rational "time-consistent" choice assume—that our future wants are knowable and comparable to our current wants. Real people cannot meet such standards.

Behavioral research also exaggerates mental lapses by ignoring differences between abstract and contextual reasoning. Worse, it treats abstract deduction as a universal gold standard when one-offs require contextual inference.

Abstract Deduction versus Contextual Inference

Abstract reasoning is a recent development of human civilization. Mathematical and syllogistic deduction goes back just a few thousand years at most, and statistical and probabilistic reasoning goes back just a few hundred years. In contrast, contextual choices and inferences go back more than three hundred thousand years to cave-dwelling humans.

The more recent advances in abstract reasoning have certainly been remarkable. Much of modern science and technology depends on the logical and mathematical manipulation of abstract constructs. And over a relatively short period in human history, competence in deductive reasoning has become widespread: high schoolers learn calculus, and college students solve partial differential equations. Moreover, as increasing scores on IQ tests (the Flynn Effect) suggest, our general capacity for abstract reasoning continues to improve.

160   UNCERTAINTY AND ENTERPRISE

But abstract reasoning isn't a be-all and end-all. As Keynes suggested in his *Treatise*, numerical probabilities amenable to mathematical treatment are exceptional, and Hayek highlighted the importance of specific contextual knowledge vis-à-vis scientific knowledge. James Flynn (progenitor of the Flynn Effect) argues that IQ tests only measure an "abstract problem-solving ability," not "real-world problem-solving."[41] Contextual inference—and what John Forrester, the Cambridge philosopher of science, calls "thinking in cases"[42]—remains ubiquitous.

Notwithstanding its impressive contributions to science and technology, abstract deduction is most dependable for entities governed by the laws of nature or, in the case of software, logical rules. Predicting and managing human conduct—to whatever degree possible—still relies mainly on informal contextual inference. Even in the natural sphere, general principles by themselves rarely get the job done. Technologies—"technical recipes" in Carliss Baldwin's evocative metaphor[43]—invariably embody extensive contextual inferences.

Similarly, discourse about subtle contextual inferences often demands natural metaphorical language rather than abstract mathematical symbols. Using algebra instead of words would not make the arguments Supreme Court justices hear and the opinions they write clearer or more logical. Even mathematical deduction requires natural language to convey practical meaning. And as philosopher Nancy Cartwright points out, "thick" verbs and metaphors enrich causal accounts even of natural phenomena and inanimate devices. Thus, the sun *attracts* planets, and the carburetor *feeds* gasoline.[44]

The ubiquity of uncertain contextual inference raises questions about many behavioral experiments and results. What do they test or demonstrate? Do they really establish widespread biases and other cognitive defects? Is it plausible that Tversky's Stanford subjects—including many students who must have aced college entrance tests and demanding calculus courses—were incapable of trivial logical deduction? An alternative interpretation suggests that the behavioral experiments deliberately mislead subjects. They posed simple reasoning problems in natural language rather than through abstract symbols in uncertain, highly contextualized settings. This tricked subjects into modes of reasoning that are useful or even unavoidable in such conditions.

As Kay and King argue, people do not "reason probabilistically" when responding to the questions of behavioral researchers. Instead, they interpret questions "in the light of their broad contextual knowledge."[45] But unlike Ellsberg, who worried about trickery and misunderstandings and regretted violations (chapter 10), K-T did not. Kahneman was explicit (as mentioned) in seeking to elicit biased responses. Contextual misdirection, which magnifies the usual extent of mistakes, is a helpful device for bias hunters.

Disregarding contextual uncertainty also exaggerates the predictability of biases as well as their severity. As Knight argued and Elster's propositions about paired mechanisms suggest, uncertain circumstances spur uncertain responses. Yet behavioral economists claim to find systematic, predictable biases regardless of context. The claim seems exaggerated, most obviously in financial markets. Like many, I believe markets can fluctuate for no rhyme or reason because of illogical mood swings. I have traded against such swings, expecting sanity to return when they pass. But I do not rely on a systematic formula or algorithm; my assessments are contextual "one-offs."

To my knowledge, legendary traders like George Soros and value investors like Warren Buffett also examine specific circumstances when they place bets. Per Forrester, they "think in cases." Their investment style does not at all require systematic biases. As Buffett has told Berkshire Hathaway's shareholders, "Occasional outbreaks of those two super-contagious diseases, fear and greed, will forever occur in the investment community. The timing of these epidemics will be *unpredictable*. And the *market aberrations* produced by them will be *equally unpredictable*, both as to duration and degree. Therefore, we never try to anticipate the arrival or departure of either disease. Our goal is more modest: we simply attempt to be fearful when others are greedy and to be greedy only when others are fearful"[46] (italics added).

Conversely, I am unaware of fortunes made from trading systematic anomalies like the January effect. The Fuller and Thaler behavioral fund has not been a runaway success.[47] Market anomalies are, at best, only temporarily persistent, and individual booms and busts have a unique, unpredictable character.[48]

That said, Gigerenzer's critique has failed to secure mainstream attention or acceptance in economics. The German psychologist has published prodigiously, attempted to create a community through extensive collaborations, and has won the respect of elite economists like Vernon Smith. But his work remains unknown to the rank-and-file economist. In contrast, behavioral economics and finance have blended into the mainstream. And their uncertainty-free popularity, like that of information economics, discussed in chapter 7, poses a daunting obstacle for my Knightian project.

As we have repeatedly seen, incorporating new ideas into economics requires alignment with its paradigmatic norms and forming cohesive communities of like-minded scholars. Once the discipline assimilates new ideas, they are nearly impossible to dislodge. Further deviations must coexist with accepted approaches. For example, information economics coexists with the earlier microeconomics, and behavioral finance coexists with—and indeed relies on—theories that assume practical omniscience.

162 UNCERTAINTY AND ENTERPRISE

Therefore, although I agree with Gigerenzer's critique, I will not take it any further. Instead, I try to demonstrate how uncertainty can provide a helpful complementary view of modern enterprise. My demonstration, following Simon's approach, also analyzes how procedures and routines affect what boundedly rational organizations do and do not do.

PART III
THE SPECIALIZATION OF ENTERPRISE

The Atlantic Telegraph Cable Fleet, 1866

From The New York Metropolitan Museum Open Access collection[1]

According to the Met's website, laying a telegraphic cable beneath the Atlantic was "one of the 19th century's great technological achievements."[2] Robert Charles Dudley's 1866 painting shows the cable-laying fleet assembled at Berehaven on the southwestern coast of Ireland. The fleet then sailed to Canada, reaching Newfoundland on July 28, 1866, after a sixteen-day voyage, having laid 1,960 miles of cable.[3]

Note the diversity of the fleet. The six-masted *Great Eastern*, five times larger than any other vessel of its time, had been converted to cable laying after losing money carrying passengers.[4] The *Great Eastern*'s support ships included HMS *Terrible*, the largest frigate built for the Royal Navy when it was designed, the *Alby*, the *Medway*, and the *William Cory*. In addition, as Dudley's painting shows, rowing boats ferried crew and provisions to the fleet. This diversity symbolizes the entrepreneurial ecosystem that produces much of modern innovation, as we will see.

13

Including Uncertainty: Recapitulation and Preview

Entrepreneurship offers a natural staging ground for renewing uncertainty-based research. Knight had called his examination of the "role of the *entrepreneur*, or enterpriser," the main "technical contribution" of *Risk, Uncertainty and Profit*.[1] Little else was "fundamentally new"[2] in the book. But as mentioned in chapter 6, the "perfectly interlocking" microeconomics that developed after the 1930s left no room for uncertainty or entrepreneurship. Both were off the paradigmatic research agenda. Later developments of industrial organization (IO) and information economics (chapter 7) could have let both back in, but the pioneering researchers and their followers had different priorities. Many targeted Big Business and the Invisible Hand.

By the end of the twentieth century, however, top business schools began recruiting large numbers of young economists to satisfy the growing demand for entrepreneurship courses. These recruits researched entrepreneurial topics but maintained the uncertainty-free focus of mainstream economics. This focus has created a gap that my uncertainty-based conjectures can help fill.

As mentioned (chapter 4), I analyze two applications—the specialization of entrepreneurial initiatives and the role of imaginative discourse. These applications have a dual purpose: (1) to improve our understanding of entrepreneurship in the modern economy and (2) to suggest an exemplary "paradigm-case" demonstrating what a broader uncertainty-based approach can reveal.

This chapter sets up the first of the two applications (on specialization) by

- Describing how economists who undertook entrepreneurship research repurposed models taken from information economics that focused on incentives rather than uncertainty.

- Recapping my conjectures about uncertainty outlined in chapter 3 and expanded in the chapters on Keynes, Ellsberg, and Simon.

- Previewing how these conjectures can add to our understanding of the specialization of entrepreneurial initiatives.

Uncertainty and Enterprise. Amar Bhidé, Oxford University Press. © Oxford University Press 2025.
DOI: 10.1093/oso/9780197688359.003.0013

166   UNCERTAINTY AND ENTERPRISE

1. Repurposing Incentives

Unexpected Boom   As mentioned in Part 1, William Baumol's 1968 article in the *American Economic Review* lamented that without entrepreneurship, economic theory was a *Hamlet* without the Prince.[3] In a 1993 book, Baumol repeated, nearly verbatim, his 1968 observations that economic theory did not "deal effectively with the description and analysis of the entrepreneurial function."[4]

Still No Prince

References to entrepreneurs in "indexes of recent writings" Baumol complained in his 1993 book, remained "scanty or, more often, totally absent."[5] "While some recent theoretical writings seem at first glance to offer a convenient place for an analysis of entrepreneurial activities, closer inspection indicates that matters have not really improved substantially on this score."[6]

Oliver Williamson's "managerial discretion model," Baumol wrote, featured "a calculating robot, a programmed mechanical component in the automatic system that constitutes the theoretical model of the firm."[7] New models of investment programs and product launches seemed to "smell more of the ingredients of entrepreneurship" but did not take us "a whit further in the analysis of entrepreneurship." They remained "mechanistic and automatic and call[ed] for no display of entrepreneurial imagination or initiative."[8]

Baumol was frank that his own book would not "discuss the activities that constitute entrepreneurship." Instead, he would focus on the "institutional arrangements that encourage the exercise of entrepreneurship and that provide incentives for it to take productive directions."[9] I argue in the chapters to follow that the same emphasis on incentives—at the expense of uncertainty—continues to constrain economic research on entrepreneurship.

Then in the 1990s, soaring demand for entrepreneurship courses ignited a boom in entrepreneurship research. Harvard Business School (HBS) offered the first-ever course in entrepreneurship in 1947. In 1991, about a dozen business schools offered entrepreneurship courses. By 1998, according to Ethan Bronner's *New York Times* story published that September, about 120 schools offered majors in entrepreneurship. "Driven by student and alumni demand," Bronner wrote, "no field is hotter today in business studies than that of entrepreneurship."[10]

INCLUDING UNCERTAINTY   167

Yet although donors were sending "truckloads of dollars" for chairs in entrepreneurship, there were "no scholars to fill them." Schools often hired part-time adjunct faculty and recent PhDs whose training and research had not emphasized entrepreneurship.[11] And many new hires had been trained in economics, even though the discipline had kept entrepreneurship outside its purview.

The young recruits nonetheless proved exceptionally enterprising and capable. Like European settlers of newly "discovered" continents, the new arrivals to entrepreneurship dominated their new terrain while keeping the core conventions and convictions of their homelands. As the first business economics PhD to secure tenure in Harvard's entrepreneurship unit—and the first (in 1990) to publish research on VCs in a top finance journal—used to say, "Entrepreneurship is not what or how I study, it's where I study it." (The declaration was likely intended to deflect scholarly skepticism).

Applying models and methods from the homeland secured publication in top journals eager for papers about the new entrepreneurial continent. The process snowballed. Publishing in top journals won the pioneers tenure in top schools, attracting more of the brightest and best young economists. Helped along by ample funding, a large, influential community of economists who researched entrepreneurship emerged. For example, the first meeting of the entrepreneurship working group at the National Bureau of Economic Research (NBER) in 2002 had 25 invitees and 20 attendees.[12] The group now invites papers from more than 400 researchers, and its fall 2021 meeting had more than 150 registered participants.[13]

A Shrewd and Ruthless Prince Expectedly, tenure-winning entrepreneurship research conformed to paradigmatic rules. Articles published in top journals contained formal models or statistical analyses—and excluded uncertainty. The rules also dictated what was and was not studied. Venture capital contracts, initial public offerings (IPOs), and patents, which provided a rich vein of statistical data and opportunities for formal modeling, attracted attention. Research on informal startups (that do not raise venture capital, expect to go public, or file for patents) was less popular and undertaken mainly from a statistical lens. Economists also avoided Baumol's "clever ruses" and "ingenious schemes"—the stuff of stories told by adjunct instructors but disdained by serious scholars.[14] Knight's main "technical contribution" was also forgotten. A 2021 NBER paper attributes to Knight the definition of entrepreneurs as "individuals who take economic risks,"[15] perhaps because the authors reject Knight's 1921 distinction between risk and uncertainty or, less charitably, because they had not read his century-old book.[16]

The uncertainty-free use of information economics is notable. Researchers studying fund-raising and contracting in entrepreneurial ventures focused on

168 UNCERTAINTY AND ENTERPRISE

information asymmetries and conflicts of interest. Signals of truthfulness and "incentive compatible" contracts to align interests became standard modes for analyzing the relationship between investors and promoters of new and fledgling businesses. Implicitly, economists researching entrepreneurship treated lying and cheating, not uncertainty or honest mistakes, as the primary problems they should study. Their entrepreneurial Prince was no wishy-washy Hamlet.

The lying and cheating path was well-trodden. As mentioned in chapter 7, information economists had emphasized such problems before entrepreneurship research took off. Yet avoiding uncertainty and mistakes was, I believe, a mistake. True, uncertainty-free models can provide insights about the dangers of dishonesty that resonate with everyday experiences, such as the benefits of a professional inspection before purchasing a property or car. Similarly, we take costly signals more seriously. A letter or roses delivered by courier service gets more attention than an email or text message. But other uncertainty-free applications rely on implausible examples.

Signaling Unobservable Quality

In an archetypal example of signaling, employees communicate their true but otherwise unobservable talents to employers by acquiring expensive educations. But why should employers trust young applicants to know their actual abilities? As it happens, educational institutions award observable uncertainty-reducing grades that employers can use to rank and screen applicants. Moreover, employers who require applicants to document their grades never ask for tuition bills to validate signals. Nor do state-subsidized fees reduce the value of degrees from selective institutions. My undergraduate college, the heavily state-subsidized Indian Institute of Technology, charged minuscule fees while admitting very few students after a three-day entrance exam. Other unsubsidized private schools charged high tuitions and levied steep "capitation fees" for admission. Guess which degrees employers favored as evidence of talent? And could merit scholarships (John Maynard Keynes, whose father had independent means, got one to go to Cambridge) diminish job prospects by reducing the potential for credible signaling (by lowering the costs of university educations)? Arguably, the tangible "weight of evidence" (chapter 8) of entrance exams and scholarships far outweighs lost signals of unobservable quality.

Moreover, as mentioned in chapter 7, information economics did not require excluding uncertainty. In the 1980s and 1990s, Raaj Sah and Joseph

Stiglitz studied problems of controlling honest mistakes. Of course, technical challenges could make combining information asymmetries and misaligned incentives with uncertainty and honest mistakes in an equilibrium model difficult. Excluding uncertainty and mistakes may also be a sensible choice for analyzing one-off, arm's-length transactions such as selling secondhand cars. When strangers—who expect each other to take whatever they can get away with—trade, concerns about mistakes may be inconsequential. Indeed, buyers may hope that sellers mistakenly underprice their offerings—and sellers hope that buyers will overpay. And even with known individuals, we often "trust but verify." Parents and children, husbands and wives, bosses and subordinates, and teachers and students cannot ignore the possibility of misrepresentations and worse.

However, common experience also supports the dictum attributed to Napoleon: "Never ascribe to malice that which can be adequately explained by incompetence." And in ongoing relationships, concerns about honest mistakes are at least as crucial as worries about lying and cheating. Concerns about mistakes may even dominate within "unitary" groups and organizations, such as families and partnerships whose members have common interests. When we first select a personal or professional partner, we may be seriously concerned about honesty. Lying and cheating can also end such relationships. Between the starting and the ending, however, mutual concerns about misjudgments will often take priority over worries about dishonesty. Mechanisms to control information asymmetries and misaligned incentives are thus not a suitable hammer for many real-life nails.

Nonetheless, the preoccupation with lying and cheating, reflected in LeRoy and Singell's 1987 creative reinterpretation of Knightian uncertainty as moral hazard (chapter 7), has endured. Asymmetric information and misaligned incentives—and to a lesser degree, behavioral defects (chapters 11 and 12)—have remained the primary lens for economists studying entrepreneurship and many other topics. The "spawning" of research on mistakes produced by limited information that Stiglitz predicted in 2001 did not proceed. The limited research on mistakes and misjudgments focuses on "screening out" individuals with poor decision-making abilities—not, as in the Sah and Stiglitz papers, on organizational routines to catch the errors that capable decision-makers occasionally make.

Excluding uncertainty seems particularly ill-suited to studying entrepreneurship—an activity in which correctness and error are critical determinants of success or failure. "Incentive-compatible" contracting models that assume away uncertainty, for example, may help explain some conditions used to secure venture capital.[17] These models do not, however, plausibly explain why so many entrepreneurs who stake all their wealth, borrow as much as they can, and are willing to sign incentive-compatible contracts cannot secure funding.

Advocates of incentive-based, uncertainty-free explanations have proposed a catch-all category of "private benefits" to include an egotistical preference for one's own opinions. Conflicts of interest can thus cover disagreements and not just the financial stakes. But, invoking private benefits can make explanations tautological or contrived, like postulating epicycles to defend the Ptolemaic, geocentric model of the universe.

I do not exclude concerns about incentives and dishonesty from my analysis, but to balance out the lopsidedness of mainstream economic research— and offer a different perspective—I stress concerns about honest mistakes as barriers to enterprise. Unlike the new behavioralists, I also disregard demonstrably illogical reasoning or foolishness. I base my analysis on conjectures, recapitulated below, that assume procedurally reasonable conduct (per Simon, chapter 9) while modernizing Knight's 1921 analysis of uncertainty (Part 1).

2. Recapitulation of Conjectures

Uncertainty as Doubt I specify uncertainty as doubt, typically produced by missing information about known unknowns, where we know what we do not know. The subjective or internal mental state of doubt thus has its source in a more objective external situation or condition. This specification, which follows research on ambiguity started by Ellsberg (chapter 10), includes incomplete prior knowledge and expertise as doubt-producing missing information. For example, I regard my ignorance of how to interpret electrocardiograms as a source of uncertainty. However, I exclude inchoate anxieties about unknown unknowns.

Like Knight's situational uniqueness, known-to-be-missing information can produce misjudgment and error. We may overestimate the prospects of an odds-on favorite winning a race if we are unaware of its jockey's mental distress. Without a radar map, we may fail to foresee a thunderstorm. Similarly, without an X-ray, orthopedists may miss hairline fractures, and without DNA evidence, prosecutors may jail the innocent.

The missing-information specification subsumes Knight's distinction between uncertainty and numerical "risks." Risk is often regarded as the numerical probability of loss—and in financial markets, as the volatility of prices. The extent of missing information—the source of uncertainty in my specification—is unrelated to the magnitude of such risks. For example, bets on long-shot horses are riskier than bets on odds-on favorites, in the common probabilistic sense. But the information from which bookmakers estimate odds may be the same, higher, or even lower (if the long-shot horses have longer track records, as it were).[18]

However, Knight's risk-uncertainty dichotomy *does not* play a significant role in my modernization project. Instead, my conjectures and applications emphasize:

Targets and Sources of Doubt Like Keynes's broad 1921 conception of probability (chapter 8), my specification of uncertainty includes but is not limited to doubts about statistical distributions. Doubts routinely have contextual or specific ("one-off") targets, such as whether a patient has heartburn or clogged coronary arteries. In fact, my applications emphasize doubts about one-offs and not statistical distributions. I likewise emphasize contextual sources of doubts (such as the ambiguity of a particular patient's symptoms) rather than statistical sources (such the inconclusive results of clinical trials).[19]

Degrees of Doubts Diverse contextual sources usually make it impossible to numericize the extent of missing information and thus the uncertainty produced. Nonetheless, my specification allows many kinds of doubts to be ranked and ordered as "more" or "less." For example, a medical diagnosis based just on patient symptoms is more uncertain than one that includes lab tests. Therefore, while "degrees," like doubts, pertain to internal mental states, observable "weights of evidence" (per Keynes's *Treatise*) affect their extent—although neither degrees nor weights are quantifiable.

Disagreements Uncertainty about what is or could be can spur discovery, innovation, and enterprise. But uncertainty can also produce disagreements by prompting quirky responses, as Knight's and Elster's analyses suggest. Differences may arise without quirks because individuals with different imaginations and prior experiences fill in gaps in their missing information differently. As Ellsberg's ambiguity research suggests, even simple missing information can produce different (yet reasonable in the ordinary sense) psychological reactions ranging from affinity to aversion. And different reactions can hinder collaboration even if there are no information asymmetries or conflicts of interest (except in some tautological "private benefits" sense).

172 UNCERTAINTY AND ENTERPRISE

Variations in Routines In Simon's decision-making theories (chapter 9), uncertainty encourages a routinized search for solutions that satisfy aspirations rather than maximize utility. My view of routines goes beyond searching for and selecting satisficing solutions. Routines also help secure uncertainty-reducing information (as in police procedures to identify the most likely perpetrators), justify claims (as in criminal trials), and reduce disagreements (as in jury deliberations). These functions influence the design of routines, such as the minimum information needed to justify choices and default rules if the necessary data is obtainable (shown in Table 3.1).

Typically, organizations specializing in high-stakes activities follow "strict" routines, requiring high levels of information (Keynes's evidentiary weight) and extensive scrutiny of choices. Strict routines, often multistage, include research to find initially missing information.

Research cannot always discover doubt-reducing information, however. Technical barriers can present insurmountable obstacles. Until about the mid-1960s, angiograms that physicians now routinely use to resolve uncertainties about heart problems would have been technically impossible. Securing missing information may also be prohibitively costly. But regardless of why the information is unavailable, strict routines discourage novel or innovative choices where the amount of missing information is irreducibly high (Figure 3.1).[20]

3. Previewing the Specialization Application

Scope, Framework, and Antecedents In principle, uncertainty is everywhere. All worldly "matters of fact," according to Hume's *Enquiry concerning Human Understanding*, warrant some doubt. We can never be absolutely certain about natural events (from sunrises to tsunamis) or human efforts (from solving jigsaw puzzles to space exploration). My scope is far narrower than of Hume's 1748 *Enquiry* (or Keynes's wide-ranging 1921 *Treatise on Probability*), however. I am mainly interested in efforts to change what would otherwise happen. My conjectures (such as the relationship between novelty, stakes, and strict routines, depicted in Figure 3.1) reflect this focus on forward-looking human enterprise.

Yet enterprising efforts to change what would otherwise happen are also diverse and commonplace. They span initiatives in, for instance, public health, environmental protection, urban planning, space exploration, politics, and the arts. Examining this vast range would weaken my demonstration of how taking uncertainty seriously can improve our understanding of entrepreneurship.

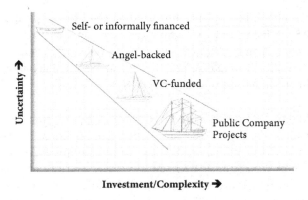

Figure 13.1 Specialization Diagonal
Source: Simplified from Figure 4.1

Therefore, following Simon's example of emphasizing *business* in his 1978 lecture, I limit my attention to contemporary commercial initiatives. Accordingly, while keeping the general conjectures about novelty, stakes, and routines (chapter 3) in mind, the following four chapters examine the more detailed map of commercial initiatives and the functional rationality (Simon, chapter 9) of its specialization diagonal (Figure 13.1).

As we will see, the coordinates of the map and its functional rationality—why the specialization on the diagonal makes sense—turn on a three-way "alignment" or "fit" between: (1) the routines used to evaluate and plan entrepreneurial initiatives; (2) The uncertainty, complexity, and resource requirement of the initiatives; and (3) The sources financing the initiatives (Figure 13.2).

My analysis follows the spirit of Sah and Stiglitz's[21] models of the relationship between organizational design and investment errors and, of course, Simon's routines. The crucial details of my analysis, particularly the influence of funding sources, adapt ideas from papers by Gene Fama and Michael Jensen.[22] The Fama and Jensen papers (which are not their most cited) relate the control mechanisms of different organizations to the complexity and capital

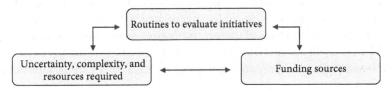

Figure 13.2 Routines, Initiatives, and Funding

174   UNCERTAINTY AND ENTERPRISE

requirements of their investments. But, as in much of standard information economics, they exclude symmetric ignorance—missing information that no one has—to focus on asymmetric information and misaligned incentives. I emphasize symmetrically incomplete—and known to be missing—information to showcase the advantages of analyzing uncertainty.

Outline Chapter 14 argues that irreducibly high uncertainty about the prospects of their ventures—arising from missing information about consumers, technologies, and competitive capabilities—forces entrepreneurs to self-finance their startups or raise money from their relatives and friends. Self-financed entrepreneurs cannot, however, start businesses with large capital requirements.

Chapter 15 explores the differences between wealthy angel investors and professional venture capitalists (VCs). Angel investors typically require more information about consumers, technologies, and competitive capabilities than self-financed founders. VCs, who follow more rigorous evaluation routines, are even less tolerant of missing information than angels. But wealthy angels and VCs can both fund and, in fact, favor businesses that require more capital and are more complex than self-financed startups.

Chapters 16 and 17 examine large public companies that invest (or reinvest) funds raised in stock markets. Their strict justification routines severely limit tolerances for market uncertainties but encourage specialization in complex mega-projects requiring vast capital and other resources.[23]

While these chapters do not question the value of "incentive-compatible contracts," they help explain some otherwise puzzling features of how entrepreneurial initiatives are financed. For example, they can explain why self-financed entrepreneurs can later raise outside financing, even though more information about customers, technologies, and competitors increases potential information-asymmetry problems. In my account, symmetrically missing information—two-sided ignorance—deters outside investors more than asymmetric information.

Exclusions and Emphases To highlight the differences between bootstrapped, angel- and VC-financed, and public-company initiatives, I gloss over differences within the categories, which can be considerable. The categories also exemplify uncertain enterprise but do not cover all its forms. For example, I exclude the enormous but "simple" bets placed by "macro" hedge funds in currency markets and the leveraged buyouts of mature businesses. Moreover, investment manias, like the 1999 internet bubble—when teenage college students started VC funds—and the 2010s "spray and pray" funding of startups[24] are also outside my purview.

Behavioral quirks may amplify misjudgments and encourage stricter due diligence and oversight, but they are not pivotal to my applications. And as before,

INCLUDING UNCERTAINTY 175

I exclude concerns about Rumsfeld's "unknown unknowns" and cataclysms such as out-of-nowhere pandemics and revolutionary possibilities, as in Keynes's examples of European wars and the seizures of private wealth.[25] I focus instead on missing information about known unknowns, such as the demand for a new product, that make the prospects of a new business uncertain.

Contextual information (about known unknowns) and its analysis are more important in my applications than statistical data and inferences. Entrepreneurial choices (including the mundane expansion of a "works" in Knight's archaic language) are situationally unique "one-offs." Any reasonable choice—or procedurally rational routine to evaluate such choices—must lean heavily on heuristics, analogies, abductive inference, and other nonstatistical consideration of contextual factors.

My entrepreneurial applications themselves use abductive inference rather than deductive reasoning. Although I have studied more than a thousand cases over the last thirty-plus years, I cannot and do not offer econometric validation for my generalizations. The credibility of my propositions depends on their fit with contextual and historical data. Methodologically, I follow the "inference to the best explanation"[26] approach implicit in Fama and Jensen's papers[27] rather than Sah and Stiglitz's equilibrium models—and I do not claim any timeless, universal validity for my results.

14

"Bootstrapping" Improvised Startups

The Case-Shiller indices, published by Standard & Poor's, have become the benchmark for US home prices. Their origins go back to 1990 when Carl "Chip" Case (1946–2016), a Wellesley College economist; Yale's Robert Shiller (yes, that Shiller); and one of Shiller's students, Allan Weiss, tried to commercialize Case and Shiller's research. The founders approached two VCs, Corning Capital and Canaan Venture Partners, for financing but were turned down. In 1991, Case, Shiller, and Weiss launched their eponymous firm through personal savings and borrowings. There were no outside investors in Case Shiller Weiss Inc. until its acquisition in 2002 by a publicly traded financial services company.

Mainstream theories (chapter 7) attribute the financing problems of entrepreneurs like Case, Shiller, and Weiss to concerns about truthfulness and incentives. One well-known model suggests that outside financing requires entrepreneurs to truthfully reveal their "type" (or roughly, their honest convictions in their ventures) by investing their own capital.[1] But Messrs. Case, Shiller, and Weiss did invest their savings and took out second mortgages on their homes. Moreover, concerns about their truthfulness and incentives should have been more severe in 2002 than in 1990. In 2002, when the business was up and running, the founders potentially had more adverse information to conceal—and were selling their entire stake. In 1990, their business plan was based more on hope than hard data—and the founders had every incentive to make the venture successful.

K-T–style behavioral theories attribute the financing problem to irrationally "overconfident" entrepreneurs. But is it plausible that Case, Shiller, and Weiss's founders were more prone to overconfidence than the entrepreneurs who VCs fund? Shiller, who coined the term "irrational exuberance," is not known for the cheery optimism of his prognostications.

In my view, irreducible uncertainties—unresolvable doubts produced by known-to-be-missing information—discouraged VCs. Case, Shiller, and Weiss wanted to use their indices to create a futures market in real estate, but they had little objective evidence of the prospects for such a market. If their scheme had been less novel—for example, if they had started an investment fund, as Thaler and Fuller did in 1993—they might have had more success raising outside

---

Uncertainty and Enterprise. Amar Bhidé, Oxford University Press. © Oxford University Press 2025.
DOI: 10.1093/oso/9780197688359.003.0014

"BOOTSTRAPPING" IMPROVISED STARTUPS   177

funding. The Case, Shiller, and Weiss venture typifies how irreducibly high uncertainty, rather than more controllable incentive problems, requires many high-potential businesses to self-finance.

The venture is, however, atypical in the following way: pathbreaking ideas usually aren't the source of the uncertainty of high-potential startups. Instead, I argue that

- High-potential businesses often have humble, improvised origins and are started by founders who lack novel ideas or deep experience.

- Hospitable markets ("habitats") improve the prospects of such businesses but also increase their irreducible uncertainties. Think of the startups as simple canoes in whitewater races. The current—the hospitable market—carries the canoeists swiftly downstream but can also throw them against rocks.

- Irreducible uncertainties discourage arm's-length financing—and present distinctive challenges. Entrepreneurs must get by without professional funding or sophisticated strategizing. Like whitewater canoeists, they have to rely on rapid reactions to avoid capsizing.*

The patterns I describe do not constitute a complete recipe for developing high-growth businesses. Nor do I mean to downplay the role of luck. Chance events were pivotal in the case histories from which I have distilled the patterns. Indeed, the crucial influence of luck is a strong deterrent for professional investors who make calculated, well-informed bets. Yet I suggest that high growth isn't simply the result of chance. Talent and temperaments matter—it takes guts (or high ambiguity tolerance, if you like) to enter a whitewater race.

1. Unlikely Origins

Promising and Unpromising Startups Erik Hurst and Benjamin Pugsley's research shows a wide gap between romanticized portrayals and the reality of startups and business founders in the United States.[2] Most new businesses "start small and stay small throughout the life of the business"; few "intend to bring a new idea to market or to enter an unserved market."[3]

---

* As we see in later chapters, professional investors favor ventures that are like entrants in America's Cup sailing competitions. Here sponsors place calculated, hundred-million-dollar-plus bets on cutting-edge boat designs, experienced crews, and sailing strategies supported by sophisticated data analytics.

178 UNCERTAINTY AND ENTERPRISE

These modest ambitions and outcomes, suggest Hurst and Pugsley, match the concentration of small businesses in industries that offer a "relatively standardized good or service to an existing customer base" and where the scale of operation is naturally low.[4] Just forty sectors, primarily "skilled craftspeople (such as plumbers, electricians, contractors, and painters), skilled professionals (such as lawyers, accountants, and architects), insurance and real estate agents, physicians, dentists, mechanics, beauticians, restaurateurs, and small shopkeepers" account for two-thirds of small businesses. Moreover, "A new plumber or a new lawyer who opens up a practice often does so in an area where plumbers and lawyers already operate" and "expects the business to remain small well into the foreseeable future and does not expect to innovate."[5]

However, exceptional businesses, memorably designated "gazelles" by David Birch, do fit the dynamic stereotype.[6] A survey of extensive academic research concludes that "a small fraction of young firms exhibit very high growth."[7] VC-backed businesses are natural candidates for gazelle status. They have ambitious growth targets, innovative business plans, and often experienced, highly qualified founding teams. But VC-backed startups are even more exceptional than gazelles.[8] What might distinguish gazelles started without VC funds?

My hypotheses emerged accidentally. I compiled case histories of indisputably gazelle-class startups through extended interviews with founders of one hundred businesses drawn from *Inc.* magazine's list of the five hundred fastest-growing privately held companies in the United States.[9] The companies had recorded a more than eighteenfold median revenue increase in the prior five years and an eightfold increase in employees. And although I had not anticipated this, most of the founders I interviewed had "bootstrapped" their startups with meager personal funds. I could, therefore, use the interviews to identify some surprising facts about high-growth, self-financed ventures and extract plausible "abductive" inferences to account for the facts.

Abductive Inferences

As mentioned in the Preface, I wrote up my research in *The Origin and Evolution of New Businesses*. Some scholars criticized the work for "selecting on the dependent variable." In an otherwise favorable review in the Boston Fed's *Quarterly*, the IO stalwart Richard Caves cautioned, "Bhidé's research strategy suffers a limitation common to studies in business administration in its reliance on a nonrandom sample of ex-post winners."[10] Sociologist Howard Aldrich bluntly asserted, "Bhide committed a fundamental methodological error: he selected only successful firms and then tried to infer what differentiated them from the (non-selected) unsuccessful ones."[11]

But what is an "unsuccessful" startup? It could range from a stillborn idea that an entrepreneur considers but rejects after introspection or consulting a few friends, to a business that gets significant traction but then implodes. Identifying a "matched sample" of "failed" startups from many possible specifications of failure seemed pointless, particularly without firm hypotheses about the exceptional successes. However, I did cross-check my inferences from my *Inc.* case histories against the results of a mail survey of self-employed HBS alums[12] and case histories written by my MBA students at HBS (instead of a final exam) of ventures the students considered successful.

After 2000, I continued to require students to write such case histories in the entrepreneurship courses I offered at the universities of Chicago, Columbia, and Tufts. I have now collected over a thousand case histories of notable successes supporting my earlier research. "Positive deviance" research has also now made what Aldrich called my "fundamental methodological error" more respectable, at least among researchers who want to discover useful patterns and practices. And unbeknownst to me until a few years ago, there is an even older case for my hypothesizing. The nineteenth-century pragmatist philosopher Charles Saunders Peirce made "abduction" a cornerstone of scientific research: Summarizing, suppose a scientist encounters an intriguing or surprising fact and can imagine an unlimited number of explanations. All cannot be explored or tested. Some criteria of plausibility—based on a common belief, context, or an accepted paradigm—must be applied. Peirce also argued that everyday reasoning also relied on abductive, contextual hypothesizing, providing the following colorful example:

> I once landed at a seaport in a Turkish province; and, as I was walking up to the house which I was to visit, I met a man upon horseback, surrounded by four horsemen holding a canopy over his head. As the governor of the province was the only personage I could think of who would be so greatly honored, I inferred that this was he. This was an hypothesis.[13]

In 1954 Stanford's George Pólya described the value of abductive-style inference (which he called "heuristic reasoning") in mathematics.[14] More

180 UNCERTAINTY AND ENTERPRISE

recently, Brewer (1996) and Walton (2014) have described applications in the law, medicine, and artificial intelligence. Abduction is thus not just a tool that can help better explain how the world works, but abduction also supports practitioners trying to make it work.

Abductive inference, however, transgresses the conventions of many social scientists—particularly economists and, increasingly, sociologists. It invites accusations of "just so" storytelling and fallacious reasoning. But outside textbooks, contextual abduction makes eminent practical sense. Inferring that "if it is a holiday, it must be Sunday" from the premise that "all Sundays are holidays" is an obvious logical fallacy. But if it's a holiday and I hear church bells ring and know it isn't Christmas or Good Friday, inferring that today is likely a Sunday is a legitimate, plausible abduction.

Certainly, contextual inference cannot yield timeless, universal truths. I spent several years in the mid-2000s with a team of researchers in Bangalore attempting to replicate my US findings. We found sharply different patterns. I attributed these differences in "What Holds Them Back in Bangalore?"[15] to local institutional dysfunctions, again relying on contextual abductive reasoning. I am, however, convinced that the patterns and inferences reported in my 2000 book remain a realistic account of entrepreneurship in the United States.

To preview: Like most low-potential businesses, promising ventures start without a proprietary idea or novel product or service. Their founders often lack deep experience or technical expertise ("human capital," as economists call it), but they can flourish in favorable habitats. Businesses started in niches with high market uncertainty are likelier to record profitable, multiyear growth than the typical new business that starts and stays small.

Unexceptional Ideas Despite all the hype about "disruption," promising self-financed startups do not usually sell breakthrough mousetraps. Ventures like Case, Shiller, and Weiss's that attempt to commercialize a novel technology or idea are exceptions. The typical *Inc.* company I studied started with products or services similar to those offered by other companies, at least in their tangible attributes. Of the one hundred *Inc.* founders we interviewed, only six claimed to have started with unique products or services. Of these, only three had applied for a patent. As indicated in Figure 14.1, 58 percent said that identical or close substitutes were available for their product or service. The rest indicated slight to moderate differences between their and their competitors' offerings.[16]

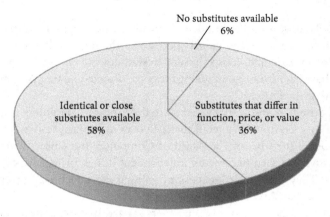

Figure 14.1 Availability of Substitutes
Source: *The Origin and Evolution of New Businesses* (Bhidé 2000, 32)

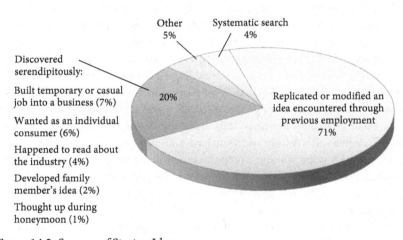

Figure 14.2 Sources of Startup Ideas
Source: *The Origin and Evolution of New Businesses* (Bhidé 2000, 54)

Seventy-one percent of the *Inc.* founders I interviewed replicated or modified an idea they had encountered through previous employment, and nearly half copied their previous employer's business model (see Figure 14.2). Any innovations were modest or easily imitated; they were too obvious to patent and too visible to protect as a trade secret.

Banal Ideas

Sean Ropko and his wife founded Excel to sell used copier equipment to wholesalers. Ropko had previously performed the same function for Xerox but started his firm after Xerox decided to shut down its in-house operation. "People have been buying and selling for years," Ropko told us. "We simply do it better than anyone else."

Carol Sosadian and Atul Tucker started Attronica Computers as a franchisee of Byte Computers, a retail chain. Byte went bankrupt two weeks later. The founders then became a World of Computers franchisee, which also folded. Attronica then became an independent dealer, primarily of AT&T's products. They grew their business by gaining more technical proficiency with the line than AT&T's direct sales force.

Robert Grosshandler and two partners started the Softa Group because they saw opportunities for "a simple software product." Their first product, Total Recall, gave the partners "market knowledge" but was otherwise unsuccessful. On the side, the Softa Group operated another mundane business—selling hardware and peripherals to generate cash flow.

Ken Dougan, who had previously worked as a dockworker, started Unique Transportation Systems. Notwithstanding the name, its business provided trucking services with "one straight truck and two vans." Dougan drove one of the trucks. "I'd talk to people in shipping and do anything they'd ask me to do."

Carol Russell and Rosalind Katz started Russell Personnel Services to provide temporary and full-time workers to employers in San Francisco—a business Russell had previously worked in. Asked what was unique about their enterprise, Russell said their company "introduced the idea of a spokesperson—Carol Russell. People will buy from you if you have a strong personality and credibility."

After working for another company in the same business, Karen Kirsch founded Best Mailing Lists, a broker of mailing lists for the direct mail industry. "My service and product were not unique, but I offered service to which no one could compare."

Mark Lavender cofounded Colter Bay to manufacture and sell sweaters and apparel under "private label" to retailers. He had previously been a senior executive in a sweater manufacturer. Lavender's experience and relationships helped Colter Bay "shave 12 to 15 percent off the cost factor" and offer "a quality product at a fair market price."

John Katzman started the Princeton Review, an SAT preparation service, by conducting classes at Hunter College in New York. Over time, Katzman differentiated his service by offering smaller classes, more computer support, and "clever teaching techniques" acquired by recruiting Adam Robinson, a highly regarded tutor.

Source: Bhidé 2000, 33

"BOOTSTRAPPING" IMPROVISED STARTUPS 183

Papers written by my HBS students showed the same pattern in high-profile startups—such as Walmart, *Rolling Stone*, Calvin Klein, and Waste Management that became household names. Few had started with a significant innovation. Like the *Inc.* 500 founders I had studied, most had imitated or slightly modified existing ideas.

Mimetic Origins of Legendary Businesses

Walmart Sam Walton, founder of the retail discounter (and now the world's largest private employer), had worked briefly in a department store, J.C. Penney, before joining the US Army. Returning to civilian life in 1945, and because his wife insisted they live in a town with fewer than ten thousand inhabitants, Walton bought a "real dog" of a franchised store in Newport, Arkansas.[17] When the landlord declined to renew the lease three years later, Walton moved to Bentonville, another small town in northwestern Arkansas. After opening a franchised "5¢ & 10¢" variety store in Bentonville, Walton started more such stores in and around Arkansas. By 1960, Walton was operating fifteen variety stores.[18]

Meanwhile, discount retailing was taking off. "You didn't have to be a genius to see discounting as a new trend that was going to sweep the country, and all kinds of folks came jumping into it," Walton later recalled. "They would take a carbon copy of somebody's store in Connecticut or Boston, hire some buyers and some supervisors who were supposed to know the business, and start opening up stores."[19] Walton visited dozens of discounters, introducing himself as a "little country boy," asking many questions, and taking notes on a yellow legal pad.[20] Convinced that "the discount idea was the future,"[21] Walton opened the first Walmart in Rogers, Arkansas (a larger town close to Bentonville) on July 2, 1962. Over time, Walmart developed a distinctive business model, mainly through a creative synthesis of ideas copied from other businesses and improvised solutions to unforeseen problems.

Rolling Stone Jann Wenner launched the iconic magazine, known for its authoritative coverage of rock-'n'-roll music, in 1967. It was not the first devoted to the genre. Paul Williams had previously started *Crawdaddy!*, which billed itself as a magazine of rock and roll criticism. It "was the first to take rock seriously as a cultural phenomenon but failed to recognize the need to cater to a popular audience. *Crawdaddy!* was elitist and could secure only limited readership." *Mojo Navigator R&R News* was the first to target a broader market and included celebrity interviews and industry gossip. It also was the first of its genre to secure advertising from the rock and roll industry. In England, there were several rock and roll newspapers, such as *Melody Maker*, which served as a model for *Rolling Stone*. Wenner's goal was simply to do "a more

184 UNCERTAINTY AND ENTERPRISE

popular and commercial magazine" that would take rock and roll "seriously on the terms that it was then coming out."[22]

Clayton Homes Now the leading producer of "manufactured" homes in the United States, Clayton Homes began as a pure imitator. Its founder, Jim Clayton, started a car dealership in 1957. Nine years later, while taking a customer on a test drive, Clayton saw a mobile home being pulled off into a lot and decided to start selling mobile homes. From 1968 to 1973, Clayton sold mobile homes from a single lot. Clayton took advantage of not having a novel product. A national retailer, Taylor Homes, was located a few blocks from Clayton's lot. "Taylor spent heavily on advertising," my students Anderson and Keller write. "Clayton succeeded at stealing many of Taylor's customers that stopped by his lot on their way to Taylor." Clayton's status as a local TV personality also helped: from 1960 to 1976, he served as a part-time host of *Startime*. In this weekly variety show, he played the guitar and sang with celebrities like Dolly Parton. In 1970, Clayton began building some of the homes he sold in an auto body shop. By 1997, the company operated over a dozen manufacturing plants, over five hundred retail centers, a financing subsidiary, and sixty-seven mobile home communities in twenty-eight states with nearly twenty thousand homesites. In 2003, Berkshire Hathaway acquired the company for $1.7 billion.

Virgin Group Founder Richard Branson started with a string of undistinguished businesses. In 1967, Branson launched a magazine called *Student*. The venture was unprofitable. Two other unprofitable and unoriginal ventures followed: a mail-order record business and a record shop. In 1973, Branson started a music publishing business, Virgin Records. The company's first album, Mike Oldfield's *Tubular Bells*, was a hit and helped finance further growth. By 1984, Virgin Records' revenues approached one hundred million pounds, and its associated retail company had become the third-largest retailer in the United Kingdom. That year, Branson started an airline, Virgin Atlantic. Branson also diversified into nightclubs, computer games software, and property development. By 1993, he had amassed a fortune of over $1 billion.[23] In 1999, Branson's group expanded into mobile telephony and, in the 2000s, into wines, trains, casinos, and space tourism.

Meager Human Capital About 40 percent of the *Inc.* founders I interviewed had no prior experience in the industry in which they launched their ventures, and among those who did, the experience often did not seem deep or well-rounded. For instance, John Katzman had been a part-time tutor in college before he launched the Princeton Review. Karen Kirsch had worked at a list broker for about a year after college before starting Best Mailing Lists. Richard Schoenberg was enrolled at the American Film Institute when he briefly worked for someone who brokered film stock before starting his own brokerage.

The founders also had limited entrepreneurial experience and social connections. Three-quarters of the founders had never previously started a business. About half had not been raised where they had started their companies—they had moved there for an education or to take a job. About 20 percent of these transplanted founders were born outside the United States.

The founders of many transformational or celebrated businesses have also lacked experience and industry knowledge. R. X. Cringely describes the entrepreneurs who built the personal computer industry as "amateurs" with "little previous work experience and no previous success." Steve Wozniak, who built the first Apple computer, "was an undistinguished engineer at Hewlett-Packard." His partner, Steve Jobs, had "worked part-time at a video game company." Neither had graduated from college.[24] Bill Gates dropped out of Harvard in his sophomore year to start Microsoft, and Michael Dell quit the University of Texas in his first year to start Dell Computers.

Inexperienced founders have also started well-known media and entertainment businesses. Jann Wenner, a dropout from the University of California at Berkeley, was a twenty-one-year-old "amateur journalist" when he started *Rolling Stone* in 1967. At Berkeley, Wenner had written a column for the *Daily Californian* and, after dropping out, had briefly worked as entertainment editor of *Sunday Ramparts*. That weekly soon folded, leaving him without a job. He "knew nothing about the magazine business" when he started *Rolling Stone,* so "the business aspects of how you created such an enterprise didn't even occur to me."[25] Richard Branson, founder of the Virgin Group, was a sixteen-year-old who had left school—with no interest in going to college—when he started his first magazine.

2. Hospitable—and Uncertain—Habitats

How Habitats Matter Seeing how "habitats" can affect the prospects of startups requires a granular bottom-up view. Statistical data alone cannot show how the nature of markets entered affects the potential for profitable growth.

Noisy Signals

On the surface, entry conditions may seem irrelevant: statistical data support the common trope that resourceful entrepreneurs can find growth opportunities anywhere, including markets where most firms are small.[26] As Haltiwanger notes, "the detailed industry of a firm accounts for only 12% of the variation in the probability that the firm has fewer than 20 employees [and] for even less variation in the dispersion in firm growth rates."[27]

Similarly, Henrekson and Johansson's meta-analysis finds that high-growth gazelles "exist in all industries" and "seem not to be overrepresented in high-tech industries," which are usually considered high-growth.[28] Azoulay et al.'s study also finds only a limited high-technology skew among high-growth companies.[29]

However, statistical results cannot preclude a role for industry or market attributes. In a dynamic economy, historical distributions of firm sizes may not correspond to current or future opportunities. In the first decades of the twentieth century, the rapid growth of emerging automobile and aircraft markets attracted many ambitious entrepreneurs. As these markets matured, barriers to entry rose, growth declined, and new business formations virtually ceased. Now the popularity of electric vehicles and drones has revived opportunities for startups. In the computing industry, high resource requirements initially excluded startups. Already large and mature companies sold early mainframe computers. Microprocessors developed in the 1970s allowed new companies like Apple and Dell (and a swarm of other startups that have since disappeared) to flourish.

Standardized industry definitions used by researchers can be unduly broad or outdated. For example, in the US Census Bureau's North American Industry Classification System, the category "Electronic Computer Manufacturing" includes mainframe and minicomputers, personal desktop computers, workstations, laptops, tablets, and computer servers. Entry and growth are unlikely to be uniform across such a wide range of new and old products. Also, exceptional opportunities in emerging subsegments (e.g., wearable devices) may not discernibly register in data for the broad general category. The Census Bureau may not even include emerging products in standardized categories until their growth has slowed.[30]

More generally, imagine that favorable markets, if complemented by exceptional entrepreneurial capacities, can help startups become gazelles, but this outcome also requires considerable luck. In other words, in the already low proportion of startups that enter the right markets, only some will have founders with the necessary talents, and even fewer will have the good luck to become gazelles. Imagine further that we cannot directly measure the required market and talent conditions and can only record their imperfect surrogates. The signal emitted by the surrogate attributes will then be statistically undetectable, incorrectly suggesting that all startups have equally low probabilities of becoming gazelles.

My case-by-case examination suggested important differences in the businesses started by my *Inc.* interviewees and popular startups. The latter originated in mature, technologically settled markets. For example, a contemporary list of the twenty most popular new businesses started in the United States included cleaning services, beauty salons, arts and crafts, painting, lawn maintenance, and landscape contracting. These categories accounted for about a quarter of the 250,000 new businesses on the popular list, but none of the *Inc.* startups I studied (and only two of the several hundred successful ventures about which my HBS students wrote papers). Conversely, 10 percent of my *Inc.* interviewees developed software, and 36 percent (including the software developers) started in computer-related fields. Software development did not appear on the popular new business list; about eleven thousand "computer service and repair" startups, accounting for just 4.5 percent of the popular total, were the only computer-related businesses on the popular list.

Crucially, computer-related *Inc.* companies were not uniformly distributed across computer and computer-related industries. None had entered mature mainframe, minicomputer, or hardware peripheral markets. Nearly all had started in niches that were then emerging around personal computers. More surprisingly, many offered decidedly low-tech, ancillary products and services to personal computer users. And as mentioned, very few *Inc.* startups—in computer-related or other fields—offered anything unique or novel. In other words, the *Inc.* companies weren't "disrupters" or "pioneers."

Instead, a majority entered new or unsettled markets that someone or something else had already stirred up. In a stable market, where competition has already eliminated weak players, entrants must take customers away from entrenched incumbents. This requires a significantly better approach or a new "combination." However, entrepreneurs do not require significant innovation in a new or changing market. Customers and suppliers take time to learn about alternatives after a change occurs. Meanwhile, entrepreneurs can buy inputs cheaply from uninformed suppliers and sell them at higher prices to uninformed customers. Moreover, meager human capital is often not a significant limitation in a market where no one has deep experience.

Riding the Personal Computer Wave

Hobbyists and "nerds" (as Cringely called them) started the personal computer industry in the 1970s. Notably, Jobs and Wozniak introduced the Apple II in 1977 as a consumer "appliance" designed and marketed for widespread home use. Two years later, my HBS classmate Dan Bricklin (MBA 1979) and Bob Frankston introduced VisiCalc, the pioneering spreadsheet. VisiCalc became a "killer app," turning the Apple II into a serious business tool. Apple's success encouraged mainframe giant IBM to develop the IBM PC, which legitimized the use of personal computers in large companies. The PC, in turn, attracted competition from "plug compatible" alternatives sold by startups, such as Compaq and Dell, and established companies, including the US TV producer Zenith and several Japanese electronics companies, such as Toshiba and NEC. This Schumpeterian "swarm of imitators" reduced prices and helped make personal computers ubiquitous.

The personal computer boom also helped create niche markets for peripherals, supplies, specialized application software, training, support, and distribution. These niches provided opportunities for entrepreneurs who did not innovate or have exceptional technical skills. More than a quarter of the *Inc.* entrepreneurs I interviewed had started businesses related to personal computers. These companies were all launched at least two years after the IBM PC came out and five years after the Apple II was first sold. Their products were mundane: training videotapes and software with features available on 1970s-era minicomputers. And buyers with limited options and knowledge were undemanding. As one midwestern dealer told me, "We have a joke slogan around here: 'We aren't as incompetent as our competitors.'"

Simple imitation in the unsettled market created "Heads I win, tails I don't lose much" opportunities. For example, two twenty-year-olds, Steve Shevlin and Robert Wilken, started Compu-Link, buying and cutting large rolls of printer-to-computer cable and selling the pieces, usually within twenty-four hours. Shevlin, who had worked briefly for a company in the same business, knew that his previous employer was making a gross margin of about 90 percent. Shevlin and Wilken made up batches of IBM printer cables and secured orders by cold-calling computer dealers. The dealers did not have many other suppliers calling them at the time—the business was new—and they could sell a printer cable for sixty dollars, which they paid Compu-Link sixteen dollars for, and which cost Compu-Link only a couple of dollars.

Another 40 percent of the *Inc.* founders entered markets that provided opportunities to differentiate offerings through personal effort. Such opportunities are not uniformly distributed across effort-intensive sectors. In commoditized goods and services, such as laundries and corner-shop retailing, customers evaluate offerings along simple, concrete dimensions and place little value on the intangible elements of the service they receive. This limits the difference in prices and profits between the best and worst providers. And because entry is easy, even the best providers earn marginal returns. In Knightian terms, market uncertainties and profit possibilities from personal differentiation are low.

However, in entertainment, fashion, and "high-touch" services, customers value "fuzzy"[31] attributes such as trendiness, elegance, and responsiveness. These hard-to-define qualities are sometimes embodied in things sold to consumers, such as clothes, handbags, and music, protected by copyrights, trademarks, design patents, and other intellectual property rules. But few of my interviewees sold such items. Instead, they customized or semicustomized services, provided mainly to businesses rather than individual consumers, through exceptional attention to unspoken wants. Some said they presented themselves as more responsive than their established competitors and played on sympathies for scrappy underdogs. While unprotected by legal intellectual property rules, this way of satisfying fuzzy wants is difficult to codify and imitate. Exceptional personal effort ("hustle") can, therefore, help entrepreneurs earn attractive profits.

Irreducible Uncertainties Startups that rely on unsettled markets or their founders' personal capacities to satisfy fuzzy wants have more promise than the typical popular startup. Yet their path to creating a saleable business, rather than just earning fleeting arbitrage profits or attractive personal incomes through their hustle, is highly uncertain.

Demand for hot products can disappear if better alternatives appear or buyers lose interest. Netflix's mail-order and video-streaming services shuttered stores renting VCR tapes. Affordable videocassette recorders had previously made such outlets ubiquitous. Technical improvements in product categories that do mature into megamarkets can eliminate the demand for once-essential components. Worldwide PC sales now exceed one hundred billion dollars, but the once-booming demand for floppy disks and drives has evaporated.[32] Moreover, as markets mature, information gaps close, sharply reducing profits, while increasing economies of scale can eliminate small competitors entirely.

Similarly, inexperienced founders cannot research their capacity to satisfy fuzzy customer wants beforehand. Nor can such founders objectively assess the prospects for turning transient early success into a profitable stand-alone business. Fuzzy wants can be fickle, and entrepreneurs may fail to adapt to changing tastes. Or buyers who value trendiness—or have sympathy for underdogs—may prefer fresh new suppliers. The difficulties of codifying the knowledge

190   UNCERTAINTY AND ENTERPRISE

that protects personal, hands-on differentiators from imitators also limit the growth of their businesses. Unless entrepreneurs can pass on their tacit skills to employees—but keep them from becoming competitors—their ventures remain unsaleable small or solo practices.

Certainly, resourceful entrants who initially seize fleeting opportunities or serve fuzzy wants may find paths to more sustainable profitability and growth. About a third of my *Inc.* interviewees had significantly altered their original business ideas. As industry "insiders," my interviewees had advantages in discovering or creating new opportunities that outsiders could not see. But there was no objective basis for assessing or researching the likelihood of finding and exploiting such opportunities. Like predictions about the demand for new products, prospects for something better turning up (as Mr. Micawber might say) could only be a highly subjective guess.

In other words, uncertainties arising from missing information about demand and differentiation prospects were irreducibly high. Statistical analysis was impossible. "Contextual" data and methods could not provide much guidance either: customer interviews and Porter's Five Force analyses could not resolve doubts about what would—or could be made to—happen. Even the identity and number of rivals that a startup would face, let alone their competitive capabilities, were unknown.

Entrepreneurs, therefore, relied on ex-post opportunistic adaptation—not ex-ante research—to correct misjudgments and discover new growth opportunities. But especially for inexperienced, "first-time" entrepreneurs, no objective information about this capacity for opportunistic adaptation existed. The entrepreneurs themselves had no evidence. And high market uncertainties magnified the role of chance. Perhaps the average or median profit earned over the life of a promising venture was no better than the profit from starting a mundane business with low profit and uncertainty.

3. Financing Constraints

Obvious and Puzzling Patterns The difficulties that new and young businesses face in raising arm's-length equity funding are well known. "Over two-thirds of businesses less than two years old were started using funds from one or more personal sources," writes Karen Mills, a former head of the US Small Business Administration. "Venture capital is important for a certain segment of startups with high-growth potential" but is "barely on the radar of most other types of new firms."[33]

The poor profit prospects of most startups offer an obvious explanation: businesses started in mature, fragmented markets without a proprietary technology or some other competitive edge cannot expect to earn a profit. Such businesses often produce lower incomes than what the owners could earn through paid employment, as research surveyed by Hurst and Pugsley also suggests. Understandably, many founders start their businesses for lifestyle benefits (as Hurst and Pugsley record) that do not interest arm's-length investors.[34] Or to put this in Knightian terms: without market or technological uncertainty, there is no possibility of profit and no outside investment.[35]

The financing problems of promising startups are more puzzling. Most of the *Inc.* founders I studied also bootstrapped their ventures with meager personal savings and borrowings or funds raised from families and friends. Twenty-six percent started with less than five thousand dollars, 21 percent raised more than fifty thousand dollars, and just two raised more than one million dollars. Most founders did not even attempt to raise outside equity. Nearly a third (32 percent) tried and failed. Just 5 percent secured venture capital and 7 percent funding from arm's-length angel investors. Yet, the *Inc.* bootstrappers were highly profitable. They could not have financed their eighteenfold, five-year median revenue increase without high profits.

Principal-agent models and "stealing theories" attribute the problems entrepreneurs face in raising capital to concerns about their truthfulness and incentives.[36] As mentioned, in one well-known model, outside financing depends on the willingness of entrepreneurs to truthfully reveal their "type" by investing their capital.[37] But the *Inc.* founders I interviewed invested their savings and borrowed whatever they could. Moreover, we should expect concerns about truthfulness and incentives to become more severe as businesses grow when the founders potentially have more adverse information to conceal. Yet my interviewees found it easier to raise equity from arm's-length investors: the proportion that secured "follow-on" equity funding (24 percent) was twice the proportion (12 percent) that raised equity at the startup stage.

My inference, which has nothing to do with cheating or misaligned incentives, attributes bootstrapping to the very conditions that make startups without unique products promising. High uncertainty limits the benefits of deep research or careful planning. Facts are hard to secure in new or changing markets, and opportunities are fleeting. In the time it takes to research buyers and competitors and formulate plans, the facts will often change, and the opportunity may have gone.

Moreover, although only a minuscule proportion of the founders I interviewed found their ideas through a systematic search for opportunities, the rest did not proceed in complete ignorance. As mentioned, 71 percent of the *Inc.* founders I interviewed replicated or modified an idea encountered through previous employment. This direct exposure gave the founders an indication about the

192 UNCERTAINTY AND ENTERPRISE

immediate prospects of their ventures as a free byproduct, without requiring additional time or effort.[38] Similarly, the founders spent little time planning. Forty-one percent of the entrepreneurs had no business plan at all. Twenty-six percent had just a rudimentary plan. Only 28 percent wrote up a full-blown business plan. The irreducible uncertainty of hospitable habitats made opportunistic adaptation a sensible choice.

Spontaneous Opportunism

When Peter Zacharkiw started Bohdan Associates in 1983, he was a Bechtel employee who invested in tax shelters on the side. He bought a computer for his tax shelter calculations, expecting to deduct the cost of the machine from his income. When Zacharkiw discovered he was overdeducted for the year, he placed an ad in the *Washington Post* to sell his computer. He got over fifty responses and sold his machine for a profit. Zacharkiw figured that he could have sold them all if he had had fifty machines. He decided to begin selling computers from his home. "At first, I just wanted to earn a little extra Christmas money," he recalls. "My wife put systems together during the day, and I delivered them at night. We grew to $300,000 per month, and I was still working full-time. I made more than I would have made the entire year at Bechtel."

Bohdan evolved into serving corporate clients. "First, we sold to individuals responding to ads. But these people were working for companies and would tell their purchasing agents, 'Hey, I know where you can get these.'" There was no business plan: "Business came to us, and we reacted."[39]

Other *Inc.* founders had to alter their plans significantly. Rich Fox and his partner, Allen Factor, who had previously worked for nonprofit organizations, started a direct mail business to raise money for causes they believed in. But direct mail solicitations require significant upfront spending on printing and mailing without any assurance of results. And prospective clients were unwilling to entrust such projects to a startup. The founders then offered telemarketing services that did not require significant up-front commitments. In telemarketing, Fox recalls, "The responses were extraordinary. So, we gave up on direct mail."[40]

Similarly, the founders of Silton-Bookman Systems had planned to sell PC-based software for human resource development. But established competitors who sold similar software on mainframes were beginning to develop PC products. Silton-Bookman then developed a training registration product. And although the founders had initially targeted small companies that could not afford mainframe solutions, their first customer was someone from IBM who happened to respond to an ad. After that, Silton-Bookman concentrated its efforts on large companies.[41]

"BOOTSTRAPPING" IMPROVISED STARTUPS   193

But for investors, judgments based on sparse information and hopes for opportunistic adaptation pose acute "winner's curse"–type problems:[*] Highly uncertain possibilities should elicit very different expectations and reactions: entrepreneurs with optimistic expectations (e.g., about how long imbalances and information gaps in an unsettled market will last and when and how many other entrants will jostle to take advantage) will want to proceed, whereas pessimists will not.

Averaging out the optimistic and (unobserved) pessimistic assessments protects investors against "winner's curse" problems but also biases them against funding highly uncertain proposals.[42] High uncertainty and transient opportunities also make independent verification by investors difficult. Yet as I show in the next chapter, professional financiers invest in developing capacities for checking founders' assumptions about, for instance, market sizes, purchasing criteria, and technologies. Underutilizing these checking capacities reduces the match between professional investors and highly uncertain yet promising startups.

Traits required to start businesses in unsettled markets (or serve fuzzy wants) may further encourage rejection. Notwithstanding the folklore, a high tolerance for monetary loss does not significantly influence the propensity to start promising businesses where entrepreneurs do not have much capital to lose, even if they stake everything they have or can borrow. Many of my interviewees had also just been fired, and others had started their businesses on the side. But starting uncertain ventures does need a high tolerance for ambiguity and confidence in hunches and guesses. Unlike investors who may average out optimistic and pessimistic assessments, founders who find an opportunity attractive cannot second-guess themselves. Unlike contestants in Keynes's metaphorical beauty contest, they do not seek to predict and bet on the average opinion. They also require the confidence to find unforeseen opportunities and solve unexpected problems and the optimism that they will.[43]

Decisiveness and confidence should attract investors. As in many other occupations, dithering and diffidence in entrepreneurship may be self-fulfilling ("If you worry that you can't, you won't"). Similarly, the psychic, nonfinancial benefits that venturesome, ambiguity-loving entrepreneurs might secure from starting an uncertain business should sharpen their motivation to find a way to make it happen. Ambivalent founders who encounter unexpected problems might give up more quickly. But confident decisiveness can also magnify

---

[*] Classic winner's-curse problems arise in auctions (e.g., of oil drilling rights) where the highest bid often exceeds the eventual value of whatever is being auctioned (Bishop 2009, 333). This is a natural consequence of incomplete information. Even if all bidders are level-headed and rational, their prior beliefs will influence their guesses of true value. And if the median guess is "correct," the bidder who most overestimates will "overpay" to win the auction.

194 UNCERTAINTY AND ENTERPRISE

winner's-curse problems. Self-assured founders are likelier to underestimate the difficulties of coping with setbacks and finding new opportunities. "Favor but investigate" is a reasonable policy for investors. But, irreducible gaps in information severely limit the possibilities for investigation.

Base-Rate Fallacies Landier and Thesmar provide a different K-T–style explanation based on cognitive defects. They assume overoptimistic agents who are "subject to a well-documented psychological bias called 'base rate neglect.'"[44] For instance, optimists observe that an idea has promise while ignoring the rate at which promising ideas fail.

But reasonably "bounded" rationality—the lack of omniscience—often makes adjusting for base rates impossible.[45] Reliable data about base rates in uncertain domains is usually unobtainable. Imagine a college student considering applying for a PhD in economics with the dream of securing a prestigious professorship. The student has earned good grades but has no knowledge of the success or failure rates of individuals in and after graduate school with similarly good grades. Moreover, there is no practical way to find this out. The uncertainty of the base rate is irreducibly high. Many applicants to graduate schools (Landier and Thesmar possibly included), therefore, rely on their grades, contextual indications of their talent, and guesses about alternative career choices. Sensibly, they spend no time researching and appropriately adjusting base rates.[46]

Similarly, many *Inc.* founders I interviewed had some knowledge of their ability vis-à-vis other entrepreneurs in the niches they targeted. As mentioned, many had direct personal experience. They could also reasonably hope that starting in an unsettled market niche might lead to larger and more lasting opportunities later. But they could not have known or discovered base rates and numerical odds. And while it is likely that only a few promising startups rise to the fastest-growing lists, reasonable yet bounded rationality (per Simon, chapter 9) makes it impossible to go further. Just defining the failure of a startup requires arbitrary specification, as mentioned.

Brooding about unknowable failure rates can also undermine confidence—precisely the opposite of visualization techniques used by star athletes. And according to the postulates that contemporary behavioral researchers use to benchmark rationality (chapters 11 and 12), rejecting ambiguous options where you cannot know the odds can be irrational. And given the low stakes (compared to say spending many years getting a PhD), ignoring base rates in starting promising businesses is as reasonable as it is unavoidable.

Coping with Constraints While high uncertainty produces opportunities with more upside than downside, the financing constraint poses significant challenges. And entrepreneurs cannot count on a breakthrough idea or stroke of luck to cope. Instead, bootstrappers rely on many expedients.

How Bootstrappers Cope

Many *Inc.* founders kept their day jobs or did consulting or other side projects to generate cash flow. Robert Grosshandler cofounded the Softa Group to develop "a simple software product." That was unsuccessful, so Softa started developing a property management program and sold hardware and peripherals. "It was low margin, but fast turnaround. Goods arrived in the morning and left in the evening." The cash generated paid for the property management software, which took nearly a year to develop.

To minimize overhead, interviewees served as the "chief cooks and bottle washers," who performed all critical tasks. Other employees, if any, performed routine or mechanical tasks for modest pay. After doing everything himself for a year, Sampler Publications' founder, Mark Nickel, hired the sister of a friend who lived across the street. Her husband had just left her, and she needed to support her kids. His second employee was "a suicidal alcoholic neighbor." John Greenwood's first employee at Micron Separations was a sixty-two-year-old, recently laid-off machine shop worker. His production manager was a Worcester Polytechnic Institute graduate who had been working as an accountant in a company he hated.

Founders who could not afford marketing campaigns tirelessly cold-called prospects. Instead of low prices, they offered early customers extensive customization or free ancillary services. Advent Software's Stephanie DiMarco "spent hours on the telephone solving problems that had nothing to do with us." George Brostoff, the cofounder of Symplex Communications, recalls that their first significant order, from Mead Data, took about four months of "consultative" selling: "We helped Mead refine their existing data network, so whether or not they bought our component, they would have an improved system."

James Odorczyk, founder of Inter-ad, described the company's future "as if it were the present" and "maintained an air of being bigger than we were" by producing quality brochures and a professionally designed logo. Marcia and Steve Plotkin, who started Real World Systems, operated out of their home for several years. When customers called, Marcia said, "Steve is in the warehouse, which meant he was in the garage!"

"We measured every penny," Russell Personnel Services' Carol Russell recalled. "We left out vowels in our classified ads. We used lots of Is and Ls because you can fit more words into a line of type. Os take up a lot of space." Mark Nickel's Sampler Publications took advantage of the free trials that copier companies offered. "We would use a copier for a few weeks and then go to another brand. We went through about six of them!"

Source: Bhidé 2000, passim

196   UNCERTAINTY AND ENTERPRISE

Managerial formularies exclude these expedients. Disregarding cash constraints, they urge preemptive, "first-to-market" investment in new technologies and market shares and hiring world-class talent, not the "suicidal, alcoholic neighbors" or unemployed machinists mentioned earlier. Entrepreneurship courses often focus on securing funding from VCs rather than looking at how bootstrappers use their wits and hustle to make do without. "Ruses" that cannot fit the standard economics model, as Baumol put it, are also not examined.

Yet because uncertainty requires it, ingenious schemes are often the "stuff of which outstanding entrepreneurship is made."[47] Conversely, the need for ingenious schemes is a source of uncertainty in businesses started by young founders: How can anyone foretell if they have the right stuff? How can the founders themselves know?

15

Calculating Capitalists: VCs and Angel Investors

Professional venture capitalists (VCs) and wealthy "business angels" have become prominent "long-tail" investors who aim for a few hits to make up for many misses. They make larger investments than friends and family members who provide informal financing, typically after more thorough evaluations. And in the standard view, thorough evaluations allow VCs and angels to "bridge the financing gap for new ventures that is *largely due* to information asymmetry"[1] (italics added). The standard view similarly attributes differences in the investments of VCs and business angels to differences in their capacity to control information asymmetries.

The alternative uncertainty-focused view in this chapter explains how and why

- Investors rely on due diligence and ongoing oversight to control entrepreneurs' honest mistakes and misjudgments.

- Professional VCs use stricter due diligence and oversight routines than angel investors.

- Stricter routines influence VCs' investment choices. As we will see, strictness limits tolerances for irreducible uncertainty produced by missing information about markets and technologies while encouraging specialization in larger, more complex initiatives.

1. Role of Due Diligence and Oversight

Controlling Winner's-Curse Problems As suggested in the previous chapter, irreducibly high uncertainty about the prospects of many promising new businesses creates winner's-curse risks, provoking summary rejections of investment proposals. But, lower uncertainty can open the door to angel and VC funding. For example, businesses in more settled markets face fewer doubts about future demand. Similarly, a proprietary technology, design, or business concept, sometimes in conjunction with experienced, well-rounded teams, reduces uncertainties about differentiation.

Uncertainty and Enterprise. Amar Bhidé, Oxford University Press. © Oxford University Press 2025.
DOI: 10.1093/oso/9780197688359.003.0015

198   UNCERTAINTY AND ENTERPRISE

In turn, "due diligence" by investors who secure and evaluate researchable information reduces the winner's curse problems. Investors don't have to accept founders' assessments mindlessly—or mindlessly average them down by imagining phantom entrepreneurs who had rejected the opportunity. Instead, investors can do their own research. For example, in ventures built around a patented technology rather than just the personal capacities of the founders, investors can evaluate the strength of patents.

I do not claim that investors ignore asymmetric information. Due diligence by VCs typically includes detailed background checks of founders. Some VCs even hire detectives to investigate possible skeletons hidden in closets, such as prior criminal records. But it is unlikely that all—or even a large part—of investors' due diligence aims to uncover lies about order backlogs or founders' criminal records. Moreover, interviewing customers and analyzing patent portfolios can produce information and insights that founders do not have and may help them rethink their strategies.

The due diligence of financiers focusing mainly on information asymmetries and lemons provides a helpful contrast. Hedge funds that specialize in short selling investigate accounting frauds. Asset-based and subprime lenders try to verify the truthfulness of borrowers' representations about titles and the value of the collateral offered. Investors in entrepreneurial ventures do not have this focus on deliberately concealed defects. Their interest typically includes sharpening their understanding of the positive aspects. Their research may even uncover information that makes investors more optimistic about a venture's prospects than its promoters.

Value of Ongoing Oversight Entrepreneurs cannot mechanically follow precisely specified plans. Unanticipated problems and opportunities inevitably arise. Again, incomplete information makes judgments about the new problems and opportunities fallible. Moreover, sound judgments combine what Isaiah Berlin called foxlike knowledge of many things, not just the hedgehog's knowledge of one big thing.[2] And in entrepreneurial ventures, as in murder trials, the many things include contextual data whose interpretation requires diverse background knowledge. Investors with complementary expertise and experience can, therefore, help control entrepreneurs' misjudgments by correcting for the blind spots and information gaps of entrepreneurs.

As a by-product, investors' oversight can help reassure potential customers and employees about the soundness of the venture. Investors can also acquire subtle, nuanced information that is difficult to discover through due diligence. For example, investors may sometimes see flaws in how entrepreneurs manage their teams that the entrepreneurs themselves miss. Through coaching, investors can help these entrepreneurs correct these flaws.

Information acquired through ongoing oversight can also give investors the confidence to add to their investments in the venture and thus help attract new investors.*

As with pre-investment evaluations, standard theories of monitoring by investors focus on controlling dishonesty and self-dealing by entrepreneurs. Yet, investors generally do not use companies' board meetings as inquisitorial checks on self-dealing. Self-assured founders may also welcome investors' sharp questioning and constructive critiques. Similarly, conflict-of-interest theories focus on how self-serving or overconfident managers may engage in empire-building and overexpansion. However, knowledgeable and experienced investors don't always hold back entrepreneurs; they sometimes encourage hesitant founders to pursue more daring strategies.

I do not mean to dismiss the possibility of conflicting interests and tense investor-entrepreneur relationships. Board meetings can get acrimonious, and VCs who typically require board control are notoriously tough-minded about replacing founder-CEOs. What's more, many entrepreneurs question the value of investor support and advice. Many of the 108 CEOs of VC-backed businesses I interviewed for my 2008 book, *The Venturesome Economy*, were deeply skeptical. Diversified investors are more reluctant to stop throwing good money after bad in struggling ventures that founders are desperate to keep going. But in the ordinary course, investors expect to cooperate with and help founders overcome problems. Financial incentives, such as stock and option grants, and reputational concerns create a common interest in avoiding mistakes and missing opportunities.[3]

Next we examine why the due diligence of professional VCs is more detailed and their oversight is closer than the due diligence and oversight of angel investors. My argument emphasizes the role of VCs as fiduciaries who pool the funds of investors—especially institutional investors like pension funds and endowments.

2. Strictness of VC Routines

Evolution of Institutional Pooling Pooling capital for long-tailed (few hits, many misses) investments is age-old: HBS historian Tom Nicholas identifies nineteenth-century whaling voyages as early examples.[4] Professional

---

* According to the OECD (2015, 110) entrepreneurs often prefer "experienced and well-connected venture capitalists" who can help "rapidly gain information about markets" and "attract highly skilled employees." Gullible or ignorant investors might more readily overlook hidden negative information and offer higher valuations. But naive investors cannot help entrepreneurs reduce their ignorance or provide credible certifications to employees and other financiers.

200 UNCERTAINTY AND ENTERPRISE

financiers have long organized such pooling. Financiers in Philadelphia raised money from investors in London for the early railroads.[5] J. Pierpont Morgan supported Thomas Edison's research and, in 1892, helped consolidate several Edison enterprises into the General Electric Company.[6] Funds raised by Morgan from British and European investors similarly helped Theodore Vail build AT&T.

The long-tailed financings of the nineteenth and early twentieth centuries were usually organized for individual projects like whaling voyages or companies like General Electric. Investing in one long-tailed venture at a time continues in initial public offerings (IPOs)—as well as in angel investment in new and fledgling businesses. Modern VCs, in contrast, pool capital to fund a series of different ventures.

In 1946, the American Research and Development Corporation (ARD), "the first true venture capital firm,"[7] raised capital from many individuals ("retail" investors) to fund a series of ventures. But ARD's funding model—issuing perpetual shares in a fund traded on the stock exchange—did not catch on. Instead, during the 1950s and 1960s, promoters targeted wealthy individuals and families, offering them shares in partnerships with a limited lifespan, usually lasting ten years.[8] Then, starting in the late 1970s, "fiduciary" institutions, including university endowments and pension funds, became prominent investors in VC partnerships.

Evolution and Institutionalization of VC Investing

ARD's promoters initially hoped to raise capital from institutional investors, but institutional investors were reluctant to back an "unproven style of investing." Instead, ARD was floated in 1946 as a closed-ended fund that marketed its shares to individuals, who "unscrupulous brokers" sometimes promised "immediate profits."[9]

The same year, Lawrence Rockefeller organized Rockefeller Brothers to invest mainly in aviation-related ventures. It was funded entirely with Rockefeller funds to benefit Rockefeller family members.[10] Like other single-family VC partnerships established around that time, the Rockefeller Brothers' "evergreen" structure created a permanent pool of capital (as did ARD's closed-ended fund).

In 1958, Draper, Gaither, and Anderson raised $6 million (now equivalent to about $50 million) for the first "proper" nonfamily VC limited partnership. Its limited partners included the Rockefellers, Edward H. Heller (a San Francisco investment banker), and Lazard Brothers (an investment banking partnership). The general partners, themselves wealthy, provided about 12 percent of the partnership's capital and received 40 percent of the profits. In contrast to prior "evergreen" structures, the 1958 partnership had a five-year life, later extended to eight years.[11] Subsequent multifamily funds had ten-year lives, which are now customary.

Rules and traditions initially discouraged many fiduciary-controlled institutions from investing in VC partnerships. Many did not invest even in publicly traded stocks.[12] In the 1970s, pension fund rules brought more institutional capital to the VC industry.[13] In 1987, just eight years after the US Department of Labor gave pension funds explicit permission, VC partnerships increased their capital nearly tenfold, from $424 million to over $4 billion, with pension funds contributing more than half of the amounts raised.[14]

University endowments, never subject to pension rules, also increased allocations to VC partnerships. For example, in 1965, William Elfers started Greylock & Company, whose limited partnerships were initially backed by "a select group of wealthy US families" and "prominent industrialists."[15] In 1978, Harvard's endowment expressed an interest in investing in Greylock. MIT, which had been considering investing in Greylock for years, wanted to invest, as did Duke and Dartmouth. From the late 1970s, these universities, and later Stanford and Yale, provided half of the capital of Greylock's partnerships.[16]

High returns earned in VC and other "alternative" asset partnerships, especially by Yale's endowment, encouraged other universities to invest.[17] The average university allocation to alternative assets, including VC, jumped from 0.5 percent in the 1980s to 27.4 percent of endowment values in the 2010s. As they previously had in stocks, Ivy League endowments led, with alternative investments increasing from 2.4 percent in the 1980s to 60.9 percent of endowment value in the 2010s.[18]

Institutional funds vastly increased the prominence and impact of VC partnerships. By the mid-1960s, there were only ten VC firms of any consequence. About eighty VC firms were active in the mid-1980s; by 2000, over eight hundred were active.[19] Institutionalization also magnified natural differences between VC partnerships (that pooled the funds of many investors) and the direct, personal investments of angels.

But before analyzing how institutionalization magnifies differences between professional VCs and angel investors, let us briefly review these differences.

Well-Known Differences An Organisation of Economic Co-operation and Development (OECD) synopsis of more than sixty practitioner and scholarly

202　UNCERTAINTY AND ENTERPRISE

publications[20] provides the following generalizations about the differences between professionally managed VC partnerships and business angels who invest on their own:[21]

- VCs favor later-stage investments, typically "after a business idea or product has been successfully test-marketed, to finance full-scale marketing and production."[22] Their preference for mature, close-to-exit businesses is especially pronounced as VC partnerships approach the end of their typical ten-year terms.[23]

- Angel investors who have no contractual time limit for exit invest at an earlier stage, often serving as a bridge to the larger growth financing that VCs later provide.[24] Moreover, as VCs are "increasingly focused on later stage investments," business angels are more prominent in "filling the financing gaps in the early stages."[25]

- VCs target businesses with "a solid market potential and prospects for high growth and high returns within a relatively short timeframe (35–40% IRR), high R&D spending, a strong and experienced management team, and the willingness of the entrepreneur to give up a significant share of ownership." These criteria result in "the concentration of VC investments in a few industries, such as the digital economy (i.e., ICT, internet, electronics) and healthcare sectors (i.e., life science, biotech, and medical device technology)."[26]

- As with VCs, capital gains "represent a common and primary objective," but "non-financial motivations" can be more significant for business angels. Many angels are "former successful entrepreneurs interested in supporting other entrepreneurs by providing both funding and expertise." Similarly, angels concentrate on "VC-preferred fields (ICT and healthcare)." However, they are willing to consider a broader range of industries, particularly those where the angel has prior experience. Angels are also "less deterred by gaps in the startup management team, because they can contribute missing expertise through their own involvement." Yet, unlike VCs, angels often "wish to remain minority shareholders," allowing founders to retain majority stakes.[27]

- VCs are "extremely selective" and "intensively scrutinize" proposals, relying on "objective information and analysis" as well as their "intuition" and "gut feelings." Out of every one hundred business plans submitted to VCs, "about ten are closely examined, and only one ends up being funded." In-house associates and analysts, sometimes assisted by outside consultants, help VC partners screen and scrutinize funding requests. Angels receive fewer funding requests and "make investment decisions based on their [own] experience," that is, without the help of paid consultants. Because of the "early stage" of their investments and "the little historic performance data on which judgements about investments can be based," angel investors place "a greater weight on the attributes of the founders."[28]

Explaining the Differences Reflecting mainstream research, the OECD survey attributes the differences between VCs and angels to problems of lying and cheating. For example, the survey says that VCs prefer IT investments because these investments play to VCs' advantages in controlling information asymmetry problems. But although the survey's attributions reflect mainstream research, I find them puzzling.

Puzzling Attributions

More than twenty years ago, Gompers and Amit, Brander, and Zott argued that the raison d'être of VCs lies in their ability to solve information asymmetry problems. These researchers attributed VCs' preferences for high-tech to VCs' ability to solve the more severe problems in that sector.[29]

But how are information asymmetries more severe in high-tech than in restaurants—a sector VCs usually avoid?[30] Suppose it is true that VCs' advantages in managing information asymmetry problems cause them to favor high-tech (more than angels do). Why, then, do angels, rather than VCs, specialize in early-stage investing (where information asymmetry problems are supposedly more severe than in later-stage investing)?

Similarly, how could information asymmetry concerns explain why VCs swiftly reject 90 percent of investment proposals they receive? The rejects could not be all lemons peddled by unscrupulous promoters. Nor can information asymmetries explain the increase in VCs' later-stage investments over the last several decades.

It is undoubtedly possible to justify information asymmetry-based attributions. For example, the OECD report, which (incorrectly, in my view) asserts that information asymmetries are more acute at the outset, suggests that angels invest earlier because their prior relationship with founders helps them control the more acute information asymmetries. But, angels often invest in founders of startups (including Starbucks, Amazon, and Google) whom they have never met. Similarly, much of the detailed VC evaluation (of proposals they do not quickly reject) has no apparent connection to uncovering information that entrepreneurs might deliberately hide.

204 UNCERTAINTY AND ENTERPRISE

I attribute differences in the investments of angels and VCs to the stricter routines that VCs use to control misjudgments. And as we see next, my explanation emphasizes uncertainty: strict routines help reduce the worries of investors in VC partnerships about the gaps in information and knowledge of VCs who manage the partnerships.

Incentive and Misjudgment Issues Professional VCs help investors who lack the expertise to evaluate private high-growth companies to diversify their portfolios. Even individuals who can manage their own deals can benefit from this help.[31]

However, investing in VC partnerships also creates incentive and misjudgment problems. In principle, angel investors who invest directly in new or fledgling businesses can secure board seats that give them a say in significant decisions. They can even replace the CEOs if they own enough of the stock. In contrast, limited partners, who provide nearly all the funds, cede investment control to VCs. According to US partnership law, any say in investment decisions jeopardizes their limited liability. Limited partners cannot replace VCs for poor investment performance—they must prove a compelling cause, such as moral turpitude. And they cannot withdraw any of their funds for the life of VC partnerships. (Hedge funds that invest in tradable assets permit withdrawals after due notice.) Yet limited partners must commit to an amount at inception and give the VCs the discretion about when to require the limited partners to fulfill their capital commitments.[32]

Several mechanisms help reduce the incentive problems. Like entrepreneurs who signal they are of a "good type" by investing in their businesses, VCs invest in their partnerships. As general partners, VCs have more personal liability than limited partners. Compensation arrangements are also said to align the interests of VCs and their limited partners. Typically, VCs receive a flat 2 percent management fee and a 20 percent "carried interest." The flat fee normally pays for operating expenses but does not provide large payoffs. Instead, the 20 percent share of the returns (over some agreed-on benchmark) provides the main reward: VCs do well if the investors in their limited partnerships do well. VC partnerships also have fixed dates for dissolution: VCs cannot permanently keep the partnership's funds. They must execute profitable exits within the fund's life to earn their 20 percent shares. Moreover, a VC that mistreats limited partners will have difficulty raising a new fund. In other words, fixed terms make VCs repeat players and produce a reputational alignment of incentives.

Well-aligned incentives do not, however, remove doubts about misjudgments. As mentioned, requiring founders to invest personal capital does not solve startup investors' winner's-curse problems. Founders who overestimate an opportunity's attractiveness are more likely to invest their funds enthusiastically and sincerely seek outside funding. Similarly, individuals who overestimate their capacities are more likely to try to start VC partnerships and contribute their own capital.[33]

Track records may not accurately reflect VCs' investment abilities. Just one or two fluky winners can significantly increase overall returns. Exit conditions that VCs cannot predict or control, make it hard to differentiate between skill and luck. Hot IPO markets can boost returns, while cold markets can depress them. Additionally, investment judgments and abilities can change. Experience can be a great teacher, but success can also go to people's heads, clouding their judgment. Therefore, even if statistical analysis could reliably differentiate between a VC's past skill and luck, this provides limited assurance about the quality of their future judgments.

Reassurance from Reviews and Routines Mutual monitoring plays a crucial role in the governance of small self-financed partnerships, according to Fama and Jensen's theory.[34] The organizational form, common in traditional law, accounting, and investment banking firms, requires partners to pool their capital and reputations and makes them all liable for the partnership's obligations. The interdependencies encourage partners to review and ratify each other's decisions (on whether to accept a controversial client, for example). Similarly, partnerships often require unanimous or supermajority approvals of decisions on matters affecting their common interest, such as whether to sign leases or admit new partners.*

In VC partnerships, limited partners have virtually no say in governance and investment decisions, as mentioned. VCs—the general partners—have nearly complete control. Limited partners nonetheless benefit from the general partners' mutual reliance and oversight. Individual VCs may have more personal discretion in committing the funds of a VC partnership than in typical professional service partnerships (which have no outside investors). Nonetheless, a common interest in a good track record—and the 20 percent carried interest—encourages methodical mutual oversight. For example, VCs often present the investments they are working on to one another at "Monday morning" meetings. VCs with diverse expertise can help fill in each other's blind spots (or dampen overenthusiasm) as evaluations of new opportunities proceed.

Eventual investment recommendations are products of comprehensive evaluations of diverse context-specific information. "Although most proposals are swiftly discarded," write HBS economists Paul Gompers and Josh Lerner,

---

* Terry O'Neill (1994), then a law school professor (she served as president of the National Organization of Women from 2009 to 2017), offers a theory reflecting "feminist thinking" and the "existence of empathy, collegiality, and group loyalty" (612) to explain phenomena such as the Uniform Partnership Act's instruction to partnerships to "make broad policy decisions by unanimous consent" (62). O'Neill's theory sees small partnerships and other closely held firms as "*unitary enterprises... characterized by commonality of interests*" (605, italics in original).

206 UNCERTAINTY AND ENTERPRISE

"serious candidates are extensively scrutinized through formal studies of technology and market strategy and informal assessment of the management team. (It is not unusual for a venture team to complete one hundred or more reference checks before deciding to invest in a firm)."[35]

VCs also, according to Lerner, "carefully analyze the prospective [financial] returns from investments, conditional on the firm's success."[36] The process results in a written analysis that the VC who sponsors an investment presents to the entire partnership group.[37] And although individual partners rarely have veto rights, consensus or overwhelming support is often the norm. This norm also encourages well-reasoned, high "weight-of-evidence" proposals.

Crucially, VC evaluations are like a murder trial rather than like the statistical analysis of the results of a drug trial. Just as murder trials include consideration of wide-ranging data—from objective forensic DNA evidence to more subjective witness cross-examination and testimony—VC evaluations draw on a mixture of facts and opinions.[38] They can include, for example, hard data about actual sales, costs, and technical specifications, as well as the views of current and potential customers and industry experts.

Comprehensive VC evaluations naturally take longer than the more ad-hoc assessments of business angels (who invest their own funds). Freear, Sohl, and Wetzel report that the median elapsed time between a VC's first meeting with an entrepreneur and the disbursement of funds is five and one-half months. The elapsed time for comparable angel investments is nearly half as long (two and one-half months).[39] In some cases, angels act even more swiftly. In September 1998, Andy Bechtolsheim, who had cofounded Sun Microsystems in the 1980s, gave the founders of Google a hundred-thousand-dollar check as he was ducking out of their first meeting. (That meeting had been arranged to demonstrate a prototype of the company's search engine.)[40]

Institutional Reinforcement As mentioned, fiduciary institutions have become a significant funding source for VC partnerships. These institutions' scrutiny *of* VC procedures and capabilities has a similar, systematic character to evaluations *by* VCs.

Vetting VCs

Many large institutional investors now employ staff to evaluate limited partnerships or retain consultants who perform such evaluations. Others invest indirectly through "funds-of-funds," which evaluate limited partnerships.

The evaluation process typically begins with VCs filling out detailed questionnaires. The International Limited Partners Association has developed a twenty-six-page template with numerical and descriptive, open-ended questions. Besides track records, the numerical questions include the total assets the VC manages, the number of years the VC has been in business, the size of its professional staff, how long the core team has worked together, and so on. The descriptive questions include the VC's strategy, what the VC has and expects to invest in, the process it has and expects to follow, and the qualifications of the investment team. The vetting of VCs who pass the questionnaire stage continues to face-to-face meetings and then to verification. For example, the investor or consultant may examine the VC's internal investment analyses to verify that the VC really follows the procedures it says it does.

Consultants also prepare lists of good VCs they can use in later client assignments. For example, a leading consultant, Cambridge Associates, holds several thousand meetings with VCs each year, "look[ing] for teams that have a clear differentiator" followed by a "full underwriting" of a few hundred VC firms. The underwriting includes background checks, visits to the VC's offices, quantitative analyses of performance, evaluation of fund terms, and investigations of fund operations.[41] Prior approvals do not however eliminate subsequent vetting. Thus, a VC typically faces double screening by consultants and investors.

The vetting aims to identify unfavorable terms and outright Madoff-like frauds and distinguish between VCs' luck and skill. But excluding luck isn't enough. Investors seek to assess whether VC firms can repeat past successes. Do they have a consistent, focused strategy for the deals they will fund, partners and other staff with complementary expertise, and repeatable, standardized routines to support investment judgments? Moreover, like the evaluations carried out *by* VCs, evaluations *of* VCs combine examining objective yet context specific data (such as the VC's investment files) and background assumptions and heuristics (for example, that standardized procedures make extrapolations from track records dependable).

The methodical evaluations used by institutional investors encourage VCs to standardize their procedures beyond what they might do if they were investing just their own capital.[42] Combining Keynes and Simon (see chapters 8 and 9), VCs who act as fiduciary agents for fiduciaries tend to use strict, high evidentiary weight routines to evaluate and justify investments. Evaluations by angels, answerable only to themselves, involve less time and effort. Or colloquially, as one VC observes, "When you are an angel representing yourself, you can be as

208   UNCERTAINTY AND ENTERPRISE

exact or inexact with your investments and your process as you want.... You can jump into things without much diligence if you want and follow your gut when the mood strikes you.... Running a fund, you are a professional manager acting as a fiduciary to LPs *based on an agreed upon set of operating constraints* [italics added]. It is much more constrained and structured and it is much more responsibility.... You have an obligation to do an appropriate level of diligence in every deal you do and to provide as much timely oversight into those companies as you can."[43]

3. How Strictness Influences VC Investments

Target Amounts Routinized strictness limits the number of investments VCs can make, as does the labor intensity of their evaluations and oversight. Unlike algorithmic credit card issuance in the United States, with preapprovals mailed out by the millions, VC investing is an artisanal, hard-to-scale activity. Interdependencies among the partners, which encourage mutual monitoring, also cap the size of VC firms and thus their collective evaluation and oversight capacities.[44]

The constrained capacities and fixed size of VC partnerships (with amounts set at inception) help set a target range for individual investment amounts. Maximums ensure diversification, precluding VCs from putting a fund's entire capital into a single investee. Minimums discourage wasting evaluation and oversight capacities on small investments that cannot justify the costs of that evaluation and oversight evaluation. Minimums also help deter VCs from skimping on their evaluation and oversight standards.[45]

Evaluation and oversight capacities and criteria also explain their summary rejections of small deals. The OECD report notes that the lower end of typical VC investments is considerably higher than the top end of angel investments.[46] If VCs screened just for dishonesty and limited their oversight to controlling self-dealing, their evaluation thresholds and minimum deal sizes would be lower and closer to the size of angel investments. More VCs would (like credit card issuers) diversify widely across more deals. This does not happen much. As VC firms become more established and can raise more capital for their funds, they invest in bigger deals instead of more deals.

Uncertainty Limits Strict evaluations also place lower and upper bounds on the uncertainties (arising from incomplete information) of VC investments. Very low or easily reducible uncertainties cannot justify the costs of VC evaluations and oversight, encouraging VCs to exit investments after their IPOs.

Why VCs Exit (When Angels May Remain)

Except during manias, IPOs typically follow the resolution of significant uncertainties about demand and competitive advantages. Securities laws require companies going public to disclose troves of information and to continue to disclose such information afterward. Under widely held beliefs in market efficiency, researching public information does not significantly improve returns, and securities laws make trading on privately secured confidential information illegal. Therefore, VC advantages in securing and analyzing information become less valuable after IPOs.

Moreover, limited partners can secure the services of stock pickers without paying a 20 percent carried interest and without locking up their capital in ten-year limited partnerships. Limited partners, therefore, encourage VCs to sell stocks after an IPO or distribute the shares to the limited partners, regardless of what the VCs might believe about the subsequent returns. In contrast, angel investors can continue to hold shares in companies that have gone public. In companies like Amazon and Google, angels have made huge returns after public offerings by holding on to their shares.

VCs also have lower tolerances for uncertainty than angels, most obviously because of stricter evaluation routines. On a hunch, an angel may back an investment that VCs will summarily reject because information about demand and competitive differentiation is highly and unavoidably incomplete. More subtly, when crucial information about known unknowns is unobtainable, careful VC evaluations add little value.

Norms for consensus or overwhelming support of partners for each others' proposals further discourage highly uncertain investments: high uncertainty requires more subjective guesses that reflect the guesser's prior knowledge and beliefs. The range of guesses is wider, increasing the possibility that a proposal won't get the necessary support. This prospect will tend to discourage VCs from proposing investments they cannot justify with adequate evidence.[*]

That said, VC uncertainty limits, which, unlike murder trials, do not impose a beyond-reasonable-doubt standard, leave considerable scope for misjudgments. Due diligence procedures to prevent errors can place too much trust in experts. VCs who consult gurus because they aren't confident about their own technical or market knowledge may treat experts' opinions as indisputable truths. And

---

[*] Similarly, prosecutors with strong but incomplete evidence against a suspect may drop charges: the strength of the evidence may persuade most jurors, but its incompleteness may preclude the unanimity necessary for a conviction.

210   UNCERTAINTY AND ENTERPRISE

experts, echoing the consensus of their small communities, can promote join-the-herd investing by VCs.*

VC investing, therefore, remains long-tailed. According to Shikhar Ghosh's study of more than two thousand VC-funded businesses about three-quarters did not return investors' capital. In addition, VCs lost nearly all their investment in about a third of the companies they funded.[47] Conversely, legendary VCs ruefully—or possibly with some pride—report turning down opportunities that later became huge successes (the "ones that got away"). Bessemer Venture Partners posts a striking "anti-portfolio" of opportunities it rejected on its website. The rejections include Federal Express (seven times in the 1970s), Google (in 1999 and 2000), Facebook (in 2004), and Zoom (in 2014).†

Reexamining Angel-VC Differences Earlier I had questioned the plausibility of claims that angels specialize in early-stage investments because (1) information asymmetry problems are then more acute and (2) angels can better control these problems. My alternative view below focuses on the strictness of evaluation routines that limit VCs' uncertainty tolerance.

Uncertainty about the prospects of new and early-stage businesses is irreducibly high, and writing up investment memos backed by convincing objective evidence is difficult if not impossible. And even if one VC strongly believes in a highly uncertain venture, a wide range of opinions makes securing the endorsement of colleagues challenging. Angels are more willing to bet on inchoate hunches, and skeptics cannot veto the choices of the believers. Entrepreneurs can, therefore, secure early-stage funding from angels even if many say no.[48] For example, Jeff Bezos, who started Amazon with personal savings and family money, approached about sixty individual angel investors (VCs, Bezos says, were "totally uninterested") for early-stage funding. Only one-third of the sixty invested. With twenty putting in about fifty thousand dollars each, Bezos raised one million dollars.[49]

Additionally, the slower and more protracted process of their evaluations and approvals makes VCs a poor fit for early-stage businesses entering rapidly changing markets.

---

* What starts as one influential "thought-leader's" guess can become an accepted truth for the expert community. Therefore, while industry and technical experts may appear to facilitate decentralized Hayekian and contextually based choices, consulting them can promote collectivized overinvestment. This overinvestment can pose systemic risks by inflating the bubbles that Janeway (2018, ch. 7) argues are a routine, even "banal" feature of innovation and technological progress.

† Note that my claims about the tolerances for uncertainty—angels more than VCs—do not rely on any "psychological" differences in their preferences for or against ambiguity. I also have no reason to believe that individual VCs are more ambiguity-averse. I merely suggest that their choices as investment agents for limited partners, especially fiduciary institutions, reflect a greater aversion to ambiguity.

As startups turn prototypes and concepts into saleable products, uncertainties about consumer demand and competitive differentiation diminish. Business models also become more settled, and the competitive picture becomes clearer. Now, interviewing customers, competitors, suppliers, and employees can provide more objective evaluations of the prospects.* Later-stage funding also better suits VC targets for deal sizes and timely exits. Entrepreneurs can document the value of investing more funds to support expansion more credibly than they can for seed-stage proposals—and later-stage businesses are closer to demonstrating the sustainability needed for an IPO.

The lore credits VCs for success stories such as Google, Amazon, and Apple, writes Ibrahim, "but each of these companies first relied on angels and might never have attracted venture capital without them." By helping startups with no operating history develop, angel funding provides "a mechanism for sorting among the countless new startups that later seek venture capital."[50] And as the OECD report notes, this interdependency has grown as VC preferences for later-stage funding have strengthened.

In my uncertainty-based framework, VCs' stronger preferences reflect their increased reliance on institutional investors. Institutions that can invest more in VC partnerships than wealthy individuals allow VCs to fund larger, later-stage deals. Concurrently, as discussed, fiduciary responsibilities encourage institutions to evaluate VCs more thoroughly than wealthy individuals might consider necessary. This encourages VCs to follow more systematized evaluation procedures that favor later-stage deals. Seed and early-stage investments are less amenable to systematized evaluations.

Later-stage funding does expose VCs to more information asymmetry problems. In the more uncertain seed stages, the ignorance of investors and founders is symmetrically high—and valuations reflect this two-sided ignorance. Then, as the venture progresses, entrepreneurs naturally secure more information about its strengths and weaknesses and, in the case of inexperienced founders, about their own managerial capacities. Now, to get higher later-stage valuations from VCs or to keep their jobs, founders have incentives to hide any adverse information they may discover. Therefore, VCs may devote more effort to checking founders' claims and require more ongoing control than angel investors (who, as mentioned, often do not demand control or board seats). But this does not mean VCs seek out ventures with information asymmetry problems in the way that subprime lenders target individuals with impaired credit histories. Contrary to the mainstream lemon accounts, my explanation

---

* Evaluations still require laborious research and subjective assessments of contextual information. In other words, the lower but not too low uncertainty of later-stage investments allows VCs to limit leaps of faith about customer demand and competitive advantages and add value through case-by-case due diligence and expert judgment.

212   UNCERTAINTY AND ENTERPRISE

suggests that VCs are more exposed to information asymmetries than angel investors because VCs have lower tolerances for uncertainty. Coping with the asymmetries is a side effect of their uncertainty preferences, not their raison d'être.

High-Tech Tilt   Lower tolerances for uncertainty, embodied in strict routines, also better explain VC preferences for high-tech investments than the usual information asymmetry–based claims. Uncertainty considerations also help explain VCs' preference for patents and avoidance of futuristic technologies.

Like VCs, angel investors also favor technology companies, and as we saw in the previous chapter, information technology is overrepresented among bootstrapped *Inc.* startups. The rising tide of high technology floats many venturesome boats. Rapid growth and unsettled conditions attract all kinds of startups, regardless of how they are financed.

But VCs have a more pronounced and somewhat different technology tilt. While angels favor high-tech, according to the OECD survey, they "consider a wider range of sectors."[51] My case subjects and student papers have also covered angel-funded businesses, such as new restaurants, that traditional VCs typically avoid. Similarly, the proportion of *Inc.* 500 companies in information technology has been about half that in VC portfolios.[52] The number of biotechnology companies, which account for nearly one-fifth of VC investments,[53] is negligible.

Objectively researchable exit prospects help make technology investments more compelling for VCs. As mentioned, VCs must exit their investments within the ten-year life of their funds, either through an IPO or acquisition. IPOs replace limited-term VC funding with permanent capital from public markets, while acquisitions by public companies do this indirectly. Public markets, in turn, favor businesses whose competitive advantages have no expiry date and do not depend on the contributions of a few individuals. Proprietary technologies can promote confidence in such sustainability. Other competitive advantages, such as brand names, purchasing economies, and ubiquity, can also sustain the long-lived profitability of a McDonald's or a Walmart. But VCs' evaluation routines can more easily assess the prospects for technology-based advantages, especially if the technology is protected by patents. A technological basis also makes the potential for reaching the scale that IPOs need more researchable.

Angels are more willing than VCs to invest in businesses that are not expected to go public. For example, they may back chic restaurants not built for IPO exits. They bet instead on recouping their investments through their share of the profits before the restaurant loses out to trendier rivals. Bootstrapped businesses often start with even more transient opportunities, as mentioned. Some angel-financed eateries (such as California Pizza Kitchen) do go public or secure attractive acquisition offers after building brand names and scale. Similarly, some bootstrapped *Inc.* 500 startups, famously Microsoft and Dell, eventually become stock market stars. But VCs avoid betting on serendipitous exits, whereas angels and bootstrappers can tolerate hazy or improbable prospects. Likewise, angels and bootstrappers are more willing to back tech ventures that have not secured patents.

Patents, Please

Catalini, Guzman, and Stern's study of more than thirteen million startups found that the proportion of firms that received venture capital and had applied for or received a patent in their first year was about nine times the proportion among all startups. Given the low ambitions of the typical startup, this is not surprising. More tellingly, the proportion of patent securers among VC firms was also more than five times higher than in the top 5 percent of all high-potential startups.[54]

Similarly, Farre-Mensa et al.'s analysis of more than thirty-four thousand US patent applications showed that getting a patent increases a startup's chances of VC funding by 47 percent over the next three years.[55]

My interviews with the CEOs of 106 VC-backed businesses (reported in my 2008 book) found that only about one-fifth had *not* invested in patents. In addition to the competitive advantages, my interviewees believed that patents helped attract VC investments. One CEO said that "overinvesting" in patents "helps you get top-tier business partners and VCs. From the VC point of view, IP [i.e., patents] is extremely important since it helps determine the exit value." Farre-Mensa et al.'s statistics support my interviewee's view: early patents, they find, double the odds of an IPO.[56]

Irreducible uncertainties also discourage investments in futuristic technologies with uncertain paths to large-scale commercialization. For instance, VCs did not invest in personal computer software companies (including Microsoft and VisiCalc) that started between 1975 and 1982. Subsequently, after the market for personal computer software had been established, they financed companies like Lotus and Intuit. Similarly, nanotechnology has been much talked about for over two decades. I supervised an MBA study on its "coming revolution" in 1991. But to date, VCs have invested only a minuscule proportion of their capital in that field. As one VC told me, he does not fund "science experiments." Angel investors and bootstrappers (like the founders of Microsoft and VisiCalc) are more willing to take chances on technologies with no verifiable prospects for rapid commercialization (and time-bound exits).

214   UNCERTAINTY AND ENTERPRISE

Episodic investment bubbles can however impel bets on futuristic fantasies. In such episodes, like the recent manias for cryptocurrency exchanges, non-fungible tokens (NFTs), and Large Language Models (LLMs) few verifiable facts about markets or technologies are necessary. The primary justificatory evidence is the confident, widespread expectation of a glorious outcome. Sometimes, expectations are self-fulfilling, although crushing disappointments are more typical. And even when investment manias help validate the technological expectation, the financial result is usually distressing, except for a lucky few.

Complexity and Coordination Issues Just as VCs that favor later-stage investments face more severe information asymmetry issues because there is more information to hide, later-stage investees confront more serious coordination problems because they are more complex.

As new businesses grow, the specialization and diversity of their staff, functions, and dedicated resources increases—in other words, they become more "complex." A larger enterprise can afford—and often requires—more specialization, but specialists may not cooperate because of conflicting interests. Or they may not coordinate their efforts effectively because of incompletely shared information: people working in different locations and performing different tasks cannot naturally know what everyone else is doing or planning. Specialists can work at cross purposes without meaning to and without explicit disagreement because of "alignment" uncertainties.

"Alignment" versus "Market" Uncertainties

In my usage, *market* uncertainties refer to doubts about the prospects of an enterprise arising from incomplete information about external factors such as the behavior of consumers and competitors. *Alignment uncertainties* refer to doubts about the consistency of internal choices arising from incomplete mutual information within groups undertaking the enterprise and whose members have a common interest in its success.

Consultation and joint planning may reduce but cannot eliminate information gaps about internal intentions and choices. We cannot be sure even about our own future wants and choices. Nor can we communicate—even to ourselves, much less to colleagues—everything we think, feel, and believe. Irreducible market uncertainties also increase alignment uncertainties: Unexpected external developments can trigger unpredictable—and inconsistent internal responses.

In the typical promising startup, where irreducible market uncertainties are high, alignment uncertainties are low and easily controlled. With one or two founders doing most of the work, the incompleteness of their information sharing is inconsequential or nonexistent. For example, Bill Gates and Paul Allen handled both the technical and business side and had no employees when they started Microsoft in 1975. The founders could, therefore, easily know or find out what each other was thinking or doing. When Michael Dell assembled PCs in his dormitory room in 1984, gaps in information sharing could not arise.[57]

Businesses that secure angel funding usually encounter more significant coordination problems and alignment uncertainties. Angels often invest in businesses that have already advanced their technology or business model using self- or informal financing. After angel financing, a greater division and specialization of labor increases the scope for internal information gaps.

VC-backed, later-stage businesses face even more significant alignment issues and uncertainties. Reduced market uncertainties encourage commitment to strategies that increase the potential for internal misalignments. Moreover, VCs emphasize rapid "scaling up" of their businesses to enable timely exits. Rapid growth adds to the coordination problems and alignment uncertainties.

Stock options and other monetary incentives that promote cooperation and and help control alignment uncertainties are standard features of VC-backed businesses. But VCs rely on more than financial incentives to control coordination problems. They help design organizational charts and recruit managers to fill newly created positions. They coach founder CEOs, or if that fails, replace them with experienced executives often hired for their managerial rather than technical expertise.

Some VCs have recently promoted the use of coordination mechanisms that also do not focus on incentives. For example, John Doerr, a VC who invested in Google and Amazon and served on their boards, has become a prominent advocate of "Objectives and Key Results" (OKR) systems.[58] By design, organizations using OKRs detach them from the compensation and evaluation of employees. Instead, they seek to align objectives, vertically and horizontally, throughout the organization.

Tellingly, OKRs originated in Management by Objectives systems first developed by Intel, a large public semiconductor company. (Doerr, a Rice University–trained electrical engineer and HBS MBA, had been a salesperson at Intel before becoming a VC.) As the next two chapters show, large public

216 UNCERTAINTY AND ENTERPRISE

companies have a comparative advantage in undertaking complex mega-initiatives. However, large, complex initiatives create potentially significant alignment uncertainties, posing severe coordination problems. Chapters 16 and 17 also demonstrate that the mechanisms that public companies have developed to control the problems also reduce tolerances for irreducible market uncertainties.

16

The Evolution of Dynamic Bureaucracies

The now-defunct East India Company seems an unlikely progenitor for the large modern public corporation. "The Company," as it was often called, started in 1600 when 218 merchants and "adventurers" secured a Royal Charter to monopolize trade with the East—and "the right to wage war when necessary." By 1803, it had "built much of London's docklands" and "generat[ed] nearly half of Britain's trade." Beyond trade, the Company ruled much of India, which it had "swiftly subdued and seized" from its boardroom in the city of London. It employed some 260,000 soldiers and had created "a vast and sophisticated administration and civil service."[1] A small headquarters staff—John Stuart Mill served as colonial administrator for seventeen years—managed the Company's sprawling colonial empire.

But power did not secure permanence. A War of Independence that erupted in 1857 ended the Company's rule in India. Although the insurrection failed, the British government took control of India, ending Company dominion (and Mill's administrator career). Even earlier, the Company had chronic financial difficulties despite monopolies, opium sales, and colonial tax impositions. In 1773, it required a bailout from the British government. A hundred years later, Parliament dissolved the now 284-year-old Company, which had once called itself "the grandest society of merchants in the Universe."[2]

Modern megacorporations like Microsoft and Walmart do not raise armies or rule colonies. But their economic role is no less influential, ranging from cutting-edge technology to traditional retailing. Like the East India Company, modern mega-corporations are controlled by career professionals. Like the Company, they are relentlessly expansionary. The popular view, however, often sees large organizations as sclerotic bureaucracies. Mainstream economics likewise ignores their relentless orchestration of uncertain initiatives. In standard theories, business firms exist to control the costs of transactions with known payoffs[3] and use sticks and carrots to control duplicitous or lazy employees. These uncertainty-free theories ignore misjudgments that can arise because of incomplete information. The theories also ignore how the strict routines that large companies use to control misjudgments affect the uncertainty, complexity, and stakes of their initiatives.

I highlight the ignored or misunderstood expansionary impulse of large public firms and explain why they favor initiatives at the southeastern end of my specialization diagonal (Figure 4.1). Differently put, large companies are carefully dynamic. Their initiatives, I show, are expensive, complex, and meticulously

Uncertainty and Enterprise. Amar Bhidé, Oxford University Press. © Oxford University Press 2025.
DOI: 10.1093/oso/9780197688359.003.0016

218   UNCERTAINTY AND ENTERPRISE

planned—like the Mars Rover or Hubble Telescope projects—and not improvised hacks or workarounds.

I examine the distinctiveness of large company dynamism through a historical and bottom-up analysis. The main sections of this chapter explore how large, professionally managed corporations

- Developed distinctive organizational structures and collectivized decision-making routines in the first half of the twentieth century.

- Consolidated their dominant position after World War II.

- Struggled in the last quarter of the twentieth century.

Although, as we will see, giant corporations have lost their aura of invincibility, many of their critical attributes have endured. These influence their distinctive entrepreneurial twenty-first century role, which I analyze in the next chapter.

1. Foundational Developments

Strategies and Structures Business historian Alfred Chandler's *Strategy and Structure* (1962) and *The Visible Hand* (1977) provide authoritative accounts of the development of large modern industrial corporations through the first half of the twentieth century. *The Visible Hand,* which won a Pulitzer in History, proposed a sometimes controversial counterpoint to Adam Smith's famous eighteenth-century metaphor.[4] Here, I want to focus on the 1962 book and some of its underappreciated ideas.

Chandler's book famously describes the progressive development of the strategies and organizational structures that culminated in large, multidivisional, professionally managed corporations like General Motors and Exxon.

Progressive Development

In the mid-1800s, Chandler observes, American industry mainly comprised very small, single-product establishments focused on a single function: manufacturing. Starting in the 1870s, the completion of railroad lines that helped unify the national market spurred empire builders to undertake ambitious strategies for geographic expansion and vertical integration. Manufacturing-focused firms also added functions such as marketing. The far-flung, vertical integration posed significant coordination problems. But many empire builders bent on expansion lacked interest in the administration of their companies—or constantly meddled in day-to-day operations.

Exceptional entrepreneurs who had an interest in orderly operations developed functionally departmentalized organizations. Geographically dispersed manufacturing was simplified into a single function controlled by a central departmental office. The new organizations also consolidated nationwide distribution networks and instituted uniform accounting procedures. By the end of the 1910s, most large US companies had adopted functionally departmentalized organizations, which smoothed day-to-day operations and supported further expansion.[5]

Continued expansion exposed the limitations of functional organization, however. When businesses had saturated their existing markets, they diversified into new products and markets. The diversification placed an "intolerable strain on existing administrative structures," according to Chandler. Manufacturing and marketing different kinds of products "made the tasks of departmental headquarters exceedingly difficult to administer."[6] Selling paint, the chemicals giant DuPont discovered, posed different problems from selling explosives, yet both were the responsibility of the same sales department. Similarly, the mass retailer Sears Roebuck had to cope with differences between buying items for its mail-order catalogs and for its stores.

Economic crises that exposed these problems led companies to establish "divisions" with dedicated resources. For instance, losses incurred in a financial crisis in 1920–1921 caused DuPont to abandon its functional structure and form product divisions with dedicated resources and more autonomy. The same crisis spurred General Motors (GM) to form the Cadillac, Buick, Oakland, Olds, and Chevrolet divisions. The reorganization helped General Motors "win the largest share of the automobile market in the United States," Chandler writes.[7]

Three features of Chandler's histories are particularly pertinent to my analysis.

1. *The dynamism of large, professionally managed corporations.* The expansionary drive of their nineteenth- and early-twentieth-century founders is self-evident. What readers sometimes overlook in Chandler's histories is how the businesses maintained their momentum after professional managers took control. Yet, as Schumpeter had earlier asserted, Chandler

portrayed the professionally managed corporation as relentlessly expansionary. Its continued investments in "scale and scope" produced "a fundamental dynamic or force for change in the capitalist economies."[8]

(Chandler's language, which is not as colorful as Schumpeter's accounts, can obscure this message. And like Schumpeter, Chandler does little to explain—as I try to do in the next chapter—why professional managers of dominant firms would attempt further expansion. Why not enjoy the "quiet life" that British economist Sir John Hicks had suggested was "the best of all monopoly profits?"[9])

2. *How new organizational structures supported enterprise.* The prominence of operational problems in spurring the development of organizational structures can hide the entrepreneurial role of the structures. But, a careful reading of Chandler's histories suggests that difficulties in undertaking new initiatives also helped catalyze some organizational innovations. Chandler also repeatedly and emphatically stresses how new organizational innovations supported new entrepreneurial initiatives and not just the greater efficiency of existing operations. The multidivisional structure that General Motors adopted after an economic crisis in the 1920s not only helped GM increase its share of existing markets in the United States. It underpinned GM's overseas expansion and enabled the company to "execute brilliantly a broad strategy of diversification into the making and selling of all types of engines, and products using engines."[10]

3. *The diverse constituents of organizational structures.* Chandler's 1962 thesis is often reduced to a simple slogan: "Strategy dictated organizational structure." A strategy of geographic expansion, for example, required creating a functional organization, and related diversification impelled a multidivisional structure. But Chandler uses "functional" and "multidivisional" merely as convenient labels while defining "structure" as the "design of organization through which the enterprise is administered." The design, which has formal and informal elements, "has two aspects. It includes, first, the lines of authority and communication between the different administrative offices and officers and, second, the information and data that flow through these lines of communication and authority. Such lines and such data are essential to assure the effective coordination, appraisal, and planning so necessary in carrying out the basic goals and policies and in knitting together the total resources of the enterprise."[11]

The Chandlerian structures implicitly include Herbert Simon's routines (chapter 4). True, Chandler does not explicitly use the "routines" to describe the "flow of information and data" in his definition. But, although Simon's name

THE EVOLUTION OF DYNAMIC BUREAUCRACIES   221

does not appear in the indices of *Strategy and Structure* and *The Visible Hand*, the spirit of Simon's routines pervades Chandler's accounts. For example, in implementing its new multidivisional structure between 1921 and 1925, General Motors, Chandler writes, worked out procedures that "facilitated forward planning and policy formulation," including the "rational allocation of funds" and "decisions as to where the corporation should expand, contract, or maintain, its activities."[12] The devil of the multidivisional structure was thus in its routines and related details.*

Role of Discourse Despite appearances, the large, professionally managed corporation was not a command-and-control hierarchy. Undoubtedly, earlier artisanal guilds, workshops, and small factories were more compact and flatter than the organizations that evolved after the nineteenth century. Earlier, most large hierarchies weren't commercial. They were found in organized religion (notably the Catholic Church and its orders), civil administration (mainly for tax collection and public works), and the military (Roman armies adopted the "manipular" system around the third century BCE). In commerce, the East India Company was an exception to compact organization, and it too was not just a business enterprise.

Many commercial enterprises then became multitiered. As Chandler records, geographic expansion, mass production, and mass marketing impelled functional organizations with more managerial and supervisory levels between the boss and frontline workers. The "lines of authority" that Chandler includes in his definition of organizational structure became longer. The multidivisional form increased the number and function of middle managers. But lines of authority weren't just channels for handing down orders. Often, middle managers sent up ideas and proposals.

Experts outside the direct chain of command were also influential. When General Motors adopted its multidivisional structure in the 1920s, it set up financial and advisory staff "to help coordinate, appraise, and plan policy." A research section "worked on improved engines, parts, bodies, fuels, and other technical improvements."[13] Even the notoriously headstrong Henry Ford (who said customers could get the Model T in any color as long as it was black and was so sure of the design's success that he discontinued every other model) took advice from experts. He hired motion study expert Frederick Taylor to improve the efficiency of his assembly line, and a sociology department helped Ford implement his revolutionary five-dollar-a-day wage plan in 1914.[14]

---

* Their perceived knowledge and expertise of the details likely allowed US-based consultants, especially McKinsey & Co. and Booz, Allen, Hamilton, to secure lucrative projects to implement multidivisional structures in Europe (as described by Christopher McKenna 2006).

222 UNCERTAINTY AND ENTERPRISE

Large organizations weren't Hobbesian Leviathans. Despite differences in rank and titular authority, they favored justificatory discourse. According to Alfred Sloan, who served as the company's chief executive from 1923 to 1946, GM developed a "tradition of selling ideas, rather than simply giving orders." All levels of management had to "make a good case" for their proposals; the manager who wanted to "operate on a hunch" would "find it hard to sell his ideas to others." But the sacrifice of possibly brilliant hunches was compensated for by the "better-than-average results" of policies that could be "strongly defended against well-informed and sympathetic criticism." GM's approach, Sloan claimed, protected the company against "ill-considered decisions by assuring that basic decisions were made only after thorough consideration by all parties concerned."[15]

Exclusions from Mainstream Economics The features and challenges of large organizations have become staples of management research and business education. Heterodox economic theories, such as evolutionary economics, also take many of these features seriously. But mainstream theories (chapters 6 and 7), which serve as my principal foil, exclude critical components of organizational designs—especially routines—along with the uncertain initiatives the organizations undertake.

Textbook microeconomics assumes perfectly competitive markets in which atomistic producers of undifferentiated commodities do not undertake any entrepreneurial activity. In industrial organization theories, businesses secure market power by investing in their scale and scope (to use Chandler's terms). But the theories assume unitary, black-box organizations whose internal designs do not affect their investments. And the information economics–style theories that claim to peer into organizational black boxes ignore critical design elements such as the routines that large corporations use to evaluate, justify, and plan uncertain initiatives. (Recall Herbert Simon's complaint, quoted in chapter 9, of "pitifully skeletonized abstraction[s].")

Oliver Williamson's theories (which won him a Nobel in Economics in 2009) are a prominent example. According to Williamson, contracting problems between independent firms lead to their joint ownership. "Thermal economies" from combining successive stages of the steelmaking process, he argues, cannot explain their integration in one steelmaker: "Were it possible to write and enforce a complex contingent claims contract between blast furnace and rolling mill stages, the integration of these activities, for thermal economy reasons, would be unnecessary."[16] But independent owners of the two stages cannot negotiate contracts that cover all possibilities, and

THE EVOLUTION OF DYNAMIC BUREAUCRACIES 223

unexpected events can produce conflicts. Williamson argues that joint ownership of both stages harmonizes interests and allows "a wider variety of sensitive incentive and control processes to be activated."[17] Papers by Oliver Hart and Bengt Holmström (who shared the Economics Nobel in 2016) claim similar advantages from "non-contractible" decision rights that ownership of an asset provides.

These theories, I believe, exaggerate the force of authority while ignoring the role of justificatory routines and other details of organizational structures. According to sociologist Mark Granovetter, Williamson "vastly overestimates the efficacy of hierarchical power ('fiat,' in his terminology) within organizations."[18] Chandler's account of the problems of nineteenth-century empire-builders supports Granovetter's assessment. "The economic advantages of integration and consolidation," writes Chandler, "were in no sense, automatically concomitant with industrial imperialism." Successful acquisitions required "careful attention to the administration of marketing, manufacturing, and the procurement of raw materials" and, above all, "coordinating and integrating these different activities into a unified whole. . . . The task appeared so difficult that many doubted the possibility of building efficient consolidated enterprises."[19]

Top-down decrees (even if dutifully obeyed, which they often are not) remain inadequate solutions to coordination and integration problems in twenty-first-century behemoths like Microsoft and Walmart. Their chief executives are not as omnipotent or omniscient as skeletonized theories—and occasionally, the executives themselves—imagine they must be.

2. Postwar Dominance

Not Quite New Innovation, Schumpeter wrote in his 1942 book *Capitalism, Socialism and Democracy*, "is being reduced to routine. Technological progress is increasingly becoming the work of trained specialists who turn out what is required to make it work in predictable ways."[20] The "perfectly bureaucratized giant industrial unit" employing the specialists could fulfill all "objective possibilities" for innovation. Ousting the individual entrepreneur, the bureaucratic giants had "come to be the most powerful engine of progress."[21]

John Kenneth Galbraith's 1967 opus, *The New Industrial State*, analyzes how this engine revved up in the quarter century after Schumpeter's book. Both books eloquently question mainstream beliefs, albeit from opposing ideological perspectives.

224   UNCERTAINTY AND ENTERPRISE

Differently Heterodox

In his Introduction to the fourth (1985) edition of Galbraith's book, Sean Wilentz calls its author "the most renowned and, arguably, most influential liberal economist in the United States during the decades after the Second World War." The book, written mainly during the years Galbraith served Presidents John F. Kennedy and Lyndon B. Johnson, continues Wilentz, describes "the vastly more sophisticated, technologically advanced business enterprises that had arisen since 1945."[22]

Galbraith, like Schumpeter, was heterodox. The two had briefly been colleagues in Harvard's economics department before Schumpeter died in 1950. Both had emigrated to the United States, Schumpeter from Austria, and Galbraith from Canada. And, according to economist-historian Deirdre McCloskey, "Both tried political power early, Schumpeter as a pro-market minister of finance in Austria's brief socialist government after World War I and Galbraith as a New Dealish deputy director of the US Office of Price Administration during World War II. Experience in government had opposite effects on the two. Schumpeter became permanently suspicious of state power. Galbraith became permanently delighted with it. These two men of clever words, both master rhetoricians, laid out the case for and the case against unregulated markets."[23]

(Chandler, also a preeminent chronicler of the rise of Big Business, kept out of politics—although his books have been criticized for their "whiggishness." While economists Schumpeter and Galbraith directly attacked the doctrines of their discipline, the business historian Chandler expressed his skepticism gently.[24] And he was far from a "master rhetorician.")

Galbraith classifies the postwar economy into two distinct parts—a "few hundred technically dynamic, massively capitalized and highly organized corporations" and "thousands of small and traditional proprietors." Their difference "invades every aspect of economic organization."[25] The first part, which Galbraith calls the "Industrial System," is "the dominant feature of the New Industrial State."[26] It has effective autonomy from shareholders. Salaried professionals control giant enterprises through a "technostructure"—"an apparatus for group decision-making—for pooling and testing the information provided by numerous individuals to reach decisions that are beyond the knowledge of anyone."[27]

But how new was Galbraith's Industrial System and its control? The power of industrial giants in 1967 was radically greater than in the nineteenth century. But

Great but Gradual Changes

Galbraith's first chapter, "Change and the Industrial System," opens with the "great" innovations and economic alterations since World War II. However, while Chandler's *Strategy and Structure* (which Galbraith does not cite) mainly covers prewar developments, the two accounts have similarities. Thus, the first change Galbraith lists is in the influence of large corporations:

> Seventy years ago the corporation was still confined to those industries— railroading, steam navigation, steelmaking, petroleum recovery and refining, some mining—where, it seemed, production had to be on a large scale. Now it also sells groceries, mills grain, publishes newspapers and provides public entertainment, all activities that were once the province of the individual proprietor or the insignificant firm. The largest firms deploy billions of dollars worth of equipment and hundreds of thousands of men in scores of locations to produce hundreds of products.[28]

Galbraith then highlights the influence of professional managers: "The men who now run the large corporations own no appreciable share of the enterprise. They are selected not by the stockholders but, in the common case, by a board of directors which, narcissistically, they selected themselves."[29] Retaining the ample, reliable profits of existing businesses reinforces managerial control over new initiatives. "A plea for larger dividend payments is occasionally heard at stockholders' meetings. But it is heard respectfully and ignored."[30] Having "a secure source of capital from its own earnings," the professionally managed enterprise "concedes no authority to outsiders. It has full control over its own rate of expansion, over the nature of that expansion and over decisions between products, plants and processes."[31]

But we can find the nucleus of both "postwar" changes in Chandler's prewar accounts. A "new form of capitalism," the "large managerial business enterprise," appeared in the last half of the nineteenth century, Chandler wrote.[32] This new form, controlled by a hierarchy of salaried executives rather than the owners, "dominated the core industries in the United States" by the end of World War I.[33]

226 UNCERTAINTY AND ENTERPRISE

Similarly—and notably for my argument—Galbraith's "technostructure" closely resembles the organizational "structures" emphasizing middle management functions in Chandler's pre–World War II histories. Like Chandler, Galbraith stresses the diffusion of decision-making. Top executives do not answer to stockholders or creditors about managing existing businesses or new initiatives. But their decision-making powers are more ceremonial than substantive. The "stereotyped organization chart"[34]—a pyramid with authority flowing down the chain of command—is fiction: "Those who hold high formal rank in an organization—the president of General Motors or General Electric—exercise only modest powers of substantive decision," Galbraith writes.[35]

Long development cycles, capital requirements, complexity, uncertainty, and technological sophistication demand careful planning and coordination. Thus, the Ford Motor Company's marketing plans must reduce and control uncertainties about demand: they must anticipate what customers will want in a new car model and devise ways to market the cars long before they roll off assembly lines. Diverse activities must also align across time and functions.

Combining Hayekian price system language and Chandlerian "organizational" analysis, Galbraith argues that planning and coordination challenges require diffusion of knowledge and expertise on the one side and joint decision-making on the other:

> Decision in the modern business enterprise is the product not of individuals but of groups. The groups are numerous, as often informal as formal, and subject to constant change in composition. Each contains the men possessed of the information, or with access to the information, that bears on the particular decision, together with those whose skill consists in extracting and testing this information and obtaining a conclusion. This is how men act successfully on matters where no single one, however exalted or intelligent, has more than a fraction of the necessary knowledge.[36]

Galbraith's joint decision-making does not rely on Hayek's "spontaneous" mutual adaptation to combine diffused knowledge. Nor does any simple top-down procedure control the combination. As in Chandler's "structure," Galbraith's technostructure relies on many formal and informal mechanisms for joint decision-making.*

---

* The mechanisms include, as in Chandler's and Alfred Sloan's accounts, committees. Notwithstanding their reputations as time wasters, committees pool information with exceptional efficiency, says Galbraith. "Association in a committee," Galbraith writes (1967, 64), "enables each member to come to know the intellectual resources and the reliability of his colleagues. Committee discussion enables members to pool information under circumstances which allow, also, of immediate probing to assess the relevance and reliability of the information offered. Uncertainty about one's information or error is revealed as in no other way."

Smooth Sailings There is one notable difference between Chandler's prewar corporations and Galbraith's postwar Industrial System. Prewar corporations encountered considerable turbulence during their evolution. Economic crises in the 1920s spurred the development of DuPont's and GM's multidivisional organizational structures, as mentioned. Big businesses also struggled in the Great Depression as demand collapsed. Automobile sales, for example, fell from a record 5 million vehicles in 1929 to just 1.33 million in 1932, requiring the Ford Motor Company to terminate over eighty thousand of its workers.[37]

In contrast, Galbraith's large corporations did not make losses. In the 1957 recession, "Not one of the one hundred largest industrial corporations failed to return a profit. Only one of the largest two hundred finished the year in the red." Seven years later, "all of the first hundred again made money; only two among the first two hundred had losses and only seven among the first five hundred. None of the fifty largest merchandising firms—Sears, Roebuck, A&P, Safeway, et al.— failed to return a profit. Nor, predictably, did any of the fifty largest utilities. And among the fifty largest transportation companies only three railroads, and the momentarily unfortunate Eastern Airlines, failed to make money."*[38]

A staunch Keynesian, Galbraith credits the postwar profitability of big businesses to an unarguably novel feature of the New Industrial State: fiscal policies aiming to steady aggregate demand. Additionally, he sees loss-free operation as a result and requirement of the "technostructure." The technostructure anticipates what will sell and formulates plans to market (often through persuasive advertising) what is produced. Big Business thus earns healthy profits in good and not-so-good economic times.

Reciprocally, an effective technostructure requires autonomy from the vagaries of the economy and the interference of stockholders. But when businesses make losses, usually impotent and passive shareholders "cannot be told to mind their own business," writes Galbraith. When earnings fail—and only then—is when "the stockholder of the large corporation can be aroused."[39] Losses also deprive the technostructure of the retained earnings used to fund its long-term investment plans.

Galbraith added two more claims in later editions of his book. First, there was "no evidence of any weakening of the trend either to larger and larger firms or to those having an ever greater share of the total output."[40] Second, there was "great

---

* Galbraith (1967, 82). He goes on to tweak the "American business liturgy" of:

a profit and loss economy. "The American competitive enterprise system is an acknowledged profit and loss system, the hope of profits being the incentive and the fear of loss being the spur." This may be so. But it is not true of that organized part of the economy in which a developed technostructure is able to protect its profits by planning. Nor is it true of the United States Steel Corporation, author of the sentence just cited, which has not had losses for a quarter of a century.

228 UNCERTAINTY AND ENTERPRISE

stability" in the position of mature corporations within the system, along with stability in earnings and growth.[41]

"The firms that comprised the largest hundred industrials ten or twenty years ago are, overwhelmingly, those that comprise that list today," Galbraith claimed. "Among the largest ten and especially the largest five, changes in membership or even in rank are comparatively rare. The fiction of the 'representative firm' growing, aging, falling behind, being replaced by younger, more vigorous specimens, once much beloved by economists is, in this part of the economy, sadly in decline. The great firm is unsparing of even the most agreeable myth."[42]

3. Struggling Behemoths

Macro and Micro Challenges As if on cue, hard times befell Galbraith's Industrial State after the publication of his book in 1967. Stagflation in the 1970s ended the consensus for Keynesian macroeconomics (chapter 8). In 1981, President Ronald Reagan, who had repeatedly cited the high "misery index" (inflation plus the unemployment rate), reappointed Paul Volcker as chair of the Federal Reserve. Volcker's Fed swiftly raised interest rates, hiking its fed funds rate to 20 percent by June.

Demand collapsed—and not just for small businesses. In the recession of 1982, eight of the top one hundred industrial companies and twenty-one of the largest two hundred ended the year with a deficit.[43] Layoffs and plant closures blighted the Rust Belt. Employment in large companies had already peaked in the 1970s. In 1979, David Birch published a study claiming that small firms generated 66 percent of all new jobs in the United States, whereas "middle sized and large firms, on balance, provided relatively few new jobs."[44]

Encountering new competition along with falling demand, entrenched incumbents lost their leading positions. As global trade expanded with falling transportation costs, Japanese goods eroded the market shares and profits of venerable US producers, including Detroit's auto companies and Pittsburgh's steelmakers. A government bailout spared Chrysler, a Big Three automaker, from bankruptcy in 1979.[45] High-quality, attractively priced Toyota and Honda cars attracted buyers even though their distribution and service networks—and US buyers' preference for large vehicles—protected Detroit's carmakers. Overall, the Big Three share of US car sales fell from over 80 percent in the early 1970s to below 64 percent by 1990.[46]

Japanese consumer electronics companies—like Sony, NEC, Toshiba, Hitachi, and Nintendo—became market leaders in home stereos, VCR and CD players, citizens' band (CB) radios, and video game machines. Sony's Walkman, first sold in Japan in 1979, quickly became a global hit, creating a new category of personal

THE EVOLUTION OF DYNAMIC BUREAUCRACIES   229

music players. Korean and Taiwanese producers followed Japanese companies into consumer electronics, as they had previously done in automobiles, steel, and shipbuilding.

Domestic upstarts also challenged entrenched incumbents. Iconic retailers Sears, Roebuck and A&P—founded in the nineteenth century—faced no new overseas competition. But they were attacked by discount and category-killing retailing models promoted by businesses like Walmart and Home Depot that started after World War II. Similarly, postwar minicomputer companies like Digital Equipment Corp. and Data General—followed by Apple, Compaq, Dell, and Gateway—eroded IBM's dominance in the computer industry. Minicomputer and many personal computer companies did not survive, and IBM's leadership in mainframe computers remained. But if the attacks didn't kill IBM, they did wound.

This was not supposed to happen in Galbraith's New Industrial State. Technological progress had made innovation prohibitively expensive; according to Galbraith, only established giants could innovate. Galbraith doubled down on this argument in the 1985 edition of his book, inserting the following: "The small competitive firm cannot afford the outlays that innovation demands. An economic system consisting of such firms would require, rather, that we reject the technology which, since earliest consciousness, we have been taught to applaud."[47]

Yet by then, VCs had already funded new and fledgling businesses in semiconductors (Intel), personal computer hardware and software (Apple, Compaq, Lotus Development Corporation), and biotechnology (Genentech). Moreover, many upstarts that challenged the Industrial System's giants had been formed before professionalized VC had appeared and before the first edition of Galbraith's book was published in 1967. Galbraith overlooked or chose to disregard the evolutionary, accretive process through which technologies improve and businesses expand their competitive capabilities. Even during the heyday of the postwar New Industrial State, and when professional VC was in its infancy, giants did not monopolize progress.

Upstart Innovators

As in previous decades, enterprising individuals and founder-controlled businesses continued to innovate after World War II. Edwin Land, Harvard College dropout (and son of a scrap dealer of Russian-Jewish ancestry), and Land's physics professor, George W. Wheelwright III, started the Polaroid Corporation in 1937. In World War II, Polaroid developed products for military use. In 1948, it introduced the world's first instant photography

230 UNCERTAINTY AND ENTERPRISE

camera. In 1951, An Wang, a Harvard PhD in applied physics, cofounded Wang Laboratories, a pioneering computer company and progenitor of the Massachusetts high-tech "miracle," within walking distance from Galbraith's Harvard office.

On the opposite coast, Bill Hewlett and David Packard bootstrapped their eponymous venture, starting in a Palo Alto garage in 1939. Varian Associates, another Silicon Valley pioneer, was formed in 1948. Martin Chase started the discount retail revolution, opening an Ann and Hope outlet in 1953. Several entrepreneurs, including Sam Walton, soon followed, as mentioned. The global fast-food empires of McDonald's and Burger King started with a handful of outlets in the 1950s. Malcolm McLean, a small-time trucking company entrepreneur, pioneered containerized shipping that transformed global trade. McLean's first containerized shipment was in April 1956. Decades later, containers would carry goods to US ports that undermined US producers' hegemony.

Once glorified, the management of US giants was now scorned. Many looked to Japan for alternatives. Harvard sociologist Ezra Vogel's 1979 book, *Japan as Number One: Lessons for America*, became a best-seller.[48] US management savants distilled wisdom from Japanese giants. *Theory Z: How American Management Can Meet the Japanese Challenge*, written by UCLA business professor William Ouchi,[49] followed Vogel's book on the best-seller list in 1981.

Then, in the 1990s, as the Japanese economy stagnated and Japanese giants (like their US counterparts) struggled, attention turned to homegrown cost-cutting remedies such as downsizing, restructuring, and reengineering.[50] Others drew inspiration from agile, young Californian high-tech companies. "Bring Silicon Valley Inside" or die, HBS research fellow Gary Hamel warned big-company readers of the *Harvard Business Review*.[51]

An Eclipse That Wasn't HBS economist Michael Jensen's "Eclipse of the Public Corporation," published in 1989, questioned the very purpose of the large, autonomous Galbraithian enterprise. "The publicly held corporation has outlived its usefulness in many parts of the economy," Jensen wrote. Takeovers by raiders and acquisitions by leveraged buyout firms symptomized the outlived usefulness, according to Jensen.[52] (Depressed stock prices had attracted swarms of raiders in the mid-1980s. "Barbarians at the gates" took over the food giant RJR-Nabisco, ending its existence as a public company in 1988.[53])

"Gross corporate waste and mismanagement," wrote Jensen, had triggered the transactions.[54] Takeovers and leveraged buyouts unlocked value destroyed by "misguided policies."[55] Jensen was especially critical of the retention of profits—a key feature of Galbraith's Industrial System: "Corporate managers generally don't disgorge cash unless they are forced to do so. In 1988, the 1,000 largest public companies (by sales) generated total funds of $1.6 trillion. Yet they distributed only $108 billion as dividends and another $51 billion through share repurchases."

Retaining and reinvesting profits increased managers' autonomy and the size of the companies they managed. Managers, Jensen argued, had many incentives to overexpand. Their pay, perquisites, and prestige increased with the size of the companies they controlled.[56] Replacing public equity with debt discouraged overexpansion by forcing businesses to pay out their operating profits to creditors, like high mortgage payments forcing individuals to forgo frivolous consumption.

Over the next thirty years, the large public corporation continued to cede public attention and substantive ground to privately owned businesses. However, their eclipse was, at best, partial. Leveraged buyout firms (as private equity firms were then called) organized fixed-term partnerships to finance their transactions. Like the VC partnerships discussed in the last chapter, buyout partnerships had to exit their deals before their terms ended, either through an IPO or sale to a (usually) public company. Just as VC firms offered (or claimed to offer) transitional nurturing and incubation services (besides just money) to fledglings, buyout firms provided (or claimed to provide) repair and reconstruction to mature businesses.

Neither VCs nor buyout firms, however, offered permanent private homes and oversight. Intense oversight was a valuable enabler of successful exits but could not add to the returns of fixed-term partnerships after that. It ceased after the ventures and businesses the partnerships had financed or acquired became public companies or returned to public ownership. Thus, if Galbraith exaggerated the powers of his Industrial System giants, Jensen exaggerated their eclipse. As we see next, the large quasi-autonomous public company has remained an economic dynamo into the third decade of the twenty-first century—and the seemingly bureaucratic routines and structures it developed through the twentieth century support rather than hinder its distinctive entrepreneurial contributions.

17

The Dominions of Giants

The large public corporation has a distinctive capacity to undertake mammoth, complex initiatives. While institutional funding of VCs has increased their capital, the investments of VC-backed businesses remain smaller and simpler. Nor has control by career professionals suppressed the expansionary tendencies of mega-corporations. Professional CEOs can be less impulsive than freewheeling founders but cannot just serve as caretakers. Stock markets demand and reward growth. As in the preindustrial East India Company, the expansionary impulse of the public company remains powerful.

Yet the dynamism of business behemoths is obscured by the very features that sustain their potency. As we saw in chapter 15, VC firms make more systematic and deliberate investment decisions than business angels and self-financed founders. The systematized routines that help VCs raise more capital and make larger investments also require more information, reducing their tolerance for uncertainty. Similarly with large public companies: for all their professed enthusiasm for de-layering and streamlining, their decision-making remains (as in Chandler's and Galbraith's twentieth-century accounts) procedure-bound and collectivized.

This is not a pathology. Seemingly bureaucratic evaluation and planning routines are both prerequisites for undertaking complex megaprojects and constraints on acceptable uncertainty. If bootstrapped startups are like canoes and VC-financed businesses are catamarans and express boats, large company initiatives are like full-rigged ships with significantly different designs and functions (see Figure 17.1).

That said, the dynamism of large corporations is subtly self-limiting. Unlike VC ownership of private companies, which ends with the time-limited existence of VC partnerships, publicly traded stocks have no expiry date. But the accumulation of successful initiatives tends to produce a debilitating sprawl. Like the East India Company and so many iconic industrial corporations dating back to the nineteenth century that disintegrated or disappeared, overextension—if nothing else—precludes immortality. Overextension also dulls enterprise, contributing to justifiable perceptions of bureaucratic stagnation.

Uncertainty and Enterprise. Amar Bhidé, Oxford University Press. © Oxford University Press 2025.
DOI: 10.1093/oso/9780197688359.003.0017

THE DOMINIONS OF GIANTS   233

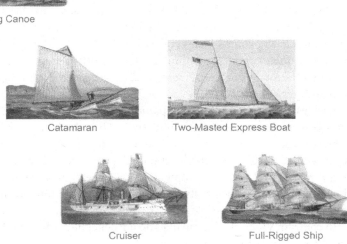

Figure 17.1 Varieties of Vessels (1889)
Source: Compiled from the New York Metropolitan Museum's *Types of Vessels* Series (N139)

My analysis of these distinctive features proceeds through sections that

- Describe the distinctive features of large public company initiatives that have endured into the twenty-first century.

- Explain the interconnectedness of the features—how their decision-making routines and practices influence and reflect the uncertainty, scale, and complexity of the initiatives the corporations specialize in.

- Explore the self-limiting nature of large-company dynamism.

The chapter concludes by recapitulating the main points of Part 3.

1. Enduringly Distinctive Features

Existing Resources As in Galbraith's *New Industrial State*, large public companies mainly use surplus cash from their mature businesses to fund new initiatives. In contrast, VC-backed firms with no internal funding sources repeatedly raise fresh capital. Young public companies also often raise capital to finance their growth by issuing more stock. But after (and if!) they mature, public companies only issue stock in dire circumstances. In fact, many large public companies retire more stock than they issue.[1]

Stock buybacks do not, however, paralyze. Even after buybacks, the surplus funds generated by existing businesses allow public companies to invest substantially larger amounts than VCs. In the 2010s the five hundred largest public companies in the United States collectively spent $2 trillion on R&D and $6.8 trillion on their capital expenditures.[2] These outlays amounted to more than ten times the total VC disbursements—which cover more than R&D and capital expenditures—in the 2010s.[3]

Besides cash, large public companies commit the intangible resources of their existing businesses to new initiatives. These include marketing and distribution channels; supplier and customer relationships; technical, financial, legal, and regulatory expertise; employees and recruiting capabilities; and brand names and corporate reputations. The seasoned public company can thus combine the custody of its mature businesses with the sponsorship of new initiatives.

In contrast, VC-backed companies do not generate surplus funds. Even if they did, VCs could not reinvest the funds in their other portfolio companies. The funds initially raised from limited partners therefore cap VC disbursements. VCs also avoid sharing intangible resources—each tub in their portfolio stands on its own bottom.[4]

Size, Complexity, and Uncertainty Public companies with reliable internal funding sources can undertake projects with much larger capital requirements than VC-backed businesses. For example, semiconductor companies like Intel now spend between $10 billion and $15 billion to build semiconductor fabrication plants and more than $4 billion to develop new generations of microprocessors. Boeing spent about $32 billion on its 787 Dreamliner.[5] AT&T, T-Mobile, and Verizon paid $81.11 billion to the US government in February 2021 to purchase spectrum rights for 5G networks.[6] Large pharmaceutical companies spend $1 billion to $4.5 billion to develop a new cancer drug. General Motors budgeted more than $5 billion for the Cruise Origin, the car company's first automated vehicle.[7] The Gorgon Liquefied Natural Gas project undertaken in Australia by a consortium of major oil companies cost $54 billion.[8]

The larger projects are naturally more complex than VC or angel-backed initiatives. They support and require a finer division of labor across a broader range of functions and locations. For example, VCs helped the previously angel-funded Starbucks expand from Seattle and other parts of the Pacific Northwest to Chicago and other midwestern cities. A 1992 IPO that raised $29 million helped Starbucks open cafés in New York and other East Coast locations, further increasing the company's geographic scope and operational complexity. In the 2010s, after the coffee retailer had become a large, profitable company, reinvested earnings helped it rapidly expand in China. By 2017, it was opening one new café a day, and by 2018, Starbucks was operating 3,600 cafés in China.[9] Besides café employees, the expansion required knowledgeable local staff for training, developing menus, negotiating leases, marketing, logistics, and so on.

The launches of IBM's personal computer (PC) and Sun's workstation in the early 1980s offer a similar contrast. IBM's historic launch, which made PCs a must-have office appliance, spanned many activities and functions. These included hardware and software design, licensing (of the operating system and the likeness of Charlie Chaplin's character the Little Tramp), development of ISVs (independent software vendors) and office product dealer networks, training and deployment of the in-house sales force, and a national advertising campaign. In contrast, the fledgling VC-financed Sun targeted a smaller, more specialized market. It focused on hardware design, enhancement of the UNIX operating system, and direct sales and support. Sun had no large-scale manufacturing and did not develop a dealer network or mount public relations or advertising campaigns.[10] And like Starbucks, Sun significantly widened its functional and geographic scope after its 1986 IPO.[11]

The complexity has a temporal dimension. Large company megaprojects take many years to complete, sometimes over a decade. After considerable research and planning, Boeing announced its 787 Dreamliner program in 2001. It eventually entered service three years behind schedule in 2011. In 2008, Intel's chief technology officer said the company saw a "clear way" to manufacturing chips under ten nanometers.[12] Expected to ship in 2015, Intel's chips actually began selling in 2019.[13] And just as tasks and activities in one function or location affect those in another, making them collectively "complex," what is done now influences what happens much later.[14] In contrast, funding constraints force bootstrapped entrepreneurs into quick payback ventures, and the exit requirements of fixed-term VC partnerships bound the duration of their projects.[15]

Large companies that undertake complex, long-gestation megaprojects also require evidence supporting the prospects for commensurately large payoffs. In my terminology, the evidentiary requirements limit tolerances for irreducible market uncertainty.

Manifestations of Uncertainty Intolerance

Large companies routinely reject uncertain ideas that VCs, angels, or informally financed entrepreneurs are willing to try out. These include internally generated ideas. Famously, scientists and engineers at the Xerox Palo Alto Research Center (PARC) prototyped local area networks and other computer technologies in the 1970s. In 1979, after Xerox refused to commercialize its local area networking technology, PARC engineer Bob Metcalfe left to co-found a company (3Com) to develop and market Xerox's invention.[16] The same year, visits by Steve Jobs and other Apple employees to Xerox PARC accelerated the use of mouse-pointing devices in Apple's computers.[17]

Large public companies similarly avoid licensing unproven technologies. Stanford University, for instance, attempted to license workstation technology (developed for the Stanford University Network project). But established minicomputer producers (Digital Equipment Corporation and Prime, now defunct) decided that the technology had no value. Stanford then assigned the rights to the graduate student who was developing the technology while working on a PhD in computer-assisted design (CAD) tools. The student, Andy Bechtolsheim (who, as mentioned, would later make an angel investment in Google), invested twenty-five thousand dollars of his own money in a prototype and sold licenses to VC-backed startups for ten thousand dollars each. Eventually, Bechtolsheim contributed the technology to Sun Microsystems (which was also VC-financed), where he became a cofounder.[18]

This is not an isolated case: Shane's study of MIT's technology licensing suggests that new firms are more likely than existing firms to license a novel technology.[19] Similarly, Kalamas, Pinkus, and Sachs record that only a third of the deals struck by large pharmaceutical companies to license new drugs from biotechnology companies occur in the preclinical stage. This proportion, they suggest, reflects "the uncertain prospects of deals made early in the development process."[20]

Moreover, uncertainty aversion goes beyond avoiding early-stage technologies and unproven markets. As mentioned, relying on easy-to-imitate ideas and the personal efforts of founders can, paradoxically, make the prospects of promising startups highly uncertain. This kind of mundane uncertainty has also apparently catalyzed "spinouts" from established high-tech employers: According to Klepper, the founders of high-tech spinouts, like the founders of many promising businesses, "begin humbly without very ambitious plans." They leave their employers "out of frustration" after failing to get support for their ideas. These initial ideas are "not very important in determining their long-term fates." Instead, their performance seems to depend on the "broad experiences of their founders." And employers are indifferent rather than aggrieved: Klepper notes that companies spawning spinouts rarely sue departing employees or challenge them competitively.[21] In my terminology, mundane yet high market uncertainty places the typical spinout outside the zone of interest of established companies.[22]

Strictness and Collectivization Large public corporations use strict, collectivized procedures for evaluating and planning initiatives. Cofounder Gordon Moore's description of Intel's allocation of its R&D budget exemplifies the strictness: "Each product group," writes Moore, "is required to submit a project list ordered in decreasing priority, explain in sometimes excruciating detail why the list is ordered as it is, and indicate where the line ought to be drawn between projects to work on and projects to put off." Only a "small group" tries to "stay abreast with what is going on more broadly in the semiconductor industry," and even this group avoids programs that will generate results only after ten years.[23] Intel's procedures have evolved since Moore's time. But it is a safe bet that as Intel's R&D expenditures have risen from under $2 billion in 1996 to more than $13 billion per year, they have not become less stringent and evidence-hungry.

Although there is no template that all large companies use, their evaluation and planning routines have some common features. According to the 2014 *Oxford Handbook of Innovation Management*, "Most products are developed following a standard sequence of activities, employing tasks and routines that are also fairly standard across different development projects."[24] According to the *Handbook*, these often include funneling many possibilities down to a few product launches. This funnel originates in routines going back to the 1960s, such as NASA's Phased Project Planning, which defined "gates" for reviewing projects: Projects that survive reviews, which include consideration of strategic fit, customer input, and technical feasibility, progress to the next stage of development. Project teams preparing for reviews commonly hold "mock-up gate meetings . . . to improve their chances to pass gate reviews. Gate reviews are also opportunities to train junior team members and expose them to senior management thinking."[25]

The process retains the collectivized traditions developed in the twentieth century. According to the Oxford *Handbook*, it is not just "senior management thinking" that decides the fate of proposed ideas. Product development is a "cross-functional activity involving input from—and creating output for—marketing, strategy, business development, finance, human resources, sales, legal, IT, and many others."[26] Product development teams include "engineers, scientists, supply chain experts, software developers, ad-hoc specialists,

238   UNCERTAINTY AND ENTERPRISE

designers, marketeers, consultants, and so on."[27] Concepts and designs are also typically reviewed by functional specialists who do not outrank members of development teams. Outside suppliers may also have a voice. The reactions of potential buyers—secured through systematic techniques, from small focus groups to large-scale market research—play a critical role.

Implementing new concepts and designs likewise entails detailed cross-functional planning and monitoring. Producing and marketing new electric vehicles, cancer drugs, airliners, or the next generation of Windows operating systems and iPhones takes several years and the contributions of tens of thousands of individuals working in several functions and locations. Project, program, and product managers help coordinate these efforts through plans that minutely specify tasks and deadlines. Progress is closely monitored; even minor deviations require multiple approvals and signoffs.

Qualifications Large businesses cannot of course expect proof "beyond reasonable doubt." Contra Galbraith's claim, big company technostructures do not have preternatural powers to divine what customers will want and persuade them to buy what planners had decided would sell. For example, a sweeter, reformulated Coca-Cola was a winner in taste tests, surveys, and focus groups. Actual sales of the reformulation fell far below expectations, and loyalist consumers of the "classic" formula organized boycotts and street protests. Eventually, seventy-seven days after launching its "New Coke," the president of The Coca-Cola Company announced the return of the classic: "The simple fact is that all of the time and money and skill poured into consumer research on a new Coca-Cola could not measure or reveal the depth and abiding emotional attachment to original Coca-Cola felt by so many people."[28]

Data-driven, data-rich digital behemoths also struggle to develop what will sell. In 2014, Facebook paid about two billion dollars to acquire Oculus, a maker of virtual reality headsets.[29] By 2022, the company had spent about one hundred billion dollars on R&D for the "metaverse"—a 3-D virtual world[30]—and renamed itself Meta Platforms. Disney, Microsoft, and Walmart also foresaw huge possibilities in virtual products and services. The rebranded Facebook, whose core offering has nearly three billion monthly active users, set a modest goal of five hundred thousand monthly active users for Horizon Worlds, its flagship metaverse product, by the end of 2022. By the spring of 2023, Horizon Worlds had well under half its modest target of active users, and the company had stopped marketing the metaverse to advertisers. Microsoft had also closed its virtual workspace platform, and Disney and Walmart had ended their metaverse projects.[31]

Pharmaceutical companies face the whims of nature. The development of a new antibiotic, for example, usually takes about a decade and can cost more than half a billion dollars. But rapidly mutating bacteria can become resistant to new drugs long before developers earn back their investments. Similarly, drugs that pass safety tests in clinical trials can produce unacceptable side effects in widespread use, sometimes discovered after decades. Ranitidine, marketed as Zantac, was until recently considered an effective antacid used to treat diseases such as peptic ulcers. The World Health Organization included the drug, introduced in 1981, in its list of essential medicines. US pharmacies filled over eighteen million prescriptions for over four million patients in 2018.[32] In 2019, however, a probable carcinogen was discovered in ranitidine products, which were withdrawn from the US market in April 2020.[33]

The possibility of drug resistance or the discovery of new side effects are not unknown unknowns. They are predictable unpredictabilities. The fallibility of market research is also well known. But a sure thing or even a nearly sure thing standard would make any investment or new initiative impossible. And while mature, professionally managed corporations have higher demands for justificatory evidence than young, founder-controlled businesses, they cannot eliminate even simple Ellsberg-style "missing information" uncertainty. Imagined possibilities that go beyond the observable evidence are inescapable. Only the groundedness of justifications varies.

Not Entirely Impersonal Just as large corporations have low but not zero tolerance for missing information, their procedures for evaluating new initiatives are not algorithmic or formulaic. The distinction between procedures for "operating" and "enterprising" choices is notable. Operating rules—using computer-generated credit scores to issue credit cards, for example—can be rigidly formulaic. Enterprising routines, which include interpreting ambiguous contextual data, aim for "procedural rationality" (per Simon, chapter 9), not substantive invariance.

While large company routines require heavy weights of evidence (Keynes, chapter 8) they also include subjective interpretations of the evidence and at least some leaps of faith. Even in the pharmaceutical industry, there is room for opinion, judgment, personal relationships, and forceful personalities to override bald facts and rigid protocols.

Personal Relationships and Personalities

As briefly mentioned (chapter 2), Eli Lilly's blockbuster drug Prozac had initially failed to outperform a placebo in clinical trials. When the trial was repeated on patients who had responded to other tranquilizers, it outperformed

240 UNCERTAINTY AND ENTERPRISE

a placebo. And this was not the first hole Prozac—"fluoxetine"—had climbed out of. Lilly's researchers had previously encountered skepticism at scientific conferences when they presented the results of animal studies. Lilly's internal committees ignored the skepticism.

Later, safety studies on rats and dogs had shown a rapid increase in fatty acids—a potentially risky side effect. The project was suspended but then (with the encouragement of the FDA) allowed to continue. It was hoped that fluoxetine might avoid the side effects in humans that it produced in animals. And indeed, it did not create the side effects. However, it did fail its initial efficacy tests in human trials, yet the fluoxetine team persuaded Lilly's management to redo the trial with a different design.

Why did Lilly's management keep supporting the project?

The personal relationships and reputation of Robert Rathbun, a key researcher on the fluoxetine project, may be one reason. Rathbun and Irwin Slater, both pharmacologists at Lilly, had once worked on a groundbreaking treatment for high blood pressure. Lilly later promoted Slater to director of pharmacological research, responsible for managing the fluoxetine project. Thus, the technical advocate had a natural managerial ally.[34]

Imperial Chemical Industries (ICI) development of tamoxifen, now a gold-standard breast cancer treatment, provides another example. UK-based ICI had attempted to develop tamoxifen as a contraceptive and as a cancer treatment. It failed as a contraceptive in clinical trials, and although it showed modest promise for cancer treatments, ICI's board of directors nearly stopped development. Arthur Walpole, a thirty-four-year ICI veteran who led the tamoxifen project, threatened to resign. He then persuaded his bosses to market tamoxifen as a palliative treatment for patients with terminal breast cancer in the United Kingdom and to sponsor human trials in the United States.[35]

Source (with detailed citations): Bhidé, Datar, and Stebbins 2021a; 2021b

2. Explaining Interconnected Distinctiveness

Simple Inferences and Extensions Strict (but not totally inflexible) routines with high demands for objective evidence directly reduce tolerances for market uncertainty, while collectivization does so indirectly. The indirect relationship between collectivization and uncertainty intolerance is implicit in my arguments (chapter 15) about VC-backed businesses: undiscoverable information

THE DOMINIONS OF GIANTS   241

increases guesswork, the role of prior experiences and predispositions, and potential disagreements. Giving many individuals with diverse expertise and job assignments (not just direct bosses) a say makes agreement particularly difficult. Therefore, initiatives supported with objective information are more likely to progress through the development funnel—and are more likely to be proposed than high-uncertainty projects that face quick rejection.[36]

Strict evaluation routines also help explain preferences for large projects: ceteris paribus, projects with lower capital requirements produce less profit and are less likely to justify high evaluation costs. Similarly, large companies' planning and monitoring capabilities are more valuable in undertaking large, multiyear projects.[37]

But why do large companies establish such elaborate and collectivized routines rather than use the more streamlined procedures of VCs and nimble pre-IPO businesses? Why did companies like General Motors, with reputations for obedient deference to organizational rank, also develop traditions for consensual decision-making? And why do high-tech companies that claim to detest bureaucracy adopt these collectivized practices as they mature? These questions do not arise in economic models focusing on information asymmetries and misaligned incentives (chapter 7). As mentioned, the models usually exclude uncertainty, honest mistakes, and genuine differences of opinion. Bosses establish optimal incentives and monitor subordinates to control self-serving conduct.

Routines do play an important role in Nelson and Winter's heterodox evolutionary theories. They assume that large organizations rely on routines because their scale and complexity make it impossible for top management to "direct or observe many of the details of the organization's functioning."[38] But reasons for consensus favoring routines (and their relationship to uncertainty and resource requirements) are outside what Nelson and Winter seek to explain.

Diffusion of Stockholders and Knowledge   Fama and Jensen's hypotheses, which I used in chapter 15, again provide a good starting point for understanding the "functional rationality" (chapter 9) of large company routines.

Fama and Jensen argue that large companies separate decision management (proposing and implementing decisions) from decision control (ratifying and monitoring decisions). The separation, they claim, reflects two kinds of diffusion. Ownership is diffused across many stockholders, and "valuable specific knowledge" is diffused across many employees.[39] Both help large companies take advantage of economies of scale, but they also amplify decision management and decision control problems.

Tiered delegation reduces these problems. At the apex, boards of directors exercise decision control on behalf of diffused stockholders: They ratify and monitor the organization's most important decisions and hire, fire, and compensate

242   UNCERTAINTY AND ENTERPRISE

the top executives. Below, a "decision hierarchy" helps utilize "decision skills throughout the organization." Bosses review and ratify their subordinates' "decision initiatives" and, in turn, submit their proposals for ratification by their superiors.[40] This arrangement allows boards and top executives to delegate decisions to subordinates they cannot directly supervise.[41]

Fama and Jensen's hypotheses allow bottom-up initiatives without the emasculating hard rules of Harvard economist, Jeremy Stein's model.[42] Although they focus on the prototypical agency problem of misaligned incentives,[43] the mechanisms Fama and Jensen analyze readily extend to controlling misjudgments and explaining uncertainty aversion. (Proposals supported by more evidence are more likely to get the boss's attention and approval.)

But puzzles about public company routines remain. VC-backed pre-IPO businesses and up-and-coming public companies also have boards of directors.[44] They too "partition and delegate" decision functions to decision hierarchies. Why are evaluation routines much more thorough in mature public companies? Why do they use widely diffused, multifunctional evaluators alongside "decision hierarchies"? Why, in other words, are large company routines for evaluating, planning, and monitoring projects so costly, clumsy, and slow—and so uncertainty averse?

My explanations below rely on governance and coordination problems that I argue are more acute in mature public companies.*

Governance Problems Diffused stockholding poses well-known governance problems in large public companies. In principle (and in the Fama and Jensen model), independent boards of directors, representing public stockholders, "direct" top managers. In practice, the independent direction is perfunctory. As Galbraith pointed out, executives control board nominations. The election of official nominees is usually automatic and Soviet-like. No domain expertise is necessary and may even disqualify.[45] Additionally, as Warren Buffett points out, handsome fees for modest effort discourage directors from asking tough questions.

Warren Buffett on Board Independence

"Director compensation has now soared to a level that inevitably makes pay a subconscious factor affecting the behavior of many non-wealthy [board] members. Think, for a moment, of the director earning $250,000–300,000

---

* The main building blocks exist in the Fama and Jensen papers, the business histories reviewed in the last chapter, Galbraith's book, and much other economic, legal, and management research. But for brevity I combine a high-level restatement of well-known prior ideas with some modest original extensions without attempting to untangle the two.

for board meetings consuming a pleasant couple of days six or so times a year. Frequently, the possession of one such directorship bestows on its holder three to four times the annual median income of US households. . . .

"Is it any wonder that a non-wealthy director ('NWD') now hopes—or even yearns—to be asked to join a second board, thereby vaulting into the $500,000–600,000 class? To achieve this goal, the NWD will need help. The CEO of a company searching for board members will almost certainly check with the NWD's current CEO as to whether NWD is a 'good' director. 'Good,' of course, is a code word. If the NWD has seriously challenged his/her present CEO's compensation or acquisition dreams, his or her candidacy will silently die. When seeking directors, CEOs don't look for pit bulls. It's the cocker spaniel that gets taken home."

Source: Berkshire Hathaway Inc. 2019 Annual Report, 13

In contrast, VCs serve on the boards of the companies they invest in—unlike the shareholders of public companies, they do not rely on kind strangers for oversight. VCs specializing in markets and technologies can provide more thoughtful direction than the titular and often inexpert overseers of public companies. And VCs don't join boards for board fees. They aim to maximize their "carried interest" through profitable exits and to build reputations as good VCs so that they can continue raising new funds as their existing partnerships terminate (chapter 15).

Moreover, the governance problems of public companies become more acute as they mature. Initially, founders and founding families with a strong interest in the success of the enterprise often own large blocks. But the blocks naturally dissipate as founders (and their heirs or charitable foundations) divest their holdings. Concurrently reinvested earnings in new initiatives increase the complexity of the enterprise and, thus, the difficulties of oversight.

Giving top executives "high-powered incentives" ("pay for performance") through stock options and bonuses is not a panacea. Without effective director oversight, incentives can encourage executives to recklessly "go for broke." Additionally, even if options and bonuses effectively align the monetary interests of executives and shareholders, they do not solve the problem of managerial misjudgment. In large public companies, these problems can be severe. As Peter Lynch, the former manager of Fidelity's Magellan Fund, once joked, "I only buy businesses a fool could run, because sooner or later one will."[*]

---

[*] Note that Lynch's quip, refers to fools, not knaves. Also recall Napoleon's dictum mentioned earlier.

244   UNCERTAINTY AND ENTERPRISE

Strict evaluation and planning routines comfort investors like Lynch that a "fool could run" the business if necessary. The routines—and their innate uncertainty aversion—also restrain CEOs from undertaking reckless initiatives. Of course, some CEOs exercise their positional authority to override standard procedures. As of this writing, corporate bigwigs are opening the spigots for any and all artificial intelligence investments. But as Galbraith pointed out fifty years ago, "technocracies" place severe limits on the discretion of bosses.

That said, controlling the misjudgments of top executives is an ancillary benefit of intricate, collectivized routines rather than their aim. Instead, Chandler's historical accounts of managerial "structures" and Galbraith's analysis of technostructures (reviewed in the last chapter) suggest that the direct purpose of the routines is to control coordination problems.

Coordination Problems As mentioned, large companies have advantages in funding and orchestrating large, complex initiatives that coordinate specialized functions and experts to create products with many valued attributes. Even in a capitalist market, organizations cannot rely just on market prices to achieve this coordination.* If this were possible, the raison d'être for the large corporation would disappear.

Partitioning complex initiatives into chunks undertaken by dedicated teams is a helpful but only partial solution.[46] In principle, partitioning enables a Hayekian decentralization of decision-making without placing an implausible burden on market prices to align decentralized choices. In small teams, everyone can easily know what everyone else is doing or planning. If necessary, the team leader can dictate the alignment of their joint efforts.

In principle, the work of each team is mainly self-contained; to the extent it is not self-contained, organizations can efficiently secure alignment using a tree structure.[47] With a tree, everyone does not have to coordinate with everyone else—or even each small team with every other small team. Instead, the "leaves" can communicate through their twigs and branches.

Partitioning can also allow a "design chief" to provide "conceptual integrity," leaving numerous others (organized into trees) to implement. The problem of

---

* While Hayekians and other economists praise market prices for coordinating independent agents, their examples focus on what has become a small part of modern economic activity. They claim that prices align the supply and demand for commodities like copper and coordinate the production of near-commodities like pencils. Relying on prices (or spontaneous order) to plan and coordinate development of new drugs, software, or airplanes is unheard of, however. High capital costs and complex technologies limit the role of price signals, even in commodity production. High copper prices may encourage metal producers to consider a new mine or smelter. But no sensible copper producer will invest in new capacity without extensive market research to assess long-run prices and demand. And prices play, at best, a modest role in the design and commissioning of a new mine or smelter.

the camel as a "horse designed by a committee" is thus avoided, creating a cohesive, usable product with well-coordinated functions.

Brooks on Conceptual Integrity

In his classic, *The Mythical Man Month* (1975), Frederick Brooks, the architect of the IBM 360 system, argues that "most programming systems reflect conceptual disunity" arising from "the separation of design into many tasks by many men."[48]

Brooks contends that "conceptual integrity is *the* most important consideration in system design. It is better to have a system omit certain anomalous features and improvements, but to reflect one set of design ideas, than to have one that contains many good but independent and uncoordinated ideas."[49] And "conceptual integrity dictates that the design must proceed from one mind, or from a very small number of agreeing resonant minds."[50] You cannot get design integrity from a committee, Brooks asserts.

"Schedule pressures, however, dictate that system building needs many hands." And one "powerful way" of "getting conceptual integrity on very large projects" is to separate "architectural effort from implementation."[51]

There is however a practical catch. Partitioning by an omniscient being would be ideal in an uncertainty-free universe. Real-world uncertainties impose severe limitations, however. Consider Brooks's recommended separation of operating system architecture (which he defines as the "complete and detailed specification of the user interface"[52]) from its implementation. Lacking omniscience, the architect responsible for the conceptual integrity of the user interface must guess what users require and what implementing teams can deliver. And a frontline salesperson or engineer may know of a crucial fact that the architect does not. Yet vertical partitioning may prevent the salesperson's or engineer's knowledge from reaching the architect. Conversely, frontline implementors can misinterpret the architect's grand design, undermining the "conceptual integrity" of the system.[53]

Horizontal specialization poses further alignment and information sharing problems. For example, operating systems combine several components, including user interfaces, command interpreters, file management modules, process management components, networks, memory, storage, input/output devices, and security measures. Designing these components requires a wide range of expertise including knowledge of assembly and machine language,

246 UNCERTAINTY AND ENTERPRISE

biometrics and accessibility design, documentation and knowledge management, industry-standard interfaces, and communication protocols and FCC regulations.

Organizing teams to develop and integrate the components of such complex systems involves trade-offs. Small teams may easily achieve "internal" coordination through direct communication between co-located team members. But coordinating across many small teams is more challenging. Yet, if what the teams produce doesn't mesh, the entire system can crash.*

In some celebrated cases, seemingly trivial misalignments that caused systemic failure have been hard to identify even after the fact. An O-ring seal that could not tolerate freezing temperatures caused the 1986 space shuttle *Challenger* disaster. It took a blue-ribboned Presidential Commission to establish the mismatch between the O-ring specifications and launch conditions as the cause.[54]

These coordination problems are absent or minor in the simple initiatives undertaken by self- or informally financed ventures, as mentioned. In 1973, software programmer Gary Kildall personally created CP/M, the first operating system for personal computers. But early versions of CP/M, like the early personal computers, were rudimentary. For example, they merely supported single-tasking on 8-bit microprocessors and no more than 64 kilobytes of memory and did not work with hard drives.[55] Similarly, Bob Frankston and Dan Bricklin programmed VisiCalc, the pioneering spreadsheet, by themselves. Frankston wrote the code at night, which Bricklin tested and debugged by day. Again, while Bricklin's conceptualization of the spreadsheet was pathbreaking, VisiCalc, which also initially ran just on 8-bit computers, had far less functionality than today's Excel. No separation of architecture and implementation was required for its development.

To summarize: Complex high-stakes initiatives, such as the Windows operating systems and Office 365—with their many possibilities for costly misalignments—impel large public companies like the 2020s Microsoft to use comprehensive, collectivized evaluation, planning, and oversight routines. The routines go far beyond Fama and Jensen's (and Knight's RUP) decision hierarchies, sometimes frustrating founder-CEOs like Jeff Bezos, under whose watch they evolve. The

---

* Alignments with outside groups and circumstances can also be critical. Operating systems must work with externally developed devices (such as printers and displays), applications (including games and productivity software), and users' "cloud" and "on-premises" servers. They must also conform to rules for Wi-Fi communications and privacy and conventions for accessibility.

routines evaluate the strategic soundness of proposals and their tactical details—far beyond anything necessary to control slacking or stealing.* They typically are set in pyramidal tree structures but include horizontal intersections (such as committees, task forces, and councils) and positions (such as product and program managers) with multiple bosses.

Strict routines that reduce internal coordination problems unintentionally reduce tolerances for external market uncertainties about customers, competitors and technologies. Reciprocally, low market uncertainties increase the reliability of plans and routines to control misaligned responses to external changes. Large companies cannot however eliminate uncertainty—a Knightian precondition for profit—or function like a Weberian bureaucracy.

Officials in Weber's idealized bureaucracy have duties and rights within a "specified sphere of competence" and make decisions "according to calculable rules."[56] Although bureaucratic procedures can impede "the discharge of business in a manner best adapted to the individuality of each case," Weber argued that in its perfectly developed form, bureaucracy eliminates "love, hatred, and all purely personal, irrational and emotional elements which escape calculation."[57]

But procedures for evaluating new commercial initiatives cannot disregard "the individuality of each case" and consideration of individuality inevitably requires at least some subjective judgments that "escape calculation." Dynamic giants somehow develop routines that leave room for such judgments. The routines do not however allow mega-corporations to grow indefinitely. As we see next, routines that support the expansion of large public companies eventually deaden their dynamism and ultimately threaten their very existence.

3. Self-Limiting Dynamism

Expansionary Impulses Jensen's 1989 *Eclipse* article attributed large-scale reinvestment of public company profits to anti-shareholder policies of top managers, as mentioned in the previous chapter. Additionally, Jensen claimed that "the tendency of companies to reward middle managers through promotions rather than annual performance bonuses also creates a cultural bias toward growth.

---

* As one Amazon project manager observes, "Let's say you want to tweak an API [an interface through which software programs communicate]. That might be a 2-line code change, which at a startup, would be deployed in a few days. At Amazon, that will take 6–7 weeks, even if I have 20 major enterprise customers who all want this change and agree on it. Amazon can't afford mistakes, so everything has to go through 4–5 layers of approval before you can get it done" (Iyer, 2020).

248 UNCERTAINTY AND ENTERPRISE

Organizations must grow to generate new positions to feed their promotion-based reward systems."[58]

But as Warren Buffett points out, Edgar Smith's 1924 book, *Common Stocks as Long-Term Investments*, had come to the opposite view about reinvestment. Buffett quotes from John Maynard Keynes's review of Smith's 1924 book:

> I have kept until last what is perhaps Mr. Smith's most important, and is certainly his most novel, point. Well-managed industrial companies do not, as a rule, distribute to the shareholders the whole of their earned profits. In good years, if not in all years, they retain a part of their profits and put them back into the business. Thus *there is an element of compound interest* (Keynes's italics) operating in favour of a sound industrial investment. Over a period of years, the real value of the property of a sound industrial is increasing at compound interest, quite apart from the dividends paid out to the shareholders.

Buffett continues, "Though investors were slow to wise up, the math of retaining and reinvesting earnings is now well understood. Today, school children learn what Keynes termed 'novel': combining savings with compound interest works wonders."[59]

But compounding requires reinvestment. Therefore, Buffett and his partner Charlie Munger have "long focused on using retained earnings advantageously." And with 99 percent of Buffett's one-hundred-billion-dollar-plus net worth held in Berkshire Hathaway stock, this reinvestment policy is unlikely to be anti-shareholder. In other large public corporations, too, stockholders prefer reinvestment; they do not see professional managers as mere harvesters of vineyards that an entrepreneurial founder planted.

Contra Jensen, middle managers—and other employees, regardless of rank—do not push top executives of public companies for growth merely because of dysfunctional "promotion-based reward systems." As HP's David Packard wrote in his memoirs, he and cofounder Bill Hewlett concluded that "continuous growth was essential" because their company "depended on attracting high caliber people" who demanded "ample opportunity for personal growth and progress."[60]

Complementary Assets To slightly repurpose the biblical parable of the Talents, stockholders of the modern public corporation are like the master who condemned the "wicked and lazy" servant for merely maintaining assets entrusted to the servant's care.[61] Like ambitious employees and customers, they expect enterprising leadership, not stewardship of the status quo.

Conditions apply, however.

THE DOMINIONS OF GIANTS   249

The corporation must have a robust system for evaluating, planning, and monitoring investments, as mentioned. Stockholders in public companies typically do not trust just the talents of the top managers. Investment geniuses like Warren Buffett and Charlie Munger, whose track records speak for themselves, are exceptions.

Moreover, just as a frigate's steering and navigational systems aren't simply scaled-up versions of a catamaran's, acceptable routines in a large public corporation aren't scaled-up versions of the routines that support a VC- or angel-financed business.[62] Inevitably, acceptable routines are cumbersome and impose high demands for supporting evidence. This can delay entry into rapidly growing markets, allowing nimbler rivals to establish first-mover advantages. Yet investments made after most uncertainties have already been eliminated— except by geniuses like Buffett—cannot produce attractive returns.

Synergies with established units can compensate for the delays. Using the intangible resources of existing businesses—and not just their cash flows—to develop new products and enter new markets ("related" diversification) has well-known benefits. For example, using existing sales forces and customer relationships can reduce the cost and difficulty of launching new products. It can also improve the cost-effectiveness of the existing sales forces, increasing profits. Business units serving different users can also benefit from shared capabilities, such as R&D labs. And expanding into related businesses concurrently uses the expertise of existing staff and gives them opportunities to acquire new skills and experiences.

Crucially, synergies allow existing businesses to enter markets after uncertainties about demand and technologies have fallen to tolerable levels. In industry after industry, we can see examples of established companies leveraging their existing resources to catch up and overtake the pioneers. These include IBM in mainframe and minicomputers; General Electric and Siemens in Computed Tomography and Magnetic Resonance Imaging; Microsoft in spreadsheets, word processing, and user-friendly operating systems; and Google in web-based email and mobile telephone operating systems. Similarly, pharmaceutical giants routinely acquire or license products from small biotech companies. Using their sales and marketing capabilities justifies paying nosebleed prices for the products—and escaping the technological uncertainties of early-stage development.

Coordination Constraints As the case of Barnes & Noble shows, existing resources cannot *ensure* successful catch-up.[63] The "relatedness" of new initiatives can also increase alignment uncertainties and coordination problems. "Cross-selling" new products to existing customers can backfire. The successful introduction of a low-cost product can reduce the sales of existing products with

250 UNCERTAINTY AND ENTERPRISE

higher profit margins, while a defective new product can erode customer loyalty. Existing channels may also lack the capacity to cross-sell. While Starbucks and some drugstore chains have successfully used their cafés and retail stores to sell packaged food, Sears's attempt to sell "socks and stocks" flopped. Promoters of new initiatives may, therefore, favor hiring their own sales personnel who will learn how to overcome buyers' misgivings about new products.

Conversely, managers and other staff of existing businesses, worried about reduced sales—and the diversion of their cash flows—may veto initiatives in adjoining or related markets.[64] Therefore, the routines and existing resources that once enabled expansion can later obstruct the growth that stockholders and ambitious employees continue demanding. And the more successfully and broadly the corporation has previously expanded its scope, the greater the obstacles.

Big Blue's Blues

IBM developed its system of collective decision-making during the 1950s and 1960s when it faced the "critical problem" of building consensus between engineers and marketers.[65] Frank Cary, an IBM executive, testified (in a 1969 antitrust trial) that IBM had developed an organization "based on checks and balances, which provide a structure to insure [sic] the representation ... of staff, line, product division, subsidiaries and headquarters viewpoints." Cary (who later served as the company's CEO) emphasized the role played by twenty-five hundred staff officers in planning new products: they had to understand the product and the marketplace and present proposals that had "been reviewed, and checked and balanced against Manufacturing, Engineering, Service, [and] both the Domestic and the World Trade Marketing Divisions, before they c[a]me forward to have it further reviewed by the Corporate Staff and the Management Review Committee."[66]

The system helped solidify IBM's global dominance in mainframe hardware, software, and peripherals and, in the 1970s, to catch up in the minicomputer market that the Digital Equipment Corporation had created. By the 1990s, however, IBM's routines became paralyzing, according to Cringely:

> Every IBM employee's ambition is apparently to become a manager, and the company helps them out in this area by making management the company's single biggest business. IBM executives don't design products and write software; they manage the design and writing of software. They go to meetings. So much effort, in fact, is put into managing all the managers who are managing things that hardly anyone is left over to do the real work. This means that most IBM hardware and nearly all IBM software is written or designed by the lowest level of people in the company—trainees. Everyone else is too

busy going to meetings, managing, or learning to be managers there is little chance to include any of their technical expertise in IBM products....

IBM has layers and layers of management to check and verify each decision as it is made and amended. The safety net is so big at IBM that it is hard to make a bad decision. In fact, it is hard to make any decision at all, which turns out to be the company's greatest problem and the source of its ultimate downfall (remember, you read it here first).[67]

This biting and undoubtedly embellished 1992 account was prophetic. The once dominant computing giant had a near-death experience and only survived after radical retrenchment that reversed decades of prior expansion.

Illusory Resolution Conglomerates seemed to sidestep the coordination problems of related diversification and the deadening reactions they evoked. According to Chandler, conglomerates had "appeared on the American business scene" in the 1960s as a "major variation of the diversified, multidivisional enterprise." Previously, the "large, diversified enterprise had grown primarily by internal expansion—that is, by direct investment of plant and personnel in industries related to its original line of products. It moved into markets where the managerial, technological, and marketing skills and resources of its organization gave it a competitive advantage. The conglomerate, on the other hand, expanded entirely by the acquisition of existing enterprises, and not by direct investment into its own plant and personnel, and it often did so in totally unrelated fields."[68]

Instead of orchestrating synergies across disparate businesses, conglomerates ran internal capital markets, transferring funds from units that did not have profitable reinvestment opportunities to those that did. Oliver Williamson constructed a theory for the advantages of internal capital markets, providing intellectual legitimacy to the form, while consulting firms like the Boston Consulting Group created tools (like the "growth-share" matrix) for their management. And stock markets encouraged conglomerates by valuing their stock for more than their constituent parts.

The advantages crumbled in the 1980s. Studies suggested that unrelated diversifiers produced worse returns on capital than related diversifiers and focused firms. Academics questioned the benefits of internal capital markets.[69] Stock markets imposed steep "conglomerate discounts," valuing conglomerates for much less than their constituent units. Discounts, in turn, attracted raiders seeking to profit from breaking up conglomerates.[70]

252 UNCERTAINTY AND ENTERPRISE

Change and Continuity Galbraith's older New Industrial State giants also retreated, along with the beleaguered 1960s conglomerates. Belying Galbraith's assertions of their invulnerability, the giants went bankrupt or were sent off to private equity firms for disassembly and repair. Soon, few will remember shopping at Sears or A&P. Flying Pan Am or Eastern Airlines is already a distant memory. Even some large corporations that gained prominence after the publication of Galbraith's 1967 book, such as HP and Intel, are struggling.

But giant corporations have not become extinct or irrelevant. At the end of 2023, the ten highest-ranked US corporations in terms of market value accounted for about 26 percent of the total value of listed US stocks (see Table 17.1). Apple alone accounted for nearly 6 percent.[71]

And as the life stories of today's top giants indicate, entrances and exits from the top ranks have quickened. Eight of the 2023 top ten were formed in or after the mid-1970s.[72] Only one (Microsoft) was in the top ten at the start of 2000.[73]

The new giants have risen swiftly into the top ranks through both internal expansion (like Apple's development of the iPhone) and acquisitions (such as Google's acquisition of YouTube and Meta/Facebook's acquisition

Table 17.1 Top Ten US Public Companies Ranked by Market Value, December 31, 2023

Rank	Company	Market Value ($ billions)	Year Founded	Year of IPO
1	Apple	2,994	1976	1980
2	Microsoft	2,795	1975	1986
3	Alphabet (Google)	1,756	1998	2004
4	Amazon	1,570	1994	1997
5	Nvidia	1,223	1993	1999
6	Meta (Facebook)	910	2004	2012
7	Tesla	790	2003	2010
8	Berkshire Hathaway	777	~1955	~1965
9	Eli Lilly	553	1876	1952
10	Broadcom	523	1991	1998
	Total	13,368		

Note: (1) The total value of 9,148 companies listed in US markets at the end of 2023 was $50,467 billion (Source: Bloomberg). (2) Berkshire Hathaway originates in a textile manufacturing company established in 1839 as the Valley Falls Company. (3) Broadcom includes a business started within Hewlett Packard in 1961.

THE DOMINIONS OF GIANTS   253

of Instagram). Chandler's older multidivisional giants relied mainly on internal development. A growing appetite for "long-tailed" investments in private and public markets has directly or indirectly financed rapid expansion. Tesla, for example, raised over $60 million from VCs and other private investors from 2004 to 2010,[74] $226 million in an initial public offering in June 2010, and about $4.5 billion in stock and bond issues in the following six years.[75] And indirectly, the giants have benefitted from acquiring companies like YouTube and Instagram that VCs and other private investors had already helped build up.

New technologies, know-how, and experienced talent have supported rapid growth by helping to control coordination problems. These include goal-alignment protocols (like OKRs) and project management techniques for developing new products, customer relationship management and logistics software, and a cadre of professionals who have managed rapid growth and the integration of acquired companies.

Yet in meaningful ways, the new giants have followed classic patterns. Their journeys have been serendipitous, with many unexpected twists and turns. When Gates and Allen started Microsoft, they could not have known that an operating system would be the cornerstone of their dominance in personal computer software. Steve Jobs could not have known that Apple's iPhone revenues would be five times its revenues from personal computers. Jeff Bezos could not have anticipated that Amazon would buy a robotics company in 2012 and, in 2014, start a cloud services business that would generate over $80 billion in revenues by 2022.[76] And initially, Google's founders had not worked out how they could monetize their search engine—they had "ruled out banner ads or pop-up ads, the standard ways in which websites earned money."[77]

The giants have also typically progressed—through some exceptional combination of entrepreneurial capacity and luck—from informal or self-funding, to angel finance, to VC, to public markets. And access to more capital and other intangible resources has encouraged larger and more complex initiatives. But giant businesses that somehow made the difficult passage from inception to maturity cannot grow to the sky. Nor can they cease to grow. Inevitably, today's giants will succumb to self-made unmanageability even if their core businesses withstand Schumpeter's "waves of creative destruction" or Christensen's disruptive innovations.

Review of Part 3 and Preview of Part 4

Routines have played a central role in this and the earlier chapters on specialization, with their strictness connecting the uncertainty (extent of doubt-producing

254 UNCERTAINTY AND ENTERPRISE

missing information), investment requirements, and complexity (including temporal complexity) of one-off entrepreneurial initiatives. Textbook microeconomics (and Knight's book) exclude routines. Routines are implicit in the Sah and Stiglitz papers comparing decentralized polyarchies and hierarchies and in the Fama and Jensen papers on organizational forms. But these papers do not explain how routines work; they merely treat routines as black boxes that model what they produce. Some old behavioralists—prominently, Simon and Nelson and Winter—explicitly gave decision-making routines a central role. But they also modeled routines mechanistically, often through computerized algorithms.

I have emphasized the rich forms and designs of routines (as in Table 3.1) and their incorporation of subjective human judgment. So far, however, I have focused on the consideration of objective justificatory evidence. In reality, organizational routines—and other collective routines such as jury deliberations—involve more than just consideration of evidence. Routines evaluate and help construct imaginative yet plausible interpretations ("meanings") of what is, was, and could be. The next and penultimate part of my book analyzes imaginative interpretations of uncertain entrepreneurial possibilities, typically produced through discourse.

Economists, including those studying entrepreneurship and innovation, do not pay much attention to constructive, imaginative discourse. In textbook microeconomics (and heterodox "Hayekian" theories), market prices, not humans, do the talking. This talk is presumptively efficient, whereas information economics and agency theories stress the distortions arising from concerns about lies.

In the old Simon-style behavioral economics (chapter 9), discourse operates invisibly, behind the scenes. It has no suggestion of imagination or emotion. It is telling that Simon modeled the mind as a computer. K-T–style behavioral economics (chapters 9 and 10), like information economics and agency theory, focuses on problems of misrepresentation but with a twist: markets fail because people can be manipulated and not because they presuppose dishonesty. And in recent behavioral finance, emotion-stoking rumors cause wild fluctuations in markets. Here, too, discourse does not promote constructive exchange or enterprise.

Yet, outside economics, discourse has long been a significant subject for systematic study. The study of rhetoric and literature goes back to antiquity. The current discourse-related scholarship, like the practical advice on the topic, is vast and disparate. And for my purposes, this is a double-edged sword. The vastness potentially provides much material to mine. But its disparateness—and the absence of a cohesive economics-like paradigm—makes any practical synthesis challenging.

And now a spoiler alert for Part 4: As we will see, psychologist Jerome Bruner's work helped me navigate the disparateness of entrepreneurial discourse and identify its key features. Bruner's work also altered my views about entrepreneurial storytelling. I had long thought of entrepreneurial pitches and proposals as stories. I still see significant storytelling elements in such pitches and proposals: they use imagined details, sequences of events, and evocative metaphors (chapter 19). But I have now come to recognize (chapters 20 and 21) that entrepreneurial proposals and plans lack crucial elements of a "proper" story, such as unexpected reversals of fortune. Instead, proper stories play a supporting role in imaginative entrepreneurial discourse: they are not the show's stars.

PART IV
IMAGINATIVE DISCOURSE

Columbus at Isabella's Court

Henry Wolf, 1897. Open Access image from the Smithsonian online collection.

18

The Aims of Discourse

Evidence alone does not establish confidence in an enterprise—that an imagined future is attainable or desirable. What and how promoters communicate—their spoken, written, and visual "conversations"—influences perceptions of their evidence, which is inevitably incomplete and subject to positive or negative interpretations. An entrepreneur's sales pitch affects the expected value of her product beyond just its technical specs. How she responds to tough questions, not just her résumé, affects investors' assessments of her capacities. Moreover, because others' confidence and doubts can make or break a venture, discourse can become a real springboard or a barrier.

This may seem trivial—who could question that discourse, not just evidence, influences interpretations and thus the perceived uncertainty? Moreover, broadly defined, discourse about uncertain matters is an integral part of our lives; it is something we all know about and experience. We talk, tell stories, argue, attend meetings, send emails, create, deliver, and endure PowerPoint presentations, and make or receive sales pitches. What could be more ordinary? But despite appearances, the territory is treacherous; therefore, I proceed slowly. In this chapter, I start with a simplifying distinction between narrative and logico-scientific thinking. I then use the distinction to examine the aims and sub-aims of discourse (which can all be subsumed under the "end" of reducing uncertainty). The following three chapters examine the "means" of uncertainty-reducing discourse.

My conjectures* lean heavily on the work of psychologist Jerome Bruner (1915–2016). Although he said little about business, Bruner's literary and legal applications provide an excellent foundation—and foil—for analyzing entrepreneurial discourse.

Specifically, the main sections of this chapter

- Review Bruner's distinction between narrative and logico-scientific modes of thought and verification.

- Use Bruner's distinction to examine the aims and sub-aims (the "ends") of entrepreneurial discourse.

---

* I cover more speculative ground than in previous chapters. I delve more deeply into the mysteries of the mind, and my accounts follow the "narrative" mode (discussed later in this chapter) to an even greater degree than before—hence "conjectures."

Uncertainty and Enterprise. Amar Bhidé, Oxford University Press. © Oxford University Press 2025.
DOI: 10.1093/oso/9780197688359.003.0018

260 UNCERTAINTY AND ENTERPRISE

- Compare the aims of entrepreneurial, literary, and legal discourse. The similarities—and even more the differences—help crystallize ideas about entrepreneurial ends and set the stage for my later analysis of the means.

I view "discourse" broadly, in the way US courts treat talk, writing, music, and imagery as "speech." Yet, to simplify, I limit my scope to discourse that (1) Has an honest, constructive intent. To emphasize problems of uncertainty rather than dishonesty, I assume promoters sincerely believe in their ventures and products but don't have incontrovertible evidence. Likewise, I assume that potential investors, customers, recruits, and suppliers worry about promoters' misjudgments and exaggerations but not outright lies. (2) Aims to create value by reducing doubts rather than bargaining over shares. Thus, I focus on cooperative, not competitive or adversarial, interactions.[1] (3) Does not rely on intimidation—"tough talk"—to secure compliance. In ad-hoc, bootstrapped ventures, the promoters are supplicants who do not have the power to threaten or bully. In established businesses, bosses can threaten or command, but as mentioned, authoritarian discourse can be ineffectual or counterproductive. Regardless, it is outside the scope of my chapters.

1. Narrative-Mode Thought

Neglect and Confusion Knight's 1921 book, which did not treat uncertainty as a mental state, did not analyze how discourse affected its extent. His chapter on "meeting uncertainty" discussed how predicting or controlling the future could reduce uncertainty but said nothing about influencing perceptions and interpretations. Subsequent economists, including those who study entrepreneurship and innovation, have also said little about how discourse affects confidence and doubt.

Outside economics, scholars have studied discourse since ancient times. Aristotle's fourth-century BCE *Poetics* and *Rhetoric* are landmark examples. Today, scholarship in literature, linguistics, psychology, philosophy, anthropology, and history includes "narratology," "systemic functional linguistics," "discourse analysis," and "conversation analysis." In practical spheres, study and teaching span script writing, journalism, psychotherapy and psychoanalysis, advertising, and public relations. But no unifying paradigm has emerged.

THE AIMS OF DISCOURSE   261

Moreover, much of the discourse of communications experts is incomprehensible to outsiders.

Bruner's Project When I intended to focus on entrepreneurial storytelling and narratives rather than more broadly on discourse, I found no consensus among narratologists (or popular writers) about basic terms. What was a "story"? And how was it different from "narrative"? Luckily, following online breadcrumbs, I discovered Bruner's 1991 article "The Narrative Construction of Reality,"[2] and then the other products of his multidecade project on narratives.

The discovery was eye-opening. Besides his own insights, Bruner, a "Pied Piper of interdisciplinary wonder" and "acrobatic meta-connector of ideas,"[3] provides a clear synthesis of wide-ranging scholarship. The insights and synthesis provided an invaluable foundation for my conjectures.

I was also embarrassed to discover Bruner's work so late, nearly a decade after his death at age one hundred in 2015. Although not as famous as Freud, Skinner, Kahneman, or Tversky, insiders consider Bruner a leader of the cognitive revolution that K-T's behavioral economics built on (chapter 11). Remarkably, Bruner began working on narratives in the 1980s, after four decades of influential contributions to cognitive psychology and child development.

Influential Contributions

As mentioned in chapter 11, a cognitive revolution overthrew the "deliberate mind-blindness"[4] of Pavlov's and Skinner's behaviorism. The revolutionaries had different views about its replacement, however. Simon and Newell modeled the mind as a computer. In contrast, other scholars undertook "an all-out effort to establish meaning as the central concept of psychology." They studied how humans, through their encounters with the world, make sense of the world and of themselves.[5]

Bruner emerged as a preeminent meaning constructionist. After his bachelor's and PhD degrees in psychology (from Duke University in 1937 and Harvard in 1941), Bruner served as an expert in psychological warfare in US Army Intelligence. He returned to Harvard in 1945 and secured a professorship in 1952. In 1960, he and George Miller cofounded Harvard's "interdisciplinary, iconoclastic Center for Cognitive Studies."[6] He was the center's codirector for the next twelve years.

Bruner's technical contributions included then-novel ideas that the mind, not just the senses, controlled perception and that structuring information

262 UNCERTAINTY AND ENTERPRISE

into categories made it more memorable. But he wasn't a conventional, objective cause-and-measurable-effect psychologist. His conception of cognition incorporated culture and history. As he wrote in his 1962 book *On Knowing*, "Man does not respond to a world that exists for direct touching. Nor is he locked in a prison of his own subjectivity. Rather, he represents the world to himself and acts on behalf of or in reaction to his representations. The representations are products of his own spirit as it has been formed by living in a society with a language, myths, a history, and ways of doing things."[7]

The cognitive revolution Bruner envisioned "required that psychology join forces with anthropology and linguistics, philosophy and history, even with the discipline of law."[8] He lamented the revolution's shift "from 'meaning' to 'information,' from the construction of meaning to the processing of information," with "computation as the ruling metaphor."[9] He criticized "scientific psychology" that excluded history, culture, and "beliefs, desires, intentions, [and] commitments."[10] And Bruner, like Gigerenzer, was skeptical of claims of widespread cognitive biases (chapters 11 and 12). Like Kay and King, Bruner saw evidence of contextual and cultural interpretations by subjects in K-T–style experiments, not reflexively defective reasoning.

Bruner's work in childhood education complemented his cognitive research. His *Process of Education* (1960), which became a "powerful stimulus" to curricular reform, argued "that any subject can be taught to any child at any stage of development if it is presented in the proper manner."[11] According to the educational luminary Howard Gardner, Bruner led a small group that developed "a brilliant curriculum, which introduced kids ages 9, 10, and 11 to gritty nutritious ideas and practices from the range of social science—from the principles of Chomskian linguistics to the evolutionary similarities between human beings and higher apes."[12]

Born blind with cataracts—an operation restored his sight at two—Bruner was a "rich kid" who tried to hide it.[13] He played a "pivotal role" in the Head Start program[14] that serves low-income children and families. His "leftwing political leanings"[15] notwithstanding, Bruner docked an "ocean-going yacht"[16] at "a glorious retreat on the southern coast of Ireland."[17]

In 1972, Bruner sailed that yacht across the Atlantic to accept the Watts Professorship in Psychology at Oxford. Bruner had thought "anything must be an improvement on Harvard," which had become "increasingly stuffy," but found that Oxford wasn't more liberal.[18]

In 1980, Bruner returned to the United States, briefly to Harvard, before settling in his New York City birthplace. He undertook his capstone project on narratives there, initially at the New School for Social Research[19] and then at New York University (NYU).

Bruner's narrative project enlisted diverse collaborators and used seemingly unscientific methodologies. For example, Bruner assembled a team of literature scholars to examine literary masterpieces. The project ignored the disdain of pedantic economists and sociologists for abductive inference from exceptional successes (chapter 14). It followed, according to Bruner, William James's example (from the *Varieties of Religious Experience*) of studying "the most religious man at his most religious moment." In another sample-of-one project, Bruner collaborated with a postdoc in educational psychology to study the recorded nighttime monologues of a child in her crib.[20]

Bruner wrote two influential books in the 1980s. *Actual Minds, Possible Worlds* (1986) examined imaginative narrative thought that makes experience meaningful. *Acts of Meaning* (1990) explored culturally shaped narrative thinking; Bruner later called himself a "cultural psychologist."[21]

In 1991, Bruner moved from NYU's psychology department to its law school. He had found "a great many psychologists to be rather dull," wanting to "turn mysteries into the obvious." Psychology also "failed to look at how societies create social norms." The law considered passions, such as vengeance, and codified them into rules about crime and punishment.[22]

Bruner teamed up with Anthony Amsterdam, a law professor who had grown interested in storytelling. They taught a seminar, nominally, on "lawyering theory," which included creative writing exercises and discussed material ranging from Greek tragedy to modern murder mysteries. Their seminar, which ran for over twenty years (until Bruner turned ninety-five), also resulted in *Minding the Law: How Courts Rely on Storytelling, and How Their Stories Change the Way We Understand the Law—and Ourselves* (2000). In *Making Stories: Law, Literature, Life* (2002), Bruner published a concise summation of his narrative project.

Bruner's declaration in the title of his 2002 summation that stories influence law and life, not just literature, poses the question: do stories reduce the uncertainty of entrepreneurial initiatives? In a later chapter, I argue that entrepreneurial proposals contain storylike elements but lack the essential attributes of a proper story. But that gets ahead of my own, not quite story. For now, let us see what Bruner's distinction between narrative and logico-scientific thinking tells us about the ends of entrepreneurial discourse.

An Important Distinction Bruner starts *Actual Minds, Possible Worlds* with a William James epigraph: "To say that all human thinking is essentially of two kinds—reasoning on the one hand, and narrative, descriptive, contemplative thinking on the other—is to say only what every reader's experience will corroborate." Bruner's book similarly distinguishes between logico-scientific and narrative modes of thought that provide "distinctive ways of ordering experience, of constructing reality."[23]

View from the Far Reaches

Invoking James's advice to study outliers, Bruner bases his characterization of narrative thought from "at its far reach: as an art form." "Great works of fiction," he suggests, "come closest to revealing "purely" the deep structure of the narrative mode." Likewise, mathematics and the physical sciences "reveal most plainly (and purely) the deep structure" of logico-scientific thought.*

The logico-scientific mode, according to Bruner, idealizes a "formal, mathematical system of description and explanation."[24] It "deals in general causes," seeking to transcend the particular by "higher and higher reaching for abstraction." In mathematics and formal logic—its ultimate abstractions—it disclaims "any explanatory value at all where the particular is concerned." Requirements of consistency and noncontradiction regulate its language. In contrast, imaginative narrative leads to "good stories, gripping drama, believable (though not necessarily 'true') historical accounts. It deals in human or human-like intention and action," and the "particulars of experience" that it locates in "time and place."[25]

Both may express or imply causality, but of "palpably different" types: "The term *then* functions differently in the logical proposition 'if x, then y' and in the narrative *recit* 'The king died, and then the queen died.' One leads to a search for universal truth conditions, the other for likely particular connections between two [particular] events—mortal grief, suicide, foul play."[26]

Most pertinently, for my purposes in this chapter, the two modes have different criteria of "well-formedness" and "differ radically in their procedures for verification." Both good stories and well-formed logical arguments "can be used as means for convincing another. Yet what they convince *of* is fundamentally different: arguments convince one of their truth, stories of their lifelikeness. The one verifies by eventual appeal to procedures for establishing formal and empirical proof. The other establishes not truth but verisimilitude."[27] Like storytellers, scientists may invent facts and worlds, but their "world-making" is of "a different order from what story-making does." Physics must "eventuate in predicting something that is testably right, however much it may speculate. Stories have no such need for testability. Believability in a

---

* Amsterdam and Bruner's (2000) *Minding the Law* also implicitly follows this approach of examining extreme cases. Their argument that "courts rely on storytelling" relies on landmark US Supreme Court judgments that set or overturned precedents.

THE AIMS OF DISCOURSE   265

story is of a different order than the believability of even the speculative parts of physical theory."[28]

2. Aims and Sub-aims

Plausibility, Not Proof An entrepreneurial proposal is far removed from a great play or novel. Yet, its underlying thought and persuasiveness conform more to Bruner's narrative mode than to a paradigmatic, logico-scientific mode. Entrepreneurial proposals project an imagined future. This future pertains to a particular state, not to any conjecture about a general scientific law or abstract mathematical result. The desirability of the particular state is likewise inferred from particular unmet wants or unsolved problems. Human intentions play a critical role in its realization. Like the now-disreputable prescientific theories of bodies "wanting" to fall to the earth's center, the causality is animistic and willful, not naturalistic or deterministic.

The "well-formedness" of the expression (the investment proposal or sales pitch) of imagined states and paths also conforms to Bruner's narrative criteria. Reducing uncertainty is an overarching goal. Discourse helps convince others—and oneself—that an imagined future is desirable and feasible, moving mental states away from doubt toward confidence. Yet promoters cannot demonstrate the desirability and feasibility of their imagined futures through logic, statistical analysis, or controlled experiments. Nor is logico-scientific verification necessary. Amsterdam and Bruner argue that good stories are "true enough if they *ring true*."[29] Likewise, a critical objective of an entrepreneurial proposal or pitch is to establish *plausibility*. A beyond-reasonable-doubt standard for commercial initiatives is impossible to satisfy and, as mentioned in the last chapter, pathological.

Attention, Alignment, and Understanding Regardless of the degree of uncertainty reduction attempted, attention must come first. But attention is never a given. David Hume's *A Treatise on Human Nature,* published in 1739 when the author was in his twenties, "fell dead-born from the press."[30] Now considered a classic of Western philosophy, it received little attention until about a century later. During Hume's lifetime, his most popular work was the bestselling six-volume *History of England*. Gregor Mendel's classic paper on heredity, published in 1865, was cited just about three times before it was rediscovered in the early 1900s, some twenty years after the friar died in 1884. John Kennedy Toole committed suicide at thirty-one after failing to secure the publication of *A Confederacy of Dunces*. The author's mother and a fellow writer got the Louisiana State University Press to publish *Dunces* eleven years after Toole's death. The

266   UNCERTAINTY AND ENTERPRISE

book became a cult classic, secured a Pulitzer Prize, and is now considered a canonical work of modern American writing.[31]

Examples of entrepreneurs who initially failed to secure the attention of investors include Steve Jobs in 1976. "Apple was an obvious candidate for venture investment," Sebastian Mallaby writes. "Yet when Apple set out to raise money, the stars in the venture capital firmament failed to recognize the opportunity.... Tom Perkins and Eugene Kleiner refused even to meet with Steve Jobs."[32] Attention or neglect sometimes derives from promoters' personalities and reputations or their products' attributes. But attention is also often a deliberate objective of discourse, as a prerequisite for its other goals.

Complexity makes two other uncertainty-reducing objectives significant. As mentioned, complex initiatives undertaken by specialized teams face coordination problems: different teams have incomplete information about what each other is doing or planning or how they will respond to unexpected issues. Joint planning and consultative discourse that reduces mutual information gaps can control these "alignment" uncertainties.

Similarly, customers face uncertainties about the functions and use of complex products. Smart modern electronics, from TVs to computers to mobile phones, can make users feel incredibly dumb and frustrated. Conversely, in "made-to-order" systems, developers often misunderstand what users really want. Communicating how complex products should be used to users—and what users want to developers—thus constitutes another uncertainty-reducing objective of discourse.

3. Comparing Aims

Similarities Literary, legal, and entrepreneurial discourse all target states of mind. They seek to shape beliefs and feelings about some imagined future state. "While fiction may begin on familiar ground," Bruner writes, "it aims to go beyond it into the realm of the possible, the might-be, could have been, perhaps will be."[33] Moreover, according to Amsterdam and Bruner's *Minding the Law*, any writing "whether of love or law, in fiction or essay, is never alien to drama, designed to enliven, not simply to inform neutrally."[34] Entrepreneurial discourse must likewise "enliven" to secure and retain attention.

Contrasts The differences in the aims of literary, legal, and entrepreneurial discourse are also, for my purposes, notable.

According to Aristotle's *Poetics*, tragedies provide catharsis—the "purgation" of the emotions of pity and fear through their experience in attending a play.

THE AIMS OF DISCOURSE 267

Modern horror movies may aim for the same effect. But the aims of literary discourse have also broadened and evolved. Literature often now attempts to instill, not purge, disturbing emotions. Writers give their fictional landscapes a "reality" of their own but do not impose interpretations. Their texts merely try to "initiate and guide a search for meanings among a spectrum of possible meanings."[35] The texts both suggest "perspectives that can be constructed to make experience comprehensible"[36] while also making "the familiar and the ordinary strange again . . . by 'alienating' the reader from the tyranny of the compellingly familiar."[37]

Entrepreneurial discourse, in contrast, does not offer the catharsis of classical tragedy or, like the modern psychological novel, intend to disturb. Far from making the unfamiliar seem strange, it aims to make to-be-created novelties seem familiar. And it does not seek to spur a variety of interpretations. Its intended message is unambiguous: *Invest! Buy!*

The legal discourse of advocates and judges is similarly unambiguous: to persuade audiences to convict or acquit the accused, reaffirm or overturn precedents, and so on. But there is a crucial difference. Legal discourse is "specialized for waging and negotiating controversy," write Amsterdam and Bruner in *Minding the Law.* "Talk becomes law-talk only when the way to do (or think about) something is contestable, when people want to settle the contest or its boundaries by ruling some of the contenders out of bounds."[38] And, adds Bruner in his 2002 book, public confidence in adversarial legal storytelling is based on the assumption that "confrontation is a good way to get to the bottom of things."[39]

An entrepreneur's discourse with investors and potential buyers has no such adversarial purpose. A dialogue starts when both sides want to get a deal done. As I remind students in sessions on selling, the job titles of commercial buyers indicate that they must buy. Similarly, VCs must invest. Buyers and investors may be skeptical, and they usually have alternatives. But like readers of novels—and unlike impartial jurors and judges—the entrepreneur's audience starts with what William James called a "will to believe," not unshakable doubt.

19

The Devices of Discourse

Our modernizing voyage has sailed far from Knight's 1921 uncertainty dock. I have treated uncertainty as doubts about known unknowns and emphasized the role of routines in evaluating uncertain claims. Such moves took us to places that Knight did not go and mainstream economics usually avoids. Thus, while Knight analyzed situational uniqueness as a precondition for entrepreneurial profit, he said nothing about the specialization of entrepreneurial initiatives analyzed in Part 3. Likewise, with entrepreneurial discourse. Knight ignored the topic, whereas I examine the role of discourse in reducing doubts and disagreements about known unknowns. Thus, as we saw in the previous chapter, entrepreneurial discourse aims for plausibility, attention, and the control of misalignments and misunderstandings. These aims derive from missing rather than concealed information. Plausibility is valuable, for example, when unobtainable information about known unknowns makes indisputable proof impossible.

This chapter offers conjectures about "means"—the devices commonly used to pursue the aims discussed in the previous chapter. Here, too, usefulness is based on the limitations of information: these devices help promoters reduce uncertainties about their initiatives by compensating for the incompleteness of their evidence. Specifically, the following sections analyze

- The content of entrepreneurial proposals and plans—how details and their ordering help reduce doubts.

- Evocative devices—the figurative language and metaphors promoters use to make imagined and hoped-for outcomes seem real.

- The performance of the discourse—the influence of its careful staging before audiences and in interactive conversations.

I again extend Bruner's analysis of literary and legal discourse and follow the narrative mode, seeking plausibility, not logico-scientific verifiability for my arguments, as I have throughout this book.

Uncertainty and Enterprise. Amar Bhidé, Oxford University Press. © Oxford University Press 2025.
DOI: 10.1093/oso/9780197688359.003.0019

THE DEVICES OF DISCOURSE 269

1. Content of Proposals and Plans

Imagined Details Details help novelists, playwrights, filmmakers, and other creative artists make their imagined worlds "ring true." Herman Melville's fantastical *Moby Dick* is full of accurate details about whaling. Honoré de Balzac's novel *Illusions Perdues* (*Lost Illusions*) describes printing and printers in nineteenth-century France, drawing on Balzac's personal experience. The details often mirror the audience's known world, although not faithfully so. For example, the "story worlds" of myth or science fiction depict creatures and rules that are both fantastical and sufficiently lifelike in such a way that the audience can relate to the imagined story world and believe in its possibility.[1]

Some but not all of the details are relevant to the tale told. As Chekhov famously advised, if you hang a gun on the wall in the first act, you must fire it in the next. Otherwise, don't put it there.[2] Yet when staged, Chekhov's plays include lifelike sets, props, and actors wearing period costumes that have nothing to do with the plot. Likewise, street scenes in movies depict traffic and pedestrians. These costly details contribute nothing to the plot, but they contribute to verisimilitude.

Real, imagined, and seemingly extraneous details also feature in historical biographies, documentaries, and journalism. Biographies, for example, often include reconstructed conversations that come from the biographer's imagination. Unlike Hollywood's *Gone with the Wind*, Ken Burns bases his epic nine-episode documentary on the Civil War on historical events. But both Burns and Hollywood rely on scripted dialogue, costumes, and props. Like novels and short stories, newspaper accounts describe the build, hair, eyes, and clothes of real-life protagonists and are now routinely supplemented with photographs. Scholarly histories, too, contain photographs and detailed descriptive color, increasing the cost of the published product—and its perceived authenticity.

Details play a similar role in entrepreneurial discourse. Like novelists, promoters construct a possible world that combines information and imagination. Imagination is unavoidable because promoters (and potential supporters) cannot logically or statistically deduce the possible world; their information, even about known unknowns, is inevitably incomplete. Given a jigsaw puzzle with missing pieces, the entrepreneur imagines its solution. However, potential investors, suppliers, customers, and other interlocutors may not readily buy into the entrepreneur's imagined world: their interpretation of the current world may be different, or they may worry about winner's-curse problems, as mentioned. And like novelists, promoters can secure plausibility by adding detail. Paradoxically, irrelevant or imagined data can increase the effectiveness of relevant, documented evidence.

The Power of Plausible Thinking

Imagine an entrepreneur who projects ten million dollars in sales for her venture based on a 10 percent share of a hundred-million-dollar market. The market size is widely accepted and supported, but the projected share is clearly speculative. The entrepreneur could make her projection more believable by constructing a spreadsheet with imagined details. The spreadsheet might, for example, show the venture reaching its sales forecast by employing twelve salespeople, each making four sales calls daily, with a one-in-seven success rate. If the assumptions are reasonable—for example, they do not specify hiring a thousand salespeople, require each salesperson to make thirty calls a day, or secure a sale on every call—the detailed model should be more believable than a bald assumption of 10 percent market share.

Using imagined details does not require gullible listeners. Assumptions can provide helpful evidence about promoters: can they construct coherent models and defend their assumptions? As with readers of novels or historical biographies, sophisticated financiers welcome fictitious details with internal consistency and justifiability. Additionally, entrepreneurial plans envision imagined paths to imagined destinations. No one really expects events to unfold exactly as planned. The challenge for entrepreneurs is to improvise around unforeseen problems. This course correction is also an act of creative imagination, not of logical deduction. And the imaginative plausibility of the initial plan provides evidence of later adaptive capacity.[3]

(I did not see the value of imagined or irrelevant detail when I was a twenty-something McKinsey & Co. management consultant in the early 1980s. I questioned the eighty-hour weeks that colleagues put into producing thick reports padded with what I believed were flimsy or pointless analyses. How could intelligent consultants and clients take the charade seriously? I now understand why.)

Familiar Categories While details can increase the plausibility of proposals and the credibility of promoters, they also have a downside. Just as four-hour movies or thousand-page books test the patience of audiences and readers, too-long proposals and pitches can turn off investors and customers. As mentioned, attention is a precondition for effective uncertainty-reducing discourse. Details also strain cognitive capacities. As George Miller, Jerome Bruner's Harvard collaborator, reported in 1956—in what would become one of the most highly cited papers in psychology—the "magical number" of seven (plus or minus two) limits the number of items we can keep in short-term

THE DEVICES OF DISCOURSE   271

memories. Detail has similar tradeoffs in improving coordination and under-standing: Disseminating detailed project plans so that different teams know what each other is doing can reduce alignment uncertainties, but excessively detailed plans can be misunderstood or ignored. Likewise, comprehensive instructions to reduce user uncertainties about complex products can create more confusion.

Grouping details into familiar categories helps reduce the downside. As mentioned, Bruner's early research suggested that grouping data in structured categories improves learning and memory. Miller's 1956 magic-number paper likewise reported that collating "bits" of information into "chunks" can "dramatically" improve what people remember. Similarly, grouping details into categories can help promoters keep the interest and attention of financiers and reduce the confusion experienced by users.

Using familiar groupings reduces the cognitive effort required to absorb detail, saves time, and reduces misunderstandings. And while jargon can be off-putting, specialized language can increase credibility. As Deaver Brown, a serial entrepreneur—who since the early 1990s has helped me teach a case about face-to-face selling—advises, "Your credibility with buyers comes from how you state your facts, knowing the way they think, talking in their language. I speak about retail stock keeping units, UPC codes, margins, space—issues that are important to them."[4]

The "rule of three" from Aristotle's *Rhetoric* has stood the test of time as a grouping principle. Likewise, in *Poetics*, Aristotle says good dramatic plots have three clear parts—a beginning, middle, and end.[5] Triads are commonly used in oral arguments, reports, articles, book chapters, or catchy slogans (including "life, liberty, and the pursuit of happiness" in the US Constitution and "A Mars a Day Helps You Work, Rest and Play" in the chocolate company's advertising jingles). While we may, on average, be able to remember Miller's magic seven (plus or minus two) chunks, threesomes are more memorable. Winston Churchill's wartime promise of "blood, toil, tears, and sweat" is commonly recalled as "blood, sweat, and tears."[6]

Ordering and Staging Like the grouping of details, how imagined events are ordered affects plausibility and attention. Aristotle's *Poetics* asserted the importance of ordering in the classical dramatic plot. It must be "necessary or probable," Aristotle wrote, "that this happens after that."[7] The worst kind of "defective plots" were "episodic," in which the succession of episodes was neither probable nor necessary.[8] In Aristotle's schema, plots also required "peripeteia"—reversals of fortune or turning points—but these could not come out of the blue. The reversals or turning points "should follow what went before; for there is a great difference between happening next and happening as a result."[9] Plots require

272 UNCERTAINTY AND ENTERPRISE

protagonists to face dilemmas, but their choices must follow naturally from their character and conform to our expectations of human nature.

Modern literature and drama often reject Aristotle's rule of a nearly inevitable progression of events. The 1998 movie *Sliding Doors* depicts two very different paths that the life of the leading character (Gwyneth Paltrow) takes, depending on whether she catches a train. An earlier Polish film, *Blind Chance* (released in 1987 after many years of suppression by Polish authorities), used the same device. But whatever the virtues of Aristotle's rule might be in the creative sphere, presenting the path to an imagined future as a nearly inevitable journey has advantages in entrepreneurial discourse.

Humans tend to believe things happen for a reason. Like Einstein, we like to think God does not play dice with the universe. Yet the kind of verifiable causality central to the logico-scientific mode is impossible in on-off imagined futures or accounts of unique events such as world wars, where we expect a distinctive constellation of circumstances to strongly influence what will or has happened. Here, we often depend on an expectation of sequential causality. If one thing follows another, we tend to believe the first event caused—often intentionally— the subsequent event.[10]

By logico-scientific standards, the tendency is irrational—a post hoc, ergo propter hoc fallacy. Precedence can be accidental. When we infer causal patterns, we may be "fooled by randomness," as Taleb's book tells us.[11] But frequently, in human affairs, there is no practical alternative to seeing sequences as intentionally causal. It is often a precondition for planned action, for any reasoned, forward-looking conduct, and an antidote to the paralyzing uncertainty that incomplete information may otherwise produce. Moreover, as Hume's unanswered skepticism about repeated sunrises suggests, causal scientific accounts of natural phenomena also rely on animal instinct, a blind faith in the uniformity of nature.

Similarly in the entrepreneurial sphere: ordering imagined events can secure plausibility for an entrepreneur's plans and proposals. For example, "Users complain about such-and-such problem. Therefore, they will want to buy our new product. Hiring and incentivizing capable sales staff will get us orders. And we can get this made at a price that will give both the supplier and us a profit margin." No one needs to truly believe that the venture will unfold according to the plan. But an artful sequence of imagined steps helps make imagined futures plausible. (Of course, the imagined links in the chain, like imagined details, need to be mimetic, to borrow from *Poetics*, of experience. Art must imitate life.)

Besides plausibility, artfully sequenced expositions help keep the attention of listeners. Aristotle's worst kind of plot—a sequence of disconnected events— is also dull, like an account of filling a shopping cart. Implying causality,

THE DEVICES OF DISCOURSE   273

combined with colorful detail, maintains interest. (Remember I told you in the last chapter that Bruner, a rich kid with a yacht, thought Harvard increasingly stuffy, sailed to Oxford, found it no better, and returned to his childhood hometown, New York. I included these details and sequence hoping to keep you engaged.)

In the interest of brevity, the entrepreneur's imagined sequence (like Aristotle's idealized plot) omits the less important details. But not always. Planning complex product launches, say, of Google's Pixel Fold phone, helps reduce coordination problems and alignment uncertainties. The discourse in the planning process is often mind-numbing. The product of the process is also tedious—and frequently an inaccurate guide to what happens. Nonetheless, the discourse that produces the plan has value in forestalling at least some crucial misalignments.[*]

Promoters often manage the detail-attention tradeoff by staging discourse. For example, first conversations with financiers can take the form of a very brief "elevator pitch." If the pitch creates interest, detailed presentations and lengthier meetings follow. Product planning starts with presentations and discussions about concepts and prototypes. The minutiae follow much later. Similarly, the first step in the full-blown sales process, especially for complex products, may be a short initial conversation to "qualify" the prospect. Many electronic devices now come with bare-bones "quick start" guides, with detailed manuals posted online.

2. Evocative Devices

Figurative Language Like logico-scientific thought, the narrative mode includes mechanisms for mapping current states to future states. However, there are critical differences in expression. In the idealized logico-scientific mode, current conditions (observed or assumed) and future states are specified in precise, objective ways, connected by unambiguous propositions. To illustrate, consider the middle-school algebra question "How long will it take a train to travel 765 miles at 85 mph?" While the problem is entirely imaginary, its variables—elapsed time, speed, and distance—are precisely specified, as is the "correct" answer. Similarly, while entities in scientific theories like "mass" and "electrical

---

[*] In complex products, complete, correctly sequenced user instructions can be crucial. IKEA's business model of selling attractively priced, self-assembled furniture requires that consumers have confidence in the instructions provided. Consumer uncertainty about the accuracy of the instructions would be as damaging for IKEA as uncertainty about the quality of the products themselves.

274 UNCERTAINTY AND ENTERPRISE

resistance" are often theoretical constructs, they have objective, measurable manifestations.

In contrast, entrepreneurial discourse—which aims for plausible groundedness, not verifiable precision—relies on fuzzy categories and suggestive relationships. Where natural scientists use measurable attributes to construct a periodic table of elements or distinguish between proteins and carbohydrates, entrepreneurs often invoke imprecise stereotypes. For example, consumers may be described as aspirational or frugal, and product designs as trendy or classic.

Evocative metaphors and other nonliteral figures of speech, typically avoided in scientific language, play a prominent role in entrepreneurial discourse. Like fictitious details that (as discussed earlier) promote plausibility, ambiguous metaphors help clarify murky future states and paths for getting there. Promoters secure this paradoxical support through the likeness, evoked by metaphor, between the familiar (observed or assumed) and an imagined state or path. For example, by 2014, after the ride-hailing company Uber had secured a valuation of $18 billion some five years after it was launched, many ventures claimed to be the Uber of some other domain or were thus labeled by the press. Instacart became the Uber of grocery delivery, SpoonRocket of food delivery, Glamsquad of women's haircuts, BloomThat of flowers, Washio of drycleaning, Saucey of alcohol, and Eaze of medical marijuana. Everywhere you looked, an Uber of "X."[12]

Similarly, instead of unambiguous formulae (such as distance = speed × time) of logico-scientific discourse, we find suggestions of causality evoked by rough-and-ready metaphorical analogy or archetype. "Sharing economy" and "platform" models are recent examples. The success of Airbnb, an online service founded in 2008 that helped owners of unused or partially used apartments and houses rent out their living spaces for short periods, shaped the metaphor of "sharing economy" ventures that would profit from renting out other similarly underutilized resources. (It also spurred investment pitches by entrepreneurs to VCs that started with "I'm the Airbnb of X, Y, Z").[13] Uber, Airbnb, and other ventures like TaskRabbit, Upwork, Thumbtack, Spotify, and most of all Amazon, created the metaphor of "platform" businesses. These would connect buyers and sellers through online marketplaces.

These suggestive analogies gain acceptance without empirical validation, deep understanding of the underlying economic theory, or even precise specification. Yet they can play a useful role in entrepreneurial discourse by providing semantic shortcuts to understanding and a starting point for detailed dialogue. Figuratively speaking, metaphors help make proposals less like WASGIJs: jigsaw puzzles in which we do not know what picture we are supposed to create when we start.[14]

Visual Metaphors Evocative art long precedes verbal metaphor. Cave art in Spain, possibly Neanderthal, has been dated to more than forty thousand years ago,[15] and in France, it dates to about thirty-three thousand years ago.[16] The first documented use of verbal metaphor, which co-evolved with human language, goes back to the Sumerian epic Gilgamesh, recorded on clay tablets, from about four thousand years ago. Both visual and verbal metaphors then flourished in literature, paintings, and sculpture. Staged theatre, opera, movies, and television combined visual and verbal evocation.

Visual metaphor did not, however, enter professional discourse until quite recently. Law firms stuck to verbal arguments and contracts. The first HBS case study I wrote (on the Irish Republic) in 1978—like nearly all other HBS case studies—had numerical exhibits but no images. When I joined McKinsey & Co. in 1980, the management consulting firm had long moved from "vertical" text reports to horizontal presentations. Every page was a chart with freehand lettering drawn by professionals using pencils, rulers, T-squares, and stencils. But the charts contained no visual metaphors. They were cut-and-dried affairs, often intended to communicate numerical information, sometimes concepts, promoting the mantra of "fact-based analysis." Metaphorical commercial imagery was mainly found in TV advertising.

HBS case studies (including the dozen or so I coauthored after 2014) now routinely contain photographs and drawings. A *Harvard Business Review* (*HBR*) article on "great presentations" advises using fewer words "complement[ing] text on slides with photos, videos, and images."[17] Apparently, professionals find less need for the respectability of precise logico-scientific discourse and are now more willing to use visual and verbal metaphors. Concurrently, PowerPoint software and other advances in information technology have made creating slide presentations, websites, videocasts—and case studies—with metaphorical imagery cheap and easy.*

Designers also use visual metaphors to reduce uncertainties about complex products. For example, user interfaces contain what designers call "signifiers"—a metaphor introduced in Don Norman's *Living with Complexity*.

---

* A Google search (on August 10, 2023) for "business metaphors" exemplifies the current state of demand and supply. The top result from the search was a webpage on "Ten Most Common Business Metaphors to Create Engaging Presentation Slides." Each metaphor (including "windows of opportunity" and "star performers / rock stars") came with a downloadable PowerPoint slide containing the corresponding image (e.g., of windows and stars). The page linked to a similar compilation of "Ten Baseball Metaphors to Help You Hit a Home Run with Your Presentations" that included "a new ball game," "swinging for the fences," and their corresponding downloadable image enhanced slides. See https://www.slideteam.net/blog/10-most-common-business-metaphors-to-create-engag ing-presentation-slides and https://www.slideteam.net/blog/10-baseball-metaphors-to-help-you- hit-a-home-run-with-your-presentations.

Signifiers, Skeuomorphs, and Bruner

"Signifiers," a term Norman repurposed from semiotics, is now commonly used in industrial design. According to Norman, a signifier is any mark (such as a red lamp) or sound (a ringing doorbell) that communicates meaningful information to users or some clue about what they can or should do—or refrain from doing.[18] For example, a light on a car dashboard tells us that we need to refill the oil and a ringing doorbell that a visitor has arrived.

The digitization of traditional services and products has increased the need for signifiers. For example, to withdraw money from my bank account, I would cash a check through a bank teller, and to file a document, I'd put it in a folder. Now I need to navigate through the user interfaces of an ATM or the file management system of a computer. And to make the navigation intuitive, designers often use folder icons in file managers or phone handset icons on mobile phone screens.

These so-called skeuomorphs are visual metaphors that evoke some traditional object or function. However, traditional things can become obsolete, falling outside current users' experience or memory. For example, how many young users have used a physical file folder or a phone handset? Yet after it has gained common acceptance, the icon can take on a life of its own, continuing to perform its signifier functions in interfaces used in new devices.

Another historical curiosity about metaphoric icons takes us back to Jerome Bruner. A colleague recalls that the "mind as computer" was antithetical to Bruner's worldview. Yet Bruner's ideas of representing information through actions, icons, and symbols inspired the computer scientist Alan Kay's pioneering and now ubiquitous graphical user interfaces that combine actions, images, and symbols.[19]

3. Carefully Rehearsed Performances

Putting On a Show Performance matters. Shakespeare's classic text does not make every staging of *Othello* memorable. Nor does Wagner's libretto and music ensure acclaim for every performance of his *Ring*. The quality of the live performance is similarly important in business presentations, although artistic standards are less demanding: According to Gene Zelazny, McKinsey & Co.'s

THE DEVICES OF DISCOURSE   277

legendary director of visual communication, presenters, not their slides, must take precedence.

Putting the Presenter First

When Gene Zelazny, who had worked at McKinsey & Co. for more than fifty years, passed away, the firm's managing partner said that "it was Gene who created the use of charts as our mode of communication and he elevated them to an art form. . . . His charts became the standard by which we all—no matter where we live and work—communicate with each other and with our clients."[20] Yet Zelazny had previously told an interviewer who had asked him how presentations had changed during his career:

> We see more visuals, more slides, than we used to because we've made it so easy to produce them. The evolution of presentation technology has led to a subtle shift in emphasis from the speaker to the visuals. . . . Today the visuals have become more important than the speaker.
>
> I maintain that it's the presenter who's the presentation, not the visuals. The visuals should continue to be "visual aids" in the true sense of the word, "aids." As such, my single most appreciated recommendation is to have speakers learn to use the period button on their laptops during the "slide show." That leaves a blank screen and forces the audience to concentrate on the speaker.[21]

Steve Jobs was no Sir Lawrence Olivier playing Othello in London's National Theatre, Martin Luther King delivering his "I Have a Dream" speech from the steps of the Lincoln Memorial in Washington, or even a John Cleese complaining about a dead parrot in *Monty Python's Flying Circus*. But in the realm of commercial presentation, Jobs was a grandmaster.

According to his biographer Walter Isaacson, Jobs "perfected the art of turning product launches into theatrical productions."[22] For the 1998 launch of his NeXT computer in San Francisco's Symphony Hall, Jobs "fretted over everything," including the "right hue of green" for the background of his slides and hired "the post-modernist theatre producer George Coates, to stage the show." Jobs was on-stage for three hours. He again "proved to be, in the words of Andrew Pollack of the *New York Times*, 'the Andrew Lloyd Webber of product introductions, a master of stage flair and special effects.' Wes Smith of the *Chicago Tribune* said the launch was "to product demonstrations what Vatican II was to church meetings."[23]

278 UNCERTAINTY AND ENTERPRISE

The NeXT computer flopped, but Jobs continued theatrical, perfectionist product launches for the iMac in 1998, the iPod in 2001, the iPhone in 2007 ("in a career of dazzling product presentations, the iPhone launch may have been his best"), and finally the iPad in 2010.[24] The launches were dramatic performances: every move, every pause, repeatedly rehearsed, the lighting and sets meticulously arranged. The stage furniture for the iPad presentation featured a leather Le Corbusier chair and an Eero Saarinen side table.[25]

Ron Popeil, founder of Ronco, occupies the other end of the tastefulness scale. Still, his over-the-top delivery also got the job done. He "invented direct-response TV sales business," according to Popeil's 2021 *New York Times* obituary. His "infomercial stardom persuaded millions of Americans to buy the Veg-O-Matic, Pocket Fisherman, and dozens of other products they had no idea they needed." His "mastery of television marketing" made him "as recognizable onscreen as the TV and movie stars of his era." His catchphrases—"But wait! There's more" and "Set it and forget it"—endured beyond his retirement. He painted in "very definable brushstrokes" that removed "every doubt in the customer's mind.[26]

Other entrepreneurs get free publicity by staging stunts.

Publicity Stunts

In 2018, Elon Musk, the founder of Tesla and Space X, put on "a stunning show" for the inaugural test flight of SpaceX's *Falcon Heavy*. Such test flights usually carry dummy payloads, such as hunks of metal. Musk, however, launched his personal, cherry red Tesla roadster with Starman, a mannequin dressed in a spacesuit, behind the wheel.[27]

Sir Richard Branson, another charismatic entrepreneur (and promoter of space travel), has used over-the-top costumes to promote his ventures. For the launch of Virgin Brides—a wedding apparel retailer—Branson shaved his beard and wore a white wedding dress. The venture failed, but his wedding dress was a "huge success," according to Branson. To inaugurate various Virgin Airlines flights, Branson has dressed as both a pilot and a stewardess, wearing bright red lipstick without shaving his beard. "It doesn't take much to drag me into a dress," he writes. Branson says he "loves playing dress-up" and has "found it to be a great way to attract attention to the Virgin message."[28]

Sir James Dyson, Branson's compatriot and founder of the eponymous household devices company, does "madcap PR stunts which he hopes will provide a bit of unusual copy" for journalists. For example, "To introduce a new handheld dryer to the press he unveiled a new hand-dryer to a roomful of expectant press. While they were busy gasping at the speed of the dryer and hearing how much more hygienic than a normal dryer the Dyson Airblade is, a few hired heavies burst on to the scene and started attacking the dryers, just to prove how sturdy they were."[29]

THE DEVICES OF DISCOURSE   279

Read and Respond Stunts and drama are not always effective, however. Standards for acceptable presentation depend on the audience and occasion. IBM's William Lowe could not have secured funding for the IBM-PC from his company's Corporate Management Committee using Popeil's infomercial sales approach. Moreover, crucial discourse often does not occur in Jobs's Symphony Hall settings. As in street-side magic, mime, or juggling shows, audiences play an active role in performances. In fact, audiences—corporate committees, VCs, or buyers—control where the conversation goes, and bored listeners can dismiss prepared presentations.

Audience participation requires calm, responsive performances. For example, "objection handling" is an important challenge for in-person selling and a staple of sales training programs.[30] It requires salespeople to have "an 'allocentric' orientation: they must look at the world through others' eyes and see what others value and how they 'frame' their choices. They must elicit information unthreateningly, listen without a confirmation bias, and be sensitive to the unspoken, to body language and nonverbal cues."[31]

Marcia Radosevich recalls what she learned before cofounding a software company, Health Payment Review. After leaving an academic job at Yale and before co-founding her business, Radosevich (a sociologist) had worked for two entrepreneurs who taught her what selling was about:

> I had imagined salespeople to be slick, fast-talkers. These guys never raised their voices. They were smart, unassuming, and their egos didn't get in the way. Clients would sometimes say to them, "Here's the language I want in the contract," and it would be totally unacceptable. They'd never say "No," they'd say, "Let me understand your concern. What's the problem you are trying to solve?"[32]

Serial entrepreneur Deaver Brown similarly advises,

> You must concentrate on what your buyers say, not what you want to say. If they say they need something, my big word is "yes." You never argue with them. Find out what they need and then give it to them. Agreeing with the buyer is not a sign of weakness.
>
> Objections are a buy sign. Until they hit you with an elbow, they're not interested. If they're polite, you've got nowhere. When they start to ask you questions that sound hostile or tough, it's because they want to find out if you're for real. When somebody says, "Your product is lousy, your price is too high, and they're not sure about you," that's the beginning of a good relationship because they're being honest with you. The buyer wants to find out in this honeymoon period how you will respond after you're married.[33]

But What about Stories? Entrepreneurial discourse is a "many splendored thing."[34] It serves multiple ends (see the previous chapter). Its means include imaginative details, evocative metaphors, and theatrical presentation to

280 UNCERTAINTY AND ENTERPRISE

compensate for missing information. Such means might suggest that entrepreneurial pitches are stories (or narratives, if you prefer). Entrepreneurs who emphasize the importance of storytelling and call themselves storytellers reinforce the impression. Richard Branson asserts, "If you want to succeed as an entrepreneur, you also have to be a storyteller."[35] Similarly, Anita Roddick, cofounder of the Body Shop, claims that "every entrepreneur is a great storyteller. It is storytelling that defines your differences."[36]

The next chapter lays out my reservations about this seemingly indisputable truism.

20
Stories as Side Dishes

As Aristotle requires of any plot, the arc of this chapter has a beginning, a middle, and an end. It starts happily: Like others, I am enthusiastic about entrepreneurial stories, but without clearly understanding their function and form. Reading Bruner's and other scholars' writing about narrative then produces a troubling Aristotelean reversal: Bruner's clarity produces doubts about the centrality of stories in entrepreneurial proposals and plans. Eventually, I find a resolution: while entrepreneurial proposals and plans do not constitute stories as Bruner defines them, they can indirectly reduce doubts about the prospects of entrepreneurial initiatives.

Accordingly, the main sections of this chapter describe

- Why I should have questioned conventional views about entrepreneurial stories—but didn't.

- How Bruner's austere definition of stories produced doubts about their centrality in entrepreneurial proposals and plans.

- "Side" stories that support the uncertainty-reducing aims of entrepreneurial discourse (examined in chapter 18).

1. Conventional Views

As mentioned, economists usually avoid analyzing discourse, including stories, but other researchers have taken storytelling on board. Their research endorses Richard Branson's and Anita Roddick's assertions that "successful entrepreneurs are great storytellers"[1] and that "effectively constructed stories . . . help entrepreneurs acquire the money they need to exploit identified opportunities."[2]

My longtime enthusiasm for stories predisposed me to accept this view. As I now realize, my teaching, research, and writing have always followed Bruner's "narrative mode." My doctoral dissertation examined stories of hostile takeovers. I then wrote and taught case studies—essentially stories—on entrepreneurs. I required my students to write up critical histories of successful entrepreneurial ventures.[3] My previous books analyzed stories gleaned from interviews.

Uncertainty and Enterprise. Amar Bhidé, Oxford University Press. © Oxford University Press 2025.
DOI: 10.1093/oso/9780197688359.003.0020

282 UNCERTAINTY AND ENTERPRISE

My current project on medical innovation involves writing and teaching case histories—again stories—of transformational advances.

The business press regularly publishes stories on effective storytelling. The cover of the November–December 2023 issue of the *Harvard Business Review* features its lead article, "Storytelling That Drives Bold Change,"[4] coauthored by an HBS professor, Frances Frei. The editor in chief's introduction to the issue (highlighting the cover article) advises *HBR* readers, "Fewer slides, and more stories!"[5]

But what, really, is a story? In my zeal for storytelling, I had ignored the Through the Looking Glass problem when Humpty Dumpty scornfully tells Alice, "When I use a word, it means just what I choose it to mean—neither more nor less." Alice then questions "whether you CAN make words mean so many different things." Similarly, might claims that "stories are an integral part of the process by which founders construct new ventures"[6] merely assume that any colorful or imaginative utterance is a "story"?

Some scholars had identified the definitional problem. Twenty years ago, organizational theorist Yiannis Gabriel observed, "Current interest in organizational storytelling and narrative is part of a broader . . . emphasis on language, scripts, metaphors, talk, stories and narratives."[7] But the meanings of the key terms, narrative, and stories have "multiplied, merged and demerged, overlapped and fragmented. Attempts to order or police their usage through definitions have not been very successful."[8]

Specification Problems

Tzvetan Todorov, a French-Bulgarian literary theorist, coined the term "narratology" in 1969.[9] The field then flourished and fragmented, with no agreement even on the term "narrative." The fourth edition of *Introduction to Narrative* calls narratology the study of the "ensemble of theories of narratives, narrative texts, images, spectacles—of cultural artifacts that tell a story"—but does not define "narrative."[10]

Attempting to cover a "prodigious variety" of narrative genres,[11] *The Cambridge Introduction to Narrative* (third edition) offers a minimalist "inclusive" definition of narrative as the *"representation of an event or a series of events."* Thus, "My dog has fleas" is a description, not a narrative. But saying, "My dog was bitten by a flea," is narrative because "it tells of an event. The event is a very small one—the bite of a flea—but that is enough to make it a narrative."[12] The *Introduction* acknowledges that other scholars use different definitions of narrative and that its use deviates from the everyday practice of treating narrative and stories as synonyms.

STORIES AS SIDE DISHES   283

Scholars now also use "narrative" for specialized purposes. Thus, Kay and King write about "reference narratives," and University College London psychoanalyst David Tuckett about "conviction narratives."[13] A "Narrative Science Project" at the London School of Economics calls narrative a "general purpose technology" used to express scientific knowledge.[14] The specialized framings often do not mention "events," and none felt right for my analysis of entrepreneurial storytelling. Attempting to distill any meaning from popular usage also seemed futile. "Narrative" is now routinely used to label any widely held belief. For example, "deflation narratives," "racist narratives," or "disinformation narratives" are used as slogans to warn about some dysfunctional possibility.

2. Eye-Opening Specification

Minimal Requirements I did not want to concoct a definition of stories and narratives to suit my purposes. Fortunately, Bruner's work provided a clear specification that combined careful scholarship, his law school teaching, and everyday experience.

Austere Specification

In *Minding the Law* (2000), Amsterdam and Bruner provide the following "austere" definition of narrative as needing "*a cast of human-like characters, beings capable of willing their own actions, forming intentions, holding beliefs, having feelings.*" Narrative "also needs a plot with a beginning, a middle, and an end, in which particular characters are involved in particular events."[15]

Plots, in turn, require "1) an initial *steady state* grounded in the legitimate ordinariness of things, 2) that gets disrupted by a *Trouble* consisting of circumstances attributable to human agency or susceptible to change by human intervention, 3) in turn evoking *efforts* at redress or transformation, which succeed or fail, so that 4) the old steady state is *restored* or a new (*transformed*) steady state is created, and 5) the story concludes . . . through some *coda*—say, for example, Aesop's characteristic *moral of the story*."[16]

More could be added to this "bare bones" outline, write Amsterdam and Bruner, but "not without getting into quarrels with some narratologist or the other."[17]

284   UNCERTAINTY AND ENTERPRISE

In his subsequent *Making Stories* (2002), Bruner offers a similar but chattier summary:

> Everyone will agree that [a story] requires a cast of characters who are free agents with minds of their own. Given a moment to think about it, they'll also agree that these characters have recognizable expectations about the ordinary state of the world, the story's world, though these expectations may be somewhat enigmatic. And again, with a moment's thought, everybody agrees that a story begins with some breach in the expected state of things—Aristotle's peripeteia. Something goes awry, otherwise there's nothing to tell about. The story concerns efforts to cope or come to terms with the breach and its consequences. And finally there is an outcome, some sort of resolution.[18]

Then, citing the literary theorist Kenneth Burke (1897–1993),[19] *Making Stories* offers an even more concise specification. A fictional or actual story must have a dramatic Pentad: an "Agent who performs an Action to achieve a Goal in a recognizable Setting by the use of certain Means." A "misfit between Agent and Action, Goal and Setting" or any of the five elements of the Pentad produces Trouble with a capital T, akin to Aristotle's peripeteia. And without Trouble (or peripeteia), there is no story.[20]

Troubling Gap   Though not as terse as "Fleas bit my dog," Bruner's minimalist specification provided a refreshing antidote to the impenetrable verbosity of some narratologists and glib popular assertions about the power of storytelling. Yet I also found the specification unsettling: it crushed my hopes of establishing the centrality of stories in entrepreneurial pitches and plans.

True, unlike logico-scientific discourse, entrepreneurial discourse has a narrative purpose: to reduce doubts by making an imagined world plausible (chapter 18). Most entrepreneurs I have known (interviewees, case-study protagonists, friends, and my father) have been engaging storytellers. As mentioned in the previous chapter, promoters of entrepreneurial initiatives use evocative language and sometimes put on a carefully rehearsed, theatrical show. And, their pitches satisfy some key story requirements: they feature human agents with intentions and beliefs and envision a sequence of events with a beginning and an end.

But there is a critical gap: the envisioned sequence flows smoothly to a happy conclusion. Narrative, in contrast, according to Bruner (using narrative as a synonym for story), "is a recounting of human plans gone off the track, expectations gone awry. It is a way to domesticate human error and surprise." But confident entrepreneurial pitches, however theatrical (think Steve Jobs), exclude error. They have no Burkean Trouble, no Aristotelean reversal of fortune, and thus no efforts at restoration or redress. There is no "shape" or "arc" to the story, no "beats" to the script. Business proposals may enumerate risks and contingency measures—but by the very fact of their anticipation, they are not "expectations gone awry."

Thanks to Bruner's generally pro-story analysis, my intended story about entrepreneurial stories was in deep Trouble. Yet I could not accept that I had naively fallen for the prevailing fashion for storytelling—my enthusiasm for stories was much older. Then, upon reflection, I found a new "steady state" that allowed me to retain stories as supporting actors, though not the stars, of entrepreneurial discourse. This resolution came from recognizing the difference between *stories* of what has already happened and *proposals* for making things happen in the future.

Of the two critical conditions (now italicized) in Bruner's specification above—*recounting* of human *plans gone off the track*—I had entirely missed the first, though I was dimly aware of the second. I knew through my case writing and teaching that engaging cases require surprising Troubles and turning points. After reading Bruner I realized that because entrepreneurial proposals try to anticipate unpleasant surprises they don't have turning points. But what's a story without a turning point?

Reading Bruner spurred another slap on the forehead realization: pitches and proposals are a foretold *chronique* or *annale* of anticipated events whereas stories *recount* resolving Troubles. Only after protagonists attempt their proposed schemes and confront surprising setbacks can they tell a bona fide Brunerian story.

Take a striking nonbusiness example: the Allies' plans for the invasion of Normandy did not constitute a story in the ordinary sense. In 1959, Cornelius Ryan reprised the invasion in *The Longest Day: June 6, 1944*.[21] Darryl F. Zanuck made Ryan's book into a movie released by 20th Century Fox in 1962. The movie, unlike the invasion plan, was unquestionably an epic drama. A *New York Times* review said that "All of the massive organization of that most salient invasion of World War II, all the hardship and bloodiness of it, all the courage and sacrifice involved, are strongly and stalwartly suggested in the mighty mosaic of episodes and battle-action details that are packed into this film." The "total effect" was of "a huge documentary report, adorned and colored by personal details that are thrilling, amusing, ironic, sad. . . . It is hard to think of a picture, aimed and constructed as this one was, doing any more or any better or leaving one feeling any more exposed to the horror of war as this one does."[22]

286 UNCERTAINTY AND ENTERPRISE

Even cocktail-party storytellers meet Bruner's two conditions—they recount (sometimes embroidered) anecdotes of some unexpected occurrence or event. Richard Branson's wearing of a wedding dress (to help launch Virgin Brides) or a stewardess's outfit (on an inaugural Virgin Airways flight) becomes a story *after* the deed is done and because of its unexpectedness. And business biographies and memoirs are engaging and plausible because they recount ups and downs.

Recounted deviations constitute the core of fiction, regardless of genre. "Once upon a time" is a stock opening for fairy tales—and futuristic sci-fi. Lucas's Star Wars movies open with, in blue text, "A long time ago in a galaxy far, far away . . . ," against a black sky background, with a few stars. Moreover, the recounting must combine the expected and the surprising. The heroes of Greek tragedies must suffer a pity-and-fear-evoking downfall. Even romantic comedies with happy, upbeat ends require things to go wrong first. Similarly, the brilliant detective of murder mysteries follows false trails before triumphantly solving the crime.

Legal stories, told before a court of law, likewise focus on some past deviation from lawful conduct. They tell, writes Bruner, "about some act that is alleged by one party to have been committed by the other, an act that did damage to the accuser and that was in violation of a statute prohibiting such acts. The other party's story seeks to rebut the accusation by presenting another version of what happened or by claiming that the act in question neither harmed the accuser nor violated a statute."[23] Witnesses are like actors in a staged drama, and adversary lawyers match their witnesses against each other.[24] And "like stories generally . . . law stories involve a subtle comparison of what was expected and what actually happened. The discrepancy between the two is then judged by criteria derived from statute and precedent."[25]

Resolution Although my rethinking put stories recounting Troubles outside the core content of forward-looking proposals and pitches, it also found ways in which Brunerian stories support uncertainty-reducing discourse. Although not the entrées of pitches and plans, stories can be valuable side dishes. And these side dishes may be stories cooked up and served by promoters to reduce the uncertainty of their initiatives. Or, to jumble metaphors, the stories may be a "free lunch" told by or about previous entrepreneurs and ventures.

I defer these free lunch stories to the next chapter. In the remainder of this chapter, I analyze three common side dish stories: (1) origin stories, about the background and motivations of promoters; (2) stories about overcoming unforeseen challenges; and (3) stories about incidents that shape organizational cultures.

3. Common Side Dish Stories

Origin Stories Except in their short, preliminary elevator pitches, promoters often start presentations to investors with human interest stories about their life histories and the reasons for starting their ventures. These stories are usually more interesting than the details about markets, competitors, and technologies. As mentioned, listeners may ignore details if speakers don't get their attention and interest first. Therefore, promoters often serve origin stories as spicy appetizers to the blander (nonstory) main courses of their investor or customer pitches.

Attention-Getting Pitches

Origin stories—"Who are you and why are you doing this?"—are staples of "pitch contests," especially those staged for TV viewers, like *Shark Tank*. They can also help entrepreneurs raise capital from professional investors. For example, a venture capitalist pitched by the founder of Kavak, an online platform for secondhand car sales in Latin America, recalls,

> The founder started by letting you know his dad was a Venezuelan general who had escorted Chavez from the presidential palace during the failed coup of 2002—this is a data point you are unlikely to forget. Then he would tell you about how his dad was a military attaché at several Venezuelan embassies around the world. They had to move a lot, and buying and selling cars was always a problem. He wanted to help people avoid that harrowing experience. The story helped the company raise over $4 billion between 2016 and 2022. Investors included celebrated names: Founders Fund, General Atlantic, Tiger Global, SoftBank, Ribbit Capital, and General Catalyst.[26]

(I would not discount the influence of the manic period, described in the next chapter, during which Kavak raised capital. In such times, emotional origin stories can overshadow substantive details.)

Besides attention, origin stories, more than the bald facts on curriculum vitae (CVs), can help reduce uncertainties about whether the promoters have the tenacity and resourcefulness to overcome unforeseen problems. By themselves, the information on LinkedIn profiles and CVs don't say much about whether the founder has the right stuff. Stories about personal experiences also help make business ideas that cannot satisfy logico-scientific verification standards seem plausible. A typical tale, of starting a business after failing to find something the

288 UNCERTAINTY AND ENTERPRISE

founder wanted, isn't just an engaging anecdote. It suggests the need for a new offering that systematic market research cannot validate.

The value of the origin stories can go far beyond their contribution to initial fundraising. For example, Microsoft's startup tale has become computer-industry folklore. In December 1974, Paul Allen visited his high school friend Bill Gates, then a sophomore at Harvard. He spotted an issue of *Popular Electronics* featuring the Altair 8080—the first-ever personal computer—on the cover at a kiosk in Harvard Square. "I bought a copy, read it, and raced back to Bill's dorm to talk to him," Allen recalled. "I told Bill, 'Well, here's our opportunity to do something with BASIC.'"[27] Allen and Gates did not write a business plan; they immediately started working on a BASIC version for the Altair. Gates writes that they "were like the characters in those Judy Garland and Mickey Rooney movies: 'Let's put on a show in the barn!' We thought there was no time to waste, and we set right to it." Gates and Allen "didn't sleep much and lost track of night and day" in order to complete their BASIC in four weeks.[28]

Certainly, the longevity of its origin story owes much to the subsequent success of Microsoft. Suppose Microsoft had not become a multitrillion-dollar market-value enterprise. Who would care how it started half a century ago? Likewise, Richard Branson's struggles with dyslexia and ending his formal education at age sixteen are memorable because of his subsequent accomplishments. At the same time, catchy origin stories can contribute to continued success, creating an enduring mystique that helps attract capital, customers, and other resource providers long after the startup stage.

Recognizing the advantages, founders often go all-out to create heroes' journey legends about their backgrounds and motivations. They may spread their stories through media interviews, blogs, TED talks, and social media. They encourage biographers and publish memoirs. They may even help professors write case studies.

Hero's Journeys

A business school classmate who had become a health care VC once encouraged me to write a case study on Physicians Sales & Service (PSS), a Florida-based medical supplies distributor my classmate had invested in. Its founder and CEO, Patrick Kelly, was charismatic, told engaging stories, and was keen on having an HBS case study written. And sure enough, Kelly flew up with his executive team on the PSS corporate jet to be interviewed for the case. I also discovered the PSS CEO had been much written about in the business and Florida press.

Four years after I wrote the PSS case, Kelly published a memoir, *Faster Company: Building the World's Nuttiest Turn-on-a-Dime Home-Grown Billion-Dollar Business*. The dust jacket described Kelly as the founder of "one of the fastest growing companies in the history of the medical supply industry."[29] Kelly's book recounted how his mother had placed him, the third of her three children, in the Virginia Home for Boys because she couldn't cope. She worked two or three low-paid jobs; her husband had left her after the birth of their third child.

The Home did not usually take boys until they were eight. But a local pastor had helped Kelly's mother find a place when her son was just five, making him the "youngest—and the scrawniest" ever to live there.

"When you start a company," Kelly writes, "the only issue you care about is whether you'll survive. When I first got to the Boys' Home, that was pretty much the only issue I cared about, too.

"I was a little red-faced Irish kid a good 20 or 30 pounds lighter than the next smallest resident of the home. And boys being boys, I took a pounding." At some point, Kelly decided to fight back. Fists weren't much use against bigger kids, so anytime a kid picked a fight with him, Kelly would "wrap my arms around him as best I could. Then I would sink my teeth into whatever part of his body was handiest. And keep them there." The kids howled, and Kelly "probably got beaten up worse than I would have otherwise. But pretty soon word got around: You can beat that kid up, but he'll make you pay. Those bites hurt. And bit by bit, they stopped beating me up." So "when I decided to sink my teeth into starting a company, I wasn't planning on giving up any too easily."[30]

Kelly left the Home after thirteen years, age eighteen. He then flunked out of Virginia Commonwealth University (VCU) and became a draftee in the Vietnam War. His experience made him an adult with self-esteem. "The army had encouraged me to learn and take responsibility. They had trusted me to do what needed to be done, and had backed me up (at least most of the time)." The experience, writes Kelly, inspired him to build a company whose people would "think and act as if they were in charge" and "make decisions with the company's best interest at heart."[31]

Returning from Vietnam, Kelly reenrolled at VCU and completed a four-year premed degree in two and a half years, with almost straight As and dean's list recognition every semester. After graduation, Kelly worked for two medical products distributors. Here, he learned how to sell—and what opportunities existing distributors were missing by failing to provide high-quality services to physicians. He used both lessons in the business he then started.

290   UNCERTAINTY AND ENTERPRISE

Kelly's personal history is arresting, and he tells it with many codas. The history also depicts a tenacious, determined, and inspiring individual who will get things done, no matter what.

Fred Smith, founder of Federal Express, is another entrepreneur with Vietnam War combat experience. Unlike Kelly, he came from a wealthy family, attended a prep school, and then college at Yale. Although he did not flunk out, Smith was a "crummy student"[32] in college. He graduated with a B-minus average, including a now famous C for a term paper describing a rudimentary version of FedEx's overnight delivery service.[33]

Smith enrolled in the US Marine Corps platoon leaders' program at Yale. After graduation, he was commissioned as a second lieutenant in the Marine Corps and sent into active duty in Vietnam. By the time Smith was discharged, he had attained the rank of captain and been awarded the Silver Star, Bronze Star, two Purple Hearts, the Navy Commendation medal, and the Vietnamese Cross of Gallantry.

Back from Vietnam in 1969, Smith used an inheritance and trust funds to purchase a controlling interest in a struggling Little Rock company, which he turned into an "aggressive business buying and selling used corporate jets." Less than two years later, when the twenty-something Smith approached bankers to start FedEx, the bankers saw a "bright, handsome, wealthy, self-confident, battle-decorated leader."[34] By 1983, after FedEx had become a billion-dollar corporation, his biographer wrote, "Smith *is* Federal Express. He is as well known as the company. Most of the rank and file employees believe it; security analysts believe it; the competition believes it; and certainly Fred Smith appears to believe it."[35] A "loyal and talented group of senior officers and managers . . . willingly accepted a secondary role when the publicity started flooding the media about Fred Smith and *his* Federal Express."[36]

The entrepreneur in my third example of a high-profile origin story, John Crowley, did not serve in Vietnam or start a billion-dollar business. Crowley was a healthcare litigation attorney before attending HBS and joined a small strategy consulting firm after his MBA. Yet Crowley and his biotech startup repeatedly made the front pages of the national press. A book about Crowley (*The Cure: How a Father Raised $100 Million—and Bucked the Medical Establishment—in a Quest to Save His Children*) inspired a movie, *Extraordinary Measures*, starring Harrison Ford and Brendan Fraser (who played Crowley).

What Crowley did was indeed extraordinary. His daughter and son were born with the rare and life-threatening Pompe disease. After starting a nonprofit organization to fund Pompe disease research, Crowley cofounded and invested his life savings in an Oklahoma venture to develop a treatment.

In March 2000, he moved to Oklahoma to become CEO of the company (renamed Novazyme) and raised $8 million in venture funding in just a few months.[37]

The following year, Crowley negotiated the sale of Novazyme to Genzyme Corporation, then the world's third-largest biotechnology company. Crowley joined Genzyme after the sale and took charge of its Pompe program. The program produced an enzyme replacement therapy that Crowley's children received in January 2003. The treatment stabilized the children's condition but wasn't a cure. His continued search for a cure prompted Crowley to co-found another biotech, Amicus, to work on Pompe and other rare diseases.[38]

Founders who don't have stirring personal stories make do with what they can. For example, Blueground has become the global leader in renting furnished apartments for over a month. In 2023, it managed fifteen thousand apartments in twenty-seven cities worldwide. According to a VC who invested in Blueground, its founder's pitch started with the following story: He (the founder) had been a consultant who had to travel a lot and stay in hotel rooms for several months because landlords wouldn't trust him. He then thought of starting a business to rent apartments for a year and sublet them for shorter periods.[39] Not quite having children with a rare disease. Nevertheless, a personal story exemplifying the want helped provide plausibility to the founder's pitch.

Recovery Stories Events often diverge from initial hopes and plans. As mentioned in chapter 14, about a third of the *Inc.* founders I interviewed significantly altered their initial business ideas. In the now-fashionable term, they "pivoted." Even when promoters stick to their basic strategies, execution difficulties may force changes in their implementation. Or unexpected external changes may demand significant alterations in what had initially worked.

Some entrepreneurs and organizations hide the changes. They fear that admitting that publicizing failures could compromise their credibility. "Microsoft watchers often cite the phrase 'the third time's the charm' in explaining how long it takes the company to turn a not-so-great first version of a product into something fairly solid," writes MaryJo Foley, a longtime Microsoft watcher.[40] For example, Microsoft released its first graphical user interface operating system, Windows 1.0, in November 1985 to compete against Apple's Lisa (released in January 1983). But Windows 1.0 was no match. Windows 2.0, released in October 1987, was more popular but was still considered inadequate. Then, finally, Windows 3.0, released in 1990, achieved commercial success, selling two million copies in the first six months.[41]

292   UNCERTAINTY AND ENTERPRISE

But Microsoft does not promote these "third time's the charm" stories. Possibly, the company may think the failure of the 1.0 versions is embarrassing. And might not publicizing such stories encourage buyers to wait for the third, good version?

Other entrepreneurs and companies, however, advertise their recoveries and rebounds. As mentioned, backstories of overcoming personal early challenges (Kelly's upbringing in a Boy's Home, Richard Branson's dyslexia) can help attract attention and establish personas of determination and resilience. Likewise with recoveries from unexpected challenges: recovery stories attract attention—the public and the media love tales of turnarounds. Recovery stories can also establish reputations of doggedness and resourcefulness and thus the confidence that when unforeseen challenges appear, the entrepreneur will somehow overcome them. Therefore, instead of hiding their setbacks, promoters tell stories of how they coped—usually, but not always, successfully.

Resourceful Recoveries

Patrick Kelly's memoir (and my case study on PSS) describe how Kelly and his team faced and neutralized an existential crisis triggered by the Clinton administration's proposals to slash healthcare costs.

Kelly recalls that in its first ten years, PSS "occupied a clearly defined niche," offering "fast, no-hassle service." Its salespeople developed personal relationships with their customers, helped solve their problems, and got them what they needed in twenty-four hours or less. PSS's costs and prices were also higher, "but it didn't seem to matter. Enough physicians valued our service that we were able to grow rapidly. We were the Mercedes of our industry, and we took pride in that fact. We didn't try to compete on price, any more than Mercedes does."[42]

Then, the Clinton administration's healthcare proposals shocked PSS. Soon, "every healthcare provider and institution in the country was nervous."[43] And customers "weren't looking to buy a Mercedes anymore, they wanted a Chevrolet. And those sales reps that they were so fond of? If the reps couldn't give them cheap product, those reps were history."[44]

"We had to change fast; and we had to change dramatically."[45]

Fortunately, PSS had "become one of the largest players in the marketplace, so we had some clout with our suppliers." The company immediately lowered prices by 20 percent on its top one hundred items, consolidated product lines, negotiated price breaks from vendors, began offering low-cost private-label products, and established a buying club that promised physicians steep price breaks if they bought most of their supplies from PSS.[46]

PSS's salespeople "howled," Kelly writes. "We had preached for ten years that PSS was the Mercedes of the industry.... Now we were saying the exact opposite. Worse still, we were threatening their incomes. Commissioned salespeople like price cuts about as much as politicians like term limits."[47]

In the next three months, after PSS's CEO and its other top executives had visited every branch to explain the new strategy, "salespeople came around." No one left, though "competitors were wooing the best of them all the time."[48] And price cuts increased PSS's market share and the utilization of its infrastructure. Soon, the incomes of the salespeople were higher than before: "The customer was buying more product from PSS reps and was more dependent than ever on the value those reps could provide."[49]

As with his origin stories, Kelly provides a lesson (a "coda" in Bruner's list of story requirements) to his "recovery from a crisis" tale. It was a "dramatic example of how the marketplace can change on you in a heartbeat.... If you think you can build a company around delivering only one kind of value to a customer—if you think you'll never have to change, you're making a big mistake." And the task "isn't just knowing when to change, it's creating a company that *can* change."[50] An unstated implication of the lesson: PSS had become such an enterprise—one that could, as in the title of Kelly's book, "turn on a dime."

In addition to his PR stunts (mentioned in the previous chapter), James Dyson has long used stories about adversity and supposed "failures" to get attention. Dyson's eponymous company, best known for its revolutionary cyclonic ("bagless") vacuum cleaner, now develops and sells several other appliances such as air purifiers, hand dryers, bladeless fans, heaters, and hair dryers. Like its vacuum cleaner, the appliances are technologically groundbreaking—and expensive. This poses uncertainties for consumers: Will the innovative products work—and justify their high prices?

Dyson likes using media coverage to reassure consumers (and get their attention). In *Invention: A Life* (his 2021 memoir), Dyson writes, "Word of mouth and editorial remain the best way to tell people what you have done. It is far more believable than advertising and a real compliment when intelligent journalists want to go off and talk about your product of their own free will. If you have new technology and a new product, a journalist's opinion and comment is far more important and believable than an advertisement."[51]

Dyson uses stories with dogged or ingenious responses to Troubles to get the attention of journalists. His memoir recounts the troubles his company faced in promoting the baglessness of its vacuum cleaners in Belgium: "Belgium had tight comparative advertising laws and our European competitors ganged up to sue us, arguing that we shouldn't say that we didn't have a bag as this gave Dyson a comparative advantage. While this seems absurd, the court found us guilty." Banned from talking about vacuum cleaner bags, the Dyson company produced an advertisement "with the word 'bagless' blanked out repeatedly and a line that read, 'Sorry, but the Belgian court won't let you know what everyone has a right to know.' This got the media interested. We were able to tell them the story of how European manufacturers, as a group, were trying to silence competition."[52]

Dyson also repeats stories about "failure." After closing a new line of contra-rotating washing machines, Dyson told *Bloomberg Business Week* that he had "really enjoyed getting into washing machines and understanding how to make them better," but "we didn't make any money on it." A "huge amount" of what his company did, said Dyson, was "wasted because it doesn't work or it's the wrong direction or whatever. That's the nature of being an engineer. That's the nature of R&D. We spend $2.5 million a week on R&D, and a lot of it is failure."[53]

The first sentence in Dyson's 2021 memoir mentions 5,126 failed handmade prototypes of his pioneering vacuum cleaner before he made one that worked to his satisfaction. "Failure" or "fail" appear more than fifty times in Dyson's book.[54] But while some of Dyson's tales recount truly failed initiatives (like the washing machine), others are about recovering from setbacks. His 5,127th vacuum prototype did, in fact, succeed. And as he once told an interviewer, "I have always found that the very moment you're ready to give up, that if you go on a little longer, you end up finding what you're looking for. It's one of life's rewards for perseverance."[55]

Without scandalous wrongdoing (as in the Theranos case) or ruinous loss (as in the WeWork wipeout), outright failures are less interesting—and less helpful in getting attention or inspiring confidence—than recovering from Troubles. Legend has it that a spider in a cave where the Scottish leader, Robert the Bruce, had taken refuge after repeated losses against English armies inspired Bruce's successful comeback. The dejected Scot saw the spider spin its web after repeatedly falling. Imagine if the persistent spider had never succeeded and Bruce had given up. What story would there be to tell?

Corporate Culture Stories As mentioned, the discourse of planning and plans produced by this discourse help control the alignment uncertainties of complex initiatives. Yet planning isn't storytelling, and plans aren't stories that recount Troubles and their resolutions. However, recounted stories can also help control alignment uncertainties through their influence on organizational cultures.

STORIES AS SIDE DISHES   295

MIT organizational psychologist Edgar Schein offered a now-classic definition of culture in his 1985 book as a "pattern of basic assumptions—invented, discovered, or developed by a given group as it learns to cope with its problems of external adaptation and internal integration—that has worked well enough to be considered valid and, therefore, to be taught to new members as the correct way to perceive, think, and feel in relation to those problems."[56] And, with strongly held assumptions, members of a group "would find behavior based on any other premise inconceivable."[57]

An earlier (1982) book by organizational consultants Terence Deal and Allen Kennedy defined organizational culture simply as "the way things get done around here."[58]

In either specification, cultures can promote coordinated effort and reduce alignment uncertainties. A culture that values and fosters cooperation encourages members of specialized teams to look out for each other. Star-centric cultures do not. Similarly, what is strongly valued—if anything—will affect how members of the organization will reflexively behave and expect each other to behave. In cultures that emphasize customer service (or safety, or low costs, or cutting-edge technology, etc.), that's what everyone, regardless of their function or training, will tend to prioritize. This common orientation also helps reduce alignment uncertainties and coordination problems.

As Deal and Kennedy make clear, stories shape organizational cultures. In some cases, the organization's leaders deliberately tell and retell stories designed to influence the "basic assumptions" of its members. By repeating stories of initiatives undertaken by frontline employees, PSS's Kelly promoted an ethos of "every man and woman a CEO."[59] Sam Walton's penny-pinching stories similarly shaped Walmart's culture of frugality. In other cases, the organization's leaders may not tell all its culture-shaping stories. Rank-and-file employees may also create and propagate stories that reflect and reinforce the organization's culture.

Google's Aristotle Project

In a 2016 *New York Times* article, later expanded into a book, Charles Duhigg reported, "Five years ago, Google—one of the most public proselytizers of how studying workers can transform productivity—became focused on building the perfect team.... The company's top executives long believed that building the best teams meant combining the best people. They embraced other bits of conventional wisdom as well, like 'It's better to put introverts together,' said Abeer Dubey, a manager in Google's People Analytics division, or 'Teams are more effective when everyone is friends away from work.' But Dubey went on, 'It turned out no one had really studied which of those were true.'"[60]

In 2012, Google started a project—code-named Aristotle and led by Dubey—to "study hundreds of Google's teams and figure out why some stumbled while others soared." Dubey "gathered some of the company's best statisticians, organizational psychologists, sociologists, and engineers." After reviewing half a century of academic studies, Project Aristotle's researchers scrutinized the composition of groups inside Google. But they could not find any evidence that team composition mattered. "We looked at 180 teams from all over the company," Dubey told the *Times* reporter. "We had lots of data, but there was nothing showing that a mix of specific personality types or skills or backgrounds made any difference." Two teams might have nearly identical compositions but very different levels of effectiveness. "At Google, we're good at finding patterns," Dubey said. "There weren't strong patterns here."[61]

The Aristotle team turned to psychology and sociology research on group norms—"the traditions, behavioral standards and unwritten rules that govern how we function when we gather." They then identified several norms—instances of behavior described as an "unwritten rule" or part of the "team's culture"—in the data they had collected. Some teams reported constant interruptions in meetings, with the example set by the team leader. Other team leaders discouraged interruptions. Some teams began meetings with chit-chat while others got right to business.[62]

After studying over a hundred groups, Project Aristotle researchers concluded that "influencing group norms were the keys to improving Google's teams." But which norms? Again, the data did not show clear patterns. Returning to academic papers, the Google researchers found that "everything fell into place" through the concept of "psychological safety"[63]—the acceptance of interpersonal risk-taking within teams.[64] The data "indicated that psychological safety, more than anything else, was critical to making a team work."[65]

In late 2014, the Aristotle team began sharing their findings with other Google employees. They hadn't yet figured out how to make psychological safety easy and hoped their colleagues could help.[66] Using the feedback of colleagues, the Aristotle team produced a guide with "actionable tips" to help managers "reinforce psychological safety on their teams."[67]

The *New York Times* article received wide publicity. Google also posted an account of Project Aristotle, with links to the psychological safety guide, on its website re:Work.[68]

Note that (1) the *New York Times* article and Google's re:Work post tell bona fide stories, with human intentions, Troubles ("couldn't find patterns in the data, didn't know how to promote psychological safety"), and ultimately their resolution (guide produced); (2) mid-level employees in the Analytics

Division, not top executives, created and spread the story; (3) the story reflects and reinforces Google's espoused norms: caring about employees, teamwork, relying on data-and-scientific research, and public-mindedness—offering the results of Project Aristotle to the world.

To summarize: origin stories, bounceback stories, and organizational culture stories can supplement the pitches and proposals that themselves lack the critical elements of a bona fide story. But the side stories do not create or tell themselves. Promoters must decide what to include and exclude, come up with a catchy ending ("coda"), and then refine and possibly embellish the plot. This requires effort. It also takes effort to spread these stories by telling them repeatedly and persuading the media to share them. Side stories are not a free resource. But promoters can also benefit without much effort from stories told by and about other entrepreneurs and ventures, as we see in the next chapter.

21

Spillovers from Popular Stories

Our collective inheritance of intangible public goods or social spillovers includes literature and the body of law created by previous generations of writers and jurists. In this chapter, and the last on imaginative discourse, I show how past entrepreneurial stories can similarly help present-day promoters reduce the perceived uncertainty of their ventures.[1]

As in earlier chapters, I return to Bruner's narrative project, drawing extensively from *Making Stories* (2002) as a starting point. Specifically, the following three sections analyze

- Spillovers from literary and legal stories.

- Stories told by and about entrepreneurs and their ventures—and drawing on literary and legal parallels—the spillovers from these stories.

- Why popular entrepreneurial stories are more dynamic—why they come and go more quickly than the canonical stories in literature and the law.

The chapter concludes by examining changes in the kinds of initiatives businesses undertake—and the knock-on effects on their discourse.

1. Literary and Legal Stories

Three Gifts Bruner's discourse—offered in the narrative, not the logico-scientific mode—invites personal interpretations. Here is my take on Bruner's propositions about spillovers from stories that have become part of the accepted canon in literature and the law.

— *Sensemaking.* Stories that become part of the accepted canon, Bruner writes are an "invitation" to "see the world as embodied in the story."[2] They help us "create meaning," so our perceptions of Life imitate prior Art. "We say of people we know in real life that they are Micawbers or characters right out of a Thomas Wolfe novel." By shaping our perceptions of how things are, stories also influence our expectations of future possibilities.[3] We expect a Micawber-like person to behave like the optimistic, kindhearted Micawber character in *David Copperfield.*

Story-based sensemaking protects us from existential angst, the torment of living in a meaningless universe. We want a coherent account of what is going

Uncertainty and Enterprise. Amar Bhidé, Oxford University Press. © Oxford University Press 2025.
DOI: 10.1093/oso/9780197688359.003.0021

on—and why. We especially crave sensemaking that gives us agency: we wish to persuade ourselves that doing this, not that, better serves a preferred end. We don't want to be the helpless pawns of pure chance.

Sensemaking has a special value in the law. Shared legal stories are "a matter of great moment," writes Bruner, "for developing a body of law, the *corpus juris*."[4] Enshrined as legal precedents, they shape interpretations of conduct as permissible or unlawful. "Wellwrought" literary stories may also influence legal judgments, writes Bruner. He offers the 1954 Supreme Court decision on school desegregation as an example of "how literature finds its way into the law's *corpus juris*."[5]

From *Plessy* (1896) to *Brown* (1954)

In its 1896 *Plessy v. Ferguson* judgment, the US Supreme Court ruled that providing "separate but equal" railroad cars for traveling blacks and whites satisfied the Constitution's equal protection clause. "If the railroad care standard also held for schools," the plaintiff in *Brown v. Board of Education* (1954) had "no case." The defendant would merely have had to show that "*de jure* segregated black schools were as just well supported materially as white ones."[6]

But, argues Bruner, in the half-century after *Plessy*, there had been an "enormous literary change" through an "inward turn" in narrative:

> Even for separate-but-equal Jim Crow railroad cars, the question had become a subjective one: How did it feel to be shunted into a separate railroad car or sent to the back of the bus? What did it do to one's self-respect and, critically, to one's will to learn and develop? The parallel question regarding schools became, What does segregation do to black children's view of themselves, their self-esteem, their readiness to learn? The landscape of consciousness had become part of the narrative of equal protection.
>
> In the years after *Plessy*, subjective themes of this nature were at the center of powerful (and successful) poetry, plays, and stories written by widely read black authors like Langston Hughes and Richard Wright. Their voices became part of the American literary tradition of consciousness and protest. They had plenty to say about what it felt like to live Jim Crow.
>
> Their voices can be heard in the background of the 1954 Supreme Court opinion that finally overruled the separate-but-equal standard of *Plessy*. The Harlem Renaissance had given equal protection its subjective story— if not in the *corpus juris*, then in the popular imagination. In the *Brown* opinion, that subjectivity is explicitly mentioned, but it had begun to make its presence felt in the appellate litigation that preceded the Supreme Court decision.[7]

300   UNCERTAINTY AND ENTERPRISE

— *Language.* Canonical stories provide the terms and images we use in everyday discourse. Our language relies heavily on evoking likeness through metaphor and figures of speech, often supplied by fiction.[8] Describing conduct as "flying too close to the sun" borrows from the ancient Greek myth of Icarus. A business journalist calling a corporate executive a "gunslinger" takes the metaphor from Wild West movies, not from personally witnessed shootouts.

"Prototypical plights" depicted in narratives "become root metaphors of the human condition–like Sisyphus forever pushing his rock uphill, a root metaphor for self-sustaining frustration," writes Bruner. "Many situations can be assimilated to the image of Sisyphus, even the tenant farmer perpetually in debt to the landlord and forever too poor to buy his plot of land."[9] Similarly, we refer to events, things, and people by metaphors taken from narrative: "Heroes and broken contracts can be referred to only by virtue of their prior existence in a narrative world."[10] Even basic descriptive categories that are not obvious metaphors are often narrative-based.

Narrative Foundations of Categories

Categories are crucial "at every level of language," Bruner observes (in his book *Minding the Law*, written with Amsterdam).[11] Simple description would be impossible without categories that put many possibilities into a single class—the millions of colors our senses can differentiate, reduced to a few dozen color categories.[12] Likewise, "Where there be law, so too must there be categories. For law defines categorically the limits of the permissible or, more often, of the impermissible. Since human imagination cannot conceive of the full variety of possible transgressions, law requires a system of categories to reduce that variety. So an innumerable array of natural and unnatural, potentially harm-wreaking temptations is dealt with under the rubric of 'attractive nuisance.'"[13]

Like our sensemaking, categories are "*made in the mind* and not found in the world"[14] (italics in the original). But they are "almost never constructed arbitrarily. Typically, they are extracted from some larger scale, more encompassing way of looking at things—either from some theory about the world or from a narrative about the human condition and its vicissitudes."[15] Thus, "'Good faith effort' is a category extracted from narrative; so is 'golden opportunity' and 'gutsy kid.' And so are 'willful ignorance' and 'informed consent' and 'malice aforethought.'"[16] Similarly, "Adultery is not defined merely by legal statute; its canonical variants take their life from . . . changing habits of thought—and of storytelling."[17]

SPILLOVERS FROM POPULAR STORIES 301

— *Collective Attitudes.* Canonical stories contain messages that influence collective norms and values. Stories, says Bruner, "always have a message," although that message may be "so well concealed that even the teller knows not what ax he may be grinding."[18]

Since time immemorial, story messages have affirmed conventions of good moral conduct. Ancient Greek myths "were intended as models for virtues and vices."[19] Filial duty is repeated throughout the twenty-four thousand verses of the *Ramayana* (eighth–fourth-century BCE Indian epic). Aesop's fables ended with an explicit "moral of the story."[20] Biblical stories and parables do not spell out their point as clearly (providing opportunities for priests and exegesis scholars to draw out their ethical implications), but they certainly carry ethical messages. Medieval morality plays featured characters who personified virtues and vices and stories of "the temptation, fall and restitution of the protagonist."[21] Modern writers like C. S. Lewis and J. R. R. Tolkien—and numerous lesser hacks—have continued to tell good-versus-evil stories with religious overtones and messages.

In turn, collective conceptions of good and evil shaped by canonical stories influence private discourse. Seemingly individual sensemaking, including causal beliefs—doing x will produce a desired effect y—cannot escape the influence of collective norms. Socially acceptable means and methods restrict the 'x's we naturally contemplate and promote. Moreover advancing views abhorrent to our targeted audiences tends to fail, while conforming to accepted norms increases the potential for agreement-producing dialogue.

Coevolution of Cultures and Stories Influential stories do not always affirm accepted values, however. Great fiction, per Bruner, is often "subversive in spirit"[22] and shows evil in what complacent readers might otherwise take for granted. By exploring "human plights through the prism of imagination,"[23] books like Harper Lee's *To Kill a Mockingbird* awaken a "sense of injustice,"[24] Bruner writes. "*Uncle Tom's Cabin* played as great a part in precipitating the American Civil War as any debate in Congress. Indeed, debates about slavery were banned from the floor of Congress after one of them led to a caning, and this lent the power of rarity to Harriet Beecher Stowe's remarkable novel, setting the travails of slavery in a narrative of suffering responded to by human kindness."[25]

Moreover, cultures often tolerate exceptional storytellers who question prevailing beliefs. Societies somehow accommodate underground writing even under totalitarian regimes. Informers and a harsh security apparatus, not cultural values, repressed *Samizdat* publications in the former Soviet Union. The state, not the culture, imprisoned Aleksandr Solzhenitsyn and then banished him from the USSR.

Therefore although culture is usually "a maker and enforcer of what is expected," Bruner observes, it also "paradoxically, compiles, even slyly treasures,

302 UNCERTAINTY AND ENTERPRISE

transgressions. Its myths and its folktales, its dramas and its pageants memorialize both its norms and notable violations of them. Eve tempts Adam to taste of the fruit of the off-limits Tree of Knowledge, and *la vraie condition humaine* begins with the Expulsion from the Garden."[26] Differently put, conventional stories—the "coin and currency"[27] of culture—stabilize and align collective expectations while challenging stories can alter social attitudes.

Creative Impulses Transformational literature deviates from stock stories not only because cultures tolerate subversive stories but also because creative storytelling is inherently dynamic. One source of the dynamism comes from the tension between the need for verisimilitude—making an imagined world seem plausible—and some departure from the expected that makes the ordinary strange. For the first, verisimilitude, the storyteller relies on a stock script or formula that audiences have internalized from stories they have previously heard. The second, at least in stories aspiring to memorability or literary greatness, demands an unexpected divergence from the stock script.

Creative Divergences

In Bruner's words, the writer or playwright's task is "to imagine, to explore [out of the ordinary] possibility. But to do that, he must first establish a familiar 'reality' given that his mission is to estrange it, to render it alien enough to make imagined deviations from it seem plausible. In Ibsen's *A Doll's House*, for example, Nora's dramatic revulsion becomes credible only against the deadening banality of her preternaturally ordinary husband. It is the playwright's genius to have captured both the tedium of her life and her rebellion against it. The challenge of literary narrative is to open possibilities without diminishing the seeming reality of the actual."[28]

Literary genres—an overarching category, such as comedy or tragedy, whose scripts follow expected conventions—have a similar dynamic. "Verisimilitude in a made-up story is intensified by adhering (often slyly) to the rules of genre," according to Bruner. "The hero-protagonist in a tragedy, for example, must suffer his downfall via the very virtues that make him a hero to start with. . . . So ingrained are such genre rules that fictional stories are made more lifelike simply by adhering to them."[29] And typically, "narratives play variations on the plights portrayed in conventional literary genres,"[30] such as the downfall of the tragic hero. But "at their most venturesome" they can also "generate new genres to achieve their ends—as did Laurence Sterne or James Joyce, with his self-styled epiphanies of the ordinary."[31]

New genres and conventions also have different Troubles with different resolutions, producing different effects on readers. "A wholesome setting-right of what the peripeteia put asunder [in the plot's turning point] may be the stuff of true adventure and other old-fashioned stories," Bruner writes, but in modern literature, "outcomes have taken an increasingly inward turn. . . . Story action in novels leads not so much to restoration of the disrupted canonical state of things as to epistemic or moral insights into what is inherent in the quest for restoration."[32]

Forgettable or trite stories stick to a standard formula or script. But memorable fiction—"great" literature—becomes canonical because it deviates. And by entering the canon, the deviant story alters the canon. It changes the conduct an audience considers normal and the scripts they accept as plausible.

External influences—new technologies, institutions, and social movements—also encourage innovative storytellers to produce new scripts and genres. The Scientific and Industrial Revolutions created the genre of science fiction, the specialization of criminal investigation led to police procedurals and detective novels, and urban immiseration and international drug dealing produced new kinds of heroes, villains, and stock plots. And reflexively, as mentioned, memorable stories helped alter the reality they portrayed, as in the abolition of child labor and slavery.

In principle, legal stories resist change because the system relies so heavily on precedent and the principle of *stare decisis*, of standing by things previously decided. Therefore, "legal stories strive to make the world seem self-evident, a 'continued story' that inherits a legitimated past," writes Bruner.[33] In practice, the legal system and its stories aren't static. Like innovative writers, creative litigators and judges find ways to modify, extend, and occasionally overturn precedents. Legal stories also change because of changes in social norms—which may themselves be altered by changes in literary stories, as in the 1954 school desegregation case.

Changes in canonical stories can also provoke reactions in an opposing direction. "The inward turn of literary narrative about race went a long way toward changing the legal interpretation of equal protection when it was given a subjective dimension in *Brown*," Bruner writes. "But no culture is about just one story. A dialectically contrary one quickly arose: the story of the black being given 'unfair advantages,' a story with roots in the Reconstruction period after the abolition of slavery, when Northern commanders of occupation troops in the Southern states of the old Confederacy even appointed some black governors."[34]

304   UNCERTAINTY AND ENTERPRISE

2. Entrepreneurial Stories

Nonfictional and Semifictional Abundance The market for stories that support the discourse of entrepreneurs who don't tell their tales themselves is well supplied, but usually not in creative literature.

Serious playwrights, novelists, and moviemakers, unlike Schumpeter, have often treated entrepreneurs as villains, not heroes. Shakespeare's best-known commercial character, Shylock, is a heartless moneylender. His nemesis, the intelligent, quick-witted, and beautiful Portia, plays a lawyer's apprentice.[35] Anthony Trollope's magnificent, one-hundred-chapter *The Way We Live Now* satirized the financial scandals of the 1870s. Its protagonist, financier Augustus Melmotte, who buys a seat in Parliament and has the aristocracy craving his favor, turns out to be a forger and a fraud. The source of the Great Gatsby's mysterious wealth in F. Scott Fitzgerald's 1925 novel turns out to be bootlegging. Orson Welles's *Citizen Kane* is about a scandal-mongering media tycoon, philanderer, and wife abuser.

Often ignoring the benefits of technological progress—the decline in hunger, infant mortality, increasing lifespans, and living standards—great literature has highlighted its dark side. Blake's "dark Satanic Mills" poem, Charles Dickens's novels on child labor, John Steinbeck's *The Grapes of Wrath*, Upton Sinclair's *The Jungle*, Charlie Chaplin's *Modern Times*, Martin Ritts's *Norma Rae*, and Steven Soderbergh's *Erin Brockovich* are celebrated examples.[36]

Physicians-turned-writers—Arthur Conan Doyle, A. J. Cronin, and W. Somerset Maugham—have authored sympathetic stories about medical practice. Lawyers Erle Stanley Gardner and John Mortimer's fiction (later turned into TV shows) portray lawyers favorably: Gardner's Perry Mason and Mortimer's Rumpole representing unjustly accused and down-and-out defendants dramatically beat the odds to secure not-guilty verdicts. I am unaware of any similarly popular pro-business fiction written by entrepreneurs or managers.

Yet other kinds of storytelling does put enterprise and innovation in a good light. Celebrated innovators and industrialists publish memoirs, which I quote or paraphrase in this text and in my earlier work. Turning to the bookshelf behind me, I see titles by Alfred Sloan (General Motors), David Packard (H-P), Sam Walton (Walmart), Richard Branson (Virgin), James Dyson (Dyson), Joe Coulombe (Trader Joe's), Patrick Kelly (PSS), and Marvin Bower (McKinsey & Co.). All easily satisfy Bruner's specification for a story—protagonists with intent, Troubles, and resolutions.

Biographies (e.g., of Jeff Bezos and Steve Jobs) and histories of noteworthy innovations (e.g., computers, container shipping, and winemaking in France) on my bookshelf also satisfy the story specification. They are neither hagiographies nor hatchet jobs. There are, of course, non-fiction bestsellers that

SPILLOVERS FROM POPULAR STORIES 305

recount downfalls—of Enron and Theranos, for instance. Serious newspapers and magazines also publish stories about enterprise with both sad and happy endings. Some are exposés ending in bankruptcies or jail sentences. Others chronicle tenacious innovators overcoming challenges to introduce a transformative technology or create a billion-dollar enterprise. Even the *New Yorker,* often skeptical of capitalism and celebrity entrepreneurs like Elon Musk,[37] publishes favorable long-form accounts in its *Annals* of Innovation, Technology, Invention, and Business. Conversely, *Inc.* magazine, which celebrates entrepreneurship, publishes cautionary tales about hubris and failure.

Business schools consume and spread stories packaged as case studies. Every business school I know of, including those whose faculty disdain "storytelling" research, uses story-infused case teaching to some degree. At HBS, cases are not only a cornerstone of teaching; their production and sale to other schools help maintain the institution's brand and earn sizable revenue. Reciprocally, HBS invests heavily in case writing and, reportedly after a hushed-up scandal, verifying the contents of the cases.

Low-cost storytelling makes the *Harvard Business Review* an especially profitable money-spinner for HBS. Although operating under a university banner— and unlike the story-rich *Business History Review* (also hosted at HBS) and the *Harvard Law Review*—*HBR* does not require contributors to document facts or acknowledge prior work.[38] It also publishes self-congratulatory pieces by business celebrities, sometimes awkwardly timed.[39] In my observation, the quality press has, historically at least, been far more careful in verifying facts and quotes and crediting the sources of their ideas than *HBR*. Well-known journalists, including Pulitzer Prize winners, have been fired for making up quotes and characters.[40] *HBR* authors risk no reckonings for peddling similar "factions."[41]

Yet with unpaid contributions and low vetting expenses, *HBR*'s story machine grinds profitably on. Like audiences of angry talk shows, readers seem to have low demands for accuracy. Operating for over a century, *HBR* has established an unbreakable lock on its oeuvre. Over the years, it has published influential articles whose storylike character would preclude publication in conventional academic journals. Such pieces have produced valuable spillovers for commercial enterprise.

Iconic Examples Two classic *HBR* articles exemplify the spillover effects. One by Michael Porter, published in 1979, introduced his Five Forces framework.[42] Porter expanded on the *HBR* article in his landmark 1980 book, *Competitive Strategy.*[43] As mentioned (chapter 7), Porter adapted his framework from economic theory and did not give it a story structure. But as also mentioned, Porter drew heavily on case studies, making his framework unsuitable for story-averse

306 UNCERTAINTY AND ENTERPRISE

economics journals. Yet Porter's framework has long provided categories for business discourse, especially in routines to evaluate large company initiatives (chapters 16 and 17).

The second, *Disruptive Technologies: Catching the Wave*, coauthored by Clay Christensen and his thesis adviser Joseph Bower, was published in 1995.[44] Like Porter, Christensen turned his *HBR* article into a landmark (1997) book: *The Innovator's Dilemma: When New Technologies Cause Great Firms to Fail*. The sources and structure of the Christensen publications were squarely in the narrative mode. They drew on a few detailed case histories, many from the disk drive industry, that Christensen had studied for his doctoral dissertation. Unlike Porter's five-force framework, Christensen's disruption model had a simple story structure with a beginning, middle, and end.

Briefly, the Christensen plot starts with an incumbent dominating its market. Entrants who cannot attack its core find a foothold on the periphery. They offer customers who do not need all the bells and whistles of the incumbent's mainline product a simpler but cheaper alternative. The incumbent either ignores the technically inferior offering because it is complacent or wants to keep the high profits of its existing products. But eventually, the entrant upgrades its product, moves out of its low-end niche, and takes over the core. The king is dead. Long live the new king.

My left-brained thinking dismissed the generality Christensen and his acolytes attributed to the disruption story. Manifestly, many landmark innovations, such as the iPhone and the Tesla, start life as expensive top-line products. The practical solution proposed to incumbents—preempt upstarts by creating nimble units that don't serve existing customers—also seems questionable: Incumbents cannot afford to be spooked by peripheral shadows. They must deal with more obvious threats from other large companies and regulators. And many of Christensen's fearless forecasts—that the iPhone would fail and that cheap alternatives would soon (as of 1999) dethrone Microsoft's Office software—turned out to be demonstrably wrong.[45]

Why, then, did people like Steve Jobs and Intel's Andy Grove take the disruption model seriously and admire Christensen's book so much?

Sensemaking, Linguistic, and Attitudinal Spillovers My mistake: I had applied the logico-scientific standard of logical or empirical validation to Christensen's narrative-mode discourse. His disruption story drew its power from its plausibility and resonance. Recall Bruner's observation that new stories seem plausible because of their similarity to familiar old stories. The disruption tale recalls well-worn stories, one from the Old Testament and the other from ancient Greek myth. Christenson's innovators evoke David using simple tech to slay Goliath,

SPILLOVERS FROM POPULAR STORIES 307

and incumbents are like tragic heroes doomed by misjudgments or character flaws.

In the business sphere, the disruption tale also offers the spillovers of literary and legal storytelling discussed earlier: it has influenced sensemaking, language, and attitudes.

We lament the "senseless" deaths of organizations and not just of fellow humans. Somehow, the implicit default seems to be eternal life, so the failure of successful organizations demands an explanation. And indeed, during the glory decades of Galbraith's New Industrial State (chapter 16), the immortality of giant businesses seemed assured. After that era ended, sensemaking started: high inflation, unions, and Japanese competitors were all blamed. Yet these explanations ran their course after the 1980s when inflation and unions retreated, and Ezra Vogel's claim of "Japan as Number One" became implausible. The 1990s demanded a new mortality tale, which Christensen's disruption successfully supplied.

Moreover, where Porter mainly analyzed, Christensen prescribed. Besides offering to explain how, as the subtitle of Christensen's book says, *New Technologies Cause Great Firms to Fail*, disruptive sensemaking explicitly promoted proactive agency. Christensen advised upstarts to target niche customers who preferred cheaper and simpler products and incumbents to forestall such attacks with their own low-end offerings. The resonance of the messages affected real-world choices and discourse. Intel's then-CEO Andrew Grove claimed inspiration from the disruption story to push Intel's launch of a low-end Celeron chip for low-end netbooks—and he repeatedly invoked it to justify the launch.[46]

Christensen's work has profoundly influenced the language used to characterize innovation. Disruption is everywhere. What might once have been called "revolutionary" or "transformational" is now disruptive. Christensen's stories and rhetoric have also influenced collective attitudes. Frequent, radical change is inevitable and good. Embrace it and help make it happen. The responses of the naturally skeptical to entrepreneurial proposals have thus been nudged from "This can't work" toward a "fear of missing out."

Few other recent business stories have had such influence. Most tell of specific entrepreneurs and advances rather than a story about a general class of innovations. Yet, taken as a whole, the impact of business stories on entrepreneurial actions and discourse—through sensemaking, linguistic, and attitudinal spillovers—has been profound. As indicated (chapter 19), entrepreneurs use metaphors ("We are the Uber of X") and figurative labels ("platform technologies" or "sharing economy") to communicate the premise of their business models—and evoke the possibilities of a large payoff—to potential

308 UNCERTAINTY AND ENTERPRISE

financiers. The metaphors and labels make sense because of some well-known story, for example, of Uber ride sharing, Amazon's online platform, or Airbnb's apartment rentals.

Seemingly mundane descriptive categories also get their meaning from the spillovers of a story rather than from technical specifications. As in the legal understanding of "adultery" mentioned by Bruner, "Software as a Service," "Minimal Viable Product," "Lean Startup," "customer journeys," and "agile programming" all take their meaning from prototypical cases that evolved through a struggle against some prior arrangements.

Memoirs and biographies that do not advance general propositions like disruption theory often suggest possibilities about specific problems and domains. Every chapter in Coulombe's *Becoming Trader Joe* tells engaging stories with a coda or moral about specialty food and wine retailing.[47] Although Coulombe makes few claims about business in general, his codas also invite readers to imagine extensions beyond retailing.

Memoirs can also stimulate big-picture thinking in unrelated domains. Bill Gates, for example, credits Alfred Sloan's *My Years with General Motors* for shaping his vision for Microsoft; he calls Sloan's memoir "probably the best book to read if you want to read only one book about business."[48]

Sloan's book—472 pages long with financial tables and organization charts— is not an easy read. Other memoirs are shorter, seemingly fluffier, and yet also influence hard-nosed entrepreneurs. For example, Sam Walton's folksy *Made in America* "clearly resonated" with Jeff Bezos. Like Gates, Bezos is a voracious reader who sometimes gave copies of Walton's book to colleagues with passages underlined (which we could consider a subtle form of discourse). One underlined passage described Walton borrowing the ideas of his competitors, implying to Bezos that successful retailers stood on the shoulders of earlier giants. So, therefore, should Amazon. Bezos also "wove the Walmart founder's credo about frugality and a 'bias for action' into the cultural fabric of Amazon."[49]

Sensemaking spillovers from memoirs and other stories affect audiences beyond high-profile founder-CEOs like Gates and Bezos. Stories about recovering from setbacks make similar recoveries in other ventures seem more plausible to audiences. And people with optimistic Micawber-like outlooks might conflate what's plausible with what's likely, given that there is no basis for calculating objective odds. Conversely, negative stories promote pessimistic expectations.[50]

3. Dynamism of Stories and Specialization

Why Stories Keep Changing Popular business stories don't have the longevity of literary or legal stories and do not become canonical to the same degree. There

SPILLOVERS FROM POPULAR STORIES   309

is no mechanism to select, preserve, and study canonical works in business schools, as exists in literature, classics, and other humanities departments. Nor are audiences' loyalties to genres and stock stories as strong in business as they are in literature.

In contrast to the law, there is no *stare decisis* reverence for precedent or an established *corpus juris* of accepted rules based on canonical results. Quite the opposite. Many in the business community take Henry Ford's view that "History is bunk" and constantly demand new Big Ideas. Business gurus and their enabling publications eagerly attempt to satisfy the demand by creating new buzz phrases, illustrated with real or made-up stories, instead of actual New Ideas. Sometimes, even the new buzz phrases are variants of old buzz phrases—"non-disruptive creation" instead of "non-destructive creation."[51]

Technological and business innovations—routinely demanded and supplied in modern economies—can also spur new stories, metaphors, and spillovers. The internet created opportunities for Amazon, whose success story produced the "platform" metaphor. New 3G wireless networks and smartphones with mapping capabilities created an opportunity for Uber's ride-hailing app—and made its model a metaphor, along with the "sharing economy." As mentioned, other startups used these metaphors to get the attention of financiers and the public.

Entrepreneurial stories can fall as quickly as they rise—sometimes because the opportunity has run its course or merely because stale stories don't sell. And as prevailing stories change, so do the kinds of opportunities they support. Who wants to write about, fund, or start ventures in the once-hot category of fast casual restaurants?

Changes in Specialization Compared to business stories—and even literary genres and foundational legal doctrines—the evolution of entrepreneurial forms (examined in chapters 13 to 17) has been slow. Two of the four primary forms we examined precede industrialization: The self- or informally financed startups and angel-funded initiatives have existed whenever and wherever there has been commerce. Only two new forms with distinctive routines for evaluating and managing entrepreneurial initiatives emerged in the twentieth century, and even their development was gradual. The large, professionally managed corporation became Schumpeter's "powerful engine[s] of progress" in the first half of the twentieth century. VC-backed businesses became prominent players in the second half.

A few variants of these forms have subsequently evolved, such as organized networks of angel investors, VCs specializing in later-stage investing, and the in-house VC operations of large public corporations. These do not entail any radical changes in the evaluation and planning routines that, in my framework, are defining features of entrepreneurial specialization. During and after the mid-2010s, some financiers invested vast sums in private "unicorns." Unlike traditional VCs, these financiers did not have or establish serious evaluation or oversight routines. Like some others,[52] I believe this kind of hands-off investing was an unfortunate, transient consequence of an unprecedented "free-money" bubble. Time will tell.

However, form-shifting by entrepreneurial ventures is an inherent feature of the modern ecosystem. Besides the ambitions of founders like Gates and Bezos, new and fledgling businesses are subject to intense pressures to expand from financiers, employees, and even customers who avoid stagnating enterprises. The grow-or-die imperative requires companies like Amazon to change their funding sources, establish more rigorous routines, and specialize in larger, less uncertain, and more complex initiatives[53] (see Figure 21.1).

Nexus Changes in discourse accompany changes in specialization. Initially, discourse is limited to discussions among the founders (which in solo ventures may be internal monologues) or customer sales pitches. High uncertainty limits the content of this discourse—often, the entrepreneurs proceed on "a wing and a prayer." Informal funding, if any, is secured through a brief pitch to friends and family. With simple products, there is not much that founders can tell potential buyers either. Moreover, not much needs to be said when the stakes are low. Buying a lottery ticket from the corner shop requires no discourse or estimation of the numerical odds.

At the other end of the specialization diagonal, discourse is more elaborate. Proposals and plans about large complex projects include extensive detail. In

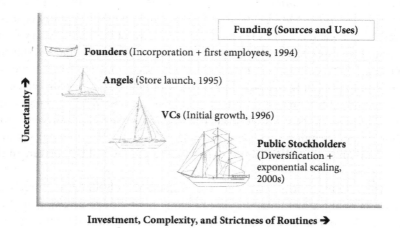

Figure 21.1 Changes in Amazon's Funding, Routines, and Initiatives

SPILLOVERS FROM POPULAR STORIES   311

Aristotelean terms, evaluations embody a preference for *logos* over *pathos*, with the *ethos* coming from the credentials of the promoters. But corporate discourse is no more just about spreadsheet numbers than Christopher Columbus's conversations were about latitudes and longitudes. As mentioned, the numerical detail includes imagined assumptions that can be challenged. And it is not a bloodless discourse. Unlike Max Weber's idealized bureaucracy, the corporate technocracy reflects the feelings and subjective interpretations of its discoursers. External discourse with users is also a many splendored thing. Conversations with customers, which can include visual metaphors on user interfaces, reflect the complexity and stakes of the offerings. But while pitches about complex products include more technical facts, they too seek to summon feelings and include imagined details to evoke imagined futures.

Like ancient sagas crafted by many bards or modern TV shows hammered out in writers' rooms, proposals and plans emerge after extensive multi-party discourse. They look much further ahead than the snap judgments and opportunistic adaptations (chapter 14) of bootstrapped entrepreneurs. And the collectively crafted "plot," as it were, is thick. It includes who will do what and when—but without the dramatic reversals and villains of a proper story.

PART V
CODA

Frontispiece of Francis Bacon's *Instauratio Magna*. 1620

Sir Francis Bacon (1561–1626) was a key figure in the Scientific Revolution, a movement that challenged the authority of ancient knowledge. The engraving on the title page of Bacon's 1620 book (above) provided "one of the most vivid iconographical statements of new optimism about the possibilities and the extent of scientific knowledge," writes Steven Shapin, a Harvard historian of science.[1]

But did the scientific method go too far—beyond overthrowing ancient authority to suppressing Bruner's narrative-mode reasoning? And does the hegemony of the logico-scientific mode, particularly in the analysis of human behavior, restrict our view of the possibilities and problems for Aristotelian *eudaimonia* (happiness, flourishing)?

22

The Case for Widening

Concluding his introduction to a 1971 edition of Knight's book, Stigler wrote that he found it

> intensely interesting for a reason somewhat removed from the theory of profit: It explains as no other work does the crucial importance of uncertainty, and its inevitable consequence, ignorance, in transforming an economic system from a beehive into a conscious social process with error, conflict, innovation, and endless spans and varieties of change. The full yield of this vision has hardly begun to be reaped by modern economics.[1]

Edmund Phelps's 2006 Nobel Prize Lecture suggested that the full yield remained remote. The "distinctive character of the modern economy," observed Phelps, involves "uncertainty, ambiguity [and] diversity of beliefs." Entrepreneurs "have to act on their 'animal spirits,'" often launching their innovations first and discovering the benefits and costs afterward.[2] Knight, Phelps wrote elsewhere, understood that "uncertainty is a hallmark of the modern economy."[3] But instead of treating the modern economy as it really is ("an evolving, unruly, open-ended system"), the "established body of economic theory" implied a "deterministic future."[4]

Another nearly twenty years have passed, yet the deterministic research that won Stigler and Phelps their Economics Nobels remains dominant. Chaos theorists hold out hopes they will provide a unified theory of complex, unruly systems, but "the full yield" of their vision has also "hardly begun to be reaped." And whatever success a mathematical chaos theory might have with the distributional and statistical uncertainties of natural systems or anonymous financial markets, I am skeptical about imminent breakthroughs in resolving the uncertainties of one-off, contextual choices. Similarly, notwithstanding its anticipated marvels, I find it difficult to imagine how artificial intelligence will tame even banal uncertainties that frustrate actual human intelligence. Nor, in a dynamic, ever-changing world, can we rely on convention or precedent to predict the consequences of our choices.

Should we surrender? In *Excessive Ambitions*, Jon Elster (chapter 12) argues that "large bodies of social science are permeated by explanatory hubris. Economists and political scientists, in particular, rely on deductive models and

---

Uncertainty and Enterprise. Amar Bhidé, Oxford University Press. © Oxford University Press 2025.
DOI: 10.1093/oso/9780197688359.003.0022

316 UNCERTAINTY AND ENTERPRISE

statistical tools that are vastly less robust and reliable than their practitioners claim."[5] In "Excessive Ambitions (II)," Elster similarly attacks "overreaching" prescriptions aimed at creating institutions that will "produce good decisions, select good decision-makers, or create good decision-making bodies."[6] Instead, Elster proposes a modest, harm-minimizing approach: "insulate decision-makers as much as possible from the influences of self-interest, passion (emotion or intoxication), prejudice and cognitive bias. Once that has been done, one should let the chips fall where they may."[7]

But chips do not just "fall where they may." Choices, no less than chance, matter. And why hold uncertain choices about one-offs hostage to the logico-scientific standards of verifiability that Elster demands? What is so wrong with Bruner's plausible narrative-mode reasoning? Recognizing the impossibility of provable certitudes, why discard the legitimacy and solidarity—Albert Hirschman's "voice"—of debating the best imaginable choice? And cannot academics—economists no less than historians—contribute to such discourse?

The applications discussed in Parts 3 and 4 suggested the possibilities for what we can learn about uncertain entrepreneurial interactions. The discussion was abductive and reasoned in the narrative mode. Its sensibility, in William James's (chapter 9) typology, was more bottom-up empiricist than top-down rationalist. Although based on some general premises and conjectures (Part 1) and supported by some classic theoretical ideas (Part 2), my inferences did not claim universality or timelessness: they pertain to current arrangements for organizing enterprise in the United States and possibly other technologically progressive, largely decentralized economies and societies. I relied on qualitative observations that others could interpret differently. For all that, I daresay that my approach offered a perspective on questions (especially about the role of routines and discourse) that mainstream economics does not usually examine.

Compared to the possibilities, however, I restricted the scope of my applications. Because I wanted to make a credible case for going beyond the standard logico-scientific approach to uncertainty, I stuck to issues of commercial entrepreneurship that I have researched for much of my academic career. Yet the possibilities and benefits of applying a broadened approach are virtually limitless. I have already hinted at these broader possibilities through several medical and legal examples (such as drug and criminal trials) in Part 1 of this book.

At the same time, I am reluctant to suggest a standardized template. While the general conjectures I outlined in chapter 3 have potential applicability beyond commercial enterprise, they are not universal. I don't believe meaningful universal rules for managing real-world uncertainties are even possible. Therefore, in the rest of this coda, I again sketch out specific puzzles that a broadened approach could help examine. And while these puzzles go beyond my comfort zone, I do not stray too far from what I have covered here and in my earlier work. I won't propose voyages through entirely unfamiliar waters. Similarly, while I am more explicit here about the public policy implications, I will not offer concrete prescriptions.

Specifically, in increasing order of distance from the ideas discussed earlier—and public policy importance—the following three sections raise questions about

- Deviations from normal patterns of entrepreneurial specialization.

- How new technologies and discourse about uncertain topics interact.

- Delegating authority about uncertain policy choices to specialists.

In discussing these questions, I revisit ideas covered in earlier chapters, making this coda a look back as well as a look forward.

1. Deviations from Normal Patterns

The entrepreneurial specialization map (Figure 4.1) framed the applications in Part 3. Organizational evaluation and planning routines, we saw, help place different organizations along a diagonal channel from the top left (high uncertainty + low investment and complexity) to the lower right (low uncertainty + high investment and complexity) corners of the map.

The map and its underlying routines help explain the normally symbiotic division of entrepreneurial labor in a modern economy. To start with, at least, the relationship between small startups and large mature businesses is harmonious. New and fledgling businesses target small, low-cost, highly uncertain opportunities, while giant enterprises place calculated bets on large, complex initiatives. The former often serve a Darwinian purpose in selecting the "fittest" new products and technologies that the latter can scale up.

Upstart businesses may also offer complementary goods and services whose revenue potential is too small or speculative to interest established companies. In the early 1980s, as IBM made its PCs a mainstream must-have, swarms of startups enhanced the value of and sales of PCs by providing installation and maintenance services, hardware add-ons, and educational videos and books. Entrepreneurial app and game developers now use and enhance the value of phones and tablets made by Apple and Samsung, the cloud services of Microsoft and Amazon, and the 4G and 5G networks of telecom oligopolists.

The specialization diagonal also describes a common trajectory of new businesses, products, and technologies. They often evolve along the diagonal, toward more scale and complexity and less uncertainty. Their pace can be fast or slow, however, and some new products and technologies (e.g., cloud computing,

318 UNCERTAINTY AND ENTERPRISE

5G networks, or anti-obesity drugs) require huge investments for their initial market introductions.

Gold rushes ("irrational exuberance") can suspend organizational demands for evidence and thus normal uncertainty limits. These suspensions can occur in "hot" sectors such as biotech in the late 1980s, the internet in the late 1990s, and recently, artificial intelligence. Manias can also be widely distributed. Years of unconventional monetary policies in the 2010s made investors "increasingly aggressive," VC and "old Cambridge" (chapter 8) economist Janeway wrote in January 2022. Bubbles formed in crypto assets and meme stocks. "Nontraditional capital," such as mutual funds, hedge funds, and sovereign wealth funds, flooded into venture-backed businesses at extreme valuations. The "extraordinary increase in the supply of capital . . . eliminated any perceived need for critically assessing business models and business plans."[8]

Manias can provide opportunities for astute—or lucky—entrepreneurs to get in and out before the music stops. During the internet bubble, entrepreneurs and investors made great fortunes in businesses, such as Marc Andreasson's Netscape, which later evaporated. And just as wars can spur significant medical advances (such as the development of penicillin in World War II), occasionally "explosions of investor exuberance have funded the deployment of innovative technologies at sufficient scale to transform the market economy, as was the case with railroads, electrification, and the internet."[9]

But, continues Janeway, they may not: "Whether a bubble is productive depends on what it leaves behind." The Dutch tulip mania of the 1630s, London's South Sea Bubble of 1720, and recent manias in non-fungible tokens and meme stocks left no identifiably productive legacies. Conversely, just as transformational medical advances do not require battlefield catalysts, technological revolutions do not require manic investments. Moreover, "All bubbles burst, so even investors in the vehicles of a productive episode inevitably will fall into one of two categories: the quick or the dead."[10]

Whether investors who deploy their personal funds choose to dance while the music plays may be a private choice. For entrepreneurs, "Taking virtually free capital from investors who have no interest in (or capacity for) firm governance is irresistible," Janeway writes.[11] But what about mutual funds, which normally invest in public companies whose routines are designed for the lower-right corner of the specialization map? Historically, US rules such as the Investment Company Act of 1940 have discouraged fiduciaries from operating outside this domain. But these rules have, in recent years, been diluted. Should they have been? Can we count on the directors of investment companies to restrict fund managers to domains where they have the necessary expertise?[12] Or does investment in multibillion-dollar private unicorns no longer require governance expertise or effort?

THE CASE FOR WIDENING   319

Normal specialization raises the opposite policy concerns: underinvestment by financiers in unproven entrepreneurs and by corporate executives in breakthrough projects. Does the "procedural rationality" (per Simon, chapter 9) of evaluation routines and their uncertainty ceilings produce socially undesirable results? And can these be corrected by government subsidies?

Schemes to subsidize startups emerge from supposed "market failures" in early-stage financing. Financing constraints likely do discourage some aspiring entrepreneurs. Self-financing undoubtedly increases the personal downside for many business founders. But the hazards of investing all their savings and incurring possibly imprudent levels of personal debt did not stop my *Inc.* list interviewees from starting their businesses (chapter 14). Moreover, individuals discouraged by financing constraints might also be less capable of coping with the uncertainties.[13] Financing constraints may not even force founders who target niche markets to start on a suboptimal scale, while bootstrapping encourages them to undertake quick, cheap, trial-and-error development.

And suppose some theoretical "market failure" in private financing does exist. Practically speaking, how could public subsidies fill the "financing gap"? What process or criteria could a public agency use to solve the uncertainty problems that discourage the private financing of low-evidence initiatives?

Similarly, at the other end of the specialization spectrum. The routines of public companies reflect their comparative advantage in undertaking large, complex projects and their fiduciary responsibility to stockholders. They strongly discourage investments in futuristic technologies and unfathomable customer wants. The hype notwithstanding, even the visionary Steve Jobs respected technical and commercial limits. Pathbreaking advances that require significant initial investments, such as CAR-T and mRNA development, must unavoidably economize and improvise to carry on, often on a smaller scale than their promoters would prefer. Some undoubtedly shut down. Typically, evaluation routines make the upper-right-hand space of Figure 22.1 a dead zone.

Is this empty space a zone of market failure? Schumpeter's analysis suggests it could be. According to Schumpeter, economically significant innovations are "large" and "spontaneous" rather than "small" and "adaptive." They so displace the "equilibrium point" that "the new one cannot be reached from the old one by infinitesimal steps. Add successively as many mail coaches as you please, you will never get a railway thereby."[14] Dramatic imagery, but how realistic? To take Schumpeter's own example, steam engines that powered railways emerged from water pumps in coal mines and gradually made their way into public transportation.

Economic historian Nate Rosenberg's careful research documents the "continuities" of innovation.[15] Unfortunately, Rosenberg's guarded language cannot compete with Schumpeter's rhetoric, and the "slow and often invisible

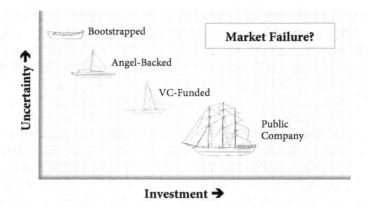

Figure 22.1 Dead Zone

accretion of individually small improvements in innovations" are often ignored because of "a preoccupation with what is technologically spectacular," as Rosenberg puts it.[16] The 2023 drama of Large Language Models captivates the public, while the earlier painstaking progress in artificial intelligence, going back to Simon and Newell's work in the 1950s, did not. Yet Charles Darwin's "endless forms most beautiful and most wonderful"[17] evolved from simple beginnings through small mutations. Similarly, the sum of modest advances routinely produces technological revolutions.

Could diverting resources from commonplace, incremental enterprise to select, radical initiatives nonetheless serve the common interest? Perhaps large, uncertain initiatives, like national security, the control of infectious disease, and basic scientific research, are legitimate public goods. But who would select such initiatives and how? Big Science funding inevitably reflects the consensus of scientific communities—and a bias against renegade ideas. Public funding agencies, like large stockholder-owned businesses, cannot rely on hunches to place big bets– their legitimacy requires structured, defensible reviews (as I argue in section 3 of this coda). They can more easily seed small, speculative projects as the US Department of Defense did in the late 1960s to get the internet started. And even that project was funded after several years of private and public evaluation of alternatives.

So is the uncertainty-investment tradeoff an avoidable pathology or a practical, desirable necessity? Let the reader decide.[18]

2. Technologies of Discourse

As mentioned, expectations of daily sunrises, according to the Scottish Enlightenment philosopher David Hume, are based on animal instinct, not

THE CASE FOR WIDENING   321

reason. Hume's skepticism included questioning the claim that our insights about cause-and-effect relationships derive from reason. He proposed instead a "naturalist conception" based on "the instinctive associative mechanism of the 'imagination.'"[19] Differently put, an unavoidably uncertain world requires the instinct of imagination.

As an ardent supporter of the scientific sensibilities emerging in his time and a staunch (in the classical tradition) empiricist, Hume also valued evidence and observation. But, evidence collaborates with and does not replace imagination. For example, expecting to like the seventh *Harry Potter* book "because" we enjoyed the first six combines empirical data (our responses to the earlier books) with imaginative extrapolation. We could plausibly expect the opposite: we could imagine that the seventh will disappoint because all long streaks must inevitably end.

Take this further. Voluntary exchange and collaboration, beyond the obligations of kinship and custom, require giving and accepting reasons that combine imagination and evidence. Promoters of entrepreneurial schemes, drawing on their observation and experience, imagine why buyers will pay for their products and investors will back their ideas. To close the deal, promoters must communicate their imagined reasons and evidence in a way that will resonate with the imaginations and experiences of potential buyers and investors and overcome their doubts about value and feasibility. So, too, outside business entrepreneurship. The claims of reformers and reactionaries, racists and antiracists, pro- and antivaxxers, prosecutors and defense lawyers, and even scientists and medical researchers originate in their imaginations and experiences.

Misaligned Imaginations

Research that conflicts with the imaginations and experiences of target audiences face rejection. Robin Warren and Barry Marshall won the 2005 Nobel Prize in Medicine for showing how H. pylori bacterial infections cause stomach and duodenal ulcers. But when they presented their initial findings in October 1982, the response was "mixed." The "standard teaching" was that "nothing grows in the stomach."[20] Marshall recalls that "most of my work was rejected for publication, and even accepted papers were significantly delayed. I was met with constant criticism that my conclusions were premature and not well supported. When the work was presented, my results were disputed and disbelieved, not on the basis of science, but because they simply could not be true. I was told that the bacteria were either contaminants or harmless commensals."[21]

322   UNCERTAINTY AND ENTERPRISE

Language and art—primal markers of human societies—are well suited for discourse that can help reduce doubts and disagreements (chapter 19). Evocative words and images enable us to align imaginations and interpretations of evidence while our capacities for imaginative discourse have advanced relentlessly throughout human history. The knock-on effects have profoundly shaped and reshaped the human condition in every sphere.

Enriched vocabularies have extended the possibilities that people can invite each other to imagine. And canonical stories and "conventionalized narrative" have converted "individual experience into collective coin which can be circulated," writes Bruner. "Being able to read another's mind need depend no longer on sharing some narrow ecological or interpersonal niche but, rather, on a common fund of myth, folktale, 'common sense.'"[22]

Technological advances in the physical devices of discourse have been momentous. Written communication, which broke our reliance on in-person speech, started on clay and stone tablets. A procession of new technologies for recording, reproducing, and transmitting the written word followed. These included papyrus scrolls, animal skins, paper, quill pens, typewriters, cylinder seals, woodblock printing, movable type, the Gutenberg printing press, rotary presses, and postal and telegraph networks. Visual and audio communication advances included the development of paint brushes, pigments added to beeswax and suspended in oil or water-soluble media, acid etching of metal plates, offset printing, photography, telephones, gramophones, radio, movies, television, tape recorders, and videocassettes. In recent decades, communications services and devices have been leading products of the digital revolution. Apple's Mac established a foothold through desktop publishing, and iPhones made Apple the world's most valuable commercial enterprise.

Besides creating new markets for companies like Apple, advances have supported the initiatives of the users of the new technologies. Upstarts and established organizations have both benefitted along the lines discussed in chapter 18 (on the aims of uncertainty-reducing discourse). Upstarts use affordable yet high-quality sound equipment, digital cameras (including traditional single-lens cameras, mobile phone cameras, camcorders, bodycams, and drone cameras), and editing software (such as Photoshop) to produce professional-class content. They distribute the content widely through platforms and social media, bypassing traditional intermediaries like newspapers, radio, and television.

Crowdsourcing platforms such as Kickstarter and Indigogo allow entrepreneurs to look beyond their own families, contacts, and local communities to fund the development of new products and projects that would not interest professional investors and which they cannot bootstrap. Similarly, "influencers" on YouTube and TikTok have attained followings that rival those of Hollywood stars, which they monetize through brand sponsorship, selling ads and merchandise, and viewer fees. In 2023, twenty-five-year-old James Stephen Donaldson (professionally, "MrBeast") had over 200 million YouTube followers[23] and an estimated net worth of $500 million.[24] On TikTok, the twenty-four-year-old Charli Grace D'Amelio, who posts her dance videos, had over 150 million followers.[25]

New communication technologies have supported insurgent political initiatives. Change.org, founded in 2007 in San Francisco, gives campaigners tools to promote petitions and collect signatures. It claims over five hundred million registered users.[26] Famously, two outsiders—Barack Obama (a first-term senator from Illinois) and Donald Trump (who had never held public office)—used online campaigns and social media to mobilize grassroots support and funds to win election to the US presidency.

Large, established organizations have also used technological advances in their uncertainty-reducing discourse. Consumer goods giants were the backbone of twentieth-century radio and TV advertising. The term "soap opera" originates in melodramas sponsored by large soap producers. Large corporations now use search engine and social media ads and sponsor influencers on YouTube and TikTok. Similarly, companies selling products whose features cannot be clearly explained in writing rely on online videos. I frequently look to YouTube to unravel the mysteries of my allegedly user-friendly iPad.*

New technologies have become integral to routines that organizations use to evaluate and plan uncertain ventures. Designers use computerized 3-D models to secure the feedback and approval of bosses and new product committees. Spreadsheets have become an indispensable tool for analyzing financial prospects. Mocking their made-up assumptions and details misses the point of discourse about imagined futures: Spreadsheet models provide valuable conversation pieces for discussing what could be made to happen and how. Project management software, data repositories, wikis, and videoconferencing help control the alignment uncertainties of complex initiatives.

Coordinating Complex Initiatives

Much is made of how large projects fail. More surprising is the smooth execution of many complex initiatives. Netflix has transitioned from mailing

---

* YouTube user instruction is another example of new technology–enabled symbiosis. Upstart producers of widely watched how-to videos earn advertising revenues that they share with Alphabet (Google), the YouTube operator. Large companies like Apple whose products are supported by the videos also benefit.

DVDs to streaming videos and has become a producer of movies. Amazon has swiftly shifted from "hub-and-spoke" fulfillment to regionalized facilities to slash shipping times. By mid-year 2023, Amazon delivered 1.8 billion packages the same or the next day to its US customers, about a fourfold increase since 2019.

The migration of computing infrastructure to the "cloud" has been comprehensive and quick. In 2020, more than 60 percent of US businesses moved their workloads to the cloud, and as of 2023, 94 percent were using cloud services.[27] Cloud computing, in turn, helped businesses adapt swiftly to the disruptions of Covid lockdowns.[28] In the public sector, the US Postal Service has implemented "end-to-end logistics tracking." It offers customers tracking services as accurate as those provided by private companies like FedEx and UPS.[29] Public agencies, like private companies, responded to the challenges of the Covid-19 pandemic rapidly. Under legislation passed in March 2020, the US government made 476 million emergency payments to qualifying individuals.[30] Apparently, public or private bureaucracies can—at least occasionally—use project management techniques and technologies to perform impressive feats of coordination.

But no rose is without its thorns. Advances in communication technologies can also increase mutual doubts and mistrust. Below, I review three doubt-and-disagreement increasing pathways: the overproduction, weakened quality control, and divisiveness of discourse.

Knight anticipated the overproduction problem in a 1949 comment (on an article by Hayek) that he wrote for the *University of Chicago Law Review*. Knight complained about the "pathetic failure to recognize the limits of intercommunication" in the "stampede" to rush "more and more billions of words onto more and more tons of paper through the printing press (now supplemented by getting them 'on the air'). We are approaching a limiting condition in which everyone writes or talks, while no one reads or listens—since no one can do both at once. . . . And while one person can communicate to a large number, and with modem facilities, to the whole world, no skill or device will enable one to receive communication *from* more than one at a time."[31]

The "modern facilities" that Knight wrote of in 1949 now seem primitive in their overproduction of communication.

Overproduction produces different harms in the workplace and public life. In the workplace, employees confront a torrent of emails and instant messages. Many are irrelevant or trivial, but recipients cannot identify the important ones

THE CASE FOR WIDENING   325

without reading them. Ironically, tech companies that enable the messaging flood also now offer software to automate prioritization and filtering. But the software has done little to reduce the problems of information overload. Low costs have also degraded person-to-person communication. The expense and effort of writing or typing out a letter, putting it in a stamped envelope, and then into a mailbox signaled (as in the Spence model mentioned in chapter 7) its potential value and seriousness. So did making a long-distance phone call. Now we expect emails from unknown senders and calls from unknown callers to be worthless junk.

Oversupply creates different difficulties for public discourse.

Technology has broken the power of traditional media oligopolies. Cable networks and now online internet streaming destroyed the stranglehold of three TV networks in the United States and state broadcasters in other countries. Low costs also made news reporting a round-the-clock affair. The intense competition for audience attention has, however, also created strong incentives to exaggerate or fabricate.

Moreover, technology has democratized the competition for attention. Anyone with a mobile phone or an internet connection can now report news or opine cheaply and widely. On the positive side, citizen-journalists can publicize grave ills. Amateur video recordings have exposed police brutality. But technology has also made doctoring images easy. And as audiences get bored, the pressure to sensationalize or fabricate intensifies.

Second, new technologies and platforms have weakened mechanisms to police the quality of discourse.[32] The internet initially produced great hopes for decentralized quality control. When eBay, the pioneering e-auctioneer, first published customer reviews, scholars praised and documented the benefits of independent evaluations of sellers.[33] But soon, sellers began paying reviewers to post glowing evaluations of their products, and entrepreneurs started "click farms" to mass-produce fake ratings and rankings.[34] E-commerce sites resisted: Amazon began ranking reviewers and identifying "verified purchasers." But that encouraged sellers to offer high-rated reviewers free goods or pay for "verified" purchases.[35]

Things are similar in the public sphere. Traditional media producers reflected what their readers wanted. Supermarket tabloids published improbable stories of extraterrestrials and celebrity scandals. In contrast, publications like the *New Yorker* and *Inc.* magazine catered to serious subscribers, ranging from literary lefties to conservative small-business owners. In my experience, both magazines checked the accuracy of their articles with great diligence, although what they covered (and how) naturally reflected the interest of their readers.

326 UNCERTAINTY AND ENTERPRISE

Google and Facebook wrecked the advertising model that supported careful reporting—and fact-checking. More competition for fewer readers and advertisers tempted traditionally staid news outlets toward tabloid sensationalism and fantasy. What the outlets now call "fact-checking" has become a partisan effort to discredit the views they oppose. Meanwhile, Section 230 of the Communications Decency Act (CDA) protects online platforms like Google and Facebook from lawsuits over falsehoods posted by their users, while sensationalist postings increase their ad revenues.[36]

Organizations like Snopes claim to objectively evaluate news and rumors. But Snopes itself relies on web-based advertising. It faces the same pressures to sensationalize and exaggerate as the targets of its investigations—refuting demonstrable falsehoods may not attract the commercially necessary web traffic. And Snopes, say its conservative critics, makes up the claims it supposedly refutes, and then tailors the results to suit the preferences of a leftist audience. Who then to trust? While independent policing of the news has prima facie appeal, it fails to answer the question posed in Juvenal's *Satires: Quis custodiet ipsos custodes?* "Who will guard the guards themselves?"

A third technologically magnified threat is divisive discourse. Twentieth-century technologies spawned media oligopolies (like TV networks and newsmagazines) that created and disseminated products for mass consumption. Here, the problem for discourse was excessive blandness and societal groupthink. Twenty-first-century advances have promoted the opposite kind of excesses. The new info-oligopolists provide platforms for content they do not themselves create. Unlike the media oligopolies they destroyed, they are protected by Section 230 rules, as mentioned. Yet platforms benefit from shrill, unpaid-for content that does not attempt to change minds. It targets preexisting prejudices and reinforces dogmatic beliefs.

Optimistically, the advantages of the new communication technologies exceed the drawbacks for private discourse. We have and will somehow continue to cope with information overload and dubious reviews on e-commerce platforms. Prospects in the public sphere seem more troubling, however. Technology has made it easy to mobilize mobs against agnostics, not just rival dogmatists, making dysfunctional spillovers from stories (chapter 21) more potent and toxic.*

---

* To borrow from William Butler Yeats's "The Second Coming": "The best lack all conviction, while the worst / are full of passionate intensity." Silence is the pragmatic choice for the best who refuse sectarian protection from mobs of the worst.

THE CASE FOR WIDENING   327

But even with public discourse, it's worth asking: Are conditions really worse than in the good old days? Horrible falsehoods that justified witch hunts and pogroms did not need social media for dissemination. Sensationalism and war-mongering marked the "yellow press" circulation wars in the 1890s. And even if technology has made public discourse more hateful and divisive, are drastic restraints on free expression a suitable remedy? Might not a measured reform of privacy and antitrust rules—and eliminating the exceptional liability protections for platform oligopolists—be sufficient?[37]

3. Balancing Justification and Authority

Agency and authority have lurked in the background for most of this book. Agency, our belief in willful choices when we can't know what will happen, stands in contrast to predetermination and fate. It creates rational anxieties (doubts, uncertainties) about our choices. If everything was predestined, why worry? At the same time, because excitement accompanies anxiety, agency makes life an adventure worth living.

Agency also encourages us to value voluntary agreement over authority. Human interdependencies, no less than nature, limit our choices. Inevitably, what we might want to do is constrained by the preferences of our fellows. In agreeing to align our choices, we exercise agency more than if some authority dictates alignment. Likewise, there is more agency in agreements about specific issues than in the Hobbesian fiction of a blanket contract with an all-powerful Leviathan.

Yet deference to authority endures. As ever, might often seems right. Force and intimidation, not debate or sweet reason, secure authority among children in schoolyards as they did in prehistoric tribes. Athenian democracy, which excluded women and slaves, was "most honoured in the breach."[38] In 416 BCE, Athenians attacked the neutral island of Melos during their war with Sparta. "The strong do what they can, and the weak suffer what they must,"[39] the invaders told the Melians. After the Melinians surrendered, Athenians executed Melinian men and enslaved the women and children. Moreover, democracy in Athens, such as it was, did not endure.

As of 2020, less than half of the world's population lived in some sort of democracy, and fewer than a tenth in fully democratic states.[40] Full democracies, too, have expanded the executive branch's powers and made legislative oversight and deliberation an empty performance. The powers of the security apparatus in democracies can also be draconian.

In the workplace, socialist workers' paradises never empowered workers. Most capitalist businesses are explicitly hierarchical. Just as pharaohs commanded the

328 UNCERTAINTY AND ENTERPRISE

construction of pyramids, Steve Jobs could order the development of the iPhone without consulting Apple's shareholders or many rank-and-file employees. Legal firms that were once governed by the consensus of their partners now vest considerable authority in small executive committees, and career administrators control once self-governing university faculties.

Although authority limits agency, it does have benefits in coping with uncertainty. Reaching consensus through reasoned discussion can pose insurmountable difficulties. Put aside simple conflicts of preference or interest: Neither logic nor evidence can eliminate ignorance about future wants or the means for securing them. Yet "imaginative instincts" about wants and means often diverge, creating disagreements that cannot be easily resolved through honest discourse. Moreover, interminable discussion can harm everyone. Therefore, empowering an authority, at least as a fallback if discourse fails or takes too long, can serve the common good. And hybrid arrangements, with authority serving as a referee or fallback, guided by the prior give-and-take of divergent views, can outperform relying entirely on authority or justificatory discourse.

As with communications technologies, combining authority and discourse poses more severe problems in the public sphere. In the private sphere, competition for customers, talent, and funding stimulates efforts to improve decision-making. Businesses keep changes in routines and structures they believe have worked in their organizations, copy or adapt what they see working in other organizations, and try to eliminate dysfunctional practices. Overcentralized organizations run by imperious bosses or organizations paralyzed by endless internal debate survive only if they have monopolistic power. Generally, the backstop of centralized authority balances justificatory discourse about uncertain matters.

In the public sphere, the functions and roles of public agencies often protect them from competitive pressures. Politicians responsible for the oversight and control of the agencies can face electoral contests, but even in full democracies, uncontested elections to "safe" seats and offices are hardly unknown. And for those politicians who face tough elections, fundraising and campaigning leave little time for the duties of their office. In either case, the practical capacity of politicians to supervise public agencies is limited. Additionally, public organizations face severe institutional constraints on organizational experiments and learning from other's experiences.

Imbalances of authority and justification can produce two kinds of public dysfunctions. Arrangements requiring excessive justification and few options for authoritative override can paralyze, producing what Philip Howard, founder of the Common Good coalition, calls the Rule of Nobody.[41] At the other end, we have Robert Moses's ruthless destruction of vibrant New York City

THE CASE FOR WIDENING   329

neighborhoods to make way for soulless public housing projects, illegal wiretaps by J. Edgar Hoover's Federal Bureau of Investigation, and the CIA's Bay of Pigs fiasco in Cuba.

In keeping with my focus on technological advances, however, I restrict my attention to controlling the authority of experts over technically uncertain matters. The problem arises because technological progress—and experts who do not explicitly coerce through violence—threatens the legitimacy of the institutions that progress requires.

There can be little doubt that technological advances create irrepressible demands for new rules and regulations. To cite uncontroversial examples: The development of automobile transport required driving rules and vehicle inspections. Air travel required a system to control traffic and certify the airworthiness of aircraft. Radio, television, mobile networks, and Wi-Fi required regulating airwaves' use to prevent signal interference. New petrochemical, pharmaceutical, textile, nano-material, and fracking technologies created new forms of air and water pollution that governments had to discourage and control. The discovery of antibiotics required rules to prevent bacteria from acquiring drug resistance, and advances in genetic engineering cry out for rules to stop the creation of deadly new viruses.

Technology cannot however resolve uncertainties about the design of good rules, as Elster's "Excessive Ambitions" essay suggests. Yet the need for new rules inevitably increases the authority of experts who implement the rules. What they say often goes: their expertise makes the experts a law unto themselves, without any serious demands to justify choices that are, at their core, highly uncertain and hit-or-miss.

Up to a point, the independence of empowered experts serves the public interest. The typical layperson or professional politician lacks the knowledge and expertise to regulate technological advances—and even imperfect rules designed by fallible experts are often better than "letting the chips fall where they may." Ceding authority to experts, however, also has drawbacks. Conformist, uncritical thinking on issues for which there can be no demonstrably correct answer is one problem. Experts who have internalized a scientific discipline's Kuhnian paradigm (chapter 5) will not question its premises or inferences. If, as often happens, all the responsible experts are committed to the same paradigm, they will not debate fundamental issues.[42]

Paradigmatic conditioning poses a further problem. As mentioned, scientists value general propositions on topics aligned with their disciplinary paradigm. Their research designs seek to remove contextual influences and exclude variables outside their paradigmatic framework. Contextual, one-off vagaries, crucial in practical recipes, are just random noise in scientific theories.[43]

330 UNCERTAINTY AND ENTERPRISE

But intellectual commitments to scientifically desirable abstractions can increase the risks of expert control. Until the 2008 financial crisis, for example, the US Federal Reserve's econometric model did not include a financial sector. Such exclusion and abstractions are acceptable, even desirable, in scientific economic research, which values precise equilibrium models. And academic approval matters to Fed economists who try to publish their research in economics journals. However, excluding important institutional variables in central banking and other regulatory arenas poses systemic risks.[44]

Scientific groupthink may, on balance, be a necessary evil. The more significant societal problem with expert rule now likely pertains to expert control of highly uncertain ends. The expert has no advantage over the public or politicians in choosing goals. As Elster's essay suggests, the social sciences provide no criteria for the goodness of policy outcomes. Natural sciences, engineering, or medicine don't either. Long-term ends are even more problematic. Stanford polymath (and previously, Simon's Carnegie collaborator) James March points out that we cannot discover long-term goals through analysis.[45]

Consider goals for public health. Immortality being out of the question, could the goal be life expectancy? But what about life expectancy and quality-of-life tradeoffs? Likewise, what about variations in death rates across time, ages, incomes, and demographics? Are low variations across these dimensions a suitable goal, and if so, which dimensions should public health authorities prioritize? Without choices about such priorities, justifiable choices of means (e.g., lockdowns during pandemics) are impossible. Yet no scientific or technical knowledge can guide the choices.

In principle, politicians are supposed to specify the ends for which experts are expected to develop appropriate means. In practice, politicians often obfuscate or avoid the question, leaving experts to choose both ends and means, as happened in the Covid-19 pandemic. Sometimes, even if politicians specify ends, experts may ignore or reinterpret their marching orders. One way or the other, experts often exercise de facto control.

Now, the very notion of choosing public policy goals implies favoring one interest, be it financial or psychic, real or perceived, over another. Pandemic lockdowns pitted the preferences and beliefs of the wealthy and old against those of the young and less well-to-do. So determining goals, inevitably without any scientific or logical basis, puts experts in the business of allocating favors, turning them from public servants into overlords or, more kindly, philosopher kings. Additionally, experts' goal choices reflect their personal financial, psychological, social, ideological, or whatever interest. Those people whose interests are sacrificed by experts are naturally aggrieved. Worse, experts rarely publicly discuss or justify goals, upsetting those who suffer no harm or may even benefit. The game is rigged, many come to believe.

THE CASE FOR WIDENING   331

Independence Beyond the Law?

Inflation targeting by the US Federal Reserve (the Fed) exemplifies the problem of expert control over ends.[46] The Fed's influence and reliance on economic expertise have grown substantially since it was formed in 1913. Hostility to centralized government, dating back to the nation's independence, had prevented the formation of a proper central bank in the United States until Congress passed the Federal Reserve Act of 1913 after several financial panics. Moreover, because of continuing fears of excessive centralization, Congress created a Federal Reserve System of twelve more or less independent regional Reserve Banks.

In the 1930s, after the decentralized system had failed to prevent widespread bank failures in the Great Depression, power shifted to the Federal Reserve Board based in Washington, DC, and its twelve-member Federal Open Market Committee (FOMC).[47]

Starting in the 1960s, economic experts began playing an increasingly significant role at the Fed. Macroeconomics and its academic promoters, many Keynesians, were gaining prestige. The academics claimed the Fed should actively steer the economy and not just prevent financial crises but that the Fed's decision-makers lacked the necessary economic expertise.[48]

Congress formalized the Fed's macroeconomic responsibilities when it passed the 1978 Full Employment Act. The act gave the Fed a "dual mandate" of full employment with price stability. Then, in 2012, the Fed officially declared a 2 percent inflation target.[49]

The Fed now enjoys exceptional independence and autonomy. Unlike other federal agencies that require legislative budgetary appropriations, the Fed is entirely self-funding. By a simple majority of its twelve-member FOMC, the Fed can—and does—conjure up trillions of new base money. No congressional or presidential approval is necessary. Economic expertise is deeply entrenched. The Fed Board employs more than four hundred PhD economists,[50] and its chair is now expected to have a similar pedigree. President Donald Trump's 2018 appointment of a lawyer, Jerome Powell, as chair raised eyebrows.[51]

So, what is the problem? As mentioned earlier, commitments to paradigmatic economics pose the risk of disciplinary groupthink. But that is mainly an issue of means—what about the Fed's 2 percent inflation target?

Paul Volcker, the late, legendary 1980s inflation-fighting Fed chair, was an outspoken opponent of the target. Two percent inflation, which might not seem like much, Volcker wrote in 2018, doubles prices in a generation. Volcker also noted that no economic theory or evidence supported the claim

332   UNCERTAINTY AND ENTERPRISE

that a little inflation greases the economic wheels or reduces the risks of depressions.[52]

As troubling is the disregard for the 1978 legislation that the Fed invokes to support its target. The legislation mandated stable *prices*, not stable *inflation*. These are not the same thing. Prices rising at 2 percent each year—and thus doubling in a generation—isn't the price stability that Congress has mandated. Moreover, the 1978 law established specified precise numerical targets—3 percent for unemployment and zero for inflation; a source for the data (the Bureau of Labor Statistics); and a target date of 1988 (thus allowing for a ten-year transitional period).[53]

Besides flouting the letter and spirit of the law, the Fed's 2 percent target implicitly infringes on the legislature's Constitutional prerogative to levy taxes. Inflation—of any magnitude—is a tax. Moreover, inflation is an iniquitous levy, falling more heavily on the less well-to-do. High-income earners— including distinguished macroeconomists who argue for even higher inflation targets—do not feel the pinch as much. If they invest astutely, they can even benefit from inflation.

The Fed has also invoked the bogeyman of inflation falling below its 2 percent target to justify aggressive, unconventional monetary policies. Openly, and by design, the policies benefitted wealthy stock- and bondholders[54]— including members of the FOMC. Some were reprimanded or even forced to resign for violating Fed rules intended to control insider trading.[55] Activist policies also make the Fed a potent force in financial markets, boosting the policymakers' egos and post-Fed speaking and consulting opportunities.[56]

Fed officials may feel that their technical expertise entitles them to disregard the zero-inflation target set by the 1978 law. They may also convince themselves that their personal financial prospects and the approval of their social and professional circles do not influence their disregard. But sizable portions of the public are not thus convinced. Activists from both sides— Tea Partiers and Occupy Wall Streeters—have made the Fed targets of street protests.

Dissatisfaction with experts who don't explain—yet complain about political interference—isn't self-correcting. Disgruntled voters cannot dismiss experts. But they can turn to demagogues who are even less public-minded and more authoritarian. Increasingly, voters have done just this, jeopardizing the institutions that produced much dynamism, prosperity, and liberty.

Economists and other scholars can help control or reverse the discontent of which they are also often targets. Practical progress usually requires new

THE CASE FOR WIDENING   333

theoretical ideas. The Federalist Papers—articles and essays that Alexander Hamilton, James Madison, and John Jay wrote and pseudonymously published between October 1787 and April 1788—had a clear, practical purpose: to promote the ratification of the Constitution of the United States. They have guided lawmakers and politicians in the United States, Latin America, and Europe ever since.[57]

Not coincidentally, these papers are also considered a landmark of political theory and political science. The authors themselves saw their work as combining the practice and theory of government.[58] A pure handbook or manual, like one for repairing muskets or horse carriages, would not have had lasting, widespread appeal. Instead, the Federalist Papers contained general theories based on broad assumptions about human societies and nature.

But even the farsighted Federalist Papers, written by authors living in a predominantly agricultural, technologically backward society, could not foresee the problems of expert power and impaired discourse that twentieth- and twenty-first-century innovations would produce. So, while we should marvel at the durability of many of their insights—about governing the un-angelic in a large republic,[59] for instance—new or updated theories incorporating the effects and uncertainties of widespread commercial and technological enterprise that pervade the modern world could have great practical value.

Economists and other scholars have much to contribute—if they can transcend their paradigmatic dogmas. Effective solutions to human problems, as exemplified by the Federalist Papers, combine, per William James, abstract, rationalist monism and down-to-earth, baroque empiricism (chapter 9). Their logic likewise reflects both logico-scientific deduction and narrative mode ("thinking in cases") reasoning (chapter 18).

Progress requires both scientific and humanistic understanding. Explanations that rejected willful intent were instrumental in understanding the natural world. Hippocratic medicine, Newtonian physics, and Darwinian biology rejected animism and divine interventions and designs. Naturalistic understanding has supported great practical advances. But practical advances, by humans and for humans, are not predestined, accidental, or deduced from scientific laws. Advances and obstacles spring from human feelings, from hopes, ambitions, love for adventure, fears, frustrations, jealousies, and disagreements. The outliers are as crucial as the averages.

The ambitious social scientist strives for simplicity, generality, and timelessness. Yet, like effective action, consequential theories and explanations of uncertain choices cannot ignore complexity, context, and impermanence. "For every complex problem there is an answer that is clear, simple, and wrong," H. L. Mencken wrote. The hedgehog, who knows just one big thing, cannot design

334 UNCERTAINTY AND ENTERPRISE

the governance of unruly enterprise without the fox's knowledge of many little things.

Contemporary scholars would do well to heed Knight's conclusion to his 1949 comment:

> So, the final word should be, "beware of absolutes." Here again the honest thinker must advert to our religious tradition, with its tendency to erect an antithesis between right and might, or between the right and the expedient, with its absurd and monstrous maxim of "do right though the heavens fall." On the other hand, Talleyrand is said to have said that the only good principle is to have none. But like most bright or poetic sayings this also is "inaccurate." The right principle is to respect all the principles, but to take care to use good judgment as to which one to follow in any particular juncture—or, still more precisely, how far to follow any one and how far its opposite principle. There is always a principle, and a good principle, to be followed in any course of action, and used to justify that particular action. The ultimate besetting sin of the "intellectuals" is oversimplification—because it is that of those who elect them to interpret and formulate their own thinking.[60]

For economists, respecting a broader range of principles—and using judgment to decide which ones to use when—carries risks. Restricting the scope of acceptable problems and solutions legitimizes assessments of scholarly contributions. Per Kuhn, it also raises the collective productivity of economists and their scientific standing. Recall Stanford economist David Kreps's observation that a strong, cohesive paradigm has secured for his disciplinary colleagues exceptional prestige and incomes. Yet, might not a broader, weaker paradigm better serve the common good?

Acknowledgments

The LSE's Hayek Uncertainty and Risk seminars catalyzed this work. I thank the organizers, Tim Besley, John Kay, and Mervyn King, for including me. I am particularly grateful to Matthew Ford, Bill Janeway, and Maurice Mason for repeated rounds of insightful and detailed suggestions. I also thank James Anderson, Florian Artinger, Angus Burgin, Yves de Balmann, Anders Barsk, Richard Bronk, Nancy Cartwright, David Chaffetz, Nick Chater, Paul Collier, Mark Fentonocreevy, Richard Friberg, Bruns Grayson, Gerd Gigerenzer, Jorge Guzman, Bob Higgins, Claudia Huntington, Vijay Joshi, Steve Kaplan, Alan Kirman, Robert Kiernan, Daniel Kim, Bob Litan, Nick Lowe, M. Ali Khan, Shanti Mackintosh, Edward Mariyani-Squire, Colin Mayer, Ashok Nimgade, Lars Östling, Michael Pakenham, Anand Phatak, Quintin Price, C. V. Ravishankar, Michael Roberts, David Robinson, Jeff Sandefer, Guy Spier, Judy Stephenson, Per Strömberg, David Tuckett, Dee Vaidya, Larry Weiss, Karl Wennberg, and two anonymous referees for valuable suggestions and information; Camilla Kapustina and Jeff Polidor for careful research assistance; and, Oxford's James Cook for commissioning the book. Gina Anjou's summaries of practical screen writing techniques kept my interest in discourse (Part 4) alive when I was frustrated with impenetrable narrative theories but had not yet discovered Jerome Bruner's work. Talented artist and Tufts ed-tech expert Freedom Baird was instrumental in designing and producing the illustrations. Research librarians Ann Cullen and especially Ellen McDonald were helpful well beyond the call of their usual responsibilities. Nigel Quinney's thoughtful queries, suggestions, and edits brought much-needed coherence to a disorganized manuscript, while David Baker's wordsmithing contributed significantly to its readability. Mark Steinmeyer orchestrated a generous grant from the Smith Richardson Foundation, providing helpful feedback and securing thoughtful reviews. Alexcee Bechthold and Jacqueline Pavlovic have been exemplary editors and managers of a difficult and complex book project.

Three sources have had a broad, deep, and fortuitous influence: Melvyn Bragg's *In Our Time* podcasts, which spurred more than a dozen ideas that I have used; Peter Millican's scholarship on Hume and Oxford lectures on General Philosophy; and Howard Stevenson's ineffable wisdom, mentorship, and comments on this book and nearly all my previous work.

These acknowledgments are frustratingly meager for the overwhelming kindness and generosity I have benefitted from. My gratitude far exceeds what my ungracious words can say. So, to borrow from John Lennon and Paul McCartney: I've gotten by with a ~~little~~ **LOT** of help from my friends!

Notes

Preface

1. The thought that starting a journal might create a home for my piece had crossed my mind. But there was much more to it than brazen self-publication. My article (Bhidé 2006) really did fit the aims of the journal. Published by the eponymous Center on Capitalism and Society that Phelps had started at Columbia in 2001, the journal sought to disseminate work that mainstream journals would reject. Abjuring anonymous refereeing it would publish provocative papers along with a reviewer's commentary that might vehemently dissent. The Kauffman Foundation provided a grant, and, after hesitating, the center's founder and director, Phelps went along. I should also point out that the hero of this book, Frank Knight, published several pieces in the *Journal of Political Economy*, which he edited and helped put on the map.
2. Solow 2006.
3. My last editorial letter reported that "the economists we [have] published ran the gamut from Akerlof to Zeckhauser with Arrow, David, Heckman, Kornai, Nelson, Phelps, Sachs, Sen, Stiglitz, and Summers in between. I am particularly proud of having persuaded the late great business historian Alfred Chandler to drop the book he was working on to write what would be his last major piece (discussed by Richard Sylla) for us. We also published work by other historians (including Ferguson, McCraw, and James), political scientists (Jon Elster wrote the provocative 'Excessive Ambitions' and 'Excessive Ambitions II'), educationists (including Harvard president emeritus Derek Bok), legal scholars, social psychologists, theologians, philosophers, and even a Nobel Prize winner in medicine (Baruch Blumberg)."

Chapter 1

1. Origins of the Longitude Prize n.d.
2. Scott and Crock 2020, 302.
3. Knight 1921, 225.
4. Knight 1921, 233.
5. Knight 1921, 233.
6. Knight 1921, 227.
7. See shaded box in chapter 14 on abductive inferences and chapter 18 on narrative mode reasoning and discourse.
8. Forrester 2017.
9. Kuhn 1970, 20.
10. Keynes 1936, 383.

338 NOTES

Chapter 2

1. Bhidé, Datar, and Stebbins 2021.
2. Lehrer 2010.
3. Friberg 2016, 8.
4. Kay and King (2020b, 87) distinguish between "resolvable" and "radical" uncertainties instead of "risk" and Knightian uncertainty. In their telling example of "resolvable," they include doubts about the capital of Pennsylvania. This doubt can be resolved by consulting an atlas, with no statistics or probability distributions required.
5. Hayek 1945, 522.
6. Hayek 1945, 522.
7. Hayek 1945, 522.
8. Hayek 1945, 524.
9. Early (seventeenth- to eighteenth-century) Enlightenment ideas on probability emphasized the broader considerations. For example, the German polymath Gottfried Leibniz noted that "in several political and legal situations there is not as much need for fine calculation as there is for the accurate recapitulation of all the circumstances" (Aristimuño and Crespo 2021, 926).
10. See Brewer 1996 and Walton 2014. Note, however, Forrester's (2017, 6) interpretation of John Stuart Mill's claims about inductive inferences—that they proceed from one particular to another particular, not from a general inductive principle (inferred from many like particulars) applied to a particular target.
11. In practice, however, we routinely extrapolate models without giving much thought to their fit with specific circumstances, just as we gloss the generalizations that lurk behind contextual justifications (e.g., that the atlas we consult remains current).
12. Hearsay is inadmissible and opinions are usually considered weak evidence.
13. Repurposing Kant's term.
14. The FDA may, however, sometimes accept a single "adequate and well-controlled efficacy study" (FDA 1998, 3).
15. Stretching our imaginations, we can think of the statistical model serving as a preliminary jury poll, evaluating the "treatment is no better than the placebo" argument. In fact, because the statistical results can be ambiguous, the FDA convenes panels of experts to evaluate the data.
16. Despite the efforts of the European subsidiaries of US credit bureaus, several European bankers I interviewed were unaware they could purchase standardized credit scores. European rules also allow branch staff to review individual loan applications—and recent "know your customer" regulations strongly encourage case-by-case approvals. See Bhidé 2017 and Bhidé 2021b.
17. See Bhidé 2017 and Bhidé 2021b.
18. Forrester 2017, 2–3.
19. Isaacson 2011, ch. 35. Jobs finally had surgery in July 2004.
20. Simler and Hanson 2018, 206.
21. Gorski 2011.

Chapter 3

1. Bhidé, Datar, and Stebbins 2020, 16.
2. Hirschman 1970.
3. Sloan 1963, 54.
4. Capurso 1998, 6.
5. Mercier and Sperber 2017.
6. Sinclair 1994.
7. The 1962 Salem trials resulted in the hanging of nineteen convicted "witches." Witch hunts had begun in Europe in the early fourteenth century and continued through the late eighteenth century, with the last known execution for witchcraft taking place in Switzerland in 1782 (Wallenfeldt 2023).
8. Abrams v. United States, 250 U.S. 616, 630 (1919). Cited in Collier 2022, 362.
9. New State Ice Co. v. Liebmann, 285 U.S. 262, 311 (1932) (Brandeis, J., dissenting). Cited in Tyler and Gerken 2022.
10. Royal Museums Greenwich 2016.
11. Wikipedia, s.v. "Reichstag building," last edited October 9, 2023, https://en.wikipe dia.org/w/index.php?title=Reichstag_building&oldid=1179286860.
12. And here, too, the stakes affect stringency. The acceptable uncertainty about the efficacy and side effects of vaccines is much higher in pandemics than in normal circumstances; regulators grant emergency approvals with less data. In principle the FDA asserts the right to regulate toothbrushes as medical devices. In practice it does not.
13. Technological innovations (such as DNA tests) can also help reduce doubts.
14. Junod 2008, 12.
15. For example, in 2022 FDA officials approved Biogen's Alzheimer's treatment, overruling the expert panel's recommendation to reject the treatment.
16. Bhidé 2014.

Chapter 4

1. Baumol 1968, 64.
2. Baumol 1968, 66–67.
3. Hiring was supported by wealthy entrepreneurial alums who endowed new chairs. I landed one at Columbia's business school in 2000.
4. An entrepreneur's earnings also often include additional components that (in Knight's scheme) aren't true profit. These are wages for the entrepreneur's labor, rents for the entrepreneur's property, and returns for the capital provided by the entrepreneur exposed to objectively calculable risks—all determined by a competitive market.
5. The figure follows the spirit of the taxonomy I used in my 2000 book, reproduced in the Preface, while recasting important particulars. Most notably this new version

340 NOTES

distinguishes between market and alignment uncertainties (see the last shaded box in chapter 15, "Alignment" versus "Market" Uncertainties).

6. Knight's *Risk, Uncertainty and Profit* does not discuss the role of stories or other forms of rich communication, although in his later work on political philosophy, Knight treated discussion (rather than voting) as the essence of a good democracy but was critical of "persuasion," which he saw as coercive (Knight 1940).

7. Recent work by Robert Shiller (2017) and (2021) on "contagious" narratives, by David Tuckett (2022) on "conviction narratives," and by Kay and King (2020a) on "reference narratives" exemplifies the advantages of taking stories more seriously.

8. Thomas Kuhn was a leading proponent of this view, according to Isaac (2012) and Forrester (2017). According to Isaac (2012, 2), "By 1960, Kuhn was inclined to conclude that the 'sample problems and applications' provided in a scientific education were what held a tradition of normal science together, even in the absence of consensus on methodological or theoretical fundamentals."

Chapter 5

1. Analogously, present-day developers of e-bikes could ask why 1890s e-bikes failed to assess problems they might now face. Historical patterns can provide valuable lessons, although the world constantly changes.

2. According to Emmett (2018), "The role that *Risk, Uncertainty and Profit* is best known for today is the contribution it made to the teaching of and theorizing about competitive markets." See also Emmett 2021.

3. Stigler 1985, 3.

4. Stigler 1985, 5.

5. Westgren and Holmes 2021, 199.

6. LeRoy and Singell 1987, 402.

7. Emmett 2015; Kuchař 2020.

8. Emmett 2015, 9.

9. Emmett 2015; Kuchař 2020.

10. Emmett 2015; Kuchař 2020.

11. Burgin 2009, 516.

12. Emmett 2015; Kuchař 2020.

13. Emmett 2021, 883–884.

14. Moreover, according to Westgren and Holmes (2021), Knight uses Francis Bacon's (1620) *pars destruens* and *pars construens* form of argumentation: first clarify the errors of an existing account (*pars destruens*), then construct a new, more correct account (*pars construens*). And Knight's clarifications of errors—and their preambles— are usually lengthy (201–202).

15. Stigler 1985, 2.

16. Emmett 2000.

17. Burgin 2009, 514.

18. Hayek 1961, as cited in Burgin 2009, 514–515.

NOTES   341

19. Knight 1922, 30, as cited in Burgin 2009, 526.
20. Burgin 2009, 514.
21. Stigler 1985, 6.
22. Knight 1940, 18.
23. Westgren and Holmes 2021, 199.
24. See O'Donnell 2021a, 1134–1135.
25. Buchanan 1982, xi.
26. Knight 1921, 7.
27. Kuhn 1970, 19.
28. Kuhn 1970, 10.
29. Kuhn 1970, 10.
30. Okasha 2016, 75.
31. Forrester 2017, 48.
32. Kuhn 1970, 47.
33. What Kuhn really meant by "paradigm" is more ambiguous than the summary I have provided. Kuhn himself may have regretted the use of the term. See Forrester 2017.
34. Axiom in *Oxford Dictionaries*, as cited in Marsay 2016, 7. See also Isaac (2012, 17–18) on the replacement of Euclid's "intuitive" axioms in geometry with abstractions axiom that have no intuitive basis.
35. Wang 2018.
36. Kreps 2004, 115.
37. Stigler 1985, 11.
38. Buchanan 1982, xi.
39. Buchanan 1982, xi.
40. Buchanan 1982, xii.
41. Buchanan 1982, xiii.
42. Knight 1921, 14
43. Kreps 2004, 125. And expanding on Kuhn's observations about academic "prestige," Kreps (2004, 115) also notes that professors of economics earn higher salaries than faculty from other social sciences.
44. Kreps 2004, 124.

Chapter 6

1. Friedman 1976, 282, as cited in LeRoy and Singell, 1987, 395.
2. Arrow 1951, 417.
3. LeRoy and Singell, who challenge Friedman's claim, cite Knight's explicit assertion that "we do estimate the value or validity or dependability of our opinions and estimates and such an estimate has the same *form* as a probability judgment; it is a ratio, expressed by a proper fraction"; and likewise that: "The individual . . . throws his estimate of the value of an opinion into the probability form of 'a successes in b trials' (a/b being a proper fraction) and 'feels' toward it as toward any other

342 NOTES

probability situation" (Knight 1921, 234, as cited in LeRoy and Singell 1987, 397–398). However, as Langlois and Cosgel (1993, 460) observe, LeRoy and Singell's rebuttal conflates "probabilistic" expressions of confidence in estimates with the estimates themselves. Knight's quote refers to estimates of the dependability of our opinions—expressions of confidence. Friedman refers to "*events* for which it [i]s not possible to specify numerical probabilities" [italics added]. Knight repeatedly distinguished between estimates of the outcomes of events and expressions of confidence in estimates. LeRoy and Singell ignore Knight's distinction.

4. Mill 1844, 138.
5. Karni 2008, 1.
6. Along with W. Allen Wallis, according to Lindley (1980, 1).
7. "Mathematician" does not do justice to von Neumann's work in physics, economics, computing, and statistics—and on the development of the atomic bomb. Citing the impact of these contributions, the *Financial Times* named him as its Person of the Century in 1999.
8. Lindley 1980, 6.
9. Price Theory and Principles Textbooks n.d.
10. Pratt, Raiffa, and Schlaifer (1964).
11. The multiperiod extension of expected utilities in the form of net present value, however, taught to us in our finance classes, remains ubiquitous in business education and practice.
12. Simon 1978c, 2.
13. Savage 1954, 16, as cited in Kay and King 2020a.
14. Savage 1954, 16, as cited in Gigerenzer, Reb, and Luhan 2022, 174.
15. Simon 1988, 286, as cited in Gigerenzer, Reb, and Luhan 2022, 174.
16. Kay and King 2020a.
17. Barreto 1989, 64.
18. Barreto 1989, 2.
19. Barreto 1989, 2, 141.
20. Kay 1984, 57, and Shackle 1969, as cited in Barreto 1989, 142–143.

Chapter 7

1. Smith 2007, 105–106.
2. Ghemawat 2002, 52–53.
3. Many Chicago economists, however, questioned this possibility—in the absence of harmful regulation—although like the Harvard economists, they too assumed profits signified an undesirable deviation from perfect competition.
4. Ghemawat 2002, 53.
5. As mentioned in the Preface, my doctoral curriculum in 1985 included Richard Caves's IO course.
6. Ghemawat 2002, 54.
7. Porter, Argyres, and McGahan 2002, 43.

NOTES 343

8. Porter, Argyres, and McGahan 2002, 44.
9. Here, we believed, was a reliable method to get objective answers to real questions, not the made-up cases of managerial economics. A rock-star professor would teach us how to use his method. What could be better? I carried my enthusiasm to management consulting (at McKinsey & Co.) but then disillusionment set in, which I wrote up in a *Harvard Business Review* article titled "Hustle as Strategy." This apparently did not endear me to my former professor.
10. By the end of the 1980s, according to Ghemawat (2002, 66), "Competition to invest in tangible and intangible assets, strategic control of information, horizontal mergers, network competition and product standardization, contracting, and numerous other settings in which interactive effects were apt to be important had all been modeled using game theory."
11. Whereas the standard microeconomic model tells us exactly what to expect under conditions of perfect competition, models of imperfect or oligopolistic competition only tell us, complains MIT economist Franklin Fisher, that "a great many outcomes are known to be possible—with outcomes depending on what variables the oligopolists use and how they form conjectures about each other" (Fisher 1989, 117). The theory generates, Fisher continues, "a large number of stories, each one an anecdote describing what might happen in some particular situation" rather than "a full, coherent formal theory of what must happen or a theory that tells us how what happens depends on well defined measurable variables" (Fisher 1989, 118). Unlike Fisher, I see the uncertain, context-laden nondeterminism as a virtue, not a defect.
12. The Royal Swedish Academy of Sciences 1982.
13. According to Ghemawat (2002, 53), Bain (1951) showed that industries where the top eight firms accounted for more than 70 percent of sales were twice as profitable as industries where the top eight's sales shares were lower).
14. Gardiner v. Gray 1815.
15. The Royal Swedish Academy of Sciences 1982.
16. Stiglitz 2002, 481.
17. LeRoy and Singell 1987.
18. To quote Stigler (1971, xiv) more fully: "The theories of economists are often identified by (and sometimes limited to!) catchwords, and tradition has assigned a distinction between risks (capable of actuarial treatment) and uncertainty (stochastic events not capable of such treatment) as Knight's contribution. Fortunately this is an extreme caricature of his work, because modern analysis no longer views the two classes as different in kind. Knight's famous result is not affected: pure profit is the difference between payments to all hired factors (including those belonging to the entrepreneur) and the realized product; and this profit, which of course may be negative or positive, arises only when there is uncertainty in the outcome of the productive process. When and to the extent that events are predictable individually or en masse, they give rise only to wages or rents (including risk premia)."
19. Bhidé, 2010, 89. Kay and King's (2020b, 74) dismissal is also summary.
20. See Bhidé 2021a, especially the Appendix.

344 NOTES

21. Emmett 2021, 8.
22. As of February 27, 2022, Google Scholar reported 420 citations, while the *Crossref* count on the JPE site was 153.
23. Akerlof 1970.
24. As of March 24, 2022, Google Scholar reported 39,479 citations.
25. LeRoy and Singell 1987, Abstract. They add however that Knight's discussion was "always informal and in places inaccurate"—and that Knight did not anticipate the use of "incentive compatible contracts."
26. The journal rarely publishes articles without math or statistics. One (highly speculative) possibility for the acceptance of L-S's dog-bites-man essay—which has neither—is that it allowed Chicago economists (who edit the journal) to overcome the dissonance of treating Knight as a father figure while rejecting his most noteworthy contribution.
27. A thoughtful scholar once told me of a definitive article in the *Journal of Political Economy* showing Knight could not have really meant what he wrote. He could not recount the details, however, making me wonder how carefully he had read either Knight's 1921 book or L-S's 1987 deconstruction.

Chapter 8

1. Bernstein 1996, 217.
2. Bernstein 1996, 222–223.
3. Skidelsky 2003, 3.
4. Skidelsky 2015, xv.
5. Knight 1951, 29.
6. Bernstein 1996, 222.
7. Bernstein 1996, 223.
8. O'Donnell 2021a, 1139.
9. Assuming that 1 GBP in 1920 was 5 USD and that 1 USD in 1920 was worth 16.65 USD in 2022.
10. Skidelsky 2003, 283.
11. Faulkner et al. 2021, 858–859.
12. The overview further notes that "while the term 'risk' does come up [in the Treatise] this is in two different technical senses, both of which differ from Knight's. . . . At no point is risk counterposed with uncertainty in the manner of Knight."
13. There is a great deal more in the *Treatise*, particularly on induction and statistical inference, that is not related to my propositions.
14. Keynes 1921, 22–24.
15. Keynes further noted that even comparison was impossible in some situations: we cannot "say that the degree of our rational belief in one conclusion [was] either equal to, greater than, or less than the degree of our belief in another" (Keynes 1921, 40).
16. Keynes 1921, 40. The *Treatise* also offered a general, if preliminary, theory that included numerical and nonnumerical estimates—with considerable mathematized

NOTES 345

specification of when and how numerical techniques should be used. But the development of subjective utility maximization doomed Keynes's ambitious project, along with Knightian uncertainty, by prescribing numerical estimation of all probabilities.

17. Keynes 1921, 15.
18. O'Donnell (2003, 73) points out that "confidence" is implicit, not explicit in the *Treatise*. I use "confidence" for ease of expository convenience. Likewise, Keynes (1921, 78) distinguishes between the weight of argument and the weight of evidence, with a "correlative" relationship between the two. For convenience—and because the distinction makes no practical difference in my exposition—I prefer weight of evidence, or evidentiary weight.
19. Keynes 1921, 345. He does not provide much justification for this precept, however, apparently regarding it as self-evident.
20. The weight of evidence also affects doubts about distributional targets. For example, a second clinical trial that shows less evidence of the efficacy of a drug nonetheless increases the FDA's confidence.
21. Wilkinson 1986, 204, quoted in Feduzi 2010, 349.
22. Schauer 2003, 81–82.
23. Keynes 1921, 83.
24. Knight 1921, 219.
25. Keynes 1921, 82.
26. Keynes 1921, 81–83.
27. Keynes 1921, 83.
28. Some readers of the *Treatise* may see that my thought experiment parallels Keynes's example of the "capricious" choice of an umbrella when the barometer is high, but the clouds are dark. This is not accidental: I prefer to hold Keynes's example for later in the chapter when I discuss his emphasis on radical uncertainty.
29. Cited in Fye 2015, 356. Other medical journals also urged going slow, Fye reports, publishing editorials with titles such as, "Surgical Treatment of Coronary Artery Disease: Too Fast, Too Soon?" and "Direct Coronary Revascularization: A Plea Not to Let the Genie Escape from the Bottle" (Fye 2015, 353–354).
30. Fye 2015, 354.
31. Operated by an agency of the US government later and renamed the National Heart, Lung and Blood Institute in 1976.
32. US Congress, Office of Technology Assessment, Health Care Technology and Its Assessment in Eight Countries, OTA-BP-H-140 (Washington, DC: US Government Printing Office, February 1995).
33. Yaeger 1984.
34. O'Donnell 2003 and Feduzi 2010 provide detailed analyses.
35. Keynes 1921, 83–84.
36. Feduzi 2010, 342.
37. Kyburg 1970, 169, cited by Feduzi 2010, 342.
38. Feduzi 2010, 341.
39. Keynes 1921, 357.
40. Nuland 2008, 23.

346 NOTES

41. Bynum 2008, 56–57.
42. Russell 1922, 119.
43. Skidelsky 2003, 290.
44. Keynes 1921, 3.
45. According to Donald Gillies (2003), Keynes did not use "objective" to refer to material things. Rather he meant "objective in the Platonic sense, referring to something in a supposed Platonic world of abstract ideas" (5).
46. As Keynes wrote in a 1922 letter, "Ramsey and other young men at Cambridge are quite obdurate, and still believe that either Probability is a definitely measurable entity, probably connected with Frequency, or is of merely psychological importance and is definitely non-logical" (cited in O'Donnell 2021b, 596).
47. "Timeline," maynardkeynes.org, accessed May 23, 2024, https://www.maynardkey nes.org/keynes-career-timeline.html.
48. Gillies 2003, 114.
49. Gillies 2003, 114.
50. Ramsey 1931, "Truth and Probability," 183.
51. Ramsey (1931, 183) did not make the reasoning for this claim, now called the Dutch Book Argument, explicit. De Finetti made the argument more precise in 1937— possibly without knowing of Ramsey's claim. (Source: MacBride, Fraser, Mathieu Marion, María José Frápolli, Dorothy Edgington, Edward Elliott, Sebastian Lutz, and Jeffrey Paris, "Frank Ramsey," The Stanford Encyclopedia of Philosophy [Summer 2020 Edition], ed. Edward N. Zalta, https://plato.stanford.edu/archives/sum2020/ entries/ramsey/.)
52. Ramsey thus answered Keynes's criticism: "No rational basis has been discovered for numerical comparison of probabilities." It was not even that the theories had prescribed unrealistic methods, Keynes had asserted: "*No* method of calculation, however impracticable, has been suggested" (Keynes 1921, 32).
53. O'Donnell 2021b, 601.
54. O'Donnell 2021b, 601.
55. Keynes 1956, 115
56. O'Donnell 2021, 592.
57. O'Donnell 2021, 595.
58. O'Donnell 2021, 592.
59. Keynes 1921, 31–32.
60. O'Donnell (2021, 587) claims Keynes used this example for the sake of completeness. "As a work claiming to break new ground in probability theory, the [*Treatise*] understandably provided little discussion of non-probabilistic situations. Nevertheless, completeness required their acknowledgement, and one clear example was given."
61. From an article written by Keynes (1937, 213–214) summarizing the argument of his *General Theory*.
62. Keynes 1937, 214.
63. Keynes 1937, 214–215.
64. Knight 1921, 347.
65. Knight 1921, 226.

NOTES   347

66. Knight 1921, 242.
67. Keynes 1937, 215.
68. Phelps 1990, 1.
69. Jahan and Papageorgiou 2014, 53.
70. Samuelson's 1946 tribute to Keynes anticipated his subsequent treatment of Keynes's *General Theory*: "Until the appearance of the mathematical models of Meade, Lange, Hicks, and Harrod there is reason to believe that Keynes himself did not truly understand his own analysis" (188). Likewise, in the sole mention of uncertainty in his tribute, Samuelson wrote, "As for expectations, the General Theory is brilliant in calling attention to their importance and in suggesting many of the central features of uncertainty and speculation. It paves the way for a theory of expectations, but it hardly provides one" (192).
71. Janeway 2018, 15–16.
72. Janeway 2018, 36.
73. Janeway 2018, 15–16.
74. Phelps 2016.
75. Bernanke 2007.
76. Mankiw 2008.
77. Institute for New Economic Thinking n.d.
78. Institute for New Economic Thinking n.d.

Chapter 9

1. Simon 1987a, 2. The *International Encyclopedia of the Social Sciences* also highlights realistic assumptions as a common distinguishing feature. The usual ('neoclassical') economic models follow Milton Friedman's 1953 rule: accurate predictions matter, but realistic assumptions do not. Behavioral economists, according to the *Encyclopedia*, believe realistic assumptions help distinguish between spurious correlations and true cause-and-effect relationships. Absurd models can produce accurate predictions by chance.
2. Knight 1921, 53.
3. Marshall 1920 cited by Robb 2009.
4. Schumpeter 1934, 93–94 (English translation of 1911 German book *Theorie der wirtschaftlichen Entwicklung*).
5. Keynes 1936, 161.
6. Rakow (2010, 458) enumerates "a host of [other] psychological insights . . . which foreshadow revolutionary advances in psychological decision theory from the latter half of the 20th century." These include Simon's bounded rationality and "key components" of Kahneman & Tversky's prospect theory, such as "the reference dependent valuation of outcomes, and the non-linear weighting of probabilities." Kahneman's comment published at the end of Rakow's article indicates, in my view, defensiveness about Kahneman's failure to cite Knight's ideas. Knight, Kahneman argues, had not been part of the recently dominant conversation. Knight's prior

348   NOTES

ideas about behavior therefore did not deserve any more attention than Kahneman's grandmother's, who had similar ideas.

7. Knight 1921, 236.
8. Knight 1921, 235.
9. Knight 1921, 11. Thus, while Knight favors the aspiration of theoretical economics to become an exact science like physics, he acknowledges that it is a "human science" focusing on "conduct" consciously adapted to ends. But because economic activities are often not "rational or planned," this imposes "notable restrictions" on theoretical economics that should be recognized in the practical domain (Knight 1921, 52).
10. Knight applies this "middle way" of following simplified abstraction with extensive qualification for his own theorizing. The "complicated" argument in the "Enterprise and Profit" chapter starts with the simple case, as mentioned, of people knowing nothing about each other's capacities before analyzing numerous more realistic possibilities.
11. Vincenti 1990.
12. Bhidé 2020.
13. Friedman 1953, 14.
14. Although variants are in fact used in the natural sciences.
15. Simon 1991c, 25.
16. Augier 2008, 5904.
17. Simon 1978a, 3.
18. The Editors of Encyclopedia Britannica 2022a.
19. Augier 2008, 5905.
20. Augier 2008, 5905.
21. Simon 1978c, 2.
22. Simon 1979, 497.
23. Simon, however, goes on to argue that in fact the differences between the rationality of economics and the other social sciences are "often differences in vocabulary more than in substance" (Simon 1978, 5).
24. Simon 1978, 3.
25. Simon 1978, 6.
26. Simon 1978, 3–4.
27. Simon 1978, 4.
28. Simon 1978, 14.
29. Simon 1979, 498.
30. Simon 1979, 500.
31. Simon 1978, 14.
32. Simon 1979, 500.
33. Simon 1978, 14.
34. A 1956 sequel in the *Psychology Review* examined how environmental variations influence the problem of "behaving approximately rationally, or adaptively" (Simon 1956, 130).
35. Simon 1955, 104.
36. Simon 1979, 502.

NOTES 349

37. Simon's satisficing also allows for adjustable aspirations. Aspirations can rise and fall "with changing experiences. In a benign environment that provides many good alternatives, aspirations rise; in a harsher environment, they fall" (Simon 1979, 503).
38. Simon 1979, 503.
39. Simon 1979, 503.
40. Simon 1979, 494.
41. Simon 1997, 20.
42. Simon 1991c, 25.
43. Simon 1997, 20.
44. Simon 1979, 501.
45. Simon 1979, 507.
46. Simon 1979, 501.
47. Simon 1979, 495.
48. Simon 1979, 509.
49. Simon 1947, xi.
50. Simon 1979, 500.
51. Barnard 1938.
52. Simon 1979, 500.
53. Simon 1979, 501.
54. Dearborn and Simon 1958.
55. Simon 1979, 501.
56. Simon 1979, 507.
57. Simon 1979, 507.
58. Simon 1979, 507.
59. Simon's Nobel Prize Lecture concluded with the declaration that despite "qualifications and reservations . . . we do understand today many of the mechanisms of human rational choice. We do know how the information processing system called Man, faced with complexity beyond his ken, uses his information processing capacities to seek out alternatives, to calculate consequences, to resolve uncertainties, and thereby . . . find ways of action that are sufficient unto the day, that satisfice" (Simon 1979, 511).
60. Sent 2004, 740.
61. This may be a stretch for some of the research, e.g., Nelson and Winter's cited by Sent.
62. Murmann 2016.
63. Sent 2004, 742.
64. Solow 1958, 84.
65. Simon 1991d, 326.
66. Questioning Buchanan's claim that economists don't campaign for the prize, McCloskey admiringly cites Simon's "amazing autobiography in which he tells, on the level, how he *did* campaign" (McCloskey 1994, 24).
67. See Simon 1991d, 319–322.
68. Simon 1991d, 326
69. Leijonhufvud 2004, 353.

350 NOTES

70. Leijonhufvud 2004, 352.
71. Leijonhufvud 2004, 353–354.
72. Although Simon had no formal training in psychology, he fit in easily. His second landmark behavioral paper was published in *Psychology Today*. The American Psychological Foundation awarded Simon its Gold Medal Award for Life Achievement in Psychological Science in 1988, and the American Psychological Association honored him with its Award for Outstanding Lifetime Contribution to Psychology in 1993 (National Academy of Sciences, "Herbert A. Simon," accessed February 23, 2021, http://www.nasonline.org/member-directory/deceased-memb ers/50445.html).
73. Simon 1991d, 326.
74. Simon 1991d, 144.
75. Simon 1991d, 320.
76. Simon 1991d, 385.
77. According to Sent's history of behavioral economics, "This is symptomatic for Simon's relative lack of lasting impact on any of the disciplinary domains through which he passed during his career. For instance, despite his criticism of the theoretical outlook in political science and management theory, Simon has not contributed extensive empirical studies. Despite his pathbreaking work on the serial symbol-processing hypothesis in cognitive psychology and artificial intelligence, Simon's contributions are rather outdated in the face of the current focus on parallelism and connectionism" (Sent 2004, 750).
78. According to a just-received email from Robert Aliber: "We just flew back from London. Initially the plane cruised by 36,000 feet, then just west of Greenland, the plane climbed to 39,000 feet—the air is thinner at 39,000 feet and a gallon of fuel moves the plane further. Why didn't the pilot continue the climb to 39,000 feet when we left Heathrow? The plane was too heavy when it was nearly full of fuel— 50,000 gallons—whose weight of 330,000 pounds was many times the weight of the passengers and luggage. Most of the cost of the flight is moving the fuel that is needed to move the passengers." Here some of the information used to calculate the optimal trajectory is known (e.g., the weight of the fuel and payload), but the calculation is also subject to the vagaries of nature that are treated as noise.
79. Indeed, Simon had proposed a "horses for courses" approach, suggesting that the mainstream model was satisfactory for simple, static choices.
80. James 1907, 22.
81. James 1898, vii.
82. Augier and March 2004, 4.
83. Simon 1968, 443.
84. Simon 1968, 445.
85. Simon 1968, 443.
86. Simon 1979, 508.
87. See Bhidé 2020 for details.
88. Klaes and Sent 2003, 17 (conference paper version, not in final 2005 paper).
89. Simon 1991d, 108–109.
90. Simon 1979, 508.

NOTES 351

Chapter 10

1. Michael Young, review of Tom Wells, *The Devil and Daniel Ellsberg* (New York: Palgrave Macmillan, 2002), *Reason*, June 2002, https://reason.com/2002/06/01/the-devil-and-daniel-ellsberg-2/.
2. Ellsberg's retrospective says that writing his 1961 paper led him to conclude that maximizing the probability weighted utilities was "inadequate, misleading and wrongheaded as a universal normative (or descriptive) principle." This is not, however, important for my purposes.
3. Ellsberg 1961, 643.
4. As it happens, as interest in Knightian uncertainty receded, Ellsberg's result is now usually cited as a violation of a critical assumption of the theory that made such uncertainty superfluous.
5. Ellsberg 2011, 223.
6. Zappia 2016.
7. Ellsberg 1961, 645.
8. Savage's 1954 book, according to Zappia (2016), provided a method for testing normative theories that distinguished between mistakes and deliberate violations of axioms: "In general, a person who has tentatively accepted a normative theory must conscientiously study situations in which the theory seems to lead him astray; he must decide for each by reflection . . . whether to retain his initial impression of the situation or to accept the implications of the theory for it" (Savage 1954, 102).
9. Ellsberg 2001, 1.
10. Zappia 2016, n. 8.
11. Ellsberg 2001, 134.
12. According to Ellsberg, violators had contrived the first two of Savage's four postulates: (1) that decision-makers have a complete, consistent ordering of their gambles or "actions," and (2) choices between two "actions" must be "unaffected by the value of pay-offs corresponding to events for which both actions have the same pay-off" (Ellsberg 1961, 648).
13. Ellsberg 1961, 646.
14. Ellsberg 1961, 655.
15. Ellsberg 2011.
16. Ellsberg 1961, 658.
17. Ellsberg 1961, 669.
18. Ellsberg 2011, 223.
19. Ellsberg 2011, 224.
20. Ellsberg 1961, 646.
21. Ellsberg 2011, 224.
22. Ellsberg 2011, 224. Ellsberg (2011, 225) adds that most of those who have become aware that the thesis existed, either before or after it was published, have had the mistaken belief that it was written before the 1961 *QJE* article, which, they suppose, represents a concise summary of the thesis. On the contrary, that article, which reflects my thinking between 1957 and 1961, represents only about 10 percent of the material covered in the thesis, which reflects very extensive reading of related

352 NOTES

references in 1962 and a much more elaborate analysis of alternative approaches, leading up to a new decision rule for choice under uncertainty.

23. Zappia 2016, 57.

24. Ellsberg was apparently responding to another criterion for challenging subjective utility theory (beyond unregretted violations of its axioms) that Milton Friedman and Savage specified in a 1952 article: The theory should be retained unless "an alternative is found that is 'better,' in the sense of being equally fruitful and less frequently contradicted" (Friedman and Savage 1952, 472).

25. Siniscalchi (2008) offers a contrary view: "Since the mid-1980s, several decision models that can accommodate ambiguity and ambiguity aversion (or appeal) have been axiomatized; other contributions have addressed the behavioural manifestations and implications of ambiguity, as well as updating and dynamic choice. Furthermore, there is an ever-growing collection of applications to contract theory, auctions, finance, macroeconomics, political economy, insurance and other areas of economic inquiry."

26. Ellsberg 2011, 221.

27. Ellsberg 2011, 221.

28. Ellsberg 2011, 223.

29. Ellsberg 2011, 220.

30. Ellsberg 2011, 223.

31. Ellsberg 2011, 223.

32. Ellsberg 2011, 225.

33. Camerer 1995, 645.

34. Camerer and Weber 1992, 330.

35. Camerer and Weber 1992, 330.

36. Camerer 1995, 645.

37. Camerer and Weber 1992, 331.

38. Zappia 2021; 2028.

39. According to Knight, "We live only by knowing something about the future; while the problems of life, or of conduct at least, arise from the fact that we know so little. This is as true of business as of other spheres of activity. The essence of the situation is action according to opinion, of greater or less foundation and value, neither entire ignorance nor complete and perfect information, but partial knowledge" (1921, 199).

40. Knight (1921, 242) refers to entrepreneurs' "conative feeling" toward uncertainty. Here Knight distinguishes between subjective or "felt" and the behavioral ("connotative") response of the entrepreneur. In chapter 4 of my previous book (Bhidé 2000), I had hypothesized that founders of high-growth startups have high tolerances for ambiguity rather than risk. Puri and Robinson's (2007; 2013) systematic research on the dispositions of a broader class of entrepreneurs supports the hypothesis of uncertainty tolerance. They measure dispositional optimism, to reflect the idea that some people think things will work out okay no matter what. Robinson (personal communication) believes their measure describes psychological comfort with Knightian uncertainty, not the miscalibration about the means of distributions.

NOTES 353

Chapter 11

1. Economics, Behavioral 2008, 499.
2. See "Macroeconomics and Individual Decision Making (Behavioral Macroeconomics)," Yale Department of Economics, December 4, 2007, http://www.econ.yale.edu/~shiller/behmacro/index.htm.
3. The American Economic Association awards the John Bates Clark medal to an under-forty economist for significant contributions. Until 2007 the association made the now-annual award every other year. Sent (2004) notes that two back-to-back medals, awarded to Harvard University's Andrei Shleifer in 1999 and to Matthew Rabin of the University of California at Berkeley in 2001, recognized their behavioral contribution. She further notes that Rabin had already won the MacArthur Foundation's five-hundred-thousand-dollar Genius Award in 2000 and another behavioral economist, MIT's twenty-nine-year-old Sendhil Mullainathan, also won this Genius Award in 2003.
4. Sent 2004, 753.
5. Michigan's Department of Psychology was, in 1959, divided into ten specialized fields: experimental, mathematical, physiological, developmental, personality, social, community, industrial organization, clinical, and counseling psychology (Heukelom 2014, 77).
6. Greenwood 2015, 454.
7. List compiled from Greenwood 2015, ch. 12, and Anastasi 2008.
8. For example, according to the *Gale Encyclopedia of Psychology*:

   Cognitive psychology is the study of mental or thought processes, including perceiving, recognizing, remembering, imagining, conceptualizing, judging, reasoning, and processing information. Humans apply these cognitive processes mainly for the purpose of planning and problem solving. Cognitive psychology determines how the processes function to produce responses. Some cognitive psychologists may study how internal cognitive functions transform signs and symbols derived from the external world, and others may focus on the interplay between human genetics and environmental influences in determining individual cognitive development and capabilities. Still other cognitive psychologists may investigate how the mind detects, selects, recognizes, and verbally represents features of a particular stimulus. Specific topics investigated by cognitive psychologists are language acquisition; visual and auditory perception; information storage and retrieval; altered states of consciousness; cognitive restructuring (how the mind mediates between conflicting, or dissonant, information); and individual styles of thought and perception. (Cognitive Psychology 2016)

9. As with my earlier analysis of Simon's contributions, I will draw heavily on Kahneman's 2002 Nobel Lecture (Kahneman 2003c) and accompanying autobiographical essay.
10. Simon 1991b, 10.
11. Kahneman 2003c, 1449.
12. His work on vision resulted in some twenty-five articles, many in prominent experimental psychology journals. Two others were in *Science* (Heukelom 2014, 106).
13. Kahneman 2003b.
14. Heukelom 2014, 98.
15. Kahneman 2003b.

354 NOTES

16. Tversky and Kahneman 1971, 105.
17. Tversky and Kahneman 1971, 110.
18. Kahneman and Tversky 1972, 430.
19. Kahneman and Tversky 1972, 451. The Oregon Research Institute published the technical report (Tversky and Kahneman 1972) which the authors summarized in their journal article on the representativeness heuristic. The quotes in this paragraph are taken from the journal article, not the technical report.
20. Kahneman 2003b.
21. Kahneman 2003c, 1460.
22. Tversky and Kahneman 1974.
23. Kahneman 2003b.
24. Similarly, the Web of Science had counted more than 20,000 citations. Downloaded on February 14, 2023, from https://scholar.google.com/scholar?hl=en&as_sdt=0%2C22&q=judgment+under+uncertainty&btnG=; and https://www-webofscience-com.ezproxy.library.tufts.edu/wos/alldb/full-record/WOS:A1974U124400009.
25. Shallow accounts of behavior may well be more accurate than deep accounts, according to behavioral scientist Nick Chater's provocative book, *The Mind Is Flat*. "The sense that behaviour is merely the surface of a vast sea, immeasurably deep and teeming with inner motives, beliefs and desires whose power we can barely sense is a conjuring trick played by our own minds," writes Chater. "The truth is not that the depths are empty, or even shallow, but that the surface is all there is. . . . The stories we tell to justify and explain our own and others' behaviour aren't just wrong in detail—they are a thoroughgoing fabrication from start to finish" (Chater 2018, 5–6).
26. Kahneman and Frederick 2002, 81.
27. See for example Newell and Simon (1961).
28. Heukelom 2012, 819.
29. Heukelom 2014, 128.
30. In fact, "The analyses did not [even] calculate an average response over experimental subjects, but instead tried to find an explanation that would cover the observed behavior of the individual experimental subjects" (Heukelom 2014, 128).
31. Kahneman 2003b.
32. Heukelom 2014, 117.
33. According to Camerer, K-T's psychology "provided a way to model bounded rationality which is more like standard economics than the more radical departure that Simon had in mind. Much of behavioral economics consists of trying to incorporate this kind of psychology into economics" (cited in Sent 2004, 743).
34. Baumol 1968, 66–67.
35. Tversky had coauthored a 1970 text, *Mathematical Psychology*, which discussed the Ellsberg Paradox, and in 1974 (the year of his *Science* article with Kahneman), a paper with Paul Slovic (then a visiting professor at Hebrew University) reporting the results of their experiments on ambiguity aversion (Slovic and Tversky 1974).
36. Gilovich and Griffin 2002, 7.

NOTES   355

37. These were: business administration; computer science; engineering; humanities and education; law; library science; medicine; physical and life sciences; and social sciences and social work.

38. Six other possibilities were unrelated and miscellaneous (e.g., elementary school teacher, psychiatric social worker).

39. Kahneman and Frederick 2002, 62.

40. Gilovich and Griffin 2002, 7.

41. Tversky and Kahneman 1974, 1124.

42. Kahneman 2003b.

43. Kahneman 2003b.

44. Sent 2004, 743.

45. Mercier and Sperber 2019, 69.

46. Mercier and Sperber 2017, 4.

47. Heukelom 2014, 111.

48. Concern with the "dark side" of persuasion, conformity, and cognitive consistency had stimulated social psychologists' research on such topics. And "the social evil with the greatest fascination for social psychologists" was "the combination of stereotyping, prejudice, and discrimination," making K-T's insights about bias "highly relevant" (Gilovich and Griffin 2002, 6–7).

49. Besides social psychology, other psychology specialties also had practical interests. The University of Pennsylvania's James McKeen Cattel (1860–1944), the first psychology professor in the United States, said that psychology aimed "to describe, to understand, and to control human conduct" (Heukelom 2014, 11). In 1946 the American Psychology Association declared its goal was to "advance psychology as a science, as a profession, and as a means of promoting human welfare" (Wolfe 1946, 3).

50. Heukelom 2014, 119.

51. Simon 1991d, 326.

52. Kahneman 2003b.

53. It explained, inter alia, the "economically irrational distinction that people draw between opportunity costs and 'real' losses," why real estate markets freeze when prices fall, and the widespread status quo bias in decision-making (Kahneman 2003b).

54. They kept the key ideas and examples and much of the wording. But the initial 1975 draft lacked "the authority that was gained during the years that [K-T] spent anticipating objections" and "would not have survived the close scrutiny that a significant article ultimately gets from generations of scholars and students" (Kahneman 2003b).

55. Kahneman 2003b.

56. Kahneman 2003b.

57. K-T's "value function" did have unconventional kinks (at the point where gains turned into losses). But mainstream theorists had played with the shapes of utility functions before—in 1948, Milton Friedman and Jimmie Savage (1948, 297) proposed a "wiggly utility curve" to explain gambling and buying insurance.

356 NOTES

58. I have often encountered this problem, starting in graduate school. Harvard economics stalwart (see chapter 1) Richard Caves repeatedly urged me to drop the topic I had chosen for my doctoral dissertation (hostile takeovers) because it did not relate to existing economic theory. I ignored the advice, fortunately in retrospect. My detailed case-by-case analysis suggested insights that I published in two articles (Bhidé 1989a and Bhidé 1990), both of which are cited in a recent book on business history (Langlois 2023).
59. Camerer and Loewenstein 2004, 3.
60. Prospect theory did include a preliminary "editing" procedure, however.
61. My own entrepreneurship research has reported the significant role of framing by the founders of new businesses (Bhidé 2000, 82–83).
62. Kahneman 2003b.
63. Tversky and Kahneman 1981, 453.
64. Greenwood 2015, 6.
65. Simon 1991, 58.
66. Greenwood 2015, 14–15.
67. Greenwood 2015, 148–149.
68. Kim 2006. Wundt also held chairs in philosophy at the Universities of Heidelberg, Zürich, and Leipzig (Greenwood 2015, 15). And although Wundt helped drive a wedge between the two disciplines—with philosophy departments, "striving to maintain their speculative purity" excluding Wundtian empiricism—Wundt had not desired this outcome. Wundt "never saw his psychological scientism as a threat to philosophy—on the contrary, he considered his psychology to be a part of philosophy" that he wished to reform (Kim 2006).
69. James's laboratory research on sensation and perception led him to develop a theory that attributed the experience of emotions to physiological responses to external events. James also conducted pioneering experiments on the inner ear and dizziness (Goodman 2022).
70. Goodman 2022.
71. Like Wundt, James had held a professorship in philosophy and was not convinced that psychology was a distinct discipline. In an 1892 survey of the field, *Psychology: Briefer Course*, James (1892, 468) wrote, "This is no science; it is only the hope of a science."
72. Mischel 2019.
73. Mill, 1844, 138.
74. Mill, 1844, 146.
75. Mill, 1844, 149. Mill, however, also "acknowledged that we do not have introspective access to the elemental visual and tactile sensations upon which our perceptual inferences are supposedly based" (Greenwood 2015, 148).
76. Edgeworth, 1877, 42. The diminishing utility theory suggests that people's satisfaction from a good or service decreases as they consume more of it. Richard Jennings and William Stanley Jevons similarly used Ernst Weber and Wilhelm Wundt's experimental research on sensory experiences in perception and cognition in their decision-making theories.

NOTES 357

77. Misak 2020, 100.
78. Misak 2020, 164.
79. Winslow 1986, 555.
80. Letters column of *The Nation and Atheneum,* cited in Winslow 1986, 555.
81. Heukelom 2014, 3.

Chapter 12

1. Kahneman 2003b.
2. Kahneman 2003b.
3. Camerer, Loewenstein, and Rabin 2004b, xxii.
4. Thaler 1991, 4.
5. Heukelom 2014, 148.
6. Camerer, Loewenstein, and Rabin 2004b, xxii–xxiii.
7. Heukelom 2014, ch. 4, passim. Heukelom also notes that Thaler would quickly become "a major recipient of, and influential voice in, the Alfred Sloan-Russell Sage behavioral economics program" (Heukelom 2014, 148).
8. Heukelom 2014, 148.
9. Shleifer's behavioral finance publications just in 1990 include Morck et al. 1990, Shleifer and Summers 1990, De Long et al. 1990a, De Long et al. 1990b, and Lee et al. 1990.
10. Heukelom 2014, 155.
11. In 1995, Richard Thaler moved to the University of Chicago's business school, now known as the Booth School.
12. Akerlof and Shiller began organizing annual conferences in behavioral macroeconomics, sponsored by the NBER, in 1994. See "Macroeconomics and Individual Decision Making (Behavioral Macroeconomics)," Yale Department of Economics, December 4, 2007, http://www.econ.yale.edu/~shiller/behmacro/index.htm.
13. Shiller even asked me to discuss a paper in the July 1994 workshop. Details at Amar Bhidé, "The Birth of Behavioral Finance," December 4, 2022, https://bhide.net/index.php/the-birth-of-behavioral-finance/.
14. Some of Shiller's research reduced this problem by focusing on the excessive size of fluctuations rather than their predictable occurrence.
15. "About," FullerThaler Asset Management, Inc., retrieved February 28, 2018, from https://www.fullerthaler.com/about.
16. Behavioural insights: Organisation for Economic Co-operation and Development, https://www.oecd.org/gov/regulatory-policy/behavioural-insights.htm and for 2018 map, https://twitter.com/faisal_naru/status/1027162896340578304.
17. See Roth 1995.
18. Smith 1994, 113.
19. Smith 1994, 118.

358 NOTES

20. Smith had expected transactions between informed traders to produce prices conforming to the asset's fundamental value. "In my original experiments for consumer final-use goods," writes Smith, "I did not expect that ordinary unsophisticated people would be so competent in market price discovery using extant institutions of exchange, and it revolutionized our understanding. Other economists and I overinterpreted the results and expected asset markets to do as well. We failed to realize that retrading creates a potential conflict between fundamental value and retrade price value" (personal communication with author, January 20, 2023).

21. Noussair 2017, 645.

22. Elster 2009.

23. Elster 2015, 26.

24. Elster 2015, 26.

25. Elster 2015, 27.

26. Elster 2015, 29.

27. Knight 1921, 235.

28. Gigerenzer 2018, 303.

29. Gigerenzer 2018, 303.

30. Gigerenzer 2018, 310.

31. Gigerenzer 2018, 303.

32. Gigerenzer 2018, 303.

33. Gigerenzer 2018, 322.

34. Gigerenzer 2018, 323.

35. Gigerenzer 2018, 324.

36. Gigerenzer, Todd, & ABC Research Group, 1999.

37. Gigerenzer, Reb, and Luan 2022, 180–181.

38. Arkes, Gigerenzer, and Hertwig 2016, 23.

39. Gigerenzer 2018, 303.

40. See March 1991, 253–265.

41. Flynn 1987, 188.

42. Forrester 2017.

43. Baldwin 2018.

44. Cartwright 2004, 814–815.

45. Kay and King 2020b, 91.

46. Buffett 1987. Buffett's views are thus not very far removed from the efficient market hypothesis (see Bhidé 2010, 110–112). And Buffett has frequently advised investors to buy and hold a low-cost index fund, instead of trying to "beat the market."

47. Fuller and Thaler managed about $17.6 billion in assets according to its June 2022 regulatory filings. This is not trivial but pales in contrast with the success of Dimensional Fund Advisors (DFA). Eugene Fama had inspired one of his students, David Booth, to start DFA in 1981. Fama also served as DFA's founding director. Guided by Fama's efficient market ideas, DFA offered low-cost, passively managed index funds. By the end of 2022, DFA was managing about $584 billion—more than thirty-three times the assets Fuller-Thaler reported to the SEC in June of that year. (In 2008, a grateful

David Booth gave $300 million to his alma mater which then renamed itself the Booth School of Business.)

48. As Princeton's Burton Malkiel put it, "I do not argue that the market pricing is always perfect. After the fact, we know that markets have made egregious mistakes, as I think occurred during the recent Internet 'bubble.' Nor do I deny that psychological factors influence securities prices. But I am convinced that Benjamin Graham (1965) was correct in suggesting that while the stock market in the short run may be a voting mechanism, in the long run it is a weighing mechanism. True value will win out in the end. Before the fact, there is no way in which investors can reliably exploit any anomalies or patterns that might exist. I am skeptical that any of the 'predictable patterns' that have been documented in the literature were ever sufficiently robust so as to have created profitable investment opportunities, and after they have been discovered and publicized, they will certainly not allow investors to earn excess returns" (Malkiel 2003, 61).

Part III

1. Robert Charles Dudley, *The Atlantic Telegraph Cable Meet, 1866*. Watercolor with touches of gouache, 32.9 × 56.2 cm. The Metropolitan Museum of Art, Gift of Cyrus W. Field, 1892 (92.10.73)
2. Robert Charles Dudley, *The Atlantic Telegraph Cable Fleet Assembled at Berehaven* (Southwest Coast of Ireland), n.d.
3. Robert Charles Dudley, *The Atlantic Telegraph Cable Fleet Assembled at Berehaven* (Southwest Coast of Ireland), n.d.
4. Dobkin 2006, 157.

Chapter 13

1. Knight 1921, ix.
2. Knight 1921, vii.
3. Baumol's (1968) article did not, however, explain why economic theory had become "entrepreneurless." Perhaps Baumol had in mind his skepticism about utility maximization contained in his 1951 *Journal of Political Economy* article (Baumol 1951) that Milton Friedman had refereed. Friedman and Savage then coauthored a rejoinder to Baumol, published in 1952 (Moscati 2016, 225–226).
4. Baumol 1993, 14.
5. Baumol 1993, 12.
6. Baumol 1993, 2.
7. Baumol 1993, 13–14.
8. Baumol 1993, 14.
9. Baumol 1993, 15. It may not be coincidental that Baumol's eminence as an economic theorist preceded his writings on entrepreneurship. He is famous for his analysis

360 NOTES

landmark theory of the "cost-disease" that bears his name, for example. We would not expect significant methodological rebellion from such a scholar.

10. Bronner 1998.

11. When HBS hired me into a three-person entrepreneurship unit in 1988, my doctoral dissertation was on hostile takeovers.

12. Via email from Josh Lerner, who launched the group.

13. Entrepreneurship Working Group Fall 2021.

14. My 2000 book on entrepreneurship analyzed the economic significance of stories, ruses, and schemes. But a Knightian framework put this analysis outside the accepted economics paradigm. A game-theoretic "prisoner's dilemma" style presentation might have attracted more notice.

15. Botelho, Fehder, and Hochberg 2021, 4, who rely on Kihlstrom and Laffont 1979.

16. Some entrepreneurship scholars did operate outside the economics paradigm. These included Austrian economists, researchers who had studied entrepreneurship before the 1990s, psychologists, sociologists, anthropologists, and cross-disciplinary management researchers. They started new journals dedicated to entrepreneurship (instead of publishing in established finance and economics journals). In 2012, two traditionally trained economists, Nicolai Foss and Peter Klein, coauthored a book (Foss and Klein 2012) reintroducing Knightian uncertainty into an Austrian-style theory of the firm. These efforts to form a mutually supportive community had some success but did not secure the influence and prestige of economists at top-ranked business schools who published in the top economics and finance journals and participated in NBER meetings.

17. Kaplan and Strömberg 2003.

18. Similarly, in financial markets, buying "out of the money" options has higher risk returns than buying "in the money" options. The uncertainty isn't particularly different. However, options on "when issued" securities with no historical trading information have higher uncertainty than options on seasoned issues, regardless of their risk returns.

19. The sources can pertain to the parts of the whole. For example, missing pieces in a jigsaw puzzle, say of a giraffe, can produce uncertainty about how the remaining pieces fit together. But WASGIJs—jigsaws for which we do not know the picture that we are creating is of a giraffe—create doubts regardless of any missing pieces.

20. Or the costs of securing the missing information are prohibitive.

21. Sah and Stiglitz 1985; 1986; 1988a; 1988b; 1991.

22. Fama and Jensen 1983a; 1983b; 1985.

23. As in Fama and Jensen 1983a; 1983b; 1985.

24. Lerner and Nanda 2020.

25. Keynes 1937, 213.

26. Peirce 1931; Lipton 1991.

27. Fama and Jensen 1983a; 1983b.

NOTES 361

Chapter 14

1. Leland and Pyle 1977, 372.
2. Hurst and Pugsley 2011, 73.
3. Hurst and Pugsley 2011, 73–74.
4. Hurst and Pugsley 2011, 74.
5. Hurst and Pugsley 2011, 74–75.
6. Birch 1979.
7. Decker et al. 2014, 4.
8. The OECD (2015, 59) reports, "Data from the Small Business Administration shows that only around 300 of the 600,000 annual startups are funded by venture capitalists annually."
9. *Inc.* ranked the sales growth of companies that wanted to be on its lists and required applicants to document (through their tax returns) sales of at least fifty thousand dollars for five years before they applied. This condition helped exclude very young companies, reporting high growth starting from a low base. In selecting interviewees from *Inc.*'s list, I added a further filter to the five-year track record condition: I excluded companies over eight years old. This reduced the possibility that interviewees would not remember how they started their businesses—and tilted my sample toward younger, smaller, and more rapidly growing companies. The average company in my sample had 1988 revenues of about nine million dollars (vs. fifteen million dollars in the complete list), 100 employees (vs. 135), and a five-year sales growth of 1,459 percent (vs. 1,407 percent).
10. Caves 2001.
11. Aldrich 2001.
12. See Bhidé 1996.
13. Peirce 1965, 375. Cited in Walton 2014, 5.
14. Pólya (1954, 19) provides the example of a mathematician trying to figure out whether condition A is true, deduces that A must imply B, and discovers that B is false. According to demonstrative logic, A must then also be false. But what if B turns out to be true? According to heuristic reasoning, that would make A more likely, although not "demonstrably" true.
15. Bhidé 2008b.
16. Another survey of *Inc.* 500 founders also suggested that most promising new ventures do not start with a unique or proprietary product. Only 12 percent of the founders attributed the success of their companies to "an unusual or extraordinary idea," and 88 percent reported their success was due to the "exceptional execution of an ordinary idea."
17. Walton 1993, 27–28.
18. Trimble 1990, 5–7
19. Walton 1993, 101–102.
20. Trimble 1990, 101–102.
21. Walton 1993, 54.

362 NOTES

22. From Andrew Hauptman and Pinny Chaviv's paper in "Tales of Successful Entrepreneurs" (Bhidé 1995, 141–153).
23. Bhidé 1995, 126.
24. Cringely 1996, 9.
25. See Andrew Hauptman and Pinny Chaviv's paper in Bhidé 1995, 141–153.
26. Hurst and Pugsley 2011, 73.
27. Haltiwanger 2011, 122.
28. Henrekson and Johansson 2009, Abstract.
29. Azoulay et al. 2020, 72. Startups in high-tech industries did, however, account for a larger (17 percent) share of the top 1 percent of high-growth companies and about 23.5 percent in the very top, one-in-one-thousand fastest-growing companies.
30. Similarly, the Bureau of Labor Statistics definition used in the Azoulay et al. (2020) study defined a high-tech industry as one with the highest proportion of STEM employment.
31. Sabini and Silver 1982.
32. Their memory endures merely as "save" and "save as" icons on software menus.
33. Mills 2018, 59.
34. Hurst and Pugsley 2011, 73.
35. Robb and Robinson (2014) report that US entrepreneurs typically borrow a dollar (from banks) for every dollar they invest in their startups. Robinson's interpretation (October 17, 2023, email correspondence with author) of their results is that bank debt is an extension of bootstrapping because the bank debt is usually backed by personal guarantees.
36. Kaplan and Strömberg 2004.
37. Leland and Pyle 1977, 372.
38. Another 20 percent discovered their ideas serendipitously—only 4 percent of my interviewees found their business ideas through a systematic search.
39. Bhidé 2000, 62.
40. Bhidé 2000, 64.
41. Bhidé 2000, 64.
42. In Bhidé (2006), I present a simple algebraic version of the winner's curse argument without any mention of uncertainty!
43. Good tennis players think a little about why they might have double-faulted but not too much.
44. Landier and Thesmar 2003, 24.
45. Outside of medical practice and contrived behavioral experiments.
46. Some disciplines do, however, have obviously dismal prospects—salaries are low, and professorships are scarce. But here, too, it is unlikely that many students would stay away if only they calculated base rates.
47. Baumol 1968, 66–67.

Chapter 15

1. OECD 2015, 121.
2. Berlin 1953.

NOTES 363

3. As mentioned in chapter 13, business school-based economists have carefully studied and documented the contracting and other investment practices of VCs. Sahlman (1990) is an early example while Gompers et al. (2020) provide more current and comprehensive information on how VCs make investment decisions.

4. Nicholas 2019, 11–39.

5. Nicholas 2019, 57.

6. Nicholas 2019, 58–59.

7. Gompers and Lerner 2001, 146.

8. Gompers and Lerner 2001, 147.

9. Gompers and Lerner 2001, 146–147.

10. Nicholas 2019, 93–94.

11. Nicholas 2019, 156, 159.

12. Until 1968, public funds in California and fifteen other states did not own any stocks (White 1990), although university endowments, led by Ivy League universities, had by then shifted allocations away from high-grade bonds to stocks (Chambers, Dimson, and Kaffe 2020, 15).

13. Specifically, US Employment Retirement and Income Act (ERISA) legislation in the mid-1970s discouraged underfunding of pension plans and increased the liability of fiduciaries that violated duties of care. Initially, ERISA rules increased investments in diversified portfolios of publicly traded stocks, but in 1979 the US Department of Labor clarified its "prudent man" rule to explicitly allow pension funds to invest in VC partnerships and other high-risk "alternative" assets.

14. Gompers and Lerner 2001, 148.

15. Nicholas 2019, 160–161.

16. Gupta 2001.

17. Many were advised by Cambridge Associates, started in 1973, which had first helped Harvard's endowment select stock managers.

18. Chambers, Dimson, and Kaffe 2020, 16.

19. Nicholas 2019, 96, 268.

20. To highlight the effects of professional VCs' "intermediary" role, my analysis (like the OECD's) focuses on VC partnerships formed to invest funds supplied by several independent sources. I exclude vehicles making direct investments on behalf of a unitary beneficiary, such as family offices. Similarly, like the OECD's survey, I focus on high-net-worth ("wealthy") angel investors. Surprisingly, however, many not-so-well-to-do individuals also provide arm's-length funding to startups: Shane reports that 41.1 percent of informal investors in the United States have household incomes of less than fifty thousand dollars per year (Shane 2008, 93).

21. Although angels may form syndicates to evaluate and fund ventures, angels who join syndicates independently decide whether to invest in particular ventures.

22. OECD 2015, 109. The report also notes, however, that VCs do invest in the early stages of biotechnology,

23. OECD 2015, 110.

24. According to the OECD (2015, 121), "Generally, the most appropriate time for companies to seek angel investment is when a product or service is developed or near completion and there exists a base of customers or potential customers that confirmed their interest in buying it. BAs [Business Angels] are usually under little

364 NOTES

pressure to make an investment to generate income or capital growth. They can afford to wait until they identify the right opportunity and the right person. This means that entrepreneurs that seek angel investments need to be able to present not only an appealing idea and business plan but also themselves effectively."

25. OECD 2015, 118.
26. OECD 2015, 111.
27. OECD 2015, 117–122.
28. OECD 2015, 110–120.
29. Gompers 1995 and Amit, Brander, and Zott 1998.
30. Gompers 1995, who reported that VCs concentrate investments in "high technology industries," assumed (like Amit, Brander, and Zott 1998) that "informational asymmetries [we]re highest" in high-tech. Gompers's assumption appeared to rely on—although he didn't explicitly state this—low debt ratios and high investment irreversibility to justify the assumption of severe information asymmetries in high technology industries. But Gompers's data also suggested that VCs avoid the restaurant industry—and Gompers provides no evidence that the information asymmetry problems in starting a restaurant are materially different than in high-technology startups.
31. For instance, by employing junior staff to leverage the time and expertise of senior professionals, VCs can afford more thorough due diligence. And VCs who sit on the boards of the companies they invest in can use their insiders' familiarity to provide follow-on funding more confidently. VCs' endorsements, powerfully offered as additional financing, help bring in new investors. VCs that can invest in multiple rounds are thus attractive to capable entrepreneurs.

    Syndicating investments—pooling deal-by-deal—can provide some of these advantages: Syndicates of angels can share some of the due diligence costs. Investing in multiple syndicates can also help investors diversify. But getting agreement for each deal and from each investor is cumbersome, involves at least some duplication of effort (even when syndicates do most of the due diligence for members), and requires the disclosure of confidential company information to many angels, some of whom may decide not to invest. And "re-syndication" requirements make follow-on funding more difficult than with VC funds.
32. Typically, VCs initially require partial contributions and "call" for further funds to make follow-on or new first-time investments later. By delaying calls, VCs can avoid stockpiling low-yielding cash, which would reduce the overall returns for the life of the partnership. However, delaying calls requires the limited partners to set aside the low-yielding cash without knowing when the VC will issue a capital call, reducing the returns of investors' portfolios.
33. History suggests that investors in VC partnerships have reason to be concerned about the capabilities of the general partners. Investors in the typical VC fund, which locks them in for ten years, cannot expect to earn higher returns than from similar portfolios of publicly traded stocks. For an extended period after 1998, the median VC fund underperformed its equivalent public market portfolio. See Harris, Jenkinson, and Kaplan 2014.

34. Fama and Jensen 1983a.
35. Gompers and Lerner 1999, 5.
36. Lerner 2009, 52.
37. Kaplan and Strömberg 2004. According to Kaplan and Strömberg's categorization, the analyses cover "internal factors" related to the management team, such as its quality and performance to date); external factors such as market size, customer adoption, and competition; and factors related to the difficulty of implementing the technology and business strategy and model. Other researchers who have studied how VCs evaluate opportunities use different categories. For example, Tyebjee and Bruno's (1984) scheme comprises (1) market attractiveness (including its size and growth); (2) differentiation of products (based on their uniqueness, patents, and technical edge); (3) capabilities of the management team; (4) "environmental" factors (such as the barriers to entry and the technological life cycles); and (5) "cash-out" potential, or the scope for exiting through a public offering or sale of the business.
38. Statistical data and inference or subjective estimates of probabilities are notably absent. Even financial projections do not attempt to estimate or justify the numerical odds of success. For example, Kaplan—who, with Strömberg, examined the investment analyses of VCs (Kaplan and Strömberg 2004)—does not recall any probability distributions or estimates. In some cases, the analyses included ranges of exit values for ranges of outcomes (Kaplan, September 26, 2021, personal communication with author).
39. Freear, Sohl, and Wetzel 1995.
40. Long 2007.
41. Gandhi, Brumme, and Schwalb 2019, 5.
42. The methodical evaluations of potential institutional investors have also prompted many large VC firms to employ professionals to market their funds and smaller VC firms to retain marketing agents.
43. Lord and Mirabile 2018, 30–31.
44. VCs can extend their own evaluation and oversight limits through informal collaborations with other VC firms, with different firms in the collaborative taking the lead on different investments. But the size of such collaboratives is limited by the need for confidence among the collaborators. Responsibilities to their investors also require VCs to do some due diligence, even for the deals others may lead.
45. Although limited partnership contracts typically do not specify the limits, prospective investors in a VC fund often ask for projections for the number of expected deals and minimum and maximum amounts).
46. According to the OECD (2015, 109), angel investments range from twenty-five thousand dollars to five hundred thousand dollars, compared to three million to five million dollars for VCs.
47. Ghosh study cited in Gage 2012.
48. In the Sah and Stiglitz frameworks, angel investors represent a decentralized project screening polyarchy.
49. Academy of Achievement 2001.

366 NOTES

50. Ibrahim 2008, 1407.
51. OECD 2015, 119.
52. Bhidé (2000, 45) reports that about 30 of the *Inc.* companies are in IT, while Gompers and Lerner (2001, 148) report that 60 percent of VC disbursements went to IT.
53. Lerner and Nanda 2020, 30.
54. Catalini et al. 2019.
55. Farre-Mensa, Hegde, and Ljungqvist 2020.
56. Farre-Mensa, Hegde, and Ljungqvist 2020.
57. Encyclopedia Britannica, s.v. "Michael Dell" (The Editors of Encyclopedia Britannica 2022b).
58. Doerr 2018.

Chapter 16

1. Dalrymple 2015.
2. Dalrymple 2015.
3. Coase (1937) is considered the foundational paper of the transaction cost view of firms.
4. Langlois 2023, for example, questions Chandler's account.
5. Chandler 1962.
6. Chandler 1962, 44.
7. Chandler 1962, 46.
8. Chandler 1990, 3–4.
9. "The best of all monopoly profits is a quiet life," Hicks (1935) wrote.
10. Chandler 1962, 46.
11. Chandler 1962, 14.
12. Chandler 1962, 152–153.
13. Chandler 1962, 153.
14. Raff and Summers 1987, 16–17.
15. Sloan 1963, 503.
16. Williamson 1975, 84.
17. Williamson 1975, 104.
18. Granovetter 1985, 499.
19. Chandler 1962, 36. GM's Alfred Sloan was similarly skeptical about the economics of vertical integration, questioning the "popular misconception that it always pays to make an item yourself rather than to buy it. . . . We purchase a large proportion of the items that go into our end products, because there is no reason to believe that by producing them we could obtain better products or service, or a lower price" (Sloan 1963, 503).
20. Schumpeter 2008, 132.
21. Schumpeter 2008, 134, 106.
22. Wilentz 1985, ix.
23. McCloskey 2007, 59.

24. I can, however, personally testify to Chandler's profound unhappiness with how Oliver Williamson had used Chandler's historical accounts to advance his transaction cost models.
25. Galbraith 1967, 9–10.
26. Galbraith 1967, 10.
27. Galbraith 1967, 77.
28. Galbraith 1967, 1.
29. Galbraith 1967, 2.
30. Galbraith 1967, 40.
31. Galbraith 1967, 39.
32. Chandler 1990, 1.
33. Chandler 1990, 2.
34. Galbraith 1967, 66.
35. Galbraith 1967, 70.
36. Galbraith 1967, 65.
37. Automobile sales, for example, fell from a record 5 million vehicles in 1929 to just 1.33 million in 1932, requiring the Ford Motor Company to terminate over eighty thousand of its workers ("The 1930s Business," May 25, 2023).
38. Galbraith 1967, 82.
39. Galbraith (1967, 81) goes on to observe, "In large corporations, battles for control have been rare in recent times. And in all notable cases involving larger corporations . . . the firm in contention was doing badly at the time."
40. Galbraith (1985, 94) cites research showing that the concentration of market shares in consumer goods industries had dramatically increased, while already high concentrations in producer goods had been sustained.
41. Galbraith 1985, 93.
42. Galbraith 1985, 93.
43. Incongruously, the 1985 edition of *The New Industrial State* continued to assert that "big corporations almost never lose money" (Galbraith 1985, 103), but without including any 1980s data.
44. Birch 1979, 8.
45. Lockheed, then the largest defense contractor in the United States, was similarly bailed out in 1971.
46. Wong 1990, 12.
47. Galbraith 1985, 40.
48. Vogel 1979.
49. Ouchi 1981.
50. According to Massello (1997), Hammer and Champy's 1993 best-seller— *Reengineering the Corporation: Manifesto for Business Revolution*—made reengineering the "next new thing" and a "catch all for layoffs and unreasonable performance expectations."
51. Hamel 1999.
52. Jensen 1989, 61.
53. As described by Burrough and Helyar 1989.

368 NOTES

54. Jensen 1989, 62.
55. Jensen 1989, 66.
56. Jensen 1989, 66.

Chapter 17

1. For example, in the 2010s, the five hundred largest public companies in the United States (ranked by their annual revenues) reported $31 trillion in gross profits, paid out $3.9 trillion as dividends and spent another $4.9 billion on buying back their stock. The rest was reinvested. Increased borrowing of $2.1 trillion and tax allowances for depreciation provided a further source of funding.
2. These amounts exclude marketing, advertising, and other expenses incurred in launching new products or entering new markets that the companies do not report as R&D or capital expenditures.
3. According to OECD data, US VCs who finance more than just the R&D and capital expenditures of their portfolio companies invested less than $750 billion from 2010 to 2019. Moreover, unusually high VC disbursements in 2018 and 2019 accounted for more than 36 percent of their disbursements over the decade. This likely reflects a flood of nontraditional capital into venture-backed private companies at historically high valuations, spurred by years of "quantitative easing" (Janeway 2022). Public companies did not report this jump; nonetheless their median annual expenditure (R&D plus capital) in the 2010s of $910 billion was more than twelve times the median VC disbursements of about $75 billion.
4. Some VC firms (e.g., Kleiner, Perkins) may occasionally broker mutually beneficial transactions between portfolio companies. But VCs do not burden one portfolio company for the benefit of another.
5. "The Eye of the Storm" 2016.
6. US C-Band Auction Becomes World's Costliest Mid-Band 5G Auction Yet 2021.
7. GM will boost EV and AV investments to $35 billion through 2025 (2021).
8. Schumpeter 2021.
9. Kumar et al. 2019 and Zakkour 2017.
10. Bhidé 1989b.
11. Suk 2008.
12. Poeter 2008.
13. Rogoway 2020.
14. "The Eye of the Storm" 2016.
15. VCs' veteran financier Yves De Balmann emailed me "tend to be more interested (and for good reasons) in business models which are not people intensive and capital intensive hence their focus on software businesses. Someone may have the best idea for the next generation of nuclear technology but the investment in capital, people, and time necessary to make this a reality would turn off most investors. Even if one ignored the capital required, just the time to realization by itself introduces additional

uncertainties which would turn off most investors (except the likes of Bill Gates who almost does it out of pure philanthropy!)" (email, December 1, 2021).

16. Metcalfe 2014.
17. The Xerox PARC Visit n.d.
18. Bhidé 1989b, 4–5.
19. Shane 2001.
20. Kalamas, Pinkus, and Sachs 2002.
21. Klepper 2001, 662. See also Klepper 2007.
22. These patterns, Klepper observes, contradict the usual agency-based theories that focus on conflicts of interest and attribute spinouts to employees stealing their employer's ideas and getting better deals from venture capitalists.
23. Moore 1996.
24. von Zedtwitz, Friesike, and Gassmann 2014, 531.
25. von Zedtwitz, Friesike, and Gassmann 2014, 532.
26. von Zedtwitz, Friesike, and Gassmann 2014, 530.
27. von Zedtwitz, Friesike, and Gassmann 2014, 543.
28. Haoues 2015.
29. Savitz 2023.
30. Hern 2022.
31. Austin 2023.
32. Ranitidine Drug Use Statistics 2020.
33. A nationwide study published in 2022 confirmed that ranitidine increased the risks of liver, lung, gastric and pancreatic cancers.
34. Bhide, Datar, and Stebbins, 2021b.
35. Bhide, Datar, and Stebbins, 2021a.
36. Kling (2023) further argues that in large company hierarchies, the attention constraints of bosses (analyzed in Simon's theories of bounded rationality) add to the uncertainty aversion.
37. Additionally, substantial internal cash flows produced by existing businesses, and the borrowing capacity they support, provide the needed financial means.
38. Nelson and Winter 1982, 97.
39. Fama and Jensen 1983a; 1983b.
40. Fama and Jensen 1983b, 332–333.
41. For instance, a salesperson or brand manager who has direct knowledge of customer needs and competitive offerings may initiate a proposal for a new product. A superior reviews the proposal and, if appropriate, forwards it up the corporate hierarchy with an endorsement. Higher-ups then decide whether to proceed, perhaps after seeking the advice of a specialized staff or outside consultants. Similarly, employees with the appropriate expertise may be given the discretion to implement the product launch, subject to monitoring and oversight by superiors and by an independent finance or control staff.
42. Stein 2002. In Stein's model, bosses command subordinates to use hard, judgment-free rules.
43. Fama and Jensen 1983a, 311.

370 NOTES

44. When outsiders invest in even small entrepreneurial organizations, Fama and Jensen (1983a, 306) note, they require boards empowered to control important decisions.

45. One director of the Scottish Mortgage Investment Trust (and now the Chair of its Board) claimed the Trust had a deliberate, long-standing policy of excluding directors with investment management experience (Agnew, McCrum, and Dunkley 2023).

46. Knight had conceptualized a "tiered" division for the specialization of judgment within large organizations—a forerunner to the more sophisticated hierarchical partitioning in Fama and Jensen's theory summarized earlier.

47. See Radner 1992.

48. Brooks 1975, 42.

49. Brooks 1975, 42.

50. Brooks 1975, 44.

51. Brooks 1975, 44.

52. Brooks 1975, 44.

53. These practical difficulties lead to uneven results from the general principle of separating the overall design and its implementation. Brooks (1975, 44–45) recalls separation being "used with great success on IBM's Stretch computer and on the System/360 computer product line" but failing on Operating System/260.

54. In other cases, attributing significant failures to minor or tactical mismatches is more ambiguous. In my view, a simple contractual omission cost IBM its dominance in personal computers: IBM did not require exclusivity for the operating system it licensed from Microsoft. But this is an unverifiable hypothesis. Microsoft, in turn, wrote off its $7.9 billion acquisition of Nokia in 2015 and then exited the smartphone business. Many attribute this failure to Microsoft's erratic development of its phone operating system and its troubled relationships with application developers, but this too is not provable.

55. See Cringely 1996, 124–125.

56. Kalberg 1980, x.

57. Weber 1947, x.

58. Jensen 1989, 66.

59. "Berkshire Hathaway Inc. 2019 Annual Report," 4.

60. Packard 1995, 141. See also "Pressures to Grow" in Bhidé 2000 (230–233).

61. Matt. 25:14–30.

62. Good routines do not naturally emerge—they evolve after considerable trial and error through a combination of entrepreneurial determination and unforeseen circumstances. See Part 2, "The Evolution of Fledgling Businesses" in Bhidé (2000).

63. Barnes & Noble, which had pioneered book superstores and discounted prices on new releases, launched a website to compete with Amazon in May 1997. According to Stone, "many seemed ready to see Amazon crushed. The CEO of Forrester Research, a widely followed technology research firm, issued a report in which he called the company 'Amazon.Toast.'" By 1999 Barnes & Noble had become the second-largest online bookseller in the United States, but it was unable to catch up. "Bezos had predicted that the chain retailer would have trouble seriously competing online, and, in the end, he was right," wrote Stone. Barnes & Noble's controlling stockholders,

the Riggio brothers, "were reluctant to lose money on a relatively small part of their business and didn't want to put their most resourceful employees behind an effort that would siphon sales away from the more profitable stores. On top of that, their company's distribution operation was well entrenched and geared toward servicing physical stores by sending out large shipments of books to a set number of locations. The shift from that to mailing small orders to individual customers was long, painful, and full of customer-service errors. For Amazon, that was just daily business" (Stone 2013, ch. 2).

64. See Henderson 1993 and Christensen 1997.
65. Olegario 1997.
66. Frank Cary, U.S. v. IBM (transcript), pp. 101, 612–101, 613, as cited in Olegario 1997.
67. Cringely 1996, 125–126.
68. Chandler 1977, 480–481.
69. I argued (Bhidé 1990, 76–79) that structural changes in stock markets after the mid-1970s had negated any advantages that internal capital markets might have once enjoyed.
70. A phenomenon I analyzed for my doctoral dissertation and published in Bhidé 1989a. Stock markets and management gurus continued, however, to applaud General Electric's unrelated acquisitions, which preceded the 1960s conglometarization wave. The conglomerate was the second-largest US public company by market capitalization at the start of 2000, and its CEO, Jack Welch, had become a cult hero. However, that more-than-a-century-old enterprise also unraveled after 2016. Buffett's Berkshire Hathaway is now virtually the only prominent well-regarded conglomerate.
71. Moreover, the US stock market is not unusually concentrated by global standards. In fact, in the major markets, only Japan has lower concentration in its biggest companies (see Dimson, Marsh and Staunton 2024).
72. The top two—Apple and Microsoft—were founded in 1976 and 1975, respectively. Three (Amazon, Nvidia, and Google/Alphabet) were 1990s-born. Two (Tesla and Facebook/Meta) are millennials.
73. The nine dropouts from the top-ten class of 2000 comprise five pre–World War II stalwarts (General Electric, Exxon, IBM, AT&T, and Pfizer) and four companies that started after the 1960s (Cisco, Walmart, Intel, and Oracle).
74. "Tesla Funding Rounds" n.d.
75. "Tesla Raises $1.46 Billion in Stock Sale—IFR," Reuters, May 20, 2016, https://www.reuters.com/article/idUSKCN0YB097/.
76. Amazon Web Services Revenue 2022 n.d.
77. Mallaby 2022, 175.

Chapter 18

1. Like Grice (1989), I assume that conversation is normally based on cooperative principles and has a common purpose. People try to be truthful, informative, relevant, and clear.

372 NOTES

2. Bruner 1991.
3. Cooper 2015.
4. "Jerome Bruner (1915–2016)" n.d.
5. Bruner 1990, 2.
6. "Jerome Bruner," Harvard University Department of Psychology, accessed May 24, 2024, https://psychology.fas.harvard.edu/people/jerome-bruner.
7. Bruner 1962, 129–30.
8. Bruner 1990, 3.
9. Bruner 1990, 4.
10. Bruner 1990, 14.
11. Tikannen 2016.
12. Gardner 2016.
13. Cooper 2015.
14. Mattingly, Lutkehaus, and Throop 2008. Cooper (2015) describes Bruner as "the brains behind Head Start."
15. Crace 2007.
16. Sylva 2016.
17. Slobin 2016.
18. According to Haste (2016), members of Oxford's psychology department regarded Bruner's views as an attack on experimental psychology. Nonetheless, he also had supporters, and in 2007 the Oxford educational studies department named its building after Bruner.
19. After 1997 the institution, founded by progressive academics, including Columbia University dissidents objecting to a loyalty oath, began calling itself the New School University.
20. Lucariello 2016.
21. Amsterdam and Bruner 2000, 4.
22. Cooper 2015.
23. Bruner 1986, 11. In my reading, Bruner's "narrative mode" reasoning resembles Forrester's (2017) *Thinking in Cases*. However, to keep things simple I avoid connecting or contrasting narrative-mode reasoning and case-based thinking.
24. Bruner 1986, 12.
25. Bruner 1986, 13.
26. Bruner 1986, 11–12.
27. Bruner 1986, 11.
28. Bruner 1986, 14.
29. Amsterdam and Bruner 2000, 30.
30. Hume 1777, 7–8.
31. Giemza 2004.
32. Mallaby 2022, 82.
33. Bruner 2002, 13.
34. Amsterdam and Bruner 2000, 11.
35. Bruner 1986, 25.
36. Bruner 1986, 37.

NOTES 373

37. Bruner 2002, 8–9.
38. Amsterdam and Bruner 2000, 11.
39. Bruner 2002, 42.

Chapter 19

1. According to David Baker (February 15, 2024, personal communication with author), details derived from "personal experience" may now have a special status. For example, there is the current fashion for commissioning fiction only from authors who have "lived experience" of what they are writing about. Even in most business presentations, a personal element to the story now seems to be a more or less obligatory part of the narrative—as a guarantee of sincerity, authenticity, and truth.
2. Hemingway's *The Art of the Short Story* questioned Chekhov's advice: "It is also untrue that if a gun hangs on the wall when you open up the story, it must be fired by page fourteen. The chances are, gentlemen, that if it hangs upon the wall, it will not even shoot. If there are no questions, shall we press on?" (Hemingway 1990, 4).
3. Matthew Ford suggested this addition.
4. Slightly adapted from HBS video, confirmed via email with the author on August 2, 2023.
5. The beginning does not necessarily follow anything, but something else does necessarily follow from it, namely the middle. Likewise, the end must follow from the middle but does not require anything to follow—it is the end!
6. Presentation Skills 3 2023.
7. Aristotle 1989, 70.
8. Aristotle 1989, 63.
9. Aristotle 1989, 64.
10. Infants are also disturbed when their expected causal sequence is violated (Bruner 1986, 18).
11. Taleb 2001.
12. Entis 2014.
13. Mikhalkina and Cabantous 2015.
14. Analogies can also, however, catalyze manic enterprises if metaphors are taken as proof rather than as suggestive possibilities.
15. Handwerk 2023 and Marti et al. 2021.
16. Ray 2017.
17. Gallo 2020.
18. Norman 2013.
19. Greenfield 2016; Kay 2016.
20. "Remembering Gene Zelazny," McKinsey & Company, accessed September 10, 2023, https://www.mckinsey.com/alumni/news-and-events/global-news/alumni-news/2023-05-remembering-gene-zelazny.
21. Gene Zelazny interview with Michael McLaughlin, accessed January 26, 2016, http://managementconsultingnews.com/interview-gene-zelazny/.

374 NOTES

22. Isaacson 2011, 232.
23. Isaacson 2011, 233.
24. Jobs's last, for the iPad in 2010, may not have been his "best." Nonetheless, "the usual excitement that Jobs was able to gin up for a product launch paled in comparison to the frenzy that built for the iPad unveiling" (Isaacson 2011, 493).
25. Isaacson 2011, 493. And for unplanned poignancy, it was commonly known that Jobs had been treated for cancer before the iPhone launch and again, after a relapse, before the iPad event.
26. Victor 2021.
27. Wattles 2018. An earlier 2010 test for Space X's *Dragon* capsule had carried a "secret" payload of a wheel of cheese, said to honor a classic Monty Python sketch of John Cleese trying to buy cheese from a cheese shop that carries no cheese (Malik 2010).
28. Weiss 2014; Branson 2014.
29. Morris 2006.
30. Bhidé and Alter 1994.
31. Bhidé 2000, 107–108.
32. Adapted from Bhidé and Mohan (1994) and confirmed by Radosevich via email, August 21, 2023. See also Philip Dogeneiro's account in Bhidé 2000, 107.
33. Slightly adapted from HBS video interview, confirmed via email with the author on August 2, 2023.
34. Borrowing from Francis Thompson's poem "In No Strange Land" (Thompson 1907).
35. Branson 2016.
36. Roddick 2000, 41.

Chapter 20

1. Martens, Jennings, and Jennings 2007, 1124–1125, citing Aldrich and Fiol 1994; Lounsbury and Glynn 2001; O'Connor 2004; Porac et al. 2002; Smith and Anderson 2004.
2. Martens, Jennings, and Jennings 2007, 1125.
3. As mentioned, I compiled selected papers in Bhidé 1995.
4. Frei and Morriss 2023, 52–71.
5. Ignatius 2023, 12.
6. Lounsbury and Glynn 2001, 545.
7. Gabriel 2004, 63.
8. Gabriel 2004, 63.
9. "Narratologie" in Todorov's (1969) French text.
10. Bal 2017, 3.
11. Abbott 2021, 1.
12. Abbott 2021, 14.
13. Kay and King (2022a, 122) call "reference narratives" an "expression of our realistic expectations." Tuckett has been writing about "conviction narratives" since about 2011. In a recent paper (Johnson, Bilovich, and Tuckett 2023, Abstract), Tuckett and

his coauthors call narratives "structured representations of causal, temporal, analogical, and valence relationships" that "arise from the interplay between individual cognition and the social environment."

14. Morgan 2022, 3.
15. Amsterdam and Bruner 2000, 113.
16. Amsterdam and Bruner 2000, 114.
17. Amsterdam and Bruner 2000, 114.
18. Bruner 2002, 16–17.
19. *The Johns Hopkins Guide to Literary Theory and Criticism* calls Burke "one of the most unorthodox, challenging, and theoretically sophisticated American-born literary critics of the twentieth century" (Dickstein 2004).
20. Bruner 2002, 34.
21. Ryan 1960.
22. Crowther 1962.
23. Bruner 2002, 37.
24. Bruner 2002, 41.
25. Bruner 2002, 37.
26. Via email from Cristobal Perdomo, August 19, 2023.
27. Wallace and Erickson 1993, 67.
28. Gates 1996, 18.
29. From the dust jacket of Kelly's (1998) book. Not long after the book's publication, PSS/World imploded.
30. Kelly 1998, 37–38.
31. Kelly 1998, 92.
32. Sigafoos 1983, 27.
33. Bhidé 2000, 170–171.
34. Sigafoos 1983, 29.
35. Sigafoos 1983, 184.
36. Sigafoos 1983, 24.
37. Bohmer and Campbell 2002.
38. Gaglani and Crowley 2022.
39. Email from Apostolos Apostolakis, August 19, 2023.
40. Foley 2022.
41. Microsoft's Timeline 2008.
42. Kelly 1998, 79.
43. Kelly 1998, 79.
44. Kelly 1998, 80.
45. Kelly 1998, 80.
46. Kelly 1998, 81.
47. Kelly 1998, 81.
48. Kelly 1998, 81.
49. Kelly 1998, 81.
50. Kelly 1998, 82.
51. Dyson 2021, 72.

376 NOTES

52. Dyson 2021, 127.
53. Harvey 2014.
54. Gallo 2021.
55. Harvey 2014.
56. Schein 1985, 9.
57. Schein 1985, 18.
58. Deal and Kennedy 1982. In their typology, organizations could have "Tough-Guy / Macho," "Work Hard / Play Hard," "Bet the Company," and "Process" cultures.
59. Kelly 1998, 86.
60. Duhigg 2016.
61. Duhigg 2016.
62. Duhigg 2016.
63. Duhigg 2016.
64. Edmondson 1999.
65. Duhigg 2016.
66. Duhigg 2015.
67. re:Work, Guide 2023.
68. The re:Work homepage describes the site as a "curated platform" to help "push forward the practice and research of data-driven HR [human relations]."

Chapter 21

1. Promoters may direct their confidence producing discourse to themselves as well as to others. Tuckett and his collaborators could call the self-directed discourse "conviction narratives" even if they don't satisfy Bruner's austere specification for a story.
2. Bruner 2002, 25.
3. Bruner 2002, 7.
4. Bruner 2002, 25.
5. Bruner 2002, 53.
6. Bruner 2002, 54.
7. Bruner 2002, 54–55.
8. But it's not a one-way street. "Natural languages are splendid instruments for representing and expressing things in story form," writes Bruner. Their "commonsense grammar . . . easily takes note of such narrative distinctions as the usual who did what to whom, with what intent, with what result, in what setting, along what time course, and by what means" (2002, 33).
9. Bruner 2002, 60.
10. Bruner 2002, 8.
11. Bruner and Amsterdam 2000, 9.
12. Bruner and Amsterdam 2000, 9.
13. Bruner and Amsterdam 2000, 8–9.
14. Bruner and Amsterdam 2000, 9.
15. Bruner and Amsterdam 2000, 11–12.

NOTES 377

16. Bruner and Amsterdam 2000, 12.
17. Bruner and Amsterdam 2000, 11.
18. Bruner 2002, 5.
19. Bruner 2002, 25.
20. I was required, as a three-year-old, to read their Marathi translations, *Isap-niti* (Isap = Aesop, *niti* = guidance or conduct from the Sanskrit), word by painful word. It was a great relief to reach the *tātparya* (= purport, intent, in the Sanskrit).
21. King 1994, 240.
22. Bruner 2002, 11.
23. Bruner 2002, 10.
24. Bruner 2002, 34.
25. Bruner 2002, 10.
26. Bruner 2002, 15.
27. Bruner 2002, 15.
28. Bruner 2002, 48.
29. Bruner 2002, 22.
30. Bruner 2002, 48.
31. Bruner 2002, 48–49.
32. Bruner 2002, 19–20.
33. Bruner 2002, 49.
34. Bruner 2002, 57.
35. A small-time tradesman, Dick the Butcher in Shakespeare's *Henry IV*, who urges first killing all the lawyers, is also portrayed as a villain.
36. Horatio Alger Jr.'s "rags to riches" young adult novels depicted the possibilities for upward mobility in the nineteenth century but did not enthuse about innovation and progress. In any case, no one would confuse the Alger stories with serious literature.
37. See Farrow 2023.
38. In April 2023, I was surprised to read an *HBR* article by two INSEAD professors announcing their discovery of a "distinct new concept" that they called "non-disruptive creation" (Kim and Mauborgne 2023). I had discussed what I believe is the same idea in my 2000 book (Bhidé 2000, 330–334). I started calling my construct "non-destructive creation" around 2004 in articles and public lectures. The *Journal of Economic Perspectives* (Taylor 2005, 235) summarized one such lecture in 2005. I had written an entire chapter on non-destructive creation in my 2008 book (Bhidé 2008b, ch. 13). The *HBR* article made no mention of this work.

I emailed *HBR*'s editor in chief asking for either an independent evaluation of my concern about plagiarism or, failing that, a brief acknowledgment of my questions about originality in the next issue of *HBR*. The editor refused to accept either option. I let the matter drop. I couldn't afford a lawsuit. Battling Harvard's legal lawyers to prove that there was no material difference between "non-disruptive" and "non-destructive" would have been difficult. And I had this book to write.
39. In 2017 *HBR* published as a Spotlight article a piece by Jeffery Immelt titled "How I Remade GE" (Immelt 2017) almost immediately after Immelt had stepped down after 17 years as GE's CEO. *HBR*'s editor in chief (Ignatius 2017) wrote an

378 NOTES

introduction to the article titled "The Great Transformer," praising Immelt as a leader who had "utterly remade the organization he inherited from Jack Welch," the previous CEO. Just a few months after the article's publication the utterly remade organization went into free fall and barely survived. Earlier, in 2002, Suzy Welch had been forced to resign as *HBR*'s editor in chief, for having an extramarital affair with Jack Welch, while preparing an interview—"Jack on Jack"—for *HBR* (DePaulo 2002).

40. See Robillard's (2012) list of ten such instances.
41. To borrow from Bruner 1986, 42.
42. Porter 1979.
43. Porter 1980.
44. Bower and Christensen 1995.
45. See Bhidé and Ghemawat 2014.
46. As it happened, cheap netbooks came and went while Apple's iPhone (which used ARM-based chips and destroyed Nokia's dominance with more expensive devices) unexpectedly emerged as the main threat to Intel's microprocessor sales. Despite his admiration for Christensen's book, Steve Jobs resolutely stuck with premium products.
47. Coulombe and Civalleri 2021.
48. DeAngelo 2021, 2.
49. Stone 2013, 75. The "frugality myth," according to David Baker (February 15, 2024, personal communication with author) was also "ingrained in The Thomson Corporation. The founder, Ken Thomson's obituary mentions: 'His private habits were extremely frugal. He flew economy class, often skipped boardroom lunches for a snack at a yoghurt bar and liked nothing more than to spot a bargain in a discount store. It was even reported that his wife cut his hair to save the cost of a barber. He did not drink or smoke.'"
50. See Brattström and Wennberg (2022) for a discussion of how stories about entrepreneurs can affect the public's perceptions of the social value of entrepreneurship. One may further presume that perceptions of "goodness" or "badness" will spill over into people's willingness—especially of the idealists and young—to start businesses or help founders.
51. See note 38 above.
52. See Janeway 2022.
53. Not all businesses progress through all the phases. Many fail along the path, or their founders find a way to remain privately owned or avoid grow-or-die pressures. And even in companies like Amazon that evolve with exceptional speed, the changes do not occur overnight. Toughening and routinizing ad-hoc decision-making poses protracted challenges that can make or break the enterprise.

Part V

1. Shapin 1998, 20.

Chapter 22

1. Stigler 1971, xiv.
2. Phelps 2006.
3. Phelps 2013, 37.
4. Edmund S. Phelps's (unsigned) summary of the Aims and Scope of the Center on Capitalism and Society posted on the Center's website, around 2002, according to my records. The most recent (as of June 1, 2024) "Mission" of the Center, posted on the Center's website (https://capitalism.columbia.edu/content/mission) uses similar language:

   The Center and the prevailing economic theory. The established body of formal economic theory—intertemporal, information-theoretic and game-theoretic—captures neither the dynamism and its rewards nor the vulnerability to crisis. That theory *cannot* capture dynamism since the theory contradicts its existence: the theory implies a deterministic future—however buffeted it may be by stochastic shocks—in which nothing is left that is not already known while capitalist systems are evolving, unruly, open-ended systems that dictate an indeterminate future. The established theory allows only the probabilistically predictable "innovations" arriving from known stochastic processes. There is no dynamism, no intuition, insight or creativity.

5. Elster 2009, 3.
6. Elster 2013, 5. What counts as a good decision, continues Elster, is often indeterminate. And "although one can make plausible qualitative arguments for how to design good decision-making bodies . . . one cannot verify empirically whether the relevant conditions obtain" (Elster 2013, 5).
7. Elster 2013, 5.
8. Janeway 2022.
9. Janeway 2022.
10. Janeway 2022. The productive and unproductive legacies of speculative excesses is also a key theme of Janeway's *Doing Capitalism in the Innovation Economy* (2018).
11. Janeway 2022.
12. My firsthand, albeit limited, experience as a board director makes me skeptical of such a possibility.
13. See Andersen and Nielsen 2012.
14. Schumpeter 1934, 64n1.
15. See Bhidé 2000, 326–328, for a summary of Rosenberg's main ideas on the issue.
16. Rosenberg 1982, 62. Richard Nelson has also emphasized its importance, and its policy implications, for decades. (See, for instance, Merges and Nelson 1994.)
17. Darwin 1859, 489–490.
18. Braunerhjelm and Henrekson 2024; Stam 2015; and Wennberg and Sandström 2022 provide detailed, thoughtful analyses of the policy issues.
19. Millican 2002, 12, summarizing Craig's (2002) interpretation of Hume's propositions about causality.
20. Warren 2005.
21. Marshall 2005.
22. Bruner 2002, 16.

380 NOTES

23. Mixerno.Space 2023.
24. Salvucci 2023.
25. TikTok n.d.
26. The World's Platform for Change n.d.
27. Flynn 2023.
28. Retailers like Walmart, who had to close their physical stores, scaled up their e-commerce platforms for online shopping. Banks, like other service-sector employers, switched to remote work to keep their operations running. Healthcare providers scaled up their telemedicine services, and schools and colleges (relying on the tele-communications clouds of vendors like Zoom) set up remote classrooms.
29. USPS Tracking—US Global Mail n.d.
30. Similarly, the US unemployment insurance system managed a surge in payments from two million claims paid in the first week of March 2020 to thirty-three million weekly claims in June 2020.
31. Knight 1949, 435n.
32. My discussion of this problem paraphrases the argument in Bhidé 2018b.
33. See, for example, Ba and Pavlou 2002; Resnick and Zeckhauser 2002; and Melnik and Alm 2002.
34. Ashcraft 2017.
35. Some reviews are hard to fake. Airbnb and Uber can police the authenticity of user reviews of hosts and drivers. But even here, users may inflate ratings because the hosts and drivers also rate users. It is also questionable whether customers necessarily provide more trustworthy certifications of quality than producers or merchants do. Yes, sellers want to persuade you to buy. Still, those with hard-won reputations have an incentive to make claims they can justify and face legal liabilities for false claims.
36. Worse, according to critics, Facebook doesn't just amplify misinformation; it funds misinformation. An *MIT Technology Review* investigation reports that "Facebook and Google are paying millions of ad dollars to bankroll clickbait actors, fueling the deterioration of information ecosystems around the world." Hao 2021.
37. Mullainathan and Shleifer (2005) analyze a model that can be interpreted optimisti-cally: the diversity of reader's beliefs and competitive efforts to satisfy them, creates in the aggregate a less biased news supply.
38. Schama 2022.
39. Ratcliffe 2018.
40. "Covid-19 Pandemic Causes a Global Democracy Slump" 2021.
41. Howard 2014.
42. There are practical pressures to avoid multidisciplinary expert control. If experts come from different disciplines, they may be unable to have a conversation, creating deadlocks.
43. Bhidé 2020.
44. The centralization of monetary policymaking makes the problems particularly se-vere. The risks of an incomplete model developed by the in-house economists of commercial or investment banks are more contained.
45. March 1991.

NOTES 381

46. My discussion of this problem paraphrases the argument in Bhidé 2013; 2016; and especially 2018a.
47. Putnam and Norland 2018.
48. See Acosta and Cherrier's (2021) historical analysis of the academic pressures to increase the role of economists at the Fed.
49. Ferguson and Lahiri 2023.
50. Board of Governors of the Federal Reserve System, "Meet the Researchers," June 3, 2024, https://www.federalreserve.gov/econres/theeconomists.htm.
51. In an earlier era, most chairs did not have PhDs in economics. The legendary William McChesney Martin Jr., the Fed's longest-serving chair whose nearly nineteen-year term spanned five presidents, had started in a stockbroking firm after studying English and Latin for his bachelor's degree.
52. Volcker 2018.
53. If it had wanted to give the Fed perpetual discretion (beyond the ten-year transition), Congress could have directed the Fed to secure the greatest possible price stability consistent with 3 percent unemployment. It did not. Instead, the 1978 bill gave the president—not the Fed—explicit, perpetual authority to propose to Congress alternative targets for inflation and unemployment.
54. In an op-ed for the *Washington Post*, Chair Ben Bernanke (2010) justified the Fed's unprecedented program of quantitative easing on the grounds it would lead to "higher stock prices" that "will boost consumer wealth and help increase confidence, which can also spur spending."
55. In January 2022, Fed vice chair (and macroeconomist) Richard Clarida stepped down before the end of his term to return to his Columbia professorship. Clarida's departure followed news about discrepancies in his trading disclosures. At the onset of the 2020 pandemic, Clarida had moved millions of dollars into a stock fund a day before Chair Jerome Powell signaled that the Fed might move to further ease monetary policy. The year before Clarida's departure, Dallas Fed president Robert Kaplan and Boston Fed president Eric Rosengren had come under fire for "revelations that they had bought and sold stocks and real estate–linked assets in 2020 as the central bank was engaged in an extensive rescue of financial markets. Both men resigned within weeks of the firestorm," according to Reuters (Guida 2022).
56. In 2008, the *Wall Street Journal* reported that former Fed chair Alan Greenspan charged "six-figure fees to answer questions for audiences, typically assemblies of financial professionals." Greenspan's consulting clients included Germany's biggest bank, the world's biggest bond-fund manager, and a hedge fund that had "made billions betting against housing" (Ip 2008).

Greenspan's successor (and former Princeton economics professor), Ben Bernanke, began meeting hedge fund managers shortly after retiring as Fed chair in 2014, according to Reuters. In April 2015, Bernanke joined Citadel LLC, becoming "the latest top central banker to join the hedge fund industry as an advisor." The previous month, FOMC member—and Harvard economics professor—Jeremy Stein had joined BlueMountain Capital Management. The hirings, Reuters noted, "underscore[d] how eager top investors are for a read on when the Federal Reserve

382 NOTES

will tighten monetary policy again following years of easy money policies aimed at boosting growth after the financial crisis" (Herbst-Bayliss 2015). Fed activism was apparently a gift that kept on giving—to the architects of its activism, if not the public.

Heads of the Office of the Comptroller of the Currency—another independent bank regulator—enjoy no similar postretirement opportunities.

57. Dietze 2019.

58. Dietze 2019.

59. *Federalist* 51 noted that, "If men were angels, no government would be necessary. If angels were to govern, neither external nor internal controls on government would be necessary. In framing a government which is to be administered by men over men, the great difficulty lies in this: You must first enable the government to control the governed; and in the next place oblige it to control itself."

Similarly, *Federalist* 10, authored by Madison, made a bold claim about large, diverse republics. Earlier theories had claimed that democracy required small, cohesive electorates. Madison's theory emphasized the problem of capture by special interests. "A landed interest, a manufacturing interest, a mercantile interest, a moneyed interest, with many lesser interests, grow up of necessity in civilized nations, and divide themselves into different classes, actuated by different sentiments and views. The regulation of these various and interfering interests forms the principal task of modern legislation." Given the proper rules (e.g., checks and balances, the division of powers, representative government rather than direct democracy), competition between rival interests in a large republic could prevent the dominance of any one interest.

60. Knight 1949, 443.

References

Abbott, H. P. (2021). *The Cambridge introduction to narrative*. Third ed. Cambridge University Press.

Abrams v. United States, 250 U.S. 616 (1919), (1919). https://supreme.justia.com/cases/federal/us/250/616/

Academy of Achievement. (2001, May 4). Jeff Bezos [In-Person]. https://web.archive.org/web/20161111185213/http://www.achievement.org/autodoc/printmember/bez0int-1

Acosta, J., & Cherrier, B. (2021). The transformation of economic analysis at the Board of Governors of the Federal Reserve System during the 1960s. *IDEAS Working Paper Series from RePEc* 43(3), 323–349. https://doi.org/10.1017/S1053837220000188

Clarke, J. S., Cornelissen, J. P., & Healey, M. P. (2019). Actions speak louder than words: How figurative language and gesturing in entrepreneurial pitches influences investment judgments. *Academy of Management Journal* 62(2), 335–360. https://doi.org/10.5465/amj.2016.1008

Agnew, H., McCrum, D., & Dunkley, E. (2023). Inside the boardroom bust-up that shook Scottish Mortgage. FT.com. https://search.proquest.com/docview/2789969308?pq-origsite=primo

Akerlof, G. A. (1970). The market for "lemons": Quality uncertainty and the market mechanism. *The Quarterly Journal of Economics* 84(3), 488–500. https://doi.org/10.2307/1879431

Aldrich, H. (2001). Customer review. Amazon. https://www.amazon.com/gp/customer-reviews/R1U7WVXQR0N7ZQ/ref=cm_cr_dp_d_rvw_ttl?ie=UTF8&ASIN=0195131444

Aldrich, H. E., & Fiol, C. M. (1994). Fools rush in? The institutional context of industry creation. *The Academy of Management Review* 19(4), 645–670. https://doi.org/10.2307/258740

Amazon Web Services Revenue 2022. (n.d.). Statista. Retrieved November 30, 2023, from https://www.statista.com/statistics/233725/development-of-amazon-web-services-revenue/

Amit, R., Brander, J., & Zott, C. (1998). Why do venture capital firms exist? Theory and Canadian evidence. *Journal of Business Venturing* 13(6), 441–466. https://doi.org/10.1016/S0883-9026(97)00061-X

Amsterdam, A. G., & Bruner, J. S. (2000). *Minding the law*. Harvard University Press.

Anastasi, J. S. (2008). Cognition. In W. A. Darity Jr. (Ed.), *International encyclopedia of the social sciences*. Second ed. Vol. 1, 596–599.

Andersen, S., & Nielsen, K. M. (2012). Ability or finances as constraints on entrepreneurship? Evidence from survival rates in a natural experiment. *The Review of Financial Studies* 25(12), 3684–3710. https://doi.org/10.1093/rfs/hhs107

Aristimuño, F., & Crespo, R. (2021). The early Enlightenment roots of Keynes' probability concept. *Cambridge Journal of Economics* 45(5), 919–932. https://doi.org/10.1093/cje/beab004

Aristotle. (1989). Aristotle: Poetics. In D. A. Russell & M. Winterbottom (Eds.), and M. E. Hubbard (Trans.), *Classical literary criticism* (pp. 51–91). Oxford University Press.

Arkes, H., Gigerenzer, G., & Hertwig, R. (2016). How bad is incoherence? *Decision* 3(1), 20–39.

Arrow, K. J. (1951). Alternative approaches to the theory of choice in risk-taking situations. *Econometrica* 19(4), 404–437. https://doi.org/10.2307/1907465

Ashcraft, B. (2017, May 17). Inside Chinese "click farms." Kotaku. https://kotaku.com/inside-chinese-click-farms-1795287821

Augier, M. (2008). Simon, Herbert A. (1916–2001). In S. Durlauf & L. Blume (Eds.), *The new Palgrave dictionary of economics*. Second ed. (pp. 5904–5908). Palgrave Macmillan.

384 REFERENCES

Augier, M., & March, J. (2004). Herbert A. Simon, Scientist. In Mie Augier & James G. March (Eds.), *Models of a man: Essays in memory of Herbert A. Simon* (pp. 3–32). MIT Press.

Austin, D. (2023, May 10). The metaverse is dead, long live generative AI. eDiscovery Today by Doug Austin. https://ediscoverytoday.com/2023/05/10/the-metaverse-is-dead-long-live-generative-ai-artificial-intelligence-trends/

Azoulay, P., Jones, B. F., Kim, J. D., & Miranda, J. (2020). Age and high-growth entrepreneurship. *American Economic Review* 2(1), 65–82.

Ba, S., & Pavlou, P. A. (2002). Evidence of the effect of trust building technology in electronic markets: Price premiums and buyer behavior. *MIS Quarterly* 26(3), 243–268. https://doi.org/10.2307/4132332

Bacon, F. (1620). *Novum Organum* (T. Fowler, Trans.). Clarendon Press.

Bain, J. S. (1951). Relation of profit rate to industry concentration: American manufacturing, 1936–1940. *The Quarterly Journal of Economics* 65(3), 293–324. https://doi.org/10.2307/1882217.

Bal, M. (2017). *Narratology: Introduction to the theory of narrative.* Fourth ed. University of Toronto Press.

Baldwin, C. Y. (2018). Design rules, volume 2: How technology shapes organizations: Chapter 7: The value structure of technologies, Part 2: Technical and strategic bottlenecks as guides for action. Harvard Business School Working Paper 19-042. https://www.hbs.edu/faculty/Pages/item.aspx?num=55140

Barnard, C. I. (1938). *The functions of the executive.* Harvard University Press.

Barreto, H. (1989). *The entrepreneur in microeconomic theory: Disappearance and explanation.* Routledge.

Baumol, W. J. (1968). Entrepreneurship in economic theory. *The American Economic Review* 58(2), 64–71.

Baumol, W. J. (1993). *Entrepreneurship, management, and the structure of payoffs.* MIT Press.

Berkshire Hathaway Inc. Annual Report 2019. (2019). Annual report. https://www.berkshirehathaway.com/2019ar/2019ar.pdf

Berlin, I. (1953). *The hedgehog and the fox: An essay on Tolstoy's view of history.* Weidenfeld & Nicolson.

Bernanke, B. S. (2007, March 28). Testimony: The economic outlook. Joint Economic Committee, U.S. Congress. https://www.federalreserve.gov/newsevents/testimony/bernanke20070328a.htm

Bernanke, B. S. (2010, November 5). Aiding the economy: What the Fed did and why. *Washington Post.*

Bernstein, P. L. (1996). *Against the gods: The remarkable story of risk.* Wiley.

Bhidé, A. (1986). Hustle as strategy. *Harvard Business Review* 64(5), 59–65.

Bhidé, A. (1989a). The causes and consequences of hostile takeovers. *Journal of Applied Corporate Finance* 2(2), 36–59. https://doi.org/10.1111/j.1745-6622.1989.tb00178.x

Bhidé, A. (1989b). Vinod Khosla and Sun Microsystems (A)—Case. Harvard Business School Publishing. https://www.hbs.edu/faculty/Pages/item.aspx?num=11608

Bhidé, A. (1990). Reversing corporate diversification. *Journal of Applied Corporate Finance* 3(2), 70–81. https://doi.org/10.1111/j.1745-6622.1990.tb00201.x

Bhidé, A. (1993). The hidden costs of stock market liquidity. *Journal of Financial Economics* 34(1), 31–51. https://doi.org/10.1016/0304-405X(93)90039-E

Bhidé, A. (1995). Tales from successful entrepreneurs. Harvard Business School. https://www.hbs.edu/faculty/Pages/item.aspx?num=12813

Bhidé, A. (1996). Road well traveled: A note on the journeys of HBS entrepreneurs. *Harvard Business Review.* https://store.hbr.org/product/road-well-traveled-a-note-on-the-journeys-of-hbs-entrepreneurs/396277

Bhidé, A. (2000). *The origin and evolution of new businesses.* Oxford University Press.

Bhidé, A. (2006). How novelty aversion affects financing options. *Capitalism and Society* 1(1). https://doi.org/10.2202/1932-0213.1002

REFERENCES   385

Bhidé, A. (2008a). *The venturesome economy: How innovation sustains prosperity in a more connected world.* Princeton University Press.

Bhidé, A. (2008b). What holds back Bangalore businesses? *Asian Economic Papers* 7(1), 120–153. https://doi.org/10.1162/asep.2008.7.1.120

Bhidé, A. (2010). *A call for judgment: Sensible finance for a dynamic economy.* Oxford University Press.

Bhide, A. (2013, August 20). Wanted: A boring leader for the Fed. *New York Times*, A19.

Bhide, A. (2014, January 30). A law unto themselves. *City Journal.* Retrieved June 7, 2024, from https://www.city-journal.org/article/a-law-unto-themselves/

Bhide, A. (2016, August 17). Easy money is a dangerous cure for a debt hangover. *Financial Times.* https://search.proquest.com/docview/1819571909?pq-origsite=primo

Bhidé, A. (2017). Formulaic transparency: The hidden enabler of exceptional U.S. securitization. *Journal of Applied Corporate Finance* 29(4), 96–111.

Bhidé, A. (2018a, November 7). Congress should set the Fed's inflation target—ideally at zero. *Wall Street Journal.* https://search.proquest.com/docview/2130147568?pq-origsite=primo

Bhidé, A. (2018b, June 8). Skepticism beats Snopes as an antidote to fake news. *Wall Street Journal.* https://www.wsj.com/articles/skepticism-beats-snopes-as-an-antidote-to-fake-news-1528497662

Bhidé, A. (2020). Making economics more useful: How technological eclecticism could help. *Applied Economics* 52(26), 2862–2881. https://doi.org/10.1080/00036846.2019.1696939

Bhidé, A. (2021a). Renewing Knightian uncertainty: Problems and possibilities. Harvard Business School Working Papers 21-129. https://papers.ssrn.com/abstract=3868219

Bhidé, A. (2021b). Symmetric ignorance: The cost of anonymous lemons. *European Financial Management* 27(3), 414–425. https://doi.org/10.1111/eufm.12298

Bhidé, A., & Alter, M. (1994). Selling as a systematic process. Retrieved August 31, 2023, from https://store.hbr.org/product/selling-as-a-systematic-process/395091

Bhidé, A., Datar, S., & Stebbins, K. (2020). HIV tests and AIDS treatments—Containing a fearsome pandemic. Harvard Business School Working Paper Series 20-007.

Bhide, A., Datar, S., & Stebbins, K. (2021a). Case histories of significant medical advances: Tamoxifen. SSRN Scholarly Paper 3679645. https://doi.org/10.2139/ssrn.3679645

Bhidé, A., Datar, S., & Stebbins, K. (2021b). SSRIs and non-SSRIs (through 1999): Case histories of significant medical advances. Harvard Business School Working Paper Series 20-135. https://doi.org/10.2139/ssrn.3866769

Bhidé, A., Datar, S., & Villa, F. (2020). Coronary artery bypass grafting: Impossible to routine. Harvard Business School Working Paper Series 20-010.

Bhidé, A., & Mohan, B. (1994). Marcia Radosevich and Health Payment Review—1989 (A). https://hbsp.harvard.edu/product/394204-PDF-ENG?Ntt=health%20payment%20review

Bhidé, A. V., & Ghemawat, P. (2014, October 9). Clay Christensen's theories are great for entrepreneurs, but not executives. Quartz. https://qz.com/278155/clay-christensens-theories-are-great-for-executives-but-not-entrepreneurs

Birch, D. L. (1979). *The job generation process.* MIT Program on Neighborhood and Regional Change.

Bishop, M. (2009). *Economics: An A–Z guide.* The Economist.

Bloomberg Anywhere. (2021). Bloomberg Finance LP. https://bba.bloomberg.net/

Boeing reports first-quarter results. (2020, April 29). Boeing. Earnings release, p. 13. https://s2.q4cdn.com/661678649/files/doc_financials/quarterly/2020/q1/1Q20-Press-Release.pdf

Boettke, P. J., & Candela, R. A. (2021). The common sense of economics and divergent approaches in economic thought: A view from Risk, Uncertainty, and Profit. *Journal of Institutional Economics* 17(6), 1–15. https://doi.org/10.1017/S1744137421000229

Bohmer, R., & Campbell, B. (2002). *Father's love: Novazyme Pharmaceuticals Inc.* Harvard Business School Publishing. https://hbsp.harvard.edu/product/603048-PDF-ENG?Ntt=a%20father%27s%20love

386 REFERENCES

Botelho, T., Fehder, D., & Hochberg, Y. (2021). Innovation-driven entrepreneurship National Bureau of Economic Research. Working Paper 28990. https://doi.org/10.3386/w28990

Bower, J. L., & Christensen, C. M. (1995, January 1). Disruptive technologies: Catching the wave. *Harvard Business Review.* https://hbr.org/1995/01/disruptive-technologies-catching-the-wave

Branson, R. (2014, October 31). Fancy dress is not just for Halloween. Virgin. https://web.archive.org/web/20141031233929/http://www.virgin.com/richard-branson/fancy-dress-is-not-just-for-halloween

Branson, R. (2016, February 8). Why entrepreneurs are storytellers. Virgin. https://virgin.com/branson-family/richard-branson-blog/why-entrepreneurs-are-storytellers

Brattström, A., & Wennberg, K. (2022). The entrepreneurial story and its implications for research. *Entrepreneurship Theory and Practice* 46(6), 1443–1468. https://doi.org/10.1177/10422587211053802

Braunerhjelm, P., & Henrekson, M. (2024). *Unleashing society's innovative capacity: An integrated policy framework* Springer International. https://doi.org/10.1007/978-3-031-42756-5

Brewer, S. (1996). Exemplary reasoning: Semantics, pragmatics, and the rational force of legal argument by analogy. *Harvard Law Review* 109(5), 923. https://doi.org/10.2307/1342258

Bronner, E. (1998, September 23). Students at B-schools flock to the E-courses. *New York Times.* https://www.nytimes.com/1998/09/23/business/students-at-b-schools-flock-to-the-e-courses.html

Brooks, F. P. (1975). *The mythical man-month: Essays on software engineering.* Addison-Wesley.

Bruner, J. (1991). The narrative construction of reality. *Critical Inquiry* 18(1), 1–21. https://doi.org/10.1086/448619

Bruner, J. S. (1962). *On knowing: Essays for the left hand.* Belknap Press of Harvard University Press.

Bruner, J. S. (1986). *Actual minds, possible worlds.* Harvard University Press.

Bruner, J. S. (1990). *Acts of meaning.* Harvard University Press.

Bruner, J. S. (2002). *Making stories: Law, literature, life.* First Harvard University Press paperback ed. Harvard University Press.

Buchanan, J. A. (1982). Foreword. In Frank H. Knight, *Freedom and reform: Essays in economics and social philosophy.* Liberty Fund.

Buffett, W. (1987). Chairman's letter—1986. https://www.berkshirehathaway.com/letters/1986.html

Burgin, A. (2009). The radical conservatism of Frank H. Knight. *Modern Intellectual History* 6(3), 513–538. https://doi.org/10.1017/S1479244309990163

Burrough, B., & Helyar, J. (1989). *Barbarians at the gate: The fall of RJR Nabisco.* HarperCollins.

Bynum, W. F. (2008). *History of medicine: A very short introduction.* Oxford University Press.

Camerer, C. (1995). Individual decision making. In J. H. Kagel & A. E. Roth (Eds.), *The Handbook of Experimental Economics* (pp. 587–704). Princeton University Press. https://doi.org/10.2307/j.ctvzsmff5.12

Camerer, C. F., & Loewenstein, G. (2004). Behavioral economics: Past, present, future. In C. F. Camerer, G. Loewenstein, & M. Rabin (Eds.), *Advances in Behavioral Economics* (pp. 3–52). Princeton University Press. https://doi.org/10.2307/j.ctvcm4j8j.6

Camerer, C. F., Loewenstein, G., & Rabin, M. (Eds.). (2004a). In C. Camerer & E. Fehr (Eds.), *Advances in Behavioral Economics* (pp. i–vi). Princeton University Press. https://doi.org/10.2307/j.ctvcm4j8j.1

Camerer, C. F., Loewenstein, G., & Rabin, M. (Eds.). (2004b). Preface. In C. Camerer & E. Fehr (Eds.), *Advances in Behavioral Economics* (pp. xxi–xxiv). Princeton University Press. https://doi.org/10.2307/j.ctvcm4j8j.4

Camerer, C. F., & Weber, M. (1992). Recent developments in modeling preferences: Uncertainty and ambiguity. *Journal of Risk and Uncertainty* 5(4), 325–370.

REFERENCES   387

Campbell, W. J. (2020, September 27). Quote of the 1990s? "If it doesn't fit, you must acquit," 25 years on. The 1995 Blog. https://1995blog.com/2020/09/27/quote-of-the-1990s-if-it-doesnt-fit-you-must-acquit-25-years-on/

Capurso, T. J. (1998). How judges judge: Theories on judicial decision making. *University of Baltimore Law Forum* 29(1), Article 2.

Cartwright, N. (2004). Causation: One word, many things. *Philosophy of Science* 71(5), 805–819. https://doi.org/10.1086/426771

Catalini, C., Guzman, J., & Stern, S. (2019). Hidden in plain sight: Venture growth with or without venture capital. National Bureau of Economic Research. Working Paper 26521. https://doi.org/10.3386/w26521

Caves, R. (2001, June 1). From our bookshelf. *Regional Review, Federal Reserve Bank of Boston* 11(Quarter 2). https://www.bostonfed.org/publications/regional-review/2001/quarter-2/from-our-bookshelf.aspx

Chambers, D., Dimson, E., & Kaffe, C. (2020). Seventy-five years of investing for future generations. *Financial Analysts Journal* 76(4), 5–21. https://doi.org/10.1080/0015198X.2020.1802984

Chandler, A. D. (1962). *Strategy and structure: Chapters in the history of the industrial enterprise*. MIT Press.

Chandler, A. D. (1977). *The visible hand: The managerial revolution in American business*. The Belknap Press of Harvard University Press.

Chandler, A. D. (1990). *Scale and scope: The dynamics of industrial capitalism*. The Belknap Press of Harvard University Press.

Change.org Statistics User Count and Facts. (2023). Retrieved October 30, 2023, from https://expandedramblings.com/index.php/changeorg-facts-statistics/

Chater, N. (2019). *The mind is flat: The illusion of mental depth and the improvised mind*. Penguin Books.

Christensen, C. M. (1997). *The innovator's dilemma: When new technologies cause great firms to fail*. Harvard Business School Press.

Coase, R. H. (1937). The nature of the firm. *Economica* 4(16), 386–405. https://doi.org/10.1111/j.1468-0335.1937.tb00002.x

Cognitive Psychology. (2016). In J. L. Longe (Ed.), *The Gale encyclopedia of psychology*. Third ed. Gale Research Inc.

Collier, C. W. (2022). The economics of information and the meaning of speech. *Catholic University Law Review* 71(2), 345–376.

Cooper, C. J. (2015). His first century. *NYU Law Magazine*. https://blogs.law.nyu.edu/magazine/2015/his-first-century/

Coulombe, J., & Civalleri, P. (2021). *Becoming Trader Joe: How I did business my way and still beat the big guys*. HarperCollins Leadership.

Covid-19 pandemic causes a global democracy slump. (2021, February 2). Economist Intelligence Unit. https://www.eiu.com/n/covid-19-pandemic-causes-a-global-democracy-slump/

Crace, J. (2007, March 27). Jerome Bruner: The lesson of the story. *The Guardian*. https://www.theguardian.com/education/2007/mar/27/academicexperts.highereducationprofile

Craig, E. (2002). The idea of necessary connexion. In Peter J. R. Millican (Ed.), *Reading Hume on human understanding: Essays on the first Enquiry* (pp. 211–230). Clarendon Press; Oxford University Press.

Cringely, R. X. (1996). *Accidental empires: How the boys of Silicon Valley make their millions, battle foreign competition, and still can't get a date*. Newly rev. and exp. ed. HarperBusiness.

Crowther, B. (1962, October 5). Screen: Premiere of "The Longest Day": Production by Zanuck opens at the Warner. *New York Times*. https://web.archive.org/web/20190414021748/https://www.nytimes.com/1962/10/05/archives/screen-premiere-of-the-longest-dayproduction-by-zanuck-opens-at-the.html

388   REFERENCES

Dalrymple, W. (2015, March 4). The East India Company: The original corporate raiders. *The Guardian.* https://www.theguardian.com/world/2015/mar/04/east-india-company-origi nal-corporate-raiders

Darwin, C. R. (1859). *On the origin of species by means of natural selection, or, The preservation of favoured races in the struggle for life.* John Murray. https://www.loc.gov/item/06017473/

Deal, T. E., & Kennedy, A. A. (1982). *Corporate cultures: The rites and rituals of corporate life.* Addison-Wesley.

DeAngelo, H. (2021). Corporate financial policy: What really matters? *Journal of Corporate Finance* 68, 101925. https://doi.org/10.1016/j.jcorpfin.2021.101925

Dearborn, D. C., & Simon, H. A. (1958). Selective perception: A note on the departmental identifications of executives. *Sociometry* 21(2), 140–144. https://doi.org/10.2307/2785898

Decker, R., Haltiwanger, J., Jarmin, R., & Miranda, J. (2014). The role of entrepreneurship in US job creation and economic dynamism. *The Journal of Economic Perspectives* 28(3), 3–24.

De Finetti, B. (1931). *Probabilismo: Saggio critico sulla teoria delle probabilità e sul valore della scienza.* Perrella.

De Long, J. B., Shleifer, A., Summers, L. H., & Waldmann, R. J. (1990a). Positive feedback in-vestment strategies and destabilizing rational speculation. *The Journal of Finance* 45(2), 379–395. https://doi.org/10.2307/2328662

De Long, J. B., Shleifer, A., Summers, L. H., & Waldmann, R. J. (1990b). Noise trader risk in fi-nancial markets. *Journal of Political Economy* 98(4), 703–738. http://www.jstor.org/stable/2937765

DePaulo, L. (2002, May 6). If you knew Suzy. *New York.* https://nymag.com/nymetro/news/media/features/5976/index.html

Dickstein, B. (2004). Kenneth Burke. Pennsylvania Center for the Book. https://pabook.librar ies.psu.edu/literary-cultural-heritage-map-pa/bios/Burke__Kenneth

Dietze, G. (2019). *The Federalist—A general appreciation* (pp. 3–38). Baltimore, MD: Johns Hopkins University Press. https://muse.jhu.edu/pub/1/oa_monograph/chapter/2412 221#chapter1_12

Dimson, E., Marsh, P., & Staunton, M. (2024). *Global investment returns yearbook 2024.* Twenty-fifth ed. UBS.

Dobkin, J. C. (2006). The laying of the Atlantic cable: Paintings, watercolors, and commemo-rative objects given to the Metropolitan Museum by Cyrus W. Field. *Metropolitan Museum Journal* 41, 155–170.

Doerr, J. (2018). *Measure what matters: OKRs: The simple idea that drives 10x growth.* Portfolio Penguin.

Duhigg, C. (2016, February 25). What Google learned from its quest to build the perfect team. *New York Times.* https://www.nytimes.com/2016/02/28/magazine/what-google-learned-from-its-quest-to-build-the-perfect-team.html

Dyson, J. (2021). *Invention: A life.* Simon & Schuster.

Economics, Behavioral. (2008). In M. Altman (Ed.), *International encyclopedia of the social sciences.* Second ed., Vol. 2 (pp. 499–502). Macmillan Reference USA.

Edgeworth, F. Y. (1877). New and old methods of ethics: Or "physical ethics" and "methods of ethics." J. Parker. http://nrs.harvard.edu/urn-3:HUL.FIG:004719231

The Editors of Encyclopedia Britannica. (2022a). Herbert A. Simon. Britannica. Retrieved August 23, 2022, from https://www.britannica.com/biography/Herbert-A-Simon

The Editors of Encyclopedia Britannica. (2022b, February 19). Michael Dell. Britannica. https://www.britannica.com/biography/Michael-Dell

Edmondson, A. (1999). Psychological safety and learning behavior in work teams. *Administrative Science Quarterly* 44(2), 350–383. https://doi.org/10.2307/2666999

Ellsberg, D. (1961). Risk, ambiguity, and the Savage axioms. *The Quarterly Journal of Economics* 75(4), 643–669. https://doi.org/10.2307/1884324

Ellsberg, D. (2001). *Risk, ambiguity, and decision.* Garland Publishing.

Ellsberg, D. (2011). Introduction to the symposium issue. *Economic Theory* 48(2/3), 219–227.

· REFERENCES   389

Elster, J. (2009a). Excessive ambitions. *Capitalism and Society* 4(2), Article 6. https://doi.org/
10.2202/1932-0213.1055

Elster, J. (2009b). Interpretation and rational choice. *Rationality and Society* 21(1), 5–33.

Elster, J. (2013). Excessive ambitions (II). *Capitalism and Society* 8(1), Article 1. https://ssrn.
com/abstract=2207111

Elster, J. (2015). *Explaining social behavior: More nuts and bolts for the social sciences.* Second
ed. Cambridge University Press. https://doi.org/10.1017/CBO9781107763111

Emmett, R. B. (2000, August 1). Annotated bibliography of Frank Knight. Econlib. https://
www.econlib.org/library/Knight/KnightBib.html

Emmett, R. B. (2015). Frank H. Knight before he entered economics (1885–1914). Social
Science Research Network. SSRN Scholarly Paper 2695954. https://doi.org/10.2139/
ssrn.2695954

Emmett, R. B. (2018, December 3). A century of *Risk, Uncertainty and Profit.* Econlib. https://
www.econlib.org/library/Columns/y2018/Emmettriskuncertaintyprofit.html

Emmett, R. B. (2020). Reconsidering Frank Knight's Risk, Uncertainty and Profit. *The
Independent Review* 24(4), 533–541.

Emmett, R. B. (2021). The writing and reception of Risk, Uncertainty and Profit. *Cambridge
Journal of Economics* 45(5), 883–900. https://doi.org/10.1093/cje/beab005

Entis, L. (2014, August 12). "We're the Uber of X!" *Entrepreneur.* https://www.entrepreneur.
com/starting-a-business/were-the-uber-of-x/236456

Entrepreneurship Working Group. (Fall 2021). National Bureau of Economic Research.
Retrieved February 17, 2022, from https://www.nber.org/conferences/entrepreneurship-
working-group-fall-2021.

The eye of the storm. (2016, May 14). The Economist. https://www.economist.com/business/
2016/05/14/the-eye-of-the-storm

Fama, E. F., & Jensen, M. C. (1983a). Agency problems and residual claims. *The Journal of Law
& Economics* 26(2), 327–349.

Fama, E. F., & Jensen, M. C. (1983b). Separation of ownership and control. *The Journal of Law
and Economics* 26(2), 301–325. https://doi.org/10.1086/467037

Fama, E. F., & Jensen, M. C. (1985). Organizational forms and investment decisions. *Journal of
Financial Economics* 14(1), 101–119. https://doi.org/10.1016/0304-405X(85)90045-5

Farre-Mensa, J., Hegde, D., & Ljungqvist, A. (2020). What is a patent worth? Evidence from
the U.S. patent "lottery." *The Journal of Finance* 75(2), 639–682. https://doi.org/10.1111/
jofi.12867

Farrow, R. (2023, August 21). Elon Musk's shadow rule. *The New Yorker.* https://www.newyor
ker.com/magazine/2023/08/28/elon-musks-shadow-rule

Faulkner, P., Feduzi, A., McCann, C. R., & Runde, J. (2021). F. H. Knight's Risk, Uncertainty
and Profit and J. M. Keynes' Treatise on Probability after 100 years. *Cambridge Journal of
Economics* 45(5), 857–882.

FDA. (1998). Guidance for Industry. Providing clinical evidence of effectiveness for human
drug and biological products (Clinical 6). Food and Drug Administration. https://www.
fda.gov/files/drugs/published/Providing-Clinical-Evidence-of-Effectiveness-for-Human-
Drug-and-Biological-Products.pdf

The Fed—Meet the Researchers. (2024, June 3). The Board of Governors of the Federal Reserve
System. Retrieved June 3, 2024, from https://www.federalreserve.gov/econres/theeconomi
sts.htm

Feduzi, A. (2010). On Keynes's conception of the weight of evidence. *Journal of Economic
Behavior & Organization* 76, 338–351.

Ferguson, R. W., Jr., & Lahiri, U. (2023, June 15). The history and future of the Federal Reserve's
2 percent target rate of inflation. Council on Foreign Relations. https://www.cfr.org/blog/
history-and-future-federal-reserves-2-percent-target-rate-inflation-0

Fisher, F. M. (1989). Games Economists Play: A Noncooperative View. *The RAND Journal of
Economics* 20(1), 113–124. https://doi.org/10.2307/2555655

390 REFERENCES

Flynn, J. R. (1987). Massive IQ gains in 14 nations: What IQ tests really measure. *Psychological Bulletin* 101(2), 171–191. https://doi.org/10.1037/0033-2909.101.2.171

Flynn, J. (2023, June 22). 25 amazing cloud adoption statistics [2023]: Cloud migration, computing, and more. Zippia. https://www.zippia.com/advice/cloud-adoption-statistics/

Foley,M.J.(2022,February3).CouldMicrosoft's"thethirdtime'sthecharm"daysbeover?ZDNET. https://www.zdnet.com/article/could-microsofts-the-third-times-the-charm-days-be-over/

Forrester, J. (2017). Thinking in cases. Polity Press.

Foss, N. J., & Klein, P. G. (2012). Organizing entrepreneurial judgment: A new approach to the firm. Cambridge University Press.

Freear, J. J., Sohl, J. E., & Wetzel, W. E., Jr. (1995). Angels: Personal investors in the venture capital market. *Entrepreneurship and Regional Development* 7, 85–94.

Frei, F. X., & Morriss, A. (2023). Storytelling that drives bold change. *Harvard Business Review* 101(6), 62–71.

Friberg, R. (2016). *Managing risk and uncertainty: A strategic approach.* MIT Press. https://public.ebookcentral.proquest.com/choice/publicfullrecord.aspx?p=4961102

Friedman, M. (1953). *Essays in positive economics.* University of Chicago Press.

Friedman, M. (1962). *Price theory: A provisional text.* Aldine.

Friedman, M. (1976). *Price theory: A provisional text.* Aldine.

Friedman, M., & Savage, L. J. (1948). The utility analysis of choices involving risk. *Journal of Political Economy* 56(4), 279–304.

Friedman, M., & Savage, L. J. (1952). The expected-utility hypothesis and the measurability of utility. *Journal of Political Economy* 60(6), 463–474.

Fye, B. (2015). *Caring for the heart: Mayo Clinic and the rise of specialization.* Oxford University Press.

Gabriel, Y. (2004). Narratives, stories, texts. In D. Grant, C. Hardy, C. Oswick, & L. L. Putnam (Eds.), *The Sage handbook of organizational discourse* (pp. 61–79). Sage.

Gage, D. (2012, September 20). The venture capital secret: 3 out of 4 start-ups fail. *Wall Street Journal.* https://online.wsj.com/article/SB10000872396390443720204578004980476429190.html

Gaglani, S., & Crowley, J. (n.d.). Making rare disease treatments a priority—John Crowley, executive chairman at Amicus Therapeutics (September 22, 2022). https://www.osmosis.org/podcasts/making-rare-disease-treatments-a-priority-john-crowley

Galbraith, J. K. (1967). *The new industrial state.* Houghton Mifflin.

Galbraith, J. K. (1985). *The new industrial state.* Revised ed. Princeton University Press. https://doi.org/10.2307/j.ctvcm4hjz

Gallo, C. (2020, January 6). What it takes to give a great presentation. *Harvard Business Review.* https://hbr.org/2020/01/what-it-takes-to-give-a-great-presentation

Gallo, C. (2021, September 9). How James Dyson's thousands of failures can help you tell a captivating founder origin story. Inc.com. https://www.inc.com/carmine-gallo/how-james-dysons-thousands-of-failures-can-help-you-tell-a-captivating-founder-origin-story.html

Gandhi, V., Brumme, C. R., & Schwalb, N. (2019). The Velux Foundations: Selecting impact funds. Harvard Business School Case Study 9-819-021 (p. 20). *Harvard Business School.* https://hbsp.harvard.edu/product/819021-PDF-ENG

Gardiner v. Gray (High Court of England and Wales). (1815, March 6). https://vlex.co.uk/vid/gardiner-v-gray-807002237

Gardner, H. (2016, December 20). Remembering Jerome Bruner. Association for Psychological Science. https://www.psychologicalscience.org/observer/remembering-jerome-bruner

Gates, B. (1996). *The road ahead.* Penguin Group USA.

Ghemawat, P. (2002). Competition and business strategy in historical perspective. *Business History Review,* 37–74.

REFERENCES   391

Giemza, B. A. (2004). Ignatius rising: The life of John Kennedy Toole (Review). *Southern Cultures* 10(1), 97–99.

Gigerenzer, G. (2018). The bias bias in behavioral economics. *Review of Behavioral Economics* 5(3–4), 303–336. https://doi.org/10.1561/105.00000092

Gigerenzer, G., Reb, J., & Luan, S. (2022). Smart heuristics for individuals, teams, and organizations. *Annual Review of Organizational Psychology and Organizational Behavior* 9, 171–198.

Gigerenzer, G., Todd, P. M., & ABC Research Group. (1999). *Simple heuristics that make us smart*. Oxford University Press.

Gillies, D. (2003). Probability and uncertainty in Keynes's The General Theory. In S. Mizuhara & J. Runde (Eds.), *The philosophy of Keynes' economics: Probability, uncertainty and convention* (pp. 108–126). Routledge.

Gilovich, T., & Griffin, D. (2002). Introduction—Heuristics and biases: Then and now. In D. Griffin, D. Kahneman, & T. Gilovich (Eds.), *Heuristics and biases: The psychology of intuitive judgment* (pp. 1–18). Cambridge University Press. https://doi.org/10.1017/CBO97 80511808098.002

Gleason, S. (2012, November 8). Consulting firm that once advised Gadhafi enters Chapter 11. *Wall Street Journal*. https://www.wsj.com/articles/BL-BANKB-18428

GM will boost EV and AV investments to $35 billion through 2025. (2021, June 16). General Motors. https://investor.gm.com/news-releases/news-release-details/gm-will-boost-ev-and-av-investments-35-billion-through-2025/

Gompers, P. A. (1995). Optimal investment, monitoring, and the staging of venture capital. *The Journal of Finance* 50(5), 1461–1489. https://doi.org/10.2307/2329323

Gompers, P. A., Gornall, W., Kaplan, S. N., & Strebulaev, I. A. (2020). How do venture capitalists make decisions? *Journal of Financial Economics* 135(1), 169–190. https://doi.org/10.1016/j.jfineco.2019.06.011

Gompers, P. A., & Lerner, J. (1999). *The venture capital cycle*. MIT Press.

Gompers, P., & Lerner, J. (2001). The venture capital revolution. *The Journal of Economic Perspectives* 15(2), 145–168. https://doi.org/10.1257/jep.15.2.145

Goodman, R. (2022, Spring). William James. In E. N. Zalta (Ed.), *The Stanford encyclopedia of philosophy*. Metaphysics Research Lab, Stanford University. https://plato.stanford.edu/archives/spr2022/entries/james/

Gorski, D. (2011, October 31). "And one more thing" about Steve Jobs' battle with cancer. Science-Based Medicine. https://sciencebasedmedicine.org/one-more-thing/

Gotrich, L. (2018). Susanna breathes air into Baudelaire's "Invitation to the Voyage." NPR. https://www.npr.org/sections/allsongs/2018/02/05/582756299/susanna-breathes-air-into-baudelaires-invitation-to-the-voyage

Granovetter, M. (1985). Economic action and social structure: The problem of embeddedness. *American Journal of Sociology* 91(3), 481–510.

Greenfield, P. M. (2016, December 20). Remembering Jerome Bruner. Association for Psychological Science. https://www.psychologicalscience.org/observer/remembering-jerome-bruner

Greenwood, J. D. (Ed.). (2015). The cognitive revolution. In *A conceptual history of psychology: Exploring the tangled web*. Second ed. (pp. 454–494). Cambridge University Press. https://doi.org/10.1017/CBO9781107414914.013

Grice, H. P. (1989). *Studies in the way of words*. Harvard University Press.

Guida, V. (2022, January 10). Fed's no. 2 official resigns amid trading scandal. Politico. https://www.politico.com/news/2022/01/10/federal-reserve-vice-chair-resigns-ethics-scandal-526849

Gupta, U. (2001, March 26). Done deals—Waite. HBS Working Knowledge. http://hbswk.hbs.edu/archive/2140.htmldone-deals-waite

392 REFERENCES

Haltiwanger, J. (2011). Comment on "What do small businesses do?" by Erik Hurst and Benjamin Wild Pugsley. Brookings Papers on Economic Activity. https://www.brookings.edu/wp-content/uploads/2011/09/2011b_bpea_hurst.pdf

Hamel, G. (1999). Bringing Silicon Valley inside. *Harvard Business Review* 77(5), 70–183.

Hammer, M., & Champy, J. (1993). *Reengineering the corporation: A manifesto for business revolution*. First ed. HarperBusiness.

Handwerk, B. (2023, June 21). Oldest known Neanderthal engravings were sealed in a cave for 57,000 years. *Smithsonian Magazine*. Retrieved August 10, 2023, from https://www.smithsonianmag.com/science-nature/oldest-known-neanderthal-engravings-discovered-in-french-cave-180982408/

Hao, K. (2021). How Facebook and Google fund global misinformation. *MIT Technology Review.Com*. https://search.proquest.com/docview/2820958524?pq-origsite=primo

Haoues, R. (2015, April 23). 30 years ago today, Coca-Cola made its worst mistake. CBS News. https://www.cbsnews.com/news/30-years-ago-today-coca-cola-new-coke-failure/

Harris, R. S., Jenkinson, T., & Kaplan, S. N. (2014). Private equity performance: What do we know? *The Journal of Finance* 69(5), 1851–1882. https://doi.org/10.1111/jofi.12154

Harvey, I. (2014, August 15). James Dyson's road to success paved with failure. *The Globe and Mail*. https://www.theglobeandmail.com/report-on-business/innovators-at-work/james-dysons-road-to-success-paved-with-failure/article20074990/

Haste, H. (2016). Jerome Bruner 1915–2016. BPS. Retrieved August 9, 2023, from https://www.bps.org.uk/psychologist/jerome-bruner-1915-2016

Hayek, F. A. (1945). The use of knowledge in society. *The American Economic Review* 35(4), 519–530.

Hayek, F. (1961). Friedrich Hayek to Dr F. A. Harper of the William Volker Fund, 22 May 1961, box 58, folder 19, Friedrich Hayek Papers, Hoover Institution Archives.

Hemingway, E. (1990). The art of the short story. In J. L. Benson (Ed.), *New critical approaches to the short stories of Ernest Hemingway* (pp. 1–13). Duke University Press.

Henderson, R. (1993). Underinvestment and incompetence as responses to radical innovation: Evidence from the photolithographic alignment equipment industry. *The Rand Journal of Economics* 24(2), 248–270. https://doi.org/10.2307/2555761

Henrekson, M., & Johansson, D. (2009). Gazelles as job creators: A survey and interpretation of the evidence. Working Paper 733. Research Institute of Industrial Economics.

Herbst-Bayliss, S. (2015, April 16). Ex-Fed chair Bernanke joins hedge fund Citadel as advisor. Reuters. https://www.reuters.com/article/hedgefunds-bernanke-idUSL2N0XD1B220150416

Howard, P. K. (2014). *The rule of nobody: Saving America from dead laws and broken government*. First ed. W. W. Norton & Company.

Hern, A. (2022, October 27). Meta shares dip is proof metaverse plan never really had legs. *The Guardian*. https://www.theguardian.com/technology/2022/oct/27/metas-shares-dip-is-proof-metaverse-plan-never-really-had-legs-facebook

Heukelom, F. (2012). Three explanations for the Kahneman-Tversky programme of the 1970s. *The European Journal of the History of Economic Thought* 19(5), 797–828. https://doi.org/10.1080/09672567.2010.540350

Heukelom, F. (2014). *Behavioral economics: A history*. Cambridge University Press.

Hicks, J. R. (1935). Annual survey of economic theory: The theory of monopoly. *Econometrica* 3(1), 1–20. https://doi.org/10.2307/1907343

Hirschman, A. O. (1970). *Exit, voice, and loyalty: Responses to decline in firms, organizations, and states*. Harvard University Press.

Hume, D. (1777). *The life of David Hume, Esq: Written by himself*. W. Strahan and T. Cadell. https://ir.vanderbilt.edu/bitstream/handle/1803/1804/Life%20of%20David%20Hume%20by%20Himself.pdf?sequence=1&isAllowed=y

Hurst, E., & Pugsley, B. W. (2011, Fall). What do small businesses do? Brookings Papers on Economic Activity, 73–142.

REFERENCES   393

Ibrahim, D. M. (2008). The (not so) puzzling behavior of angel investors. *Vanderbilt Law Review* 61(5), 1405–1452.

Ignatius, A. (2017). The great transformer. *Harvard Business Review*, September–October, 10.

Ignatius, A. (2023). Leaders, what's your story. *Harvard Business Review* 101(6), 12.

Immelt, J. R. (2017). How I remade GE. *Harvard Business Review* 95(5), 2–11

Institute for New Economic Thinking. (n.d.) "Knightian Uncertainty Economics (KUE)." (n.d.) accessed July 15, 2022, https://www.ineteconomics.org/research/programs/knightian-uncertainty-economics-kue.

Ip, G. (2008, April 8). His legacy tarnished, Greenspan goes on defensive. *Wall Street Journal.* https://www.wsj.com/articles/SB120760341392296107

Isaac, J. (2012). *Working Knowledge.* First ed. Harvard University Press.

Isaacson, W. (2011). *Steve Jobs.* First Simon & Schuster hardcover ed. Simon & Schuster.

Iyer, H. (2020, August 10). Life as a product manager at Amazon, Google, and Microsoft. The Org. https://theorg.com/insights/life-as-a-product-manager-at-amazon-google-and-microsoft

Jahan, Ahmed Saber Mahmud, & Chris Papageorgiou. (2014). What is Keynesian economics? *Finance & Development* 51(3), 53–54.

James, W. (1898). *The will to believe, and other essays in popular philosophy.* Longmans, Green, and Co. https://hdl.handle.net/2027/hvd.HNJBYV

James, W. (1892). *Psychology: Briefer course.* Henry Holt and Company.

James, W. (1907). *Pragmatism: A new name for some old ways of thinking: Popular lectures on philosophy.* First ed. Longmans, Green. https://hdl.handle.net/2027/hvd.32044009965229

Janeway, W. H. (2018). *Doing capitalism in the innovation economy: Reconfiguring the three-player game between markets, speculators and the state.* Second ed. Cambridge University Press.

Janeway, W. H. (2022, January 6). Capital is not a strategy. Project Syndicate. https://www.project-syndicate.org/commentary/attracting-nontraditional-capital-is-not-a-business-plan-by-william-h-janeway-2022-01

Jensen, M. C. (1989). Eclipse of the public corporation. *Harvard Business Review* 5, 61–75.

Jensen, M. C. (1993). The modern industrial revolution, exit, and the failure of internal control systems. *The Journal of Finance* 48(3), 831–880. https://doi.org/10.2307/2329018

Jerome Bruner (1915–2016). (n.d.). Harvard University Department of Psychology. Retrieved June 2, 2024, from https://psychology.fas.harvard.edu/people/jerome-bruner

Johnson, S. G. B., Bilovich, A., & Tuckett, D. (2023). Conviction narrative theory: A theory of choice under radical uncertainty. *Behavioral and Brain Sciences* 46, e82. https://doi.org/10.1017/S0140525X22001157

Jones, D. S. (2000). Visions of a cure: Visualization, clinical trials, and controversies in cardiac therapeutics, 1968–1998. *Isis* 91(3), 504–541.

Junod, S. W. (2008). FDA and clinical drug trials: A short history. In Madhu Davies & Faiz Kerimani (Eds.), *A quick guide to clinical trials* (pp. 25–55). Bioplan, Inc. https://www.fda.gov/media/110437/download

Kahneman, D. (2003a). A psychological perspective on economics. *The American Economic Review* 93(2), 162–168.

Kahneman, D. (2003b). Daniel Kahneman autobiographical essay. The Nobel Prize. Retrieved June 2, 2024, from https://www.nobelprize.org/prizes/economic-sciences/2002/kahneman/biographical/

Kahneman, D. (2003c). Maps of bounded rationality: Psychology for behavioral economics. *The American Economic Review* 93(5), 1449–1475.

Kahneman, D., & Frederick, S. (2002). Representativeness revisited: Attribute substitution in intuitive judgment. In D. Griffin, D. Kahneman, & T. Gilovich (Eds.), *Heuristics and biases: The psychology of intuitive judgment* (pp. 49–81). Cambridge University Press. https://doi.org/10.1017/CBO9780511808098.004

394 REFERENCES

Kahneman, D., & Tversky, A. (1972). Subjective probability: A judgment of representativeness. *Cognitive Psychology* 3(3), 430–454. https://doi.org/10.1016/0010-0285(72)90016-3

Kahneman, D., & Tversky, A. (1973). On the psychology of prediction. *Psychological Review* 80(4), 237–251. https://doi.org/10.1037/h0034747

Kahneman, D., & Tversky, A. (1982a). On the study of statistical intuitions. *Cognition* 11(2), 123–141. https://doi.org/10.1016/0010-0277(82)90022-1

Kahneman, D., & Tversky, A. (1982b). Variants of uncertainty. *Cognition* 11(2), 143–157. https://doi.org/10.1016/0010-0277(82)90023-3

Kalamas, J., Pinkus, G. S., & Sachs, K. (2002, Autumn). The new math for drug licensing (current research). *The McKinsey Quarterly*, 9–14.

Kalberg, S. (1980). Max Weber's types of rationality: Cornerstones for the analysis of rationalization processes in history. *The American Journal of Sociology* 85(5), 1145–1179.

Kaplan, S. N., & Strömberg, P. (2001). Venture capitalists as principals: Contracting, screening, and monitoring. *American Economic Review* 91(2), 426–430. https://doi.org/10.1257/aer.91.2.426

Kaplan, S., & Strömberg, P. (2003). Financial contracting theory meets the real world: An empirical analysis of venture capital contracts. *Review of Economic Studies* 70(2), 281–315.

Kaplan, S. N., & Strömberg, P. (2004). Characteristics, contracts, and actions: Evidence from venture capitalist analyses. *The Journal of Finance* 59(5), 2177–2210.

Karni, E. (2008). Savage's subjective expected utility model. In Palgrave Macmillan (Ed.), *The new Palgrave dictionary of economics* (pp. 1–5). Palgrave Macmillan. https://doi.org/10.1057/978-1-349-95121-5_2467-1

Kay, A. (2016, December 20). Remembering Jerome Bruner. Association for Psychological Science. https://www.psychologicalscience.org/observer/remembering-jerome-bruner

Kay, J., & King, M. (2020a). Probability and optimization. In *Radical uncertainty: Decision-making beyond the numbers*. W. W. Norton & Company.

Kay, J., & King, M. (2020b). *Radical uncertainty: Decision-making beyond the numbers*. W. W. Norton & Company.

Kay, N. M. (1984). *The emergent firm: Knowledge, ignorance, and surprise in economic organisation*. St. Martin's Press.

Kelly, P. (1998). *Faster company*. John Wiley & Sons.

Keynes, J. M. (1921). *A treatise on probability*. Macmillan and Co.

Keynes, J. M. (1936). *The general theory of employment, interest and money*. Macmillan and Co.

Keynes, J. M. (1937). The general theory of employment. *The Quarterly Journal of Economics* 51(2), 209–223. https://doi.org/10.2307/1882087

Keynes, J. M. (1956). *Essays and sketches in biography: Including the complete text of Essays in biography and Two memoirs*. Meridian Books.

Kihlstrom, R. E., & Laffont, J.-J. (1979). A general equilibrium entrepreneurial theory of firm formation based on risk aversion. *Journal of Political Economy* 87(4), 719–748.

Kim, A. (2006). Wilhelm Maximilian Wundt. Stanford Encyclopedia of Philosophy Archive. https://plato.stanford.edu/archives/fall2016/entries/wilhelm-wundt

Kim, A. (2022, Winter). Wilhelm Maximilian Wundt. In Edward N. Zalta & Uri Nodelman (Eds.), *The Stanford encyclopedia of philosophy*. Metaphysics Research Lab, Stanford University. https://plato.stanford.edu/archives/win2022/entries/wilhelm-wundt/

Kim, W. C., & Mauborgne, R. (2023, May 1). Innovation doesn't have to be disruptive. *Harvard Business Review*. https://hbr.org/2023/05/innovation-doesnt-have-to-be-disruptive

King, P. M. (1994). Morality plays. In R. Beadle (Ed.), *The Cambridge companion to Medieval English theatre* (pp. 240–264). Cambridge University Press. https://doi.org/10.1017/CCOL0521366704.009

Klaes, M., & Sent, E.-M. (2005). A conceptual history of the emergence of bounded rationality. *History of Political Economy* 37(1), 27–59. https://doi.org/10.1215/00182702-37-1-27

Klahr, D., & Simon, H. A. (2001). What have psychologists (and others) discovered about the process of scientific discovery? *Current Directions in Psychological Science* 10(3), 75–79.

REFERENCES   395

Klepper, S. (2001). Employee startups in high-tech industries. *Industrial and Corporate Change* 10(3), 639–674. https://doi.org/10.1093/icc/10.3.639

Klepper, S. (2007). Disagreements, spinoffs, and the evolution of Detroit as the capital of the U.S. automobile industry. *Management Science* 53(4), 616–631.

Kling, A. (2023, May 3). Big firms need to be sluggish. In My Tribe. https://arnoldkling.subst ack.com/p/big-firms-need-to-be-sluggish

Knight, F. H. (1921). *Risk, uncertainty and profit.* Houghton Mifflin.

Knight, F. H. (1922). Ethics and the economic Interpretation. In F. H. Knight, *The Ethics of Competition* (1997). Transaction Publishers.

Knight, F. H. (1940). "What is truth" in economics? *Journal of Political Economy* 48(1), 1–32.

Knight, F. H. (1942). Profit and entrepreneurial functions. *The Journal of Economic History* 2, 126–132.

Knight, F. H. (1949). World justice, socialism, and the intellectuals. *The University of Chicago Law Review* 16(3), 434–443. https://doi.org/10.2307/1597904

Knight, F. H. (1951). The rôle of principles in economics and politics. *The American Economic Review* 41(1), 1–29.

Kreps, D. (2004). Beliefs and tastes: Confessions of an economist. In Mie Augier & James G. March (Eds.), *Models of a man: Essays in memory of Herbert Simon* (pp. 113–142). MIT Press.

Kuchař, P. (2020, May 4). A conversation with Ross Emmett. Conversations on the history of economics. https://medium.com/extended-present/a-conversation-with-ross-emmett-b4eda0973c1a

Kuhn, T. S. (1970). *The structure of scientific revolutions.* Second ed. University of Chicago Press.

Kumar, N., Mittal, D. S., & Chu, S. E. (2019). *Starbucks China: Facing Luckin, the local disruptor.* Singapore Management University. Retrieved February 26, 2022, from https://rcoe.smu.edu.sg

Kyburg, H. E. (1970). *Probability and inductive logic.* Macmillan.

Landier, A., & Thesmar, D. (2003). Financial contracting with optimistic entrepreneurs: Theory and evidence. *SSRN Electronic Journal.* https://doi.org/10.2139/ssrn.479581

Langlois, R. N. (2023). *The corporation and the twentieth century: The history of American business enterprise.* Princeton University Press.

Langlois, R. N., & Cosgel, M. M. (1993). Frank Knight on risk, uncertainty, and the firm: A new interpretation. *Economic Inquiry* 31(3), 456–465.

Lee, C. M. C., Shleifer, A., & Thaler, R. H. (1990). Anomalies: Closed-end mutual funds. *The Journal of Economic Perspectives* 4(4), 153–164. http://www.jstor.org/stable/1942727

Lehrer, J. (2010, December 10). The truth wears off: Is there something wrong with the scientific method? *The New Yorker.* http://www.newyorker.com/reporting/2010/12/13/10121 3fa_fact_lehrer

Leijonhufvud, A. (2004). Herb Simon. In Mie Augier & James G. March (Eds.), *Models of a man: Essays in memory of Herbert A. Simon* (pp. 351–354). MIT Press.

Leland, H. E., & Pyle, D. H. (1977). Informational asymmetries, financial structure, and financial intermediation. *The Journal of Finance* 32(2), 371–387. https://doi.org/10.2307/2326770

Lerner, J. (2009). *Boulevard of broken dreams: Why public efforts to boost entrepreneurship and venture capital have failed, and what to do about it.* Princeton University Press. https://www.jstor.org/stable/10.2307/j.ctt7t2br

Lerner, J., & Nanda, R. (2020). Venture capital's role in financing innovation: What we know and how much we still need to learn. *The Journal of Economic Perspectives* 34(3), 237–261. https://doi.org/10.1257/jep.34.3.237

LeRoy, S. F., & Singell, L. D. (1987). Knight on risk and uncertainty. *Journal of Political Economy* 95(2), 394–406. https://doi.org/10.1086/261461

Lindley, D. V. (1980). L. J. Savage—His work in probability and statistics. *The Annals of Statistics* 8(1), 1–24.

396 REFERENCES

Lipton, P. (1991). *Inference to the best explanation*. Routledge.

Long, T. (2007, September 7). Sept. 7, 1998: If the check says "Google Inc.," we're "Google Inc." *Wired*. Retrieved October 4, 2021, from https://www.wired.com/2007/09/dayintech-0907/

Lord, H., & Mirabile, C. (2018). *Venture capital: A practical guide to fund formation and management*. CreateSpace Independent Publishing Platform.

Lounsbury, M., & Glynn, M. A. (2001). Cultural entrepreneurship: Stories, legitimacy, and the acquisition of resources. *Strategic Management Journal* 22(6/7), 545–564.

Lucariello, J. (2016, December 20). Remembering Jerome Bruner. Association for Psychological Science. https://www.psychologicalscience.org/observer/remembering-jerome-bruner

Machina, M., Ritzberger, K., Yannelis, N., & Ellsberg, D. (2011). Introduction to the symposium issue. *Economic Theory* 48(2/3), 219–227.

Malik, T. (2010, December 9). Wheel of cheese launched into space on private spacecraft. Space. https://www.space.com/10459-wheel-cheese-launched-space-private-spacecraft.html

Malkiel, B. G. (2003). The efficient market hypothesis and its critics. *The Journal of Economic Perspectives* 17(1), 59–82.

Mallaby, S. (2022). *The power law: Venture capital and the making of the new future*. Penguin Press.

Mankiw, N. G. (2008, November 28). What would Keynes have done? *New York Times*. https://www.nytimes.com/2008/11/30/business/economy/30view.html

March, J. G. (1991). The technology of foolishness. In J. G. March (Ed.), *Decisions and organizations*. Paperback ed. (pp. 253–265 [Chapter 12]). Basil Blackwell. Original work published 1988.

Marsay, D. (2016). Decision-making under radical uncertainty: An interpretation of Keynes' Treatise. *Economics: The Open-Access, Open-Assessment E-Journal*. https://doi.org/10.5018/economics-ejournal.ja.2016-1

Marshall, A. (1920). *Principles of economics: An introductory volume*. Macmillan and Co.

Marshall, B. (2005). Barry Marshall autobiographical essay. The Nobel Prize. http://www.nobelprize.org/nobel_prizes/medicine/laureates/2005/marshall-bio.html

Martens, M. L., Jennings, J. E., & Jennings, P. D. (2007). Do the stories they tell get them the money they need? The role of entrepreneurial narratives in resource acquisition. *The Academy of Management Journal* 50(5), 1107–1132.

Martí, A. P., Zilhão, J., d'Errico, F., Cantalejo-Duarte, P., Domínguez-Bella, S., Fullola, J. M., Weniger, G. C., & Ramos-Muñoz, J. (2021). The symbolic role of the underground world among Middle Paleolithic Neanderthals. *Proceedings of the National Academy of Sciences* 118(33), e2021495118. https://doi.org/10.1073/pnas.2021495118

Massello, D. J. (1997). People: Overlooked by re-engineering. *Administrative Radiology Journal: AR* 16(1), 12–16.

Mattingly, C., Lutkehaus, N. C., & Throop, C. J. (2008). Brune's search for meaning: A conversation between psychology and anthropology. *Ethos* 36(1), 1–28.

McCloskey, D. N. (1994). *Knowledge and persuasion in economics*. Cambridge University Press.

McCloskey, D. N. (2007). Creative destruction vs. the new industrial state. *Reason* 39(5), 59–63.

McKenna, C. D. (2006). *The world's newest profession: Management consulting in the twentieth century*. Cambridge University Press. https://doi.org/10.1017/CBO9780511511622

Meet the Economists. (n.d.). Retrieved November 8, 2023, from https://www.federalreserve.gov/econres/theeconomists.htm

Melnik, M. I., & Alm, J. (2002). Does a seller's eCommerce reputation matter? Evidence from eBay auctions. *The Journal of Industrial Economics* 50(3), 337–349. https://doi.org/10.1111/1467-6451.00180

Mercier, H., & Sperber, D. (2017). *The enigma of reason*. Harvard University Press.

Mercier, H., & Sperber, D. (2019). Précis of The Enigma of Reason. *Teorema* 38(1), 69–76.

Merges, R. P., & Nelson, R. R. (1994). On limiting or encouraging rivalry in technical progress: The effect of patent scope decisions. *Journal of Economic Behavior & Organization* 25(1), 1–24. https://doi.org/10.1016/0167-2681(94)90083-3

Metcalf, B. (2014). Serial innovator: Bob Metcalfe. *The Henry Ford Magazine*, June–December, 36–39.

REFERENCES   397

Microsoft's Timeline 1975–1998. (2008, May 14). https://www.landley.net/history/mirror/ms/microsoft_company.htm

Mikhalkina, T., & Cabantous, L. (2015). Business model innovation: How iconic business models emerge. *Academy of Management Proceedings* 33, 59–95. https://doi.org/10.1108/S0742-332220150000033024

Mill, J. S. (1844). *Essay on some unsettled questions of political economy.* John W. Parker.

Millican, Peter. J. R. (2002). Introduction. In Peter J. R. Millican (Ed.), *Reading Hume on human understanding: Essays on the first Enquiry* (pp. 1–26). Clarendon Press; Oxford University Press.

Mills, K. G. (2018). *Fintech, small business and the American dream: How technology is transforming lending and shaping a new era of small business opportunity.* First ed. Palgrave Macmillan.

Misak, C. J. (2020). *Frank Ramsey: A sheer excess of powers.* First ed. Oxford University Press.

Mischel, W. (2019). Psychology. Britannica. https://www.britannica.com/science/psychology

Mixerno.Space. (2023). YouTube live subscriber counter for MrBeast. Retrieved November 11, 2023, from https://mixerno.space/youtube-channel-counter/UCX6OQ3DkcsbYNE6H8uQQuVA

Moore, G. E. (1996). Some personal perspectives on research in the semiconductor industry. In R. S. Rosenbloom & W. J. Spencer (Eds.), *Engines of innovation: U.S. industrial research at the end of an era.* Harvard Business School Press.

Morck, R., Shleifer, A., Vishny, R. W., Shapiro, M., & Poterba, J. M. (1990). The stock market and investment: Is the market a sideshow? *Brookings Papers on Economic Activity* 1990(2), 157–215. https://doi.org/10.2307/2534506

Morgan, M. S. (2022). Narrative: A general-purpose technology for science. In D. J. Berry, K. M. Hajek, & M. S. Morgan (Eds.), *Narrative science: Reasoning, representing and knowing since 1800* (pp. 3–30). Cambridge University Press; https://doi.org/10.1017/9781009004329.002

Morris, S. (2006, December 11). James Dyson: Why bother with advertising if you can get editorial? *The Independent.* https://www.independent.co.uk/news/media/james-dyson-why-bother-with-advertising-if-you-can-get-editorial-427933.html

Moscati, I. (2016). Retrospectives: How economists came to accept expected utility theory: The case of Samuelson and Savage. *The Journal of Economic Perspectives* 30(2), 219–236.

Mullainathan, S., & Shleifer, A. (2005). The market for news. *The American Economic Review* 95(4), 1031–1053.

Murmann, J. P. (2016). Nelson, Richard R. (born 1930). In M. Augier & D. J. Teece (Eds.), *The Palgrave encyclopedia of strategic management* (pp. 1–4). Palgrave Macmillan. https://doi.org/10.1057/978-1-349-94848-2_646-1

National Academy of Sciences. (2021, February 23). Herbert A. Simon. http://www.nasonline.org/member-directory/deceased-members/50445.html

Nelson, R. R., & Winter, S. G. (1982). *An evolutionary theory of economic change.* The Belknap Press of Harvard University Press.

Newell, A., & Simon, H. A. (1961). Computer simulation of human thinking. *Science* 134(3495), 2011–2017.

Nicholas, T. (2019). *VC: An American history.* Harvard University Press.

The 1930s business and the economy. (2023). Topics in the News. Encyclopedia.com. https://www.encyclopedia.com/social-sciences/culture-magazines/1930s-business-and-economy-topics-news

Norman, D. A. (2013). *The design of everyday things.* Rev. and exp. ed. Basic Books.

Noussair, C. (2017). The discovery of bubbles and crashes in experimental asset markets and the contribution of Vernon Smith to experimental finance. *Southern Economic Journal* 83(3), 644–658.

Nuland, S. B. (2008). *Doctors: The illustrated history of medical pioneers.* Black Dog & Leventhal.

O'Connor, E. (2004). Storytelling to be real: Narrative, legitimacy building, and venturing. IDEAS Working Paper Series from RePEc. https://www.proquest.com/docview/1698233

398 REFERENCES

743?parentSessionId=HFgmoVcVtcy8gZNPuBsRENjesSa5IAjzPUhshN8tVzk%3D&pq-origsite=primo&

O'Donnell, R. (2003). *Keynes as a writer: Three case studies (first)*. Macquarie University, Department of Business.

O'Donnell, R. (2021a). Keynes and Knight: Risk-uncertainty distinctions, priority, coherence and change. *Cambridge Journal of Economics* 45(5), 1127–1144. https://doi.org/10.1093/cje/beab034

O'Donnell, R. (2021b). Keynes's treatise on probability: The first century. *Review of Political Economy* 33(4), 585–610. https://doi.org/10.1080/09538259.2021.1936926

OECD. (2015). New approaches to SME and entrepreneurship financing: Broadening the range of instruments. https://doi.org/10.1787/9789264240957-en

OECD. (2021, November 12). Venture Capital Investments. OECD.Stat. https://stats.oecd.org/Index.aspx?DataSetCode=VC_INVEST

Ogilvy, D. (1963). *Confessions of an advertising man*. First ed. Atheneum.

Okasha, S. (2016). Scientific change and scientific revolutions. In *Philosophy of science: A Very Short Introduction* (pp. 71–88). Second ed. Oxford University Press.

Olegario, R. (1997). IBM and the two Thomas J. Watsons. In T. K. McCraw (Ed.), *Creating modern capitalism: How entrepreneurs, companies, and countries triumphed in three industrial revolutions*. Harvard University Press.

O'Neill, T. A. (1994). Toward a new theory of the closely-held firm. *Seton Hall Law Review* 24(2), 603–652.

Origins of the Longitude Prize. (n.d.). Longitude Prize. Retrieved May 3, 2022, from https://longitudeprize.org/the-history/

Ouchi, W. G. (1981). *Theory Z: How American business can meet the Japanese challenge*. Addison-Wesley.

Packard, D. (1995). *The HP way: How Bill Hewlett and I built our company*. First ed. HarperBusiness.

Pearson, R. (2002). Moral hazard and the assessment of insurance risk in eighteenth- and early-nineteenth-century Britain. *Business History Review* 76(1), 1–35. https://doi.org/10.2307/4127750

Peden, W. (2018). Imprecise probability and the measurement of Keynes's "Weight of Arguments." *Journal of Applied Logics—IfCoLog Journal* 5(3), 677–708.

Peirce, C. S. (1878, April 12). Illustrations of the logic of science: Fourth paper—The probability of induction. *The Popular Science Monthly* 12, 705–737.

Peirce, C. S. (1931). *Collected papers of Charles Sanders Peirce*. The Belknap Press of Harvard University Press.

Peirce, C. S. (1965). *Collected Papers of Charles Sanders Peirce, Vol. 5, Pragmatism and Pragmaticism* (C. Hartshorne & P. Weiss, Eds.). Harvard University Press.

Phelps, E. S. (1990). *Seven schools of macroeconomic thought: The Arne Ryde Memorial Lectures*. Clarendon Press; Oxford University Press.

Phelps, E. S. (2006). Nobel Prize lecture. Nobel Prize. https://www.nobelprize.org/uploads/2018/06/phelps_lecture.pdf

Phelps, E. S. (2013). *Mass flourishing: How grassroots innovation created jobs, challenge, and change*. Princeton University Press.

Phelps, E. S. (2016, September 8). Hard truths about easy money: The Fed's reluctance to raise interest rates is eerily similar to its precrisis policies a decade ago. *Wall Street Journal*.

Poeter, D. (2008, June 30). Intel's Gelsinger sees clear path to 10nm chips. Channel Web. https://web.archive.org/web/20090425061704/http://www.crn.com/hardware/208801780

Pólya, G. (1954). *Mathematics and plausible reasoning*. Princeton University Press.

Porac, J. F., Mishina, Y., & Pollock, T. G. (2002). Entrepreneurial narratives and the dominant logics of high-growth firms. In A. Huff and M. Jenkins (Eds.), *Mapping Strategic Knowledge*. SAGE Publications Ltd. https://doi.org/10.4135/9781446220443.n6

REFERENCES 399

Porter, M. E. (1979, March 1). How competitive forces shape strategy. *Harvard Business Review*. https://hbr.org/1979/03/how-competitive-forces-shape-strategy

Porter, M. E. (1980). *Competitive strategy: Techniques for analyzing industries and competitors*. Free Press.

Porter, M., Argyres, N., & McGahan, A. M. (2002). An interview with Michael Porter. *The Academy of Management Executive* 16(2), 43–52.

Pratt, J. W., Raiffa, H., & Schlaifer, R. (1964). The foundations of decision under uncertainty: An elementary exposition. *Journal of the American Statistical Association* 59(306), 353–375. https://doi.org/10.2307/2282993

Presentation Skills 3: The Rule of Three. (2009). *Presentation Magazine*. https://www.presentationmagazine.com/presentation-skills-3-the-rule-of-three-7283.htm

Price Theory and Principles Textbooks. (n.d.). Econlib. Retrieved March 20, 2022, from https://www.econlib.org/library/Topics/principlestexts.html

Puri, M., & Robinson, D. T. (2007). Optimism and economic choice. *Journal of Financial Economics* 86(1), 71–99. https://doi.org/10.1016/j.jfineco.2006.09.003

Puri, M., & Robinson, D. T. (2013). The economic psychology of entrepreneurship and family business. *Journal of Economics & Management Strategy* 22(2), 423–444. https://doi.org/10.1111/jems.12013

Putnam, B., & Norland, E. (2018, February 2). Fed: End of an era of economists at the helm? CME Group. https://www.cmegroup.com/content/cmegroup/en/education/featured-reports/fed-end-of-an-era-of-economists-at-the-helm.html

Radner, R. (1992). Hierarchy: The economics of managing. *Journal of Economic Literature* 30(3), 1382–1415.

Raff, D. M. G., & Summers, L. H. (1987). Did Henry Ford pay efficiency wages? *Journal of Labor Economics* 5(4), S57–S86. http://www.jstor.org/stable/2534911

Rakow, T. (2010). Risk, uncertainty, and prophet: The psychological insights of Frank H. Knight. *Judgment and Decision Making* 5(6), 458–466.

Ramsey, F. P. (1931). *Foundations of mathematics and other logical essays*. Routledge. https://doi.org/10.4324/9781315887814

Ranitidine Drug Use Statistics, United States, 2013–2020. (2020). ClinCalc. https://clincalc.com/DrugStats/Drugs/Ranitidine

Ratcliffe, S. (2018). *Thucydides*. Oxford University Press. https://doi.org/10.1093/acref/9780191866692.013.q-oro-ed6-00010932

Ray, C. C. (2017, September 25). Clues to prehistoric cave painters remain scant. *New York Times*. https://www.nytimes.com/2017/09/25/science/prehistoric-cave-paintings.html

Re:Work, Guide. (2023). Google. https://rework.withgoogle.com/print/guides/5721312655135/

Reichstag building. (2023). Wikipedia. https://en.wikipedia.org/w/index.php?title=Reichstag_building&oldid=1179286860

Remembering Gene Zelazny | McKinsey & Company. (n.d.). Retrieved September 10, 2023, from https://www.mckinsey.com/alumni/news-and-events/global-news/alumni-news/2023-05-remembering-gene-zelazny

Remembering Jerome Bruner. (2016). *APS Observer* 30(2): 33–40. https://www.psychologicalscience.org/observer/remembering-jerome-bruner

Resnick, P., & Zeckhauser, R. (2002). Trust among strangers in internet transactions: Empirical analysis of eBay's reputation system. In M. R. Baye (Ed.), *The economics of the internet and e-commerce* (*Advances in Applied Microeconomics,* Vol. 11, pp. 127–157). Emerald Group. https://doi.org/10.1016/S0278-0984(02)11030-3

Robb, A. M., & Robinson, D. T. (2014). The capital structure decisions of new firms. *Review of Financial Studies* 27(1), 153–179. https://doi.org/10.1093/rfs/hhs072

Robb, R. (2009). Nietzsche and the economics of becoming. *Capitalism and Society* 4(1). https://doi.org/10.2202/1932-0213.1051

Robert Charles Dudley. (n.d.). "The Atlantic Telegraph Cable Fleet Assembled at Berehaven (Southwest Coast of Ireland): Ships, the Great Eastern, H.M.S. Terrible, the Alby, the

400 REFERENCES

Medway and the William Cory." The Metropolitan Museum of Art. Retrieved December 19, 2023, from https://www.metmuseum.org/art/collection/search/383832

Robillard, K. (2012, July 31). Ten journos caught fabricating. *Politico.* https://www.politico.com/story/2012/07/10-journos-caught-fabricating-079221

Roddick, A. (2000). *Business as unusual.* Thorsons.

Rogoway, M. (2020, July 24). Investors roast Intel over manufacturing failures, stock sheds $42 billion in value. *The Oregonian.* https://www.oregonlive.com/silicon-forest/2020/07/investors-roast-intel-over-manufacturing-failures-stock-sheds-44-billion-in-value.html

Rosenberg, N. (1982). *Inside the black box: Technology and economics.* Cambridge University Press.

Roth, A. E. (1995). Introduction to experimental economics. In A. E. Roth & J. H. Kagel (Eds.), *The handbook of experimental economics* (pp. 3–110). Princeton University Press. https://doi.org/10.2307/j.ctvzsmff5.5

Royal Museums Greenwich. (2016, July 9). Anniversary of the Longitude Act—What was it? https://www.rmg.co.uk/stories/blog/anniversary-longitude-act-what-was-it

The Royal Swedish Academy of Sciences. (1982, October 20). Press release. The Nobel Prize. https://www.nobelprize.org/prizes/economic-sciences/1982/press-release/

Russell, B. (1922). Review of *A Treatise on Probability,* by John Maynard Keynes. *The Mathematical Gazette* 11(159), 119–125. https://doi.org/10.2307/3603283

Ryan, C. (1960). *The longest day: June 6, 1944.* Victor Gollancz.

Sabini, J., & Silver, M. (1982). Some senses of subjective. In P. F. Second (Ed.), *Explaining human behavior: Consciousness, human action and social structure* (pp. 71–91). Sage.

Sah, R. K. (1991). Fallibility in human organizations and political systems. *The Journal of Economic Perspectives* 5(2), 67–88.

Sah, R., & Stiglitz, J. (1985). Human fallibility and economic organization. *American Economic Review* 75(2), 292–297.

Sah, R. K., & Stiglitz, J. E. (1986). The architecture of economic systems: Hierarchies and polyarchies. *The American Economic Review* 76(4), 716–727.

Sah, R. K., & Stiglitz, J. E. (1988a). Committees, hierarchies and polyarchies. *The Economic Journal* 98(391), 451–470. https://doi.org/10.2307/2233377

Sah, R. K., & Stiglitz, J. E. (1988b). Qualitative properties of profit-maximizing k-out-of-n systems subject to two kinds of failures. *IEEE Transactions on Reliability* 37(515–520). https://papers.ssrn.com/abstract=2085855

Sah, R. K., & Stiglitz, J. E. (1991). The quality of managers in centralized versus decentralized organizations. *The Quarterly Journal of Economics* 106(1), 289–295. https://doi.org/10.2307/2937917

Sahlman, W. A. (1990). The structure and governance of venture-capital organizations. *Journal of Financial Economics* 27(2), 473–521. https://doi.org/10.1016/0304-405X(90)90065-8

Salvucci, J. (2023, November 7). MrBeast's net worth: How much does YouTube's top creator make? TheStreet. https://www.thestreet.com/money/mrbeast-net-worth

Samuelson, P. A. (1946). Lord Keynes and the general theory. *Econometrica* 14(3), 187–200. https://doi.org/10.2307/1905770

Savage, L. J. (1954). *The foundations of statistics.* Wiley.

Savitz, E. J. (2023, May 12). How Google took back the narrative around AI. *Barron's.* https://www.barrons.com/articles/netflix-password-sharing-stock-family-8cd2a296

Schama, S. (2022, May 6). When history is weaponised for war. *Financial Times.*

Schauer, F. F. (2003). *Profiles, probabilities, and stereotypes.* Belknap Press of Harvard University Press.

Schein, E. H. (1985). *Organizational culture and leadership.* First ed. Jossey-Bass.

Schumpeter, J. (1934). The theory of economic development—Joseph A. Schumpeter. https://www.hup.harvard.edu/catalog.php?isbn=9780674879904

Schumpeter, J. A. (1934). *The theory of economic development: An inquiry into profits, capital, credit, interest, and the business cycle.* Harvard University Press.

Schumpeter, J. A. (2008). *Capitalism, socialism, and democracy.* First ed. Harper Perennial Modern Thought.

REFERENCES 401

Schumpeter, J. A. (2021, November 6). The supermajors have an LNG problem. *The Economist*. https://www.economist.com/business/2021/11/06/the-supermajors-have-an-lng-problem

Scott, I. A., & Crock, C. (2020). Diagnostic error: Incidence, impacts, causes and preventive strategies. *Medical Journal of Australia* 213(7), 302–305. https://doi.org/10.5694/mja2.50771

Sent, E.-M. (2004). Behavioral economics: How psychology made its (limited) way back into economics. *History of Political Economy* 36(4), 735–760. https://doi.org/10.1215/00182702-36-4-735

Shackle, G. L. S. (1969). *Decision, order, and time in human affairs*. Second ed. Cambridge University Press.

Shane, S. (2001). Technological opportunities and new firm creation. *Management Science* 47(2), 205–220. https://doi.org/10.1287/mnsc.47.2.205.9837

Shane, S. A. (2008). *The illusions of entrepreneurship: The costly myths that entrepreneurs, investors, and policy makers live by*. Yale University Press.

Shapin, S. (1998). *The scientific revolution*. Paperback ed. University of Chicago Press.

Shiller, R. J. (2017). Narrative economics. *The American Economic Review* 107(4), 967–1004.

Shiller, R. J. (2021). The Godley-Tobin Memorial Lecture. *Review of Keynesian Economics* 9(1), 1–10. https://doi.org/10.4337/roke.2021.01.01

Shleifer, A., & Summers, L. H. (1990). The noise trader approach to finance. *The Journal of Economic Perspectives* 4(2), 19–33. http://www.jstor.org/stable/1942888

Sigafoos, R. A. (1983). *Absolutely, positively, overnight! Wall Street's darling inside and up close*. St. Luke's Press.

Simler, K., & Hanson, R. (2018). *The elephant in the brain: Hidden motives in everyday life*. Oxford University Press.

Simon, H. A. (1946). The proverbs of administration. *Public Administration Review* 6(3), 53–67.

Simon, H. A. (1947). *Administrative behavior: A study of decision-making processes in administrative organization*. First ed. Macmillan and Co.

Simon, H. A. (1951). A formal theory of the employment relationship. *Econometrica* 19(3), 293–305. https://doi.org/10.2307/1906815

Simon, H. A. (1955). A behavioral model of rational choice. *The Quarterly Journal of Economics* 69(1), 99–118. https://doi.org/10.2307/1884852

Simon, H. A. (1956). Rational choice and the structure of the environment. *Psychological Review* 63(2), 129–138. https://doi.org/10.1037/h0042769

Simon, H. A. (1968). On judging the plausibility of theories. In B. Van Rootselaar & J. F. Staal (Eds.), *Studies in logic and the foundations of mathematics* (Vol. 52, pp. 439–459). Elsevier. https://doi.org/10.1016/S0049-237X(08)71211-4

Simon, H. A. (1978a). Herbert Simon autobiographical essay. The Nobel Prize. https://www.nobelprize.org/prizes/economic-sciences/1978/simon/biographical/

Simon, H. A. (1978b). On how to decide what to do. *The Bell Journal of Economics* 9(2), 494–507. https://doi.org/10.2307/3003595

Simon, H. A. (1978c). Rationality as process and as product of thought. *The American Economic Review* 68(2), 1–16.

Simon, H. A. (1979). Rational decision making in business organizations. *The American Economic Review* 69(4), 493–513.

Simon, H. A. (1988). The science of design: Creating the artificial. *Design Issues* 4(1/2), 67–82. https://doi.org/10.2307/1511391

Simon, H. A. (1991a). Bounded rationality and organizational learning. *Organization Science* 2(1), 125–134.

Simon, H. A. (1991b). Not so stupid. *Scientific American* 265(2), 10.

Simon, H. A. (1991c). Organizations and markets. *The Journal of Economic Perspectives* 5(2), 25–44.

Simon, H. A. (1991d). *Models of my life*. Basic Books.

Simon, H. A. (1997). *Administrative behavior*. Fourth ed. Free Press.

Simon, H. A., & Newell, A. (1958). Heuristic problem solving: The next advance in operations research. *Operations Research* 6(1), 1–10.

402 REFERENCES

Sinclair, U. (1994). *I, candidate for governor: And how I got licked.* University of California Press.

Siniscalchi, M. (2008). Ambiguity and ambiguity aversion. In Palgrave Macmillan (Ed.), *The new Palgrave dictionary of economics* (pp. 1–7). Palgrave Macmillan.

Skidelsky, R. (2003). *John Maynard Keynes, 1883–1946: Economist, philosopher, statesman.* Penguin Books.

Skidelsky, R., & Keynes, J. M. (2015). *John Maynard Keynes: The essential Keynes.* Penguin Classics.

Sloan, A. P. (1963). *My years with General Motors.* First ed. Doubleday.

Slobin, D. (2016, December 20). Remembering Jerome Bruner. Association for Psychological Science. https://www.psychologicalscience.org/observer/remembering-jerome-bruner

Slovic, P., & Tversky, A. (1974). Who accepts Savage's axiom? *Behavioral Science* 19(6), 368–373. https://doi.org/10.1002/bs.3830190603

Smith, A. (2007). *An inquiry into the nature and causes of the wealth of nations.* MetaLibri. https://www.ibiblio.org/ml/libri/s/SmithA_WealthNations_p.pdf

Smith, R., & Anderson, A. R. (2004). The devil is in the e-tale: Forms and structures in the entrepreneurial narratives. In D. Hjorth & C. Steyaert (Eds.), *Narrative and Discursive Approaches in Entrepreneurship.* Edward Elgar Publishing. https://doi.org/10.4337/978184 5421472.00012

Smith, V. (1994). Economics in the laboratory. *Journal of Economic Perspectives* 8(1), 113–131.

Solow, R. M. (1958). Review of *Models of man: Social and rational,* by H. A. Simon. *The Review of Economics and Statistics* 40(1), 81–84. https://doi.org/10.2307/1926487

Solow, R. M. (2006). Comments on papers by Saint-Paul, Aghion, and Bhidé. *Capitalism and Society* 1(1), Article 3. https://doi.org/10.2202/1932-0213.1001

Sorkin, A. R. (2003, July 31). Buffett wins battle to buy Clayton Homes. *New York Times,* 3.

Spadafora, F. (2023). U.S. unemployment insurance through the Covid-19 crisis. *Journal of Government and Economics* 9, 100069. https://doi.org/10.1016/j.jge.2023.100069

Stam, E. (2015). Entrepreneurial ecosystems and regional policy: A sympathetic critique. *European Planning Studies* 23(9), 1759–1769. https://doi.org/10.1080/09654313.2015.1061484

Stein, J. C. (2002). Information production and capital allocation: Decentralized versus hierarchical firms. *The Journal of Finance* (New York) 57(5), 1891–1921. https://doi.org/10.1111/ 0022-1082.00483

Stigler, G. J. (1971). Introduction. In F. H. Knight, *Risk, uncertainty and profit,* 1971 ed. (pp. xii–xiv). University of Chicago Press.

Stigler, G. J. (1985). Frank Hyneman Knight. Center for the Study of the Economy and the State. Working Paper 37. https://econpapers.repec.org/paper/fthchices/37.htm

Stiglitz, J. E. (2002). Information and the change in the paradigm in economics. *The American Economic Review* 92(3), 460–501.

Stone, B. (2013). *The everything store: Jeff Bezos and the age of Amazon,* illustrated ed. Little, Brown and Company.

Suk, P. (2008, September 10). Offshoring software development. OECD. https://web.archive. org/web/20080910041023/http:/www.oecd.org/dataoecd/32/9/37846828.pdf

Sylva, K. (2016, December 20). Remembering Jerome Bruner. Association for Psychological Science. https://www.psychologicalscience.org/observer/remembering-jerome-bruner

Taleb, N. N. (2001). *Fooled by randomness: The hidden role of chance in the markets and in life.* Texere.

Taylor, T. (2005). Recommendations for further reading. *The Journal of Economic Perspectives* 19(3), 233–240. https://doi.org/10.1257/089533005774357770

Tesla Funding Rounds. (n.d.). Start-up rankings. https://www.startupranking.com/startup/ tesla/funding-rounds

Tesla raises $1.46 billion in stock sale—IFR. (2016, May 20). Reuters. https://www.reuters. com/article/idUSKCN0YB097

Thaler, R. (1991). *Quasi rational economics.* Russell Sage Foundation.

Thompson, F. (1907). In no strange land. *Blue Ridge Journal.* https://www.blueridgejournal. com/poems/ft-strange.htm

Tikkanen, A. (2016). Jerome Bruner. Britannica Academic. https://academic-eb-com.ezproxy. library.tufts.edu/levels/collegiate/article/Jerome-Bruner/16778

TikTok: Most-followed influencers worldwide 2023. (n.d.). Statista. Retrieved November 11, 2023, from https://www.statista.com/statistics/1078315/most-followers-tiktok-global/

Todorov, T. (1969). *Grammaire du Décaméron*. Mouton.

Trimble, V. (1990). *Sam Walton: The inside story of America's richest man*. Penguin Books.

Tuckett, D. (2022). Conviction, narratives, ambivalence, and constructive doubt: Reflections on six expert commentaries. *Futures and Foresight Science*. https://doi.org/10.1002/ffo2.131

Tversky, A., & Kahneman, D. (1971). Belief in the law of small numbers. *Psychological Bulletin* 76(2), 105–110. https://doi.org/10.1037/h0031322

Tversky, A., & Kahneman, D. (1972). Availability as a determinant of frequency and probability judgments. *Oregon Research Institute Technical Reports*, 12(1).

Tversky, A., & Kahneman, D. (1973). Availability: A heuristic for judging frequency and probability. *Cognitive Psychology* 5(2), 207–232. https://doi.org/10.1016/0010-0285(73)90033-9

Tversky, A., & Kahneman, D. (1974). Judgment under uncertainty: Heuristics and biases. *Science* 185(4157), 1124–1131.

Tversky, A., & Kahneman, D. (1981). The framing of decisions and the psychology of choice. *Science* 211(4481), 453–458. https://doi.org/10.1126/science.7455683

Tversky, A., & Kahneman, D. (1986). Rational choice and the framing of decisions. *The Journal of Business* 59(4), S251–S278.

Tversky, A., & Kahneman, D. (2002). Extensional versus intuitive reasoning: The conjunction fallacy in probability judgment. In D. Griffin, D. Kahneman, & T. Gilovich (Eds.), *Heuristics and biases: The psychology of intuitive judgment* (pp. 19–48). Cambridge University Press. https://doi.org/10.1017/CBO9780511808098.003

Tyebjee, T. T., & Bruno, A. V. (1984). A model of venture capitalist investment activity. *Management Science* 30(9), 1051–1066. https://doi.org/10.1287/mnsc.30.9.1051

Tyler, C. W., & Gerken, H. K. (2022). The myth of the laboratories of democracy. *Columbia Law Review* 122(8), 2187–2240.

US C-band auction becomes world's costliest mid-band 5G auction yet. (2021, April 22). S&P Global Market Intelligence. https://www.spglobal.com/marketintelligence/en/news-insig hts/research/us-c-band-auction-becomes-worlds-costliest-mid-band-5g-auction-yet

USPS Tracking—US Global Mail. (n.d.). Retrieved October 30, 2023, from https://www.usglo balmail.com/blog/usps-tracking/

Victor, D. (2021, July 29). Ron Popeil, inventor and ubiquitous infomercial pitchman, dies at 86. *New York Times*. https://www.nytimes.com/2021/07/29/business/ron-popeil-dead.html

Vincenti, W. G. (1990). *What engineers know and how they know it: Analytical studies from aeronautical history*. Johns Hopkins University Press.

Vogel, E. F. (1979). *Japan as number one: Lessons for America*. Seventh print. Harvard University Press.

Volcker, P. (2018, October 24). What's wrong with the 2 percent inflation target. Bloomberg. https://www.bloomberg.com/view/articles/2018-10-24/what-s-wrong-with-the-2-perc ent-inflation-target

von Zedtwitz, M., Friesike, S., & Gassmann, O. (2014). *Managing R&D and new product development*. Oxford University Press. https://doi.org/10.1093/oxfordhb/9780199694 945.013.022

Wallace, J., & Erickson, J. (1993). *Hard drive: Bill Gates and the making of the Microsoft empire*. Harper Business.

Wallenfeldt, J. (2023). Salem witch trials. Encyclopedia Britannica. https://www.britannica. com/event/Salem-witch-trials#ref1228978

Walton, D. (2014). *Abductive reasoning*. University of Alabama Press. http://muse.jhu.edu/ book/31258

Walton, S. (1993). *Sam Walton: Made in America*. Paperback ed. Bantam Books.

404 REFERENCES

Wang, J. (2018, October 1). Study: Pressure to publish in top journals stifles creativity in economic research. University of Chicago News. Accessed on June 7, 2024, from https://news.uchicago.edu/story/study-pressure-publish-top-journals-stifles-creativity-economic-research

Warren, R. J. (2005). Robin J. Warren autobiographical essay. The Nobel Prize. http://www.nobelprize.org/nobel_prizes/medicine/laureates/2005/warren-bio.html

Wattles, J. (2018, February 10). NASA is keeping tabs on Elon Musk's Tesla Roadster. CNNMoney. https://money.cnn.com/2018/02/10/technology/future/nasa-elon-musk-spacex-tesla-roadster/index.html

Weber, M. (1947). *The theory of social and economic organization*. First American ed. Oxford University Press.

Weiss, G. (2014, October 31). Richard Branson says costumes can be a boon for business. *Entrepreneur*. https://www.entrepreneur.com/growing-a-business/richard-branson-says-costumes-can-be-a-boon-for-business/239227

Wells, T. (2001). *Wild man: The life and times of Daniel Ellsberg*. First ed. Palgrave.

Wennberg, K., & Sandström, C. (Eds.). (2022). *Questioning the entrepreneurial state: Status-quo, pitfalls, and the need for credible innovation policy*. Springer International. https://doi.org/10.1007/978-3-030-94273-1

Westgren, R. E., & Holmes, T. L. (2021). Entrepreneurial beliefs and agency under Knightian uncertainty. *Philosophy of Management*. https://doi.org/10.1007/s40926-021-00183-z

White, J. A. (1990E., June 28). Giant pension funds' explosive growth concentrates economic assets and power. *Wall Street Journal*.

Wilentz, S. (1985). General editor's introduction. In *The New Industrial State*, rev. ed. (pp. ix–x). Princeton University Press. https://doi.org/10.2307/j.ctvcm4hjz.3

Wilkinson, A. B. (1986). *The Scottish law of evidence*. Butterworths; Law Society of Scotland.

William James. (n.d.). Retrieved December 15, 202, from https://psychology.fas.harvard.edu/people/william-james

Williamson, O. E. (1975). *Markets and hierarchies: Analysis and antitrust implications, a study in the economics of internal organization*. Free Press.

Winslow, E. G. (1986). Keynes and Freud: Psychoanalysis and Keynes's account of the "animal spirits" of capitalism. *Social Research* 53(4), 549–578.

Witynski, M. (2021, August 11). What is behavioral economics? uchicagonews. https://news.uchicago.edu/explainer/what-is-behavioral-economics

Wolfe, D. W. (1946). The re-organized American Psychological Association. *American Psychologist* 1, 3–6.

Wong, D. (1990). The U.S. auto industry in the 1990s. *The Business Review* (Philadelphia), 11–20.

The world's platform for change. (n.d.). Change.org. Retrieved October 30, 2023, from https://www.change.org/

The Xerox PARC Visit. (n.d.). Making the Macintosh: Technology and culture in Silicon Valley. Retrieved February 26, 2022, from https://web.stanford.edu/dept/SUL/sites/mac/parc.html

Yaeger, D. (1984, July 2). Improved tests help doctors diagnose disease earlier, attempt to avoid surgery—Search for a "silent enemy." *Wall Street Journal*.

Young, M. (2002, June). The devil and Daniel Ellsberg: From archetype to anachronism [Review of *Wild man: The life and times of Daniel Ellsberg*, by Tom Wells]. Reason. https://reason.com/2002/06/01/the-devil-and-daniel-ellsberg-2/

Zakkour, M. (2017, August 24). Why Starbucks succeeded in China: A lesson for all retailers. *Forbes*. https://www.forbes.com/sites/michaelzakkour/2017/08/24/why-starbucks-succeeded-in-china-a-lesson-for-all-retailers/

Zappia. C (2016). Daniel Ellsberg and the validation of normative propositions. *OEconomia* 6(1), 57–79. https://doi.org/10.4000/oeconomia.2276

Zappia, C. (2021). From Knightian to Keynesian uncertainty: Contextualizing Ellsberg's ambiguity. *Cambridge Journal of Economics* 45(5), 1027–1046. https://doi.org/10.1093/cje/beab024

Index

For the benefit of digital users, indexed terms that span two pages (e.g., 52–53) may, on occasion, appear on only one of those pages.

Note: Tables, figures, and boxes are indicated by an italic *t*, *f*, and *b* following the page number.

abduction, 7, 179*b*–80*b*
abstraction, 108*b*, 159*b*–60*b*
acquisitions, 230–31, 252–53
Acts of Meaning (Bruner), 263
Actual Minds, Possible Worlds (Bruner), 263
actuarial data, 17n
Administrative Behavior (Simon), 99–100, 101*b*
Advances in Behavioral Economics (Camerer, Lowenstein, and Rabin), 127*b*–31*b*, 141*b*–42*b*, 149*b*–50*b*
Advent Software, 195*b*
advertising, 4, 64n, 275, 326
Aesop, 283*b*
Aesop's fables, 301
African Americans, 17n
Against the Gods: The Remarkable Story of Risk (Bernstein), 69
agency, 327–28, 329, 334
agnosticism, 11–12
air travel industry, 329
Airbnb, 3–4, 274, 380n.35
Akerlof, George, 65, 67, 128*b*–31*b*
Alan Turing, 79–80n
Alby (ship), 163
Aldrich, Howard, 178*b*–79*b*
alignment uncertainty, 214*b*
Allais, Maurice, 120
Allen, Paul, 215, 288
Alphabet, 252*t*, 323n. *See also* Google
Altair, 288
alternative medicine, 22
Amazon
  and angel vs. VC funding, 210, 211
  and complex projects, 323*b*–24*b*
  and coordination issues of large public companies, 247n
  and declining quality of discourse, 325
  and dynamism of business stories, 309
  and entrepreneurial specialization, 310
  growth and evolution of, 253, 310*f*
  and information asymmetry problems, 203*b*
  and limited partnerships, 209*b*

market value, 252*t*
  and "platform" business metaphor, 274, 309
  and scope of recent innovations, 3–4
  and spillovers from literary storytelling, 307–8
  and VC coordination mechanisms, 215
ambiguity, 109, 110, 115–16, 116*b*–17*b*, 118*b*, 118, 119–20, 121*b*–22*b*, 121, 122–25, 170
American Civil War, 301
American Economic Association, 56n, 70*b*–71*b*, 95
American Economic Review, 33, 166
American Film Institute, 184–85
American Research and Development Corporation (ARD), 200
America's Cup, 177n
Amicus, 291*b*
Amit, R., 203*b*
Amsterdam, Anthony, 263, 275, 283*b*
analogical reasoning, 15, 16, 269, 274
anchoring, 159
Andreasson, Marc, 318
angel investors
  and advantages of large public companies, 232
  complexity and coordination issues, 215
  differences among VC types, 197, 201–4, 210–12
  due diligence and oversight, 199
  and entrepreneurial specialization, 35–36
  evaluation methods contrasted with VCs, 207–8
  funding, routines, and initiatives, 310*f*
  incentive and misjudgment issues, 204
  and information asymmetry problems, 203*b*
  information requirements of, 174
  and institutionalized investing, 200, 201
  and mutual monitoring, 206
  and overview of author's model, 174
  and target funding levels, 208
  and uncertainty limits, 209, 210n
  and VC exit decisions, 209*b*

406 INDEX

angel investors (*cont.*)
  and VC's preference for high-tech industries, 212–13
  and winner's-curse problem, 197
animal instinct, 12
anthropology, 101*b*, 141*b*
antibiotic resistance, 329
antipoverty programs, 14
antipsychotic drugs, 13*b*
antitrust legislation, 63, 250*b*, 327
A&P, 227
Apple
  and advances in communication technology, 322
  and agency/authority dynamic, 327–28
  and angel vs. VC funding, 211
  and business recovery stories, 291
  and challenges facing established industry leaders, 229
  and competitive markets, 26, 27
  and disagreements over business model, 22
  and entrepreneurial specialization, 317
  growth and value of, 252–53
  growth of, 252–53
  and growth of new industrial giants, 253
  and growth of personal computing, 188*b*
  and human capital challenges, 185
  and Jobs's background, 186*b*
  and justificatory routines, 31
  and large companies' intolerance for uncertainty, 236*b*
  market value, 252*t*
  and neglect of VC firms, 266
  and technology–enabled symbiosis, 323n
apps developers, 317
Aquinas, Thomas, 67–68
"Are There Uncertainties That Are Not Risks?" (Ellsberg), 110–11
Aristotle, 23, 67–68, 145, 260–61, 271, 272–73, 275, 281, 284–85
Aristotle Project, 295*b*–97*b*
Arrow, Kenneth, 52, 112
artificial intelligence (AI), 28, 97, 319–20
Assange, Julian, 112*b*
assembly lines, 221
Atacama Desert, 18
Athenian democracy, 327
The Atlantic Telegraph Cable Fleet, 1866 (Dudley), 163
AT&T, 199–200, 234
attention, 265–66
attention-getting pitches, 287*b*
attitudinal differences, 22

Attronica Computers, 182*b*
auctions, 193n
audience for study, 7–9
Augustine of Hippo, Saint, 145
authority and authoritarianism, 4, 8, 24–25, 26, 27, 29, 31, 32*t*, 327–30
authority structures, 223. *See also* hierarchical structures
automobile industry, 228, 329. *See also specific companies*
autonomous decision-making, 29
availability heuristic, 137*b*
axioms, 49*b*, 49, 114*b*–15*b*, 114, 117*b*–18*b*
Azoulay, P., 186*b*

Bacon, Francis, 313, 340n.1
Bain, Joe, 61, 343n.13
Baldwin, Carliss, 160*b*
Barnard, Chester, 101*b*, 108*b*
Barnes & Noble, 249–50
Barreto, Humberto, 57*b*
base-rate fallacies, 194
BASIC, 288
Baudelaire, Charles, 1
Baumol, William, 33–34, 166*b*, 166, 167, 169–70, 359n.3, 359n.9
Bay of Pigs invasion, 328–29
Bayes, Thomas (Bayes' theorem), 54
Bechtel, 192*b*
Bechtolsheim, Andy, 206, 236*b*
Becker, Gary, 56, 95, 98
Becoming Trader Joe (Coulombe), 308
behavioral economics
  and "bias bias," 157*b*, 157
  and context of study, xn
  heuristics and biases, 130
  and Knight's rejection of purely rational explanations, 91–92n
  and multidisciplinary approaches, 93–94
  and muted influence of Simon's work, 102, 103–4, 105, 109
  and "nudges," 90n
  origins and impact of, 126, 127
  and prospect theory, 140*b*, 140
  relationship with academic psychology, 145–47
  and Simon's academic background, 90, 95*b*
  and Simon's theories, 103*b*
  transition from psychology to economics, 148
  and uncertainty in modern economic theory, 6
behavioral finance, 151–53, 152*b*, 161, 254

"Behavioral Macroeconomics and Macroeconomic Behavior" (Akerlof), 128b–31b
"A Behavioral Model of Rational Choice" (Simon), 98–99
behaviorism, 91–92n, 93–94n, 129b, 145, 146–47, 261b
Behavioural Insights Team (BIT), 153–54
Belgium, 293b–94b
Berkshire Hathaway, 161, 184b, 248, 252t
Berlin, Isaiah, 198
Bernanke, Ben, 88, 381n.54, 381n.56
Bernoulli, Daniel, 53, 77, 79
Bernstein, Peter, 69, 71b
Bessemer Venture Partners, 210
Best Mailing Lists, 184–85
betting odds, 83
Bezos, Jeff, 210, 246–47, 253, 304–5, 308, 310
biases
    and base-rate fallacies, 194
    and behavioral finance research, 151, 152–53
    "bias bias," 157b, 157
    and "bias-bias" critique, 157b
    and Big Science funding, 320
    Bruner's critique of cognitive biases, 262b
    and case for narrative-mode reasoning, 315–16
    and competitive markets, 27
    and critiques of K-T research, 156–57, 158, 160–61
    and evidence/belief nexus, 76–77
    and expansionary impulse of large public companies, 247–48
    heuristics and bias research, 130, 134, 135, 136b–37b, 137–38n, 139
    and Knight's rejection of purely rational explanations, 92
    and K-T's academic backgrounds, 130b–32b, 136b
    and origins of behavioral economics, 130
    and performative element of entrepreneurial discourse, 279
    and prospect theory, 140, 141b–42b, 142, 143
    and role of justificatory discourse, 26
    and Simon's academic background, 90
    and Smith's experimental economics, 154–55
    and spillovers from literary storytelling, 308
    and split within behavioral economics, 126
    and startup financing constraints, 193
    and uncertainty in modern economic theory, 6
Biblical stories, 301–2
bicycles, x–xi, 6, 10

Big Business, 63. *See also* large public corporations; monopoly power; oligopoly power
Big Science, 320
big-data, 3–4
biographies, 304–5
biotechnology, 229, 236b, 290b–91b, 318
Birch, David, 178, 228
black swan events, 114
Blanchard, Olivier, 88
Bletchley Park, 80n
Blind Chance (film), 272
Bloomberg Business Week, 294b
Bloomsbury Group, 70
Blue Bus Company, 75
Blueground, 291b
boards of directors, 31, 225b, 240b, 241–43, 318
The Body Shop, 279–80
Boeing, 29, 234, 235
Boettke, P. J., 385
Bohdan Associates, 192b
bootstrapped ventures
    and advantages of large public companies, 232, 235
    and comparative advantage of public companies, 320f
    and content of entrepreneurial proposals, 311
    coping with financing constraints, 194–96, 195b
    and crowdsourcing, 322–23
    and entrepreneurial discourse, 260
    and entrepreneurial specialization, 319
    and "gazelle" businesses, 178
    Hewlett Packard, 230b
    and overview of author's model, 174
    and startup financing constraints, 191
    and VC's preference for high-tech industries, 212–13
Booz, Allen, Hamilton, 221
Boston Consulting Group, 251
Boston Globe, 78b
bounded rationality
    and base-rate fallacies, 194
    and computational constraints on certainty, 98
    and critiques of K-T research, 158
    and heuristics and bias research, 138
    and origins of behavioral economics, 129–30
    and Simon's academic background, 90
    and Simon's global rationality, 98–99
    and Smith's experimental economics, 154–55
Bower, Joseph, 306
Bower, Marvin, 304
Brandeis, Louis D., 27
Brander, J., 203b

408 INDEX

Branson, Richard, 184b, 185, 278b, 279–80, 281, 286, 288, 304
Braunerhjelm, P., 379n.18
Braunwald, Eugene, 79b
Brewer, S., 179b–80b
Bricklin, Dan, 188b, 246
Broadcom, 252t
Bronner, Ethan, 166
Brooks, Frederick, 245b, 245, 370n.53
Brostoff, George, 195b
Brown, Deaver, 271, 279
Brown v. Board of Education, 299b, 303
Bruner, Jerome
    and aims of entrepreneurial discourse, 268
    and aims of various forms of discourse, 266, 267
    and author's teaching style, 281–82
    and case for narrative-mode reasoning, 316
    and contents of entrepreneurial proposals, 270–71, 272–73
    on conventionalized narrative, 322
    definitions and features of narrative, 281, 283b–84b, 283, 284, 293b
    and entrepreneurial discourse, 259
    influence of, 261b–62b
    on logico-scientific mode, 264b
    and narrative gap in entrepreneurial discourse, 284–86
    and narrative mode, 261–65
    and spillovers from popular stories, 298, 299b, 299, 300b, 300–2, 302b–3b, 303, 304, 306–7, 308
    and visual metaphors, 276b
bubbles, 155, 214, 318
Buchanan, James, 43, 46n, 50
Buffett, Warren, 152–53, 161, 242–43b, 248, 249, 358n.46
Bundy, McGeorge, 112b
Bureau of Labor Statistics, 332b
bureaucracy, 232, 241, 247
Burger King, 230b
Burke, Kenneth, 284b, 284–85, 375n.19
business models, 211
"buyer beware" (caveat emptor), 65
Byte Computers, 182b

cable television, 325
California Pizza Kitchen, 212–13
A Call for Judgment (Bhidé), x
Cambridge Associates, 207b
The Cambridge Introduction to Narrative, 282b
Cambridge Journal of Economics, 72
Cambridge University, 70b
Camerer, Colin, 120, 121b, 122–23, 127b, 141b–42b, 149b–50b, 150b, 150, 354n.33

Canaan Venture Partners, 176
cancer diagnoses, 22
Candela, R. A., 385
Candler, Asa Griggs, 64n
capital costs and expenditures, 62n, 234, 244n
capital gains, 202
capital markets, 251
Capitalism, Socialism and Democracy (Schumpeter), 223
Capitalism and Society (Bhidé), x
cardioplegic drugs, 79b
Carnegie Mellon University, 95b, 103b, 105
Carnegie School, 103
CAR-T, 319
Cartwright, Nancy, 160b
Cary, Frank, 250b
Case, Carl "Chip," 176–77, 180
Case-Shiller indices, 176
Cassileth, Barrie, 22
Catalini, C., 213b
categories and categorization, 300b, 302b
catharsis, 275
Catholic Church, 221
causality, 272
Caves, Richard, ix, 178b–79b, 356n.58
Center for Cognitive Studies (Harvard), 261b
Central Intelligence Agency (CIA), 328–29
chain of command, 221
Challenger space shuttle disaster, 35, 246
challenges of uncertainty, 3–5
Chandler, Alfred, 35, 218b–19b, 218–21, 222, 223, 224b, 224–25, 225b, 226, 227, 232, 244, 251, 252–53
Change.org, 323
chaos theory, 315
Chase, Martin, 230b
Chicago school of economics, 5, 46n, 67
Chicago Tribune, 277
Chile, 18
Christensen, Clay, 253, 306–7
Christensen, Michael, 66
Churchill, Winston, 271
Citizen Kane (film), 304
citizen-journalists, 325
civil administration, 221
civil law, 75
Clark, William, 148
Clayton, Jim, 184b
Clayton Antitrust Act, 63
Clayton Homes, 184b
Cleese, John, 277
Cleveland Clinic, 78b
clickbait, 142–43
click farms, 325

clinical trials, 75
cloud computing, 317, 324*b*
Coase, Ronald H., 43, 366n.3
Coates, George, 277
Coca-Cola, 238
Cochran, Johnnie, 28n
codebreaking, 80n
cognitive biases and illusions, 130*b*, 138n, 156–57, 262*b*. *See also* biases
cognitive psychology, 97, 127, 128–29, 129*b*, 138–39, 353n.8
Cognitive Science Series, 150*b*
collective attitudes, 301
collective decision-making, 250*b*–51*b*
Colter Bay, 182*b*
Columbia University, 179*b*
Columbus, Christopher, 310–11
Columbus and Isabella's Court (Wolf), 259
committee discussions, 205, 226n, 239*b*–40*b*, 244–45, 245*b*, 246–47, 250*b*, 279, 323, 327–28
Committee on Social Thought, 43
commoditized goods, 188–89
commodity prices, 244n
Common Good coalition, 328–29
common law, 24, 65
Common Stocks as Long-Term Investments (Smith), 248
Communications Decency Act (CDA), 326
communication technology, 323, 324–25
Communist Club (University of Chicago), 46–47
Compaq, 188*b*
comparative advantage, 65, 215–16, 293*b*–94*b*, 319
compensatory damages, 75
competition, 26–27
Competitive Strategy (Porter), 61, 305–6
complexity
    advantages of large corporations, 232
    and complex products, 273n
    complex projects, 319, 323*b*–24*b*
    and distinctive features of large public companies, 234–39
    and entrepreneurial specialization, 36*f*
    and financing of ventures, 214–16
    and justifications for choices, 28
    and Simon's global rationality, 98–99
    and venture capitalist funding, 214–16
Compu-Link, 188*b*
computational power, 97, 98*b*, 98
computer operating systems, 246–47
computer-related industries, 182*b*, 185, 186*b*, 188*b*, 192*b*, 195*b*, 229*b*–30*b*, 234, 235. *See also* personal computers; *specific companies*

computer simulations, 102*b*, 108–9, 138–39
conceptual integrity, 244–45, 245*b*
conceptualist view of probability, 75n
Confessions of an Advertising Man (Ogilvy), 8n
confirmation bias, 137*b*
conflict-of-interest, 199
conjunction fallacy, 136*b*
conservatism, 28–29
consulting firms, 207*b*
consumer electronics industry, 228–29
Consumer Sentiment Index, 103
consumer tastes, 64n
containerized shipping industry, 230*b*
contextual inference, 160*b*, 160–61, 175, 180*b*
contextual knowledge/information, 13–14, 15–16, 17, 18, 19*f*, 161
contracting problems, 222–23
controlled trials, 14
conventions, 49. *See also* paradigms and paradigmatic methodologies
conviction narratives, 283*b*
Coombs, Clyde, 131*b*
coordination issues, 214, 215–16, 244, 249–50
Cornell University, 45*b*, 46, 151
Corning Capital, 176
Coronary Artery Surgery Study (CASS), 78*b*–79*b*
corporate culture stories, 294–95
corporate technocracy, 310–11
corroboration of testimony, 75
Cosgel, M. M., 342n.3
Coulombe, Joe, 304, 308
Cournot, Antoine, 60–61
Covid-19 pandemic, 25, 78, 88, 324*b*, 330
CP/M operating system, 246
Crawdaddy!, 183*b*–84*b*
creativity, 36–37, 302–3
credit cards, 18
criminal prosecutions, 12–13, 21, 22, 28, 29, 75, 80–81
criminology, 15–16
Cringely, R. X., 185, 188*b*, 250*b*
Cronin, A. J., 304
crossover problem, 79*b*
Crow, Jim, 299
crowdsourcing, 322–23
Crowley, John, 290*b*–91*b*
Cruise Origin, 234
cryptocurrencies, 214, 318
cultural influences, 28–29, 301–2
The Cure (Anand), 290*b*
curriculum vitae (CVs), 287–88
Cyert, Richard, 101*b*

410   INDEX

Daily Californian, 185
D'Amelio, Charli Grace, 322–23
Darwin, Charles, 130*b*, 319–20, 333
data-driven enterprises, 238
David Copperfield, 298
dead reckoning, 3
Deal, Terrence, 295
Dearborn, DeWitt, 101*b*–2*b*
Debreu, Gerard, 116
decision making
  and computational constraints on
    certainty, 97
  decision theory, 55*b*, 123
  decision trees, 55*b*–56*b*
  and Ellsberg's academic background,
    111*b*–12*b*
  and Ellsberg's uncertainty/ambiguity
    research, 110–11, 113, 114, 123, 124
  and Knight's rejection of rational
    explanations, 91
  and muted influence of Simon's work, 103,
    105–6, 107
  and origins of behavioral economics, 127
  and prospect theory, 140*b*
  and Simon's academic background, 94*b*, 95*b*
  and Simon's research, 98–101, 101*b*–2*b*, 108*b*
  and startup financing constraints, 193–94
  and structure of large public corporations,
    222–23, 224, 226
  and systemic learning, 98*b*
  and varied forms of rationality, 97
deductive equilibrium, 49
De Finetti, Bruno, 54, 83–84, 113
Dell, Michael, 185, 215
Dell Computers, 185, 186*b*, 188*b*
demagoguery, 4
demand, 27–29, 189–90
democracy, 327, 328
Descartes, René, 145
descriptive propositions, 114*b*–15*b*, 114–15
detail-attention tradeoff, 273
Dewey, John, 25
diagnostic criteria, 20
diagnostic imaging, 4
Digital Equipment Corporation, 236*b*, 250*b*
digital revolution, 322
DiMarco, Stephanie, 195*b*
"diminished marginal utility" theory, 146
direct mail business, 192*b*
director compensation, 242*b*–43*b*
direct-response TV sales, 278
disagreement, 20–21, 22, 23–24, 57–59
discount retailing business, 183*b*, 229

discourse-related scholarship, 254–55. *See also*
    entrepreneurial discourse
discrimination lawsuits, 76
Disney, 238
Disraeli, Benjamin, 31
disruption, 180, 187, 253, 283*b*, 306–7, 308,
    324*b*
Disruptive Technologies: Catching the Wave
    (Christensen), 306
distribution functions, 234
dividends, 230–31
DNA, 3–4, 16–17
Doerr, John, 215–16
A Doll's House (Ibsen), 302*b*
Donaldson, James Stephen ("MrBeast"),
    322–23
doubt
  and degrees of disagreement, 21–22
  and honest disagreement, 20–21
  and interpersonal differences, 21
  and missing information, 18–20, 19*f*
  and novelty/prior validation, 20
  resulting from missing information, 170–72
  and significance of disagreements, 22
Dougan, Ken, 182*b*
Doyle, Arthur Conan, 304
Draper, Gaither, and Anderson, 200*b*–1*b*
Dreamliner, 235
drug development, 16–17, 18–19, 20, 22, 23–24,
    29, 30*b*–31*b*, 206, 239*b*–40*b*
Dubey, Abeer, 296*b*
Dudley, Robert Charles, 163
due diligence, 197–99, 209–10
due process, 25
Duhigg, Charles, 295*b*
DuPont, 219*b*, 227
Dutch tulip mania, 318
dynamism of business stories, 308–11
Dyson, James, 278*b*, 293*b*–94*b*, 304
Dyson Company, 293*b*–94*b*

Eastern Airlines, 227
East India Company, 217, 221, 232
eBay, 325
e-bikes, x–xi, 6, 10
eclectic methodologies, 101*b*–2*b*
Eclipse, 247–48
"Eclipse of the Public Corporation" (Jensen),
    230
Econometrica, 85n, 104, 127, 140*b*, 141*b*
econometrics, 87–88, 133n, 135
economic policy, 87
Economics Journal, 111*b*

INDEX 411

Edgeworth, Francis Ysidro, 146
Edison, Thomas, 199–200
Edwards, Ward, 127, 131*b*
efficacy testing, 30*b*–31*b*
efficient markets hypothesis, 65, 152*b*, 152–53
Einstein, Albert, 54–55, 272
elevator pitches, 273, 287*b*, 287, 291*b*, 297,
    310–11
Elfers, William, 201*b*
Eli Lilly, 13*b*, 239*b*–40*b*, 252*t*
elitism, 51
Ellsberg, Daniel
    academic legacy of, 110
    and affinity for ambiguity, 121*b*–22*b*
    and ambiguity aversion, 121*b*
    and author's modernization project, 109
    background and research interests, 110–11
    career trajectory, 111*b*–12*b*
    and critiques of behavioral economics, 158,
        160–61
    Ellsberg Paradox, 120*b*
    and heuristics and bias research, 134
    and Keynes's one-off choice thought
        experiment, 76*b*
    preferences thought experiment, 116*b*–18*b*
    and prescriptions, 114*b*–15*b*
    and prospect theory, 142
    uncertainty/ambiguity research, 119–20, 122–25
Ellsberg Paradox, 110–11, 120*b*
Elster, Jon, 155–56, 161, 171, 315–16, 329,
    330, 379n.6
eminent utility, 14*b*–15*b*
Emmett, Ross, 45*b*, 67, 340n.2
empiricism, 107*b*–8*b*, 107, 133, 321
Encyclopedia Britannica, 145
endowment funds, 201*b*
English law, 75
The Enigma of Reason (Sperber), 26, 138
Enquiry concerning Human Understanding
    (Hume), 172
Enron, 304–5
entertainment industries, 189
entrepreneurial discourse
    aims and sub-aims, 265–66
    comparing aims, 266–67, 268
    contents of proposals and plans, 269
    described, 259–60
    evocative devices, 273–75
    and figurative language, 273–74
    and narrative-mode thought, 260–61
    and origin stories, 287*b*
    rehearsed performances, 276–77
    and visual metaphors, 275

See also entrepreneurship; stories and
    storytelling
entrepreneurship
    complementary potential, 34
    and consumer tastes, 63–64n
    and creativity, 36–37
    demand for courses, 166–67
    disagreement of application in economic
        models, 57–59
    and doubt resulting from missing
        information, 171
    and Ellsberg's uncertainty/ambiguity
        research, 123–25
    exclusion from microeconomics, 52–53,
        57*b*, 57
    as focus of uncertainty-based research,
        167–70
    and heuristics and bias research, 134
    and Knight's *Risk, Uncertainty and Profit*,
        86–87
    and limitations imposed by uncertainty, 174
    and overview of author's model, 172–74, 175
    role in uncertainty-based research, 165
    surging interest in, 33–34
    See also entrepreneurial discourse; startups
Epic of Gilgamesh, 275
epidemiology, 15–16
equilibrium models, 50, 106–7
"equilibrium" solutions, 54–55
Espionage Act, 112*b*
ethnic prejudice, 17n
Euclidean geometry, 49*b*
evaluation functions, 32*t*, 237, 249, 319
evidence and evidentiary standards, 4, 16–17,
    23–24, 32*t*, 75n, 79–81
evolution, 26, 241
evolutionary economics, 103, 222
An Evolutionary Theory of Economic Change
    (Nelson and Winter), 103
Excel, 182*b*
Excessive Ambitions (Elster), 315–16, 329
executive education programs, 305
Exit, Voice, and Loyalty (Hirschman), 25
exit decisions, 209*b*
expansionist pressures, 217–18
expected outcomes, 142n
expected utility, 53, 55, 102, 342n.11
experiential influences on information, 17–18
experimental economics, 154–55
experimental psychology, 145, 146–47. *See also*
    behavioral economics
Extraordinary Measures (film), 290*b*
Exxon, 218

412 INDEX

Facebook, 3–4, 210, 238, 252–53, 252t, 326, 380n.36
fact-checking, 326
Factor, Allen, 192b
failure, 294b
Fama, Eugene, 152–53, 152b, 173–74, 175, 205, 241, 242, 246–47, 253–54, 370n.44
Farre-Mensa, J., 213b
fashion industry, 189
Faster Company (Kelly), 332b
Favaloro, René, 78b, 79b
Fechner, Gustav Theodor, 146
Federal Bureau of Investigation (FBI), 328–29
Federal Express, 210, 290b
federalism, 27
Federalist Papers, 332–33
Federal Open Market Committee (FOMC), 331b, 332b
Federal Reserve System, 228, 331b–32b
Federal Trade Commission (FTC), 63
feminism, 205n
fiduciaries, 199, 200, 207–8, 318
field observation, 108–9
figurative language, 273–74
filial duty, 301
finance, 15–16, 148, 190–92, 319
financial markets, 332b
fingerprint evidence, 16–17
fiscal policy, 70, 87
Fitzgerald, F. Scott, 304
Five Forces framework (Porter), 61, 65, 80, 153, 190, 305–6
flood insurance, 96b
fluoxetine (Prozac), 239b–40b
Flynn Effect, 159b, 160b
Foley, MaryJo, 291
Fooled by Randomness (Taleb), 272
Ford, Henry, 221, 309
Ford Motor Company, 221, 226, 227
forensic evidence, 20, 23–24
Forrester, John, 19f, 161
Foss, Nicolai, 360n.16
The Foundations of Statistics (Savage), 53, 115
founding of companies, 310f. *See also* bootstrapped ventures; startups
Fox, Rich, 192b
framing, ix–x, 126, 130, 139–40, 142–43, 143b, 144, 151, 157, 157b, 159, 283b
Frankston, Bob, 188b, 246
Frederick, Shane, 132–33
Freear, J. J., 206
free/open markets, 27
freethinking, 44b–45b
Free to Choose (book and TV show), 47, 57b

Frei, Frances, 282
Freud, Sigmund, 135n, 145, 146–47
Friberg, R., 390
Friedman, Milton
  and decision-making in business firms, 99
  and exclusion of entrepreneurship from microeconomics, 57b
  and heuristics and bias research, 135
  and information economics, 65
  on Knightian uncertainty, ix
  and Knight's influence, 46–47
  and Knight's "middle way" methodology, 93
  and Knight's risk/uncertainty construct, 52–53
  and shift from Kuhnian paradigm in statistics, 55
  and subjective utility theories, 53
Friedman, Walter, 17n
Full Employment Act, 331b
Fuller & Thaler Asset Management, 153, 161
functionally departmentalized organizations, 219b
functional rationality, 31, 96b, 241
The Functions of the Executive (Barnard), 101b, 108b

Gabriel, Yiannis, 282
Gaddafi, Muammar, 63n
Galbraith, John Kenneth
  and advantages of large public companies, 233–34, 238
  and challenges facing established industry leaders, 228, 229, 230–31
  and decline of New Industrial State giants, 252
  and governance issues of large public companies, 244
  heterodoxy of, 224b
  on innovations since World War II, 225b
  and Jensen's "Eclipse of the Public Corporation," 230
  and postwar Industrial System, 223–26, 227–28
  and spillovers from literary storytelling, 307
gambling, 58
game developers, 317
games of chance, 53
game theory, 62–63, 65
Gandhi Peace Award, 112b
Gardner, Erle Stanley, 304
gate reviews, 237
Gates, Bill, 185, 215, 253, 288, 308, 310
"gazelle" startups, 178, 186b–87b
General Electric, 199–200, 226, 249
General Motors, 25, 218, 219b, 220, 226, 227, 234, 241

The General Theory of Employment, Interest and Money (Keynes), 71, 76b, 85n, 86, 87n, 89, 91, 347n.70
genetics, 3–4
Genzyme Corporation, 291b
geocentrism, 119–20
Ghemawat, Pankaj, 60–61, 343n.10, 343n.13
Ghosh, Shikhar, 210
Gigerenzer, Gerd, 156–57, 157b, 158–59, 161, 162, 262b
Gilded Age, 63
Gilovich, Thomas, 135–36, 136b–37b
global financial collapse/crisis (2008), x, 69, 88
global warming, 20
goal-alignment protocols, 253
Gompers, Paul, 203b, 205–6, 364n.30
Good, Irving John, 80n
good-versus-evil stories, 301
Google
 and angel vs. VC funding, 210, 211
 Aristotle Project, 295b–97b
 and competitive markets, 26, 27
 and declining quality of discourse, 326
 growth and value of, 252–53
 and growth of new industrial giants, 253
 and information asymmetry problems, 203b
 and large companies' intolerance for uncertainty, 236b
 and limited partnerships, 209b
 market value, 252t
 and planning for complex product launches, 273
 and scope of recent innovations, 3–4
 and synergies in large public companies, 249
 and technology-enabled symbiosis, 323n
 and uncertainties in modern marketplace, 4
 and unique products, 28
 and VC coordination mechanisms, 215
 and VC financing, 206
Gorgon Liquefied Natural Gas, 234
Gorski, David, 22
gossip, 58
government interventions, 66. *See also* fiscal policy
Granovetter, Mark, 223
grassroots activism, 332b
Great Depression, 70, 86–87, 227
Great Eastern (ship), 163
The Great Gatsby (Fitzgerald), 304
Greek mythology, 300, 301, 306–7
Greek philosophy, 12, 80
Greenwood, John, 195b
Gresham's Law, 65

Greylock & Company, 201b
Griffon, Dale, 135–36, 136b–37b
Griliches, Ziv, 158
Grosshandler, Robert, 182b, 195b
groupthink, 26, 326, 330, 331b
Grove, Andrew, 306, 307
Guzman, J., 213b

HAART standard of care, 24
Haltiwanger, J., 186b
Hamel, Gary, 230
Hamilton, Alexander, 332–33
Harlem Renaissance, 299b
Harris, R. S., 364n.33
Harrison, John, 3
Hart, Oliver, 65, 222–23
Harvard Business Review, 230, 275, 282, 305–6
Harvard Business School (HBS), ix, 55b–56b, 60–61, 113, 116, 166, 167, 275, 282, 288b, 290b, 292, 305, 332b
Harvard College, 111b, 229b–30b
Harvard Medical School, 78b–79b
Harvard University, 46, 87–88, 145, 185, 224b, 261b
Harvard University Press, 150b
Hayek, Friedrich, 14, 14b, 15, 32t, 37, 46, 88–89, 226, 244n, 244, 324
Hayek Seminars, x
Head Start, 262b
healthcare legislation, 288
health insurance, 64, 66
Health Payment Review, 279
Hebrew University, Jerusalem, 130b–31b
Heckman, James, 50
heliocentrism, 119–20
Heller, Edward H., 200b–1b
Henrekson, M., 186b, 379n.18
hero's journeys, 286, 288, 288b–91b
Heukelom, Floris, 147, 357n.7
heuristics
 and abductive inference, 180b
 and behavioral finance research, 152
 and Gigerenzer's critique of K-T research, 158
 and information processing psychology, 102b
 and K-T's academic backgrounds, 131b, 132b
 and K-T's heuristics and bias research, 130, 136b–37b, 141b
 and prospect theory, 142, 143
Hewlett, Bill, 230b, 248
Hewlett-Packard, 230b
Hicks, John, 220
hierarchical structures, 37, 223, 241–42, 253–54, 327–28

414 INDEX

highly active antiretroviral therapy (HAART) standard of care, 24
high-tech industries, 212–14, 230
high-touch services, 189
Hippocrates, 80, 333
Hirschman, Albert, 25, 316
History of Political Economy, 103b
HMS *Terrible*, 163
Holmes, Oliver Wendell, 25–26
Holmström, Bengt, 65, 222–23
home prices, 176
Homo economicus, 50–51, 56
Honda Prize, 103–4
Hoover, J. Edgar, 328–29
Horizon Worlds, 238
hostile takeovers, 281–82
Howard, Philip, 328–29
H. pylori bacterial infections, 321
human capital, 180, 184–85
human engineering, 139
humanism, 44b–45b
humanities, 38
Hume, David, 12, 145, 172, 272, 320–21
Hunter College, 182b
Hurst, Erik, 177–78, 190–91

IBM, 188b, 229, 235, 249, 250b–51b, 279, 317
Ibrahim, D. M., 211
Ibsen, Henrik, 302b
"I Have a Dream" (King), 277
IKEA, 273n
imagination, 36–37, 320–21, 322, 323
imperfect market theories, 60, 63, 64–67
Imperial Chemical Industries (ICI), 240b
incentives, 64–65, 67–68, 176, 204–5
Inc. magazine, 178, 181f, 325. *See also* startups
incomplete information, 106, 154, 193n. *See also* known unknowns; missing information; unknown unknowns
Index of Leading Economic Indicators, 103
Indian Institute of Technology, 56b, 168b
Indian philosophy, 12
indifference, 116b, 117b, 124
Indigogo, 322–23
industrial organization (IO), 64n, 64, 65–67, 68
Industrial Revolution, 3, 303
Industrial System (Galbraith), 224–25, 225b, 227, 228, 229, 230–31
inference, 159b–60b
inflation, 87
influencers, 322–23
informally-financed entrepreneurs, 35–36

"Information and the Change in the Paradigm in Economics" (Stigler), 65–66
information asymmetry
and aims of entrepreneurial discourse, 268
and angel vs. VC funding, 210, 211–12, 215
and decision-making routines of large public companies, 241
and entrepreneurship in uncertainty-based research, 169
and information economics, 64–65, 66
and reinterpretation of Knight's thesis, 67
and VC funding, 198, 203, 203b, 211–12, 214
information economics, 60, 64–67, 84
information processing theories, 102b, 138–39
initial public offerings (IPOs), 167, 209b, 212, 231, 241
innovation, 3–4, 124, 223, 229, 304–5, 309, 319–20
The Innovator's Dilemma (Christensen), 306
insanity defenses, 28
Institute for New Economic Thinking (INET), 88–89
institutionalized investing, 199–201, 200b–1b. *See also* angel investors; venture capitalists (VCs)
institutional reinforcement, 206, 207–8
insurance, 64, 66, 73, 96b
Intel, 29, 215–16, 235, 307
intellectual property, 213b
Inter-ad, 195b
interest rates, 228
internal capital markets, 251
International Aids Conference (Vancouver, 1996), 24
International Encyclopedia of the Social Sciences, 126, 347n.1
International Limited Partners Association, 207b
internet, 318, 320, 325
interpersonal differences, 21
Introduction to Narrative, 282b
Intuit, 213
intuition
background beliefs and information, 16–17
and behavioral economics, 130, 131b
and Ellsberg's uncertainty/ambiguity research, 115–16, 118
and heuristics and bias research, 132–34, 138n
and Knight's influence, 6
and VC financing of startups, 202–3
Invention: A Life (Dyson), 293b–94b
invention and inventiveness, 98b
investing strategies, 151, 152–53, 161, 173–74

INDEX 415

Investment Company Act, 318
investment criteria of VCs, 208
invisible hand, 55, 60, 63, 165
iPhone, 253, 306, 327–28
IQ tests, 159b–60b
Iraq War, 112b
irreducible uncertainties, 189–90
Isaacson, Walter, 277

James, William, 107, 107b–8b, 133, 145, 263,
    264b, 316, 333, 356n.69, 356n.71
Janeway, William, 87–88, 318, 379n.10
January effect, 151, 152–53, 161
Japan, 228–29, 230
Japan as Number One: Lessons for America
    (Vogel), 230, 307
Jay, John, 332–33
J.C. Penney, 183b
Jenkinson, T., 364n.33
Jensen, Michael, 173–74, 175, 205, 230–31, 241,
    242, 246–48, 253–54, 370n.44
Jim Crow segregation, 299
Jobs, Steve, 22, 27, 185, 188b, 236b, 277, 279,
    304–5, 306, 319, 327–28
Johansson, D., 186b
John Bates Clark medal, 151
John Maynard Keynes (Skidelsky), 70b–71b
Johnson, Lyndon B., 112b, 224b
Johnson, W. E., 71–72
Journal of Economic Perspectives, 149b–50b, 151
Journal of Political Economy, 47, 51, 60
Joyce, James, 302b
"Judgment under Uncertainty: Heuristics and
    Biases" (Kahneman and Tversky), 135
juries and jury deliberations, 24
Justice Department, 63
justifications for decisions, 23–26, 27–30, 32t
Juvenal, 326

Kahneman, Daniel
    academic background, 130b–32b
    and base-rate fallacies, 194
    and behavioral finance research, 150, 151–52
    and Bruner's critique of cognitive biases, 262b
    critiques of K-T research, 137b, 156–57,
        157b, 158, 160–61
    and extension of behavioral research to
        economics, 154
    and heuristics and bias research, 130
    and irrationality in financing, 176
    and muted influence of Simon's work, 109
    and origins of behavioral economics, 128–30,
        148

and prospect theory, 140–44
and Simon's bounded rationality, 98
and Smith's experimental economics,
    154–55
and split within behavioral economics, 126
and Thaler's academic background, 148
and tribute to Thaler, 149b–50b
and Wanner's academic background, 150b
Kant, Immanuel, 16–17, 145
Kaplan, S. N., 364n.33, 365n.37, 365n.38
Katona, George, 103–4, 103b
Katz, Rosalind, 182b
Katzman, John, 182b, 184–85
Kavak, 287b
Kay, John, x, 14, 57, 105–6, 158, 160–61, 283b,
    338n.4, 340n.7, 374n.13
Kellogg, Miner Kilbourne, 41
Kelly, Patrick, 288b–90b, 292, 292b, 293b, 295, 304
Kelvin, William Thomson, Baron, 47
Kennedy, Allen, 295
Kennedy, John F., 112b, 224b
Keynes, Florence Ada, 70
Keynes, John Maynard
    on abstract reasoning, 160b
    background, 70b–71b
    biographical sketch, 70b–71b
    and broadening mainstream views, 38n
    and critiques of behavioral economics, 158
    critiques of classical theories, 69
    and Ellsberg's uncertainty/ambiguity
        research, 110–11, 115n, 123
    and evidence/belief nexus, 75n
    and evidentiary weight, 74–77
    on expansionary impulse of large public
        companies, 248
    and extreme and macro uncertainties, 69,
        84–89
    and extreme/macro uncertainty, 84–88
    father's education, 168b
    and Federal Reserve policies, 331b
    and Freudian psychology, 146–47
    and Galbraith's postwar Industrial System,
        227
    influence on model, 33
    and information economics, 65
    legacy of *Treatise on Probability*, 69, 81–84
    modern relevance of theories, 69, 88–89
    and nonnumerical probabilities, 72–73
    one-off choice thought experiment, 76–77, 76b
    and overview of author's model, 174–75
    publication of *Treatise on Probability*, 71–72
    and relevance and sufficiency of evidence,
        77–78, 79–80

416   INDEX

Keynes, John Maynard (*cont.*)
  and routines and conventions, 80–81
  skepticism of numerical measurement,
    73*b*–74*b*
  and specification of probabilities, 73*b*–74*b*
  and subjective utility theories, 54
  and sufficiency/relevance of evidence, 77, 80n
  and value of scientific research, 8
  See also Treatise on Probability (Keynes)
Keynes, John Neville, 70
Keynesian Revolution, 70
Kickstarter, 322–23
Kildall, Gary, 246
King, Martin Luther, 277
King, Mervyn, x, 14, 57, 105–6, 158, 160–61,
    283*b*, 338n.4, 340n.7, 374n.13
King's College, 71–72
Kipling, Rudyard, 38
Kirsch, Karen, 182*b*, 184–85
Kissinger, Henry, 112*b*
Klein, Peter, 360n.16
Klepper, S., 236*b*, 369n.22
Knight, Frank
  and agency/authority dynamic, 334
  and author's modernization project, 7, 9, 10,
    93, 109
  background, 5–6, 44*b*–45*b*, 70*b*–71*b*
  and broadening mainstream views, 38n
  and Coase, 43
  and context of study, ix–xi
  and critiques of behavioral economics, 158
  definition of entrepreneurs, 167
  and disagreements on uncertainty, 171
  dislike of Keynes, 71, 71*b*
  and doubt resulting from missing
    information, 170–71
  early education, 44
  and Ellsberg's academic background, 111*b*
  and Ellsberg's uncertainty/ambiguity
    research, 110–11, 112–13, 115, 116,
    123–24
  and entrepreneurship in uncertainty-based
    research, 33, 165, 169
  failure to gain influence, 46–47
  and imaginative discourse, 36–37
  and industrial organization (IO)
    economics, 62n
  and James's radical empiricism, 108*b*
  and justification for modernizing
    uncertainty, 23
  and Keynes's *General Theory*, 86–87
  life insurance pricing models, 17
  and mental vs. situational specification, 11n, 13

  and "middle way" methodologies, 92–93
  and Mill's rationality assumption, 146n
  and missing information, 18, 20
  and modern relevance of Keynesian theory,
    88–89
  modifications to model construct, 10*t*
  and multidisciplinary approaches, 93–94
  and muted influence of Simon's work, 105–6,
    107
  and origins of uncertainty concept, 43–44
  and overproduction of communication
    problem, 324
  and overview of author's model, 175
  paradigmatic barriers faced by, 48, 50–51
  and role of contextual evidence, 13–14,
    15–16
  and Simon's study of decision-making, 100–1
  and "target" uncertainty, 15
  and uncertainty/doubt model, 19*f*
  and uncertainty/risk distinction, 34
  and unpredictable responses to uncertainty,
    91–92
  writing style problems, 44
  See also Risk, Uncertainty and Profit (Knight)
Knight, Lev, 45*b*
known unknowns, 57, 176–77
Knudsen, Thorbjom, 66
Korea, 228–29
Kreps, David, 50, 51, 334, 341n.43
Kuhn, Thomas
  and agency/authority dynamic, 334
  on audience for scientific research, 7–8
  and cognitive psychology revolution, 129*b*
  and industrial organization (IO) economics,
    61–63
  and information economics, 65–66
  and muted influence of Simon's work, 106
  and origins of behavioral economics, 128
  and paradigmatic barriers faced by Knight,
    48, 51
  and prospect theory, 141*b*
  and Savage's subjective utility theory, 54, 55
  and scientific paradigms, 48*b*–49*b*, 341n.33

labor economics, 153–54
Laibson, David, 152*b*
Lancet, 78*b*
Land, Edwin, 229*b*–30*b*
Landier, A., 194
Langlois, R. N., 342n.3, 366n.4
language and linguistics, 214, 273–74, 300,
    319–23
Large Language Models (LLMs), 214, 319–20

INDEX   417

large public corporations
  challenges facing, 228–29
  and director compensation, 242*b*–43*b*
  distinctive features of, 232–35
  and entrepreneurial specialization, 35, 317, 319
  explaining interconnected distinctiveness, 240–42
  funding, routines, and initiatives, 310*f*
  governance problems, 242–44
  origins of, 217–18
  and overview of author's model, 174
  postwar dominance of, 223
  self-limiting dynamism, 247–50
  strategies and structures of, 218–21
  top ten US companies, 252*t*
Lavender, Mark, 182*b*
law and legal discourse, 75, 275, 300*b*, 303
laws of motion, 54–55
Lee, Harper, 301
Leijonhufvud, Alex, 104, 104*b*–5*b*, 106
lemon market problems, 65
lending practices, 18
Lerner, Josh, 205–6
LeRoy, Stephen, 44, 67–68, 169, 341n.3, 344n.25
Les Fleurs du mal (Baudelaire), 1
leveraged buyouts, 230–31
Lewis, C. S., 301
Lewis, Meriwether, 148
Lexington Home Telephone Company, 45*b*
licensing of technologies, 236*b*
life insurance, 17n, 64, 66
Lighthouse, Civitavecchia (Kellogg), 41
limited partnerships, 206*b*–7*b*, 209*b*
Lincoln, Edmund, 45*b*
"Linda" experiment, 136*b*–37*b*
Lintner, John, 152*b*
"L'Invitation au voyage" (Baudelaire), 1
Lisa operating system, 291
literary genres, 302*b*
"lives saved-lives lost" framework, 143*b*, 157*b*
Living with Complexity (Norman), 275
Loewenstein, George, 127*b*, 141*b*–42*b*, 149*b*–50*b*, 150, 150*b*
logico-scientific thought, 37, 259, 263, 264*b*, 265, 268, 272, 273–74, 275, 284, 287–88, 306–7, 313, 316, 333
London School of Economics, x, 283*b*
The Longest Day: June 6, 1944 (Ryan), 285
longitude competition, 27
loss aversion, 91–92, 140*b*, 141*b*
lotteries, 310
Lotus, 213

Lowe, William, 279
Lynch, Peter, 243–44

macroeconomics, 15–16, 70*b*, 86–87, 153–54, 331*b*
macro uncertainty, 84–89
Made in America (Walton), 308
Madison, James, 332–33, 382n.59
Making Economics More Useful (Bhidé), 54–55
Making Stories: Law, Literature, Life (Bruner), 263, 284*b*, 298
Mallaby, Sebastian, 266
Management by Objectives systems, 215–16
managerial discretion model, 166*b*
Managerial Economics (course), 61
manias, 318
manipulation, 117*b*–18*b*
Mankiw, Greg, 88
Manning, Chelsea, 112*b*
manufactured home industry, 184*b*
"Maps of Bounded Rationality: Psychology for Behavioral Economics" (Kahneman), 129
March, James, 101*b*, 330
marginal utility, 146
market anomalies, 161
market competition, 222
market efficiency, 209*b*
market failures, 319, 320*f*
market habitats, 177
marketing functions, 218*b*–19*b*, 234
market prices, 244n, 254
market research, 239
market uncertainty, 214*b*
Marsay, D., 49*b*
Marshall, Alfred, 107*b*–8*b*, 158
Marshall, Barry, 321
masking protocols, 25
Mason, Edward, 60–61
Massachusetts General Hospital, 78*b*
Massachusetts Institute of Technology (MIT), 201*b*, 295
Massachusetts Supreme Judicial Council, 76
mass-energy equivalence, 54–55
materialist view of probability, 74–75n
Mathematical Gazette, 81
Mathematical Psychology, 140*b*
mathematics, 180*b*
Maugham, W. Somerset, 304
MBA programs, 63
McArthur, John H., ix, 56*b*
McCloskey, Deirdre, 104, 224*b*, 349n.60
McDonald's, 29, 212, 230*b*
McKinsey & Co., 221, 275, 276, 277*b*

418 INDEX

McLean, Malcolm, 230*b*
Mead Data, 195*b*
medical research and knowledge, 3, 4, 12–13, 13*b*, 14, 20, 22, 24, 27–28, 75
medical supply industry, 28, 288*b*–90*b*
Medicare, 78*b*
Medway (ship), 163
megaprojects, 29, 35, 232, 235
Melody Maker, 183*b*–84*b*
Melos, 327
memes, 318
memoirs, 304, 308
Memorial Sloan Kettering Cancer Center, 22
Mencken, H. L., 333–34
mental state specification, 10–13
The Merchant of Venice (Shakespeare), 304
Mercier, H., 137–38
Merck, 29
merit scholarships, 168*b*
Meta, 238, 252–53, 252*t*. *See also* Facebook
metaphors, 275n, 300, 307–8
Meta Platforms, 238
Metcalfe, Bob, 236*b*
microeconomics, 52–53, 57*b*, 134, 222, 254
Micron Separations, 195*b*
Microsoft
    and advantages of large public companies, 238
    business origin story, 288
    and business recovery stories, 291–92
    and coordination issues of large public companies, 246–47
    and disruptive technology narrative, 306
    and entrepreneurial specialization, 317
    growth and value of, 252
    growth of, 252
    and growth of new industrial giants, 253
    and human capital challenges, 185
    market value, 252*t*
    size and influence of, 217
    and spillovers from literary storytelling, 308
    and synergies in large public companies, 249
    top-down authority, 223
    and VC coordination mechanisms, 215
    and VC's preference for high-tech industries, 212–13
middle management, 226, 247–248
"middle way" methodologies, 92–93, 101, 348n.10
military organization, 221
Mill, John Stuart, 49*b*, 53, 133, 146n
Miller, George, 261*b*, 270–71
Miller, Merton, 152*b*
Milligan College, 45*b*

Mills, Karen, 190
Mind: A Quarterly Review of Psychology and Philosophy, 145
Minding the Law (Amsterdam and Bruner), 263, 264n, 274, 275, 283*b*, 300*b*
minority shareholders, 202
Minsky, Hy, 88
misjudgment, 13, 204–5
missing information
    and degree of doubt, 18–20
    and Ellsberg's uncertainty/ambiguity research, 122–25
    and financing of ventures, 174, 176–77
    implications for entrepreneurship, 52–53
    and interpersonal differences, 21
    large corporations' tolerance levels for uncertainty, 238, 239
    and Smith's experimental economics, 154
    and uncertainty/doubt model, 19*f*
    See also incomplete information
Models of Man—Social and Rational (Solow), 104
modernization, x–xi, 9, 10, 93, 109, 123–25
Modigliani, Franco, 152*b*
Mojo Navigator R&R News, 183*b*–84*b*
monetary incentives, 215, 243
monetary policy, 70, 87–88, 318
Monitor Company, 63n, 152–53
monopoly power, 60–61, 63, 64, 66, 217, 220, 328
Mont Pelerin Society, 46
Monty Python's Flying Circus, 277
Moore, Gordon, 237
moral hazard, 64–65, 67–68
Morgan, J. Pierpont, 199–200
Morgenstern, Oskar, 54, 111*b*, 113
mortality statistics, 17n
Mortimer, John, 304
Moses, Robert, 328–29
Mossin, Jan, 152*b*
mRNA, 319
Mullainathan, Sendhil, 152*b*, 380n.37
Munger, Charlie, 248, 249
murder trials, 16–17, 20, 21, 28, 28n, 30*b*–31*b*, 81, 206
Musk, Elon, 31, 278*b*, 304–5
mutually beneficial transactions, 64–65
"myside" biases, 26
The Mythical Man Month (Brooks), 245*b*
My Years with General Motors (Sloan), 308

Napoleon I, 169
"The Narrative Construction of Reality" (Bruner), 261

INDEX 419

narrative mode, 7, 273–74, 316. *See also* stories
and storytelling
Narrative Science Project, 283*b*
narrative thought, 264*b*. *See also*
entrepreneurial discourse
narratology, 282*b*
National Aeronautics and Space Administration
(NASA), 237
National Bureau of Economic Research
(NBER), 38n, 128*b*, 149*b*, 151, 152*b*, 167
National Heart and Lung Institute, 78*b*
NEC, 188*b*
Nelson, Richard, 30, 103–4, 103*b*, 241, 379n.16
neoclassical economics, 99, 100–1
Netflix, 323*b*–24*b*
Netscape, 318
Newell, Allen, 95*b*, 102*b*, 129*b*, 133, 139n, 261*b*,
319–20
New England Journal of Medicine, 79*b*
New Industrial State, 252, 307
The New Industrial State (Galbraith), 223–24,
224*b*, 227, 229, 233–34, 252, 307
New Palgrave Dictionary of Economics, 94*b*, 95, 95*b*
New School for Social Research, 262*b*
New Technologies Cause Great Firms to Fail
(Christensen), 307
Newton, Isaac, 54–55, 333
New York City, 328–29
New Yorker, 304–5, 325
New York Times, 88, 112*b*, 166, 277, 278, 285,
295*b*–96*b*
New York University, 262*b*, 263
NeXT computer, 277–78
Nicholas, Tom, 199–200
Nickel, Mark, 195*b*
Nixon, Richard, 87
Nobel Prize in Economics
and behavioral economics, 127, 127n, 128*b*,
129, 130, 137*b*, 151
and behavioral finance research, 151
Hart and Holmström, 222–23
and information economics, 65–66
and Kahneman's tribute to Thaler, 152*b*
and Knight, 43–44, 46, 52
and paradigmatic barriers faced by Knight, 50
and rationality in finance, 152*b*
and shift from Kuhnian paradigm in
statistics, 56
Simon, 90, 93–94, 95, 95*b*, 99, 101*b*, 102,
103–5, 104*b*–5*b*, 106, 107, 108*b*
Smith's experimental economics, 154
Stigler and Phelps, 315
Stiglitz Nobel Lecture, x

Nobel Prize in Literature, 81
Nobel Prize in Medicine, 321
"noisy" models, 21
non-fungible tokens (NFTs), 214
nonnumerical probabilities, 72–73
nonstatistical information, 58
Norman, Don, 275
normative questions, 114*b*–15*b*
North American Industry Classification
System, 186*b*
North-Easter (Wolf), 41
Northwestern University, 116
Novazyme, 290*b*–91*b*
novelty of information, 20, 21, 28–30, 30*f*
nudges, 90n, 92, 93, 153–54, 156–57
Nvidia, 252*t*

Obama, Barack, 323
Objectives and Key Results (OKR) systems,
215–16
Oculus, 238
Odean, Terry, 152*b*
O'Donnell, R., 83, 84, 345n.18, 356n.60
Odorczyk, James, 195*b*
Office 365, 246–47
Ogilvy, David, 8n
Oldfield, Mike, 184*b*
Old Testament, 306–7
oligopoly power, 60–61, 64, 66, 325, 326
O'Neill, Terry, 205n
one-off choices
and agency/authority dynamic, 329
background beliefs and information, 16–17
and case for narrative-mode reasoning, 316
and conflicts with author's modernization
project, 58
and critiques of K-T research, 158, 159, 161
and decision-making routines of large public
companies, 253–54
and doubt resulting from missing
information, 171
and entrepreneurship in uncertainty-based
research, 168–69
and entrepreneurs in economic theory, 34
and evidence/belief nexus, 75, 76, 77
and interpersonal differences, 21
and justification for modernizing
uncertainty, 23
and Keynes's nonnumerical probabilities,
72–73
and Knight's risk/uncertainty construct,
52–53
and limitations of chaos theory, 315

420 INDEX

one-off choices (*cont.*)
 and mental vs. situational specification,
  11–12
 and missing information, 18–19
 and narrative foundations of categories, 300b
 and overview of author's model, 175
 and prospect theory, 142
 and Ramsay's critique of Keynes's *Treatise*, 83
 and role of contextual evidence, 15–16
 and role of justificatory discourse, 23–24
 and subjective utility theories, 53
 technological, social, and experiential
  influences, 17
 and uncertainty/doubt model, 19f
On Knowing (Bruner), 261b–62b
operating systems, 246
operations research, 97
opportunism, spontaneous, 192b
opportunistic adaptation, 190
Organisation of Economic Co-operation and
 Development (OECD), 153–54, 199n,
 201–2, 208, 212
The Origin and Evolution of New Businesses
 (Bhidé), ix, 178b–79b
origin stories, 287–88, 287b
orthodoxy in economic theory, 51
Othello (Shakespeare), 276–77
Ouchi, William, 230
outliers, 109, 264b, 333
overconfidence, 91–92, 176
oversight, 197–99
Oxford, 103b
Oxford Handbook of Innovation Management,
 237–38

Packard, David, 230b, 248, 304
Palo Alto Research Center (PARC), 236b
pancreatic cancer, 22
paradigms and paradigmatic methodologies
 and abductive, contextual hypothesizing,
  179b
 and agency/authority dynamic, 329
 and broadening mainstream views, 38
 and industrial organization (IO) economics,
  61–64
 and information economics, 65–66
 Kuhn's establishment of concept, 48b–49b
 paradigmatic barriers faced by Knight, 48
 paradigmatic conflict, 105
 Savage's impact on Kuhnian paradigm,
  52–53, 54–55, 57, 60
partitioning, 244–46
partnership laws, 204

patents, 167, 213b
Pavlov, Ivan, 91–92n, 94n, 129b
Pearson, Robin, 17
Peden, W., 74–75n
Peirce, Charles Saunders, 75n, 179b
pension funds, 200, 201b
Pentagon Papers, 110–11, 112b
perceptual biases, 138n
performance, 276–77
personal computers, 188b, 213, 229, 235, 279, 317
personal probability, 52
personality types, 22
pharmaceutical industry, 234, 236b, 238–39,
 239b–40b
Phased Project Planning (NASA), 237
Phelps, Edmund, x, 67n, 87, 87n, 88, 315,
 337n.1, 379n.4
photography industry, 229b–30b
Physicians Sales & Service (PSS), 288b–89b,
 292b–93b
pitches, 259, 263, 265, 270–71, 273, 279–80,
 284–85, 286, 287
placebo, 23–24
planetary motion, 20, 119–20
planning functions, 249
Plessy v. Ferguson, 299b
Plotkin, Marcia, 195b
Plotkin, Steve, 195b
Poetics (Aristotle), 260–61, 271–72, 275
Polaroid Corporation, 229b–30b
political activism, 323
Pollack, Andrew, 277
pollution, 329
Pólya, George, 180b, 361n.14
polyarchies, 253–54
Pompe disease, 290b–91b
Popeil, Ron, 278, 279
Popper, Karl, 88–89
Popular Electronics, 288
populism, 25
Porter, Michael, 61–62, 63, 65, 152–53, 305–6, 307
poverty, 150b
Powell, Jerome, 331b, 422n.55
PowerPoint, 275
practical omniscience, 53–54, 57–58, 66, 105–6, 161
Pratt, John, 55b–56b
prejudice, 17n
"preponderance of evidence" standard, 75–76
prescriptive rules, 114–15, 114b–15b
prices and pricing strategies, 244n, 292b–93b,
 331b, 332b
Princeton Review, 182b, 184–85
principle-agent model, 191

Principles of Economics (Marshall), 91
prior validation of information, 20
private benefits, 170
private equity firms, 252
probability
  and abstract reasoning, 160*b*
  and doubt resulting from missing
    information, 171
  and Ellsberg's uncertainty/ambiguity
    research, 114
  Keynes's skepticism of numerical
    measurement, 73*b*–74*b*
  Keynes's *Treatise on Probability*, 71–72
  and Knight's view of uncertainty, 5–6
  materialist view of, 75n
  and mental vs. situational specification, 11n
  nonnumerical, 72–73
  and Ramsay's critique of Keynes's *Treatise*,
    82–84
  See also statistical data and modeling;
    Treatise on Probability (Keynes)
"The Probability of Induction"
  (Peirce), 75n
Process of Education (Bruner), 262*b*
product planning and launches, 273, 277–78
profits and profitability, 62n, 100, 190–91,
  230–31
prospect theory
  and behavioral finance research, 152
  development of, 140*b*–42*b*
  and heuristics and bias research, 140
  and Kahneman's tribute to Thaler, 149*b*–52*b*
  and origins of behavioral economics, 130
  and prospect theory, 142–43
  and split within behavioral economics, 126
"prototypical plights," 300
Prozac, 13*b*, 239*b*–40*b*
psychoanalysis, 135, 146–47
Psychological Review, 141*b*, 348n.34
psychology, 91–92n, 105, 115, 128–29, 296*b*–97*b*
Psychology Review, 141*b*
Public Administration Review, 156n
public companies, 234
public good, 124
public health, 330
public policy, 317
publishing industry, 183*b*–84*b*
Pugsley, Benjamin, 177–78, 190–91
Pure Food and Drug Act, 65

quantitative methods, 108–9
Quarterly Journal of Economics (QJE), 85, 98–
  99, 104, 110–11, 112, 118, 118*b*, 119, 121*b*

Rabin, Matthew, 127*b*, 149*b*–50*b*, 150, 150*b*
racial identity and racism, 17n, 303
radical empiricism, 108*b*
Radical Uncertainty (Kay and King), x, 14, 57,
  105–6
Radosevich, Marcia, 279
Raiffa, Howard, 55*b*, 116, 117*b*, 118–19, 120*b*, 134
railroad industry, 63, 199–200
Ramayana, 301
Ramsey, Frank, 54, 82–84, 113, 146–47,
  346n.51, 346n.52
RAND Corporation, 111*b*–12*b*, 116, 120*b*
randomized controlled trials, 4–5, 14, 18–19
ranitidine, 238–39
Rappaport, David, 135
Rathbun, Robert, 240*b*
"Rational Decision Making in Business
  Organizations" (Simon), 99
rationality
  and behavioral economics, 126, 127, 129–30,
    137*b*
  and behavioral finance research, 151–53,
    152*b*
  and computational constraints on certainty,
    97, 98
  and heuristics and bias research, 132, 134,
    135, 137, 138
  and Knight's "middle way" methodology, 92
  and Knight's rejection of purely rational
    explanations, 91, 92
  and muted influence of Simon's work, 104,
    105–6, 107
  and Ramsay's critique of Keynes's *Treatise*, 83
  rational choice, 97, 113, 119, 132
  and Simon's academic background, 90
  Simon's global rationality, 98–99
  and Simon's Nobel Prize Lecture, 102
  Simon's rationalization theories, 96*b*
  and Simon's study of decision-making, 100
  and Simon's theories, 101*b*
  and systemic learning, 98*b*
  varied forms of, 95–97
  See also bounded rationality
Reagan, Ronald, 228
Real World Systems, 195*b*
reasonable doubt standard, 16–17, 80–81
reasonableness, 31
recessions, 228
recovery stories, 291–92, 292*b*–94*b*
reinvestment strategies, 248
relevance of evidence, 77–78, 79–80
religious faith, 11–12
religious organizations, 221

422 INDEX

representation hypothesis, 131*b*, 138n
representativeness heuristic, 135n, 136*b*
research and development, 234, 294*b*
"The Results of Municipal Electric Lighting in Massachusetts" (Lincoln), 45*b*
retailing business, 229
returns on investments, 202
revealed preference theory, 147
rhetoric, 23
Rhetoric (Aristotle), 260–61, 271
Ricardo, David, 65
Richard T. Ely Lectures, 56n, 95
Right Livelihood Award, 112*b*
"Risk, Ambiguity and the Savage Axioms," 110
Risk, Uncertainty and Profit (Knight), ix–xi, 5–6, 43, 44, 45*b*, 47, 50, 71–72, 75, 86, 315
risk vs. uncertainty, 5–6, 113
RJR-Nabisco, 230
Robbins, Lionel, 43–44
Robert I, King of the Scots (Robert the Bruce), 294*b*
Robinson, Adam, 182*b*
Robinson, Joan, 88
Rockefeller, Lawrence, 200*b*
Rockefeller Brothers, 200*b*
Roddick, Anita, 279–80, 281
Rolling Stone, 183*b*–84*b*, 185
Ronco, 278
Ropko, Sean, 182*b*
Rosenberg, Nate, 319–20
Ross, Steve, 152*b*
roulette wheels, 12
routines
    advantages of large corporations, 232, 233, 237, 239, 240–41, 242, 244, 246–47
    and collective decision-making, 250*b*–51*b*
    and entrepreneurial specialization, 35, 319
    and heuristics and bias research, 138
    impact on novel deviations, 30*f*
    justificatory routines, 29–30
    and muted influence of Simon's work, 106–7
    and overview of author's model, 172
    risk-reducing function of, 80, 80n
    and VC financing, 199–200, 205–6
rule of law, 25
Rule of Nobody, 328–29
rule of three, 271
Rumsfeld, Donald, 20, 174–75
Russell, Bertrand, 12n, 81
Russell, Carol, 182*b*, 195*b*
Russell Personnel Services, 182*b*, 195*b*
Russell Sage Foundation, 139, 148, 150, 150*b*, 151
Ryan, Cornelius, 285

Safeway, 227
Sah, Raaj K., 66, 173–74, 253–54
Samizdat publications, 301
Sampler Publications, 195*b*
sampling theory, 131*b*
Samsung, 317
Samuelson, Paul, 47, 85n, 87, 116, 117*b*, 147, 152*b*, 347n.70
Sandström, C., 379n.18
SAT preparation services, 182*b*
Savage, L. J. "Jimmie"
    and behavioral finance research, 151–52
    conflicts with author's modernization project, 57–58
    and Ellsberg's academic background, 111*b*
    and Ellsberg's uncertainty/ambiguity research, 113, 114, 114*b*–15*b*, 115, 116, 117*b*–18*b*, 118, 120, 121–22*b*
    and heuristics and bias research, 134, 135
    and Knight's risk/uncertainty construct, 52–53
    and K-T's academic backgrounds, 131*b*
    and Ramsay's critique of Keynes's *Treatise*, 83–84
    and shift from Kuhnian paradigm in statistics, 55
    and subjective utility theory, 53–54, 55, 60
scaling issues, 208, 215, 219–20, 317
Schein, Edgar, 295
schizophrenia, 28
Schlaifer, Robert, 55*b*
Schoenberg, Richard, 184–85
Schultz, Howard, 64n
Schumpeter, Joseph, 33, 91, 158, 219–20, 223, 224*b*, 253, 304, 309, 319
Schumpeter Prize, 103–4
Science, 132, 132*b*, 133–34, 135, 137, 139, 140*b*, 143*b*
scientific advances, 3–4, 77–78, 124, 321, 333
Scientific American, 129
scientific economics, 38
scientific methodologies, 7–8, 23
scientific psychology, 262*b*
Scientific Revolution, 38, 303, 313
scope issues, 219–20
Scottish Enlightenment, 10–11
Scottish law, 75, 80–81
scripts, 269, 282, 284–85, 302, 302*b*, 303
Sears Roebuck, 219*b*, 227
Secrets: A Memoir of Vietnam and the Pentagon Papers (Ellsberg), 112
securities laws, 209*b*
self-financed entrepreneurs, 35–36, 174, 232, 253, 319
self-interest, 26
semiconductor companies, 234

sensemaking, 298–99, 308
Sent, Esther-Mirjam, 102, 103–4, 103*b*, 137–38
sequencing discourse, 271–73
Shakespeare, William, 276, 304
Shapin, Steven, 313
Shark Tank, 287*b*
Sharpe, William, 152*b*
Sherman Antitrust Act, 63
Shevlin, Steve, 188*b*
Shiller, Robert, 128*b*, 151, 176–77, 180, 340n.7
Shleifer, Andrei, 151, 380n.37
side-dish stories, 287
Siemens, 249
signaling, 168–69, 168*b*
"signifiers," 275, 276*b*
Silent Witness, 80
Silicon Valley, 230, 230*b*
Silton-Bookman Systems, 192*b*
Simon, Herbert
 academic background, 90
 and artificial intelligence advances, 319–20
 and artificial intelligence models, 139n
 and behavioral finance research, 151
 and bounded rationality, 129–30
 and Chandlerian organizational structures, 220–21
 and critiques of behavioral economics, 158
 and critiques of K-T research, 156n, 158
 and decision-making routines of large public companies, 261*b*
 education background, 94*b*–95*b*
 and Ellsberg's uncertainty/ambiguity research, 110–11, 125
 on experimental psychology, 145
 and heuristics and bias research, 133n, 134, 137, 138–39
 influence on model, 33
 and justificatory routines, 30
 memorial and legacy, 104*b*–5*b*
 muted influence of, 102
 and origins of behavioral economics, 127, 129*b*, 130
 and overview of author's model, 172–73
 and realistic reasonableness, 93–94
 and shift from Kuhnian paradigm in statistics, 56n
 and Smith's experimental economics, 155
 and types of rationality, 95–98
Simpson, O. J., 28n, 81
Sinclair, Upton, 26
Singell, Larry, 44, 67–68, 169, 341n.3, 344n.25
situational specification, 10–13
situational uncertainty, 10–13, 10*t*, 18

situational vs. statistical sources, 13–14
Six Sigma, 3–4
skeuomorphs, 276*b*
Skidelsky, Robert, 70*b*–71*b*
Skinner, Burrhus Frederick, 91–92n, 129*b*, 145
Slater, Irwin, 240*b*
Sliding Doors (film), 272
Sloan, Alfred, 25, 222, 304, 308, 366n.19
Sloan Foundation, 150*b*, 151
Smith, Adam, 92, 141*b*, 158
Smith, Edgar, 248
Smith, Fred, 290*b*
Smith, Vernon, 154–55, 161
Smith, Wes, 277
Smith v. Rapid Transit, 75, 76
Snopes, 326
social engineering, 139
social influences on information, 17–18
socialism, 327–28
social media, 3–4, 288, 322–23, 327
social sciences, 315–16. *See also specific disciplines*
sociology, 296*b*
Softa Group, 182*b*, 195*b*
software companies, 195*b*
Sohl, J. E., 206
Solow, Robert, x, 104, 105–6, 138n
Solzhenitsyn, Aleksandr, 301
Sophists, 23
Soros, George, 161
Sosadian, Carol, 182*b*
Soviet Union, 301
SpaceX, 278*b*
Sparta, 327
specialization
 and entrepreneurial discourse, 34–38
 entrepreneurial specialization, 36*f*, 317, 318–19
 of labor, 215
 organizational, 29
 and spillovers from popular business stories, 309–10
specification in storytelling, 282*b*–84*b*, 283
Spence, Michael, 65
Sperber, D., 137–38
stagflation, 228
staging discourse, 271–73
stakes, 27–28, 29–31, 30*f*, 36*f*
Stam, E., 379n.18
Standard & Poor's, 176
standardization, 186*b*
Stanford University, 142–43, 143*b*
Stanford University Network, 236*b*
Starbucks, 234–35, 249–50

424 INDEX

stare decisis, 303
Starman publicity stunt, 278*b*
startups
  and base-rate fallacies, 194
  Case-Shiller indices example, 176–77
  coping with financing constraints, 194–96
  and entrepreneurial specialization, 317
  and financing constraints, 190–92
  habitats of, 185
  and human capital challenges, 180, 184–85
  investment, uncertainty, and profit, ix*f*
  and irreducible uncertainties, 189–90
  and market habitats, 185
  promising vs. unpromising, 177–80
  and unexceptional ideas, 180–83, 182*b*
  and spontaneous opportunism, 192*b*
  See also bootstrapped ventures
Star Wars, 286
statistical data and modeling, 4–6, 7, 13–14, 16, 17, 75, 133. *See also* probability
steam engines, 319
Stein, Jeremy, 242, 369n.22, 381n.56
stereotypes, 274
Stern, S., 213*b*
Sterne, Laurence, 302*b*
Stigler, George, 43–44, 46n, 50, 65–66, 67, 99, 315, 343n.18
Stiglitz, Joseph, x, 65, 66, 168–69, 173–74, 253–54
Stirling University, 103*b*
stock buybacks, 234
stockholders, 242, 249
stock options, 215, 243
stories and storytelling
  attention-getting pitches, 287*b*
  and categories, 300*b*
  conventional views, 281–82
  creative divergences, 302*b*–3*b*
  dynamism of business stories, 308–11
  entrepreneurial stories, 304–8
  and evocative devices in entrepreneurial discourse, 279–80
  Google's Aristotle Project, 295*b*–97*b*
  hero's journeys, 288*b*–91*b*
  literary and legal stories, 298–99, 299*b*
  recovery stories, 292*b*–94*b*
  and side-dish stories, 287
  and specification, 282*b*–84*b*, 283
  spillovers from popular stories, 298–311
"Storytelling That Drives Bold Change" (Frei and Morriss), 281–82
Stowe, Harriet Beecher, 301
Strategy and Structure (Chandler), 218, 220–21, 225*b*

Strömberg, P., 365n.37, 365n.38
Student magazine, 184*b*
stunts, 278, 278*b*, 293*b*
subjective interpretations, 310–11
subjective utility, 53–54, 55, 55*b*, 56, 60
subsidies, 319
substantive rationality, 97
Sudden Infant Death Syndrome (SIDS), 28
sufficiency of evidence, 77–78, 79–80
Sunday Ramparts, 185
Sun Microsystems, 206, 236*b*
Sunstein, Cass, 153–54
Superior Court of the Commonwealth of Massachusetts, 75
supply and demand, 27–29, 244n
sure-thing principle, 117*b*
Symplex Communications, 195*b*
Symposium on the 50th Anniversary of the Ellsberg Paradox, 120*b*, 121
systemic biases, 130
systemic learning, 98*b*

tabloid journalism, 325
Taiwan, 228–29
takeovers, 230–31
Taleb, N. N., 272
tamoxifen, 240*b*
target funding levels, 208
"target" uncertainty, 15–16, 18–19, 19*f*
Taylor, Frederick, 221
Taylor Homes, 184*b*
team structures, 244, 245, 246
technology and technological advances
  balancing justification and authority, 327–30
  and challenges facing established industry leaders, 229
  and declining quality of discourse, 325
  and dynamism of business stories, 309
  and Ellsberg's uncertainty/ambiguity research, 124
  and entrepreneurial specialization, 319
  and entrepreneurial stories, 304–5
  Galbraith's technostructure, 224, 226, 227n, 227, 233, 244
  and growth of new industrial giants, 253
  influences on information, 17–18
  and scope of recent innovations, 3–4
  and spillovers from literary storytelling, 309
  technocracy, 244
  and technologies of discourse, 320–23
  technology-enabled symbiosis, 323n
  See also high-tech industries
TED talks, 288

telecom industry, 317
telegraph cables, 163
television and telemarketing, 192*b*, 287*b*
Tesla, 31, 252–53, 252*t*, 278*b*, 306
testimony, 75
Thaler, Richard, 148, 149*b*–50*b*, 151, 152, 357n.7, 357n.11
"Theories of Rational Choice under Uncertainty: The Contributions of von Neuman and Morgenstern" (Allberg), 111*b*
"A Theory of Business Profit" (Knight), 45*b*
Theory of Economic Development (Schumpeter), 91
Theory of Games and Economic Behavior (Von Neumann and Morgenstern), 54
theory of the firm, 134
theory of the future, 86
Theory Z: How American Management Can Meet the Japanese Challenge (Ouchi), 230
Theranos, 294*b*, 304–5
thermal economies, 222–23
Thesmar, D., 194
3Com, 236*b*
tiered delegation, 241–42
TikTok, 322–23
time-series regression, 104*b*–5*b*
Tirole, Jean, 65
T-Mobile, 234
To Kill a Mockingbird (Lee), 301
Todorov, Tzvetan, 282*b*
Tolkien, J. R. R., 301
"Tom W" experiment, 136*b*
top-down authority, 223
Toshiba, 188*b*
Total Recall, 182*b*
Treatise on Probability (Keynes)
  and abstract reasoning, 160*b*
  and author's model, 69, 73, 77
  and Ellsberg's uncertainty/ambiguity research, 115n
  and evidentiary standards, 74–77, 79–80n
  and extreme and macro uncertainties, 69, 84–89
  Keynes's skepticism of numerical measurement, 73*b*–74*b*
  legacy of, 81–84
  and overview of author's model, 172
  and probability, 71–73
  Ramsay's critique of, 82–84
  and relevance and sufficiency of evidence, 77–78, 79–80
  and routines and conventions, 80–81

triadic organization, 271
trials, 16–17
Trollope, Anthony, 304
Trump, Donald, 323, 331*b*
Tubular Bells (Oldfield), 184*b*
Tucker, Atul, 182*b*
Tuckett, David, 283*b*, 340n.7, 374n.13
Tufts University, 179*b*
tuition rates, 168*b*
TV advertising, 275
Tversky, Amos
  academic background, 131*b*–32*b*
  and base-rate fallacies, 194
  and behavioral finance research, 151–52
  and Bruner's critique of cognitive biases, 262*b*
  and critiques of bias research, 137*b*
  and critiques of K-T research, 156–57, 157*b*, 158, 160–61
  and extension of behavioral research to economics, 154
  and heuristics and bias research, 130
  and irrationality in financing, 176
  and Kahneman's tribute to Thaler, 149*b*–50*b*
  and muted influence of Simon's work, 109
  and origins of behavioral economics, 128–29, 130, 148
  and prospect theory, 140–44
  and Simon's academic background, 90
  and Simon's bounded rationality, 98
  and Smith's experimental economics, 154–55
  and split within behavioral economics, 126
  and Thaler's academic background, 148
  and Wanner's academic background, 150*b*
Twachtman, John Henry, 1

Uber, 3–4, 274, 309, 380n.35
UK Parliament, 27, 217
Uncertainty Economics program, 88–89
Uncle Tom's Cabin (Stowe), 301
uncontested decisions, 24
uniformity of nature, 12
Uniform Partnership Act, 205n
unilateral decision-making, 31
uniqueness of situations, 28–30, 30*f*, 31
Unique Transportation Systems, 182*b*
University of British Columbia, 143*b*, 150*b*
University of California, Berkeley, 130*b*–31*b*, 185
University of Cambridge, 111*b*
University of Chicago, 43, 45*b*, 46–47, 50, 51, 53, 60, 71*b*, 94*b*, 99, 116, 151, 152*b*, 179*b*
University of Chicago Law Review, 324
University of Iowa, 45*b*

426 INDEX

University of Michigan, 103, 103b, 105, 131b
University of Munich, 156–57
University of Texas, 185
UNIX operating system, 235
unknown unknowns, 5, 20, 118, 174–75
unsettled markets, 187, 188b
US Air Force, 111b
US Army Intelligence, 261b
US Census Bureau, 186b
US Commerce Department, 103
US Congress, 63, 65, 111b–12b
US Constitution, 332–33
"US Decision-Making in Vietnam, 1945–68"
    (report), 111b–12b
US Department of Defense, 111b–12b, 320
US Department of Justice, 112b
US Department of Labor, 200b–1b
US Department of State, 111b–12b
US Federal Reserve, 330, 331b–32b
US Food and Drug Administration, 4–5, 17, 22,
    28, 29, 30b–31b, 75, 240b
US Marine Corps, 111b, 290b
US Office of Price Administration, 224b
US Postal Service, 324b
US Senate, 24
US Small Business Administration, 190
US Supreme Court, 4–5, 24, 264–65, 298, 299b
US Veterans Administration, 78b–79b
utility maximization
    and behavioral finance research, 151–52
    and exclusion of entrepreneurship form
        microeconomics, 57–58
    and muted influence of Simon's work, 106
    practical benefits of, 106–7
    and Ramsay's critique of Keynes's Treatise,
        83–84
    and shift from Kuhnian paradigm in
        statistics, 55–56
    and Simon's Administrative Behavior, 102b
    and Simon's global rationality, 99
    and Simon's study of decision-making, 102b
    and subjective utility theories, 55
    and types of rationality, 95
    See also subjective utility
utility theory, 53, 140b, 142n. See also subjective
    utility; utility maximization

vaccine hesitancy, 20, 25
Vail, Theodore, 199–200
value theory, 140b–41b
Varian Associates, 230b
Varieties of Religious Experience (James), 263

venture capitalists (VCs)
    and advantages of large public companies,
        232, 233–35
    "alignment" and "market" uncertainties,
        214b
    angel investors contrasted with, 210–12
    and Case-Shiller indices, 176
    and challenges facing established industry
        leaders, 229
    complexity and coordination issues, 214–16
    coping with financing constraints, 196
    and decision-making routines of large public
        companies, 240–41, 242
    differences among, 201–4
    due diligence and oversight, 197–99
    and entrepreneurial specialization, 35–36,
        309–10
    and entrepreneurs in economic theory, 34
    and evocative devices in entrepreneurial
        discourse, 274
    and exit decisions, 209b
    as focus of research, 167
    funding, routines, and initiatives, 310f
    and "gazelle" businesses, 178
    and governance issues of large public
        companies, 243, 249
    and growth of new industrial giants, 252–53
    and high-tech industries, 212–14
    incentive and misjudgment issues, 204–5
    information requirements of, 174
    and institutionalized investing, 199–201,
        200b–1b
    and institutional reinforcement, 206, 207–8
    and irrationality in financing, 176–77
    and irreducible uncertainties, 189
    and large companies' intolerance for
        uncertainty, 236b
    and mutual monitoring, 205–6
    overview of, 197
    and overview of author's model, 174
    and patents, 213b
    and startup financing constraints, 190, 191
    strictness of investment criteria, 208
    strict routines, 199–200
    target funding levels, 208
    and uncertainties in modern marketplace, 4
    and uncertainty limits, 208–10
    vetting criteria, 206b–7b
    and winner's curse problem, 197–98
The Venturesome Economy (Bhidé), x, 199
Verizon, 234
vertical integration, 218b–19b

vetting criteria for venture capitalists, 206b–7b
Vietnam War, 110, 289b, 290b
Vincenti, Walter, 93
Virgin Airlines, 278b, 286
Virgin Brides, 278b, 286
Virgin Group, 184b, 185
Virginia Commonwealth University (VCU), 289b
The Visible Hand (Chandler), 218, 220–21
VisiCalc, 188b, 213, 246
Visser, Bauke, 66
visual metaphors, 275
Vogel, Ezra, 230, 307
Volcker, Paul, 228, 331b–32b
Von Mises, Ludwig, 67n
Von Neumann, John, 54, 111b, 113, 342n.7

Wagner, Richard, 276
Wallot, Paul, 27
Walmart, 183b, 212, 217, 230b, 238
Walpole, Arthur, 240b
Walton, D., 179b–80b
Walton, Sam, 183b, 230b, 295, 304, 308
Wang, An, 229b–30b
Wang Laboratories, 229b–30b
Wanner, Eric, 150, 150b, 151
Warren, Robin, 321
Washington Post, 192b
Watson, John Broadus, 91–92n, 145
Watts Professorship in Psychology, 262b
Wayne State University, 22
The Way We Live Now (Trollope), 304
weather forecasting, 20
Webber, Andrew Lloyd, 277
Weber, Max, 31, 120, 239, 310–11
"weight-of-evidence" proposals, 205–6
Weiss, Allan, 176–77, 180
Welles, Orson, 304
Wennberg, K., 378n.50, 379n.18
Wenner, Jann, 183b–84b, 185
Wetzel, W. E., Jr., 206
WeWork, 294b

Wheelwright, George W., III, 229b–30b
Whitehead, A. N., 71–72
WikiLeaks, 112b
Wilentz, Sean, 224b
Wilken, Robert, 188b
The Will to Believe (James), 145
William Cory (ship), 163
Williams, Paul, 183b–84b
Williamson, Oliver, 65, 166b, 222–23, 251
Windows operating system, 246–47, 291–92
winner's curse problem, 193n, 197–98
Winter, Sidney, 30, 103–4
wireless technology, 309, 317
Wolf, Henry, 41, 259
Wolfe, Thomas, 298
Woman on the Quay, Honfleur (Twachtman), 1
Worcester Polytechnic Institute, 195b
World Health Organization, 238–39
World of Computers, 182b
World War I, 225b
World War II, 87, 93–94, 139, 224b, 229,
   229b–30b, 285
Wozniak, Steve, 185, 188b
Wright, Richard, 299b
Wrigley, William, 64n
Wundt, Wilhelm Maximilian, 145, 356n.68

Xerox, 182b

Yale University, 103b, 116, 151, 201b, 290b
yellow press, 327
YouTube, 323n

Zacharkiw, Peter, 192b
Zantac, 238–39
Zanuck, Darryl F., 285
Zelazny, Gene, 276, 277b
Zenith, 188b
zoning laws, 328–29
Zoom, 210
Zott, C., 203b